LISTENING CLEAR

중학영어듣기 모의고사 20회

2

▌핵심만 골라 담은 중학 영어듣기능력평가 완벽 대비서 LISTENING CLEAR

- 더 완벽하게! 최신 중학 영어듣기능력평가 출제 유형 100% 반영

- 더 풍부하게! 유형별 문제 해결 전략 및 풍부한 기출 표현 수록

- 더 편리하게! 1.0배속, 1.2배속, 받아쓰기용 QR코드로 학습 편의성 강화

- 더 정확하게! 잘 안 들리는 영어 발음 현상과 영국식 발음 반복 훈련

학습자의 마음을 읽는 **동아영어콘텐츠연구팀**

동아영어콘텐츠연구팀은 동아출판의 영어 개발 연구원, 현장 선생님, 그리고 전문 원고 집필자들이
공동연구를 통해 최적의 콘텐츠를 개발하는 연구조직입니다.

원고 개발에 참여하신 분들

고미라   강윤희   이정은   이지현   김영선   전혜래나

유경연   박석완   배윤경   윤소영   김지형   강남숙

LISTENING
CLEAR

중학영어듣기
모의고사 20회

2

STRUCTURES 구성과 특징

STEP 1   유형별 기출문제로 기본 다지기

〈전국 16개 시·도 교육청 영어듣기능력평가〉에 출제된 유형별 기출문제를 학습하며 기본기를 다집니다.

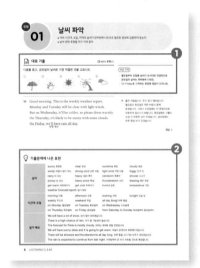

대표 기출 | 해결 전략 ❶

유형별 대표 기출문제를 풀어 보며 유형에 대한 감을 익힐 수 있어요.
해결 전략에는 어느 부분을 집중해서 들어야 하는지, 무엇을 주의해야 하는지 설명되어 있어요.
문제 푸는 요령을 터득할 수 있으니 꼭 짚어 보세요.

기출문제에 나온 표현 ❷

실제 시험에 출제되었던 필수 어휘와 필수 표현을 한눈에 볼 수 있어요.
매 시험마다 반복적으로 출제되는 표현이 많으므로 암기해 두는 것이 좋아요.

STEP 2   모의고사로 실전 감각 기르기

실제 시험과 유사한 소재와 유형, 출제 경향을 완벽히 반영한 모의고사 20회를 풀며 실전 감각을 기릅니다.

실전 모의고사

실제 시험보다 약간 어려운 난이도로 구성되어
있어서 실전에 효과적으로 대비할 수 있어요.

고난도 모의고사

실전 모의고사보다 어려운 문제를 통해 실력을
더욱 향상시킬 수 있어요.

1.0배속

1.2배속

★ 1.0배속 / 1.2배속 녹음 파일: 각자 수준에 맞는 속도를 선택하여 문제를 풀어 보세요.

STEP 3   받아쓰기로 실력 높이기

모의고사 문제를 다시 듣고 받아쓰면서 듣기 실력을 향상시킵니다.

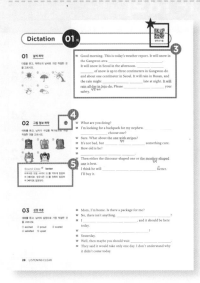

정답 단서 / 함정 ❸

정답 단서와 함정이 표시되어 있어서 문제를 더욱 잘 이해할 수 있고, 반복되는 출제 패턴을 파악할 수 있어요.

❇ 영국식 발음 ❹

매회 다섯 문항이 영국식 발음으로 녹음되어 있어서 영국식 발음에 익숙해질 수 있어요.

Sound Clear ☆ ❺

듣기 어려운 발음과 주의해야 하는 발음 현상을 학습할 수 있어요.

★ 받아쓰기용 녹음 파일: 문장마다 받아쓰기 시간이 확보되어 있어서 편리하게 학습할 수 있어요.

STEP 4   필수 어휘·표현 정리하기

모의고사에 나온 필수 어휘와 표현을 점검하며 학습한 내용을 마무리합니다.

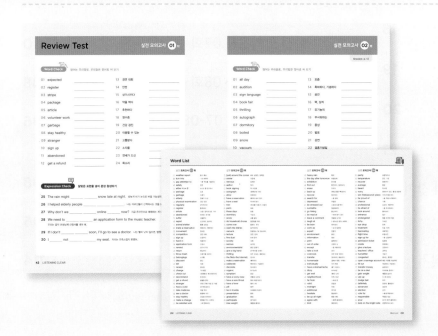

Review Test

모의고사에 나온 단어, 숙어, 관용 표현 문제를 풀며 복습할 수 있어요.

Word List

부록으로 제공된 어휘 목록을 암기장으로 활용해 보세요.

CONTENTS 차례

PART 3 고난도 모의고사 19-20회

PART

1

유형 분석 &
주요 표현

날씨 파악

■ 여러 시간대, 요일, 지역의 날씨가 한꺼번에 나오므로 필요한 정보에 집중하여 듣는다.
■ 날씨 관련 표현을 미리 익혀 둔다.

대표 기출

🔊 MP3 유형 01

다음을 듣고, 금요일의 날씨로 가장 적절한 것을 고르시오.

①    ②   ③   ④   ⑤

해결 전략

- 월요일부터 요일별 날씨가 순서대로 언급되므로 금요일의 날씨는 뒷부분에 나와요.
- On Friday로 시작하는 문장에 정답이 드러나요.

W　Good morning. This is the weekly weather report.
　　Monday and Tuesday will be clear with light winds.
　　But on Wednesday, it'll be colder, so please dress warmly.
　　On Thursday, it's likely to be sunny with some clouds.
　　On Friday, we'll have rain all day.
　　　　　　　　정답 단서

여　좋은 아침입니다. 주간 일기 예보입니다. 월요일과 화요일은 약한 바람과 함께 맑겠습니다. 그러나 수요일에는 더 추워지므로 따뜻하게 입으시기 바랍니다. 목요일에는 구름이 조금 낀 화창한 날이 되겠습니다. 금요일에는 하루 종일 비가 오겠습니다.

정답 ①

기출문제에 나온 표현

날씨	sunny 화창한	clear 맑은	sunshine 햇빛	cloudy 흐린
	windy 바람이 많이 부는	strong wind 강한 바람	light wind 약한 바람	foggy 안개 낀
	rainy 비 오는	heavy rain 폭우	rainstorm 폭풍우	shower 소나기
	snowy 눈 오는	heavy snow 폭설	thunderstorm 뇌우	freezing 매우 추운
	get warm 따뜻해지다	get cold 추워지다	humid 습한	temperature 기온
	weather forecast(report) 일기 예보			

시간대·요일	morning 아침	afternoon 오후	evening 저녁	tonight 오늘 밤
	weekly 주간의	weekend 주말	all day (long) 하루 종일	
	on Monday 월요일에	on Tuesday 화요일에	on Wednesday 수요일에	
	on Thursday 목요일에	on Friday 금요일에	from Saturday to Sunday 토요일부터 일요일까지	

일기 예보	We will have a lot of snow. 눈이 많이 내리겠습니다.
	There is a high chance of rain. 비가 올 가능성이 높습니다.
	The forecast for Paris is mostly cloudy. 파리는 대체로 흐릴 전망입니다.
	We will have sunny skies and it is going to get warm. 하늘이 맑겠으며 따뜻해지겠습니다.
	There will be showers and thunderstorms all day long. 하루 종일 소나기와 뇌우가 내리겠습니다.
	The rain is expected to continue from last night. 어젯밤부터 온 비가 계속될 것으로 예상됩니다.

그림 정보 파악

- 그림을 보고, 각 그림의 특징과 차이점을 미리 파악한다.
- 그림을 묘사하는 모양, 위치, 특징 등의 표현에 주의를 기울여 듣는다.
- 중간에 다른 선택지로 오답을 유도하는 단어가 나올 수 있으므로 끝까지 집중해서 듣는다.

📄 대표 기출

🔊 MP3 유형 02

대화를 듣고, 여자가 만든 필통으로 가장 적절한 것을 고르시오.

①   ②   ③   ④   ⑤

해결 전략

- 대화를 듣기 전에 필통의 특징을 나타내는 표현을 생각해 두세요.
- 여자가 만든 필통을 보고 있는 남자의 말에 정답이 드러나요.

W Surprise! Here is your new pencil case.

M Wow! It looks really nice. Did you buy it, Mom?

W No, I made it myself. Do you like it?

M Of course! The banana on it is very cute.

W I wanted to draw a pineapple at first, but it was too difficult for me.
   정답 단서 *함정*

M It's okay, Mom. I like bananas much better. Thank you!
   정답 단서

여 짜잔! 여기 네 새 필통이야.
남 와! 정말 좋아 보여요. 이거 사신 거예요, 엄마?
여 아니, 내가 만들었어. 마음에 드니?
남 당연하죠! 필통에 있는 바나나가 정말 귀여워요.
여 처음에는 파인애플을 그리고 싶었는데, 나에겐 너무 어렵더라.
남 괜찮아요, 엄마. 저는 바나나를 훨씬 더 좋아해요. 고마워요!

정답 ①

💡 기출문제에 나온 표현

모양	circle 동그라미, 원　　square 사각형　　triangle 삼각형　　star 별 모양 heart 하트 모양　　heart-shaped 하트 모양의 Which one do you like better, circle or square? 둥근 것과 네모난 것 중 어느 것이 더 좋으세요? What about putting these three heart-shaped stickers under it? 그것 아래에 이 하트 모양의 스티커 세 개를 붙이는 것은 어떨까요?
위치	in front of ~ 앞에　　behind ~ 뒤에　　next to ~ 옆에　　in the middle 중앙에 at the top 맨 위에　　on the left(right) (side) of ~의 왼쪽(오른쪽)에 Put the fork to the right of the spoon. 숟가락의 오른쪽에 포크를 놓으세요. I put the title at the top. Now I want to put a picture under the title. 나는 맨 위에 제목을 넣었어. 이제 제목 아래에 그림을 넣고 싶어.
특징	space 공간　　picture 그림　　title 제목　　no ~ ~가 없는 number 숫자　　handle 손잡이 There's still some space under the picture. 여전히 그림 아래에 공간이 좀 있어요. There are no numbers on the watch. 시계에 숫자가 없네요.

심정 추론

■ 지시문을 읽고, 누구의 심정을 묻는 문제인지 확인한다.
■ 화자의 어조와 감탄사 등에 주목하면서 전체적인 상황과 분위기를 통해 화자의 심정을 추론한다.
■ 선택지가 영어로 출제되므로 심정을 나타내는 영어 단어를 미리 익혀 둔다.

📄 대표 기출 🔊 MP3 유형 03

대화를 듣고, 여자의 심정으로 가장 적절한 것을 고르시오.

① shy   ② bored   ③ scared
④ happy   ⑤ upset

(해결 전략)

• 여자의 심정을 묻는 문제이므로 여자의 말을 주의 깊게 들으세요.
• 여자의 말 Wow!, I'm so glad to be here today.를 통해 긍정적인 감정을 파악할 수 있어요.

W Dad, we finally got to the top of the mountain.
M It took a long time, but the air is so fresh up here, isn't it?
W Yeah. It's so different from downtown.
M Look at the beautiful view down there, Anna.
W Wow! It's really beautiful.
    정답 단서
M I knew you would love this view.
W Yeah, I'm so glad to be here today.
    정답 단서
M Let's take a picture together.
W Sure.

여 아빠, 우리가 드디어 산 정상에 도착했어요.
남 오래 걸렸지만, 여기 공기가 아주 상쾌하지, 그렇지 않니?
여 네. 시내와는 아주 달라요.
남 저 아래 아름다운 경치를 봐, Anna.
여 우와! 정말 아름다워요.
남 난 네가 이 풍경을 좋아할 줄 알았어.
여 네, 오늘 여기 오게 돼서 정말 기뻐요.
남 같이 사진 찍자.
여 좋아요.

정답 ④

💡 기출문제에 나온 표현

긍정적 심정	happy 행복한	excited 신난	satisfied 만족하는	proud 자랑스러운
	peaceful 평화로운	relaxed 느긋한	calm 침착한	surprised 놀란
	I really want to see it. I can't wait. 저는 정말로 그것이 보고 싶어요. 너무 기다려져요.			
	Wow, congratulations! 와, 축하해!			
	I'm so happy for you. 네가 잘 되어서 나도 기뻐.			
부정적 심정	angry 화가 난	shy 부끄러운	upset 속상한	bored 지루해하는
	nervous 긴장한	scared 무서워하는	worried 걱정하는	disappointed 실망한
	My hands are shaking now. 지금 제 손이 떨리고 있어요.			
	I get afraid when I speak in front of many people. 저는 많은 사람들 앞에서 말을 할 때 겁이 나요.			
	I will try my best, but this contest makes me uncomfortable. 저는 최선을 다할 거지만, 이 경연 대회가 저를 부담스럽게 하네요.			

장소 추론

- 장소를 짐작할 수 있는 특정 어휘나 표현을 통해 장소를 추론한다.
- 장소를 나타내는 표현이 직접 언급되지 않은 경우에는 전체적인 상황을 통해 추론한다.
- 특정 장소에서 나눌 수 있는 대화에서 자주 쓰이는 표현을 미리 익혀 둔다.

📄 대표 기출
🔊 MP3 유형 04

대화를 듣고, 두 사람이 대화하는 장소로 가장 적절한 곳을 고르시오.

① 약국　　　② 우체국　　　③ 소방서
④ 동물 병원　　⑤ 분실물 센터

(해결 전략)

- 여자의 첫 번째 말에 나오는 send this package를 통해 물건을 보낼 수 있는 장소임을 알 수 있어요.
- 이어서 나오는 Which country, by airplane, take about five days를 통해 두 사람이 대화하는 장소를 파악할 수 있어요.

M Hello. How may I help you?

W Hi. I want to send this package to my friend in another country.
　　정답 단서

M All right. Which country do you want to send it to?
　　　정답 단서

W To Russia, please.

M What's in it?

W There are some books in it. How much will it cost?

M It'll cost $60 by airplane.
　　　정답 단서

W Here you are. How long will it take?

M It will take about five days.
　　　정답 단서

남 안녕하세요. 무엇을 도와드릴까요?

여 안녕하세요. 이 소포를 다른 나라에 있는 친구에게 보내고 싶어요.

남 알겠습니다. 어느 나라로 보내고 싶은가요?

여 러시아요.

남 그 안에 뭐가 들어 있나요?

여 책이 몇 권 들어 있어요. 비용이 얼마나 들까요?

남 항공 우편으로 60달러 들 겁니다.

여 여기 있습니다. 얼마나 걸릴까요?

남 5일 정도 걸릴 거예요.

정답 ②

💡 기출문제에 나온 표현

기차역	train ticket 기차표	take (시간이) 걸리다	leave 떠나다, 출발하다	
분실물 센터	lost (lose의 과거형) 잃어버렸다		contact 연락하다	find 찾다
관광 안내소	look around the city 시내를 둘러보다 famous places to visit 방문할 만한 유명한 장소		city tour map 시내 관광 지도 Have a nice trip. 즐거운 여행하세요.	
영화관	movie 영화	ticket 표	seat 좌석	sold out 매진된, 다 팔린
햄버거 가게	order 주문하다	coke 콜라	chicken burger 치킨버거	
상점	look for ~을 찾다 on sale 세일 중인	exchange 교환하다 discount 할인	refund 환불하다 membership 회원	receipt 영수증
서점	picture book 그림책	page 페이지, 쪽	best-selling book 베스트셀러	
도서관	check out a book 책을 대출하다 library card 도서관 카드		return a book 책을 반납하다 make a copy 복사하다	

관계 추론

■ 대화의 앞부분에 결정적인 단서가 나오는 경우가 많으므로 처음부터 집중해서 듣는다.
■ 두 사람의 관계를 짐작할 수 있는 여러 단서들을 종합하여 답을 고른다.

📄 대표 기출   🔊 MP3 유형 05

대화를 듣고, 두 사람의 관계로 가장 적절한 것을 고르시오.

① 요리사 – 고객   ② 미용사 – 고객
③ 소설가 – 독자   ④ 은행원 – 고객
⑤ 미술 교사 – 학생

M How can I help you?

W I'd like to get a haircut, please. How much will it cost?

M It's $10.   _{정답 단서}

W That's good. And can you change my hair color, too?

M What color do you want?   _{정답 단서}

W Hmm… I can't decide. What color is popular these days?

M Brown is trendy now.

W That'll be nice.

(해결 전략)

• How can I help you?라는 남자의 말에서 남자가 손님을 맞이하고 있음을 알 수 있어요.
• 이어서 나오는 여자의 말을 통해 두 사람의 관계를 파악할 수 있어요.

남 무엇을 도와드릴까요?
여 머리를 자르고 싶어요. 얼마죠?
남 10달러입니다.
여 좋아요. 그리고 제 머리색도 바꿀 수 있을까요?
남 어떤 색을 원하세요?
여 음… 결정을 못 하겠어요. 요즘 무슨 색이 인기 있나요?
남 갈색이 지금 유행이에요.
여 그거 좋겠네요.

정답 ②

💡 기출문제에 나온 표현

매표소 직원 – 손님	buy a ticket 표를 사다 children under 7 7세 미만 아동	adult ticket 어른 표 enter for free 무료로 입장하다
호텔 직원 – 손님	make a reservation 예약하다 ask for ~을 요청하다 a room with two single beds 1인용 침대가 두 개 있는 방	reserve a room 방을 예약하다 breakfast coupon 조식 쿠폰
택배 기사 – 고객	deliver 배달하다 be at home 집에 있다	security office 경비실 leave the package 택배를 두다
시험 감독 교사 – 응시 학생	clear off a desk 책상을 치우다 test booklet 시험지	answer sheet 답안지
미용사 – 고객	get a haircut 머리를 자르다 change one's hair color 머리색을 바꾸다	have a reservation 예약이 되어 있다
도서관 사서 – 이용객	borrow a book 책을 빌리다 3 days late 3일 늦은	return a book 책을 반납하다 pay a fine 연체료를 내다
문구점 점원 – 학생	sketchbook 스케치북 12-color paint set 12색 물감 세트	paint brush 미술용 붓

특정 정보 파악

- 날짜, 음식, 수업, 동아리 등 다양한 소재가 출제된다.
- 대화의 앞부분에서 다른 선택지로 오답을 유도하는 경우가 많으므로 주의해야 한다.
- 끝까지 집중해서 들으면서 대화 속 인물이 최종적으로 선택하는 것을 답으로 고른다.

📄 대표 기출

🔊 MP3 유형 06

대화를 듣고, 여자가 가입하고자 하는 동아리를 고르시오.

① 바둑　　　② 컴퓨터　　　③ 축구
④ 배드민턴　　⑤ 요가

(해결 전략)

- 남자가 가입한 동아리를 정답으로 혼동하지 않도록 주의하세요.
- 여자가 거절한 동아리를 하나씩 지워 나가세요.
- 끝까지 집중해서 들어야 여자가 최종적으로 선택한 동아리를 고를 수 있어요.

W	Chris, have you decided on your school club?
M	Yes. I signed up for the *baduk* club last week.
W	Sounds interesting.
M	Will you join the computer club again this year?
W	Well, I want to try something different.
M	Then how about a sports club like the badminton club?
W	Hmm... badminton is difficult for me.
M	Oh, I see. Well, why don't you join the yoga club?
W	Sounds better for me. I'll do that.

여 Chris, 학교 동아리 정했니?
남 응. 난 지난주에 바둑 동아리에 가입했어.
여 재미있겠다.
남 넌 올해도 컴퓨터 동아리에 들 거니?
여 글쎄, 난 다른 걸 해 보고 싶어.
남 그럼 배드민턴 동아리 같은 운동 동아리는 어때?
여 음… 배드민턴은 내게 어려워.
남 아, 알겠어. 그럼 요가 동아리에 드는 건 어때?
여 내게는 그게 더 좋을 것 같아. 그걸 해야겠다.

정답 ⑤

💡 기출문제에 나온 표현

사물	I made a name tag. Look! 제가 이름표를 만들었어요. 보세요!
날짜	Let me check. May 11th will be fine. 확인해 볼게요. 5월 11일이 좋겠어요.
도시	Namwon sounds good. I've never been there. 남원 좋겠다. 나는 그곳에 가 본 적이 없어.
음식	I'm going to have a chicken burger. 저는 치킨버거를 먹을게요.
수업	I'd like to learn how to play the guitar this summer. 나는 이번 여름에 기타 치는 법을 배우고 싶어.
악기	I'd love to play the piano. 나는 피아노를 연주하고 싶어.
동물	I really liked the penguins. They were so cute. 나는 펭귄들이 정말 좋았어. 펭귄들이 정말 귀여웠어.
동아리	I signed up for the *baduk* club last week. 나는 지난주에 바둑 동아리에 가입했어.

의도 파악

- 지시문을 읽고, 마지막 말을 하는 사람이 누구인지 확인한다.
- 마지막 말의 의도를 파악하는 문제이므로 특히 마지막 말을 집중해서 들어야 한다.
- 의도를 나타내는 다양한 상황별 표현을 미리 익혀 둔다.

📄 대표 기출

🔊 MP3 유형 07

대화를 듣고, 여자의 마지막 말의 의도로 가장 적절한 것을 고르시오.

① 감사 ② 거절 ③ 격려
④ 허락 ⑤ 충고

해결 전략

- 마지막 말을 하는 사람이 여자이므로 여자가 하는 말을 주의 깊게 들으세요.
- I'm really sorry.는 상대방의 제안을 거절할 때 쓰는 표현이에요.

M Kate, do you like any Korean pop groups?

W Yes. I love the group, "Dreamers." Their music is really fantastic.

M Yeah, then how about coming with me to a K-pop festival this Friday?

W I'd love to, but I can't. I have a family dinner.

M How about Saturday then?

W I'm really sorry. Every Saturday I have to take a violin lesson. *정답 단서*

남 Kate, 너 한국 팝 그룹 좋아해?
여 응. 나는 Dreamers라는 그룹을 좋아해. 그들의 음악은 정말 환상적이야.
남 맞아, 그럼 이번 주 금요일에 나랑 케이 팝 축제에 가는 거 어때?
여 그러고 싶지만, 그럴 수가 없어. 저녁에 가족 식사가 있어.
남 그럼 토요일은 어때?
여 정말 미안해. 매주 토요일에 바이올린 수업이 있어.

정답 ②

💡 기출문제에 나온 표현

동의	I agree (with you). (네 말에) 동의해. That could be a good idea. 좋은 생각이야.	You can say that again. 동감이야.
반대	I'm against it. 나는 그것에 반대해.	I don't think that's a good idea. 그건 좋은 생각이 아닌 것 같아.
승낙	Okay, I will. 알았어, 그렇게 할게.	That sounds great. 그거 좋다.
거절	I'm afraid I can't. 난 안 되겠어. Maybe next time. 다음에 할게.	I'm sorry, but I can't. 미안하지만, 안 돼.
칭찬	That's my boy! You did a great job! 역시 내 아들이야! 잘했어!	
격려	I'm sure you'll get on the team next time. Cheer up! 다음번에는 네가 그 팀에 합류할 거라고 확신해. 기운 내!	
부탁·요청	Can you take these cookies to her? 그녀에게 이 쿠키들 좀 가져다 줄 수 있니? Can you help me set the table? 식탁 차리는 것 좀 도와줄래?	
조언·충고	You should not give our snacks to animals. 동물들에게 우리의 간식을 주어서는 안 돼. You should make eye contact during the speech. 너는 연설하는 동안에 눈을 마주쳐야 해.	
감사	I appreciate your help. 도와주셔서 감사합니다.	
축하	Wow, congratulations! 와, 축하해!	

주제 파악

- 선택지를 읽고, 어떤 내용이 나올지 예상해 본다.
- 앞부분에 주제를 나타내는 말이 명확히 언급되는 경우가 많으므로 처음부터 집중해서 듣는다.
- 마지막에 내용을 정리하는 문장으로 주제가 언급되는 경우도 있다.

📄 대표 기출

◁) MP3 유형 08

다음을 듣고, 여자가 하는 말의 내용으로 가장 적절한 것을 고르시오.

① 수영 대회 준비
② 화재 대피 훈련
③ 할인 쿠폰 사용
④ 방학 일정 공지
⑤ 승강기 작동 원리

해결 전략

- 앞부분에 주제가 명확히 드러났어요.
- 앞부분을 놓쳤다면, 뒤에 이어지는 내용을 종합하여 전체적인 내용을 파악하세요.
- 중간에 한두 문장만 듣고 정답을 고르지 않도록 주의하세요.

W   Attention, please! We'll now practice what to do in a fire. You'll learn how to be safe in a real fire. When you hear the fire alarm, find the nearest exit and get out of the building. Also, remember to take the stairs. Elevators can be dangerous during a fire.

정답 단서

한정

여   주목해 주세요! 우리는 이제 화재가 발생하면 무엇을 해야 하는지 연습해 보겠습니다. 여러분은 실제 화재 시 어떻게 안전할 수 있는지 배울 것입니다. 화재 경보를 들으면, 가장 가까운 출구를 찾아 건물 밖으로 나가세요. 또한, 계단을 이용하는 것을 기억하세요. 엘리베이터는 화재 시 위험할 수 있습니다.

정답 ②

💡 기출문제에 나온 표현

일정 안내	Let me tell you about today's schedule. 여러분께 오늘의 일정에 대해 말씀드리겠습니다.
수상 소감	I'm very happy to receive the award for Player of the Year. 제가 올해의 선수상을 받게 되어 매우 기쁩니다.
회원 모집	We're looking for new members to join our volunteer club. 우리는 자원봉사 동아리에 가입할 새 회원을 찾고 있습니다.
행사 안내	To celebrate the victory, we've canceled afternoon classes today. 승리를 축하하기 위해, 우리는 오늘 오후 수업을 취소했습니다.
올바른 휴대 전화 사용법	Let me tell you how to use your cell phone wisely. 휴대 전화를 현명하게 사용하는 방법을 말씀드리겠습니다.
환경 보호 방법	Let's remember these things to protect our environment. 우리의 환경을 보호하기 위해 이것들을 기억합시다.
기차 이용 예절	For a convenient and comfortable journey for all passengers, please remember the following. 모든 승객들을 위한 편리하고 편안한 여행을 위해, 다음 사항을 기억하십시오.
수영장 안전 수칙	I'd like to tell you about some important rules for using the swimming pool. 저는 여러분께 수영장 이용에 있어 몇 가지 중요한 규칙에 대해 말씀드리고 싶습니다.
분실물 습득 안내	We have found a coat and a scarf in the women's restroom on the fifth floor. If you have lost a coat and a scarf, please come to the customer service center. 우리는 5층 여자 화장실에서 코트와 스카프를 발견했습니다. 코트와 스카프를 분실하신 분은 고객 서비스 센터로 오십시오.

이유·목적 파악

■ 이유를 묻는 문제는 직접적으로 이유를 묻는 경우가 많으므로 그에 대한 대답을 집중해서 듣는다.
■ 목적을 묻는 문제는 인사말 바로 뒤나 대화의 앞부분에서 목적을 밝히는 경우가 많으므로 처음부터 집중해서 듣는다.

📄 대표 기출

🔊 MP3 유형 09

대화를 듣고, 여자가 헤드폰을 사지 <u>못한</u> 이유로 가장 적절한 것을 고르시오.

① 가격이 비싸서
② 가게가 문을 닫아서
③ 인터넷 연결이 안돼서
④ 원하는 색상이 모두 팔려서
⑤ 쇼핑 시간이 부족해서

(해결 전략)

• 남자의 말 Why not? 이후의 대화를 주의 깊게 들으세요.

W Hi, Roy. How was your weekend?
M Good, thanks. So did you buy the headphones for your brother?
W No, I couldn't.
M Why not?
W They didn't have the ones I wanted in the shop.
M What kind of headphones were you looking for?
W I wanted black ones, but they were sold out.
M Then maybe you can buy them online.
W Yeah. I'll try that.

여 안녕, Roy. 주말 어떻게 보냈어?
남 좋았어, 고마워. 남동생을 위한 헤드폰을 샀니?
여 아니, 못 샀어.
남 왜 못 샀어?
여 가게에 내가 원하던 헤드폰이 없었어.
남 어떤 종류의 헤드폰을 찾고 있었는데?
여 검정색을 원했는데, 그것들은 다 팔렸어.
남 그럼 아마 온라인에서 살 수 있을 거야.
여 그래. 한번 시도해 볼게.

정답 ④

💡 기출문제에 나온 표현

갈 수 없는 이유	A Wait, Bella! The bowling center is closed today. 잠깐만, Bella! 볼링 센터가 오늘 문을 닫았어. B Oh, no! Are you sure? 오, 이런! 정말이에요? A Yeah, it closes every first Sunday of the month. 응, 매달 첫째 주 일요일은 문을 닫는대.
거절한 이유	A Yuna, why don't we go to the movies tomorrow? 유나야, 우리 내일 영화 보러 가는 게 어때? B I'd love to, but I can't. I need to go to Mokpo with my family. 그러고 싶지만, 안 돼. 나는 가족들과 목포에 가야 하거든.
전화 목적	A Hello. Blue Star Tours. May I help you? 안녕하세요. Blue Star Tours입니다. 무엇을 도와드릴까요? B Hi, I'd like to change my flight schedule, please. 안녕하세요, 제 비행 일정을 변경하고 싶습니다.
방문 목적	A What brings you back to Korea? 한국에는 무슨 일로 다시 온 거니? B I'm here to meet the main actor of the movie, *Great Love*. 나는 영화 〈Great Love〉의 주연 배우를 만나기 위해 여기에 왔어.

유형 10

할 일·한 일 파악

- 지시문을 읽고, 누가 언제 할 일 또는 한 일을 묻는 문제인지 확인한다.
- 할 일을 파악하는 문제는 미래를 나타내는 동사에 유의하며 듣는다.
- 한 일을 파악하는 문제는 과거를 나타내는 동사에 유의하며 듣는다.

대표 기출
◁》 MP3 유형 10

대화를 듣고, 남자가 대화 직후에 할 일로 가장 적절한 것을 고르시오.

① 김치 담그기
② 저녁 준비하기
③ 점심 식사하기
④ 축구 하러 가기
⑤ 달걀 사러 가기

해결 전략

- 남자가 할 일이므로 남자의 말을 주의 깊게 들으세요.
- 대화 직후에 할 일은 주로 마지막 부분에 나오므로 끝까지 듣고 나서 답을 고르세요.

M Mom, we are going to have a class party tomorrow.

W Sounds interesting. What are you going to do?

M We're planning to play soccer first, and then make lunch for ourselves. *한정*

W Really? You're going to cook lunch? Do you need to bring anything?

M I need to bring some *kimchi* and eggs. We're making *kimchi* fried rice. *한정*

W We have *kimchi*, but no eggs at home. You should go and buy some. *정답 단서*

M Okay. I'll go now.

남 엄마, 우리는 내일 학급 파티를 열 거예요.
여 재미있겠다. 무엇을 할 예정이니?
남 먼저 축구를 하고, 그러고 나서 우리가 직접 점심을 만들 계획이에요.
여 정말? 점심을 요리할 거라고? 뭐 가져가야 하니?
남 김치와 달걀을 좀 가져가야 해요. 우리는 김치볶음밥을 만들 거예요.
여 집에 김치는 있지만, 달걀은 없구나. 네가 가서 좀 사 와야겠다.
남 알겠어요. 지금 갈게요.

정답 ⑤

기출문제에 나온 표현

할 일	A She runs a blog on Korean food. 그녀는 한국 음식에 대한 블로그를 운영해.
	B Then I need to visit her blog right now. 그럼 지금 당장 그녀의 블로그를 방문해봐야겠다.
	A How about cleaning your desk first? It's so dirty. 우선 네 책상을 치우는 게 어떠니? 너무 지저분하구나.
	B Okay. I'll clean it now. 알았어요. 지금 치울게요.
한 일	A How was your weekend? 주말 어땠니?
	B I went shopping with my mom last Sunday. 나는 지난주 일요일에 엄마랑 쇼핑했어.
	A What did you do during the lunch break? Did you play badminton again? 너 점심시간에 뭐 했니? 또 배드민턴을 쳤니?
	B No, not today. I went to the class farm to water the tomatoes. It's my turn today. 아니, 오늘은 안 했어. 나는 토마토에 물을 주려고 학급 농장에 갔어. 오늘 내가 당번이거든.

숫자 정보 파악

- '지불해야 할 금액'이나 '~할 시각'을 고르는 두 가지 형태의 문제로 출제된다.
- 금액을 묻는 문제는 물건의 가격이나 개수, 할인, 쿠폰 등의 정보를 종합하여 총액을 계산한다.
- 시각을 묻는 문제는 시각 정보가 여러 번 등장하므로 필요한 정보의 시각을 주의 깊게 듣는다.

대표 기출

🔊 MP3 유형 11

대화를 듣고, 여자가 지불해야 할 금액으로 가장 적절한 것을 고르시오.

① $5   ② $10   ③ $15
④ $18   ⑤ $20

(해결 전략)

- 주문하는 음식과 가격을 메모하면서 들으세요.
- 마지막에 여자가 쿠폰을 사용했으므로 남자가 말한 총액에서 쿠폰 가격을 빼세요.

M Hi. May I take your order?

W Yes. I want one seafood pizza, please.

M It's $18. Something to drink?

W Um... I'd like an orange juice, please.

M That's $2. So one seafood pizza and one orange juice, right?

W Yes. That's correct.

M Okay. The total comes to $20.

W Oh, wait! Can I use this $5 discount coupon? 한정

M Of course. Then it's $15 in total. 정답 단서

W All right. Here you are.

남 안녕하세요. 주문하시겠습니까?
여 네, 해산물 피자 하나 주세요.
남 18달러입니다. 뭐 마실 것을 드릴까요?
여 음… 오렌지 주스 주세요.
남 그건 2달러입니다. 그럼 해산물 피자 하나와 오렌지 주스 한 잔, 맞죠?
여 네, 맞아요.
남 좋아요. 총 금액은 20달러입니다.
여 오, 잠깐만요! 이 5달러 할인 쿠폰을 사용할 수 있나요?
남 물론이죠. 그럼 총 15달러입니다.
여 알겠어요. 여기 있습니다.

정답 ③

💡 기출문제에 나온 표현

금액	총액	The total comes to $20. 총 금액은 20달러입니다. It's $15 in total. 총 15달러입니다.
	쿠폰/할인	Can I use this $5 discount coupon? 이 5달러 할인 쿠폰을 사용할 수 있나요? Everything is 30% off. 모든 제품은 30퍼센트 할인됩니다. If you buy two, we will give you a 10% discount. 두 개를 사시면, 10퍼센트를 할인해 드립니다.
	가격	One dollar each for black and white or two dollars each for color. 흑백은 각 1달러, 컬러는 각 2달러입니다.
시각		How about 5:30? 5시 30분은 어때요? How about the 4 o'clock show? 4시 공연은 어때요? Let's meet here at 4 o'clock this afternoon. 오늘 오후 4시 정각에 여기서 만납시다. The repair person will be there at 5. 수리 기사가 5시에 그곳에 갈 겁니다. It takes 30 minutes to get there. 그곳에 도착하는 데 30분이 걸립니다.

부탁·요청한 일 파악

■ 지시문을 읽고, 누가 누구에게 하는 부탁·요청인지 확인한다.
■ 주로 대화의 마지막 부분에 부탁이나 요청하는 내용이 드러나므로 뒷부분을 주의 깊게 듣는다.
■ 부탁·요청하는 표현을 미리 익혀 둔다.

📄 대표 기출

🔊 MP3 유형 12

대화를 듣고, 남자가 여자에게 부탁한 일로 가장 적절한 것을 고르시오.

① 버스표 구입하기
② 입장료 알아보기
③ 식사 장소 알아보기
④ 미술 작품 알아보기
⑤ 미술관 위치 확인하기

해결 전략

• 남자가 부탁한 일을 고르는 문제이므로 남자의 말을 집중해서 들으세요.
• Can you ~?로 시작하는 남자의 마지막 말에 정답이 드러나요.

W Junkyu, how about going to the Modern Art Gallery for our field trip?

M How long does it take to get there from the school?

W It takes about one hour by bus. 함정

M Can we have lunch there?

W Hmm... I don't think so. Maybe we need to find a place to eat.

M Can you find a good restaurant nearby? 정답 단서

W All right. I'll look for one.

여 준규야, 우리 현장 학습으로 현대 미술관에 가는 게 어때?
남 학교에서 거기까지 가는 데 얼마나 걸리니?
여 버스로 한 시간 정도 걸려.
남 거기서 우리가 점심을 먹을 수 있을까?
여 음… 안 될 것 같아. 아마도 식사할 곳을 찾아야 할 것 같아.
남 근처에 괜찮은 식당을 찾아 줄 수 있어?
여 알았어. 내가 찾아볼게.

정답 ③

💡 기출문제에 나온 표현

부탁·요청하기 전에 상대방의 의사 묻기	Can I ask you a favor? 부탁 하나 해도 될까?
	Could you do me a favor? 부탁 하나 들어주시겠어요?
	Can you give me a hand? 좀 도와줄래?
부탁·요청하기	Can you tell me the website address? 나한테 웹사이트 주소를 알려 줄 수 있어?
	Can you carry my bag to the classroom for me? 교실까지 내 가방을 들어 줄 수 있어?
	Could you pass me some more cookies? 쿠키를 좀 더 건네주실 수 있어요?
	Please help me to set the table. 식탁 차리는 것 좀 도와주세요.
	Could you buy me her new comic book at the festival? 축제에서 그녀의 새 만화책을 내게 사다 줄 수 있어?
	Can you send him this package at the post office? 우체국에서 이 소포를 그에게 보내 줄 수 있어?
	Could you bring me some of your comic books? 나한테 네 만화책 몇 권을 가져다줄 수 있어?

언급하지 않은 것 찾기

- 선택지 순서대로 내용이 언급되는 경우가 많다.
- 선택지와 비교해 가면서 화자가 언급한 내용을 하나씩 지워 나간다.
- 끝까지 들은 후에 남아 있는 선택지를 답으로 고른다.

📄 대표 기출

🔊 MP3 유형 13

대화를 듣고, 남자가 금붕어에 대해 언급하지 <u>않은</u> 것을 고르시오.

① 구입 시기
② 어항 세척 횟수
③ 수온 유지
④ 먹이 주는 횟수
⑤ 산란기 주의 사항

(해결 전략)

- 남자가 언급하지 않은 것을 고르는 문제이므로 남자의 말을 주의 깊게 들으세요.
- 금붕어 구입 시기, 어항 세척 횟수, 수온 유지, 먹이 주는 횟수가 언급될 때마다 선택지를 하나씩 지우세요.

W Wow! Tom, you have beautiful goldfish.
M Yes. I bought them two weeks ago. *정답 단서*
W Oh, I want to raise some, too. Can you give me some tips?
M Well, firstly, you need to clean the fishbowl once a month. *정답 단서*
W Okay. Anything else?
M Keep the water temperature around 22 degrees. *정답 단서*
W Then how often should I feed them?
M Twice a day is enough. *정답 단서*
W Thanks. I'll keep those in mind.

여 와! Tom, 넌 아름다운 금붕어들을 가지고 있구나.
남 응. 2주 전에 샀어.
여 오, 나도 좀 키우고 싶은데. 조언 좀 해 줄래?
남 음. 우선 한 달에 한 번 어항을 청소해야 해.
여 알겠어. 또 다른 건?
남 수온을 약 22도로 유지해.
여 그럼 얼마나 자주 먹이를 줘야 해?
남 하루에 두 번이면 충분해.
여 고마워. 그것들을 명심할게.

정답 ⑤

💡 기출문제에 나온 표현

주제·화제	It'll be about how to recycle trash to make new things. 그것은 새로운 것을 만들기 위해 쓰레기를 재활용하는 방법에 대한 거야.
	I'd like to tell you about our school bus service. 저는 여러분께 학교 버스 서비스에 대해 말씀드리고 싶습니다.
개최 장소	It was held at Clean-Nature Center. 그것은 Clean-Nature Center에서 열렸어.
	We will have Job Experience Day in the student hall this Friday. 이번 주 금요일에 학생회관에서 Job Experience Day 행사가 열립니다.
일시·시각	The event will start at 9 a.m. 행사는 오전 9시에 시작합니다.
	Friday, April 19 is the grand opening of Electronic Plaza, our new store. 4월 19일 금요일에 저희의 새 가게인 Electronic Plaza가 개점합니다.
신청 방법	To sign up, fill out the form and give it to your class leader by this Wednesday. 신청하려면, 이번 주 수요일까지 신청서를 작성하여 반장에게 내세요.
요금	The bus fare is free for our students. 저희 학생들에게는 버스 요금이 무료입니다.
참가 대상	All second-year students can sign up. 2학년 학생들은 모두 신청할 수 있어.
사은품	All shoppers will get water bottles as welcoming gifts. 모든 쇼핑객들은 사은품으로 물병을 받을 것입니다.

일치하지 않는 것 찾기

- 선택지 순서대로 내용이 언급되는 경우가 많다.
- 선택지와 비교해 가면서 일치하는 내용을 하나씩 지워 나간다.
- 일치하지 않는 내용의 선택지는 일부 특정 정보가 다르게 제시되므로 세부 사항을 집중해서 듣는다.

📄 대표 기출

🔊 MP3 유형 14

다음을 듣고, 벼룩시장에 대한 내용과 일치하지 <u>않는</u> 것을 고르시오.

① 금요일에 실시된다.
② 아픈 아이들을 돕기 위한 행사이다.
③ 중고품을 판매한다.
④ 학교 강당에서 열린다.
⑤ 수요일까지 참가 신청이 가능하다.

해결 전략

- 선택지의 내용이 언급될 때마다 선택지를 하나씩 지우세요.
- 선택지에 제시된 요일, 목적, 장소 등의 특정 정보가 담화의 내용과 완전히 일치하는지 꼼꼼히 확인하세요.

W Hello, students. We're going to hold a school flea market this Friday. This event is to help the sick children in our town hospital. You can bring your used items to sell such as bags and books. It'll be held on the school playground. If you have any items to sell, please tell Ms. Brown by this Wednesday.

정답 단서 (throughout)

여 안녕하세요, 학생 여러분. 우리는 이번 주 금요일에 학교 벼룩시장을 열 예정입니다. 이 행사는 우리 동네 병원의 아픈 아이들을 돕기 위한 것입니다. 여러분은 가방이나 책과 같이 판매할 수 있는 중고품들을 가져올 수 있습니다. 벼룩시장은 학교 운동장에서 열릴 것입니다. 만약 팔 물건들이 있다면, 이번 주 수요일까지 Brown 선생님께 말씀드리세요.

정답 ④

💡 기출문제에 나온 표현

제품	It's for children from 3 to 5 years old. 3세에서 5세까지의 아이들을 위한 것입니다.
	It comes in two colors. 그것은 두 가지 색상으로 나옵니다.
	It's delivered for free. 배송료는 무료입니다.
강좌	There are two courses this spring, mornings and evenings. 올봄에 아침과 저녁, 두 가지 강좌가 있습니다.
	Each class takes only seven people. 반별 수강 인원은 7명입니다.
	The courses are free for students. 학생은 무료로 수강할 수 있습니다.
행사	It'll be held on the school playground. 그것은 학교 운동장에서 열릴 것입니다.
	There will be performances such as dancing, singing, and a magic show. 춤, 노래, 마술쇼와 같은 공연이 있을 것입니다.
시설 이용	We are open from 9 a.m. to 6 p.m. 저희는 오전 9시부터 오후 6시까지 엽니다.
	We are closed every Monday. 저희는 매주 월요일에 문을 닫습니다.
	There are free children's classes from 10 to 11 a.m. on Wednesdays. 매주 수요일 오전 10시에서 11시까지 무료 어린이 강좌가 있습니다.

그림의 상황에 적절한 대화 찾기

- 그림 속 상황, 장소, 두 사람의 관계 등을 빠르게 파악한다.
- 대화를 하나씩 들으면서 그림과 관련 없는 선택지를 지워 나간다.
- 그림과 관련된 대화의 선택지에 표시해 두었다가 끝까지 듣고 나서 알맞은 답을 골랐는지 확인한다.

📄 대표 기출

🔊 MP3 유형 15

다음 그림의 상황에 가장 적절한 대화를 고르시오.

① ② ③ ④ ⑤

① **W** Can I take your order?

　 M One chicken burger, please.

② **W** What time do you want to meet?

　 M Let's meet at five.

③ **W** Can I try this T-shirt on?   *정답 단서*

　 M Sure, go ahead.

④ **W** What's wrong with your arm?

　 M I broke it during a basketball game.

⑤ **W** Can you give me a ride?

　 M I'm sorry, but I can't.

(해결 전략)

- 대화를 듣기 전에 옷 가게에서 손님이 옷을 입어 보려는 상황임을 미리 파악할 수 있어요.
- 옷 가게와 관련 없는 대화를 순서대로 지워 나가세요.
- 옷 가게와 관련된 대화의 선택지에 표시를 한 후, 마지막 대화까지 듣고 답을 고르세요.

① 여 주문하시겠어요?
　남 치킨버거 하나 주세요.
② 여 몇 시에 만나고 싶니?
　남 5시에 만나자.
③ 여 이 티셔츠 입어 봐도 되나요?
　남 물론이죠, 그러세요.
④ 여 너 팔이 왜 그래?
　남 농구 경기 하다가 부러졌어.
⑤ 여 나 좀 태워 줄 수 있니?
　남 미안하지만, 안 돼.

정답 ③

💡 기출문제에 나온 표현

길을 묻고 답하는 상황	A Where is the nearest subway station? 가장 가까운 지하철역이 어디인가요? B It's next to the hospital over there. 저기 병원 옆에 있어요.
물을 엎지른 상황	A I'm so sorry. Let me clean that up for you. 정말 죄송해요. 제가 치울게요. B No worries. Anyone can make a mistake. 괜찮아요. 누구나 실수할 수 있죠.
사진 촬영을 금지하는 상황	A Can I take pictures of this painting? 이 그림의 사진을 찍어도 될까요? B Sorry. You are not allowed to take pictures here. 죄송합니다. 여기에서는 사진을 찍으실 수 없어요.

마지막 말에 이어질 응답 찾기

- 지시문을 읽고, 마지막 말을 하는 사람이 누구인지 확인한다.
- 각 선택지 문장에서 핵심이 되는 단어를 미리 파악해 둔다.
- 마지막 말에 이어질 응답을 찾는 문제이므로 마지막 말을 놓치지 않도록 주의한다.

대표 기출
🔊 MP3 유형 16

대화를 듣고, 남자의 마지막 말에 이어질 여자의 말로 가장 적절한 것을 고르시오.

Woman: _____

① I have a fever.
② It took 40 minutes by bus.
③ I play the piano very well.
④ My favorite food is spaghetti.
⑤ They're blue with white stripes.

M	Julia, you look worried. What happened?
W	I think I lost my new running shoes.
M	Sorry to hear that. Where did you put them last?
W	I think I put them in the locker this morning.
M	Are you sure?
W	Not really. I was in a hurry for the next class.
M	Okay. I'll help you to find them. What do your shoes look like?
W	_____

해결 전략

- 대화의 흐름을 따라가다가 뒷부분으로 갈수록 남자가 하는 말을 더욱 집중해서 들으세요.
- 남자가 마지막에 여자의 신발이 어떻게 생겼는지 물었으므로 이에 대한 응답을 답으로 고르세요.

남	Julia, 너 걱정스러워 보여. 무슨 일 있니?
여	새 운동화를 잃어버린 것 같아.
남	안됐구나. 마지막으로 어디에 두었니?
여	오늘 아침에 사물함에 넣어 둔 것 같아.
남	확실해?
여	그렇지는 않아. 내가 다음 수업 때문에 서둘렀거든.
남	그렇구나. 내가 운동화 찾는 걸 도와줄게. 신발이 어떻게 생겼니?
여	<u>흰색 줄무늬가 있는 파란색이야.</u>

정답 ⑤

 기출문제에 나온 표현

약속 시간 정하기	**A** Then do you want to meet in front of the post office at 7 p.m.? 그럼 오후 7시에 우체국 앞에서 만날까? **B** Yes, <u>see you there</u>. 그래, 거기에서 봐.
소요 시간 답하기	**A** How long will it take to get there by bus? 버스로 그곳까지 얼마나 걸릴까? **B** <u>It'll take about 15 minutes</u>. 15분 정도 걸릴 거야.
동의하기	**A** You should take him to Hanok Village. 그를 한옥 마을로 데리고 가 봐. **B** <u>That sounds good</u>. 그거 좋겠다.
조언하기	**A** He didn't answer my call. What should I do? 그가 내 전화를 안 받아. 어떻게 해야 하지? **B** <u>Text him that you are sorry</u>. 그에게 미안하다고 문자를 보내 봐.

PART

2

실전
모의고사
01-18회

1.0배속

1.2배속

01 다음을 듣고, 제주도의 날씨로 가장 적절한 것을 고르시오.

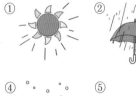

02 대화를 듣고, 남자가 구입할 책가방으로 가장 적절한 것을 고르시오.

03 대화를 듣고, 남자의 심정으로 가장 적절한 것을 고르시오.

① excited   ② proud   ③ scared
④ satisfied   ⑤ upset

04 대화를 듣고, 여자가 어제 한 일로 가장 적절한 것을 고르시오.

① 공원 청소하기   ② 울타리 칠하기
③ 친구들과 산책하기   ④ 할머니 댁 방문하기
⑤ 양로원에서 봉사하기

05 대화를 듣고, 두 사람이 대화하는 장소로 가장 적절한 곳을 고르시오.

① 병원   ② 학교   ③ 우체국
④ 수영장   ⑤ 도서관

06 대화를 듣고, 남자의 마지막 말의 의도로 가장 적절한 것을 고르시오.

① 동의   ② 염려   ③ 감사
④ 후회   ⑤ 거절

07 대화를 듣고, 두 사람이 연극을 볼 날짜와 요일을 고르시오.

① 11일 금요일   ② 12일 토요일
③ 13일 일요일   ④ 19일 토요일
⑤ 20일 일요일

08 대화를 듣고, 남자가 대화 직후에 할 일로 가장 적절한 것을 고르시오.

① 기차역 가기   ② 어머니 배웅하기
③ 휴대 전화 고치기   ④ 앱 다운로드하기
⑤ 할아버지 댁 방문하기

09 대화를 듣고, 두 사람이 밴드 경연 대회에 대해 언급하지 않은 것을 고르시오.

① 대회 날짜   ② 밴드 구성원
③ 참가자 수   ④ 신청 기한
⑤ 신청서 제출처

10 다음을 듣고, 여자가 하는 말의 내용으로 가장 적절한 것을 고르시오.

① 분실물 공지   ② 환경 정화 활동
③ 도서 대출 방법   ④ 도서관 폐관 시간
⑤ 서점 영업시간

11 대화를 듣고, 여자가 지불해야 할 금액으로 가장 적절한 것을 고르시오.

① $2   ② $4   ③ $6
④ $8   ⑤ $10

12 대화를 듣고, 여자가 주문할 음식을 고르시오.

① 더블 치즈버거   ② 샌드위치

③ 토마토 스파게티   ④ 매운맛 치킨

⑤ 불고기 피자

13 다음을 듣고, 아프리카코끼리에 대한 내용으로 일치하지 <u>않는</u> 것을 고르시오.

① 세계에서 가장 큰 육지 동물이다.

② 키가 3미터에 달한다.

③ 무게가 6,000킬로그램 정도 나간다.

④ 풀, 과일, 나무 등을 먹는다.

⑤ 귀가 커서 어깨를 따뜻하게 해 준다.

14 대화를 듣고, 두 사람의 관계로 가장 적절한 것을 고르시오.

① 교사 – 학생   ② 식당 종업원 – 손님

③ 은행원 – 고객   ④ 호텔 직원 – 투숙객

⑤ 여행사 직원 – 고객

15 대화를 듣고, 남자가 여자에게 요청한 일로 가장 적절한 것을 고르시오.

① 문법책 빌려주기

② 영어 숙제 알려 주기

③ 함께 문법 강의 듣기

④ 문자 메시지 확인하기

⑤ 웹 사이트 주소 보내 주기

16 대화를 듣고, 남자가 스웨터를 환불받지 <u>못한</u> 이유로 가장 적절한 것을 고르시오.

① 훼손되어서

② 이미 착용해서

③ 환불 기간이 지나서

④ 할인받은 품목이라서

⑤ 영수증을 잃어버려서

17 다음 그림의 상황에 가장 적절한 대화를 고르시오.

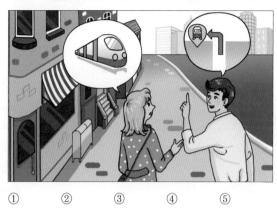

①   ②   ③   ④   ⑤

18 대화를 듣고, 두 사람이 감기를 낫게 하기 위한 방법으로 언급하지 <u>않은</u> 것을 고르시오.

① 약 먹기   ② 충분히 쉬기

③ 과일 먹기   ④ 물 많이 마시기

⑤ 병원 가기

[19-20] 대화를 듣고, 남자의 마지막 말에 이어질 여자의 말로 가장 적절한 것을 고르시오.

19 Woman: _____

① My favorite food is salad.

② That's exactly what I mean.

③ You should exercise every day.

④ I don't understand what you just said.

⑤ Eat more fruits and vegetables and less fast food.

20 Woman: _____

① I had a really great time.

② It was my favorite musical.

③ I already bought a ticket.

④ Luckily, yes. I'll never forget their voices.

⑤ I'm planning to go to another musical soon.

01 날씨 파악

다음을 듣고, 제주도의 날씨로 가장 적절한 것을 고르시오.

①   ②   ③

④   ⑤

W Good morning. This is today's weather report. It will snow in the Gangwon area _____ _____ _____ _____.
It will snow in Seoul in the afternoon. _____ _____ _____ of snow is up to three centimeters in Gangwon-do and about one centimeter in Seoul. It will rain in Busan, and the rain might _____ _____ _____ late at night. It will rain all day in Jeju-do. Please _____ _____ _____ your safety.
정답 단서

02 그림 정보 파악

대화를 듣고, 남자가 구입할 책가방으로 가장 적절한 것을 고르시오.

①   ②   ③

④   ⑤

Sound Clear ☆ **better**
미국식은 모음 사이의 [t]를 약하게 발음하여 [베러]로, 영국식은 [t]를 정확히 발음하여 [베터]로 발음된다.

W What are you doing?
M I'm looking for a backpack for my nephew. _____ _____ _____ _____ choose one?
W Sure. What about the one with stripes?
M It's not bad, but _____ _____ _____ something cute. *한정*
W How old is he?
M _____ _____ _____ _____.
W Then either the dinosaur-shaped one or the monkey-shaped one is best. *한정*
M I think he will _____ _____ _____ _____ better. ☆
I'll buy it.

03 심정 추론

대화를 듣고, 남자의 심정으로 가장 적절한 것을 고르시오.

① excited ② proud ③ scared
④ satisfied ⑤ upset

M Mom, I'm home. Is there a package for me?
W No, there isn't anything. _____ _____ _____ _____?
M I _____ _____ _____ _____, and it should be here today.
W _____ _____ _____ _____ _____?
M Yesterday.
W Well, then maybe you should wait _____ _____ _____.
M They said it would take only one day. I don't understand why it didn't come today.

04 한 일 파악

대화를 듣고, 여자가 어제 한 일로 가장 적절한 것을 고르시오.

① 공원 청소하기
② 울타리 칠하기
③ 친구들과 산책하기
④ 할머니 댁 방문하기
⑤ 양로원에서 봉사하기

W Where did you visit to do volunteer work yesterday?
M I visited the park near my house.
W Did you _____ _____ _____ and fallen leaves and branches?
M No. I helped paint a fence at the park. _____ _____ _____?
W I did volunteer work at a nursing home.
M What did you do there?
W I _____ _____ _____ take a walk.
M Sounds good.

05 장소 추론

대화를 듣고, 두 사람이 대화하는 장소로 가장 적절한 곳을 고르시오.

① 병원   ② 학교   ③ 우체국
④ 수영장   ⑤ 도서관

Sound Clear ☆ **examination**
ex 뒤에 모음이 오면 주로 [igz]로 소리 나서 [이그재미네이션]으로 발음된다.

M Hi, Jane. I'm sorry I'm late.
W That's okay.
M Are you all right? _____ _____ _____.
W I'm a little worried. It's my first time to have a physical examination.
M Just relax. _____ _____ _____ _____ because you exercise regularly.
W But I don't anymore. I _____ _____ _____ _____ _____ for two months.
M Oh, don't worry so much. Let's _____ _____ _____ _____ and register first.

06 의도 파악

대화를 듣고, 남자의 마지막 말의 의도로 가장 적절한 것을 고르시오.

① 동의   ② 염려   ③ 감사
④ 후회   ⑤ 거절

W Hi, Kevin. What are you doing?
M _____ _____ _____ _____ about abandoned animals.
W You mean street dogs and cats.
M Yeah. Many of them _____ _____ _____ on the streets. It's really sad.
W Maybe we can do _____ _____ _____ _____.
M What do you think we can do?
W When we _____ _____ _____, we can report them to animal shelters.
M That's a good idea.

07 특정 정보 파악

대화를 듣고, 두 사람이 연극을 볼 날짜와 요일을 고르시오.

① 11일 금요일 ② 12일 토요일
③ 13일 일요일 ④ 19일 토요일
⑤ 20일 일요일

Sound Clear ☆ **want to**
동일한 발음의 자음이 연이어 나오면 앞 자음 소리가 탈락하여 [원투]로 발음된다.

W Look at this poster! I want to watch this play.
M Me, too! Why don't we _____ _____ _____ _____ now?
W Good. How about Saturday, the 12th?
M Let me see. (*Pause*) _____ _____ _____ _____ _____ on the 12th.
W How about the next day?
M I have a family gathering on that day.
W _____ _____ _____ _____ _____? There are lots of seats available on Sunday.
M Okay. The 20th is fine for me, too.

08 할 일 파악

대화를 듣고, 남자가 대화 직후에 할 일로 가장 적절한 것을 고르시오.

① 기차역 가기
② 어머니 배웅하기
③ 휴대 전화 고치기
④ 앱 다운로드하기
⑤ 할아버지 댁 방문하기

M Mom, are you visiting Grandfather this Saturday?
W Yes. I'll _____ _____ in the morning to take the train.
M Did you already buy a ticket?
W No, not yet. I think I'll buy one at the station.
M _____ _____ _____ _____ the mobile app to buy your ticket? It's really convenient.
W Great. Will you download the app for me?
M Sure. I'll _____ _____ _____ _____.

09 언급하지 않은 것 찾기

대화를 듣고, 두 사람이 밴드 경연 대회에 대해 언급하지 않은 것을 고르시오.

① 대회 날짜   ② 밴드 구성원
③ 참가자 수   ④ 신청 기한
⑤ 신청서 제출처

W Do you know there's a band competition on September 13?
M Yes. I'll sing and Mike will play the keyboard. _____ _____ _____ a guitarist and a drummer.
W Can I join you? I can play the guitar.
M Really? Great! Then we only _____ _____ _____.
W Let's ask some other people in our class. When is the deadline to sign up?
M By this Friday. We need to _____ _____ _____ _____ _____ to the music teacher.
W I see. I'm sure we'll find a drummer before then.

10 주제 파악

다음을 듣고, 여자가 하는 말의 내용으로 가장 적절한 것을 고르시오.

① 분실물 공지
② 환경 정화 활동
③ 도서 대출 방법
④ 도서관 폐관 시간
⑤ 서점 영업시간

W May I have your attention, please? Thank you for visiting the library today. We'd like to _____ _____ that the library is going to close in 30 minutes. Please return the books to _____ _____ _____ _____ _____. Please throw your trash in the trash cans. Make sure you _____ _____ _____ _____ with you when you leave. Thank you for spending time with us here today.

11 숫자 정보 파악

대화를 듣고, 여자가 지불해야 할 금액으로 가장 적절한 것을 고르시오.

① $2 　　② $4 　　③ $6
④ $8 　　⑤ $10

W Hi. I'd like to _____ _____ _____ _____.
M All right. These books are $4 each.
W Can I get a bookstore membership discount?
M Yes, you can. Please _____ _____ _____ _____
_____.
W Here you are.
M Okay. You get a $1 discount _____ _____ _____.
W Great. Here's a $10 bill.
M Here are _____ _____ _____ _____.

12 특정 정보 파악

대화를 듣고, 여자가 주문할 음식을 고르시오.

① 더블 치즈버거　　② 샌드위치
③ 토마토 스파게티　　④ 매운맛 치킨
⑤ 불고기 피자

Sound Clear ☆ **What about**
[t]가 모음 사이에서 약화되고 뒤 단어의 첫 모음과 연음되어 [와러바웃]으로 발음된다.

W What _____ _____ _____ _____ _____?
M A double cheeseburger and a coke. What about you?
W I'm not sure. What do you recommend?
M I heard _____ _____ _____ _____ is very good, especially the spicy kind. Try it.
W Well, I had some chicken last night. I _____ _____
_____.
M The tomato spaghetti is good, too. Do you like spaghetti?
W I do. _____ _____ _____ _____.

13 일치하지 않는 것 찾기

다음을 듣고, 아프리카코끼리에 대한 내용으로 일치하지 <u>않는</u> 것을 고르시오.

① 세계에서 가장 큰 육지 동물이다.
② 키가 3미터에 달한다.
③ 무게가 6,000킬로그램 정도 나간다.
④ 풀, 과일, 나무 등을 먹는다.
⑤ 귀가 커서 어깨를 따뜻하게 해 준다.

M African elephants are the _____ _____ _____
_____. They can reach 3 meters tall and weigh about 6,000 kilograms. Because of their massive size, they need to _____ _____ _____ _____ _____. They can eat as much as 150 kilograms of food a day, which includes grasses, fruits, and trees. They are famous for their very large ears. The large ears cover their shoulders and _____
_____ _____ under the hot African sun.

14 관계 추론

대화를 듣고, 두 사람의 관계로 가장 적절한 것을 고르시오.

① 교사 – 학생
② 식당 종업원 – 손님
③ 은행원 – 고객
④ 호텔 직원 – 투숙객
⑤ 여행사 직원 – 고객

W Good morning. How can I help you?
M I'd like to check out now. Here is my key.
W Okay. Please wait a moment, and I'll _____ _____
_____ _____. (*Pause*) Here you are.
M Thank you. _____ _____ _____ a gift shop near here?
W We have a souvenir shop on the second floor. You can _____ _____ _____ _____ there.
M That's good to know. Thank you.
W You're welcome. Enjoy shopping and _____ _____
_____ _____ back home.

15 요청한 일 파악

대화를 듣고, 남자가 여자에게 요청한 일로 가장 적절한 것을 고르시오.

① 문법책 빌려주기
② 영어 숙제 알려 주기
③ 함께 문법 강의 듣기
④ 문자 메시지 확인하기
⑤ 웹 사이트 주소 보내 주기

(*Cellphone rings.*)

W Hello, Hajun. What's up?

M Hey, _____ _____ _____ because you didn't answer my message.

W Oh, I'm sorry. I didn't see your message. _____ _____ _____ _____ ?

M I'm worried about my English essay because _____ _____ _____ grammar. I need your help.

W Well, there's a website that can check your grammar for you.

M Oh, that will help. Can you send me the address?

W Sure. I'll _____ _____ _____ 정답 단서 _____ right away.

M Thanks a lot.

16 이유 파악

대화를 듣고, 남자가 스웨터를 환불받지 <u>못한</u> 이유로 가장 적절한 것을 고르시오.

① 훼손되어서
② 이미 착용해서
③ 환불 기간이 지나서
④ 할인받은 품목이라서
⑤ 영수증을 잃어버려서

Sound Clear ☆ **coupon**
'쿠폰'은 실제로 [쿠판]으로 발음된다.

W Charles, _____ _____ _____. Anything wrong?

M I wanted to get a refund for this sweater, but I couldn't.

W Why not? _____ _____ _____ your receipt?

M Of course, I did.

W Then _____ _____ _____ _____ ?

M The person said there are no refunds or exchanges on discounted items. 정답 단서

W Right. You bought it with a discount ☆ coupon, didn't you?

M Yes. But the cashier didn't tell me that _____ _____ _____ _____ .

17 그림의 상황에 적절한 대화 찾기

다음 그림의 상황에 가장 적절한 대화를 고르시오.

① ② ③ ④ ⑤

① W Do you mind if I open the window?
　 M No, _____ _____ _____. Go ahead.

② W How many more stops should I go to get to Grand Park?
　 M I'm sorry, but _____ _____ _____ _____ .

③ W Your eyes are red. Are you all right?
　 M I'm just _____ _____ _____ .

④ W How was your trip to London?
　 M It was great. I visited many places.

⑤ W Can you tell me how to get to the subway station?
　 M Go straight down this street and _____ _____ _____ _____ .

18 언급하지 않은 것 찾기 ✳

대화를 듣고, 두 사람이 감기를 낫게 하기 위한 방법으로 언급하지 않은 것을 고르시오.

① 약 먹기   ② 충분히 쉬기
③ 과일 먹기   ④ 물 많이 마시기
⑤ 병원 가기

> **Sound Clear** ☆ **vitamin**
> 미국식은 [바이러민]으로, 영국식은 [비터민]으로 발음된다.

W   I have a terrible cold.
M   Did you _____ _____ _____?
W   Yes. I'm also taking vitamin C.
M   Are you _____ _____ _____?
W   That's the problem. I have a lot of work to do every day.
M   Getting enough rest is important. You also need to _____ _____ _____ _____ _____.
W   Okay. I'll try. If I don't get better soon, I'll _____ _____ _____ _____ _____.
M   Yeah. You probably should.

19 마지막 말에 이어질 응답 찾기

대화를 듣고, 남자의 마지막 말에 이어질 여자의 말로 가장 적절한 것을 고르시오.

Woman: _____

① My favorite food is salad.
② That's exactly what I mean.
③ You should exercise every day.
④ I don't understand what you just said.
⑤ Eat more fruits and vegetables and less fast food.

W   What's your favorite food?
M   Hamburgers. I _____ _____ _____ _____ every day.
W   Every day? That's not good for your health.
M   I know. But I love eating them, and _____ _____ _____.
W   But you might not stay healthy. You should _____ _____ _____.
M   _____ _____ _____ _____ by that?
W   Eat more fruits and vegetables and less fast food.

20 마지막 말에 이어질 응답 찾기

대화를 듣고, 남자의 마지막 말에 이어질 여자의 말로 가장 적절한 것을 고르시오.

Woman: _____

① I had a really great time.
② It was my favorite musical.
③ I already bought a ticket.
④ Luckily, yes. I'll never forget their voices.
⑤ I'm planning to go to another musical soon.

M   Hi, Julie. Did you _____ _____ _____ _____ yesterday?
W   Yes, I did.
M   How was it? Did you like it?
W   I really enjoyed it, but _____ _____ _____ _____ my seat.
M   What was wrong with it?
W   It was hard to see the actors _____ _____ _____.
M   Oh, then were you able to hear their voices well?
W   Luckily, yes. I'll never forget their voices.

1.0배속

1.2배속

01 다음을 듣고, 크리스마스의 날씨로 가장 적절한 것을 고르시오.

①   ②   ③

④   ⑤

02 대화를 듣고, 남자가 구입할 스마트폰 케이스로 가장 적절한 것을 고르시오.

①   ②   ③

④   ⑤

03 대화를 듣고, 남자의 심정으로 가장 적절한 것을 고르시오.

① sorry   ② excited   ③ scared
④ nervous   ⑤ satisfied

04 대화를 듣고, 여자가 도서 박람회에서 한 일로 가장 적절한 것을 고르시오.

① 도서 구입하기   ② 물품 판매하기
③ 기념사진 찍기   ④ 작가의 사인 받기
⑤ 롤 모델 인터뷰하기

05 대화를 듣고, 두 사람이 대화하는 장소로 가장 적절한 곳을 고르시오.

① 식당   ② 호텔   ③ 옷 가게
④ 미용실   ⑤ 사진관

06 대화를 듣고, 여자의 마지막 말의 의도로 가장 적절한 것을 고르시오.

① 사과   ② 불평   ③ 감사
④ 거절   ⑤ 제안

07 대화를 듣고, 여자가 구입할 식품을 고르시오.

① 빵   ② 달걀   ③ 마요네즈
④ 과일   ⑤ 우유

08 대화를 듣고, 여자가 대화 직후에 할 일로 가장 적절한 것을 고르시오.

① 장보기   ② 청소하기   ③ 빨래하기
④ 책 읽기   ⑤ 설거지하기

09 다음을 듣고, 남자가 하는 말의 내용으로 가장 적절한 것을 고르시오.

① 미세 먼지 해결책
② 환경 오염의 심각성
③ 한중 교류의 중요성
④ 오늘의 미세 먼지 수치
⑤ 강연 주제와 강사 소개

10 대화를 듣고, 남자가 스카이다이빙에 대해 언급하지 않은 것을 고르시오.

① 체험 시기   ② 체험 장소   ③ 체험 소감
④ 예약 방법   ⑤ 할인 방법

11 대화를 듣고, 두 사람이 준비할 파티에 대한 내용으로 일치하지 않는 것을 고르시오.

① 부모님의 결혼기념일을 위한 것이다.
② 사진첩을 만들 것이다.
③ 편지를 쓸 것이다.
④ 케이크를 주문할 것이다.
⑤ 풍선으로 집을 장식할 것이다.

12 대화를 듣고, 여자가 전화를 건 목적으로 가장 적절한 것을 고르시오.

① 주문을 취소하기 위해서
② 환불을 요청하기 위해서
③ 주문 품목을 추가하기 위해서
④ 주문 수량을 변경하기 위해서
⑤ 배송 날짜를 문의하기 위해서

13 대화를 듣고, 남자가 지불해야 할 금액으로 가장 적절한 것을 고르시오.

① $10   ② $13   ③ $15
④ $18   ⑤ $20

14 대화를 듣고, 두 사람의 관계로 가장 적절한 것을 고르시오.

① 의사 – 간호사   ② 약사 – 환자
③ 학부모 – 교사   ④ 식당 종업원 – 손님
⑤ 마트 직원 – 손님

15 대화를 듣고, 남자가 여자에게 부탁한 일로 가장 적절한 것을 고르시오.

① 발표 자료 만들기
② USB 가져다주기
③ 이메일로 파일 보내 주기
④ 발표 연습 도와주기
⑤ 책상 정리하기

16 대화를 듣고, 여자가 독서 동아리에 가입한 이유로 가장 적절한 것을 고르시오.

① 장래 희망과 관련이 있어서
② 친한 친구가 권유해서
③ 책을 더 많이 읽기 위해서
④ 책 읽는 습관을 갖기 위해서
⑤ 책에 대해 토론하는 것을 좋아해서

17 다음을 듣고, 여자가 졸업 음악 축제에 대해 언급하지 않은 것을 고르시오.

① 날짜   ② 장소
③ 참가 대상   ④ 공연 제한 시간
⑤ 참가 학급 수

18 다음 그림의 상황에 가장 적절한 대화를 고르시오.

①   ②   ③   ④   ⑤

[19-20] 대화를 듣고, 여자의 마지막 말에 이어질 남자의 말로 가장 적절한 것을 고르시오.

19 Man: _____

① I'm looking forward to it.
② You have to learn English.
③ No. I don't think she can come.
④ Sure. Sign up before Wednesday.
⑤ Sign language is difficult to learn.

20 Man: _____

① I prefer rice noodles, too.
② No. We'll have to look it up.
③ You don't have to lose weight.
④ I'm sorry. You have the wrong number.
⑤ Okay. It'll take more than 30 minutes.

01 날씨 파악 ❋

다음을 듣고, 크리스마스의 날씨로 가장 적절한 것을 고르시오.

①
②
③
④
⑤

Sound Clear ☆ **around the**

자음 세 개가 연속으로 나오면 중간 자음의 발음이 약화되어 [어롸운더]로 발음된다.

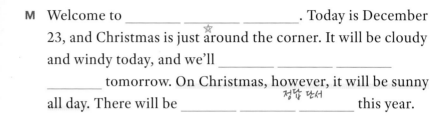

M Welcome to _____ _____ _____. Today is December 23, and Christmas is just around the corner. It will be cloudy and windy today, and we'll _____ _____ _____ _____ tomorrow. On Christmas, however, it will be sunny all day. There will be _____ _____ _____ this year.

02 그림 정보 파악

대화를 듣고, 남자가 구입할 스마트폰 케이스로 가장 적절한 것을 고르시오.

①
②
③
④
⑤

W Hello. How may I help you?
M _____ _____ _____ a smartphone case.
W Okay. How about this striped one?
M Actually, it's for my younger sister. _____ _____ _____ _____ _____ a striped phone case.
W I see. What about this one with the big heart in the center?
M I think _____ _____ _____.
W Then how about this one with three small hearts and the word "HAPPY" below?
M Oh, that's cute. _____ _____ _____.

03 심정 추론

대화를 듣고, 남자의 심정으로 가장 적절한 것을 고르시오.

① sorry ② excited ③ scared
④ nervous ⑤ satisfied

W How was your audition for the student singing club?
M _____ _____ _____.
W Good for you! But you don't look happy. What's the matter?
M My best friend, Somin, _____ _____ _____.
W Oh, didn't you two practice together all the time?
M Yeah. She is the one who _____ _____ _____ _____ _____ well.
W I know.
M She has to _____ _____ _____ for the next audition. That's too long.

04 한 일 파악

대화를 듣고, 여자가 도서 박람회에서 한 일로 가장 적절한 것을 고르시오.

① 도서 구입하기　　② 물품 판매하기
③ 기념사진 찍기　　④ 작가의 사인 받기
⑤ 롤 모델 인터뷰하기

> **Sound Clear ☆ hour**
> h가 묵음이라서 [아워]로 발음된다.

M　Sue, how was the book fair last weekend?
W　It was so great. You know, Suzanne Jones, my favorite author.
M　You said she is your role model. Did you meet her?
W　Yes! She was _____ _____ _____ at the fair.
M　Great. Did you get her autograph?
W　Yes! I waited for an hour, but _____ _____ _____
　　_____.
M　Awesome. Did you take a picture with her, too?
W　No. The line was too long, so they _____ _____
　　_____.

05 장소 추론　　❄

대화를 듣고, 두 사람이 대화하는 장소로 가장 적절한 곳을 고르시오.

① 식당　　② 호텔　　③ 옷 가게
④ 미용실　　⑤ 사진관

M　Hello. I _____ _____ _____ for 2 p.m.
W　Your name is?
M　Steve Kim.
W　Okay, Mr. Kim. _____ _____ _____ _____, please. (*Pause*) So how do you want your hair done?
M　I just want a trim.
W　_____ _____ _____ _____? Perms for men are popular these days.
M　Not this time. Keep the same hairstyle and just trim it, please.

06 의도 파악

대화를 듣고, 여자의 마지막 말의 의도로 가장 적절한 것을 고르시오.

① 사과　　② 불평　　③ 감사
④ 거절　　⑤ 제안

W　You look very tired. What's wrong?
M　_____ _____ _____ _____ these days.
W　Why not?
M　I'm staying in the school dormitory, but my roommate _____ _____ _____.
W　That sounds terrible. Have you talked to him about it?
M　I have. He _____ _____ _____ _____, but there is not much he can do.
W　Why don't you use earplugs? They will help.

07 특정 정보 파악

대화를 듣고, 여자가 구입할 식품을 고르시오.

① 빵　　② 달걀　　③ 마요네즈
④ 과일　　⑤ 우유

W　What are you making, Dad?
M　I'm making fruit salad for the picnic. Is there _____ _____ _____ _____ _____?
W　Um, I want an egg sandwich.
M　I can _____ _____ _____ _____. Bring me some boiled eggs, the mayonnaise, and some bread.
W　Okay. (*Pause*) I have _____ _____ _____ _____ _____ here, but there's no bread left. I'll go out to get some now.
M　Great. Thanks.

08 할 일 파악

대화를 듣고, 여자가 대화 직후에 할 일로 가장 적절한 것을 고르시오.

① 장보기 ② 청소하기
③ 빨래하기 ④ 책 읽기
⑤ 설거지하기

M Honey, ________ ________ ________ ________?
W No, I'm just reading. Why?
M We have to ________ ________ ________ ________. My parents are coming over.
W You're right. I'll wash the dishes.
M ________ ________ ________ ________. I already did them.
W Then what do you want me to do?
M Will you vacuum the house? ________ ________ ________ ________ at the store.
W Okay. I'll do that now.

09 주제 파악

다음을 듣고, 남자가 하는 말의 내용으로 가장 적절한 것을 고르시오.

① 미세 먼지 해결책
② 환경 오염의 심각성
③ 한중 교류의 중요성
④ 오늘의 미세 먼지 수치
⑤ 강연 주제와 강사 소개

M Welcome to today's special lecture. Nowadays, ________ ________ ________ ________ ________ fine dust, one of our society's serious problems. I hope today's lecture can ________ ________ ________ ________ ________ better. Julie Parker is an environmentalist who has been studying this issue ________ ________ ________ ________ ________. Let's give a big hand for today's guest lecturer, Julie Parker.

10 언급하지 않은 것 찾기

대화를 듣고, 남자가 스카이다이빙에 대해 언급하지 않은 것을 고르시오.

① 체험 시기 ② 체험 장소
③ 체험 소감 ④ 예약 방법
⑤ 할인 방법

Sound Clear☆ try
[t]와 [r]이 연달아 나와 [츄라이]로 발음된다.

W Eric, ________ ________ ________ ________ skydiving?
M Yes, I have. Actually, I did it last month.
W Really? How was it?
M It was so thrilling! You must try☆ it.
W Awesome. I really ________ ________ ________ ________.
M Check out "Freefall Skydiving" on the Net. You can ________ ________ ________ on the website.
W Cool. Send me the address later.
M I will. Oh, don't forget to ________ ________ ________ ________, too.
W That's a good tip. Thanks.

11 일치하지 않는 것 찾기

대화를 듣고, 두 사람이 준비할 파티에 대한 내용으로 일치하지 않는 것을 고르시오.

① 부모님의 결혼기념일을 위한 것이다.
② 사진첩을 만들 것이다.
③ 편지를 쓸 것이다.
④ 케이크를 주문할 것이다.
⑤ 풍선으로 집을 장식할 것이다.

Sound Clear ☆ **love it**
앞 단어의 끝 자음과 뒤 단어의 모음이 만나 연음되어 [러빗]으로 발음된다.

W ________ ________ ________ ________ Mom and Dad's wedding anniversary?
M ________ ________ ________ ________ a photo album for them?
W That's a great idea. They will love☆ it.
M Let's write a letter and make a special cake, too.
W Make a cake? ________ ________ ________ ________? (정답 단서)
M I have baked a cake with my baking club. I think I can do it.
W Good. Then I will ________ ________ ________ with balloons.
M Fantastic.

12 목적 파악

대화를 듣고, 여자가 전화를 건 목적으로 가장 적절한 것을 고르시오.

① 주문을 취소하기 위해서
② 환불을 요청하기 위해서
③ 주문 품목을 추가하기 위해서
④ 주문 수량을 변경하기 위해서
⑤ 배송 날짜를 문의하기 위해서

(*Telephone rings.*)
M Best T-shirt. How may I help you?
W Hello. I want to ________ ________ ________.
M Your name, please?
W Michelle Miller. I ordered thirty Wonder Woman T-shirts.
M Okay, let me check. (*Typing sound*) ________ ________ ________ ________ ________ change it?
W I want to order twenty, not thirty.
M All right. ________ ________ ________ ________ ________. (정답 단서) Anything else?
W That's it. Thank you.

13 숫자 정보 파악

대화를 듣고, 남자가 지불해야 할 금액으로 가장 적절한 것을 고르시오.

① $10 ② $13 ③ $15
④ $18 ⑤ $20

M Hi. I'd like to buy some kiwis. How much are they?
W A pack of kiwis is $8. There are ________ ________ ________ ________ ________.
M I'll take one pack.
W Okay. Anything else?
M ________ ________ ________ ________ ________?
W These are $1 each, and those organic ones are ________ ________ ________.
M I'll buy the organic ones. ________ ________ ________, please.
W So a pack of kiwis and five organic apples, right?
M That's correct. Here you are.

14 관계 추론

대화를 듣고, 두 사람의 관계로 가장 적절한 것을 고르시오.

① 의사 – 간호사　　② 약사 – 환자
③ 학부모 – 교사　　④ 식당 종업원 – 손님
⑤ 마트 직원 – 손님

Sound Clear ☆ **symptoms**
자음 세 개가 연속으로 나오면 중간 자음의 발음이 약화되어 [심텀스]로 발음된다.

M　Hi. I think I've got a cold. _____ _____ _____ _____ _____ for it?
W　What are your symptoms?
M　I have a runny nose and a sore throat.
W　Do you _____ _____ _____?
M　No, I don't.
W　Okay. I can give you these pills. Take two _____ _____ _____ _____.
M　All right. How much is it?
W　It's $5.

15 부탁한 일 파악

대화를 듣고, 남자가 여자에게 부탁한 일로 가장 적절한 것을 고르시오.

① 발표 자료 만들기
② USB 가져다주기
③ 이메일로 파일 보내 주기
④ 발표 연습 도와주기
⑤ 책상 정리하기

(*Cellphone rings.*)
M　Hello, Mom. It's me. I'm _____ _____ _____.
W　Oh, Martin, what's wrong?
M　I saved my presentation file on my USB, but _____ _____ _____ _____ _____. It's on my desk.
W　Oh, do you want me to bring it to school?
M　Can you just email me the file? The file name is "Science Project."
W　No problem. I'll _____ _____ _____ _____.
M　Thank you so much, Mom.

16 이유 파악

대화를 듣고, 여자가 독서 동아리에 가입한 이유로 가장 적절한 것을 고르시오.

① 장래 희망과 관련이 있어서
② 친한 친구가 권유해서
③ 책을 더 많이 읽기 위해서
④ 책 읽는 습관을 갖기 위해서
⑤ 책에 대해 토론하는 것을 좋아해서

M　Susan, _____ _____ _____ _____ _____ _____?
W　I'm in the book club. I like reading.
M　_____ _____ _____ _____ do you read in the club?
W　We read all kinds of books, but mostly novels.
M　Did you join so you would _____ _____ _____?
W　No. I joined it because I like to discuss the books I read with others.
M　It sounds like _____ _____ _____ _____ _____.

17 언급하지 않은 것 찾기

다음을 듣고, 여자가 졸업 음악 축제에 대해 언급하지 않은 것을 고르시오.

① 날짜　　② 장소
③ 참가 대상　　④ 공연 제한 시간
⑤ 참가 학급 수

W　Hello, students. The graduation music festival for this year _____ _____ _____ _____ _____ on February 15 in the auditorium. This festival is for everyone _____ _____ _____ _____ Narae Middle School this year. All third-grade students will participate. Each class will do a singing and dancing performance. It _____ _____ _____ _____ five minutes. Prepare well and see you at the festival!

18 그림의 상황에 적절한 대화 찾기

다음 그림의 상황에 가장 적절한 대화를 고르시오.

① ② ③ ④ ⑤

Sound Clear ☆ **Have you**
[v]가 뒤의 반모음 [j]를 만나 연음되어 [해뷰]로 발음된다.

① W Have you been to Namsan Seoul Tower?
  M No, I haven't.
② W Let's take a picture here.
  M Good. _____ _____ _____ my smartphone camera.
③ W Can I take pictures during the concert?
  M I'm sorry. You're _____ _____ _____ _____ that.
④ W _____ _____ _____ _____ in your free time?
  M I usually watch Korean dramas.
⑤ W _____ _____ _____ to take pictures here?
  M No. Taking pictures is not allowed in this museum.

19 마지막 말에 이어질 응답 찾기

대화를 듣고, 여자의 마지막 말에 이어질 남자의 말로 가장 적절한 것을 고르시오.

Man: _____

① I'm looking forward to it.
② You have to learn English.
③ No. I don't think she can come.
④ Sure. Sign up before Wednesday.
⑤ Sign language is difficult to learn.

M _____ _____ _____ _____ sign language. Are you interested in joining me?
W Sign language? What for?
M I think _____ _____ _____ for my volunteer work next semester.
W Where are you going to learn it?
M At the community center. There is _____ _____ _____ _____.
W Sounds like _____ _____ _____ _____. Can I take the class?
M Sure. Sign up before Wednesday.

20 마지막 말에 이어질 응답 찾기

대화를 듣고, 여자의 마지막 말에 이어질 남자의 말로 가장 적절한 것을 고르시오.

Man: _____

① I prefer rice noodles, too.
② No. We'll have to look it up.
③ You don't have to lose weight.
④ I'm sorry. You have the wrong number.
⑤ Okay. It'll take more than 30 minutes.

W I don't want to cook. Let's just _____ _____.
M Good idea. What do you want to eat?
W _____ _____ _____ fried chicken or hamburgers.
M Well, you know, _____ _____ _____ _____ _____.
W All right. Then what should we eat?
M How about *bibimbap*? It's _____ _____ _____.
W Okay. Do you know the number for the delivery service?
M No. We'll have to look it up.

Review Test

Word Check 영어는 우리말로, 우리말은 영어로 써 보기

01	expected	13	경연 대회
02	register	14	안전
03	stripe	15	상기시키다
04	package	16	약을 먹다
05	article	17	추천하다
06	volunteer work	18	영수증
07	garbage	19	건강 검진
08	stay healthy	20	이용할 수 있는
09	stranger	21	고통받다
10	sign up	22	소지품
11	abandoned	23	연세가 드신
12	get a refund	24	목소리

Expression Check 알맞은 표현을 넣어 문장 완성하기

25 The rain might _____ _____ snow late at night. 밤늦게 비가 눈으로 바뀔 가능성이 있습니다.

26 I helped elderly people _____ _____ _____. 나는 어르신들이 산책하시는 것을 도왔어.

27 Why don't we _____ _____ online _____ now? 지금 온라인으로 예매하는 게 어때?

28 We need to _____ _____ an application form to the music teacher.
우리는 음악 선생님께 신청서를 내야 해.

29 If I don't _____ _____ soon, I'll go to see a doctor. 나는 빨리 낫지 않으면, 병원에 가 볼 거야.

30 I _____ not _____ _____ my seat. 자리는 만족스럽지 못했어.

Answers p.12

Word Check 영어는 우리말로, 우리말은 영어로 써 보기

01 all day _____

02 audition _____

03 sign language _____

04 book fair _____

05 thrilling _____

06 autograph _____

07 dormitory _____

08 boiled _____

09 snore _____

10 vacuum _____

11 look up _____

12 fine dust _____

13 요즘 _____

14 축하하다, 기념하다 _____

15 공연 _____

16 팩, 상자 _____

17 유기농의 _____

18 무서워하는 _____

19 증상 _____

20 발표 _____

21 강연 _____

22 결혼기념일 _____

23 맞는, 정확한 _____

24 강당 _____

Expression Check 알맞은 표현을 넣어 문장 완성하기

25 Today is December 23, and Christmas is just _____ _____ _____.
오늘은 12월 23일로, 크리스마스가 임박했습니다.

26 I _____ _____ _____ for 2 p.m. 저는 오후 2시에 예약되어 있어요.

27 _____ _____ "Freefall Skydiving" on the Net. 인터넷에서 'Freefall Skydiving'을 찾아봐.

28 I _____ a runny nose and a _____ _____ _____. 저는 콧물이 나오고 목이 따끔거려요.

29 I'm _____ big _____. 저 큰일 났어요.

30 This festival is for everyone who will _____ _____ Narae Middle School this year.
이 축제는 올해 나래중학교를 졸업하는 모두를 위한 것입니다.

01 다음을 듣고, 내일 오후의 날씨로 가장 적절한 것을 고르시오.

 ①   ②   ③

 ④   ⑤

02 대화를 듣고, 남자가 그린 그림으로 가장 적절한 것을 고르시오.

 ①   ②   ③

 ④   ⑤

03 대화를 듣고, 여자가 마지막에 느꼈을 심정으로 가장 적절한 것을 고르시오.

① scared   ② bored   ③ frustrated
④ relieved   ⑤ curious

04 대화를 듣고, 두 사람이 대화하는 장소로 가장 적절한 곳을 고르시오.

① 서점   ② 도서관   ③ 미술관
④ 우체국   ⑤ 컴퓨터실

05 대화를 듣고, 여자의 마지막 말의 의도로 가장 적절한 것을 고르시오.

① 조언   ② 거절   ③ 감사
④ 허락   ⑤ 위로

06 대화를 듣고, 여자가 여행 중 가장 좋았던 것을 고르시오.

① 일광욕   ② 수영   ③ 등산
④ 석양   ⑤ 숙소

07 대화를 듣고, 남자가 대화 직후에 할 일로 가장 적절한 것을 고르시오.

① 친구를 만나러 간다.
② 친구에게 선물을 보낸다.
③ 친구에게 전화를 한다.
④ 친구의 블로그에 들어간다.
⑤ 친구에게 사과 편지를 쓴다.

08 다음을 듣고, 여자가 사촌에 대해 언급하지 <u>않은</u> 것을 고르시오.

① 이름   ② 나이   ③ 출생지
④ 직업   ⑤ 성격

09 다음을 듣고, 남자가 하는 말의 내용으로 가장 적절한 것을 고르시오.

① 겨울 방학 계획   ② 스노보드의 장점
③ 동아리 회원 모집   ④ 스포츠 강습 홍보
⑤ 건강 관리의 중요성

10 대화를 듣고, 여자가 전화를 건 목적으로 가장 적절한 것을 고르시오.

① 숙제를 물어보기 위해서
② 약속 시간을 정하기 위해서
③ 숙제 출력을 부탁하기 위해서
④ 이메일 주소를 물어보기 위해서
⑤ 프린터 수리를 요청하기 위해서

11 대화를 듣고, 남자가 지불해야 할 금액으로 가장 적절한 것을 고르시오.

① $72   ② $80   ③ $90
④ $92   ⑤ $100

12 다음을 듣고, 동물원에 대한 설명으로 일치하지 <u>않는</u> 것을 고르시오.

① 국내에서 가장 큰 동물원이다.
② 전 세계의 다양한 동물들이 있다.
③ 판다는 특정 기간에만 볼 수 있다.
④ 사파리 버스 투어는 주말에 할 수 있다.
⑤ 매일 오전 10시부터 오후 6시까지 개장한다.

13 대화를 듣고, 두 사람의 관계로 가장 적절한 것을 고르시오.

① 교사 – 학생   ② 의사 – 환자
③ 경찰관 – 시민   ④ 식당 종업원 – 손님
⑤ 비행기 승무원 – 탑승객

14 대화를 듣고, 여자가 이용할 교통수단을 고르시오.

① 버스   ② 택시   ③ 지하철
④ 자전거   ⑤ 버스와 지하철

15 대화를 듣고, 여자가 남자에게 부탁한 일로 가장 적절한 것을 고르시오.

① 쿠키 만들기   ② 함께 자원봉사하기
③ 쿠키 포장하기   ④ 쿠키 재료 사 오기
⑤ 봉사 활동 홍보하기

16 다음 그림의 상황에 가장 적절한 대화를 고르시오.

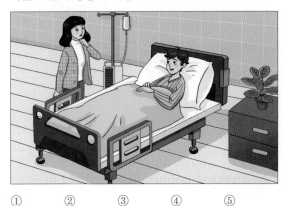

①   ②   ③   ④   ⑤

17 대화를 듣고, 두 사람이 뷔페에 가지 <u>못한</u> 이유로 가장 적절한 것을 고르시오.

① 시간이 부족해서
② 쿠폰을 잃어버려서
③ 영화관에서 너무 멀어서
④ 쿠폰 사용 시간이 지나서
⑤ 남자가 해산물을 좋아하지 않아서

18 다음을 듣고, 여자가 파티에 대해 언급하지 <u>않은</u> 것을 고르시오.

① 일시   ② 장소   ③ 입장료
④ 경품 행사   ⑤ 문의 방법

[19-20] 대화를 듣고, 여자의 마지막 말에 이어질 남자의 말로 가장 적절한 것을 고르시오.

19 Man: _____

① I'm sorry to hear that.
② I'm sure you can do it.
③ That's too late. Let's meet at 4.
④ The game has already started.
⑤ I'm afraid I can't. I have to do my homework.

20 Man: _____

① Maybe next time.
② You can do better the next time.
③ I don't know what I should do.
④ If I were you, I would go to see a doctor.
⑤ That's a good idea. Then he'll use his phone less.

받아쓰기용

01 날씨 파악

다음을 듣고, 내일 오후의 날씨로 가장 적절한 것을 고르시오.

① ② ③
④ ⑤

W Good morning. This is Sandra Kim with the weather forecast. Today will be _____ _____ _____ all day long. It's perfect weather for a picnic. But tomorrow, it will be cloudy in the morning, and we expect heavy rain in the afternoon. So _____ _____ _____ your umbrella when you go out. The rain will continue _____ _____ _____ _____ _____.

02 그림 정보 파악 ✽

대화를 듣고, 남자가 그린 그림으로 가장 적절한 것을 고르시오.

① ② ③
④ ⑤

Sound Clear ☆ **vase**
미국식은 [베이스]로, 영국식은 [바스]로 발음된다.

M Thank you for _____ _____ _____ _____ _____.
W You're welcome. There are so many beautiful paintings.
M All of the members of the Maestro Art Club worked so hard.
W _____ _____ _____ _____?
M I like nature, so I drew many flowers.
W Oh, is that one yours? The red flowers in the vase?
M No, _____ _____ _____ _____. I drew a rose garden with a few butterflies.
W I found it. I like your painting!

03 심정 추론

대화를 듣고, 여자가 마지막에 느꼈을 심정으로 가장 적절한 것을 고르시오.

① scared   ② bored   ③ frustrated
④ relieved   ⑤ curious

W _____ _____ _____ _____ what was wrong with my computer?
M Yes. It was a computer virus.
W Thank you. Is my computer clean now?
M Yes, but I'm afraid the virus erased _____ _____ _____ _____.
W Really? But I didn't _____ _____ _____ _____. Can you recover any of them?
M There's _____ _____ _____ _____ any of the files.
W Oh, no! There are so many important files that I need tomorrow!

04 장소 추론 ✱

대화를 듣고, 두 사람이 대화하는 장소로 가장 적절한 곳을 고르시오.

① 서점　　② 도서관　　③ 미술관
④ 우체국　　⑤ 컴퓨터실

W Excuse me. Can you help me find some books?
M You can search for books on the computer.
W I don't know _____ _____ _____ _____.
M It's very simple. Just enter a few key words, and _____ _____ _____ _____ will show up.
W Oh, I see.
M And the book code _____ _____ _____ _____.
W Thank you. How many books can I borrow?
M You can borrow _____ _____ _____ _____ for two weeks.

05 의도 파악

대화를 듣고, 여자의 마지막 말의 의도로 가장 적절한 것을 고르시오.

① 조언　　② 거절　　③ 감사
④ 허락　　⑤ 위로

Sound Clear ☆ stressed out
[t]와 [r]이 연달아 나오고, 앞 단어의 끝 자음과 뒤 단어의 첫 모음이 만나 연음되어 [스츄레스다웃]으로 발음된다.

W You don't look good. What's wrong?
M I'm upset with my mom. She always _____ _____ _____ _____.
W Most parents talk like that.
M I think I study enough. I _____ _____ _____ _____ _____ _____ on weekends. But my mom wants me to study more.
W You must _____ _____ _____ _____.
M I'm really stressed out about it. What should I do?
W _____ _____ _____ _____ your dad about how you feel?

06 특정 정보 파악

대화를 듣고, 여자가 여행 중 가장 좋았던 것을 고르시오.

① 일광욕　　② 수영　　③ 등산
④ 석양　　⑤ 숙소

M Sandy, how was your trip?
W I wanted to stay there longer. It was _____ _____ _____ _____.
M Sounds good. What did you do there?
W I _____ _____ _____ _____ _____ sunbathing and swimming. I also went hiking in the mountains.
M Wow, it seems like you had such a great time.
W Yeah. But _____ _____ _____ _____ _____ was the beautiful sunset. I'll never forget the setting sun.
M Wonderful.

07 할 일 파악

대화를 듣고, 남자가 대화 직후에 할 일로 가장 적절한 것을 고르시오.

① 친구를 만나러 간다.
② 친구에게 선물을 보낸다.
③ 친구에게 전화를 한다.
④ 친구의 블로그에 들어간다.
⑤ 친구에게 사과 편지를 쓴다.

Sound Clear☆ laugh
gh가 [f]로 소리 나서 [래프]로 발음된다.

W You look so worried. What's up?
M ________ ________ ________ ________ ________ is mad at me.
W What happened?
M I ________ ________ ________ ________ her blog, and she didn't like it.
W What did you write?
M Nothing special. It was ________ ________ ________. I thought she would laugh at it.
W I think you should call or ________ ________ ________ ________ ________.
M You're right. I have to call her right now.
정답 단서

08 언급하지 않은 것 찾기

다음을 듣고, 여자가 사촌에 대해 언급하지 않은 것을 고르시오.

① 이름 ② 나이 ③ 출생지
④ 직업 ⑤ 성격

W Today, I'd like to introduce my cousin Grace. ________ ________ ________ in the U.S. She studied design at university and is now working as a wedding dress designer. She's very passionate about her job. She wants to ________ ________ ________ ________ someday. She is outgoing, humorous, and very ________ ________ ________. I like her very much.

09 주제 파악

다음을 듣고, 남자가 하는 말의 내용으로 가장 적절한 것을 고르시오.

① 겨울 방학 계획
② 스노보드의 장점
③ 동아리 회원 모집
④ 스포츠 강습 홍보
⑤ 건강 관리의 중요성

M Are you planning to learn how to snowboard this winter? It is very important to ________ ________ ________ ________. We have snowboarding experts who have more than ________ ________ ________ ________ ________. Join our snowboarding programs and learn the basics of snowboarding ________ ________ ________ ________. For more information, visit our website at www.snowlover.com.

10 목적 파악

대화를 듣고, 여자가 전화를 건 목적으로 가장 적절한 것을 고르시오.

① 숙제를 물어보기 위해서
② 약속 시간을 정하기 위해서
③ 숙제 출력을 부탁하기 위해서
④ 이메일 주소를 물어보기 위해서
⑤ 프린터 수리를 요청하기 위해서

(*Cellphone rings.*)
M Hi, Jina. What's up?
W Hey, Brian. Have you seen my text?
M No, I haven't. ________ ________ ________ ________?
W Can you print my homework? My printer is ________ ________ ________.
정답 단서
M No problem. Send it to me by email. When do you need it?
W By tomorrow morning. I have to ________ ________ ________ ________ ________.
M Okay. I'll bring it to school tomorrow.
W Thank you.

11 숫자 정보 파악

대화를 듣고, 남자가 지불해야 할 금액으로 가장 적절한 것을 고르시오.

① $72   ② $80   ③ $90
④ $92   ⑤ $100

M Excuse me. Could you _____ _____ _____ _____? I want to take a closer look.

W Sure. This is the newest model, the GX34.

M _____ _____ _____. How much is this?

W It's $100.

M Do you _____ _____ _____ _____?

W The GX23 here is $80. This one is a little bigger than the GX34.
정답 단서

M It's okay. I'll take the GX23.
정답 단서

W Okay. Are you _____ _____ _____ _____ _____? You can get 10% off.
정답 단서

M That's good to hear. Here's my membership card.

---

12 일치하지 않는 것 찾기

다음을 듣고, 동물원에 대한 설명으로 일치하지 않는 것을 고르시오.

① 국내에서 가장 큰 동물원이다.
② 전 세계의 다양한 동물들이 있다.
③ 판다는 특정 기간에만 볼 수 있다.
④ 사파리 버스 투어는 주말에 할 수 있다.
⑤ 매일 오전 10시부터 오후 6시까지 개장한다.

M Welcome to ABC Animal Kingdom, the largest zoo in the country. Many different animals _____ _____ _____ _____ _____ welcome you. In a special animal exhibit, you can see pandas from China until June 23. On weekends, you can _____ _____ _____ _____ _____ _____ such as the Safari Bus Tour or the Baby Animal Encounters. We are open from 10 a.m. to 6 p.m. every day except Mondays. _____ _____ _____ _____ _____ at the zoo. Thank you.
정답 단서

---

13 관계 추론

대화를 듣고, 두 사람의 관계로 가장 적절한 것을 고르시오.

① 교사 – 학생
② 의사 – 환자
③ 경찰관 – 시민
④ 식당 종업원 – 손님
⑤ 비행기 승무원 – 탑승객

Sound Clear ☆ **next to**
동일한 발음의 자음이 연이어 나오면 앞 자음 소리가 탈락하여 [넥스투]로 발음된다.

W Excuse me.

M Yes. How may I help you?

W I ordered my steak medium, but this one is overcooked.

M Oh, I'm sorry. I'll _____ _____ _____ _____ _____.

W Thank you. And the people at the table next to me are too loud.

M Do you want to _____ _____ _____?

W That would be nice.

M Just wait a moment, please. I'll _____ _____ _____ _____ _____.

---

14 특정 정보 파악

대화를 듣고, 여자가 이용할 교통수단을 고르시오.

① 버스   ② 택시   ③ 지하철
④ 자전거   ⑤ 버스와 지하철

W Dad, can I _____ _____ _____ _____ today? I want to buy some books.

M Are you going to the one in Gangnam Station?

W No. I'm going to Gwanghwamun.

M Why? The bookstore in Gangnam Station is nearer.

W I don't want to transfer _____ _____ _____ _____ _____ _____ .

M But it will take too long to get there.

W I _____ _____ _____ _____ . I will read a book in the subway. 정답 단서

M Okay. Take care.

15 부탁한 일 파악 ✿

대화를 듣고, 여자가 남자에게 부탁한 일로 가장 적절한 것을 고르시오.

① 쿠키 만들기   ② 함께 자원봉사하기
③ 쿠키 포장하기   ④ 쿠키 재료 사 오기
⑤ 봉사 활동 홍보하기

Sound Clear ☆ **Could you**
[d]가 뒤의 반모음 [j]를 만나 동화되어 [쿠쥬]로 발음된다.

W _____ _____ _____ ?

M Not really. Why?

W I'm going to volunteer _____ _____ _____ _____ and bring some homemade cookies.

M _____ _____ _____ ! Do you want me to help you bake the cookies?

W No. I've already 한정 baked them. Could you just help me wrap each cookie individually? ☆

M Sure. 정답 단서

16 그림의 상황에 적절한 대화 찾기

다음 그림의 상황에 가장 적절한 대화를 고르시오.

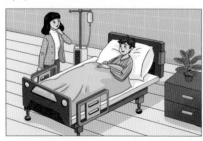

① ② ③ ④ ⑤

① **W** May I _____ _____ _____ ?
  M I'd like to have a steak with a salad.

② **W** I _____ _____ _____ and feel dizzy.
  M Take these pills three times a day.

③ **W** I hope _____ _____ _____ _____ .
  M Thanks. The doctor said I have to stay here for another week.

④ **W** May I help you?
  M I'm looking for a present for my girlfriend.

⑤ **W** Excuse me. _____ _____ _____ _____ near here?
  M Sorry. I don't know this neighborhood well.

17　이유 파악

대화를 듣고, 두 사람이 뷔페에 가지 <u>못한</u> 이유로 가장 적절한 것을 고르시오.

① 시간이 부족해서
② 쿠폰을 잃어버려서
③ 영화관에서 너무 멀어서
④ 쿠폰 사용 시간이 지나서
⑤ 남자가 해산물을 좋아하지 않아서

W Let's get _____ _____ _____ before the movie starts.
M Sounds good.
W I have coupons for a seafood buffet restaurant. Do you like seafood?
M I love seafood. That place is _____ _____ _____ _____ the theater. Let's go.
W Oh, wait. These coupons are only valid at lunchtime. 정답 단서
M That means we can't use them. It's 5 p.m. now.
W Yeah. What about the pizza place _____ _____ _____ ?
M All right then.

18　언급하지 않은 것 찾기

다음을 듣고, 여자가 파티에 대해 언급하지 <u>않</u>은 것을 고르시오.

① 일시　　② 장소　　③ 입장료
④ 경품 행사　⑤ 문의 방법

W The Summer Night Party is on Saturday, August 1, between 7 p.m. and midnight. It will be held in the main plaza of our resort. _____ _____ _____ _____ _____ can attend the party for free. Please show us your room key _____ _____ _____ . Enjoy the live music with free snacks and drinks. If you need _____ _____ _____ , please do not hesitate to contact our reception desk.

19　마지막 말에 이어질 응답 찾기

대화를 듣고, 여자의 마지막 말에 이어질 남자의 말로 가장 적절한 것을 고르시오.

Man: _____

① I'm sorry to hear that.
② I'm sure you can do it.
③ That's too late. Let's meet at 4.
④ The game has already started.
⑤ I'm afraid I can't. I have to do my homework.

M _____ _____ _____ _____ baseball?
W Yes. I'm a big fan of the Black Eagles.
M Me, too! That's _____ _____ _____ _____ .
W They will play the Blue Hats this weekend for the league championship.
M I know. _____ _____ _____ _____ to the game together?
W Great. Let's meet at 5.
M That's too late. Let's meet at 4.

20　마지막 말에 이어질 응답 찾기

대화를 듣고, 여자의 마지막 말에 이어질 남자의 말로 가장 적절한 것을 고르시오.

Man: _____

① Maybe next time.
② You can do better the next time.
③ I don't know what I should do.
④ If I were you, I would go to see a doctor.
⑤ That's a good idea. Then he'll use his phone less.

M _____ _____ _____ my little brother. He uses his smartphone too much.
W How old is he?
M He's only eleven. Last night, _____ _____ _____ _____ playing with his phone.
W He should find a way to control himself.
M I _____ _____ _____ .
W He can download a smartphone control app. It'll help him _____ _____ _____ _____ .
M That's a good idea. Then he'll use his phone less.

1.0배속　 1.2배속

01 다음을 듣고, 화요일의 날씨로 가장 적절한 것을 고르시오.

02 대화를 듣고, 여자의 올해 담임 선생님을 고르시오.

03 대화를 듣고, 남자의 심정으로 가장 적절한 것을 고르시오.
① proud　② nervous　③ ashamed
④ confused　⑤ unsatisfied

04 대화를 듣고, 여자가 우도에서 한 일로 가장 적절한 것을 고르시오.
① 사진 찍기　　② 말 타기
③ 자전거 타기　④ 일출 보기
⑤ 전동 스쿠터 타기

05 대화를 듣고, 두 사람이 대화하는 장소로 가장 적절한 곳을 고르시오.
① 병원　② 안경원　③ 수영장
④ 옷 가게　⑤ 놀이공원

06 대화를 듣고, 남자의 마지막 말의 의도로 가장 적절한 것을 고르시오.
① 격려　② 수락　③ 감사
④ 거절　⑤ 제안

07 다음을 듣고, 여자가 하는 말의 내용으로 가장 적절한 것을 고르시오.
① 안약의 종류
② 눈에 좋은 음식
③ 눈이 가려운 원인
④ 시력을 보호하는 방법
⑤ 눈이 가려울 때 대처 방법

08 대화를 듣고, 두 사람이 함께 여행을 가기로 한 나라를 고르시오.
① 한국　② 일본　③ 영국
④ 프랑스　⑤ 브라질

09 대화를 듣고, 남자가 대화 직후에 할 일로 가장 적절한 것을 고르시오.
① 팩스 보내기
② 홈페이지 가입하기
③ 영어책 읽어 주기
④ 전화번호 검색하기
⑤ 자원봉사 활동 신청하기

10 대화를 듣고, 여자가 에어쇼에 대해 언급하지 않은 것을 고르시오.
① 볼거리　　② 입장권 가격
③ 입장권 할인 방법　④ 개최 장소
⑤ 행사 기간

11 대화를 듣고, 작가와의 만남 행사에 대한 내용으로 일치하지 <u>않는</u> 것을 고르시오.

① 다음 주 수요일에 열린다.
② 학교 도서관에서 열린다.
③ Julia Harrington이 강의를 한다.
④ 책 사인회가 있을 것이다.
⑤ 온라인으로 참가 신청을 할 수 있다.

12 대화를 듣고, 여자가 전화를 건 목적으로 가장 적절한 것을 고르시오.

① 가습기를 빌리기 위해서
② 생수를 주문하기 위해서
③ 수건을 요청하기 위해서
④ 방 청소를 부탁하기 위해서
⑤ 룸서비스에 대해 문의하기 위해서

13 대화를 듣고, 택시가 남자의 집에 도착할 시각을 고르시오.

① 6:00 a.m.   ② 6:15 a.m.   ③ 6:30 a.m.
④ 6:45 a.m.   ⑤ 7:00 a.m.

14 대화를 듣고, 두 사람의 관계로 가장 적절한 것을 고르시오.

① 경찰관 – 시민
② 은행원 – 고객
③ 택시 기사 – 승객
④ 환전소 직원 – 여행객
⑤ 지하철 역무원 – 지하철 이용객

15 대화를 듣고, 남자가 저녁을 먹지 <u>않은</u> 이유로 가장 적절한 것을 고르시오.

① 너무 피곤해서
② 일이 너무 바빠서
③ 다이어트 중이라서
④ 내일 건강 검진이 있어서
⑤ 내일 맛있는 것을 먹기 위해서

16 대화를 듣고, 여자가 남자에게 요청한 일로 가장 적절한 것을 고르시오.

① 치약 사 오기   ② 칫솔 주문하기
③ 함께 쇼핑하기   ④ 개 사료 구입하기
⑤ 개 산책시키기

17 다음을 듣고, 남자가 체육 주간에 대해 언급하지 <u>않은</u> 것을 고르시오.

① 경기 종목   ② 경기 시간
③ 준비물   ④ 결승전 일시
⑤ 우승 상품

18 다음 그림의 상황에 가장 적절한 대화를 고르시오.

①   ②   ③   ④   ⑤

[19-20] 대화를 듣고, 여자의 마지막 말에 이어질 남자의 말로 가장 적절한 것을 고르시오.

19 Man: _____

① Sure. People can vote online.
② The election is not tomorrow.
③ Don't forget to vote tomorrow.
④ I think you should vote for her.
⑤ I'm not sure. I haven't decided yet.

20 Man: _____

① At least it'll be less crowded.
② Everything will turn out fine.
③ Can you think of a bright side?
④ It'll be dangerous to go on a tour.
⑤ You don't have to wear a raincoat.

01 날씨 파악

다음을 듣고, 화요일의 날씨로 가장 적절한 것을 고르시오.

①   ②   ③

④   ⑤

Sound Clear ☆ **-5°C**
영하는 minus[마이너스]로, °C는 degree (s) Celsius[디그뤼-쎌시어스]로 발음한다.

M Good morning. It is a _____ _____ _____ _____ Sunday. However, it will rain starting tomorrow morning, and _____ _____ _____ _____ to -5°C during the day. The rain will turn into snow at night, and it will snow on Tuesday. Please be careful on the icy roads. _____ _____ _____ _____ on Wednesday with temperatures recovering to average, and there will be sunny skies.

정답 단서

02 그림 정보 파악

대화를 듣고, 여자의 올해 담임 선생님을 고르시오.

①   ②   ③

④   ⑤

M Julie, who is your homeroom teacher this year?
W Mr. Brown, _____ _____ _____ _____.
M Mr. Brown? I don't know him.
W He's right over there with some other teachers. _____ _____ _____.
M There are two men wearing glasses. Do you mean the man with a beard?
한정
W No, he's the science teacher.
M Now I can see him. _____ _____ _____ _____, and he's wearing a black suit, right?
W That's right.

03 심정 추론

대화를 듣고, 남자의 심정으로 가장 적절한 것을 고르시오.

① proud   ② nervous
③ ashamed   ④ confused
⑤ unsatisfied

W Peter, _____ _____ _____ _____ _____ of the singing contest?
M I won second place.
W Really? Congratulations! You must be _____ _____ _____ _____.
M Not really, but thanks.
W _____ _____ _____ _____? Because you didn't win first place? Second place is also great!
M Only the first-place winner _____ _____ _____ _____ to meet some professional singers.
W Oh, I see.

04 한 일 파악

대화를 듣고, 여자가 우도에서 한 일로 가장 적절한 것을 고르시오.

① 사진 찍기   ② 말 타기
③ 자전거 타기   ④ 일출 보기
⑤ 전동 스쿠터 타기

Sound Clear ☆ **the island**
모음 앞의 the는 [디]로 발음된다. island의 s는 묵음이라서 [아일랜드]로 발음된다.

W   I went to Udo with my family last week.
M   Oh, do you mean the island _____ _____ _____ _____ Jeju-do?
W   That's right. _____ _____ _____ _____?
M   I've been there, too. I went horse riding there.
W   Great! I wanted to do that, but I couldn't. My younger sister _____ _____ _____ _____.
M   So what did you do there? Cycling?
W   We rode an electric scooter and _____ _____ _____ _____. The island is so beautiful.

05 장소 추론

대화를 듣고, 두 사람이 대화하는 장소로 가장 적절한 곳을 고르시오.

① 병원   ② 안경원   ③ 수영장
④ 옷 가게   ⑤ 놀이공원

M   Excuse me, ma'am. _____ _____ is your child?
W   About 110 centimeters. Is anything wrong?
M   Children under 150 centimeters in height _____ _____ _____ _____ _____. You and your child should play in the kid's zone.
W   Oh, I didn't know that.
M   And even children must _____ _____ _____ _____. There's a rental shop _____ _____ _____ _____.
W   I got it. Thank you.

06 의도 파악

대화를 듣고, 남자의 마지막 말의 의도로 가장 적절한 것을 고르시오.

① 격려   ② 수락   ③ 감사
④ 거절   ⑤ 제안

W   Thomas, _____ _____ _____ _____ going to this photo exhibition?
M   What is it about?
W   It's _____ _____ _____ all around the world.
M   Oh, I'm interested in that issue. Are you going there?
W   Yes, with Min tomorrow. Do you want to join us? I have a spare ticket.
M   Tomorrow? _____ _____ _____ _____ _____?
W   This Sunday, but Min and I only have time to go tomorrow.
M   Maybe next time. I have to _____ _____ _____ _____ _____ tomorrow.

07 주제 파악

다음을 듣고, 여자가 하는 말의 내용으로 가장 적절한 것을 고르시오.

① 안약의 종류
② 눈에 좋은 음식
③ 눈이 가려운 원인
④ 시력을 보호하는 방법
⑤ 눈이 가려울 때 대처 방법

W   Many people experience itchy eyes _____ _____ _____ _____. When your eyes are itchy, simply using eye drops _____ _____ _____. However, when eye drops don't help your eyes feel better and your eyes are getting redder, _____ _____ _____ _____ _____ so that you can get proper treatment right away. _____ _____ _____, do not touch red itchy eyes with your hands.

08 특정 정보 파악

대화를 듣고, 두 사람이 함께 여행을 가기로 한 나라를 고르시오.

① 한국　　② 일본　　③ 영국
④ 프랑스　⑤ 브라질

Sound Clear ☆ flight time

flight의 gh는 묵음이고, 동일한 발음의 자음이 연이어 나와서 [플라잇타임]으로 발음된다.

M We have to plan our summer vacation. Where are we going?
W We went to Korea last year, so I want to go _____ _____ _____ _____ this time.
M How about South America? I think Brazil would be fascinating. 한정
W Isn't it too far? The flight time will be very long. ☆
M Okay. Is there a country you _____ _____ _____?
W I'd like to _____ _____ either England or France. What do you think? 한정
M England! It'll be so exciting to watch soccer games there!
W Great. Let's _____ _____ _____ _____ first. 정답 단서

09 할 일 파악

대화를 듣고, 남자가 대화 직후에 할 일로 가장 적절한 것을 고르시오.

① 팩스 보내기
② 홈페이지 가입하기
③ 영어책 읽어 주기
④ 전화번호 검색하기
⑤ 자원봉사 활동 신청하기

M Semi, _____ _____ _____ _____ _____ some volunteer work?
W Sure. You can check the website called Volunteer Together.
M Volunteer Together?
W I can _____ _____ _____ _____ _____. What kind of volunteer work do you want to do?
M Well, I like children. So I _____ _____ _____ _____ _____ with kids.
W How about this one? Reading English books to kids.
M That sounds interesting. _____ _____ _____ 한정 _____ for this volunteer work?
W You should call this number to sign up.
M Okay. I'll do that right now.

10 언급하지 않은 것 찾기

대화를 듣고, 여자가 에어쇼에 대해 언급하지 않은 것을 고르시오.

① 볼거리　　　　　② 입장권 가격
③ 입장권 할인 방법　④ 개최 장소
⑤ 행사 기간

M Did you visit the air show yesterday? It was opening day.
W Yes, I did. It was really impressive. _____ _____ _____ _____ _____!
M Awesome! What else did you see?
W _____ _____ _____ _____ of drones.
M Great. How much is an admission ticket?
W It's $20 onsite, but _____ _____ _____ _____ _____ _____, it costs only $15.
M That's nice. I think I should go, too. When does the show end?
W It lasts for four days. It _____ _____ _____ _____.

11 일치하지 않는 것 찾기

대화를 듣고, 작가와의 만남 행사에 대한 내용으로 일치하지 <u>않는</u> 것을 고르시오.

① 다음 주 수요일에 열린다.
② 학교 도서관에서 열린다.
③ Julia Harrington이 강의를 한다.
④ 책 사인회가 있을 것이다.
⑤ 온라인으로 참가 신청을 할 수 있다.

W Bentley, _____ _____ _____ _____ _____ the meeting with the author event?
M The one that is next Wednesday at the student hall?
W It's not at the student hall but at the school library.
M Oh, is it? _____ _____?
W Julia Harrington. _____ _____ _____ _____ about her bestseller. There'll be a book-signing event, too.
M Do we sign up online?
W _____ _____ _____ _____. But this year, you have to do it in the teachers' office. *정답 단서*
M I see.

12 목적 파악

대화를 듣고, 여자가 전화를 건 목적으로 가장 적절한 것을 고르시오.

① 가습기를 빌리기 위해서
② 생수를 주문하기 위해서
③ 수건을 요청하기 위해서
④ 방 청소를 부탁하기 위해서
⑤ 룸서비스에 대해 문의하기 위해서

Sound Clear ☆ towels

towel은 [타우얼]처럼 발음된다. [r]로 끝나는 tower(타워)와 구분하여 알아 둔다.

(*Telephone rings.*)
M Hello. Front Desk. How may I help you?
W Hello. My room is too dry now.
M _____ _____ _____ _____ the humidifier?
W Yes, but it's still dry. I'd like to wet some towels and hang them up. So could you bring me _____ _____ _____?
M Sure. How many towels do you need?
W I think _____ _____ _____ _____.
M Anything else?
W Not now. Thank you.

13 숫자 정보 파악   �֎

대화를 듣고, 택시가 남자의 집에 도착할 시각을 고르시오.

① 6:00 a.m.   ② 6:15 a.m.
③ 6:30 a.m.   ④ 6:45 a.m.
⑤ 7:00 a.m.

(*Telephone rings.*)
W Fast and Safe Taxi Service. How may I help you?
M Hello. I need a taxi to _____ _____ _____ _____ _____ tomorrow morning.
W Where and what time _____ _____ _____ _____ _____?
M 215 K Street at 6:30, please. I _____ _____ _____ *정답 단서* _____ _____ _____ by 7:00.
W It's often congested there. Can we go there 15 minutes early? *한정*
M That would be great. Thank you. *정답 단서*

14 관계 추론

대화를 듣고, 두 사람의 관계로 가장 적절한 것을 고르시오.

① 경찰관 – 시민
② 은행원 – 고객
③ 택시 기사 – 승객
④ 환전소 직원 – 여행객
⑤ 지하철 역무원 – 지하철 이용객

Sound Clear ☆ **fill out**
앞 단어의 끝 자음과 뒤 단어의 첫 모음이 만나 연음되어 [필라웃]으로 발음된다.

M Hello. I'd like to open a savings account and put some money into it.
W Okay. Do you _____ _____ _____ _____ ?
M Yes, I do.
W _____ _____ _____ _____ and fill out this form, please.
M Okay. (*Pause*) Here you are.
W Thank you. Would you like to _____ _____ _____ from your original account into your new one?
M Yes, please.

15 이유 파악 ✧

대화를 듣고, 남자가 저녁을 먹지 <u>않은</u> 이유로 가장 적절한 것을 고르시오.

① 너무 피곤해서
② 일이 너무 바빠서
③ 다이어트 중이라서
④ 내일 건강 검진이 있어서
⑤ 내일 맛있는 것을 먹기 위해서

W Hi, Michael. _____ _____ _____ . Is everything okay?
M I didn't eat dinner. I'm just so hungry.
W Why? _____ _____ _____ _____ _____ ?
M No, I'm not. You know I'm trying to gain weight.
W Are you _____ _____ _____ _____ ?
M Nope. I have a medical checkup in the morning. I cannot eat anything the night before.
W I see. _____ _____ _____ _____ after your checkup.

16 요청한 일 파악

대화를 듣고, 여자가 남자에게 요청한 일로 가장 적절한 것을 고르시오.

① 치약 사 오기
② 칫솔 주문하기
③ 함께 쇼핑하기
④ 개 사료 구입하기
⑤ 개 산책시키기

(*Cellphone rings.*)
M Honey, I'm going home now. Is there _____ _____ _____ for Max?
W Yeah, I bought some last week.
M All right. _____ _____ _____ _____ .
W Hold on. We don't have any toothpaste left.
M Are you sure? _____ _____ _____ _____ from the market yesterday?
W No, I only bought toothbrushes. I realized today that we've _____ _____ _____ _____ . So can you pick some up?
M Got it.

17 언급하지 않은 것 찾기

다음을 듣고, 남자가 체육 주간에 대해 언급하지 않은 것을 고르시오.

① 경기 종목
② 경기 시간
③ 준비물
④ 결승전 일시
⑤ 우승 상품

M Attention, students. Next week is sports week at Hanguk Middle School. There is going to be a dodge ball tournament. Each class is going to _____ _____ _____ every morning from 8:00 to 8:30 a.m. _____ _____ _____ _____ _____ next Friday at 3:00 p.m. The winning class will be given fried chicken _____ _____ _____ . It's going to be a lot of fun.

18 그림의 상황에 적절한 대화 찾기

다음 그림의 상황에 가장 적절한 대화를 고르시오.

① ② ③ ④ ⑤

Sound Clear ☆ **definitely**

[t]가 [l] 앞에서 약화되어 [데피닛리]로 발음된다.

① W What is _____ _____ _____?
   M It's definitely winter because I love winter sports.
② W When did you learn to ski?
   M When I was an elementary school student, _____
      _____ _____ _____.
③ W Is that ski lift for beginners?
   M No, it's for advanced skiers. It goes directly to the top.
④ W I'm thinking of _____ _____ _____ _____.
   M Oh, really? What sport do you like the most?
⑤ W Which do you prefer, skiing or snowboarding?
   M I prefer snowboarding.

19 마지막 말에 이어질 응답 찾기

대화를 듣고, 여자의 마지막 말에 이어질 남자의 말로 가장 적절한 것을 고르시오.

Man: _____

① Sure. People can vote online.
② The election is not tomorrow.
③ Don't forget to vote tomorrow.
④ I think you should vote for her.
⑤ I'm not sure. I haven't decided yet.

W Tomorrow is election day for the school president.
M _____ _____ _____ who you're going to vote for?
W Yes. I'm going to vote for Sandra.
M Can I _____ _____ _____ _____?
W She was our class leader last year. She's very responsible. I'm sure she'll be _____ _____ _____ _____, too.
M I see. I don't know her well, but my friends also said they're going to vote for her.
W Oh, really? _____ _____ _____?
M I'm not sure. I haven't decided yet.

20 마지막 말에 이어질 응답 찾기

대화를 듣고, 여자의 마지막 말에 이어질 남자의 말로 가장 적절한 것을 고르시오.

Man: _____

① At least it'll be less crowded.
② Everything will turn out fine.
③ Can you think of a bright side?
④ It'll be dangerous to go on a tour.
⑤ You don't have to wear a raincoat.

W _____ _____ _____. We can't go on the walking tour.
M But walking along the Great Wall of China will _____
   _____ _____ _____ _____.
W In this rain? I don't think so. Let's look for some other things to do.
M Like what?
W What about _____ _____ _____ _____ _____?
M Isn't the traffic bad? Let's just do the walking tour with raincoats on. _____ _____ _____ _____ _____.
W The bright side? What's good about walking in the rain?
M At least it'll be less crowded.

Review Test

Word Check 영어는 우리말로, 우리말은 영어로 써 보기

01 relieved   _____

02 adventure   _____

03 back up   _____

04 recover   _____

05 sunbathe   _____

06 key word   _____

07 up to   _____

08 depressed   _____

09 laugh at   _____

10 exhibition   _____

11 fancy   _____

12 passionate   _____

13 외향적인   _____

14 전문가   _____

15 유효한   _____

16 제출하다   _____

17 만남, 접촉   _____

18 친절한, 상냥한 _____

19 각각 따로   _____

20 갈아타다, 환승하다 _____

21 꺼내다   _____

22 지역, 인근   _____

23 환경   _____

24 망설이다   _____

Expression Check 알맞은 표현을 넣어 문장 완성하기

25 You can _____ _____ books on the computer. 컴퓨터에서 책을 검색하실 수 있어요.

26 I'm _____ _____ my mom. 나는 우리 엄마한테 화가 났어.

27 I'm really _____ _____ about it. 나는 그것 때문에 정말 스트레스를 받아.

28 My printer is _____ _____ _____. 내 프린터가 고장 났어.

29 She is now _____ _____ a wedding dress designer.
그녀는 현재 웨딩드레스 디자이너로서 일하고 있습니다.

30 He was _____ _____ _____ playing with his phone.
그는 휴대 전화를 가지고 노느라 밤을 샜어.

Answers p.23

Word Check 영어는 우리말로, 우리말은 영어로 써 보기

01 spare _____

02 electric _____

03 beard _____

04 ashamed _____

05 confused _____

06 unsatisfied _____

07 experience _____

08 rental shop _____

09 endangered _____

10 temperature _____

11 upside down _____

12 humidifier _____

13 가까운 _____

14 인상 깊은 _____

15 가려운 _____

16 현장에서 _____

17 치료, 처치 _____

18 원래의 _____

19 상급의 _____

20 (비가) 마구 쏟아지다 _____

21 신분증 _____

22 선거 _____

23 책임감 있는 _____

24 당연히, 틀림없이 _____

Expression Check 알맞은 표현을 넣어 문장 완성하기

25 I'm going to _____ _____ Sandra. 나는 Sandra에게 투표할 거야.

26 You should call this number to _____ _____. 신청하려면 이 번호로 전화해야 해.

27 I'd like to wet some towels and _____ them _____. 저는 수건을 적셔서 걸어 두고 싶어요.

28 I want to go somewhere _____ _____ Asia this time. 나는 이번엔 아시아가 아닌 곳으로 가고 싶어.

29 I'd like to _____ _____ _____ _____. 저는 예금 계좌를 개설하고 싶어요.

30 I realized today that we've _____ _____ the toothpaste.
저는 우리가 치약을 다 써 버린 걸 오늘 알았어요.

01 다음을 듣고, 내일의 날씨로 가장 적절한 것을 고르시오.

02 대화를 듣고, 남자의 가방으로 가장 적절한 것을 고르시오.

03 대화를 듣고, 남자의 심정으로 가장 적절한 것을 고르시오.

① angry   ② proud   ③ lonely
④ thankful   ⑤ disappointed

04 대화를 듣고, 두 사람이 관심을 가지고 있는 동아리를 고르시오.

① 영화 동아리   ② 축구 동아리
③ 영어 회화 동아리   ④ 코딩 동아리
⑤ 컴퓨터 게임 동아리

05 대화를 듣고, 두 사람이 대화하는 장소로 가장 적절한 곳을 고르시오.

① 병원   ② 공항   ③ 영화관
④ 기차역   ⑤ 지하철역

06 대화를 듣고, 남자의 마지막 말의 의도로 가장 적절한 것을 고르시오.

① 후회   ② 칭찬   ③ 거절
④ 수락   ⑤ 감사

07 대화를 듣고, 여자가 먹을 음식을 고르시오.

① 스테이크   ② 샐러드   ③ 볶음밥
④ 쌀국수   ⑤ 카레

08 대화를 듣고, 남자가 대화 직후에 할 일로 가장 적절한 것을 고르시오.

① 잠자기   ② 공부하기
③ 음악 듣기   ④ 진료 받기
⑤ 교과서 복습하기

09 대화를 듣고, 여자가 좋은 피부를 유지하는 방법으로 언급하지 <u>않은</u> 것을 고르시오.

① 시간을 들여 세수함
② 수제 비누를 사용함
③ 패스트푸드를 전혀 먹지 않음
④ 피부를 건조하지 않게 유지함
⑤ 유기농 원료의 오일을 사용함

10 다음을 듣고, 여자가 하는 말의 내용으로 가장 적절한 것을 고르시오.

① 체리의 효능
② 반짝세일 안내
③ 식료품 위치 안내
④ 감자를 활용한 식단
⑤ 식품의 원산지 소개

11 대화를 듣고, 남자에 대한 설명으로 일치하지 <u>않는</u> 것을 고르시오.

① 작년부터 테니스 동아리 회원이었다.
② 현재 테니스 동아리의 회장이다.
③ 테니스를 매일 연습한다.
④ 테니스를 꽤 잘 친다.
⑤ 주로 학교에서 테니스를 친다.

12 대화를 듣고, 여자가 게시판을 만들고 있는 목적으로 가장 적절한 것을 고르시오.

① 칭찬을 주고받기 위해서
② 가족 행사를 기록하기 위해서
③ 집안일 목록을 적어 두기 위해서
④ 구입할 물품들을 적어 두기 위해서
⑤ 학교 과제를 잊지 않기 위해서

13 대화를 듣고, 여자가 부산에 도착할 시각을 고르시오.

① 2:15 p.m.   ② 6:00 p.m.
③ 8:00 p.m.   ④ 8:30 p.m.
⑤ 10:45 p.m.

14 대화를 듣고, 두 사람의 관계로 가장 적절한 것을 고르시오.

① 편집장 – 기자   ② 소설가 – 독자
③ 리포터 – 가수   ④ 음악 교사 – 학생
⑤ 사진작가 – 모델

15 대화를 듣고, 여자가 남자에게 요청한 일로 가장 적절한 것을 고르시오.

① Mike에게 연락하기
② Mike의 친구들 초대하기
③ 전학 갈 학교 알아보기
④ 송별회 장소 알아보기
⑤ 송별회 비용 모금하기

16 대화를 듣고, 남자가 뮤지컬을 보러 갈 수 <u>없는</u> 이유로 가장 적절한 것을 고르시오.

① 표를 못 구해서
② 병문안을 가야 해서
③ 할아버지의 생신이어서
④ 아르바이트를 가야 해서
⑤ 같이 갈 사람이 없어서

17 다음을 듣고, 남자가 대왕고래에 대해 언급하지 <u>않은</u> 것을 고르시오.

① 몸의 길이   ② 무게   ③ 서식지
④ 수명   ⑤ 먹이

18 다음 그림의 상황에 가장 적절한 대화를 고르시오.

①   ②   ③   ④   ⑤

[19-20] 대화를 듣고, 여자의 마지막 말에 이어질 남자의 말로 가장 적절한 것을 고르시오.

19 Man: _____

① It's just beginning.
② I don't like baseball.
③ The game is really boring.
④ I need to focus on studying.
⑤ Baseball isn't a popular game.

20 Man: _____

① Sure. Go ahead.
② That will be no problem.
③ I've never been to L.A. before.
④ I will travel to Europe next summer.
⑤ My aunt has lived in L.A. for 10 years.

받아쓰기용

01 날씨 파악

다음을 듣고, 내일의 날씨로 가장 적절한 것을 고르시오.

①   ②   ③

④   ⑤

M Good morning. This is Jacob O'connell with your London weather report. Right now it's 10°C and very clear. We're expecting _____ _____ _____ _____ _____. This good weather won't last long, however. There is _____ _____ _____ _____ _____ starting tonight. It will _____ _____ tomorrow, and the temperature will drop to as low as 3°C.

02 그림 정보 파악

대화를 듣고, 남자의 가방으로 가장 적절한 것을 고르시오.

①   ②   ③

④   ⑤

Sound Clear ☆ **have it**
앞 단어의 끝 자음과 뒤 단어의 모음이 만나 연음되어 [해빗]으로 발음된다.

(*Telephone rings.*)
W J Mall Lost and Found. How may I help you?
M _____ _____ _____ _____ this afternoon. Do you have it by any chance? ☆
W There are several bags here. Could you tell me _____ _____ _____ _____?
M It is square, and it has a handle on the top. 정답 단서
W _____ _____ _____ _____ _____, too?
M Yes. It has a long strap.
W I think _____ _____ _____ _____. 정답 단서
M What a relief! I will visit the mall tomorrow.

03 심정 추론

대화를 듣고, 남자의 심정으로 가장 적절한 것을 고르시오.

① angry ② proud ③ lonely
④ thankful ⑤ disappointed

W Did _____ _____ _____ to you?
M I've just finished *The Old Man and the Sea*.
W Do you mean the novel?
M You're right. _____ _____ _____ _____ in English.
W Really? Wasn't it hard to read?
M Well, it wasn't easy. It _____ _____ _____ _____ _____.
W You did a good job.
M I think my English _____ _____ _____ _____. I'll try a more difficult book the next time.

04 특정 정보 파악

대화를 듣고, 두 사람이 관심을 가지고 있는 동아리를 고르시오.

① 영화 동아리　　② 축구 동아리
③ 영어 회화 동아리　④ 코딩 동아리
⑤ 컴퓨터 게임 동아리

Sound Clear ☆ **kind of**
앞 단어의 끝 자음과 뒤 단어의 모음이 만나 연음되어 [카인더브]로 발음된다.

W　Dave, which club are you going to join?
M　_____ _____ _____ _____.
W　Aren't you interested in playing computer games?
M　Yeah, but as you know, there aren't any clubs _____ _____ _____ _____.
W　What about the coding club? I'm thinking of joining it.
M　What kind of club is it?
W　You can learn basic programming skills and _____ _____ _____ _____.
M　That sounds interesting.

05 장소 추론 ✳

대화를 듣고, 두 사람이 대화하는 장소로 가장 적절한 곳을 고르시오.

① 병원　　② 공항　　③ 영화관
④ 기차역　⑤ 지하철역

M　Hello. How may I help you?
W　Hi. I'd like to _____ _____ _____. It's too close to the screen.
M　Sure. Where do you want to sit?
W　_____ _____ _____ _____ _____ in the back?
M　Let me see. (*Pause*) We have one seat in the back row, but it's right _____ _____ _____ _____.
W　That's okay with me. _____ _____ _____ _____ _____ to the front row.
M　Okay. Here's your new ticket.

06 의도 파악

대화를 듣고, 남자의 마지막 말의 의도로 가장 적절한 것을 고르시오.

① 후회　　② 칭찬　　③ 거절
④ 수락　　⑤ 감사

W　Mike, do you have a large backpack?
M　I do. Do you need one?
W　Yeah. _____ _____ _____ _____? I'm going hiking this week.
M　Don't you have your own?
W　I don't have a large one. I can't put _____ _____ _____ _____ _____ in it.
M　Okay. When do you need it?
W　This Friday. Thanks. Can I _____ _____ _____ _____ _____ _____ in a few hours?
M　Call me just before you get here.

07 특정 정보 파악

대화를 듣고, 여자가 먹을 음식을 고르시오.

① 스테이크   ② 샐러드   ③ 볶음밥
④ 쌀국수   ⑤ 카레

Sound Clear ☆ **Vietnamese**

Vietnam(베트남)은 실제로 [뷔엣남]으로 발음되며, Vietnamese(베트남의)는 [뷔엣나미즈]로 발음된다.

M I'm hungry. Why don't we _____ _____ _____ _____?

W Sure, but I want to have something light for dinner.

M Why? _____ _____ _____ _____ _____?

W No. I had too much steak for lunch today.

M Then _____ _____ _____ to a Vietnamese restaurant?

W That's good. I will have rice noodles.

M Okay. I will have pineapple fried rice.

---

08 할 일 파악

대화를 듣고, 남자가 대화 직후에 할 일로 가장 적절한 것을 고르시오.

① 잠자기   ② 공부하기
③ 음악 듣기   ④ 진료 받기
⑤ 교과서 복습하기

W What's wrong with you? You don't look good today.

M _____ _____ _____ my English test next week.

W When is it?

M It's next Monday, but I can't focus on studying _____ _____ _____ _____ _____.

W Oh, dear. I think you _____ _____ _____ _____.

M Yeah, maybe. What can I do?

W Why don't you get some sleep first and then study?

M Okay. _____ _____ _____ _____.

---

09 언급하지 않은 것 찾기

대화를 듣고, 여자가 좋은 피부를 유지하는 방법으로 언급하지 않은 것을 고르시오.

① 시간을 들여 세수함
② 수제 비누를 사용함
③ 패스트푸드를 전혀 먹지 않음
④ 피부를 건조하지 않게 유지함
⑤ 유기농 원료의 오일을 사용함

M I keep getting pimples! How come you have such clean skin?

W Well, I take time to wash my face every night.

M Is that all? Do you use regular soap _____ _____ _____ _____ _____?

W Actually, I use handmade soap that my mom made.

M _____ _____ _____ _____?

W Sure. I also don't eat fast food at all.

M Really? Please give me more tips.

W I always try to _____ _____ _____ _____ _____ _____.

---

10 주제 파악

다음을 듣고, 여자가 하는 말의 내용으로 가장 적절한 것을 고르시오.

① 체리의 효능
② 반짝세일 안내
③ 식료품 위치 안내
④ 감자를 활용한 식단
⑤ 식품의 원산지 소개

W Welcome to Fresh Grocery. Now our special discount time will begin _____ _____ _____ _____ _____. In the fruit section, buy one pack of cherries and get a second pack _____ _____ _____. In the vegetable section, all potatoes and sweet potatoes are 40% off. Hurry up and _____ _____ _____ _____ _____.

11 일치하지 않는 것 찾기

대화를 듣고, 남자에 대한 설명으로 일치하지 <u>않는</u> 것을 고르시오.

① 작년부터 테니스 동아리 회원이었다.
② 현재 테니스 동아리의 회장이다.
③ 테니스를 매일 연습한다.
④ 테니스를 꽤 잘 친다.
⑤ 주로 학교에서 테니스를 친다.

W Josh, which club do you _____ _____ ?
M I have belonged to the tennis club _____ _____
   _____ .
W Really? I didn't know you like tennis.
M In fact, I'm _____ _____ _____ _____ _____ .
   I play tennis at least three times a week.
W You must be _____ _____ _____ _____ .
M I'm pretty good, but I still need to practice more.
W I'm also interested in playing tennis. Where do you play?
M I usually play _____ _____ _____ _____ .

12 목적 파악 ✲

대화를 듣고, 여자가 게시판을 만들고 있는 목적으로 가장 적절한 것을 고르시오.

① 칭찬을 주고받기 위해서
② 가족 행사를 기록하기 위해서
③ 집안일 목록을 적어 두기 위해서
④ 구입할 물품들을 적어 두기 위해서
⑤ 학교 과제를 잊지 않기 위해서

M Claire, what are you doing?
W I'm _____ _____ _____ _____ .
M For what?
W It's for managing our housework. _____ _____
   _____ the chores, and I'm the one who does all the
   housework.
M Sorry. _____ _____ _____ .
W That's why I'm making this board. I will write down _____
   _____ _____ _____ you have to do every day.
M That will be helpful.

13 숫자 정보 파악

대화를 듣고, 여자가 부산에 도착할 시각을 고르시오.

① 2:15 p.m.   ② 6:00 p.m.
③ 8:00 p.m.   ④ 8:30 p.m.
⑤ 10:45 p.m.

W _____ _____ _____ _____ _____ to Busan this
   evening?
M What time do you want to leave?
W Around 6:00 p.m.
M All the tickets from 6:00 p.m. to 8:00 p.m. are _____
   _____ .
W Then when is _____ _____ _____ _____ after 8:00?
M There is a train ticket for 8:30. Do you want to get that one?
W Yes, give me that one, please. _____ _____ _____
   _____ _____ to Busan?
M It takes two hours and fifteen minutes.

14 관계 추론

대화를 듣고, 두 사람의 관계로 가장 적절한 것을 고르시오.

① 편집장 – 기자 ② 소설가 – 독자
③ 리포터 – 가수 ④ 음악 교사 – 학생
⑤ 사진작가 – 모델

Sound Clear ☆ **didn't you**
[t]가 뒤의 반모음 [j]를 만나 동화되어 [디든츄]로 발음된다.

W Hello, Josh. Nice to meet you. I'm Judy Baker with New Stars.
M Nice to meet you, too.
W Your new album is ________ ________ ________. Congratulations!
M Thank you very much. I can't believe it.
W You ________ ________ ________ on the album, ☆didn't you?
M That's right.
W You're amazing. Do you want to ________ ________ ________ ________ ________?
M Thank you so much for your generous support. ________ ________ ________ ________!

15 요청한 일 파악

대화를 듣고, 여자가 남자에게 요청한 일로 가장 적절한 것을 고르시오.

① Mike에게 연락하기
② Mike의 친구들 초대하기
③ 전학 갈 학교 알아보기
④ 송별회 장소 알아보기
⑤ 송별회 비용 모금하기

M Did you hear that Mike is going to ________ ________ ________ ________?
W Really? I didn't know that. When is he going to leave?
M Next month.
W How about ________ ________ ________ ________ ________?
M That sounds nice. When will Mike be free?
W I'll ask him about it. Can you find a good place to throw a party? (정답 단서)
M No problem. ________ ________ ________ ________ ________.

16 이유 파악

대화를 듣고, 남자가 뮤지컬을 보러 갈 수 없는 이유로 가장 적절한 것을 고르시오.

① 표를 못 구해서
② 병문안을 가야 해서
③ 할아버지의 생신이어서
④ 아르바이트를 가야 해서
⑤ 같이 갈 사람이 없어서

M Do you have any plans for next weekend?
W No. Why?
M I can ________ ________ ________ ________ for *The Phantom of the Opera* on Sunday afternoon.
W Wow, I have wanted to see it for a long time. ________ ________ ________ ________?
M I have to visit my grandpa. He is in the hospital. (정답 단서)
W I'm sorry to hear that. ________ ________ ________ ________ for the tickets.
M You don't need to. I cannot go anyway.

17 언급하지 않은 것 찾기

다음을 듣고, 남자가 대왕고래에 대해 언급하지 않은 것을 고르시오.

① 몸의 길이 ② 무게 ③ 서식지
④ 수명 ⑤ 먹이

M ________ ________ ________ ________ blue whales? They are the largest animals in the world. They can grow to over 30 meters long. That's ________ ________ ________ ________. They weigh more than 130 tons, and they can live for about 80 years. You may think they eat big fish because of their size, but that's not true. ________ ________ ________ ________ called krill.

18　그림의 상황에 적절한 대화 찾기

다음 그림의 상황에 가장 적절한 대화를 고르시오.

①　②　③　④　⑤

Sound Clear ☆　film
'필름'이라고 발음하지 않고 [피엄]에 가깝게 발음된다.

① W　Do you enjoy playing soccer?

　 M　Yes, I do. How about you?

② W　This room is _____ _____ _____.

　 M　Let me turn on the air conditioner.

③ W　What do you think of _____ _____ _____
　　　_____?

　 M　I think it's great.

④ W　Your room is too messy. 정답 단서

　 M　Sorry, Mom. _____ _____ _____ _____.

⑤ W　Let's go to the film festival tomorrow.

　 M　_____ _____ _____, but I have to meet my uncle.

19　마지막 말에 이어질 응답 찾기

대화를 듣고, 여자의 마지막 말에 이어질 남자의 말로 가장 적절한 것을 고르시오.

Man: _____

① It's just beginning.

② I don't like baseball.

③ The game is really boring.

④ I need to focus on studying.

⑤ Baseball isn't a popular game.

W　Can you turn off the TV? _____ _____ _____
　 _____.

M　I'm sorry. I really can't. My favorite team is playing an important baseball game.

W　But I'm _____ _____ _____ my science exam tomorrow.

M　_____ _____ _____ _____ your door?

W　I did, but the sound is still bothering me.

M　Okay. I'll _____ _____ _____ _____.

W　Thanks. When will the game be over anyway?

M　It's just beginning.

20　마지막 말에 이어질 응답 찾기

대화를 듣고, 여자의 마지막 말에 이어질 남자의 말로 가장 적절한 것을 고르시오.

Man: _____

① Sure. Go ahead.

② That will be no problem.

③ I've never been to L.A. before.

④ I will travel to Europe next summer.

⑤ My aunt has lived in L.A. for 10 years.

W　_____ _____ _____ _____ _____ this winter?

M　Yes. I'm going to L.A. to meet my aunt.

W　Wow, you must be _____ _____ _____ _____.

M　That's true.

W　What are you going to do in L.A.?

M　I'm going to go to Hollywood. It will be really exciting.

W　Great. _____ _____ _____ _____ _____ and send them to me?

M　That will be no problem.

1.0배속

1.2배속

01 다음을 듣고, 부산의 날씨로 가장 적절한 것을 고르시오.

02 대화를 듣고, 여자가 만들 티셔츠로 가장 적절한 것을 고르시오.

03 대화를 듣고, 남자의 심정으로 가장 적절한 것을 고르시오.

① bored   ② excited   ③ envy
④ upset   ⑤ worried

04 대화를 듣고, 남자가 얼음 축제에서 한 일로 가장 적절한 것을 고르시오.

① 스키 타기   ② 스케이트 타기
③ 얼음낚시 하기   ④ 눈사람 만들기
⑤ 얼음 조각하기

05 대화를 듣고, 두 사람이 대화하는 장소로 가장 적절한 곳을 고르시오.

① 서점   ② 도서관   ③ 독서실
④ 슈퍼마켓   ⑤ 관광 안내소

06 대화를 듣고, 여자의 마지막 말의 의도로 가장 적절한 것을 고르시오.

① 제안   ② 위로   ③ 거절
④ 사과   ⑤ 축하

07 대화를 듣고, 남자가 가입한 동아리를 고르시오.

① 로켓 동아리   ② 환경 보호 동아리
③ 과학 동아리   ④ 우주 관측 동아리
⑤ 봉사 동아리

08 대화를 듣고, 두 사람이 대화 직후에 할 일로 가장 적절한 것을 고르시오.

① 산책을 한다.
② 서점에 간다.
③ 다른 식당에 간다.
④ 커피숍에 간다.
⑤ 줄을 서서 기다린다.

09 다음을 듣고, 남자가 수영 대회에 대해 언급하지 <u>않은</u> 것을 고르시오.

① 개최 요일   ② 신청 방법
③ 참가비   ④ 참가자 증정품
⑤ 우승자 상금

10 대화를 듣고, 남자가 전화를 건 목적으로 가장 적절한 것을 고르시오.

① 품절을 알리기 위해서
② 수리 일정을 잡기 위해서
③ 고장을 접수하기 위해서
④ 재고량을 확인하기 위해서
⑤ 배송 시각을 확인하기 위해서

11 다음을 듣고, 여자가 하는 말의 내용으로 가장 적절한 것을 고르시오.

① 휴무일 공지
② 신제품 소개
③ 영업시간 안내
④ 할인 행사 공지
⑤ 회원 가입 방법 안내

12 대화를 듣고, 여자가 내일 오후에 할 일로 가장 적절한 것을 고르시오.

① 남자와 쇼핑하기
② 친구 만나기
③ 수영 수업 받기
④ 도서관 가기
⑤ 전시회 관람하기

13 대화를 듣고, 남자가 지불해야 할 금액으로 가장 적절한 것을 고르시오.

① $108
② $120
③ $144
④ $160
⑤ $184

14 대화를 듣고, 두 사람의 관계로 가장 적절한 것을 고르시오.

① 이웃 – 이웃
② 아들 – 엄마
③ 교사 – 학부모
④ 간호사 – 환자
⑤ 배달원 – 고객

15 대화를 듣고, 여자가 남자에게 부탁한 일로 가장 적절한 것을 고르시오.

① 교실 청소하기
② 화분 가지고오기
③ 학급 문고 만들기
④ 선생님께 의견 여쭤보기
⑤ 도서관에 책 반납하기

16 대화를 듣고, 남자가 자전거를 타러 갈 수 <u>없는</u> 이유로 가장 적절한 것을 고르시오.

① 발목을 다쳐서
② 날씨가 좋지 않아서
③ 축구 경기가 있어서
④ 기말고사를 준비해야 해서
⑤ 숙제를 끝내지 못해서

17 대화를 듣고, 두 사람의 대화가 <u>어색한</u> 것을 고르시오.

① ② ③ ④ ⑤

18 대화를 듣고, 기부 운동에 대한 내용으로 일치하지 <u>않</u>는 것을 고르시오.

① 다음 달에 열린다.
② 2주 동안 진행된다.
③ 돈은 기부할 수 없다.
④ 통조림 식품은 기부할 수 있다.
⑤ 학교의 각 층에 기부함이 마련될 것이다.

[19-20] 대화를 듣고, 남자의 마지막 말에 이어질 여자의 말로 가장 적절한 것을 고르시오.

19 Woman: _____

① I'm glad you like it.
② Well, try it with your friends.
③ I want to join the tennis club.
④ What about swimming then?
⑤ Why don't you play basketball?

20 Woman: _____

① I can lend you the book.
② No thanks. I'm going to buy it.
③ Because I don't want to read it.
④ Yes. I've met the author before.
⑤ Thanks, but you should finish it first.

Dictation 06 회

01 날씨 파악

다음을 듣고, 부산의 날씨로 가장 적절한 것을 고르시오.

W Hello, everyone. This is the _____ _____ _____.
Seoul is sunny right now, and most of Gyeonggi-do is the
same. However, _____ _____ _____ _____
_____ heavy clouds in Busan and Ulsan, and rain will start
soon in Dokdo and Pohang. Lastly, Jeju-do _____ _____
_____ _____ due to a storm.

02 그림 정보 파악

대화를 듣고, 여자가 만들 티셔츠로 가장 적절한 것을 고르시오.

M Emma, what are you doing?
W _____ _____ _____ for my family. We're going to
wear them during our trip.
M Wow, that's nice. Did you draw these stars?
W Yes. These three stars _____ _____ _____ _____:
Dad, Mom, and me.
M Cool. So _____ _____ _____ _____ now?
W I'm going to write "We Are Family" below the stars.
M That's cute.

03 심정 추론

대화를 듣고, 남자의 심정으로 가장 적절한 것을 고르시오.

① bored   ② excited   ③ envy
④ upset   ⑤ worried

Sound Clear ☆ **Actually**
1음절에 강세가 있고, 2음절의 [t]가 약화되어 [액츄얼리] 또는 [액슈얼리]로 발음된다.

W Hey, did _____ _____ _____ to you? You look
different today.
M Do I? Actually, _____ _____ _____ _____!
W Are you serious? Let me guess. Is it Yumi?
M You're right! I _____ _____ _____ _____ _____,
but she does.
W Amazing. I'm happy for you!
M Thanks. We'll _____ _____ _____ _____ _____
tomorrow. I can't wait!
W Good luck on your first date.

04 한 일 파악

대화를 듣고, 남자가 얼음 축제에서 한 일로 가장 적절한 것을 고르시오.

① 스키 타기 ② 스케이트 타기
③ 얼음낚시 하기 ④ 눈사람 만들기
⑤ 얼음 조각하기

W Kyle, you look tired. Are you okay?
M I'm fine. I just ________ ________ ________ ________ throughout the weekend.
W Right, you said you were going to the ice festival. How was it?
M I had so much fun. It was a great experience.
W What did you do? Skiing or ice skating? 함정
M Neither. I ________ ________ ________ ________ ________.
W Sounds interesting. Did you catch anything?
M Yes. I ________ ________ ________ ________ ________.

05 장소 추론

대화를 듣고, 두 사람이 대화하는 장소로 가장 적절한 곳을 고르시오.

① 서점 ② 도서관 ③ 독서실
④ 슈퍼마켓 ⑤ 관광 안내소

Sound Clear ☆ **bestseller**
자음 세 개가 연속으로 나오면 중간 자음의 발음이 약화되어 [베스셀러]로 발음된다.

M Excuse me. Can you ________ ________ ________ ________ ________? It's a novel.
W The novels are in section B.
M I went there, but I couldn't find the book that I'm looking for.
W Oh, really? ________ ________ ________?
M *Demian.*
W Oh, *Demian* is ________ ________ ________ ________. So it should be in the ☆bestseller section. 정답 단서
M Where is it?
W It's right ________ ________ ________ ________ ________ over there.

06 의도 파악

대화를 듣고, 여자의 마지막 말의 의도로 가장 적절한 것을 고르시오.

① 제안 ② 위로 ③ 거절
④ 사과 ⑤ 축하

M Do you have ________ ________ ________ ________?
W Nothing special. How about you?
M Mike and I are going to watch a movie tonight. Do you want to join us?
W Maybe. ________ ________ ________ ________ are you going to watch?
M *The Avengers*. It's the number-one movie right now.
W Isn't it ________ ________ ________?
M Yes. People say that it's very spectacular, and there is also a message behind it.
W I'm afraid I don't really want to see it. ________ ________ ________ ________ ________.

07 특정 정보 파악

대화를 듣고, 남자가 가입한 동아리를 고르시오.

① 로켓 동아리　② 환경 보호 동아리
③ 과학 동아리　④ 우주 관측 동아리
⑤ 봉사 동아리

W Brian, why do you have ________ ________ ________ ________?
M I'm going to make water rockets with them.
W Water rockets?
M In my club, ________ ________ ________ ________ ________ every month. This month, the project is flying rockets.
W Oh, you mean your science club. Do you enjoy it?
정답 단서
M I really do. ________ ________ ________ ________ ________?
W I'm sorry, I can't. I joined the volunteering club yesterday.

08 할 일 파악

대화를 듣고, 두 사람이 대화 직후에 할 일로 가장 적절한 것을 고르시오.

① 산책을 한다.
② 서점에 간다.
③ 다른 식당에 간다.
④ 커피숍에 간다.
⑤ 줄을 서서 기다린다.

M The restaurant is ________ ________ ________.
W Dinner starts at 6:00. What time is it?
M It's 5:30. We have to wait for 30 minutes.
W Is there ________ ________ ________ ________ that we can spend some time at?
M I don't think it's a good idea. We'll have dinner soon. ________ ________ ________ ________ ________?
W It's cold outside. Why don't we go to the bookstore? It's on the second floor of this building.
정답 단서
M That's a good idea. We'll come back here at 6 o'clock.

09 언급하지 않은 것 찾기

다음을 듣고, 남자가 수영 대회에 대해 언급하지 않은 것을 고르시오.

① 개최 요일　② 신청 방법
③ 참가비　④ 참가자 증정품
⑤ 우승자 상금

Sound Clear ☆ **souvenir**
마지막 음절에 강세를 두어 [수베니얼]로 발음된다.

M Hello, Potomac Swimming Pool users. ________ ________ ________ ________ is next Saturday. This is the right time to show off your swimming skills. ________ ________ ________ ________ ________, it's not too late. Please tell any staff member that you want to take part in the contest. The entry fee is 5,000 won per person. All participants will ________ ________ ________ ________ and a souvenir T-shirt. Sign up now and have fun!

10 목적 파악

대화를 듣고, 남자가 전화를 건 목적으로 가장 적절한 것을 고르시오.

① 품절을 알리기 위해서
② 수리 일정을 잡기 위해서
③ 고장을 접수하기 위해서
④ 재고량을 확인하기 위해서
⑤ 배송 시각을 확인하기 위해서

(Cellphone rings.)
M Hello. Is this Noelle Miller?
W ________. ________ ________?
M Neil Smith, the air conditioner repairman. Can I ________ ________ ________ around 2 p.m. tomorrow?
W I think I'll be ________ ________ ________ at that time.
M Then how about the day after tomorrow?
W I ________ ________ ________ ________ ________ as soon as possible. Can you come tomorrow evening?
M I'm busy until 9 o'clock. Is that too late?
W 9 o'clock is fine. Thank you.

11 주제 파악

다음을 듣고, 여자가 하는 말의 내용으로 가장 적절한 것을 고르시오.

① 휴무일 공지　　② 신제품 소개
③ 영업시간 안내　④ 할인 행사 공지
⑤ 회원 가입 방법 안내

W The holiday season is fast approaching. So we at Home Furniture will _____ _____ _____ _____ _____ to save up to 50% on our products. It will be on this Sunday, December 23, from 10 a.m. to 3 p.m. _____ _____ _____ _____ _____ on all our furniture only if you are a member of our store. Don't miss this great chance. See you on that day.

12 할 일 파악

대화를 듣고, 여자가 내일 오후에 할 일로 가장 적절한 것을 고르시오.

① 남자와 쇼핑하기　② 친구 만나기
③ 수영 수업 받기　④ 도서관 가기
⑤ 전시회 관람하기

M Haley, do you want to _____ _____ _____ _____ this afternoon?
W I'm sorry, but I can't. I'm going to meet my friends in the library. *함정*
M *함정* How about tomorrow then?
W I'm _____ _____ _____ _____ _____. I have a swimming class in the afternoon.
M Then I guess I have to *정답 단서* _____ _____ _____ this time.
W What about Saturday? I'm free this weekend.
M Okay. See you on Saturday.

13 숫자 정보 파악 ✦

대화를 듣고, 남자가 지불해야 할 금액으로 가장 적절한 것을 고르시오.

① $108　② $120　③ $144
④ $160　⑤ $184

M I'd like four tickets for the first floor. I want all the seats to be _____ _____ _____ _____.
W There are only two seats on the first floor _____ _____.
M Then give me two on the first floor and two on the second floor, please.
W Okay. _____ _____ _____ _____ _____ _____ is $50, and one for the second floor is $30.
M Then it comes to $160.
W If *정답 단서* _____ _____ _____ _____ _____, you can get a 10% family discount.
M *정답 단서* Yes, we are. That's good to hear.

14 관계 추론

대화를 듣고, 두 사람의 관계로 가장 적절한 것을 고르시오.

① 이웃 – 이웃　② 아들 – 엄마
③ 교사 – 학부모　④ 간호사 – 환자
⑤ 배달원 – 고객

Sound Clear ☆ **Don't worry**
축약된 't는 거의 발음되지 않아 [돈워뤼]로 발음된다.

M Mrs. Wilson, _____ _____ _____ _____?
W Yes, much better. I had a bad cold.
M I'm glad you got better. By the way, _____ _____ _____ _____ _____ sometimes?
W Ah, it's mostly okay. But when they _____ _____ _____ _____ at night, it's a little hard for me to rest.
M I'm really sorry. We _____ _____ _____ _____.
W Most of the time it's fine. ☆ Don't worry too much.
M Thank you for your understanding.

15 부탁한 일 파악

대화를 듣고, 여자가 남자에게 부탁한 일로 가장 적절한 것을 고르시오.

① 교실 청소하기
② 화분 가지고오기
③ 학급 문고 만들기
④ 선생님께 의견 여쭤보기
⑤ 도서관에 책 반납하기

M Don't you think _____ _____ _____ _____ in our classroom?
W Yes, I do. _____ _____ _____ _____ by the window?
M That's good. I can bring some.
W Thanks. I'm also thinking of _____ _____ _____ _____.
M A class library? Where are you going to get all the books?
W I can tell everyone to _____ _____ _____ _____.
M Good idea.
W Can you tell our teacher about this and ask his opinion?
M No problem.

16 이유 파악

대화를 듣고, 남자가 자전거를 타러 갈 수 없는 이유로 가장 적절한 것을 고르시오.

① 발목을 다쳐서
② 날씨가 좋지 않아서
③ 축구 경기가 있어서
④ 기말고사를 준비해야 해서
⑤ 숙제를 끝내지 못해서

Sound Clear ☆ **As you know**
[s]가 뒤의 반모음 [j]와 연음되고 know의 k는 묵음이라서 [애쥬노우]로 발음된다.

W Have you finished your English essay?
M Yes. I _____ _____ _____ _____.
W Good. Why don't we go biking this afternoon?
M _____ _____ _____ _____.
W Why not? Come on! It's perfect weather today.
M Because of my ankle. As you know, I sprained it while _____ _____ _____ _____.
W Oh, does it still hurt?
M Yeah. I need to be careful _____ _____.

17 어색한 대화 찾기 ✷

대화를 듣고, 두 사람의 대화가 어색한 것을 고르시오.

① ② ③ ④ ⑤

① W May I _____ _____ _____?
  M I'm sorry, but you cannot try sweaters on.
② W Long time, no see. How have you been?
  M I didn't have time _____ _____ _____ _____.
③ W How did you like the musical?
  M I didn't like it. _____ _____ _____.
④ W Is there a post office nearby?
  M Yes. _____ _____ _____ from here.
⑤ W Thank you for coming to my party.
  M It's my pleasure.

18 일치하지 않는 것 찾기

대화를 듣고, 기부 운동에 대한 내용으로 일치하지 <u>않는</u> 것을 고르시오.

① 다음 달에 열린다.
② 2주 동안 진행된다.
③ 돈은 기부할 수 없다.
④ 통조림 식품은 기부할 수 있다.
⑤ 학교의 각 층에 기부함이 마련될 것이다.

Sound Clear ☆ **put it in**
각 [t]가 모음 사이에서 약화되고 뒤에 나오는 모음과 연음되어 [푸리린]으로 발음된다.

M There is a donation drive next month.
W Oh, I almost forgot. It's for _____ _____ _____ _____ _____, right?
M Yes. What are you going to donate?
W I don't know. I _____ _____ _____ my piggy bank.
M You cannot donate money. You can only donate canned food or _____ _____.
W Oh, right. I need to think about it.
M _____ _____ _____ _____, you can put it in one of the donation boxes on each floor of our school.
W I got it.

19 마지막 말에 이어질 응답 찾기

대화를 듣고, 남자의 마지막 말에 이어질 여자의 말로 가장 적절한 것을 고르시오.

Woman: _____

① I'm glad you like it.
② Well, try it with your friends.
③ I want to join the tennis club.
④ What about swimming then?
⑤ Why don't you play basketball?

W Semin, do you exercise regularly?
M No, but I feel like I should do something. I _____ _____ _____ _____ these days.
W Then you really _____ _____ _____ _____.
M What kind of exercise do you think is good for me?
W How about tennis? I play it _____ _____ _____ _____. It's a good sport.
M I'm not good at ball sports.
W What about swimming then?

20 마지막 말에 이어질 응답 찾기

대화를 듣고, 남자의 마지막 말에 이어질 여자의 말로 가장 적절한 것을 고르시오.

Woman: _____

① I can lend you the book.
② No thanks. I'm going to buy it.
③ Because I don't want to read it.
④ Yes. I've met the author before.
⑤ Thanks, but you should finish it first.

M Jina, what kinds of books do you like?
W _____ _____ _____ _____. How about you?
M So do I! Then you might like *The Garden*.
W I think _____ _____ _____ _____ _____.
M The story takes place in the Middle Ages.
W That's interesting.
M I've already finished reading it. Do you want me to _____ _____ _____ _____?
W No thanks. I'm going to buy it.

Word Check
영어는 우리말로, 우리말은 영어로 써 보기

01 belong to _____

02 regular _____

03 strap _____

04 improve _____

05 related to _____

06 row _____

07 Vietnamese _____

08 advice _____

09 pimple _____

10 throughout _____

11 section _____

12 lost and found _____

13 에어컨 _____

14 반값 _____

15 신경 쓰이게 하다 _____

16 습한 _____

17 지지 _____

18 이용할 수 있는 _____

19 송별회 _____

20 후한, 관대한 _____

21 지저분한, 엉망인 _____

22 관리하다 _____

23 몇 시간 후에 _____

24 (돈이) 들다 _____

Expression Check
알맞은 표현을 넣어 문장 완성하기

25 I need to _____ _____ studying. 나는 공부하는 데 집중해야 해.

26 Do you have it _____ _____ _____? 그것이 혹시 거기에 있을까요?

27 I have wanted to see it _____ _____ _____ _____. 나는 오랫동안 그것을 보고 싶었어.

28 Can you find a good place to _____ _____ _____? 너는 파티를 열 좋은 장소를 찾아봐 줄래?

29 Can I _____ it _____ at your house in a few hours?
몇 시간 후에 너희 집에서 그것을 가져가도 될까?

30 All the tickets from 6:00 p.m. to 8:00 p.m. are _____ _____.
저녁 6시부터 8시까지는 모든 표가 매진이에요.

Answers p.33

Word Check 영어는 우리말로, 우리말은 영어로 써 보기

01 miss _____

02 below _____

03 serious _____

04 experience _____

05 spectacular _____

06 annual _____

07 take a walk _____

08 staff member _____

09 entry fee _____

10 get a discount _____

11 one another _____

12 nationwide _____

13 다가오다 _____

14 가구 _____

15 기념품 _____

16 시끄러운 _____

17 사용하지 않은 _____

18 공유하다, 나누다 _____

19 삐다, 접지르다 _____

20 수리하다 _____

21 근처에 _____

22 기부 _____

23 장식 _____

24 기진맥진한 _____

Expression Check 알맞은 표현을 넣어 문장 완성하기

25 The sky _____ _____ _____ heavy clouds in Busan and Ulsan.
부산과 울산에는 짙은 구름이 잔뜩 끼어 있습니다.

26 These three stars _____ _____ my family. 이 별 세 개는 우리 가족을 상징해.

27 I caught _____ _____ _____ fish. 나는 물고기 두어 마리를 잡았어.

28 _____ not _____ action movies. 나는 액션 영화에 관심 없어.

29 You really should start _____ _____. 너는 정말 운동을 시작해야겠다.

30 The story _____ _____ in the Middle Ages. 그 이야기는 중세 시대에서 일어나.

1.0배속

1.2배속

01 다음을 듣고, 내일 아침의 날씨로 가장 적절한 것을 고르시오.

02 대화를 듣고, 여자가 구입할 머그 컵으로 가장 적절한 것을 고르시오.

03 대화를 듣고, 여자의 마지막 말에 드러난 심정으로 가장 적절한 것을 고르시오.
① sad   ② proud   ③ excited
④ nervous   ⑤ upset

04 대화를 듣고, 두 사람이 대화하는 장소로 가장 적절한 곳을 고르시오.
① 서점   ② 학원   ③ 공연장
④ 문구점   ⑤ 도서관

05 대화를 듣고, 남자의 마지막 말의 의도로 가장 적절한 것을 고르시오.
① 허가   ② 조언   ③ 거절
④ 동의   ⑤ 추천

06 대화를 듣고, 여자가 배우고자 하는 악기를 고르시오.
① 기타   ② 드럼   ③ 피아노
④ 바이올린   ⑤ 플루트

07 대화를 듣고, 남자가 대화 직후에 할 일로 가장 적절한 것을 고르시오.
① 점심 식사하기   ② 영화 관람하기
③ 대기 줄 서기   ④ 식당 찾아보기
⑤ 영화표 구입하기

08 대화를 듣고, 여자가 책에 대해 언급하지 않은 것을 고르시오.
① 제목   ② 장르   ③ 작가
④ 내용   ⑤ 출판 연도

09 다음을 듣고, 남자가 하는 말의 내용으로 가장 적절한 것을 고르시오.
① 정전 안내   ② 단수 안내
③ 물청소 안내   ④ 정수기 교체 안내
⑤ 온수 이용 시간 안내

10 대화를 듣고, 버스에 대한 두 사람의 의견으로 일치하지 않는 것을 고르시오.
① 등교 시 지하철보다 편리하다.
② 운행 시간이 오래 걸린다.
③ 아침에 너무 혼잡하다.
④ 자리가 잘 나지 않는다.
⑤ 막차가 일찍 끊겨서 불편하다.

11 대화를 듣고, 남자가 전화를 건 목적으로 가장 적절한 것을 고르시오.
① 예약을 취소하기 위해서
② 영업시간을 확인하기 위해서
③ 의사에게 물어볼 것이 있어서
④ 예약된 일정을 변경하기 위해서
⑤ 여자와 만날 시간을 정하기 위해서

12 대화를 듣고, 여자가 파티에 가져갈 음식을 고르시오.

① 쿠키　　　　　② 샐러드
③ 케이크　　　　④ 아이스크림
⑤ 스파게티

13 대화를 듣고, 여자가 받을 거스름돈으로 가장 적절한 것을 고르시오.

① $1　　　② $2　　　③ $3
④ $4　　　⑤ $5

14 대화를 듣고, 두 사람의 관계로 가장 적절한 것을 고르시오.

① 약사 – 환자
② 의사 – 환자
③ 경비원 – 주민
④ 경찰관 – 시민
⑤ 식당 종업원 – 손님

15 대화를 듣고, 여자가 남자에게 요청한 일로 가장 적절한 것을 고르시오.

① 사진 찍기
② 머리 염색하기
③ 머리 짧게 자르기
④ 좋은 샴푸 추천해 주기
⑤ 헤어스타일 사진 보여 주기

16 대화를 듣고, 남자가 화가 난 이유로 가장 적절한 것을 고르시오.

① 침대가 지저분해서
② 방에 벌레가 있어서
③ 냉방이 되지 않아서
④ 승강기가 고장 나서
⑤ 온수가 나오지 않아서

17 다음을 듣고, 여자가 하는 말의 내용으로 가장 적절한 것을 고르시오.

① 흡연의 폐해
② 감기 예방 수칙
③ 채식 위주의 식단
④ 건강을 유지하는 방법
⑤ 스트레스를 해소하는 방법

18 다음 그림의 상황에 가장 적절한 대화를 고르시오.

①　　②　　③　　④　　⑤

[19-20] 대화를 듣고, 여자의 마지막 말에 이어질 남자의 말로 가장 적절한 것을 고르시오.

19 Man: _____

① No, thank you.
② Most women love roses.
③ Say happy birthday to her.
④ Your wife will be very happy.
⑤ Good choice. They're on sale today.

20 Man: _____

① It costs a dollar.
② No. I already have a pen.
③ Yes, but I couldn't find it.
④ I looked it up in the dictionary.
⑤ How about using a computer?

01 날씨 파악

다음을 듣고, 내일 아침의 날씨로 가장 적절한 것을 고르시오.

① ② ③

④ ⑤

W This is CKNY, and I'm Anita with the weather. Right now, _____ _____ _____, and the sky is covered with thick clouds. There is a 70% chance of rain this afternoon. _____ _____ _____ _____ when you go out. Staring tomorrow morning, however, it's going to be clear, and we will _____ _____ _____ _____ _____ _____ all day.

02 그림 정보 파악

대화를 듣고, 여자가 구입할 머그 컵으로 가장 적절한 것을 고르시오.

① ② ③

④ ⑤

Sound Clear ☆ **writing**
w는 묵음이고, [t]가 모음 사이에서 약화되어 [롸이링]으로 발음된다.

M What can I do for you?
W I want to buy a mug. _____ _____ _____ _____ ?
M Our mugs are all very popular, but this one with the big heart is the most popular.
W Well, I'm not sure.
M Do you want _____ _____ _____ _____ on it?
W I'd like a mug with writing as well as the heart.
M Okay. This one has "Love" written _____ _____ _____.
W I like it. I'll take that one.

03 심정 추론

대화를 듣고, 여자의 마지막 말에 드러난 심정으로 가장 적절한 것을 고르시오.

① sad ② proud ③ excited
④ nervous ⑤ upset

M Do you know _____ _____ _____ _____ _____ this weekend?
W I didn't know that. Where will it be held?
M At Central Park. _____ _____ _____ _____ _____ there.
W Are the Blue Boys playing there?
M Yes, they are.
W They're _____ _____ _____ _____.
M Do you want to go with me then?
W I'd love to. I'm really _____ _____ _____ _____.

04 장소 추론 ✳

대화를 듣고, 두 사람이 대화하는 장소로 가장 적절한 곳을 고르시오.

① 서점　　② 학원　　③ 공연장
④ 문구점　⑤ 도서관

M This place is huge.

W It has _____ _____ _____ in the city.

M It has lecture rooms, too.

W Yes. I heard it has _____ _____ _____ _____.

M Do you come here often?

W Yes. I come here to check out books and to study.

M I see. I want to check out some books, but I _____ _____ _____ _____ _____ first.

05 의도 파악

대화를 듣고, 남자의 마지막 말의 의도로 가장 적절한 것을 고르시오.

① 허가　　② 조언　　③ 거절
④ 동의　　⑤ 추천

Sound Clear ☆ **dress**
[d]와 [r]이 연달아 나와 [쥬레스]에 가깝게 발음된다.

W Excuse me. Do you have this dress _____ _____ _____ _____?

M Yes, here it is. Would you like to try this on?

W Actually, _____ _____ _____ _____ yesterday. I'll take it.

M All right. It's $49.

W $49? _____ _____ _____ _____?

M I'm sorry. The sale ended yesterday.

W Oh, my. Can you sell it _____ _____ _____ _____ today? It is only one day later.

M I'm sorry. You have to wait for the next sale.

06 특정 정보 파악

대화를 듣고, 여자가 배우고자 하는 악기를 고르시오.

① 기타　　② 드럼　　③ 피아노
④ 바이올린　⑤ 플루트

W David, I heard you are taking piano lessons.

M Yes, I am. They're really fun.

W I want to _____ _____ _____ _____, too.

M Let's take piano lessons together.

W I can already play the piano. I want to _____ _____ _____.

M Then what about the violin?

W The violin? I think _____ _____ _____ _____.

M How about the guitar? You can play and sing. You like singing.

W That's a good idea. I'll _____ _____ _____ _____ now.

07 할 일 파악 ✳

대화를 듣고, 남자가 대화 직후에 할 일로 가장 적절한 것을 고르시오.

① 점심 식사하기　② 영화 관람하기
③ 대기 줄 서기　④ 식당 찾아보기
⑤ 영화표 구입하기

M How about having lunch before watching the movie?
W Okay. _____ _____ _____ _____ _____ _____ _____?
M Let's try the new Chinese restaurant over there.
W Sounds good. Oh, there is a line of people waiting.
M Yeah, we need to _____ _____ _____.
W Then _____ _____ _____ _____ to buy movie tickets first?
M Good idea. I'll go and buy tickets.
W Okay. Then _____ _____ _____ _____ _____.

08 언급하지 않은 것 찾기

대화를 듣고, 여자가 책에 대해 언급하지 <u>않은</u> 것을 고르시오.

① 제목　② 장르　③ 작가
④ 내용　⑤ 출판 연도

Sound Clear ☆ **heard of**
앞 단어의 끝 자음과 뒤 단어의 모음이 만나 연음되어 [헐더브]로 발음된다.

M What are you reading?
W I'm reading *Great Expectations*. 정답 단서
M _____ _____ _____ _____? ☆
W Haven't you heard of *Great Expectations*? It's a novel _____ _____ Charles Dickens. 정답 단서
M No, I haven't. What's the story about? 정답 단서
W It is a story of a boy who learns valuable lessons in life. 정답 단서
M Sounds interesting. _____ _____ _____ _____ after you read it.

09 주제 파악

다음을 듣고, 남자가 하는 말의 내용으로 가장 적절한 것을 고르시오.

① 정전 안내　② 단수 안내
③ 물청소 안내　④ 정수기 교체 안내
⑤ 온수 이용 시간 안내

M Due to repairs on the water pipe, you'll not be able to use the water starting at 2:30 p.m. tomorrow. Unfortunately, we're not sure _____ _____ _____ _____ _____ 정답 단서 _____. We will do our best to finish it _____ _____ _____ _____. You should fill buckets of water to use at night in case the repairs _____ _____ _____ _____. If you have any questions, please contact the management office at 250-357-9433.

10 일치하지 않는 것 찾기

대화를 듣고, 버스에 대한 두 사람의 의견으로 일치하지 <u>않는</u> 것을 고르시오.

① 등교 시 지하철보다 편리하다.
② 운행 시간이 오래 걸린다.
③ 아침에 너무 혼잡하다.
④ 자리가 잘 나지 않는다.
⑤ 막차가 일찍 끊겨서 불편하다.

W How do you get to school?
M I usually take the bus. _____ _____ _____ than going to school by subway.
W Right. But sometimes I don't like to take the bus.
M Why not?
W It takes much longer than the subway because _____ _____ _____ _____ _____.
M You're right. And it's too crowded in the morning. It's hard to _____ _____ _____.
W Yeah, but one good thing is that buses _____ _____ _____ _____.
M I agree.

11 목적 파악 ✳

대화를 듣고, 남자가 전화를 건 목적으로 가장 적절한 것을 고르시오.

① 예약을 취소하기 위해서
② 영업시간을 확인하기 위해서
③ 의사에게 물어볼 것이 있어서
④ 예약된 일정을 변경하기 위해서
⑤ 여자와 만날 시간을 정하기 위해서

(*Telephone rings.*)

M Hello. I made an appointment with Dr. Smith, but I have to change it.

W _____ _____ _____ _____ _____, please?

M My name is James Harper. I have an appointment at 3:00 p.m. on Wednesday.

W All right, Mr. Harper. When do you want to change it to?

M _____ _____ _____ _____ next Tuesday at 3 o'clock?

W 3 o'clock _____ _____ _____, but 3:30 is available.

M 3:30 is okay.

W Okay. I will _____ _____ _____ for that time.

12 특정 정보 파악

대화를 듣고, 여자가 파티에 가져갈 음식을 고르시오.

① 쿠키   ② 샐러드
③ 케이크   ④ 아이스크림
⑤ 스파게티

Sound Clear ☆ **dessert**
2음절에 강세를 두어 [디절트]로 발음된다. 1음절에 강세를 두어 [데절트]로 발음되는 desert(사막)와 구분하여 알아 둔다.

M Mina, _____ _____ _____ to my party tomorrow?

W I'm going. Everyone is bringing _____ _____ _____, right?

M Yes, they are.

W _____ _____ _____ _____?

M Jenny said she would bring some salad, and I'll make some spaghetti. 〔한정〕

W I see. Is there someone who is bringing a dessert? 〔한정〕

M Yes, Jisu is _____ _____ _____. Why don't you bring some ice cream? 〔정답 단서〕

W All right. I will.

13 숫자 정보 파악

대화를 듣고, 여자가 받을 거스름돈으로 가장 적절한 것을 고르시오.

① $1   ② $2   ③ $3
④ $4   ⑤ $5

M Are you ready to order?

W Yes. I'd like _____ _____ _____ _____ _____ _____ _____, please.

M Coffee and donuts are $1 each. Do you want anything else? 〔정답 단서〕

W The banana muffins look delicious. How much is one?

M Muffins are usually $4 each, but they're only $3 each today.

W What about _____ _____ _____ _____? 〔한정〕 〔한정〕

M It's $2.

W Hmm... I'll just _____ _____ _____ _____ _____. Here's a $5 bill. 〔한정〕

M All right. Here's your change. 〔정답 단서〕

14 관계 추론

대화를 듣고, 두 사람의 관계로 가장 적절한 것을 고르시오.

① 약사 – 환자
② 의사 – 환자
③ 경비원 – 주민
④ 경찰관 – 시민
⑤ 식당 종업원 – 손님

Sound Clear ☆ **backache**

ch가 [k]로 소리 나서 [배케이크]로 발음된다.

M Hi. I need something for a backache.
W What happened?
M _____ _____ _____ when I slipped while hiking today.
W Did you go to see a doctor?
M It's too late. _____ _____ _____ _____ _____ now, so I have to go tomorrow morning.
W I see. Apply this cream on your back several times a day. It will _____ _____ _____ _____ .
M Thank you.

15 요청한 일 파악

대화를 듣고, 여자가 남자에게 요청한 일로 가장 적절한 것을 고르시오.

① 사진 찍기
② 머리 염색하기
③ 머리 짧게 자르기
④ 좋은 샴푸 추천해 주기
⑤ 헤어스타일 사진 보여 주기

M _____ _____ _____ _____ your hair done?
W I want to change my hairstyle, but I'm not sure which style will _____ _____ _____ _____ .
M I think you will look lovely with short hair.
W Really? I've always had long hair. Could you show me _____ _____ _____ _____ _____ _____ ?
M Sure. I'll bring them right away.
W Thank you.
M Here you are. _____ _____ _____ .

16 이유 파악

대화를 듣고, 남자가 화가 난 이유로 가장 적절한 것을 고르시오.

① 침대가 지저분해서
② 방에 벌레가 있어서
③ 냉방이 되지 않아서
④ 승강기가 고장 나서
⑤ 온수가 나오지 않아서

M I'm in 507. _____ _____ _____ !
W What is the problem, sir?
M There is a big brown bug in the room. It's crawling on my bed. It's so creepy.
W Oh, I'm sorry. _____ _____ _____ _____ . Would you like me to bring you some bug spray?
M No. Just give me another room. I _____ _____ _____ _____ in this room any longer.
W Okay. We'll _____ _____ _____ _____ immediately. Let me check now.

17 주제 파악

다음을 듣고, 여자가 하는 말의 내용으로 가장 적절한 것을 고르시오.

① 흡연의 폐해
② 감기 예방 수칙
③ 채식 위주의 식단
④ 건강을 유지하는 방법
⑤ 스트레스를 해소하는 방법

W Do you want to stay healthy? I'll give you some basic tips. First, eat more vegetables and less meat. Avoid food _____ _____ _____ _____ _____ . Second, work out regularly. Doing 30 minutes of exercise every day is good for your health as well as helpful to _____ _____ _____ . Third, if you smoke, stop smoking. It's not only _____ _____ _____ _____ _____ , but it also hurts your family and friends' health.

18 그림의 상황에 적절한 대화 찾기

다음 그림의 상황에 가장 적절한 대화를 고르시오.

① ② ③ ④ ⑤

① W Would you like to order now?
   M Yes. _____ _____ _____ _____.
② W What are you going to cook?
   M I'm going to make an omelet.
③ W Do you know _____ _____ _____ _____?
   M You should add some pepper.
④ W _____ _____ the salad bowl? 정답 단서
   M Sure. Here you are.
⑤ W ☆ Can you recommend a dish on the menu?
   M The mushroom cream pasta is _____ _____ _____ _____ _____.

19 마지막 말에 이어질 응답 찾기

대화를 듣고, 여자의 마지막 말에 이어질 남자의 말로 가장 적절한 것을 고르시오.

Man: _____

① No, thank you.
② Most women love roses.
③ Say happy birthday to her.
④ Your wife will be very happy.
⑤ Good choice. They're on sale today.

M I'd like to _____ _____ _____ for my wife. It's her birthday.
W What flowers does your wife like?
M She loves roses.
W Roses _____ _____ _____ _____: red, pink, and yellow.
M I'd like some red roses. How much are they?
W You can _____ _____ _____ for only $20.
M That sounds good. _____ _____ _____ _____.
W Very good. Would you like anything else?
M No, thank you.

20 마지막 말에 이어질 응답 찾기

대화를 듣고, 여자의 마지막 말에 이어질 남자의 말로 가장 적절한 것을 고르시오.

Man: _____

① It costs a dollar.
② No. I already have a pen.
③ Yes, but I couldn't find it.
④ I looked it up in the dictionary.
⑤ How about using a computer?

W Jake, _____ _____ _____ _____ _____?
M I lost my new pen. I bought it yesterday!
W _____ _____ _____ _____ _____ _____?
M I remember I used it in English class.
W And then?
M Then, I went to P.E. class. After that, it was lunch. And now I can't find it.
W It should be _____ _____ _____ _____. Did you look everywhere?
M Yes, but I couldn't find it.

1.0배속

1.2배속

01 다음을 듣고, 목요일의 날씨로 가장 적절한 것을 고르시오.

① ② ③

④ ⑤

02 대화를 듣고, 여자가 가리키는 인물을 고르시오.

① ② ③

④ ⑤

03 대화를 듣고, 남자의 심정으로 가장 적절한 것을 고르시오.

① angry   ② happy   ③ nervous
④ bored   ⑤ proud

04 대화를 듣고, 남자가 할머니 댁에서 한 일로 가장 적절한 것을 고르시오.

① 집 청소하기   ② 점심 차리기
③ 이삿짐 정리하기   ④ 앞마당 가꾸기
⑤ 공원 산책하기

05 대화를 듣고, 두 사람이 대화하는 장소로 가장 적절한 곳을 고르시오.

① 공원   ② 유치원   ③ 약국
④ 과학실   ⑤ 기차역

06 대화를 듣고, 여자의 마지막 말의 의도로 가장 적절한 것을 고르시오.

① 불평   ② 부탁   ③ 감사
④ 위로   ⑤ 동의

07 다음을 듣고, 여자가 두리안에 대해 언급하지 않은 것을 고르시오.

① 서식 환경   ② 무게   ③ 색깔
④ 별명   ⑤ 냄새

08 대화를 듣고, 여자가 대화 직후에 할 일로 가장 적절한 것을 고르시오.

① 꽃 배달시키기   ② 선물 사러 가기
③ 케이크 찾아오기   ④ 생일상 차리기
⑤ 엄마에게 전화하기

09 대화를 듣고, 남자가 요리에 사용할 재료가 아닌 것을 고르시오.

① 빵   ② 달걀   ③ 설탕
④ 우유   ⑤ 버터

10 다음을 듣고, 남자가 하는 말의 내용으로 가장 적절한 것을 고르시오.

① 건강 관리 비결
② 감기 예방 수칙
③ 실내 식물의 효용성
④ 실내 공기 정화 방법
⑤ 식물을 잘 기르는 방법

11 대화를 듣고, 중국어 수업에 대한 내용으로 일치하지 않는 것을 고르시오.

① 초급자를 대상으로 한다.
② 월요일부터 금요일까지 한다.
③ 방학 첫째 날에 시작한다.
④ 오후에 한 시간씩 한다.
⑤ 수강료는 무료이다.

12 대화를 듣고, 여자가 전화를 건 목적으로 가장 적절한 것을 고르시오.

① 예약을 확인하기 위해서
② 다른 방 배정을 요청하기 위해서
③ 체크아웃 시각을 확인하기 위해서
④ 객실 관리 서비스에 대해 항의하기 위해서
⑤ 발견된 분실물이 있는지 확인하기 위해서

13 대화를 듣고, 두 사람이 이용할 교통수단을 고르시오.

① 버스   ② 택시   ③ 지하철
④ 자가용   ⑤ 자전거

14 대화를 듣고, 두 사람의 관계로 가장 적절한 것을 고르시오.

① 점원 – 손님   ② 운동선수 – 코치
③ 체육 교사 – 학생   ④ 연예인 – 매니저
⑤ 요가 강사 – 수강생

15 대화를 듣고, 여자가 남자에게 부탁한 일로 가장 적절한 것을 고르시오.

① 다림질하기   ② 장보기
③ 옷 찾아오기   ④ 빨래하기
⑤ 블로그 홍보하기

16 대화를 듣고, 남자가 도서관에 가는 이유로 가장 적절한 것을 고르시오.

① 책을 반납하기 위해서
② 책을 대출하기 위해서
③ 친구와 만나기 위해서
④ 필요한 자료를 찾기 위해서
⑤ 잃어버린 물건을 찾기 위해서

17 다음 그림의 상황에 가장 적절한 대화를 고르시오.

①   ②   ③   ④   ⑤

18 대화를 듣고, 여자가 제과점에 대해 언급하지 않은 것을 고르시오.

① 이름   ② 위치
③ 분위기   ④ 추천 메뉴
⑤ 영업시간

[19-20] 대화를 듣고, 여자의 마지막 말에 이어질 남자의 말로 가장 적절한 것을 고르시오.

19 Man: _____

① Yes. I love reading.
② I went to bed early last night.
③ What kinds of stories do you like?
④ I started writing them when I was 9.
⑤ There are more than 100 stories in this book.

20 Man: _____

① There will be four of us.
② We'll arrive at 7 o'clock.
③ My name is Henry Johnson.
④ We'd like to have lunch on Saturday.
⑤ Could you recommend a good dessert?

01 날씨 파악

다음을 듣고, 목요일의 날씨로 가장 적절한 것을 고르시오.

① ② ③
④ ⑤

Sound Clear ☆ **Wednesday**
d가 묵음이라서 [웬즈데이]로 발음된다.

M Good morning. This is _____ _____ _____ _____.
It will be rainy or snowy on Monday and Tuesday. On
☆
Wednesday, there will be a lot of clouds. The weather will
be clear from Thursday _____ _____ _____ _____ 정답 단서

_____ _____. As the weather continues to be clear,
the atmosphere will get dry. Please pay special attention to
_____ _____.

02 그림 정보 파악

대화를 듣고, 여자가 가리키는 인물을 고르시오.

① ② ③
④ ⑤

W I _____ _____ _____ _____! Did you see her?
M Who are you talking about?
W The young woman over there. She's my favorite singer, Kate.
She _____ _____ _____ _____ _____.
M I don't know her. Do you mean the woman with sunglasses? 한정
W No, the woman _____ _____ _____ who is wearing a
short-sleeved, striped T-shirt.
M Now I see her. _____ _____ _____ _____ _____.
W That's her.

03 심정 추론

대화를 듣고, 남자의 심정으로 가장 적절한 것을 고르시오.

① angry   ② happy   ③ nervous
④ bored   ⑤ proud

W Andy, you don't look well. What's wrong?
M _____ _____ _____ _____ _____ my class
presentation.
W Do you mean the presentation of the group project?
M Yes. I'm the presenter tomorrow. _____ _____ _____
_____ _____ to make a presentation in front of many
people.
W Don't worry. _____ _____ _____ _____ _____.
You'll do well.
M Thanks, but I feel like I'll forget _____ _____ _____
_____ _____.

04 한 일 파악

대화를 듣고, 남자가 할머니 댁에서 한 일로 가장 적절한 것을 고르시오.

① 집 청소하기   ② 점심 차리기
③ 이삿짐 정리하기   ④ 앞마당 가꾸기
⑤ 공원 산책하기

W   Ron, how was your weekend?
M   I visited my grandma. She _____ _____ _____ _____ _____ last Saturday.
W   Did you _____ _____ _____ _____ things?
M   No, my parents did. Grandma is too old to do it all by herself.
W   What did you do then?
M   I _____ _____ _____ _____ _____ in the front yard with Grandma. She loves gardening.
W   That's great.

05 장소 추론

대화를 듣고, 두 사람이 대화하는 장소로 가장 적절한 곳을 고르시오.

① 공원   ② 유치원   ③ 약국
④ 과학실   ⑤ 기차역

M   Can I have a fever reducer for babies? _____ _____ _____ _____.
W   Yes, you can. _____ _____ _____ _____ _____ when her body temperature is above 38°C.
M   I got it.
W   Read and _____ _____ _____ on the label over here.
M   Okay. Thanks a lot.

06 의도 파악

대화를 듣고, 여자의 마지막 말의 의도로 가장 적절한 것을 고르시오.

① 불평   ② 부탁   ③ 감사
④ 위로   ⑤ 동의

Sound Clear ☆ **enough**
gh가 [f]로 소리 나서 [이너프]로 발음된다.

M   Liz, why are you so late?
W   I _____ _____ _____ a school project.
M   Really? You _____ _____ _____ _____.
W   And extremely hungry.
M   _____ _____ _____ _____ _____?
W   I had a sandwich, but it wasn't enough at all.
M   Oh, no. There _____ _____ _____ at home right now.
W   Then can you order some fried chicken while I change my clothes?

07 언급하지 않은 것 찾기

다음을 듣고, 여자가 두리안에 대해 언급하지 않은 것을 고르시오.

① 서식 환경   ② 무게   ③ 색깔
④ 별명   ⑤ 냄새

W   Today, _____ _____ _____ _____ a very interesting fruit, durian, to you. Durian is a tropical fruit. It grows only in humid, hot places. It can grow up to thirty centimeters long and usually _____ _____ _____ _____ _____.
The flesh is _____ _____ _____ _____ in Southeast Asia. People call it the "King of Fruits." It _____ _____ _____ _____, so many hotels and public transportation systems do not let people carry it.

08 할 일 파악

대화를 듣고, 여자가 대화 직후에 할 일로 가장 적절한 것을 고르시오.

① 꽃 배달시키기　② 선물 사러 가기
③ 케이크 찾아오기　④ 생일상 차리기
⑤ 엄마에게 전화하기

W　Dad, it's Mom's birthday today. Do you have any special plans?
M　Of course. I _____ _____ _____ _____. I'll pick up the cake at 5 o'clock.
W　What about the flowers?
M　_____ _____ _____ to our home.
W　Sounds like a perfect plan. Is there anything I can do?
M　Can you call her and check _____ _____ _____ _____ _____?
W　Okay. I'll do that right away.

09 특정 정보 파악

대화를 듣고, 남자가 요리에 사용할 재료가 아닌 것을 고르시오.

① 빵　　② 달걀　　③ 설탕
④ 우유　⑤ 버터

Sound Clear ☆ **pan**
fan(선풍기)과 혼동하지 않도록 [p]와 [f]를 잘 구분하여 듣는다.

M　Mom, I'll make you French toast for breakfast.
W　That sounds good. Do you know _____ _____ _____ _____?
M　Of course. It's very easy to make. _____ _____ _____ _____, eggs, and milk?
W　Yes. You also need butter to put on the pan.
M　I know it. Do you want me to add _____ _____ _____ _____?
W　No. It will make the toast too sweet.
M　Okay. _____ _____ _____ _____ _____, Mom.

10 주제 파악

다음을 듣고, 남자가 하는 말의 내용으로 가장 적절한 것을 고르시오.

① 건강 관리 비결
② 감기 예방 수칙
③ 실내 식물의 효용성
④ 실내 공기 정화 방법
⑤ 식물을 잘 기르는 방법

M　Plants can purify the air at your home and they are also good for decorations. Then what can you do to _____ _____ _____ _____? First, do not water your plants too often. Too much water can kill your plants. Second, let your plants _____ _____ _____ during the day. Third, do not move your plants around a lot. _____ _____ _____ _____ _____.

11 일치하지 않는 것 찾기

대화를 듣고, 중국어 수업에 대한 내용으로 일치하지 않는 것을 고르시오.

① 초급자를 대상으로 한다.
② 월요일부터 금요일까지 한다.
③ 방학 첫째 날에 시작한다.
④ 오후에 한 시간씩 한다.
⑤ 수강료는 무료이다.

M　Are you going to take any classes during vacation?
W　_____ _____ _____ _____. What about you?
M　I'll take a Chinese class for beginners at school.
W　Sounds interesting. When is it?
M　It's from Monday to Friday, and it _____ _____ _____ _____ of vacation.
W　_____ _____ _____ _____ _____ _____?
M　The class lasts for an hour at 9 every morning, and the class is free.
W　Great! _____ _____.

12 목적 파악

대화를 듣고, 여자가 전화를 건 목적으로 가장 적절한 것을 고르시오.

① 예약을 확인하기 위해서
② 다른 방 배정을 요청하기 위해서
③ 체크아웃 시각을 확인하기 위해서
④ 객실 관리 서비스에 대해 항의하기 위해서
⑤ 발견된 분실물이 있는지 확인하기 위해서

(*Telephone rings.*)

M Green Wood Hotel. How may I help you?
W Hello. My name is Linda Brown. I _____ _____ _____ Room 1307 two hours ago.
M Yes, Ms. Brown. Is there anything wrong?
W I think I _____ _____ _____ in the room. _____ _____ _____ _____ in the room?
M I will check with lost and found and call you back. Our housekeeping staff _____ _____ _____ _____ to the lost and found desk.
W Okay. Thank you. Call me at this number, please.

13 특정 정보 파악

대화를 듣고, 두 사람이 이용할 교통수단을 고르시오.

① 버스   ② 택시   ③ 지하철
④ 자가용   ⑤ 자전거

Sound Clear ☆ **because of**
앞 단어의 끝 자음과 뒤 단어의 모음이 만나 연음되어 [비커저브]로 발음된다.

M It's already 6:30.
W Really? We're going to _____ _____ _____. Are you going to drive?
M No. The restaurant doesn't have a parking lot. Let's take a taxi.
W It's rush hour, so _____ _____ _____ _____ _____ _____. How about taking the subway?
M The subway station isn't really _____ _____ _____ _____.
W But I think the subway is the fastest way we can get there. We can't take a taxi or bus because of ☆ _____ _____ _____ _____. *정답 단서*
M You're right. Let's hurry.

14 관계 추론

대화를 듣고, 두 사람의 관계로 가장 적절한 것을 고르시오.

① 점원 – 손님
② 운동선수 – 코치
③ 체육 교사 – 학생
④ 연예인 – 매니저
⑤ 요가 강사 – 수강생

M Excuse me. _____ _____ _____ _____.
W What can I do for you?
M Do you have _____ _____ _____ _____ in a large size?
W Yes. They're right over here. These pants come in both black and gray. *정답 단서*
M I like the black ones. _____ _____ _____ _____ _____?
W Sure. The fitting room is over there. _____ _____ _____ *정답 단서*, so try on an extra-large, too.
M Okay. Thank you.

15 부탁한 일 파악

대화를 듣고, 여자가 남자에게 부탁한 일로 가장 적절한 것을 고르시오.

① 다림질하기 ② 장보기
③ 옷 찾아오기 ④ 빨래하기
⑤ 블로그 홍보하기

M What are you doing?
W I'm _____ _____ _____ on my blog. Where are you going?
M I'm going to the supermarket to _____ _____ _____. Do you need anything?
W Not really. But could you _____ _____ _____ _____?
M Sure. What is it?
W _____ _____ _____ _____, can you pick up my clothes from the dry cleaner's? I had my shirts cleaned.
M Okay. No problem.

16 이유 파악

대화를 듣고, 남자가 도서관에 가는 이유로 가장 적절한 것을 고르시오.

① 책을 반납하기 위해서
② 책을 대출하기 위해서
③ 친구와 만나기 위해서
④ 필요한 자료를 찾기 위해서
⑤ 잃어버린 물건을 찾기 위해서

Sound Clear ☆ **dropped it**
앞 단어의 끝 자음과 뒤 단어의 모음이 만나 연음되어 [드랍딧]으로 발음된다.

W Harry, where are you going?
M I'm going to the library.
W Are you going to _____ _____ _____?
M No. I just _____ _____ _____.
W Then why are you going there?
M I lost my wallet. I think I dropped it _____ _____ _____ _____ _____ in the library.
W Do you want me to go with you? I can _____ _____ _____ _____.
M Really? Thank you.

17 그림의 상황에 적절한 대화 찾기

다음 그림의 상황에 가장 적절한 대화를 고르시오.

① ② ③ ④ ⑤

① M _____ _____ _____ _____?
  W Sure. Go ahead.
② M What's your favorite animal?
  W _____ _____ _____ _____.
③ M How often do you walk your dog?
  W _____ _____ _____ _____.
④ M Is this your painting?
  W Yes. Do you like it?
⑤ M Excuse me. We _____ _____ _____ _____ _____.
  W Oh, I'm sorry. I didn't see the sign.

18 언급하지 않은 것 찾기 ❇

대화를 듣고, 여자가 제과점에 대해 언급하지 않은 것을 고르시오.

① 이름　　　　② 위치
③ 분위기　　　④ 추천 메뉴
⑤ 영업시간

Sound Clear ☆ **can't**

미국식은 a를 [애]로 발음하여 [캔트]로, 영국식은 [아]로 발음하여 [칸트]로 발음된다. 축약된 't는 거의 발음되지 않는다.

M Emily, can you ＿＿＿ ＿＿＿ ＿＿＿ ＿＿＿ for desserts?
W My favorite around here is Jackie's Bakery.
　　　　　　　　　　　　　　　　　정답 단서
M Where is it?
W It's on Baker Street. It's ＿＿＿ ＿＿＿ ＿＿＿
　　정답 단서
＿＿＿ ＿＿＿.
M It's close. Why is it your favorite?
W Because the waffles there are so good. They're crispy on the outside and ＿＿＿ ＿＿＿ ＿＿＿. You should try one.
　　　　　　　　정답 단서
M Oh, I can't wait! What time does it open?
　　　　☆
W It opens from 8 a.m. to 7 p.m.
　　　　　　정답 단서

19 마지막 말에 이어질 응답 찾기

대화를 듣고, 여자의 마지막 말에 이어질 남자의 말로 가장 적절한 것을 고르시오.

Man: ＿＿＿＿＿＿＿＿＿＿＿＿＿＿＿

① Yes. I love reading.
② I went to bed early last night.
③ What kinds of stories do you like?
④ I started writing them when I was 9.
⑤ There are more than 100 stories in this book.

W Mike, I ＿＿＿ ＿＿＿ ＿＿＿ your short story in the school newspaper.
M Oh, did you? What did you think?
W It is a really interesting story. ＿＿＿ ＿＿＿ ＿＿＿ ＿＿＿!
M Thank you.
W I didn't know ＿＿＿ ＿＿＿ ＿＿＿ ＿＿＿.
M It is my favorite hobby.
W ＿＿＿ ＿＿＿ ＿＿＿ ＿＿＿ ＿＿＿ ＿＿＿ short stories?
M I started writing them when I was 9.

20 마지막 말에 이어질 응답 찾기

대화를 듣고, 여자의 마지막 말에 이어질 남자의 말로 가장 적절한 것을 고르시오.

Man: ＿＿＿＿＿＿＿＿＿＿＿＿＿＿＿

① There will be four of us.
② We'll arrive at 7 o'clock.
③ My name is Henry Johnson.
④ We'd like to have lunch on Saturday.
⑤ Could you recommend a good dessert?

W Rose Restaurant. How may I help you?
M Hi. I would like to ＿＿＿ ＿＿＿ ＿＿＿.
W ＿＿＿ ＿＿＿ ＿＿＿ are you making the reservation?
M It's for Friday.
W What time would you like to come?
M Is 7 p.m. available?
W We have ＿＿＿ ＿＿＿ ＿＿＿ ＿＿＿ at 7. How many people will be ＿＿＿ ＿＿＿ ＿＿＿?
M There will be four of us.

Review Test

실전 모의고사 **07** 회

Word Check 영어는 우리말로, 우리말은 영어로 써 보기

01	crowded	13	외출하다
02	dozen	14	요통
03	medium	15	피하다
04	take a lesson	16	소중한, 가치 있는
05	convenient	17	기어가다
06	creepy	18	지폐
07	regularly	19	즉시, 바로
08	unfortunately	20	극도로, 매우
09	contact	21	(약 등을) 바르다
10	several	22	(우묵한) 그릇
11	dessert	23	통증
12	a piece of	24	매우 놀란, 겁먹은

Expression Check 알맞은 표현을 넣어 문장 완성하기

25 I'll be _____ _____ _____. 나는 줄을 서서 기다리고 있을게.

26 Isn't it _____ _____? 그건 할인 중 아닌가요?

27 Doing exercise is good for your health _____ _____ _____ helpful to relieve your stress. 운동하는 것은 스트레스 해소에 도움이 될 뿐 아니라 건강에도 좋습니다.

28 _____ _____ repairs on the water pipe, you'll not be able to use the water.
수도관 수리로 인해, 물을 사용하실 수 없습니다.

29 I'm not sure which style will _____ _____ _____ me.
어떤 스타일이 제게 어울릴지 모르겠어요.

30 We will do our best to finish the _____ _____ _____ _____.
가능한 한 빨리 끝내도록 최선을 다하겠습니다.

Answers p.44

Word Check
영어는 우리말로, 우리말은 영어로 써 보기

01	flesh		13	정화하다
02	continue		14	초급자
03	ponytail		15	세탁소
04	short-sleeved		16	소유물
05	presentation		17	대중교통
06	presenter		18	정리하다
07	extra-large		19	(글을) 올리다
08	fever reducer		20	표지판
09	unpack		21	바삭바삭한
10	tropical		22	예방하다
11	deliver		23	재능 있는
12	atmosphere		24	일행, 단체

Expression Check
알맞은 표현을 넣어 문장 완성하기

25 She has just _____ _____ us.   그녀가 방금 우리를 지나쳐 갔어.

26 _____ these things _____ _____.   이 사항들을 명심하세요.

27 I _____ _____ I'll forget what I need to say.   내가 말해야 할 것을 잊어버릴 것 같은 느낌이야.

28 Please _____ special _____ _____ prevent fires.
화재 예방에 특별히 주의를 기울이시기 바랍니다.

29 I had a sandwich, but it _____ enough _____ _____.
저는 샌드위치를 먹긴 했는데, 전혀 충분하지 않았어요.

30 I think I dropped it when I _____ _____ someone in the library.
내가 도서관에서 누군가에게 부딪혔을 때 그것을 떨어뜨린 것 같아.

01 다음을 듣고, 일요일의 날씨로 가장 적절한 것을 고르시오.

①
②
③

④
⑤

02 대화를 듣고, 남자가 구입할 곰 인형으로 가장 적절한 것을 고르시오.

①
②
③

④
⑤

03 대화를 듣고, 여자가 마지막에 느꼈을 심정으로 가장 적절한 것을 고르시오.

① upset　　② lonely　　③ curious
④ relieved　　⑤ surprised

04 대화를 듣고, 여자가 지난 주말에 한 일로 가장 적절한 것을 고르시오.

① 낚시하기　　　② 등산하기
③ 수영장 가기　　④ 파도타기
⑤ 집에서 쉬기

05 대화를 듣고, 두 사람이 대화하는 장소로 가장 적절한 곳을 고르시오.

① 방송국　　　② 운동장
③ 악기 매장　　④ 컴퓨터실
⑤ 밴드 동아리방

06 대화를 듣고, 여자의 마지막 말의 의도로 가장 적절한 것을 고르시오.

① 허가　　② 거절　　③ 후회
④ 감사　　⑤ 칭찬

07 다음을 듣고, Dr. Baker의 강연 내용으로 가장 적절한 것을 고르시오.

① 적절한 TV 시청 시간
② 청소년 권장 수면 시간
③ 숙면을 취하기 위한 조언
④ 효율적인 시간 관리 방법
⑤ 바람직한 휴대 전화 사용법

08 대화를 듣고, 남자가 도서를 대출할 수 <u>없는</u> 기간을 고르시오.

① 1 day　　② 2 days　　③ 3 days
④ 4 days　　⑤ 5 days

09 대화를 듣고, 여자가 대화 직후에 할 일로 가장 적절한 것을 고르시오.

① 서점 가기
② 선물 사기
③ 콘서트 표 예매하기
④ Mary에게 전화하기
⑤ Rebecca에게 전화하기

10 대화를 듣고, 여자가 이구아나에 대해 언급하지 <u>않은</u> 것을 고르시오.

① 색깔　　② 길이　　③ 무게
④ 수명　　⑤ 먹이

11 대화를 듣고, 여자가 미용실에 간 목적으로 가장 적절한 것을 고르시오.

① 예약을 변경하기 위해서
② 머리를 염색하기 위해서
③ 환불을 요청하기 위해서
④ 머리 손질을 요청하기 위해서
⑤ 미용사 친구를 만나기 위해서

12 대화를 듣고, 두 사람이 만날 시각을 고르시오.

① 6:00 p.m.   ② 6:30 p.m.   ③ 7:00 p.m.
④ 7:30 p.m.   ⑤ 8:00 p.m.

13 대화를 듣고, 두 사람의 관계로 가장 적절한 것을 고르시오.

① 의사 – 환자
② 식당 종업원 – 손님
③ 면세점 직원 – 관광객
④ 호텔 직원 – 투숙객
⑤ 비행기 승무원 – 탑승객

14 대화를 듣고, 여자가 남자에게 요청한 일로 가장 적절한 것을 고르시오.

① 쿠키 굽기   ② 요리책 찾기
③ 우유 사 오기   ④ 달걀 가져오기
⑤ 물건 계산하기

15 대화를 듣고, 여자가 운동화를 사지 <u>못한</u> 이유로 가장 적절한 것을 고르시오.

① 너무 비싸서
② 원하는 색상이 없어서
③ 신발 가게를 찾지 못해서
④ 쇼핑하러 갈 시간이 없어서
⑤ 자신에게 맞는 크기의 신발이 없어서

16 다음 그림의 상황에 가장 적절한 대화를 고르시오.

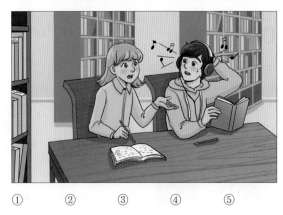

① ② ③ ④ ⑤

17 대화를 듣고, 두 사람이 어머니의 날에 할 일이 <u>아닌</u> 것을 고르시오.

① 편지 쓰기   ② 아침상 차리기
③ 꽃 사기   ④ 케이크 주문하기
⑤ 노래 부르기

18 다음을 듣고, 피트니스 센터에 대한 내용으로 일치하지 <u>않는</u> 것을 고르시오.

① 24시간 이용할 수 있다.
② 일주일 내내 이용할 수 있다.
③ 회원들에게는 요가 강좌가 무료이다.
④ 규모가 큰 사우나가 있다.
⑤ 이번 달에 등록하면 할인을 해 준다.

[19-20] 대화를 듣고, 여자의 마지막 말에 이어질 남자의 말로 가장 적절한 것을 고르시오.

19 Man: _____

① Thank you very much.
② Yes. The weekend is fine.
③ The delivery charge is $25.
④ Yes. We'll deliver it on Thursday.
⑤ I'll check the schedule one more time.

20 Man: _____

① Thanks for visiting me.
② I'll refund your money.
③ No. I don't want to pay for it.
④ I'm sorry for the inconvenience.
⑤ I hope there's nothing wrong with the new one.

받아쓰기용

01 날씨 파악

다음을 듣고, 일요일의 날씨로 가장 적절한 것을 고르시오.

①  ②  ③ 

④  ⑤ 

M So this is what the weather will look like this weekend. We'll ________ ________ ________ ________ on Friday and Saturday. It will also be quite windy on these days. On Saturday night, ________ ________ ________ ________ ________, and the showers will stop. And on Sunday, it's going to be quite foggy. Fog can ________ ________ ________, so please be careful.

02 그림 정보 파악

대화를 듣고, 남자가 구입할 곰 인형으로 가장 적절한 것을 고르시오.

①  ②  ③ 

④  ⑤ 

Sound Clear ☆ **ribbon**
'리본'은 실제로 [리븐]으로 발음된다.

M Hi. I'd like to buy a teddy bear for my daughter.
W ________ ________ ________ ________. Which one would you like?
M I guess a teddy bear with a ribbon☆ will be good.
W Here's one with a ribbon ________ ________ ________.
M Well, I think it's too ordinary. Do you have one ________ ________ ________ ________?
W Yes, we do. This one is ________ ________ ________, and that one over there is wearing a hat.
M I'll take the one with the hat. That's cute.

03 심정 추론

대화를 듣고, 여자가 마지막에 느꼈을 심정으로 가장 적절한 것을 고르시오.

① upset ② lonely ③ curious
④ relieved ⑤ surprised

W Wait a minute. Where are we now?
M Oh, no. I think we ________ ________ ________ ________ ________ ________.
W Didn't you say this was the right stop?
M I thought so, but we had to ________ ________ ________ ________. I'm sorry.
W That's okay. But the next bus comes in 15 minutes. I think ________ ________ ________ for the concert.
M If we take a taxi, we'll ________ ________ ________ ________. I'll pay for the ride.
W We won't be late then. Thank you.

04 한 일 파악

대화를 듣고, 여자가 지난 주말에 한 일로 가장 적절한 것을 고르시오.

① 낚시하기　　　② 등산하기
③ 수영장 가기　④ 파도타기
⑤ 집에서 쉬기

Sound Clear ☆ **next time**
동일한 발음의 자음이 연이어 나오면 앞 자음 소리가 탈락하여 [넥스타임]으로 발음된다.

M　Jane, you _____ _____ _____ _____.
W　Do I? The reason is probably that I have a suntan.
M　Oh, now I see that. _____ _____ _____ _____ during the weekend?
W　_____ _____ _____ _____ in such hot weather. I went to the beach.
M　And you swam all day.
W　No. I went surfing.
M　Really? I've always wanted to try that. _____ _____ _____ _____ _____ the next time you go.
W　Okay.

05 장소 추론

대화를 듣고, 두 사람이 대화하는 장소로 가장 적절한 곳을 고르시오.

① 방송국　　　② 운동장
③ 악기 매장　④ 컴퓨터실
⑤ 밴드 동아리방

M　Hello. Is your band auditioning _____ _____ _____?
W　That's right. Come on in. (*Pause*) I'm Beth. What's your name?
M　I'm Daniel. I'm in the first grade. I play the guitar. Do you want to _____ _____ _____ _____?
W　Oh, there already is a guitarist in our band. Can you _____ _____ _____ _____?
M　No. I only play the guitar and sing.
W　That's great. We need a lead singer, too. Are you interested?
M　Yeah, sure.
W　Good. _____ _____ _____ _____ _____.

06 의도 파악

대화를 듣고, 여자의 마지막 말의 의도로 가장 적절한 것을 고르시오.

① 허가　　② 거절　　③ 후회
④ 감사　　⑤ 칭찬

M　Excuse me. Can I get a refund for a musical ticket? I bought it through an app.
W　Yes. Please _____ _____ _____ _____.
M　Here you are.
W　I am sorry, but _____ _____ _____ _____ _____ on the day of the concert.
M　Really? I didn't know that.
W　The refund policy is _____ _____ _____ _____ _____. Look here.
M　Oh, well, who can read _____ _____ _____?
W　I'm sorry, but it's the policy.

07 주제 파악

다음을 듣고, Dr. Baker의 강연 내용으로 가장 적절한 것을 고르시오.

① 적절한 TV 시청 시간
② 청소년 권장 수면 시간
③ 숙면을 취하기 위한 조언
④ 효율적인 시간 관리 방법
⑤ 바람직한 휴대 전화 사용법

W Today, we had Dr. Baker with us in the studio. He _____ _____ _____ _____ for getting a good night's sleep. Don't go to bed with the TV on. Don't think too much before bedtime. Don't play games before you go to sleep and _____ _____ _____ _____ when you go to bed. Dr. Baker, thank you for _____ _____ _____ to our listeners.

08 특정 정보 파악

대화를 듣고, 남자가 도서를 대출할 수 <u>없는</u> 기간을 고르시오.

① 1 day   ② 2 days   ③ 3 days
④ 4 days   ⑤ 5 days

M I want to return these two books.
W Okay. (*Pause*) _____ _____ _____ _____ _____.
M Oh, I didn't know that. Do I have to pay a late fee?
W _____ _____ _____ _____, but you may not 정답 단서
borrow a book for four days.
M For four days?
W Yes. You can't check out books _____ _____ _____ _____ _____ that each book is overdue.
M Oh, I see.

09 할 일 파악 ✲

대화를 듣고, 여자가 대화 직후에 할 일로 가장 적절한 것을 고르시오.

① 서점 가기
② 선물 사기
③ 콘서트 표 예매하기
④ Mary에게 전화하기
⑤ Rebecca에게 전화하기

W _____ _____ _____ _____ what to buy Mary for her birthday. Do you have any good ideas?
M What about buying her some books? She likes reading.
W Well, I'd like to _____ _____ _____ _____.
M How about a concert ticket? She said she likes rock music.
W That's a good idea. Do you know _____ _____ _____?
M No. I think her roommate Rebecca might know though.
W I guess so. _____ _____ _____ _____ _____ right now.

10 언급하지 않은 것 찾기

대화를 듣고, 여자가 이구아나에 대해 언급하지 <u>않은</u> 것을 고르시오.

① 색깔   ② 길이   ③ 무게
④ 수명   ⑤ 먹이

Sound Clear ☆ **weigh**
gh가 묵음이라서 [웨이]로 발음된다.

M You have an iguana _____ _____ _____, don't you?
W Yes. Why?
M I _____ _____ _____ _____, too. Can you give me some tips?
W Hmm... if you want a baby iguana, choose a green one. That means it is young.
M Interesting.
W And _____ _____ _____ _____ _____ two meters long and weigh about ten kilograms.
M That's amazing. Is there anything I should know?
W You need to _____ _____ _____ _____ and vegetables every day.

11 목적 파악

대화를 듣고, 여자가 미용실에 간 목적으로 가장 적절한 것을 고르시오.

① 예약을 변경하기 위해서
② 머리를 염색하기 위해서
③ 환불을 요청하기 위해서
④ 머리 손질을 요청하기 위해서
⑤ 미용사 친구를 만나기 위해서

Sound Clear ☆ **appointment**
자음 세 개가 연속으로 나오면 중간 자음의 발음이 약화되어 [어포인먼트]로 발음된다.

M Hello. Do you have an ☆appointment?
W No. I _____ _____ _____ _____ yesterday, but it's not the same length _____ _____ _____.
M Do you remember the hair stylist's name?
W Yes. Her name was Rosie.
M Oh, _____ _____ _____ today. Can I trim your sides for you?
W Sure. Just make sure _____ _____ _____ _____ _____, please.
M All right. Please sit here.

12 숫자 정보 파악

대화를 듣고, 두 사람이 만날 시각을 고르시오.

① 6:00 p.m. ② 6:30 p.m.
③ 7:00 p.m. ④ 7:30 p.m.
⑤ 8:00 p.m.

M Julie, do you want to have dinner _____ _____ _____ _____?
W That sounds good to me. Let's go to the Italian restaurant next to the concert hall.
M Good. _____ _____ _____ _____ _____?
W The concert starts at 8 o'clock. So how about meeting at 6:30?
M Maybe we should meet _____ _____ _____ 한정 _____. The restaurant might be crowded.
W I see. Will it be okay if we meet two hours before the concert starts? 정답 단서
W I guess it'll be fine. See you then.

13 관계 추론

대화를 듣고, 두 사람의 관계로 가장 적절한 것을 고르시오.

① 의사 – 환자
② 식당 종업원 – 손님
③ 면세점 직원 – 관광객
④ 호텔 직원 – 투숙객
⑤ 비행기 승무원 – 탑승객

W Excuse me. Could you bring me one more blanket? It's _____ _____ _____ _____.
M Sure. Wait a moment, please. (*Pause*) Here you are. Would you like anything else?
W Not for now. Thank you. By the way, when do you _____ _____ _____?
M After we hand these out. _____ _____ _____ _____ your arrival card?
W Yes, I have. 정답 단서
M Okay. We'll begin our in-flight duty-free sales shortly. 정답 단서
W Thank you.

14 요청한 일 파악

대화를 듣고, 여자가 남자에게 요청한 일로 가장 적절한 것을 고르시오.

① 쿠키 굽기 ② 요리책 찾기
③ 우유 사 오기 ④ 달걀 가져오기
⑤ 물건 계산하기

Sound Clear ☆ **flour**

flour(밀가루)와 flower(꽃)는 [플라워]로 발음이 같으므로 맥락을 통해 의미를 파악해야 한다.

W Let's see. Did we buy everything?
M I think so. Oh, do you want to buy some cookies, too?
W I think homemade cookies are better. _____ _____
_____ _____ _____.
M That's great. Do we _____ _____ _____ _____?
W No. We need flour, sugar, and butter. Oh, we also need eggs.
M Let's get some chocolate chips, too.
W Good! _____ _____ _____ _____ _____? I'll get
the other ingredients.
M Okay. Let's meet at the checkout counter.

15 이유 파악

대화를 듣고, 여자가 운동화를 사지 못한 이유로 가장 적절한 것을 고르시오.

① 너무 비싸서
② 원하는 색상이 없어서
③ 신발 가게를 찾지 못해서
④ 쇼핑하러 갈 시간이 없어서
⑤ 자신에게 맞는 크기의 신발이 없어서

M Jane, did you buy _____ _____ _____ _____?
W No, I didn't.
M Why not? You really wanted to buy them.
W I did. I went to all of the shoe stores in town, but _____
_____ _____ _____ _____.
M Why don't you just order them online?
W When I buy sneakers, I _____ _____ _____ _____.
M I see. I hope you find the sneakers in your size soon.
정답 단서

16 그림의 상황에 적절한 대화 찾기

다음 그림의 상황에 가장 적절한 대화를 고르시오.

① ② ③ ④ ⑤

① W How much are these headphones?
  M They're $70. 함정
② W Who's _____ _____ _____?
  M I love Taylor Swift.
③ W Would you _____ _____ _____ _____?
  M Sure, no problem. I'm sorry.
④ W Can I _____ _____ _____ for a moment?
  M Of course. Go ahead.
⑤ W Can I borrow some headphones from the library? 함정
  M _____ _____ _____ _____ _____.

17 할 일 파악

대화를 듣고, 두 사람이 어머니의 날에 할 일이 아닌 것을 고르시오.

① 편지 쓰기   ② 아침상 차리기
③ 꽃 사기   ④ 케이크 주문하기
⑤ 노래 부르기

Sound Clear ☆ **favorite**
1음절에 강세가 있고, 2음절의 [ə]가 약화되어 [페이브릿]에 가깝게 발음된다.

M   Let's write Mom a letter for Mother's Day.
W   Of course. That's what we do every year. But I want to ＿＿＿＿ ＿＿＿＿ ＿＿＿＿ ＿＿＿＿ this time.
M   Why don't we make breakfast for her?
W   Good. ＿＿＿＿ ＿＿＿＿ ＿＿＿＿ ＿＿＿＿, let's sing her favorite song.
M   Sure, we can do that. How about buying some flowers?
W   Flowers are good. What about ordering a cake, too?
M   We ＿＿＿＿ ＿＿＿＿ ＿＿＿＿ buy both flowers and a cake.
W   You're right. Let's just get some flowers.

18 일치하지 않는 것 찾기

다음을 듣고, 피트니스 센터에 대한 내용으로 일치하지 않는 것을 고르시오.

① 24시간 이용할 수 있다.
② 일주일 내내 이용할 수 있다.
③ 회원들에게는 요가 강좌가 무료이다.
④ 규모가 큰 사우나가 있다.
⑤ 이번 달에 등록하면 할인을 해 준다.

M   Do you want to ＿＿＿＿ ＿＿＿＿? Come and join our fitness center. We're open 24 hours a day, ＿＿＿＿ ＿＿＿＿ ＿＿＿＿ ＿＿＿＿. For our members, we provide yoga classes at a discounted price. We have a large sauna for you to use, too. If you sign up before ＿＿＿＿ ＿＿＿＿ ＿＿＿＿ ＿＿＿＿ ＿＿＿＿, you can get a 30% discount. So hurry up.

19 마지막 말에 이어질 응답 찾기

대화를 듣고, 여자의 마지막 말에 이어질 남자의 말로 가장 적절한 것을 고르시오.

Man: ＿＿＿＿＿＿＿＿＿＿＿＿＿＿＿＿

① Thank you very much.
② Yes. The weekend is fine.
③ The delivery charge is $25.
④ Yes. We'll deliver it on Thursday.
⑤ I'll check the schedule one more time.

M   Thank you for shopping at Best Furniture.
W   My pleasure. I really like my new sofa.
M   Would you ＿＿＿＿ ＿＿＿＿ ＿＿＿＿ ＿＿＿＿ and address here for the delivery?
W   Okay. When can I ＿＿＿＿ ＿＿＿＿ ＿＿＿＿ ＿＿＿＿ ＿＿＿＿?
M   In three days. This Thursday.
W   Can you ＿＿＿＿ ＿＿＿＿ ＿＿＿＿ ＿＿＿＿?
M   I'll check the schedule one more time.

20 마지막 말에 이어질 응답 찾기

대화를 듣고, 여자의 마지막 말에 이어질 남자의 말로 가장 적절한 것을 고르시오.

Man: ＿＿＿＿＿＿＿＿＿＿＿＿＿＿＿＿

① Thanks for visiting me.
② I'll refund your money.
③ No. I don't want to pay for it.
④ I'm sorry for the inconvenience.
⑤ I hope there's nothing wrong with the new one.

M   Hi. I bought this smartphone yesterday.
W   Is there a problem?
M   ＿＿＿＿ ＿＿＿＿ ＿＿＿＿ ＿＿＿＿. It keeps turning off although it is fully charged.
W   Will you ＿＿＿＿ ＿＿＿＿ ＿＿＿＿ ＿＿＿＿? I'll check it out.
M   Here you are.
W   (Pause) Hmm... it really does. I'll ＿＿＿＿ ＿＿＿＿ ＿＿＿＿ ＿＿＿＿ ＿＿＿＿ ＿＿＿＿.
M   I hope there's nothing wrong with the new one.

1.0배속

1.2배속

01 다음을 듣고, 다음 주 목요일의 날씨로 가장 적절한 것을 고르시오.

02 대화를 듣고, 여자가 구입할 스웨터로 가장 적절한 것을 고르시오.

03 대화를 듣고, 여자의 심정으로 가장 적절한 것을 고르시오.

① scared ② bored ③ nervous
④ satisfied ⑤ annoyed

04 대화를 듣고, 여자가 지난 주말에 한 일로 가장 적절한 것을 고르시오.

① 숙제하기 ② 콘서트 가기
③ 영화관 가기 ④ 집에서 쉬기
⑤ 도서관 가기

05 대화를 듣고, 두 사람이 대화하는 장소로 가장 적절한 곳을 고르시오.

① 공원 ② 호텔 ③ 식당
④ 공연장 ⑤ 기숙사

06 대화를 듣고, 여자의 마지막 말의 의도로 가장 적절한 것을 고르시오.

① 칭찬 ② 동의 ③ 조언
④ 사과 ⑤ 거절

07 대화를 듣고, 남자가 잡지에서 가장 좋아하는 부문을 고르시오.

① 영화 ② 여행 ③ 게임
④ 만화 ⑤ 스포츠

08 대화를 듣고, 남자가 대화 직후에 할 일로 가장 적절한 것을 고르시오.

① 날씨 확인하기
② 누나에게 연락하기
③ 자전거 대여소 가기
④ 누나와 자전거 타기
⑤ 자전거 바퀴 교체하기

09 다음을 듣고, 남자가 하는 말의 내용으로 가장 적절한 것을 고르시오.

① 나비의 특징
② 나방의 서식지
③ 나비와 나방의 공통점
④ 나비와 나방의 차이점
⑤ 나비와 나방의 활동 시간

10 대화를 듣고, 여자가 증상으로 언급하지 <u>않은</u> 것을 고르시오.

① 열이 난다. ② 으슬으슬 춥다.
③ 목이 아프다. ④ 기침이 난다.
⑤ 콧물이 난다.

11 대화를 듣고, 두 사람이 이야기하는 식당에 대한 내용으로 일치하지 <u>않는</u> 것을 고르시오.

① 일식당이다.
② 어제 개업했다.
③ 일주일 동안 할인 행사를 한다.
④ 할인 행사는 모든 메뉴에 해당된다.
⑤ 할인 행사는 저녁 시간대에 한다.

12 대화를 듣고, 남자가 샌드위치를 만드는 목적으로 가장 적절한 것을 고르시오.

① 도시락을 싸기 위해서
② 파티에 가져가기 위해서
③ 바자회에서 팔기 위해서
④ 재능 기부를 하기 위해서
⑤ 요리 경연 대회에 나가기 위해서

13 대화를 듣고, 여자가 지불해야 할 금액으로 가장 적절한 것을 고르시오.

① $10   ② $13   ③ $16
④ $20   ⑤ $22

14 대화를 듣고, 두 사람의 관계로 가장 적절한 것을 고르시오.

① 친구 – 친구
② 마트 직원 – 손님
③ 주방장 – 웨이터
④ 요리 강사 – 수강생
⑤ 음식점 직원 – 손님

15 대화를 듣고, 여자가 남자에게 부탁한 일로 가장 적절한 것을 고르시오.

① 안약 사 오기
② 안과에 같이 가기
③ 안과 진료 예약해 주기
④ 렌즈 착용법 알려 주기
⑤ 안과 전화번호 알려 주기

16 대화를 듣고, 남자가 할인을 받지 <u>못한</u> 이유로 가장 적절한 것을 고르시오.

① 학생이 아니라서   ② 쿠폰을 잃어버려서
③ 학생증이 없어서   ④ 구입 금액이 적어서
⑤ 할인 기간이 지나서

17 대화를 듣고, 두 사람의 대화가 <u>어색한</u> 것을 고르시오.

①   ②   ③   ④   ⑤

18 다음을 듣고, 여자가 하는 말의 내용으로 가장 적절한 것을 고르시오.

① 르누아르의 생애   ② 전시회 관람 안내
③ 워크숍 일정 공지   ④ 미술관 이용 예절
⑤ 유명한 여행지 추천

[19-20] 대화를 듣고, 남자의 마지막 말에 이어질 여자의 말로 가장 적절한 것을 고르시오.

19 Woman: _____

① I don't like to travel.
② I will stay here for three months.
③ I've never visited America before.
④ I have to go back to school in a week.
⑤ I will go to Disney World with my cousins.

20 Woman: _____

① My hobby is reading novels.
② He likes the book *Gorilla*.
③ He likes reading by himself.
④ I can take care of him now.
⑤ He went to bed an hour ago.

받아쓰기용

01 날씨 파악

다음을 듣고, 다음 주 목요일의 날씨로 가장 적절한 것을 고르시오.

① ② ③

④ ⑤

W Hello. I'm Amanda Jones. Here is the weather for next week. Tomorrow will be _____ _____ _____ with lots of sunshine nationwide. On Tuesday and Wednesday, however, it will be cold again. Thursday will be very windy, so please don't _____ _____ _____ _____ _____. On Friday and Saturday, it will be cloudy, and _____ _____ _____.

정답 단서

02 그림 정보 파악

대화를 듣고, 여자가 구입할 스웨터로 가장 적절한 것을 고르시오.

① ② ③

④ ⑤

Sound Clear ☆ **totally**
[t]가 모음 사이에서 약화되어 [토럴리]로 발음된다.

W Look at this sweater. The polka dots on it are so cute! I will buy this.
정답 단서
M Don't you already _____ _____ _____ _____?
W Oh, that one has smaller polka dots. It's totally different. ☆
M _____ _____ _____ _____ _____ over there?
W That's too simple. I also don't like V-shaped necklines.
M All right. _____ _____ _____ _____.
정답 단서
W Okay. I'll buy the one I picked out first.
정답 단서

03 심정 추론

대화를 듣고, 여자의 심정으로 가장 적절한 것을 고르시오.

① scared ② bored ③ nervous
④ satisfied ⑤ annoyed

(Telephone rings.)
M Hello. Lion Electronics Service Center.
W Hi. My vacuum cleaner doesn't work. I hope I can _____ _____ _____ for free.
M When did you buy the product?
W I bought it about _____ _____ _____ _____ _____ ago.
M I'm afraid that all our products only have a one-year warranty.
W Only one year? That's too short.
M I'm sorry. _____ _____ _____.
W I don't want to spend any money to repair it. I'd rather _____ _____ _____ _____.

04 한 일 파악

대화를 듣고, 여자가 지난 주말에 한 일로 가장 적절한 것을 고르시오.

① 숙제하기   ② 콘서트 가기
③ 영화관 가기   ④ 집에서 쉬기
⑤ 도서관 가기

M How was your weekend?
W _____ _____ _____.
M What happened?
W I planned to go to an outdoor concert, but it was canceled
_____ _____ _____.
M Oh, yeah. It was a heavy storm. So did you just _____
_____ _____?
W No, I went to a movie. But _____ _____ _____
_____.
M That's too bad.

---

05 장소 추론

대화를 듣고, 두 사람이 대화하는 장소로 가장 적절한 곳을 고르시오.

① 공원   ② 호텔   ③ 식당
④ 공연장   ⑤ 기숙사

M Good afternoon. What can I help you with?
W Good afternoon. My name is Linda Johnson. I _____
_____ _____ last week.
M _____ _____ _____ _____, please. (*Pause*)
Okay, Ms. Linda Johnson. You booked a single room with a
mountain view _____ _____ _____ for a three-night
stay.
W That's correct.
M Your room is 501. _____ _____ _____.
W Thank you.

---

06 의도 파악

대화를 듣고, 여자의 마지막 말의 의도로 가장 적절한 것을 고르시오.

① 칭찬   ② 동의   ③ 조언
④ 사과   ⑤ 거절

Sound Clear ☆ **new**
미국식은 [누]로, 영국식은 [뉴]로 발음한다.

M What are you going to do this weekend, Rachel?
W I don't have any plans, but _____ _____ _____
_____ _____. I like reading.
M Do you also like watching movies?
W _____ _____ _____.
M Then how about _____ _____ _____ _____ with
me?
W Is there a good new one to watch?
M A new movie about the Olympics is going to open this
weekend.
W Well, I'm _____ _____ _____ _____ _____.
I will just read at home.

07 특정 정보 파악

대화를 듣고, 남자가 잡지에서 가장 좋아하는 부문을 고르시오.

① 영화　　② 여행　　③ 게임
④ 만화　　⑤ 스포츠

M Do you know this magazine?
W Yes. I ＿＿＿＿ ＿＿＿＿ because of the travel section.
M Oh, do you? Their travel section has ＿＿＿＿
＿＿＿＿ ＿＿＿＿ ＿＿＿＿.
W I know. I think it's better than any other travel guidebooks. What's your favorite section?
M My favorite section is the cartoon section. The stories are ＿＿＿＿ ＿＿＿＿ ＿＿＿＿ ＿＿＿＿.
W I agree.
M I'm already waiting for the next issue.

08 할 일 파악

대화를 듣고, 남자가 대화 직후에 할 일로 가장 적절한 것을 고르시오.

① 날씨 확인하기
② 누나에게 연락하기
③ 자전거 대여소 가기
④ 누나와 자전거 타기
⑤ 자전거 바퀴 교체하기

M Do you want to ＿＿＿＿ ＿＿＿＿ with me?
W I'd like to, but I can't. One of my tires is flat.
M You can ＿＿＿＿ ＿＿＿＿ ＿＿＿＿ ＿＿＿＿. I think that will be okay with her. I'll call and ask her.
W Thanks. By the way, where are we going?
M I'm thinking of ＿＿＿＿ ＿＿＿＿ ＿＿＿＿ ＿＿＿＿. What do you think?
W That'll be nice.
M Okay. ＿＿＿＿ ＿＿＿＿ ＿＿＿＿ ＿＿＿＿ ＿＿＿＿ after I ask my sister.

09 주제 파악

다음을 듣고, 남자가 하는 말의 내용으로 가장 적절한 것을 고르시오.

① 나비의 특징
② 나방의 서식지
③ 나비와 나방의 공통점
④ 나비와 나방의 차이점
⑤ 나비와 나방의 활동 시간

M Butterflies are typically larger and ＿＿＿＿ ＿＿＿＿ ＿＿＿＿ on their wings. We can see them in the daytime. On the other hand, moths are typically smaller ＿＿＿＿ ＿＿＿＿ ＿＿＿＿, and they fly at night. The easiest way to ＿＿＿＿ ＿＿＿＿ ＿＿＿＿ ＿＿＿＿ ＿＿＿＿ is to look at their antennae because they look very different.

10 언급하지 않은 것 찾기

대화를 듣고, 여자가 증상으로 언급하지 <u>않은</u> 것을 고르시오.

① 열이 난다.　　② 으슬으슬 춥다.
③ 목이 아프다.　　④ 기침이 난다.
⑤ 콧물이 난다.

Sound Clear ☆ **wr**ong
w가 묵음이라서 [롱]으로 발음된다.

W Dad, I ＿＿＿＿ ＿＿＿＿ ＿＿＿＿ today.
M Oh, dear. What's wrong?
W I have a fever and ＿＿＿＿ ＿＿＿＿.
M You must have a cold. Do you have any other symptoms?
W I ＿＿＿＿ ＿＿＿＿ ＿＿＿＿ ＿＿＿＿ and a runny nose, too. But I just took some medicine. I'll be fine.
M It sounds like ＿＿＿＿ ＿＿＿＿ ＿＿＿＿ ＿＿＿＿ ＿＿＿＿. Let's go to see a doctor. I'll take you there.
W Okay. Thank you, Dad.

11 일치하지 않는 것 찾기

대화를 듣고, 두 사람이 이야기하는 식당에 대한 내용으로 일치하지 않는 것을 고르시오.

① 일식당이다.
② 어제 개업했다.
③ 일주일 동안 할인 행사를 한다.
④ 할인 행사는 모든 메뉴에 해당된다.
⑤ 할인 행사는 저녁 시간대에 한다.

M A new Japanese restaurant opened yesterday.
W I heard that, too. It's next to the bank, right?
M Yes. It is ________ ________ ________ ________ ________ for a week. It's offering 20% off all menu items.
W Oh, that's great! I love Japanese food. Why don't we ________ ________ ________ ________?
M The special is ________ ________ ________.
W How about going there for lunch tomorrow?
M Okay. Let's meet at 12 in front of the restaurant.

12 목적 파악

대화를 듣고, 남자가 샌드위치를 만드는 목적으로 가장 적절한 것을 고르시오.

① 도시락을 싸기 위해서
② 파티에 가져가기 위해서
③ 바자회에서 팔기 위해서
④ 재능 기부를 하기 위해서
⑤ 요리 경연 대회에 나가기 위해서

W Sweetie, what are you doing in the kitchen?
M I'm making sandwiches, Mom.
W ________ ________ ________ ________. Are you still hungry?
M No, I'm not. I will take them to Tommy's.
W ________ ________ ________?
M There'll be a party, and everyone needs to ________ ________ ________ ________ ________ to share. (정답 단서)
W I see. Let me know if you need my help.

13 숫자 정보 파악

대화를 듣고, 여자가 지불해야 할 금액으로 가장 적절한 것을 고르시오.

① $10 ② $13 ③ $16
④ $20 ⑤ $22

W I'd like to ________ ________ ________ ________, please.
M Two shirts and one coat. Is that right?
W Yes. How much is it?
M It's $3 for each shirt and $7 for the coat. You can ________ ________ ________ in three days. (정답 단서)
W ________ ________ ________ ________ I can get them back by tomorrow?
M It's possible, but there is a $3 extra fee ________ ________ ________. (정답 단서)
W Okay. I'll pick them up tomorrow.

14 관계 추론

대화를 듣고, 두 사람의 관계로 가장 적절한 것을 고르시오.

① 친구 – 친구 ② 마트 직원 – 손님
③ 주방장 – 웨이터 ④ 요리 강사 – 수강생
⑤ 음식점 직원 – 손님

Sound Clear☆ instead of
앞 단어의 끝 자음과 뒤 단어의 모음이 만나 연음되어 [인스테더브]로 발음된다.

W ________ ________ ________ ________ ________?
M Yes. I'd like to have two hamburgers and French fries, please.
W ________ ________ ________?
M A large coke and a coffee, please.
W We have a special event on ice cream. If you buy one, ________ ________ ________ ________.
M Then I'd like to have an ice cream ☆instead of coffee.
W Okay. ________ ________ ________ ________ ________?
M For here.

15 부탁한 일 파악

대화를 듣고, 여자가 남자에게 부탁한 일로 가장 적절한 것을 고르시오.

① 안약 사 오기
② 안과에 같이 가기
③ 안과 진료 예약해 주기
④ 렌즈 착용법 알려 주기
⑤ 안과 전화번호 알려 주기

W I can't read my book anymore. _____ _____ _____ _____ _____ .

M Are you wearing contact lenses?

W No, I'm not.

M Why don't you try putting in some eye drops?

W _____ _____ _____ _____ _____ , but my eyes didn't get better.

M How about _____ _____ _____ _____ ? You may have another problem.

W Maybe I should. Will you make an appointment for me?

M Sure, I will.

16 이유 파악

대화를 듣고, 남자가 할인을 받지 못한 이유로 가장 적절한 것을 고르시오.

① 학생이 아니라서   ② 쿠폰을 잃어버려서
③ 학생증이 없어서   ④ 구입 금액이 적어서
⑤ 할인 기간이 지나서

Sound Clear ☆ **exhibit**
ex는 [igz]로 발음되고, h는 묵음이라서 [이그지빗]으로 발음된다.

M _____ _____ _____ _____ _____ for the Picasso exhibit?

W Sure. It's $30.

M Okay. Oh, wait. _____ _____ _____ , "50% Discount for Students."

W That's right. Are you a student?

M Yes, I am.

W Do you have your student ID card?

M No. _____ _____ _____ _____ right now.

W Sorry, but you need to show me your student ID _____ _____ _____ _____ .

17 어색한 대화 찾기 ✽

대화를 듣고, 두 사람의 대화가 어색한 것을 고르시오.

①   ②   ③   ④   ⑤

① **W** What do you do for a living?
   M I _____ _____ _____ _____ _____ .
② **W** We have to get new shoes for Tom.
   M Yeah. He is growing so fast.
③ **W** _____ _____ _____ _____ _____ to go to school?
   M It's 7:20.
④ **W** I'm calling to _____ _____ _____ _____ to London.
   M What day do you want to leave?
⑤ **W** _____ _____ _____ _____ . These are your size.
   M Okay, thanks.

18 주제 파악

다음을 듣고, 여자가 하는 말의 내용으로 가장 적절한 것을 고르시오.

① 르누아르의 생애 　② 전시회 관람 안내
③ 워크숍 일정 공지 　④ 미술관 이용 예절
⑤ 유명한 여행지 추천

Sound Clear ☆ **brochure**

ch가 [ʃ]로 소리 나서 [브로슈얼]로 발음된다.

W Hello, everyone. Thank you for visiting Getty Gallery. Renoir's special exhibition is being held only in our gallery. There are over _____ _____ _____ _____ _____ 정답 단서 _____. We have useful programs you can enjoy, such as workshops and audio-guided tours. 정답 단서 _____ _____ _____, please see the brochure for the details. We hope you _____ _____ _____. Thank you.

19 마지막 말에 이어질 응답 찾기

대화를 듣고, 남자의 마지막 말에 이어질 여자의 말로 가장 적절한 것을 고르시오.

Woman: _____

① I don't like to travel.
② I will stay here for three months.
③ I've never visited America before.
④ I have to go back to school in a week.
⑤ I will go to Disney World with my cousins.

M Anna, _____ _____ _____ _____ _____ during vacation?
W I'm going to Florida. My uncle's family lives there.
M Cool! I want to go there.
W I'm _____ _____ _____ _____ _____.
M How long are you going to stay there?
W _____ _____ _____.
M Do you have any plans there?
W I will go to Disney World with my cousins.

20 마지막 말에 이어질 응답 찾기

대화를 듣고, 남자의 마지막 말에 이어질 여자의 말로 가장 적절한 것을 고르시오.

Woman: _____

① My hobby is reading novels.
② He likes the book *Gorilla*.
③ He likes reading by himself.
④ I can take care of him now.
⑤ He went to bed an hour ago.

M Honey, how was Mike today?
W He was much better. He seems fine now.
M _____ _____ _____ _____ _____?
W Not yet, but he's ready for bed. Could you take care of him now?
M Okay, I will. _____ _____ _____ _____ _____.
W Thank you. I think he'll be happy _____ _____ _____ _____ _____ _____ before he goes to bed.
M No problem. Just tell me his favorite book.
W He likes the book *Gorilla*.

Review Test

Word Check

영어는 우리말로, 우리말은 영어로 써 보기

01	trim	13	이유
02	properly	14	제공하다
03	concert hall	15	면세의
04	audition	16	기내의
05	instrument	17	배송, 배달
06	lead singer	18	취침 시간
07	through	19	안개가 낀
08	ingredient	20	안내 데스크
09	ordinary	21	기한이 지난
10	late fee	22	밀가루
11	fitness center	23	연락처
12	shortly	24	꽤, 상당히

Expression Check

알맞은 표현을 넣어 문장 완성하기

25 Would you _____ _____ the volume? 볼륨 좀 줄여 주시겠어요?

26 I _____ my hair _____ here yesterday. 저는 어제 여기서 머리를 잘랐어요.

27 Have you _____ _____ your arrival card? 입국 신고서는 작성하셨나요?

28 Can I borrow your pen _____ _____ _____? 잠깐 네 펜을 빌려도 될까?

29 We can't afford to buy _____ flowers _____ a cake. 우리는 꽃과 케이크를 둘 다 살 여유가 없어.

30 On Saturday night, the winds will _____ _____, and the showers will stop.
토요일 밤에는 바람이 잔잔해지고 소나기가 그치겠습니다.

Answers p.55

Word Check   영어는 우리말로, 우리말은 영어로 써 보기

01 creative _____

02 pick out _____

03 polka dot _____

04 plain _____

05 warranty _____

06 similar _____

07 occasion _____

08 cancel _____

09 get rest _____

10 grand opening _____

11 extra fee _____

12 on display _____

13 정책, 방침 _____

14 일반적으로, 대체로 _____

15 유용한 _____

16 정보 _____

17 차라리 _____

18 안내 책자 _____

19 반면에 _____

20 바람이 빠진 _____

21 만화 _____

22 조식 포함의 _____

23 세부 사항 _____

24 제품 _____

Expression Check   알맞은 표현을 넣어 문장 완성하기

25 Please don't let your hat _____ _____. 모자가 날아가지 않게 주의하시기 바랍니다.

26 I hope I can get it repaired _____ _____. 저는 이것을 무상으로 수리 받고 싶어요.

27 How about _____ _____ _____ _____ with me? 나랑 같이 영화 보러 가는 게 어때?

28 Let's meet at 12 _____ _____ _____ the restaurant. 식당 앞에서 12시에 만나자.

29 I will _____ them _____ Tommy's. 저는 그것들을 Tommy네 집에 가져갈 거예요.

30 Could you _____ _____ _____ him now? 이제 당신이 그를 좀 돌봐 줄래요?

01 다음을 듣고, 일요일 아침의 날씨로 가장 적절한 것을 고르시오.

①
②
③
④
⑤

02 대화를 듣고, 여자가 구입할 접시로 가장 적절한 것을 고르시오.

①
②
③
④
⑤

03 대화를 듣고, 여자의 심정으로 가장 적절한 것을 고르시오.

① amazed　　　　② confused
③ grateful　　　　④ satisfied
⑤ disappointed

04 대화를 듣고, 남자가 어제 방과 후에 한 일로 가장 적절한 것을 고르시오.

① 심부름하기　　　② 야구 연습하기
③ 수학 학원 가기　　④ 시험공부 하기
⑤ 인터넷 강의 듣기

05 대화를 듣고, 두 사람이 대화하고 있는 장소로 가장 적절한 곳을 고르시오.

① 식물원　　② 박물관　　③ 수족관
④ 영화관　　⑤ 놀이공원

06 대화를 듣고, 여자의 마지막 말의 의도로 가장 적절한 것을 고르시오.

① 칭찬　　　　② 수락　　　　③ 부탁
④ 격려　　　　⑤ 제안

07 대화를 듣고, 남자가 여자를 위해 구입할 물건을 고르시오.

① 운동복　　② 축구공　　③ 모자
④ 축구화　　⑤ 가방

08 대화를 듣고, 남자가 대화 직후에 할 일로 가장 적절한 것을 고르시오.

① 선물 사기　　　　② 초콜릿 만들기
③ 케이크 고르기　　④ 케이크 시식하기
⑤ 여동생에게 전화하기

09 대화를 듣고, 여자가 스페인 여행에 대해 언급하지 않은 것을 고르시오.

① 동행자　　　　② 여행 기간
③ 여행 경비　　　④ 여행한 도시
⑤ 좋았던 음식

10 다음을 듣고, 남자가 하는 말의 내용으로 가장 적절한 것을 고르시오.

① 한식의 세계화　　② 한국의 길거리 음식
③ 전통 문화의 우수성　④ 한국의 전통 시장 홍보
⑤ 한국적인 기념품 추천

11 다음을 듣고, A Week of Thanks에 대한 내용으로 일치하지 않는 것을 고르시오.

① 다음 주에 있을 행사이다.
② 누군가에게 감사를 전하는 주간이다.
③ 학교 각 층에 카드를 넣을 상자가 마련될 것이다.
④ 감사 카드는 학생끼리만 주고받아야 한다.
⑤ 감사 카드는 금요일 오후에 배달된다.

12 대화를 듣고, 여자가 제주도에 가는 목적으로 가장 적절한 것을 고르시오.

① 친구를 만나기 위해서
② 제주도에서 살기 위해서
③ 편찮으신 할머니를 뵙기 위해서
④ 할머니의 팔순 잔치에 가기 위해서
⑤ 할머니와 여행을 하기 위해서

13 대화를 듣고, 남자가 지불해야 할 금액으로 가장 적절한 것을 고르시오.

① $60   ② $81   ③ $90
④ $108   ⑤ $120

14 대화를 듣고, 두 사람의 관계로 가장 적절한 것을 고르시오.

① 약사 – 환자
② 미용사 – 손님
③ 의사 – 간호사
④ 수의사 – 강아지 주인
⑤ 유치원 선생님 – 학부모

15 대화를 듣고, 남자가 여자에게 요청한 일로 가장 적절한 것을 고르시오.

① 영화 예매하기   ② 팝콘 구입하기
③ 좌석 변경하기   ④ 음료 리필하기
⑤ 영화표 출력하기

16 대화를 듣고, 여자가 오페라를 보러 갈 수 없는 이유로 가장 적절한 것을 고르시오.

① 표가 비싸서
② 너무 피곤해서
③ 다른 일정이 있어서
④ 졸업식에 가야 해서
⑤ 과학 숙제를 해야 해서

17 다음 그림의 상황에 가장 적절한 대화를 고르시오.

①   ②   ③   ④   ⑤

18 다음을 듣고, 여자가 마라톤에 대해 언급하지 않은 것을 고르시오.

① 개최 날짜   ② 개최 장소   ③ 코스 종류
④ 참가 자격   ⑤ 신청 방법

[19-20] 대화를 듣고, 여자의 마지막 말에 이어질 남자의 말로 가장 적절한 것을 고르시오.

19 Man: _____

① Good idea. I'll do that.
② Gloves can be a good gift.
③ Yes. I think it can be warmer.
④ You should make them thinner.
⑤ I also made my house by myself.

20 Man: _____

① I like this restaurant.
② No. You can't do that.
③ You're always welcome.
④ I do not agree with him.
⑤ Thank you for saying that.

01 날씨 파악

다음을 듣고, 일요일 아침의 날씨로 가장 적절한 것을 고르시오.

① 　② 　③

④

W Good morning. This is the weekend weather forecast. It's raining hard right now, and the rain _____ _____ _____ _____. However, tomorrow, on Saturday, _____ _____ _____ _____, and it'll be sunny all day. You can _____ _____ _____ only on Saturday because the rain will be back again on Sunday morning.
정답 단서

02 그림 정보 파악

대화를 듣고, 여자가 구입할 접시로 가장 적절한 것을 고르시오.

① 　② 　③

④ 　⑤

Sound Clear ☆ **patterns**
[t]가 모음 사이에서 약화되어 [패런스]로 발음된다.

M Hello. How may I help you?
W I want to buy a plate.
M Okay. Do you like flower patterns?
W Yes, I do. _____ _____ _____ _____ to me?
M All right. This one with one big flower is _____ _____ _____.
W Not bad, but I think it's too simple.
M Then how about this one with two flowers and _____ _____ _____ _____?
W That's nice. I'll take it.

03 심정 추론

대화를 듣고, 여자의 심정으로 가장 적절한 것을 고르시오.

① amazed　② confused
③ grateful　④ satisfied
⑤ disappointed

M Judy, do you have any special plans for this weekend?
W Yes. I'm going to Busan with my family.
M _____ _____ _____ _____. But you don't look happy.
W Well, last night, my dad said he couldn't come. He has to go to Japan _____ _____.
M Why don't you _____ _____ _____ _____?
W We can't cancel all the hotels and trains. So it's a family trip without Dad.
정답 단서
M That's too bad _____ _____ _____ _____.

04 한 일 파악 ✤

대화를 듣고, 남자가 어제 방과 후에 한 일로 가장 적절한 것을 고르시오.

① 심부름하기　　② 야구 연습하기
③ 수학 학원 가기　④ 시험공부 하기
⑤ 인터넷 강의 듣기

W Jake, _____ _____ _____ _____ to baseball practice yesterday?
M My mom _____ _____ _____ _____.
W Why? What did you do?
M She got upset because of my poor grade in math. She thinks it happened _____ _____ _____ _____ _____ _____ playing baseball.
W Oh, no!
M So she made me _____ _____ _____ _____ _____ after school yesterday.
W You must do better on the next exam.

05 장소 추론

대화를 듣고, 두 사람이 대화하고 있는 장소로 가장 적절한 곳을 고르시오.

① 식물원　　② 박물관　　③ 수족관
④ 영화관　　⑤ 놀이공원

Sound Clear ☆ **w**hole
w가 묵음이라서 [호울]로 발음된다.

W _____ _____ _____ _____, isn't it?
M Yes. I heard that it's the largest one in the country.
W I can see that. Hey, look at this. This whole tunnel is _____ ☆ _____ _____ _____.
M Wow, it's amazing. I feel like I'm deep in the ocean.
W Me, too. Let's keep going. The map says we get to the Whale Zone _____ _____ _____ _____ _____ _____. _정답 단서_
M Okay. Maybe we can see the whale sharks there.
W I want to see them. Let's go. _정답 단서_

06 의도 파악

대화를 듣고, 여자의 마지막 말의 의도로 가장 적절한 것을 고르시오.

① 칭찬　　② 수락　　③ 부탁
④ 격려　　⑤ 제안

M Mom, can you help me? I missed the school bus.
W You missed the school bus again?
M I went to bed late last night _____ _____ _____ _____.
W You said the same thing _____ _____ _____.
M But that's the truth. Can you take me to school? Mom, please.
W Promise me this will be _____ _____ _____.
M Okay. It will never happen again.
W All right. I'll _____ _____ _____ _____ _____.

07 특정 정보 파악 ✳

대화를 듣고, 남자가 여자를 위해 구입할 물건을 고르시오.

① 운동복　② 축구공　③ 모자
④ 축구화　⑤ 가방

W Dad, I'd like to go to the soccer shop this weekend.
M What do you ＿＿＿ ＿＿＿ ＿＿＿ ?
W I need a soccer ball and soccer shoes.
M A soccer ball? ＿＿＿ ＿＿＿ ＿＿＿ ＿＿＿ .
W No, look at this. It's flat.
M You can just ＿＿＿ ＿＿＿ ＿＿＿ ＿＿＿ . You don't need a new one.
W Okay, but I really need new shoes. ＿＿＿ ＿＿＿ ＿＿＿ ＿＿＿ are too small now.
M I see. I'll buy you some shoes.
정답 단서

08 할 일 파악

대화를 듣고, 남자가 대화 직후에 할 일로 가장 적절한 것을 고르시오.

① 선물 사기　② 초콜릿 만들기
③ 케이크 고르기　④ 케이크 시식하기
⑤ 여동생에게 전화하기

Sound Clear ☆ **allergy**
'알레르기'는 실제로 [앨러쥐]로 발음된다.

M Hello. I'd like to buy a birthday cake for my niece.
W Okay. Do you have ＿＿＿ ＿＿＿ ＿＿＿ ＿＿＿ ?
M Not really. Can you recommend one to me?
W All right. How about ＿＿＿ ＿＿＿ ＿＿＿ ? It's very popular.
M It looks delicious. I'll take it. Oh, wait.
W Yes?
M She might have a nut allergy. ＿＿＿ ＿＿＿ ＿＿＿ by calling my sister.
W Sure. Go ahead.

09 언급하지 않은 것 찾기

대화를 듣고, 여자가 스페인 여행에 대해 언급하지 <u>않은</u> 것을 고르시오.

① 동행자　② 여행 기간
③ 여행 경비　④ 여행한 도시
⑤ 좋았던 음식

M Sylvia, what did you do ＿＿＿ ＿＿＿ ＿＿＿ ＿＿＿ ?
W I went to Spain with my family.
M That's awesome! How long was the trip?
W It was 10 days. We ＿＿＿ ＿＿＿ many beautiful cities.
M That's quite long! Which city was the most impressive?
W Barcelona. There were ＿＿＿ ＿＿＿ ＿＿＿ ＿＿＿ Gaudi.
M How did you like Spanish food?
W Excellent. I loved ＿＿＿ ＿＿＿ ＿＿＿ the most.

10 주제 파악

다음을 듣고, 남자가 하는 말의 내용으로 가장 적절한 것을 고르시오.

① 한식의 세계화
② 한국의 길거리 음식
③ 전통 문화의 우수성
④ 한국의 전통 시장 홍보
⑤ 한국적인 기념품 추천

M One of the most important parts of traveling is to see how ＿＿＿ ＿＿＿ ＿＿＿ ＿＿＿ live. Therefore, in order to see how Korean people live, you should visit several Korean traditional markets. In the markets, you can try *정답 단서* ＿＿＿ ＿＿＿ ＿＿＿ ＿＿＿ such as *tteokbokki* and *sundae*. You can also buy various traditional Korean souvenirs ＿＿＿ ＿＿＿ ＿＿＿ . So make sure you visit traditional markets during your trip!

11 일치하지 않는 것 찾기

다음을 듣고, A Week of Thanks에 대한 내용으로 일치하지 <u>않는</u> 것을 고르시오.

① 다음 주에 있을 행사이다.
② 누군가에게 감사를 전하는 주간이다.
③ 학교 각 층에 카드를 넣을 상자가 마련될 것이다.
④ 감사 카드는 학생끼리만 주고받아야 한다.
⑤ 감사 카드는 금요일 오후에 배달된다.

W Attention, students. We are going to _____ _____ _____ _____ next week called A Week of Thanks. A Week of Thanks is a week when you _____ _____ _____ _____ who help you. There will be a special box _____ _____ _____ of our school. Write thank-you cards to your friends and teachers and put them in the box. The cards _____ _____ _____ on Friday afternoon. We hope every student participates in the event.

12 목적 파악

대화를 듣고, 여자가 제주도에 가는 목적으로 가장 적절한 것을 고르시오.

① 친구를 만나기 위해서
② 제주도에서 살기 위해서
③ 편찮으신 할머니를 뵙기 위해서
④ 할머니의 팔순 잔치에 가기 위해서
⑤ 할머니와 여행을 하기 위해서

Sound Clear ☆ **quite**
[콰잇]으로 발음된다. [콰이엇]으로 발음되는 quiet(조용한)과 구분하여 알아 둔다.

M Tom told me that you are going to stay in Jeju-do for a while.
W Yes. _____ _____ _____.
M How long are you going to stay there?
W _____ _____ _____. I'm not sure.
M That's quite long. Why are you going to _____ _____ _____ _____ _____?
W I'm going there to see my grandma. She lives in Jeju-do.
M Didn't you see her last month for her eightieth birthday?
W Right. But now, she's _____ _____ _____ _____. I'm so worried about her.

13 숫자 정보 파악

대화를 듣고, 남자가 지불해야 할 금액으로 가장 적절한 것을 고르시오.

① $60   ② $81   ③ $90
④ $108   ⑤ $120

M Hello. How much is a ticket for the museum?
W It's $30 _____ _____ _____.
M How about a child?
W _____ _____ _____ _____ of an adult ticket.
M I see. Two adults and two children, please.
W All right. Today is Culture Day, so you also get 10% off _____ _____ _____.
M Good. _____ _____ _____. Here's my card.

14 관계 추론

대화를 듣고, 두 사람의 관계로 가장 적절한 것을 고르시오.

① 약사 – 환자
② 미용사 – 손님
③ 의사 – 간호사
④ 수의사 – 강아지 주인
⑤ 유치원 선생님 – 학부모

W Hello. _____ _____ _____ _____ _____?
M She doesn't eat well and keeps sleeping.
W How long has she _____ _____ _____?
M It's been two days.
W _____ _____ _____ _____ _____ _____. (Pause) She has a mild fever. I think she has a cold. Has she had a dog flu vaccination shot?
M Yes. She had one last month.
W Okay. I'm going to _____ _____ _____ _____.

15 요청한 일 파악

대화를 듣고, 남자가 여자에게 요청한 일로 가장 적절한 것을 고르시오.

① 영화 예매하기   ② 팝콘 구입하기
③ 좌석 변경하기   ④ 음료 리필하기
⑤ 영화표 출력하기

M The movie starts in 10 minutes. We _____ _____ _____.

W Yeah. Do you need popcorn or anything?

M I want _____ _____ _____ _____ _____.

W Okay. I'll buy them. Why don't you get the movie tickets? 정답 단서

M Sure, but from where?

W The ticket machines are over there. Enter the booking number, and the tickets _____ _____ _____.

M All right.

16 이유 파악

대화를 듣고, 여자가 오페라를 보러 갈 수 <u>없는</u> 이유로 가장 적절한 것을 고르시오.

① 표가 비싸서
② 너무 피곤해서
③ 다른 일정이 있어서
④ 졸업식에 가야 해서
⑤ 과학 숙제를 해야 해서

Sound Clear ☆ **Absolutely**
[t]가 [l]에 앞에서 약화되어 [앱솔룻리]로 발음된다.

M Carol, you like operas, don't you?

W Absolutely. Why?

M I _____ _____ _____ _____ _____ at the opera house this Saturday. Why don't you go with me?

W At the opera house? Aren't the tickets expensive?

M I bought them _____ _____ _____ _____. Can you go?

W I'd love to, but _____ _____ _____ _____ _____.

M Oh, no! The opera starts at 7 p.m. Is that due to your science homework? 한정

W No. _____ _____ _____ _____ _____ _____ to celebrate my brother's graduation. 한정

17 그림의 상황에 적절한 대화 찾기

다음 그림의 상황에 가장 적절한 대화를 고르시오.

①   ②   ③   ④   ⑤

① W Did you call the customer service center?
  M Yes, but _____ _____ _____ _____ every time.

② W How long does it take?
  M Look. The sign says it's a 30-minute walk from here.

③ W Hey, you just _____ _____ _____.
  M Oops, I didn't know. Sorry.

④ W I hope we won't have to stand in line for a long time.
  M I _____ _____ _____ _____.

⑤ W Look at those endless cars.
  M Yeah, _____ _____ _____ today.

18 언급하지 않은 것 찾기 ✱

다음을 듣고, 여자가 마라톤에 대해 언급하지 않은 것을 고르시오.

① 개최 날짜 ② 개최 장소 ③ 코스 종류
④ 참가 자격 ⑤ 신청 방법

Sound Clear ☆ **20,000**
숫자는 쉼표를 기준으로 앞에서부터 끊어 읽으므로 twenty thousand[트웬티싸우전드]로 읽는다.

W: The 10th Sejong Marathon is _____ _____ _____ _____. On Sunday, March 24, more than 20,000 runners _____ _____ _____ along Sejong Street. There are five-kilometers, ten-kilometers, and half-marathon courses. If you want to participate, _____ _____ _____ at www.sejongmarathon.com by Friday, March 1. We encourage you to take part in this event. Thank you.

정답 단서 (×4)

---

19 마지막 말에 이어질 응답 찾기

대화를 듣고, 여자의 마지막 말에 이어질 남자의 말로 가장 적절한 것을 고르시오.

Man: _____

① Good idea. I'll do that.
② Gloves can be a good gift.
③ Yes. I think it can be warmer.
④ You should make them thinner.
⑤ I also made my house by myself.

W: What are you doing?
M: I'm making a doghouse for Max.
W: Wow. Are you building it _____ _____ _____?
M: Yeah. It's almost finished now. It _____ _____ _____ _____ _____.
W: Awesome. It looks warm and cozy.
M: Thanks, but I think it's too simple.
W: Hmm... why don't you _____ _____ _____ _____ _____?
M: Good idea. I'll do that.

---

20 마지막 말에 이어질 응답 찾기

대화를 듣고, 여자의 마지막 말에 이어질 남자의 말로 가장 적절한 것을 고르시오.

Man: _____

① I like this restaurant.
② No. You can't do that.
③ You're always welcome.
④ I do not agree with him.
⑤ Thank you for saying that.

W: I can't believe it's already _____ _____ _____ _____.
M: Oh, I didn't know it was this late.
W: Thank you _____ _____ _____ _____ _____ tonight.
M: My pleasure. I had a great time, too.
W: Dinner was really good.
M: I'm _____ _____ _____ _____.
W: You're an excellent cook. Seriously, you could _____ _____ _____.
M: Thank you for saying that.

01 다음을 듣고, 토요일의 날씨로 가장 적절한 것을 고르시오.

02 대화를 듣고, 남자가 찾고 있는 인물을 고르시오.

03 대화를 듣고, 두 사람의 심정으로 가장 적절한 것을 고르시오.

① sad   ② proud   ③ scared
④ pleased   ⑤ envy

04 대화를 듣고, 남자가 주말에 한 일로 가장 적절한 것을 고르시오.

① 영화 관람   ② 미술관 관람   ③ 공원 산책
④ 집 안 청소   ⑤ 보드게임

05 대화를 듣고, 두 사람이 대화하는 장소로 가장 적절한 곳을 고르시오.

① 식당   ② 은행   ③ 여행사
④ 기숙사   ⑤ 관광 안내소

06 대화를 듣고, Tom의 생일 파티 날짜를 고르시오.

① 12월 1일   ② 12월 2일
③ 12월 3일   ④ 12월 4일
⑤ 12월 5일

07 다음을 듣고, 여자가 학교 식당의 문제점으로 언급하지 않은 것을 고르시오.

① 학생들이 한꺼번에 몰려서 혼잡하다.
② 음식이 부족할 때가 많다.
③ 음식을 받기 위해 오래 기다려야 한다.
④ 자리를 내주기 위해 빨리 먹어야 한다.
⑤ 서너 명이 함께 앉을 자리를 찾기 힘들다.

08 대화를 듣고, 두 사람이 대화 직후에 할 일로 가장 적절한 것을 고르시오.

① 옷 가게 가기   ② 음식 주문하기
③ 식당 예약하기   ④ 층별 안내도 보기
⑤ 인터넷 검색하기

09 다음을 듣고, 남자가 하는 말의 내용으로 가장 적절한 것을 고르시오.

① 수면 부족의 원인
② 숙면을 취하는 방법
③ 충분한 수면의 중요성
④ 규칙적인 생활의 중요성
⑤ 수업 시간에 집중하는 방법

10 대화를 듣고, 남자에 대한 설명으로 일치하지 않는 것을 고르시오.

① 매일 피아노 연습을 한다.
② 피아노 치는 것을 좋아한다.
③ 피아노를 친 지 8년 되었다.
④ 어머니에게 피아노를 배웠다.
⑤ 대학교에서 피아노를 전공했다.

11 대화를 듣고, 여자가 전화를 건 목적으로 가장 적절한 것을 고르시오.

① 숙제를 알려 주기 위해서
② 함께 병원에 가기 위해서
③ 진료를 예약하기 위해서
④ 약속 시간을 정하기 위해서
⑤ 수학 문제를 물어보기 위해서

12 대화를 듣고, 남자의 현재 키를 고르시오.

① 153cm   ② 155cm   ③ 160cm
④ 165cm   ⑤ 170cm

13 대화를 듣고, 두 사람의 관계로 가장 적절한 것을 고르시오.

① 의사 – 환자   ② 간호사 – 환자
③ 변호사 – 의뢰인   ④ 담임 교사 – 학생
⑤ 보건 교사 – 학생

14 대화를 듣고, 두 사람이 하는 말의 내용으로 가장 적절한 것을 고르시오.

① 유용한 앱 추천   ② 스마트폰의 시초
③ 스마트폰 없는 생활   ④ 새로 출시된 스마트폰
⑤ 여가 시간을 즐기는 법

15 대화를 듣고, 남자가 여자에게 요청한 일로 가장 적절한 것을 고르시오.

① 물건 환불   ② 물건 교환
③ 지퍼 수선   ④ 영수증 재발급
⑤ 재고 수량 확인

16 대화를 듣고, 복사기에 대한 내용으로 일치하지 않는 것을 고르시오.

① 1층 출입구 옆에 있다.
② 이용하려면 복사 카드가 필요하다.
③ 옆에 동전 교환기가 있다.
④ 컬러 복사는 장당 50센트이다.
⑤ 사용 설명서가 붙어 있다.

17 다음 그림의 상황에 가장 적절한 대화를 고르시오.

① ② ③ ④ ⑤

18 대화를 듣고, 여자가 웹 사이트에 대해 언급하지 않은 것을 고르시오.

① 물건 종류가 많다.
② 주문이 간편하다.
③ 배송이 빠르다.
④ 가격이 적당하다.
⑤ 고객 서비스가 좋다.

[19-20] 대화를 듣고, 남자의 마지막 말에 이어질 여자의 말로 가장 적절한 것을 고르시오.

19 Woman: _____

① I can't stand it.
② What a surprise!
③ I'm really happy to see you.
④ We're not supposed to do that.
⑤ Okay. I'll post about straws then.

20 Woman: _____

① Sure. I'll be on time.
② I'm really curious about it.
③ Cheer up. Things will be better.
④ Maybe you're right. I'll call her.
⑤ Don't worry. She will get well soon.

01 날씨 파악 ✦

다음을 듣고, 토요일의 날씨로 가장 적절한 것을 고르시오.

① ② ③ ④ ⑤

W Good morning. Today is Monday, July 21. The weather is going to be pleasant _____ _____ _____ _____ _____. Across the nation, it will be hot and humid during the workweek and on Saturday. *정답 단서* _____ _____ _____ _____ 30°C. You will experience tropical nights from Thursday to Saturday. On Sunday, there is _____ _____ _____ _____ _____ in northern Gyeonggi-do and in northern Gangwon-do.

02 그림 정보 파악

대화를 듣고, 남자가 찾고 있는 인물을 고르시오.

① ② ③ ④ ⑤

Sound Clear ☆ **a minute ago**
[t]가 모음 사이에서 약화되고 뒤 단어의 첫 모음과 연음되어 [어미너러고]로 발음된다.

M I _____ _____ _____ just a minute ago. He is a 6-year-old boy who _____ _____, _____ _____.
W What's his name?
M Mike Robinson.
W What is he wearing?
M He is _____ _____ _____ _____ _____, jeans, and glasses.
W Okay, Mr. Robinson. We will _____ _____ _____ right away.

03 심정 추론

대화를 듣고, 두 사람의 심정으로 가장 적절한 것을 고르시오.

① sad　② proud　③ scared
④ pleased　⑤ envy

M Is it true that you're moving to Daegu?
W Yes. I was going to tell you soon. It was a sudden decision.
M Why are you moving there?
W My mother _____ _____ _____ _____ there.
M Oh, I'll miss you a lot.
W Me, too. *정답 단서* But we can _____ _____ _____ _____, and you can visit me during summer vacation.
M You're right. Things will change, but _____ _____ _____ _____ _____.
W Of course.

04   한 일 파악

대화를 듣고, 남자가 주말에 한 일로 가장 적절한 것을 고르시오.

① 영화 관람   ② 미술관 관람
③ 공원 산책   ④ 집 안 청소
⑤ 보드게임

> **Sound Clear** ☆ **sold out**
> 앞 단어의 끝 자음과 뒤 단어의 첫 모음이 만나 연음되어 [솔다웃]으로 발음된다.

W   What did you do last Saturday?
M   Nothing special. I just _____ _____ _____.
W   Why? _____ _____ _____ _____?
M   No. Actually, I went to the theater with my brother, but all the tickets were sold out.
W   That's too bad.
M   So we went to the art museum next to the park, but _____ _____ _____ _____ _____.
W   Oh, that's bad timing.
M   We went back home and played board games until midnight.

---

05   장소 추론

대화를 듣고, 두 사람이 대화하는 장소로 가장 적절한 곳을 고르시오.

① 식당   ② 은행   ③ 여행사
④ 기숙사   ⑤ 관광 안내소

W   Good afternoon, sir. How may I help you?
M   Good afternoon. _____ _____ _____ _____ some U.S. dollars into Korean won.
W   _____ _____ _____ would you like to exchange?
M $500. Here you are.
W   Okay. Are you going to Korea on holiday?
M   No, I'm going _____ _____ _____ _____.
W   I see. It comes to 600,000 won _____ _____ _____ _____ _____.
M   Thank you.

---

06   특정 정보 파악   �֎

대화를 듣고, Tom의 생일 파티 날짜를 고르시오.

① 12월 1일   ② 12월 2일
③ 12월 3일   ④ 12월 4일
⑤ 12월 5일

W   _____ _____ _____. It's already December.
M   December? Is it December 1 today?
W   Yes. Why?
M   _____ _____ _____. Tom's birthday party is tomorrow.
W   Isn't Tom's birthday December 3?
M   Right, but _____ _____ _____ _____ _____ _____ with his family on his birthday.
W   Oh, I remember that.

---

07   언급하지 않은 것 찾기

다음을 듣고, 여자가 학교 식당의 문제점으로 언급하지 않은 것을 고르시오.

① 학생들이 한꺼번에 몰려서 혼잡하다.
② 음식이 부족할 때가 많다.
③ 음식을 받기 위해 오래 기다려야 한다.
④ 자리를 내주기 위해 빨리 먹어야 한다.
⑤ 서너 명이 함께 앉을 자리를 찾기 힘들다.

W   I'd like to talk about the school cafeteria during lunchtime. There are some problems with the cafeteria. All the students come _____ _____ _____ _____, so it is very crowded. Most students have to wait for a long time to get their food. But then they _____ _____ _____ _____ so that others can sit down. In addition, when three or four students want to sit together, it is _____ _____ _____.

08 할 일 파악

대화를 듣고, 두 사람이 대화 직후에 할 일로 가장 적절한 것을 고르시오.

① 옷 가게 가기 　② 음식 주문하기
③ 식당 예약하기 　④ 층별 안내도 보기
⑤ 인터넷 검색하기

Sound Clear ☆ **little**
[t]가 모음 사이에서 약화되어 [리를]로 발음된다.

W This mall is huge! _____ _____ _____ _____ before?
M No. It's my first time here, too. I'm so excited.
W Me, too. _____ _____ _____ _____ _____ _____? Clothing stores?
M Actually, I'm a little hungry. How about _____ _____ _____ _____ _____ before shopping?
W Sure. Let's check where the food court is.
M There's a floor map over there. Let's check it out.
W Okay.

09 주제 파악

다음을 듣고, 남자가 하는 말의 내용으로 가장 적절한 것을 고르시오.

① 수면 부족의 원인
② 숙면을 취하는 방법
③ 충분한 수면의 중요성
④ 규칙적인 생활의 중요성
⑤ 수업 시간에 집중하는 방법

M Sleep affects everything. _____ _____ _____ _____ can affect how well you learn. Students who sleep well _____ _____ _____ _____ on tests. However, students who get less sleep have a harder time concentrating in class. _____ _____ _____ _____ can also affect your behavior and mood. Therefore, it's important to _____ _____ _____. Turn off the lights and go to bed at the same time every day.

10 일치하지 않는 것 찾기

대화를 듣고, 남자에 대한 설명으로 일치하지 <u>않는</u> 것을 고르시오.

① 매일 피아노 연습을 한다.
② 피아노 치는 것을 좋아한다.
③ 피아노를 친 지 8년 되었다.
④ 어머니에게 피아노를 배웠다.
⑤ 대학교에서 피아노를 전공했다.

W _____ _____ _____ _____ _____ the piano. I was so impressed.
M Thank you. I practice the piano every day. I enjoy playing it.
W _____ _____ _____ _____ the piano?
M I've played the piano for eight years. My mom taught me how to play when I was five.
W Oh, so she plays it really well, too.
M Yes. She _____ _____ _____ in university.
W Oh, I see.

11 목적 파악

대화를 듣고, 여자가 전화를 건 목적으로 가장 적절한 것을 고르시오.

① 숙제를 알려 주기 위해서
② 함께 병원에 가기 위해서
③ 진료를 예약하기 위해서
④ 약속 시간을 정하기 위해서
⑤ 수학 문제를 물어보기 위해서

(Cellphone rings.)
M Hello, Mina.
W Hey, Tom. It seems you _____ _____ _____. Are you okay?
M I feel much better now. Thanks. I went to see a doctor and _____ _____ _____ _____ _____.
W It's good to hear that. By the way, I called you because of the math homework. You _____ _____ _____ _____ _____ on page 26.
M Page 26? Okay. Thanks.
W You're welcome. _____ _____ and see you tomorrow!

12 특정 정보 파악

대화를 듣고, 남자의 현재 키를 고르시오.

① 153cm ② 155cm ③ 160cm
④ 165cm ⑤ 170cm

W Jack, why are you depressed?
M Mom, I'm ________ ________ ________ ________ in my class.
W Did you have a physical examination at school?
M Yes. Tony is five centimeters taller than me. ________ ________ ________ ________ ________ last year. (정답 단서)
W How tall is he now?
M He is 165 centimeters. He grew ten centimeters last year, but I ________ ________ ________ ________. (정답 단서)
W Don't worry. You will be much taller next year.

13 관계 추론

대화를 듣고, 두 사람의 관계로 가장 적절한 것을 고르시오.

① 의사 – 환자 ② 간호사 – 환자
③ 변호사 – 의뢰인 ④ 담임 교사 – 학생
⑤ 보건 교사 – 학생

M Hello, Ms. Lee. I have a fever, and I have the chills.
W I see. Let me ________ ________ ________.
M Okay.
W (*Pause*) Oh, you have a high fever. Since when have you had a fever?
M ________ ________ ________ ________ ________, I think.
W Take this pill, and you'd better go to the hospital right away. There's ________ ________ ________ ________ ________ these days.
M Do you mean I should ________ ________ ________?
W Yes, after telling your homeroom teacher.

14 주제 파악

대화를 듣고, 두 사람이 하는 말의 내용으로 가장 적절한 것을 고르시오.

① 유용한 앱 추천
② 스마트폰의 시초
③ 스마트폰 없는 생활
④ 새로 출시된 스마트폰
⑤ 여가 시간을 즐기는 법

Sound Clear☆ **without it**
[t]가 모음 사이에서 약화되고 뒤 단어의 모음과 연음되어 [위다우릿]으로 발음된다.

W ________ ________ ________ even one day without my smartphone.
M Living without a smartphone isn't bad. (정답 단서)
W What do you mean?
M A week ago, ________ ________ ________ ________, so I had to spend the whole day without☆ it.
W How was it?
M I enjoyed it. I had more free time and ________ ________ ________ ________ ________.
W Really? I feel so bored even when my battery's dead.
M Why don't you ________ ________ ________ ________ without your smartphone?
W Hmm... I'll think about it.

15 요청한 일 파악

대화를 듣고, 남자가 여자에게 요청한 일로 가장 적절한 것을 고르시오.

① 물건 환불 ② 물건 교환
③ 지퍼 수선 ④ 영수증 재발급
⑤ 재고 수량 확인

W May I help you?
M Yes. I _____ _____ _____ yesterday, but the zipper doesn't work.
W I apologize for your inconvenience. _____ _____ _____ _____ _____?
M No. I'd like to exchange it for another one. I want the same color and style. 정답 단서
W I'm afraid this is _____ _____ _____ _____ _____ _____. We have it in gray and navy blue.
M Then I'll go with the gray one.
W All right. Here it is. Make sure _____ _____ _____ _____.

16 일치하지 않는 것 찾기

대화를 듣고, 복사기에 대한 내용으로 일치하지 않는 것을 고르시오.

① 1층 출입구 옆에 있다.
② 이용하려면 복사 카드가 필요하다.
③ 옆에 동전 교환기가 있다.
④ 컬러 복사는 장당 50센트이다.
⑤ 사용 설명서가 붙어 있다.

W Excuse me. Where can I _____ _____?
M The copy machine is next to the entrance on the first floor.
W Do I need _____ _____ _____ _____ _____ _____?
M No, you can just pay in cash. There's a coin-exchange machine next to the copy machine. 정답 단서
W How much is it?
M _____ _____ _____ _____ _____ per page, and black and white copies cost ten cents per page.
W Can you show me how to use the machine?
M _____ _____ _____ _____ on the machine. Just follow them.

17 그림의 상황에 적절한 대화 찾기

다음 그림의 상황에 가장 적절한 대화를 고르시오.

① ② ③ ④ ⑤

① W I don't know _____ _____ _____ _____.
   M It's very simple. I'll tell you how.
② W What are you planning to do this weekend?
   M I'm planning to _____ _____ _____ _____.
③ W Is it okay if I take a picture?
   M Sure. Go ahead.
④ W _____ _____ _____ _____ _____ the museum?
   M Go straight two blocks and turn right.
⑤ W I'm so nervous. _____ _____ _____ _____ _____? 정답 단서
   M Don't worry. You'll do well.

18 언급하지 않은 것 찾기 ✳

대화를 듣고, 여자가 웹 사이트에 대해 언급하지 <u>않은</u> 것을 고르시오.

① 물건 종류가 많다.
② 주문이 간편하다.
③ 배송이 빠르다.
④ 가격이 적당하다.
⑤ 고객 서비스가 좋다.

> **Sound Clear** ✩ **check out**
> 앞 단어의 끝 자음과 뒤 단어의 첫 모음이 만나 연음되어 [체카웃]으로 발음된다.

M I like your hat. Where did you get it?
W I _____ _____ _____ bestclothes.com. It has all kinds of clothes and accessories.
M Cool. Does it deliver quickly?
W Yes. It delivers everything _____ _____ _____.
M Wow, that's surprising. How about the prices?
W _____ _____ _____ _____. It also has the best customer service.
M I should check out the site.

19 마지막 말에 이어질 응답 찾기

대화를 듣고, 남자의 마지막 말에 이어질 여자의 말로 가장 적절한 것을 고르시오.

Woman: _____

① I can't stand it.
② What a surprise!
③ I'm really happy to see you.
④ We're not supposed to do that.
⑤ Okay. I'll post about straws then.

W Plastic pollution is terrible these days. Every year a huge amount of plastic _____ _____ _____.
M Yes. I've heard that.
W It threatens humans and animals' lives. We _____ _____ _____ _____.
M What can we do?
W We have to _____ _____ _____ _____ _____ _____. For example, we shouldn't use plastic straws.
M Good idea. I think we _____ _____ _____ _____ _____ on our social networks.
W Okay. I'll post about straws then.

20 마지막 말에 이어질 응답 찾기

대화를 듣고, 남자의 마지막 말에 이어질 여자의 말로 가장 적절한 것을 고르시오.

Woman: _____

① Sure. I'll be on time.
② I'm really curious about it.
③ Cheer up. Things will be better.
④ Maybe you're right. I'll call her.
⑤ Don't worry. She will get well soon.

W Dad, I don't want to go to school tomorrow.
M _____ _____ _____ _____?
W My friend Rachel talked about me _____ _____ _____ today. I thought we were good friends.
M That's too bad. Did you ask her _____ _____ _____ _____?
W No. I didn't want to talk to her.
M There must be a misunderstanding. _____ _____ _____ _____ _____ how you feel?
W Maybe you're right. I'll call her.

Review Test

Word Check 영어는 우리말로, 우리말은 영어로 써 보기

01	nowadays		13	감사	
02	participate		14	아늑한	
03	mild fever		15	예방 접종	
04	on business		16	사실	
05	plate		17	점수	
06	whole		18	둘러싸다	
07	for a while		19	인상 깊은	
08	get ready		20	끝없는	
09	particular		21	격려하다, 권장하다	
10	awesome		22	졸업	
11	various		23	짓다, 만들어 내다	
12	reasonable		24	진지하게, 진심으로	

Expression Check 알맞은 표현을 넣어 문장 완성하기

25 I made my house _____ _____. 나는 내 집을 나 혼자 만들었어.

26 I'd love to, but _____ _____ it's before dinner. 나는 가고 싶지만, 저녁 전에만 돼.

27 You just _____ _____ _____. 당신은 방금 새치기하셨어요.

28 Why don't you _____ _____ the trip? 여행을 미루는 게 어때?

29 This whole tunnel _____ all _____ _____ glass. 이 터널 전체가 유리로 만들어져 있어.

30 I hope we won't have to _____ _____ _____ for a long time.
우리가 오랫동안 줄을 안 서도 되면 좋겠다.

Answers p.66

Word Check 영어는 우리말로, 우리말은 영어로 써 보기

01 theater _____

02 average _____

03 long-sleeved _____

04 tropical night _____

05 video chat _____

06 threaten _____

07 timing _____

08 according to _____

09 exchange rate _____

10 absolutely _____

11 clothing store _____

12 floor map _____

13 영향을 미치다 _____

14 빨대 _____

15 집중하다 _____

16 행동 _____

17 감동받은 _____

18 쾌적한 _____

19 복사기 _____

20 가능성 _____

21 환불 _____

22 오염 _____

23 오한, 한기 _____

24 자정, 한밤중 _____

Expression Check 알맞은 표현을 넣어 문장 완성하기

25 Are you going to Korea _____ _____? 한국에 휴가 가시는 거예요?

26 My mom _____ _____ piano in university. 우리 엄마는 대학교에서 피아노를 전공하셨어.

27 I _____ _____ your inconvenience. 불편함을 겪게 해 드려서 죄송합니다.

28 Students who sleep well _____ _____ score higher on tests.
잠을 푹 자는 학생들은 시험에서 더 높은 점수를 받는 경향이 있습니다.

29 My friend Rachel talked about me _____ _____ _____ today.
오늘 제 친구 Rachel이 저의 험담을 했어요.

30 All the students come _____ _____ _____ _____, so it is very crowded.
모든 학생들이 동시에 와서, 아주 혼잡합니다.

1.0배속

1.2배속

01 다음을 듣고, 수요일의 날씨로 가장 적절한 것을 고르시오.

① ② ③ ④ ⑤

02 대화를 듣고, 남자가 구입할 앞치마로 가장 적절한 것을 고르시오.

① ② ③ ④ ⑤

03 대화를 듣고, 두 사람의 심정으로 가장 적절한 것을 고르시오.
① pleased   ② annoyed
③ excited   ④ ashamed
⑤ depressed

04 대화를 듣고, 여자가 지난 주말에 한 일로 가장 적절한 것을 고르시오.
① 콘서트 가기   ② 전시회 관람하기
③ 노래 연습하기   ④ 연예인과 사진 찍기
⑤ 연예인 사진 구입하기

05 대화를 듣고, 두 사람이 대화하는 장소로 가장 적절한 곳을 고르시오.
① 은행   ② 여행사   ③ 도서관
④ 우체국   ⑤ 옷 가게

06 대화를 듣고, 여자의 마지막 말의 의도로 가장 적절한 것을 고르시오.
① 비난   ② 칭찬   ③ 동의
④ 충고   ⑤ 반대

07 다음을 듣고, 남자가 하는 말의 내용으로 가장 적절한 것을 고르시오.
① 기차역 개통   ② 열차 시간 변경
③ 도착역 알림   ④ 도난 사고 주의
⑤ 지하철 요금 인상

08 대화를 듣고, 여자가 내일 할 일로 가장 적절한 것을 고르시오.
① 박람회 가기   ② 자료 조사하기
③ 미술 학원 가기   ④ 봉사 활동 하기
⑤ 재활용품 모으기

09 대화를 듣고, 남자가 화천 산천어 얼음 축제에 대해 언급하지 <u>않은</u> 것을 고르시오.
① 시기   ② 장소   ③ 입장료
④ 체험 활동   ⑤ 교통편

10 대화를 듣고, 여자가 좋아하는 분야를 고르시오.
① 춤   ② 노래   ③ 등산
④ 요리   ⑤ 게임

11 대화를 듣고, 여자에 대한 설명으로 일치하지 <u>않는</u> 것을 고르시오.
① 남자와 처음 만난 사이이다.
② 남자네 가족의 집에서 머물 예정이다.
③ 한국에 두 번 방문했다.
④ 경복궁에 가장 가 보고 싶어 한다.
⑤ 여러 나라의 전통 건축물에 관심이 있다.

12 대화를 듣고, 여자가 책을 읽는 목적으로 가장 적절한 것을 고르시오.

① 발표를 준비하기 위해서
② 중국 문화에 관심이 생겨서
③ 중국에 여행을 가기 위해서
④ 중국인 친구를 사귀기 위해서
⑤ 중국어 시험을 대비하기 위해서

13 대화를 듣고, 남자가 지불해야 할 금액으로 가장 적절한 것을 고르시오.

① 12,000원 ② 13,000원 ③ 14,000원
④ 15,000원 ⑤ 16,000원

14 대화를 듣고, 남자가 여자에게 부탁한 일로 가장 적절한 것을 고르시오.

① 함께 줄넘기하기 ② 파스 사다 주기
③ 병원 데려다주기 ④ 얼음찜질 해 주기
⑤ 진료 예약해 주기

15 다음을 듣고, 여자가 하는 말의 내용으로 가장 적절한 것을 고르시오.

① 건강 관리 비결
② 저칼로리 식단
③ 사과 재배 방법
④ 사과가 인기 있는 이유
⑤ 사과를 이용한 요리법

16 대화를 듣고, 남자가 작가를 만나고 싶어 하는 이유로 가장 적절한 것을 고르시오.

① 작가의 팬이라서
② 사인을 받고 싶어서
③ 조언을 구하고 싶어서
④ 사진을 찍고 싶어서
⑤ 책 내용에 대해 토론하고 싶어서

17 다음 그림의 상황에 가장 적절한 대화를 고르시오.

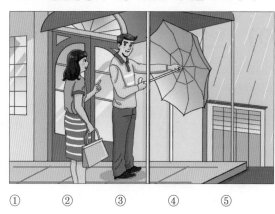

①　②　③　④　⑤

18 다음을 듣고, 여자가 에바 알머슨에 대해 언급하지 않은 것을 고르시오.

① 국적　　　　② 직업
③ 유년 시절　　④ 화풍
⑤ 작품의 주제

[19-20] 대화를 듣고, 여자의 마지막 말에 이어질 남자의 말로 가장 적절한 것을 고르시오.

19 Man: _____

① He really taught me a lot.
② I thought I saw John do it.
③ I'll teach you how to do it.
④ I want to break my bad habits.
⑤ My homeroom teacher last year.

20 Man: _____

① I don't have a tablet PC.
② Thank you for your help.
③ Sure. I'll lend you my note.
④ He did not answer the phone.
⑤ Okay. I'll tell him when he comes back.

받아쓰기용

01 날씨 파악

다음을 듣고, 수요일의 날씨로 가장 적절한 것을 고르시오.

① ② ③

④ ⑤

Sound Clear ☆ **A bit of**
앞 단어의 끝 자음과 뒤 단어의 모음이 만나 연음되어 [어비러브]로 발음된다.

M I'm Mitch with the weekly weather report. The city still _____ _____ _____ _____ _____, but starting on Tuesday night, strong winds will help _____ _____ _____ _____ completely. So the temperature will go down on Wednesday, but you can enjoy _____ _____ _____ _____ throughout the day. A bit of rain is expected on Thursday morning, and _____ _____ _____ _____ _____ turning into snow on Friday.

02 그림 정보 파악

대화를 듣고, 남자가 구입할 앞치마로 가장 적절한 것을 고르시오.

① ② ③

④ ⑤

M I'd like to _____ _____ _____ for my son.
W Okay. How about this one with stars on it?
M Do you _____ _____ _____ _____?
W Yes. This one has a big star in the middle.
M I think the star is too big. I would also _____ _____ _____ _____.
W Then what about the one with vertical stripes hanging over there? 정답 단서
M That's nice. I'll take it.
W Okay. I hope _____ _____ _____ _____.

03 심정 추론 ✚

대화를 듣고, 두 사람의 심정으로 가장 적절한 것을 고르시오.

① pleased   ② annoyed
③ excited   ④ ashamed
⑤ depressed

M _____ _____ _____ _____ the air cleaner? The air in here is not fresh.
W It's already on. I think there is a problem.
M Do you know _____ _____ _____ _____?
W I think we need to change the filter.
M _____ _____ _____ _____ last month?
W You're right. Exactly three weeks ago.
M A filter _____ _____ _____. I'll call the customer service center. 정답 단서
W You need to complain strongly. 정답 단서

04　한 일 파악

대화를 듣고, 여자가 지난 주말에 한 일로 가장
적절한 것을 고르시오.

① 콘서트 가기　　　② 전시회 관람하기
③ 노래 연습하기　　④ 연예인과 사진 찍기
⑤ 연예인 사진 구입하기

M _____ _____ _____ _____, Jenny?
W It was a perfect weekend. I met Brian _____ _____!
M Brian the singer?
W Yes. Look at this picture. I took some pictures with him.
M Wow, _____ _____ _____. Where did you go?
W I went to Wilson's Department Store. He was shopping alone.
M Weren't there _____ _____ _____ _____?
W No one recognized him except me. He was covering his face with his hat.

05　장소 추론

대화를 듣고, 두 사람이 대화하는 장소로 가장
적절한 곳을 고르시오.

① 은행　　　② 여행사　　　③ 도서관
④ 우체국　　⑤ 옷 가게

W Customer number 26. Please come to counter B.
M Hi. I want to send this to Japan.
W _____ _____ _____ _____? You cannot send food, drugs, plants, sprays, and so on.
M They're clothes.
W Okay. You can choose _____ _____ _____ _____ _____.
M I'll go with airmail. How long will it take to get there?
W It will _____ _____ _____ _____ _____ _____.

06　의도 파악

대화를 듣고, 여자의 마지막 말의 의도로 가장
적절한 것을 고르시오.

① 비난　　② 칭찬　　③ 동의
④ 충고　　⑤ 반대

Sound Clear ☆ **bottles**
[t]가 [l] 앞에서 약화되어 [바를스]로 발음
된다.

M Look at the trash can!
W Some people haven't separated their trash.
M _____ _____ _____ _____?
W Yes. The recycling bins are right there.
M _____ _____ _____ _____ the paper and plastic? I'll take out the cans and bottles.
W Okay. I don't understand why people are so irresponsible.
M Me neither. They should care about the environment.
W _____ _____ _____ _____ _____.

07　주제 파악

다음을 듣고, 남자가 하는 말의 내용으로 가장
적절한 것을 고르시오.

① 기차역 개통　　　② 열차 시간 변경
③ 도착역 알림　　　④ 도난 사고 주의
⑤ 지하철 요금 인상

M Ladies and gentlemen, _____ _____ _____ _____ the platform. We'll arrive at Gwangmyeong Station shortly. If this is your destination, please be prepared to _____ _____ _____ _____. This train's final destination is Seoul Station. Please _____ _____ _____ _____ with you when you get off the train. Thank you for traveling with us and have a good day.

08 할 일 파악

대화를 듣고, 여자가 내일 할 일로 가장 적절한 것을 고르시오.

① 박람회 가기 　② 자료 조사하기
③ 미술 학원 가기 　④ 봉사 활동 하기
⑤ 재활용품 모으기

M Why do you have all these boxes and cans?
W I'm _____ _____ _____ _____ _____. I need to create an artwork using them.
M What are you going to make?
W I have no idea.
M _____ _____ _____ the Internet for ideas?
W I did, but it wasn't helpful. I want to make _____ _____ _____.
M Then how about visiting the Eco Design Expo? _____ 정답 단서 _____ _____ _____.
W That's a good idea. I'll go there tomorrow.

09 언급하지 않은 것 찾기 ✳

대화를 듣고, 남자가 화천 산천어 얼음 축제에 대해 언급하지 않은 것을 고르시오.

① 시기 　② 장소 　③ 입장료
④ 체험 활동 　⑤ 교통편

M Do you know about the Hwacheon Sancheoneo Ice Festival?
W _____ _____ _____ _____. What is it?
M It's a winter festival held in Hwacheon in January. You can _____ _____ _____ _____ such as ice fishing and ice sledding.
W That sounds interesting. _____ _____ _____ _____ _____ before?
M No. But I'm going there this weekend. Do you want to go with me?
W I'd love to. But how can we get there? _____ _____ _____.
M There's a shuttle bus at Myeongdong Station.
W Great. That's convenient.

10 특정 정보 파악

대화를 듣고, 여자가 좋아하는 분야를 고르시오.

① 춤 　② 노래 　③ 등산
④ 요리 　⑤ 게임

Sound Clear ☆ **climber**
b가 묵음이라서 [클라이머]로 발음된다.

W _____ _____ _____ _____ _____ _____ in the future?
M I want to be a professional mountain climber. My dream is to climb Mt. Everest. What about you?
W I _____ _____ _____ _____ _____. I don't know what I want to do in the future.
M _____ _____ _____ _____ _____ to do.
W Hmm... I enjoy singing, but I don't know _____ _____ 정답 단서 _____ _____ _____.
M Practice every day, and you will be a professional someday.
W I'll have to think about it. Thanks.

11 일치하지 않는 것 찾기

대화를 듣고, 여자에 대한 설명으로 일치하지 <u>않는</u> 것을 고르시오.

① 남자와 처음 만난 사이이다.
② 남자네 가족의 집에서 머물 예정이다.
③ 한국에 두 번 방문했다.
④ 경복궁에 가장 가 보고 싶어 한다.
⑤ 여러 나라의 전통 건축물에 관심이 있다.

Sound Clear ☆ **first time**
동일한 발음의 자음이 연이어 나오면 앞 자음 소리가 탈락하여 [퍼스타임]으로 발음된다.

M Hello. I'm Jinho. Nice to meet you!
W My name is Jennifer. Nice to meet you, too.
M My family's house is your homestay. _____ _____ _____ _____ now.
W Thank you. I'm really _____ _____ _____ _____ everyone.
M It's your first time in Korea. 정답 단서 Where do you want to visit the most?
W Gyeongbokgung Palace. I'm _____ _____ _____ _____ _____ of every country I visit.
M Good. Gyeongbokgung Palace is near our house.
W That's great.

12 목적 파악 ✳

대화를 듣고, 여자가 책을 읽는 목적으로 가장 적절한 것을 고르시오.

① 발표를 준비하기 위해서
② 중국 문화에 관심이 생겨서
③ 중국에 여행을 가기 위해서
④ 중국인 친구를 사귀기 위해서
⑤ 중국어 시험을 대비하기 위해서

M What are you reading?
W I'm reading _____ _____ _____ _____ _____.
M Chinese culture? I didn't know you're interested in China.
W I'm not really interested in China. I'm reading it _____ _____ _____ _____.
M Why?
W I need to _____ _____ _____ _____ about Chinese culture next week.
M I see. Do your best.

13 숫자 정보 파악

대화를 듣고, 남자가 지불해야 할 금액으로 가장 적절한 것을 고르시오.

① 12,000원 ② 13,000원 ③ 14,000원
④ 15,000원 ⑤ 16,000원

(*Telephone rings.*)
W Han's Chicken. How may I help you?
M I want to order one fried chicken. I'm at 213 Green Road.
W Okay. Do you want _____ _____ _____ or the spicy one?
M _____ _____ _____ _____ _____?
W The original is 14,000 won. You have to pay 1,000 won more for the spicy one.
M _____ _____ _____ _____ _____. Is there a delivery fee?
W Yes, it's 1,000 won.
M I see. _____ _____ _____ _____.

14 부탁한 일 파악

대화를 듣고, 남자가 여자에게 부탁한 일로 가장 적절한 것을 고르시오.

① 함께 줄넘기하기　② 파스 사다 주기
③ 병원 데려다주기　④ 얼음찜질 해 주기
⑤ 진료 예약해 주기

Sound Clear ☆ **right away**
앞 단어의 끝 자음과 뒤 단어의 첫 모음이 만나 연음되어 [롸이러웨이]로 발음된다.

W　What's wrong, Michael?
M　_____ _____ _____. I think I sprained it while jumping rope.
W　Oh, no. Do you want me to put an ice pack on your ankle?
M　I already did that, _____ _____ _____ _____.
W　Let's go to see a doctor right away.
M　I think just putting on some pain relief patches will do. _____ _____ _____ _____ some patches for me?
W　I see. But if it still hurts tomorrow, you should see a doctor.
M　Okay, I will.

15 주제 파악

다음을 듣고, 여자가 하는 말의 내용으로 가장 적절한 것을 고르시오.

① 건강 관리 비결
② 저칼로리 식단
③ 사과 재배 방법
④ 사과가 인기 있는 이유
⑤ 사과를 이용한 요리법

W　Apples are one of _____ _____ _____ _____ in the world. There are several reasons apples are so popular. First, they are good for your health. Remember the saying, "_____ _____ _____ _____ keeps the doctor away." Second, apples can be grown all over the world. Third, they taste good. Lastly, they are effective at _____ _____ _____ _____ because they are low in calories.

16 이유 파악

대화를 듣고, 남자가 작가를 만나고 싶어 하는 이유로 가장 적절한 것을 고르시오.

① 작가의 팬이라서
② 사인을 받고 싶어서
③ 조언을 구하고 싶어서
④ 사진을 찍고 싶어서
⑤ 책 내용에 대해 토론하고 싶어서

M　Did you hear that _____ _____ _____ _____ _____ at the community center today?
W　No, I didn't. What's the lecture about?
M　Jordan Peterson will _____ _____ _____.
W　Wow, isn't he the writer of the book *12 Rules for Life*? I'll go and _____ _____ _____.
M　I will go, too. I've always wanted to meet him.
W　Why?
M　I want to _____ _____ how to be a good writer.
W　Then today will be a great chance for you.

17 그림의 상황에 적절한 대화 찾기

다음 그림의 상황에 가장 적절한 대화를 고르시오.

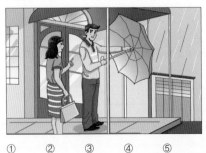

① ② ③ ④ ⑤

① W　What's wrong? You look tired today.
　 M　I think _____ _____ _____ _____.
② W　What do you think of this umbrella?
　 M　It looks okay, but it's heavy.
③ W　I don't feel well these days. What should I do?
　 M　I think you should _____ _____ _____.
④ W　What do you want to _____ _____ _____?
　 M　I want to eat seafood spaghetti.
⑤ W　_____ _____ _____ _____ with me?
　 　I don't have one.
　 M　Sure, I can.

18 언급하지 않은 것 찾기

다음을 듣고, 여자가 에바 알머슨에 대해 언급하지 <u>않은</u> 것을 고르시오.

① 국적　　　　② 직업
③ 유년 시절　　④ 화풍
⑤ 작품의 주제

Sound Clear ☆ characters

ch가 [k]로 소리 나서 [캐럭털스]로 발음된다.

W　Eva Armisen is a Spanish artist. ＿＿＿＿ ＿＿＿＿ ＿＿＿＿ ＿＿＿＿ her childlike style. The characters in her artwork all have ＿＿＿＿ ＿＿＿＿ ＿＿＿＿ ＿＿＿＿ on their faces. They ＿＿＿＿ ＿＿＿＿ ＿＿＿＿ ＿＿＿＿ ＿＿＿＿ in the small and simple moments in our everyday lives. The subjects of her artwork are family, love, and togetherness.

19 마지막 말에 이어질 응답 찾기

대화를 듣고, 여자의 마지막 말에 이어질 남자의 말로 가장 적절한 것을 고르시오.

Man: ＿＿＿＿＿＿＿＿＿＿＿＿＿＿

① He really taught me a lot.
② I thought I saw John do it.
③ I'll teach you how to do it.
④ I want to break my bad habits.
⑤ My homeroom teacher last year.

W　Hey, ＿＿＿＿ ＿＿＿＿ ＿＿＿＿ ＿＿＿＿ ＿＿＿＿?
M　I'm working on my habit tracker.
W　Habit tracker? I've never heard of it. What is it?
M　It's a list for ＿＿＿＿ ＿＿＿＿ ＿＿＿＿ every day.
W　Sounds interesting. Why are you doing that?
M　It helps me to ＿＿＿＿ ＿＿＿＿ ＿＿＿＿ ＿＿＿＿ and build good ones.
W　＿＿＿＿ ＿＿＿＿ ＿＿＿＿ ＿＿＿＿ ＿＿＿＿?
M　My homeroom teacher last year.

20 마지막 말에 이어질 응답 찾기

대화를 듣고, 여자의 마지막 말에 이어질 남자의 말로 가장 적절한 것을 고르시오.

Man: ＿＿＿＿＿＿＿＿＿＿＿＿＿＿

① I don't have a tablet PC.
② Thank you for your help.
③ Sure. I'll lend you my note.
④ He did not answer the phone.
⑤ Okay. I'll tell him when he comes back.

(Telephone rings.)
M　Hello.
W　Hello. This is Cheryl. Is David at home?
M　No, he's out. He ＿＿＿＿ ＿＿＿＿ ＿＿＿＿ ＿＿＿＿.
W　I see. That's why he didn't answer either my phone calls or text messages.
M　Do you want to ＿＿＿＿ ＿＿＿＿ ＿＿＿＿?
W　Yes, please. He has my tablet PC, but I need it tomorrow.
M　Your tablet PC?
W　Yes. Would you please ＿＿＿＿ ＿＿＿＿ ＿＿＿＿ ＿＿＿＿ ＿＿＿＿ tomorrow?
M　Okay. I'll tell him when he comes back.

01 다음을 듣고, 런던의 날씨로 가장 적절한 것을 고르시오.

①   ②   ③

④   ⑤

02 대화를 듣고, 여자가 구입할 그림으로 가장 적절한 것을 고르시오.

①   ②   ③

④   ⑤

03 대화를 듣고, 남자가 마지막에 느꼈을 심정으로 가장 적절한 것을 고르시오.

① satisfied   ② excited
③ frightened   ④ relaxed
⑤ disappointed

04 대화를 듣고, 남자가 지난 주말에 한 일을 고르시오.

① 쇼핑하기   ② 요리하기
③ 영화 보기   ④ 사진 찍기
⑤ 수족관 가기

05 대화를 듣고, 두 사람이 대화하는 장소로 가장 적절한 곳을 고르시오.

① 식당   ② 호텔   ③ 공항
④ 편의점   ⑤ 쇼핑몰

06 대화를 듣고, 여자의 마지막 말의 의도로 가장 적절한 것을 고르시오.

① 제안   ② 동의   ③ 수락
④ 불평   ⑤ 위로

07 다음을 듣고, 남자가 하는 말의 내용으로 가장 적절한 것을 고르시오.

① 운동의 필요성
② 스트레스의 원인
③ 건강을 해치는 습관
④ 건강한 식습관의 중요성
⑤ 효과적인 다이어트 방법

08 대화를 듣고, 여자가 집들이를 위해 만들 음식을 고르시오.

① 햄버거   ② 불고기   ③ 피자
④ 잡채   ⑤ 김치전

09 대화를 듣고, 남자가 대화 직후에 할 일로 가장 적절한 것을 고르시오.

① 요리 돕기   ② 양파 사 오기
③ 옆집 들르기   ④ 팬케이크 먹기
⑤ 설거지하기

10 대화를 듣고, 여자가 수영 강좌에 대해 언급하지 <u>않은</u> 것을 고르시오.

① 수업 난이도   ② 수업 일정
③ 수업료 할인 조건   ④ 사은품
⑤ 준비물

11 대화를 듣고, 할인 행사에 대한 내용으로 일치하지 않는 것을 고르시오.

① 노트북을 할인 판매한다.
② 제품에 따라 할인율이 다르다.
③ 온라인에서만 진행한다.
④ 오늘부터 사흘 동안 진행한다.
⑤ 두 개 이상 사면 배송비가 무료이다.

12 대화를 듣고, 여자가 서비스 센터를 방문한 목적으로 가장 적절한 것을 고르시오.

① 두고 간 물건을 찾기 위해서
② 스마트폰을 고치기 위해서
③ 가격을 문의하기 위해서
④ 요금제를 변경하기 위해서
⑤ 휴대 전화 케이스를 구입하기 위해서

13 대화를 듣고, 여자가 지불해야 할 금액으로 가장 적절한 것을 고르시오.

① $22　　② $25　　③ $30
④ $33　　⑤ $35

14 다음을 듣고, 여자가 자신의 롤 모델에 대해 언급하지 않은 것을 고르시오.

① 이름　　② 하는 일　　③ 나이
④ 자서전 내용　　⑤ 별명

15 대화를 듣고, 두 사람의 관계로 가장 적절한 것을 고르시오.

① 작가 – 독자
② 서점 직원 – 손님
③ 호텔 직원 – 투숙객
④ 컴퓨터 수리공 – 고객
⑤ 도서관 사서 – 이용객

16 대화를 듣고, 남자가 여자에게 부탁한 일로 가장 적절한 것을 고르시오.

① 호텔 예약하기　　② 식당 예약하기
③ 앱 다운로드하기　　④ 스마트폰 추천해 주기
⑤ 여행 계획 세우기

17 대화를 듣고, 여자가 기차를 놓친 이유로 가장 적절한 것을 고르시오.

① 늦게 일어나서　　② 차가 많이 막혀서
③ 길을 잃어버려서　　④ 경찰에게 잡혀서
⑤ 누군가를 도와주느라고

18 대화를 듣고, 두 사람의 대화가 어색한 것을 고르시오.

①　　②　　③　　④　　⑤

[19-20] 대화를 듣고, 남자의 마지막 말에 이어질 여자의 말로 가장 적절한 것을 고르시오.

19 Woman: _____

① Anytime you want.
② I don't know who he is.
③ I'm not sure. Let's hurry.
④ Of course. You can buy it.
⑤ Put them next to the lockers.

20 Woman: _____

① I'm sure you have a cold.
② I haven't been vaccinated yet.
③ You should see a doctor right now.
④ The reason is that you keep sneezing.
⑤ I think you have an allergy to something.

01 날씨 파악

다음을 듣고, 런던의 날씨로 가장 적절한 것을 고르시오.

①   ②   ③

④   ⑤

W Good morning. I'm Clara with the worldwide weather report. We _____ _____ _____ _____ _____ _____ here in Seoul because of the high level of fine dust. Due to _____ _____ _____ _____ across Japan, rain is pouring in Tokyo at this moment. In London, _____ _____ _____ _____ _____, many flights have been canceled. Finally, in Moscow, it is windy today. That's all for today.

02 그림 정보 파악

대화를 듣고, 여자가 구입할 그림으로 가장 적절한 것을 고르시오.

①   ②   ③

④   ⑤

Sound Clear ☆ **landscape**
자음 세 개가 연속으로 나오면 중간 자음의 발음이 약화되어 [랜스케이프]로 발음된다.

M Hello. How can I help you?
W I'd like to _____ _____ _____ for my living room.
M What kind of painting are you looking for?
W _____ _____ _____ a landscape painting.
M All right. How about this one? Doesn't _____ _____ _____ _____?
W Yes, it does. But one with a sky would be better.
M Then you'll like this one. A clear sky is _____ _____ _____ _____. 정답 단서
W That is beautiful. I'll take it.

03 심정 추론

대화를 듣고, 남자가 마지막에 느꼈을 심정으로 가장 적절한 것을 고르시오.

① satisfied ② excited
③ frightened ④ relaxed
⑤ disappointed

M I can't believe this! I think I'll _____ _____ _____ _____! I won a prize!
W Are you serious?
M Yes, look at this email. I _____ _____ _____ in a shopping mall event.
W Let me see. Well, did you check the date here?
M What date?
W It says _____ _____ _____ _____ until January 3. Wasn't that a week ago?
M Oh, my! _____ _____ _____ _____? No way!

04 한 일 파악

대화를 듣고, 남자가 지난 주말에 한 일을 고르시오.

① 쇼핑하기　　② 요리하기
③ 영화 보기　　④ 사진 찍기
⑤ 수족관 가기

M: I went to Sky Mall last weekend. There are lots of big stores there.

W: Oh, ＿＿＿＿＿ ＿＿＿＿＿ ＿＿＿＿＿ ＿＿＿＿＿. Did you buy anything?

M: No. I went there to watch the movie *Enemy*.

W: ＿＿＿＿＿ ＿＿＿＿＿ ＿＿＿＿＿ ＿＿＿＿＿ in the mall?

M: Yeah. It's on the ninth floor.

W: That's good. Can you recommend a good restaurant there?

M: Try the seafood restaurant ＿＿＿＿＿ ＿＿＿＿＿ ＿＿＿＿＿ ＿＿＿＿＿. People say the food there is very good.

05 장소 추론

대화를 듣고, 두 사람이 대화하는 장소로 가장 적절한 곳을 고르시오.

① 식당　　② 호텔　　③ 공항
④ 편의점　　⑤ 쇼핑몰

Sound Clear ☆ level

'레벨'이라고 발음하지 않고 [레블]에 가깝게 발음된다.

M: Excuse me. Is there a convenience store nearby?

W: Yes. At the main entrance, turn right and it's ＿＿＿＿＿ ＿＿＿＿＿ ＿＿＿＿＿ ＿＿＿＿＿ ＿＿＿＿＿ ＿＿＿＿＿.

M: I see. When does breakfast start in the morning?

W: It's from 7:30 to 10:30. The restaurant is on the first basement level.

M: Okay. Can I ＿＿＿＿＿ ＿＿＿＿＿ ＿＿＿＿＿ ＿＿＿＿＿ tomorrow at 8:30?

W: Of course. What is your room number?

M: ＿＿＿＿＿ ＿＿＿＿＿ ＿＿＿＿＿ 905. Thank you.

06 의도 파악

대화를 듣고, 여자의 마지막 말의 의도로 가장 적절한 것을 고르시오.

① 제안　　② 동의　　③ 수락
④ 불평　　⑤ 위로

W: Junho, is there anything wrong? ＿＿＿＿＿ ＿＿＿＿＿ ＿＿＿＿＿.

M: Never mind. I'm fine.

W: Come on. ＿＿＿＿＿ ＿＿＿＿＿ ＿＿＿＿＿ ＿＿＿＿＿?

M: Well, I feel bad because of my musical audition. I was so nervous that I ＿＿＿＿＿ ＿＿＿＿＿ ＿＿＿＿＿ ＿＿＿＿＿ at the climax of the song.

W: Oh, I'm sorry to hear that.

M: I'm so ＿＿＿＿＿ ＿＿＿＿＿ ＿＿＿＿＿.

W: Don't be. I'm sure you'll do better the next time.

07 주제 파악

다음을 듣고, 남자가 하는 말의 내용으로 가장 적절한 것을 고르시오.

① 운동의 필요성
② 스트레스의 원인
③ 건강을 해치는 습관
④ 건강한 식습관의 중요성
⑤ 효과적인 다이어트 방법

M: People are interested in staying healthy. Many of them exercise regularly and have an annual physical checkup. However, they seem to overlook ＿＿＿＿＿ ＿＿＿＿＿ ＿＿＿＿＿ ＿＿＿＿＿ ＿＿＿＿＿ ＿＿＿＿＿. I think having healthy food is the most effective way to stay healthy. Eat as many fruits and vegetables as possible. ＿＿＿＿＿ ＿＿＿＿＿ ＿＿＿＿＿ ＿＿＿＿＿ ＿＿＿＿＿. If you eat lots of unhealthy food, it's important to change your diet ＿＿＿＿＿ ＿＿＿＿＿ ＿＿＿＿＿. Then, you'll be successful.

08 특정 정보 파악 ❄

대화를 듣고, 여자가 집들이를 위해 만들 음식을 고르시오.

① 햄버거 ② 불고기 ③ 피자
④ 잡채 ⑤ 김치전

W David, _____ _____ _____ _____ would be good for the housewarming party?
M How about *bulgogi*? Our friends like Korean food, you know.
W But Sarah is a vegetarian. 한정
M Oh, you're right. Then how about potato pizza? _____ 한정 _____ _____.
W Not bad. But I _____ _____ _____ a Korean dish.
M Hmm... what about *japchae*? We can _____ _____ 정답 단서 _____ _____.
W That's a good idea. Let's make it.

09 할 일 파악

대화를 듣고, 남자가 대화 직후에 할 일로 가장 적절한 것을 고르시오.

① 요리 돕기   ② 양파 사 오기
③ 옆집 들르기   ④ 팬케이크 먹기
⑤ 설거지하기

M What are you going to cook for dinner?
W I'm going to make spaghetti. (*Pause*) Oh, we don't have _____ _____.
M Let me get some from the grocery store. 한정
W Thanks. And _____ _____ _____ to the Smiths next door. I borrowed some from them last week.
M Okay. I'll stop by before I go to the market.
W _____ _____ 정답 단서 _____ _____ thank you for the pancakes they gave us last weekend, too.
M I will. _____ _____ _____ _____ when I get home.

10 언급하지 않은 것 찾기

대화를 듣고, 여자가 수영 강좌에 대해 언급하지 않은 것을 고르시오.

① 수업 난이도   ② 수업 일정
③ 수업료 할인 조건   ④ 사은품
⑤ 준비물

Sound Clear ☆ **sign up**
sign의 g는 묵음이고, 두 단어가 연음되어 [싸이넙]으로 발음된다.

M Hello. I'd like to _____ _____ _____ _____.
W We have beginner, intermediate, and advanced classes.
M I'll take the class for beginners.
W The beginner's class _____ _____ _____ in the morning every Tuesday and Thursday.
M Okay. How much does it cost?
W It's $50 per month, but there's a 10% discount when you sign ☆ up _____ _____ _____ _____ _____.
M I'll sign up for three months.
W Okay. _____ _____ _____ _____ _____ as a gift when you first sign up, too.
M Good. Thanks.

11 일치하지 않는 것 찾기

대화를 듣고, 할인 행사에 대한 내용으로 일치하지 <u>않는</u> 것을 고르시오.

① 노트북을 할인 판매한다.
② 제품에 따라 할인율이 다르다.
③ 온라인에서만 진행한다.
④ 오늘부터 사흘 동안 진행한다.
⑤ 두 개 이상 사면 배송비가 무료이다.

M There's a big sale on laptops at ABC Electronics. Don't you need a new one?

W I do! How much of a discount is the store offering?

M It _____ _____ _____ _____, but most models are 30 to 50% off. Discounts apply to _____ _____ _____.

W Fantastic. For how long does the sale last?

M _____ _____ _____ _____ _____.

W What about the delivery fee?

M _____ _____ _____ for purchases over $500.

W I got it. I think I should order one right away.

12 목적 파악

대화를 듣고, 여자가 서비스 센터를 방문한 목적으로 가장 적절한 것을 고르시오.

① 두고 간 물건을 찾기 위해서
② 스마트폰을 고치기 위해서
③ 가격을 문의하기 위해서
④ 요금제를 변경하기 위해서
⑤ 휴대 전화 케이스를 구입하기 위해서

M Hello. AP Service Center. How may I help you?

W Hello. You _____ _____ _____ last night.

M Is there still a problem?

W No, no. I left my shopping bag, and I'm here to pick it up.

M Oh, I see. What does your bag look like?

W It's a paper bag _____ _____ _____ in it.

M Okay. Let me check if one of our staff members _____ _____ _____ _____ _____.

13 숫자 정보 파악

대화를 듣고, 여자가 지불해야 할 금액으로 가장 적절한 것을 고르시오.

① $22 ② $25 ③ $30
④ $33 ⑤ $35

Sound Clear ☆ **curry**
'카레'는 실제로 [커뤼]로 발음된다.

W Hi. I'd like to order a chicken curry and a salad, please.

M Do you want to _____ _____ _____ on your curry?

W Yes. One cheese topping, please.

M The total is $22. Anything else?

W I'll have a large sweet potato chips and a medium coke. I'll _____ _____ _____ _____, too.

M Then it's only $8 _____ _____ _____.

W Okay. Here's my card.

14 언급하지 않은 것 찾기

다음을 듣고, 여자가 자신의 롤 모델에 대해 언급하지 <u>않은</u> 것을 고르시오.

① 이름   ② 하는 일
③ 나이   ④ 자서전 내용
⑤ 별명

W Let me introduce my role model, Scarlet Choi. She not only _____ _____ _____ but also designs dance performances for idol groups. I read her autobiography, *Dance Is My Life*. In the book, she _____ _____ _____ _____ and how hard her life was. She overcame difficulties by dancing. I could understand _____ _____ _____ "Practice Queen."

15 관계 추론

대화를 듣고, 두 사람의 관계로 가장 적절한 것을 고르시오.

① 작가 – 독자
② 서점 직원 – 손님
③ 호텔 직원 – 투숙객
④ 컴퓨터 수리공 – 고객
⑤ 도서관 사서 – 이용객

W Hello. I'd like to check out this book.
M Can I ________ ________ ________ ________?
W I don't have one. It's my first visit here.
M You need a card to ________ ________ ________. Would you like to make one?
W Yes.
M Do you see the computer over there? Fill out ________ ________ ________ on the library's homepage first.
W Okay.
M Then, print it and ________ ________ ________ ________ with your ID card.
W All right. Thanks.

16 부탁한 일 파악

대화를 듣고, 남자가 여자에게 부탁한 일로 가장 적절한 것을 고르시오.

① 호텔 예약하기
② 식당 예약하기
③ 앱 다운로드하기
④ 스마트폰 추천해 주기
⑤ 여행 계획 세우기

Sound Clear☆ **Give me**
[v]가 [m]에 동화되어 [김미]로 발음된다.

W Do you have any plans for the holiday?
M I'm going to Gyeongju for a family trip.
W That's good. ________ ________ ________ ________ for it?
M I ________ ________ ________ ________, but I haven't decided what to eat there.
W Check out the app Yummy Time. It shows a list of the fine restaurants ________ ________.
M That's good. Will you download the app for me? ________ ________ ________ ________ (정답 단서) my new smartphone.
W Okay. ☆Give me yours.

17 이유 파악

대화를 듣고, 여자가 기차를 놓친 이유로 가장 적절한 것을 고르시오.

① 늦게 일어나서
② 차가 많이 막혀서
③ 길을 잃어버려서
④ 경찰에게 잡혀서
⑤ 누군가를 도와주느라고

M Why are you so late?
W I'm sorry. ________ ________ ________ ________.
M Did you get up late again? (함정)
W ________ ________ ________. I woke up at 7 a.m.
M Then why were you late? Was there a traffic jam (함정) on the way to the train station?
W Nope. On the way to the station, I met ________ ________ ________ ________ ________.
M Oh, no.
W He was crying, so I took him to the nearest police station. It took me (정답 단서) ________ ________ ________ ________.

18 어색한 대화 찾기

대화를 듣고, 두 사람의 대화가 어색한 것을 고르시오.

① ② ③ ④ ⑤

Sound Clear ☆ **second floor**
자음 세 개가 연속으로 나오면 중간 자음의 발음이 약화되어 [세컨플로어]로 발음된다.

① **M** Excuse me. The elevator is full now.

  W Oops, _____ _____ _____.

② **M** Let's get some ice cream. Which flavor do you like?

  W I like vanilla. What about you?

③ **M** You cannot take that cart _____ _____ _____ _____.

  W I didn't know that. I'm sorry.

④ **M** I'd like to exchange these jeans.

  W There is _____ _____ _____ on the second floor.

⑤ **M** Can you fix this copy machine?

  W I'm not sure. Let me _____ _____ _____.

19 마지막 말에 이어질 응답 찾기

대화를 듣고, 남자의 마지막 말에 이어질 여자의 말로 가장 적절한 것을 고르시오.

Woman: _____

① Anytime you want.
② I don't know who he is.
③ I'm not sure. Let's hurry.
④ Of course. You can buy it.
⑤ Put them next to the lockers.

W _____ _____ _____. I don't have an umbrella.

M Me neither. What should we do? I don't think it will stop soon.

W Hmm... _____ _____ _____ _____!

M Tell me.

W I heard the student council _____ _____ _____ when it rains.

M Student council?

W Yes! _____ _____ _____ _____ _____ our name and phone number.

M I didn't know that. I hope there are still some umbrellas left.

W I'm not sure. Let's hurry.

20 마지막 말에 이어질 응답 찾기

대화를 듣고, 남자의 마지막 말에 이어질 여자의 말로 가장 적절한 것을 고르시오.

Woman: _____

① I'm sure you have a cold.
② I haven't been vaccinated yet.
③ You should see a doctor right now.
④ The reason is that you keep sneezing.
⑤ I think you have an allergy to something.

W Hello. _____ _____ _____ _____ the problem?

M I think I have a cold. I have a runny nose and keep sneezing.

W Okay. _____ _____ _____ _____ _____.

M All right.

W Now I'll _____ _____ _____ _____.

M Okay.

W You don't have a fever, and your nose looks fine. I don't think you have a cold.

M Then why do I _____ _____ _____?

W I think you have an allergy to something.

Word Check
영어는 우리말로, 우리말은 영어로 써 보기

01 fine dust _____

02 completely _____

03 text message _____

04 vertical _____

05 palace _____

06 filter _____

07 complain _____

08 strongly _____

09 recognize _____

10 except _____

11 in person _____

12 airmail _____

13 분리하다 _____

14 강의 _____

15 다가가다 _____

16 경고 _____

17 소지품 _____

18 목적지 _____

19 미술품 _____

20 무책임한 _____

21 효과적인 _____

22 속담, 격언 _____

23 삐다, 접지르다 _____

24 등장인물 _____

Expression Check
알맞은 표현을 넣어 문장 완성하기

25 You can choose _____ airmail _____ ship delivery. 항공 우편과 선박 배송 중에 선택하실 수 있어요.

26 They should _____ _____ the environment. 그 사람들은 환경에 대해 신경 써야 해.

27 An apple a day _____ the doctor _____. 하루에 사과 한 알이면 의사가 필요 없다.

28 I need to _____ _____ a presentation about Chinese culture next week.
나는 다음 주에 있을 중국 문화에 대한 발표를 준비해야 해.

29 They _____ us _____ the joy in the simple moments in our everyday lives.
그들은 우리에게 일상생활에서 소박한 순간의 기쁨을 생각나게 합니다.

30 It helps me to _____ my bad _____ and build good ones.
그것은 나의 나쁜 습관을 고치고 좋은 습관을 만들도록 도와줘.

Answers p.77

Word Check
영어는 우리말로, 우리말은 영어로 써 보기

01 worldwide _____

02 autobiography _____

03 landscape _____

04 peaceful _____

05 importance _____

06 recently _____

07 wakeup call _____

08 climax _____

09 vegetarian _____

10 frightened _____

11 stop by _____

12 little by little _____

13 간과하다 _____

14 중급의; 중급자 _____

15 상급의 _____

16 극복하다 _____

17 구입, 구매 _____

18 건강에 해로운 _____

19 공연 _____

20 취소하다 _____

21 전자 제품 _____

22 진찰하다 _____

23 유년기 _____

24 재채기하다 _____

Expression Check
알맞은 표현을 넣어 문장 완성하기

25 I'm so _____ _____ myself. 나는 내 자신이 정말 실망스러워.

26 _____ _____ the application form first. 우선 신청서를 작성하세요.

27 I'm not _____ _____ my new smartphone. 나는 내 새로운 스마트폰에 익숙하지 않아.

28 It _____ _____ the product, but most models are 30 to 50% off.
제품에 따라 다르지만, 대부분의 모델은 30~50퍼센트 할인이야.

29 She _____ _____ dances in musicals _____ _____ designs dance
performances for idol groups. 그녀는 뮤지컬에서 춤을 출 뿐 아니라 아이돌 그룹을 위해 춤 공연도 설계합니다.

30 The student council lends us umbrellas _____ _____ _____ we leave our name
and phone number. 우리가 이름이랑 전화번호를 남기기만 하면 학생회에서 우리에게 우산을 빌려줘.

01 다음을 듣고, 추석 아침의 날씨로 가장 적절한 것을 고르시오.

① ② ③
④ ⑤

02 대화를 듣고, 여자가 구입할 손거울로 가장 적절한 것을 고르시오.

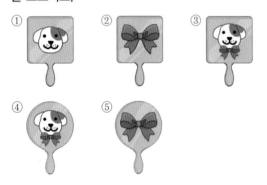

① ② ③
④ ⑤

03 대화를 듣고, 남자의 심정으로 가장 적절한 것을 고르시오.
① jealous　② bored　③ excited
④ annoyed　⑤ depressed

04 대화를 듣고, 남자가 모터쇼에서 한 일을 고르시오.
① 엔진 원리 배우기
② 차량용품 구입하기
③ 스포츠카 사진 찍기
④ 신형 자동차 시운전하기
⑤ 자동차 디자이너 만나기

05 대화를 듣고, 두 사람이 대화하는 장소로 가장 적절한 곳을 고르시오.
① 컴퓨터 매장　　② 가전제품 매장
③ 휴대 전화 대리점　④ 자동차 정비소
⑤ 전자 제품 수리점

06 대화를 듣고, 여자의 마지막 말의 의도로 가장 적절한 것을 고르시오.
① 제안　　② 동의　　③ 수락
④ 불평　　⑤ 위로

07 대화를 듣고, 남자가 구입할 물건을 고르시오.
① 책상　　② 다이어리　③ 탁상용 달력
④ 복주머니　⑤ 건강식품

08 대화를 듣고, 여자가 대화 직후에 할 일로 가장 적절한 것을 고르시오.
① 꽃 구입하기　　② 선물 고르기
③ 스테이크 굽기　④ 식당 예약하기
⑤ 졸업식 참석하기

09 대화를 듣고, 남자가 학교 문학 여행에 대해 언급하지 않은 것을 고르시오.
① 여행 주제　　② 여행지
③ 교통편　　　④ 참가 인원
⑤ 신청 방법

10 다음을 듣고, 여자가 하는 말의 내용으로 가장 적절한 것을 고르시오.
① 오디션 공지　　② 영화 관람 예절
③ 신작 영화 소개　④ 최초의 우주 비행사
⑤ 리메이크 앨범 홍보

11 대화를 듣고, 남자에 대한 설명으로 일치하지 않는 것을 고르시오.
① 다음 달에 전학 간다.
② 포항으로 이사를 간다.
③ 포항에 가 본 적이 없다.
④ 포항에 친척들이 살고 있다.
⑤ 친구 문제를 걱정하고 있다.

12 대화를 듣고, 남자가 전화를 건 목적으로 가장 적절한 것을 고르시오.

① 표를 구매하기 위해서
② 예약을 취소하기 위해서
③ 예약 날짜를 변경하기 위해서
④ 배송 시각을 변경하기 위해서
⑤ 모임 약속 시간을 정하기 위해서

13 대화를 듣고, 두 사람의 관계로 가장 적절한 것을 고르시오.

① 경비원 – 입주민
② 편의점 직원 – 손님
③ 심리 상담가 – 상담자
④ 매표소 직원 – 관광객
⑤ 분실물 보관소 직원 – 지하철 이용객

14 대화를 듣고, 여자가 공연장에 도착한 시각을 고르시오.

① 7:00 p.m. ② 7:05 p.m. ③ 7:10 p.m.
④ 7:15 p.m. ⑤ 7:20 p.m.

15 대화를 듣고, 남자가 여자에게 부탁한 일로 가장 적절한 것을 고르시오.

① 자료 수집하기 ② 영어 번역하기
③ 사진 촬영하기 ④ 동영상 촬영하기
⑤ 동영상 짧게 편집하기

16 대화를 듣고, 여자가 자리를 바꾸고 싶어 하는 이유로 가장 적절한 것을 고르시오.

① 자리가 너무 추워서
② 칠판이 잘 안 보여서
③ 에어컨 바람이 안 와서
④ 짝과 사이가 좋지 않아서
⑤ 친한 친구와 함께 앉고 싶어서

17 다음을 듣고, 남자가 한국 문화 축제에 대해 언급하지 않은 것을 고르시오.

① 개최 장소 ② 개최 요일
③ 개최 시간 ④ 행사 내용
⑤ 입장료

18 다음 그림의 상황에 가장 적절한 대화를 고르시오.

① ② ③ ④ ⑤

[19-20] 대화를 듣고, 여자의 마지막 말에 이어질 남자의 말로 가장 적절한 것을 고르시오.

19 Man: _____

① We have a similar custom.
② The game is really exciting.
③ We played *Yunnori* together.
④ I will take part in a special event.
⑤ We had a big dinner on Thanksgiving Day.

20 Man: _____

① You should see a doctor.
② I'm fine. Thank you for asking.
③ Air pollution is a serious issue.
④ It'll be as terrible as it is today.
⑤ I like winter better than summer.

받아쓰기용

01 날씨 파악

다음을 듣고, 추석 아침의 날씨로 가장 적절한 것을 고르시오.

① ② ③

④  ⑤

Sound Clear ☆ **holiday**
모음 i는 강세가 없을 때 [어]로 소리 나서 [할러데이]로 발음된다.

W Good morning, listeners. It's finally the *chuseok* holiday. Today, _____ _____ _____ _____ is expected. However, on *chuseok* morning, it will start to rain. So don't forget to _____ _____ _____ on *chuseok*. The sky will clear up in the evening, and we'll be able to _____ _____ _____ _____ at night.

정답 단서

02 그림 정보 파악

대화를 듣고, 여자가 구입할 손거울로 가장 적절한 것을 고르시오.

① ② ③

④ ⑤

W Hello. Do you have a hand mirror?
M Yes, we do. _____ _____ _____ _____ _____, a square or a circle?
W I like square shapes better.
M Good. I'd like to recommend this one. Isn't the puppy cute?
W It's cute, but can you show me one _____ _____ _____ _____ _____ _____?
한정
M Okay. What about this one? It has a big ribbon on the back.
W That's pretty. _____ _____ _____.
정답 단서

03 심정 추론

대화를 듣고, 남자의 심정으로 가장 적절한 것을 고르시오.

① jealous ② bored ③ excited
④ annoyed ⑤ depressed

(*Cellphone rings.*)
W Hey, _____ _____ _____. How is the soccer game going?
M It's only the beginning of the first half, but _____ _____ _____ _____ _____!
W Really? _____ _____ _____?
M Marcus did it. He's a really good player.
W _____ _____ _____ I missed that.
M We had a good start. Come quickly and watch it with me.
W Okay. See you soon.

04 한 일 파악

대화를 듣고, 남자가 모터쇼에서 한 일을 고르시오.

① 엔진 원리 배우기
② 차량용품 구입하기
③ 스포츠카 사진 찍기
④ 신형 자동차 시운전하기
⑤ 자동차 디자이너 만나기

W Eric, how was the motor show?
M It was so much fun.
W It's good to hear that. _____ _____ _____ any brand-new cars?
M Sadly, no. I missed the event _____ _____ _____ _____ _____. I got there too late.
W That's too bad. Then what did you do?
M I met _____ _____ _____ _____ and took some pictures with him.
W That's awesome.

05 장소 추론

대화를 듣고, 두 사람이 대화하는 장소로 가장 적절한 곳을 고르시오.

① 컴퓨터 매장   ② 가전제품 매장
③ 휴대 전화 대리점   ④ 자동차 정비소
⑤ 전자 제품 수리점

Sound Clear ☆ **at all**
[t]가 모음 사이에서 약화되고 뒤 단어의 모음과 연음되어 [애롤]로 발음된다.

M Hi. I'm looking for a wireless vacuum cleaner.
W Please come this way. (*Pause*) This model is _____ _____ _____.
M It looks good.
W It is very powerful but light. _____ _____ _____.
M It's not heavy at all, but it's _____ _____ _____ _____ _____.
W Aren't you interested in robot vacuum cleaners?
M I was using one, but it broke down. I'd like to try something different.
W I see. _____ _____ _____ and look around.

06 의도 파악

대화를 듣고, 여자의 마지막 말의 의도로 가장 적절한 것을 고르시오.

① 제안   ② 동의   ③ 수락
④ 불평   ⑤ 위로

W Excuse me. I have waited for a long time, but I _____ _____ _____ _____ _____.
M Oh, let me check. Hold on a moment, please.
W Okay.
M Your food is ready now. Here you are.
W This is not _____ _____ _____.
M Didn't you order a chicken salad?
W No. I ordered an avocado salad.
M I'm sorry. _____ _____ _____ _____.
W The service is so slow, and you make mistakes. I'm never coming here again.

07　특정 정보 파악

대화를 듣고, 남자가 구입할 물건을 고르시오.

① 책상　　② 다이어리　③ 탁상용 달력
④ 복주머니　⑤ 건강식품

M　I want to _____ _____ _____ for my family. Can you recommend anything?

W　_____ _____ _____ _____ _____?

M　It's just a New Year's gift.

W　_____ _____ _____ _____! Desk calenders might be good. 한정

M　We already have several calendars at home.

W　Then _____ _____ _____? They're practical and not very expensive.

M　That sounds good. I'll buy them.

08　할 일 파악

대화를 듣고, 여자가 대화 직후에 할 일로 가장 적절한 것을 고르시오.

① 꽃 구입하기　　② 선물 고르기
③ 스테이크 굽기　④ 식당 예약하기
⑤ 졸업식 참석하기

Sound Clear ☆ **really**

'리얼리'라고 명확하게 발음하지 않고 [륄리]에 가깝게 발음된다.

W　Tomorrow is Lisa's graduation ceremony.

M　I know. I can't believe she _____ _____ _____ 한정 elementary school.

W　Time really☆ flies. Let's buy some flowers tomorrow morning.

M　Sure. Where should we _____ _____ _____ _____ 한정 _____?

W　Charley's Steak House is her favorite place. Let's go there.

M　Great. I think we need to make a reservation. _____ 정답 단서 _____ _____ _____ _____.

W　Okay. I'll get right on it.

09　언급하지 않은 것 찾기

대화를 듣고, 남자가 학교 문학 여행에 대해 언급하지 <u>않은</u> 것을 고르시오.

① 여행 주제　　② 여행지
③ 교통편　　　④ 참가 인원
⑤ 신청 방법

M　Mom, can I sign up for the school literary tour?

W　School literary tour? What is it?

M　It's _____ _____ _____ _____ _____ in a literary work. The author of this year is Lee Hyo-seok.

W　_____ _____ _____ _____ _____?

M　To Bongpyeong.

W　_____ _____ _____ _____ _____?

M　About thirty students and a teacher. Mom, please.

W　Okay. You can go. How can you _____ _____?

M　I can sign up on our school homepage. Thank you, Mom.

10 주제 파악

다음을 듣고, 여자가 하는 말의 내용으로 가장 적절한 것을 고르시오.

① 오디션 공지
② 영화 관람 예절
③ 신작 영화 소개
④ 최초의 우주 비행사
⑤ 리메이크 앨범 홍보

W *Space Kingdom* _____ _____ _____ _____ in a week! *Space Kingdom* is a story about the life of an astronaut in the future. Susan Smith _____ _____ _____ Wendy, a strong and powerful female hero. This is her first action movie, so many people are _____ _____ _____ _____ her act. Let's visit the future by watching *Space Kingdom* this summer.

11 일치하지 않는 것 찾기

대화를 듣고, 남자에 대한 설명으로 일치하지 않는 것을 고르시오.

① 다음 달에 전학 간다.
② 포항으로 이사를 간다.
③ 포항에 가 본 적이 없다.
④ 포항에 친척들이 살고 있다.
⑤ 친구 문제를 걱정하고 있다.

Sound Clear ☆ **live in**
앞 단어의 끝 자음과 뒤 단어의 모음이 만나 연음되어 [리빈]으로 발음된다.

M I'm _____ _____ _____ _____ next month.
W I heard about that. Where are you moving to?
M To Pohang. _____ _____ _____ _____.
W Really? My hometown is Pohang, and _____ _____ _____ _____. It's a beautiful city.
M I heard Pohang is a good city to live in, but I'm worried because I don't have any friends there.
W I'm sure you will _____ _____ _____ _____ _____. They'll like you.

12 목적 파악

대화를 듣고, 남자가 전화를 건 목적으로 가장 적절한 것을 고르시오.

① 표를 구매하기 위해서
② 예약을 취소하기 위해서
③ 예약 날짜를 변경하기 위해서
④ 배송 시각을 변경하기 위해서
⑤ 모임 약속 시간을 정하기 위해서

(*Telephone rings.*)
W White Teeth Dental Clinic. What can I do for you?
M Hello. I _____ _____ _____ at 5 p.m. today.
W Could you tell me your name, please?
M My name is Robert Wilson. I'm afraid _____ _____ _____ _____ today.
W Do you want to cancel your appointment?
M No. I want to change it to _____ _____ _____ _____ _____.
W All right. You're all set now. See you on Thursday.

13 관계 추론

대화를 듣고, 두 사람의 관계로 가장 적절한 것을 고르시오.

① 경비원 – 입주민
② 편의점 직원 – 손님
③ 심리 상담가 – 상담자
④ 매표소 직원 – 관광객
⑤ 분실물 보관소 직원 – 지하철 이용객

W Hi. I left my briefcase when I got off the subway.
M Which subway station did you _____ _____ _____?
W Greenville Station.
M Do you remember when you got off?
W It was _____ _____ _____ _____.
M Okay. Can you tell me _____ _____ _____ _____ _____?
W It's dark brown, and there's a small pocket on the back.
M All right. Please write down your name and number here. I'll call you _____ _____ _____ _____ _____.

14 숫자 정보 파악

대화를 듣고, 여자가 공연장에 도착한 시각을 고르시오.

① 7:00 p.m.　② 7:05 p.m.
③ 7:10 p.m.　④ 7:15 p.m.
⑤ 7:20 p.m.

Sound Clear ☆ **scene**
c가 묵음이라서 [씬]으로 발음된다.

M Maria, how was the musical yesterday?
W It was perfect except that I was late for it.
M You were late? How late were you?
W I _____ _____ _____ _____ at 7:05. The musical started at 7.
M So you only missed the first five minutes.
W Actually, _____ _____ _____ _____ until 7:15, so I missed the opening scene.
M Oh, no.
W But _____ _____ _____, it was good.

15 부탁한 일 파악

대화를 듣고, 남자가 여자에게 부탁한 일로 가장 적절한 것을 고르시오.

① 자료 수집하기
② 영어 번역하기
③ 사진 촬영하기
④ 동영상 촬영하기
⑤ 동영상 짧게 편집하기

W Noah, are you all ready for your presentation?
M Not yet. I _____ _____ _____ _____, but I haven't finished editing the video.
W Let me help you. I love making and editing videos.
M Do you? That's very sweet of you!
W It's not a big deal. So how do you _____ _____ _____ _____ _____ ?
M Can you _____ _____ _____ than 30 seconds?
W Sure. Just let me know _____ _____ _____ _____ _____ .
M Okay. Thanks!

16 이유 파악

대화를 듣고, 여자가 자리를 바꾸고 싶어 하는 이유로 가장 적절한 것을 고르시오.

① 자리가 너무 추워서
② 칠판이 잘 안 보여서
③ 에어컨 바람이 안 와서
④ 짝과 사이가 좋지 않아서
⑤ 친한 친구와 함께 앉고 싶어서

W Mr. Lee, _____ _____ _____ _____ _____ ?
M Of course, Claire. What is it?
W Could you change my seat in the classroom?
M Do you have a problem with Soyun next to you?
W _____ _____ _____. She and I are doing great.
M Then why do you want to change your seat?
W I'm so cold in my seat. The air conditioner is too close.
M In that case, I'll see _____ _____ _____ _____ _____ with you.

17 언급하지 않은 것 찾기

다음을 듣고, 남자가 한국 문화 축제에 대해 언급하지 <u>않은</u> 것을 고르시오.

① 개최 장소　② 개최 요일
③ 개최 시간　④ 행사 내용
⑤ 입장료

M The 7th Korean Culture Festival is going to be held in Sejong Park this Saturday and Sunday. You can see a _____ _____ _____ _____ and the *Hanbok* fashion show. You'll also have _____ _____ _____ _____ various Korean foods. The admission fee is 5,000 won. Come and _____ _____ _____ _____ _____ !

18 그림의 상황에 적절한 대화 찾기

다음 그림의 상황에 가장 적절한 대화를 고르시오.

① ② ③ ④ ⑤

Sound Clear ☆ **balle**t
'발레'는 실제로 [밸레이]로 발음된다. t는 묵음이다.

① M Where are my glasses?
   W _____ _____ _____ them on your desk?
② M Can you tell me where the shoe store is?
   W _____ _____ _____ and go to the third floor.
③ M Excuse me. Can I try these pants on?
   W Sure. _____ _____ _____ _____ _____ ?
④ M What do you want for your birthday?
   W Well, can you buy me some new ballet shoes?
⑤ M These shoes are too small for me.
   W _____ _____ _____. They're bigger.

19 마지막 말에 이어질 응답 찾기

대화를 듣고, 여자의 마지막 말에 이어질 남자의 말로 가장 적절한 것을 고르시오.

Man: _____

① We have a similar custom.
② The game is really exciting.
③ We played *Yunnori* together.
④ I will take part in a special event.
⑤ We had a big dinner on Thanksgiving Day.

W _____ _____ _____ _____ your first New Year's Day in Korea?
M I visited my homestay family's hometown and met their relatives.
W That's nice. _____ _____ _____ _____ _____.
M I had *tteokguk* for breakfast. _____ _____ _____.
W What did you do after breakfast?
M I bowed to my homestay parents and grandparents and _____ _____ _____.
W That's interesting. Did you do anything else?
M We played *Yunnori* together.

20 마지막 말에 이어질 응답 찾기

대화를 듣고, 여자의 마지막 말에 이어질 남자의 말로 가장 적절한 것을 고르시오.

Man: _____

① You should see a doctor.
② I'm fine. Thank you for asking.
③ Air pollution is a serious issue.
④ It'll be as terrible as it is today.
⑤ I like winter better than summer.

M _____ _____ _____ is terrible today.
W Yeah. I can't see the buildings across the river.
M I _____ _____ _____ the last time I saw a clear sky.
W Right. I need to buy some more masks on my way home.
M Me, too. I _____ _____ _____ _____.
W Even my eyes are sore. Do you know _____ _____ _____ _____ _____ ?
M It'll be as terrible as it is today.

01 다음을 듣고, 금요일의 날씨로 가장 적절한 것을 고르시오.

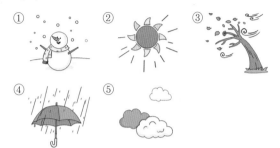

① ② ③
④ ⑤

02 대화를 듣고, 여자가 주문한 케이크로 가장 적절한 것을 고르시오.

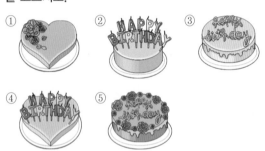

① ② ③
④ ⑤

03 대화를 듣고, 남자의 심정으로 가장 적절한 것을 고르시오.

① happy ② excited ③ nervous
④ satisfied ⑤ disappointed

04 대화를 듣고, 두 사람이 대화하는 장소로 가장 적절한 곳을 고르시오.

① 여행사 ② 미술관
③ 관광 안내소 ④ 버스 정류장
⑤ 분실물 보관소

05 대화를 듣고, 여자의 마지막 말의 의도로 가장 적절한 것을 고르시오.

① 후회 ② 거절 ③ 칭찬
④ 격려 ⑤ 요청

06 대화를 듣고, 남자의 장래 희망을 고르시오.

① 앱 개발자 ② 디자이너
③ 프로 게이머 ④ 보안 전문가
⑤ 컴퓨터 엔지니어

07 대화를 듣고, 여자가 오늘 저녁에 할 일로 가장 적절한 것을 고르시오.

① 연극 관람하기 ② 동아리 모임 가기
③ 요가 수업 가기 ④ 남자와 저녁 먹기
⑤ 여행 계획 세우기

08 대화를 듣고, 여자가 항공편에 대해 언급하지 않은 것을 고르시오.

① 연착 이유 ② 출발 시각
③ 현지 도착 시각 ④ 비행시간
⑤ 목적지 날씨

09 다음을 듣고, 남자가 하는 말의 내용으로 가장 적절한 것을 고르시오.

① 층별 안내 ② 공사 안내
③ 조식 안내 ④ 편의 시설 안내
⑤ 체크인 시각 안내

10 다음을 듣고, 사진 동아리에 대한 내용으로 일치하지 않는 것을 고르시오.

① 1학년 학생은 누구나 가입할 수 있다.
② 사진을 더욱 잘 찍는 방법을 가르쳐 준다.
③ 매주 목요일 방과 후에 모인다.
④ 본인의 카메라를 가져와야 한다.
⑤ 동아리방에서 가입 신청을 받는다.

11 대화를 듣고, 남자가 서점에 간 이유로 가장 적절한 것을 고르시오.

① 경품을 받기 위해서
② 휴대 전화를 찾기 위해서
③ 주문한 책을 찾기 위해서
④ 중고 서적을 판매하기 위해서
⑤ 신간 도서를 구입하기 위해서

12 대화를 듣고, 여자가 대화 직후에 할 일로 가장 적절한 것을 고르시오.

① 대본 수정하기
② 작품 제출하기
③ 동영상 촬영하기
④ 이메일 확인하기
⑤ 선생님께 연락하기

13 대화를 듣고, 남자가 지불해야 할 금액으로 가장 적절한 것을 고르시오.

① $30
② $39
③ $69
④ $79
⑤ $99

14 대화를 듣고, 두 사람의 관계로 가장 적절한 것을 고르시오.

① 영화배우 – 팬
② 작가 – 독자
③ 서점 직원 – 손님
④ 교사 – 학부모
⑤ 도서관 사서 – 학생

15 대화를 듣고, 남자가 강원도 여행 계획에 대해 언급하지 않은 것을 고르시오.

① 낚시하기
② 수영하기
③ 텐트 치기
④ 등산하기
⑤ 바비큐 해 먹기

16 대화를 듣고, 남자가 전화를 건 목적으로 가장 적절한 것을 고르시오.

① 상품을 주문하기 위해서
② 환불을 요청하기 위해서
③ 배송비를 문의하기 위해서
④ 주소지를 변경하기 위해서
⑤ 배송 문제를 항의하기 위해서

17 대화를 듣고, 남자가 여자에게 요청한 일로 가장 적절한 것을 고르시오.

① 화장실 청소하기
② 수건 가져다주기
③ 강아지 목욕시키기
④ 강아지 사료 사 오기
⑤ 드라이어 가져다주기

18 다음 그림의 상황에 가장 적절한 대화를 고르시오.

①　　②　　③　　④　　⑤

[19-20] 대화를 듣고, 남자의 마지막 말에 이어질 여자의 말로 가장 적절한 것을 고르시오.

19 Woman: _____

① I don't do it frequently.
② You don't need any money.
③ Every machine is out of order.
④ Nope. It's pretty simple, isn't it?
⑤ I don't know how to use the machine.

20 Woman: _____

① Gwangju is far from here.
② That's too long for express mail.
③ I'm sorry, but it's too expensive.
④ We don't have a delivery service.
⑤ It's too long. I'll send it by express mail.

받아쓰기용

01 날씨 파악

다음을 듣고, 금요일의 날씨로 가장 적절한 것을 고르시오.

①   ②   ③

④   ⑤

M Welcome to this week's weather forecast. _____ _____ _____ _____, the weather will be partly cloudy. On Wednesday afternoon, _____ _____ _____ _____.
By Thursday, it will fall to -7°C, and it will begin to snow. The snow will _____ _____ _____ _____. Three inches of snow are expected.

02 그림 정보 파악 ✲

대화를 듣고, 여자가 주문한 케이크로 가장 적절한 것을 고르시오.

①   ②   ③

④   ⑤

W I'd like to order a birthday cake for my mom.
M Okay. _____ _____ _____ _____ from these samples?
W I like this one with flowers.
M You have to choose _____ _____ _____ _____ _____, too. It can be round or heart-shaped.
W I'd like a round one. Can you _____ _____ _____ _____ _____ 정답 단서, too?
M Sure. What message do you want me to write?
W Can you write "Happy Birthday" with flowers around it?
M No problem. 정답 단서

03 심정 추론

대화를 듣고, 남자의 심정으로 가장 적절한 것을 고르시오.

① happy ② excited ③ nervous
④ satisfied ⑤ disappointed

Sound Clear ✩ **weeke**nd
-nd로 끝나는 단어는 끝 자음 [d]가 거의 발음되지 않는다.

W What did you do during the weekend?
M I went to Dream World, _____ _____ _____ _____.
W Great! You really wanted to go there, didn't you?
M Yes, but it was _____ _____ _____ _____ _____ _____.
W Why? It has many fun rides.
M The lines were so long that I could _____ _____ _____ _____ _____. Even worse, those rides were boring.
W That's too bad.

04 장소 추론 ✳

대화를 듣고, 두 사람이 대화하는 장소로 가장 적절한 곳을 고르시오.

① 여행사　　　　② 미술관
③ 관광 안내소　　④ 버스 정류장
⑤ 분실물 보관소

> **Sound Clear** ☆ **often**
> [오픈] 또는 [오프튼]으로 발음된다.

W Welcome. How may I help you?

M Hi. ＿＿＿＿ ＿＿＿＿ ＿＿＿＿ ＿＿＿＿ ＿＿＿＿ the National Art Museum?

W Do you see the bus stop across the street? Take bus number 17 there and ＿＿＿＿ ＿＿＿＿ ＿＿＿＿ ＿＿＿＿ ＿＿＿＿.

M I see. How often does the bus come?

W There's a bus ＿＿＿＿ ＿＿＿＿ ＿＿＿＿.

M Okay. Thank you so much.

W You're welcome. Have a nice day.

05 의도 파악

대화를 듣고, 여자의 마지막 말의 의도로 가장 적절한 것을 고르시오.

① 후회　　② 거절　　③ 칭찬
④ 격려　　⑤ 요청

W Sam, ＿＿＿＿ ＿＿＿＿ ＿＿＿＿ ＿＿＿＿ on your math exam?

M Unfortunately, no. I don't feel good about it.

W Was it difficult?

M Yes, it was! And I couldn't ＿＿＿＿ ＿＿＿＿ ＿＿＿＿ ＿＿＿＿ on my science exam either.

W Don't be so upset.

M I ＿＿＿＿ ＿＿＿＿ ＿＿＿＿ ＿＿＿＿ ＿＿＿＿ ＿＿＿＿, so it's very disappointing.

W Final exams are all over. So just ＿＿＿＿ ＿＿＿＿ ＿＿＿＿ and get some rest.

06 특정 정보 파악

대화를 듣고, 남자의 장래 희망을 고르시오.

① 앱 개발자　　　② 디자이너
③ 프로 게이머　　④ 보안 전문가
⑤ 컴퓨터 엔지니어

M What's wrong, Jenny?

W My computer ＿＿＿＿ ＿＿＿＿ ＿＿＿＿!

M Let me help you. (*Typing sound*) It's working now.

W Wow, thanks! I think you know a lot about computers.

M I'm good with computers. ＿＿＿＿ ＿＿＿＿ ＿＿＿＿ ＿＿＿＿ ＿＿＿＿.

W ＿＿＿＿ ＿＿＿＿ ＿＿＿＿ ＿＿＿＿?

M No. I want to be a computer engineer, so I read a lot of books about computers.

W Oh, I see.

07 할 일 파악

대화를 듣고, 여자가 오늘 저녁에 할 일로 가장 적절한 것을 고르시오.

① 연극 관람하기　　② 동아리 모임 가기
③ 요가 수업 가기　　④ 남자와 저녁 먹기
⑤ 여행 계획 세우기

Sound Clear ☆ **Not today**
동일한 발음의 자음이 연이어 나오면 앞 자음 소리가 탈락하여 [나투데이]로 발음된다.

M Liz, are you going to your yoga class today?
W ☆Not today. I have a class _____ _____ _____ _____.
M Then why don't you have dinner with me?
W _____ _____ _____ _____. Let's eat tomorrow.
M Tomorrow is fine. But why not today?
W My friend John is _____ _____ _____ _____ _____ _____, so I'm going to watch it.
M I see. Have a great time.

08 언급하지 않은 것 찾기

대화를 듣고, 여자가 항공편에 대해 언급하지 않은 것을 고르시오.

① 연착 이유　　② 출발 시각
③ 현지 도착 시각　　④ 비행시간
⑤ 목적지 날씨

M Excuse me. I didn't hear the announcement. Was it about the plane for Chicago?
W Yes. The plane for Chicago at 9:00 a.m. is delayed _____ _____ _____ _____ _____.
M Oh, no. What time is it going to leave now?
W At 10:30 a.m. from gate number 5.
M _____ _____ _____ _____ in Chicago then?
W It _____ _____ _____ _____, so it will arrive at 9:30 p.m. local time.
M I see. Thank you.

09 주제 파악

다음을 듣고, 남자가 하는 말의 내용으로 가장 적절한 것을 고르시오.

① 층별 안내　　② 공사 안내
③ 조식 안내　　④ 편의 시설 안내
⑤ 체크인 시각 안내

M This is an announcement for all guests at the Windsor Hotel. We're very _____ _____ _____ _____ caused by the construction of our new escalator. Please be careful near the construction areas _____ _____ _____ _____ _____ _____. The construction hours are from 10 a.m. to 4 p.m. There will be construction for the next three days. _____ _____ _____ for the inconvenience.

10 일치하지 않는 것 찾기

다음을 듣고, 사진 동아리에 대한 내용으로 일치하지 않는 것을 고르시오.

① 1학년 학생은 누구나 가입할 수 있다.
② 사진을 더욱 잘 찍는 방법을 가르쳐 준다.
③ 매주 목요일 방과 후에 모인다.
④ 본인의 카메라를 가져와야 한다.
⑤ 동아리방에서 가입 신청을 받는다.

W Do you love taking pictures? Do you want _____ _____ _____ _____ _____? Join our club. Any first grader can join. We'll give you many good tips on how to take better photographs. We _____ _____ _____ after school. You don't have to pay anything. You just have to bring your camera. There is a sign-up paper in our club room. _____ _____ _____ before this Friday.

11 이유 파악

대화를 듣고, 남자가 서점에 간 이유로 가장 적절한 것을 고르시오.

① 경품을 받기 위해서
② 휴대 전화를 찾기 위해서
③ 주문한 책을 찾기 위해서
④ 중고 서적을 판매하기 위해서
⑤ 신간 도서를 구입하기 위해서

M Hi. I heard you buy ☆used books.
W Yes, we do. We _____ _____ _____ _____ _____ .
M Then could you look at these books?
W Sure. (*Pause*) Wow, these books are _____ _____ _____ .
M Yeah, I bought them _____ _____ _____ _____ _____ . How about these magazines?
W Sorry. We don't buy magazines.
M Okay. Then how much can I get for the books?
W Let me check how much 정답 단서 _____ _____ _____ _____ .

12 할 일 파악

대화를 듣고, 여자가 대화 직후에 할 일로 가장 적절한 것을 고르시오.

① 대본 수정하기
② 작품 제출하기
③ 동영상 촬영하기
④ 이메일 확인하기
⑤ 선생님께 연락하기

W Minho, _____ _____ _____ _____ our video by Sunday night.
M Do you mean the one for the school video contest?
W Yes. I think we need to hurry. We should revise our script.
M Did you ask the teacher to _____ _____ _____ 한정 _____ on the script?
W Yes. She already gave us some feedback by email.
M Okay. What did she tell us to do? 정답 단서
W I _____ _____ _____ _____ yet. I'll read it now. 정답 단서

13 숫자 정보 파악

대화를 듣고, 남자가 지불해야 할 금액으로 가장 적절한 것을 고르시오.

① $30
② $39
③ $69
④ $79
⑤ $99

W How can I help you?
M Hi. I'm looking for some headphones. How much are these black ones?
W They are $79. They are _____ _____ _____ at our store.
M They are _____ _____ _____ _____ _____ .
W How about these ones then? They are similar to the black ones, and _____ _____ _____ _____ .
M How much are they?
W They were originally $99, but _____ _____ _____ _____ $30 now. They are a very popular item.
M That's great. I'll take them.

14 관계 추론

대화를 듣고, 두 사람의 관계로 가장 적절한 것을 고르시오.

① 영화배우 – 팬 ② 작가 – 독자
③ 서점 직원 – 손님 ④ 교사 – 학부모
⑤ 도서관 사서 – 학생

Sound Clear ☆ **read**
현재형(읽다)은 [뤼드]로, 과거형(읽었다)은 [뤠드]로 발음된다.

W It is very nice to meet you! I'm _____ _____ _____
_____ _____.
M Nice to meet you, too.
W _____ _____ _____ _____ since I read your first
정답 단서
novel.
M Thank you so much.
W I brought the first edition of your first novel. Can I _____
_____ _____ _____ _____?
M Of course. What is your name?
W I'm Helen.
M Here you are, Helen.
W Thanks. _____ _____ _____ _____.

15 언급하지 않은 것 찾기

대화를 듣고, 남자가 강원도 여행 계획에 대해 언급하지 <u>않은</u> 것을 고르시오.

① 낚시하기 ② 수영하기
③ 텐트 치기 ④ 등산하기
⑤ 바비큐 해 먹기

W David, do you have any plans for the weekend?
M Yes. I'm going to Gangwon-do with my family.
W Great! What are you going to do there?
M My family _____ _____ _____, so we'll hike in the
mountains. We'll also _____ _____ _____ _____.
W Sounds good. Where will you stay?
M We will set up a tent _____ _____ _____.
W Are you going to cook, too?
M Yes. We're going to _____ _____ _____. And we'll eat
some seafood at a restaurant there.
W Sounds fun. Have a great time.

16 목적 파악

대화를 듣고, 남자가 전화를 건 목적으로 가장 적절한 것을 고르시오.

① 상품을 주문하기 위해서
② 환불을 요청하기 위해서
③ 배송비를 문의하기 위해서
④ 주소지를 변경하기 위해서
⑤ 배송 문제를 항의하기 위해서

(*Telephone rings.*)
W Hello. What can I do for you?
M Hello. I'm calling about a delivery problem.
W What is the problem?
M My order is late. I paid for quick delivery, but _____
정답 단서
_____ _____ _____ _____.
W I'm very sorry. I'll check it right away. What is your name?
M My name is James Park.
W Your order will arrive today. We'll _____ _____ _____
_____ _____ on your credit card.
M I hope _____ _____ _____ _____ _____.

17 요청한 일 파악 ✳

대화를 듣고, 남자가 여자에게 요청한 일로 가장 적절한 것을 고르시오.

① 화장실 청소하기 ② 수건 가져다주기
③ 강아지 목욕시키기 ④ 강아지 사료 사 오기
⑤ 드라이어 가져다주기

> **Sound Clear** ☆ **bath**
> 미국식은 [배쓰]로, 영국식은 [바쓰]로 발음된다.

M Amy, did you walk the puppies today?
W Yes, I _____ _____ _____ _____. And I just gave some food to them.
M Good. Then I'll give them a bath now.
W All right. Do you need any help?
M No, thank you. I can _____ _____ _____ _____.
  Oh, can you bring me some towels?
W Sure. _____ _____ _____ the dryer, too?
M I already brought it to the bathroom. Thanks.

18 그림의 상황에 적절한 대화 찾기

다음 그림의 상황에 가장 적절한 대화를 고르시오.

① ② ③ ④ ⑤

① W Take an umbrella with you, or _____ _____ _____.
  M Oh, is it raining? Okay.
② W _____ _____ _____ _____?
  M It's Nancy's. Let me take it to her.
③ W Watch out! _____ _____ _____ _____.
  M Oops! Thanks for letting me know.
④ W May I take your order now?
  M I need a little more time.
⑤ W _____ _____ _____ _____ last night?
  M I'm sorry. I lost my phone.

19 마지막 말에 이어질 응답 찾기

대화를 듣고, 남자의 마지막 말에 이어질 여자의 말로 가장 적절한 것을 고르시오.

Woman: _____

① I don't do it frequently.
② You don't need any money.
③ Every machine is out of order.
④ Nope. It's pretty simple, isn't it?
⑤ I don't know how to use the machine.

M It's my first time here. Can you _____ _____ _____ _____ _____ the washing machine?
W Sure. _____ _____ _____ and some detergent in the machine. Now, close the door and put in 50 cents here.
M Okay.
W Then, set the water temperature and _____ _____ _____ _____.
M Is there anything else to do?
W Nope. It's pretty simple, isn't it?

20 마지막 말에 이어질 응답 찾기

대화를 듣고, 남자의 마지막 말에 이어질 여자의 말로 가장 적절한 것을 고르시오.

Woman: _____

① Gwangju is far from here.
② That's too long for express mail.
③ I'm sorry, but it's too expensive.
④ We don't have a delivery service.
⑤ It's too long. I'll send it by express mail.

W I'd like to _____ _____ _____ to Gwangju.
M Okay. Please put that on the scale. _____ _____?
W Books.
M Do you want to send it _____ _____ _____ _____ _____?
W How long does regular mail take?
M It usually _____ _____ _____.
W It's too long. I'll send it by express mail.

Review Test

Word Check
영어는 우리말로, 우리말은 영어로 써 보기

01	release	13	보름달
02	first half	14	실용적인
03	score a goal	15	여성의
04	brand-new	16	발레
05	relative	17	외관, 겉모습
06	wireless	18	입장료
07	a big deal	19	심지어
08	relative	20	장면
09	switch	21	편집하다
10	literary	22	들다
11	bow	23	졸업식
12	author	24	거의 ~ 않다(없다)

Expression Check
알맞은 표현을 넣어 문장 완성하기

25 Take your time and _____ _____. 천천히 둘러보세요.

26 I will _____ _____ _____ a special event. 나는 특별한 행사에 참여할 거야.

27 I was using one, but it _____ _____. 하나 쓰고 있었는데, 고장 났어요.

28 The service is so slow, and you _____ _____. 서비스는 아주 느리고 당신은 실수를 하는군요.

29 Actually, they wouldn't _____ me _____ until 7:15.
사실은, 그들이 나를 7시 15분까지 들여보내 주지 않더라고.

30 Many people are _____ _____ _____ watching her act.
많은 사람들이 그녀의 연기를 보는 것을 기대하고 있어요.

Answers p.88

Word Check
영어는 우리말로, 우리말은 영어로 써 보기

01 watch out _____

02 feedback _____

03 sample _____

04 drop _____

05 even worse _____

06 art museum _____

07 disappointing _____

08 a big deal _____

09 main character _____

10 frequently _____

11 local time _____

12 construction _____

13 야기하다 _____

14 세제 _____

15 저울 _____

16 중고의 _____

17 수정하다 _____

18 미루다, 연기하다 _____

19 제출하다 _____

20 원래 _____

21 눈보라 _____

22 국립의 _____

23 불편 _____

24 대본 _____

Expression Check
알맞은 표현을 넣어 문장 완성하기

25 I'll _____ them _____ _____ now. 내가 지금 그 애들을 목욕 시킬게.

26 You _____ my _____. 당신 덕분에 즐거운 하루가 됐어요.

27 Gwangju is _____ _____ here. 광주는 여기에서 멀어요.

28 These books are _____ _____ _____. 이 책들 상태가 좋은데요.

29 We _____ again _____ the inconvenience. 불편을 드려 다시 사과드립니다.

30 I couldn't _____ a _____ _____ on my science exam.
나는 과학 시험에서 높은 점수를 받지 못했어.

01 다음을 듣고, 목요일의 날씨로 가장 적절한 것을 고르시오.

① 　② 　③

④ 　⑤

02 대화를 듣고, 두 사람이 보고 있는 사진으로 가장 적절한 것을 고르시오.

① 　②

③ 　④

⑤

03 대화를 듣고, 남자의 심정으로 가장 적절한 것을 고르시오.
① satisfied　② excited　③ relieved
④ annoyed　⑤ pleased

04 대화를 듣고, 남자가 World Water Forum에서 한 일로 가장 적절한 것을 고르시오.
① 발표하기　　　② 길 안내하기
③ 강의 듣기　　　④ 기념품 나눠 주기
⑤ 봉사 활동 찾기

05 대화를 듣고, 두 사람이 대화하는 장소로 가장 적절한 곳을 고르시오.
① 보석상　　② 식물원　　③ 옷 가게
④ 꽃 가게　　⑤ 결혼식장

06 대화를 듣고, 여자의 마지막 말의 의도로 가장 적절한 것을 고르시오.
① 제안　　② 동의　　③ 수락
④ 불평　　⑤ 위로

07 대화를 듣고, 여자가 가입하고자 하는 동아리를 고르시오.
① 야구　　② 영어　　③ 음악
④ 수학　　⑤ 독서

08 대화를 듣고, 남자가 대화 직후에 할 일로 가장 적절한 것을 고르시오.
① 영어 숙제하기　　② 방 청소하기
③ 저녁 준비하기　　④ 컴퓨터 게임하기
⑤ 쓰레기 내다 버리기

09 대화를 듣고, 여자가 구입한 무선 이어폰에 대한 내용으로 일치하지 않는 것을 고르시오.
① 할인된 가격이 80달러이다.
② 한 가지 색상으로 출시되었다.
③ 스마트폰과 연결된다.
④ 노트북과 연결된다.
⑤ 배터리가 완전히 충전되어 있을 때 10시간 동안 지속된다.

10 다음을 듣고, 여자가 하는 말의 내용으로 가장 적절한 것을 고르시오.
① 주차장 폐쇄 공지　② 도서관 휴관 공지
③ 공사장 위치 설명　④ 자동차 점검 권장
⑤ 대중교통 이용 홍보

11 다음을 듣고, 남자가 Smart Cooking Center에 대해 언급하지 <u>않은</u> 것을 고르시오.

① 설립 연도　　② 강사 수　　③ 수업 시간
④ 수업료　　　⑤ 연락처

12 대화를 듣고, 여자가 전화를 건 목적으로 가장 적절한 것을 고르시오.

① 예약을 취소하기 위해서
② 메뉴를 변경하기 위해서
③ 창가 자리를 예약하기 위해서
④ 예약 인원을 변경하기 위해서
⑤ 대기자 명단에 이름을 올리기 위해서

13 대화를 듣고, 여자가 지불해야 할 금액으로 가장 적절한 것을 고르시오.

① $30　　　② $40　　　③ $50
④ $60　　　⑤ $70

14 대화를 듣고, 두 사람의 관계로 가장 적절한 것을 고르시오.

① 친구 – 친구　　　② 의사 – 환자
③ 가수 – 작곡가　　④ 경찰관 – 시민
⑤ 담임 교사 – 학생

15 대화를 듣고, 여자가 남자에게 부탁한 일로 가장 적절한 것을 고르시오.

① 문서 스캔하기
② 스캐너 고치기
③ 이메일에 답장하기
④ 서비스 센터에 연락하기
⑤ 스마트폰으로 이메일 보내는 방법 보여 주기

16 대화를 듣고, 여자가 이사를 한 이유로 가장 적절한 것을 고르시오.

① 넓은 집에 살고 싶어서
② 조용한 곳에 살고 싶어서
③ 통근 시간이 오래 걸려서
④ 이웃들이 마음에 안 들어서
⑤ 새로운 동네에서 살고 싶어서

17 다음 그림의 상황에 가장 적절한 대화를 고르시오.

①　　②　　③　　④　　⑤

18 대화를 듣고, 여자가 다녀온 콘서트에 대한 내용으로 일치하지 <u>않는</u> 것을 고르시오.

① 아이돌 그룹들이 참여했다.
② 공원에서 열렸다.
③ 큰 스크린이 설치되어 있었다.
④ 표가 매진이었다.
⑤ 약 3만 명의 관객들이 왔다.

[19-20] 대화를 듣고, 남자의 마지막 말에 이어질 여자의 말로 가장 적절한 것을 고르시오.

19 Woman: _____

① I don't like TV dramas.
② Can I change the channel now?
③ I know who your favorite actor is.
④ You're right. It's on channel thirteen.
⑤ I don't know his name. He's a new face.

20 Woman: _____

① We didn't make it on time.
② I made an appointment at 6 p.m.
③ Your Internet connection is down.
④ I'm afraid you'll have to wait until tomorrow.
⑤ I'd like to connect my computer to the Internet.

01 날씨 파악

다음을 듣고, 목요일의 날씨로 가장 적절한 것을 고르시오.

①
②
③
④
⑤

W Good morning. This is the weather forecast for this week. _____ _____ _____ _____ _____, but it will be sunny tomorrow. It is expected to continue until Friday. On Friday and Saturday, it will be cloudy and windy. So if you plan to _____ _____ _____ _____ this weekend, you need to wait until Sunday because we'll have _____ _____ _____ _____ .

02 그림 정보 파악

대화를 듣고, 두 사람이 보고 있는 사진으로 가장 적절한 것을 고르시오.

M Clara, _____ _____ _____ ?
W Yes. I'm 15 years old in this picture.
M I _____ _____ _____ _____ . I've never seen you with short hair like this.
W Yeah, I didn't like long hair _____ _____ _____ _____ .
M And is this your younger sister Emma next to you?
W Right. She _____ _____ _____ _____ than me.
M I can see that. You two are so cute in those dresses.

03 심정 추론

대화를 듣고, 남자의 심정으로 가장 적절한 것을 고르시오.

① satisfied   ② excited   ③ relieved
④ annoyed   ⑤ pleased

Sound Clear ☆ **either**
[이더] 또는 [아이더]로 발음된다.

M _____ _____ _____ _____ _____ _____ this morning.
W Good. Do you like it?
M The color and the size are okay, but _____ _____ _____ _____ on the top.
W Really? We should _____ _____ _____ _____ it.
M Yes. So I called the customer center several times, but nobody answered the phone.
W Oh, no. Why don't you _____ _____ _____ on the homepage?
M I already did! Nobody has answered that either.

04 한 일 파악

대화를 듣고, 남자가 World Water Forum에서 한 일로 가장 적절한 것을 고르시오.

① 발표하기 ② 길 안내하기
③ 강의 듣기 ④ 기념품 나눠 주기
⑤ 봉사 활동 찾기

Sound Clear☆ directions
미국식은 주로 [디렉션스]로, 영국식은 주로 [다이렉션스]로 발음된다.

W Andy, what did you do last weekend?
M I ________ ________ the World Water Forum.
W Oh, what is that?
M It is a forum about water pollution, so people ________ ________ ________ ________ ________.
W What kind of volunteer work did you do there?
M I gave directions☆ ________ ________ ________ in English.
W Wow, that sounds interesting.

05 장소 추론

대화를 듣고, 두 사람이 대화하는 장소로 가장 적절한 곳을 고르시오.

① 보석상 ② 식물원 ③ 옷 가게
④ 꽃 가게 ⑤ 결혼식장

M Hi. I'm looking for something special for my wife.
W ________ ________ ________ ________ ________?
M Ah, yes. It's our wedding anniversary.
W ________ ________! How about red roses? They are popular for wedding anniversaries. 정답 단서
M Hmm... I'm not sure. I ________ ________ ________.
W Then what about these dried flowers? You can ________ ________ ________ ________. 정답 단서
M That sounds good. I'll take them.

06 의도 파악

대화를 듣고, 여자의 마지막 말의 의도로 가장 적절한 것을 고르시오.

① 제안 ② 동의 ③ 수락
④ 불평 ⑤ 위로

W Steve, do you know Ms. Taylor?
M Yes. She was my homeroom teacher last year.
W What a coincidence! She is ________ ________ ________ ________ ________!
M Good for you! She's a really good teacher.
W I like her class because she always ________ ________ ________ to show us.
M Me, too. She's the most passionate person I've ever met.
W ________ ________ ________ ________ ________.

07 특정 정보 파악

대화를 듣고, 여자가 가입하고자 하는 동아리를 고르시오.

① 야구 ② 영어 ③ 음악
④ 수학 ⑤ 독서

W ________ ________ ________ ________ your school club?
M Yes. I'll join the baseball club. What about you? 함정
W Well, ________ ________ ________ ________.
M You were in the math club last year, weren't you? 함정
W Yeah, so I want to ________ ________ ________ ________.
M Then why don't you join the music club? ________ ________ ________ ________ these days. 정답 단서
W I love that idea. I'll do that.

08 할 일 파악

대화를 듣고, 남자가 대화 직후에 할 일로 가장 적절한 것을 고르시오.

① 영어 숙제하기　　② 방 청소하기
③ 저녁 준비하기　　④ 컴퓨터 게임하기
⑤ 쓰레기 내다 버리기

Sound Clear ☆ take out
앞 단어의 끝 자음과 뒤 단어의 첫 모음이 만나 연음되어 [테이카웃]으로 발음된다.

W Josh, what are you doing?
M I'm playing a game, Mom.
W Did you finish your English homework? _____ _____
_____ _____ _____ _____.
M Of course, I did. It was pretty easy.
W Good. Then can I _____ _____ _____ _____?
M Sure. What is it?
W _____ _____ _____ _____ and take out the trash?
I have to prepare dinner right now.
M All right. I'll do it right away.

09 일치하지 않는 것 찾기

대화를 듣고, 여자가 구입한 무선 이어폰에 대한 내용으로 일치하지 않는 것을 고르시오.

① 할인된 가격이 80달러이다.
② 한 가지 색상으로 출시되었다.
③ 스마트폰과 연결된다.
④ 노트북과 연결된다.
⑤ 배터리가 완전히 충전되어 있을 때 10시간 동안 지속된다.

M You bought wireless earphones!
W Yeah, _____ _____ _____ _____. I bought them at the discounted price of $80.
M Good deal! Do they only come in white?
W No, they come in two colors: white and black.
M I see. _____ _____ _____ your smartphone, right?
W Yes. They can also be connected to my laptop computer.
M _____ _____ _____ does the battery last?
W If it is fully charged, it _____ _____ _____ _____.

10 주제 파악

다음을 듣고, 여자가 하는 말의 내용으로 가장 적절한 것을 고르시오.

① 주차장 폐쇄 공지
② 도서관 휴관 공지
③ 공사장 위치 설명
④ 자동차 점검 권장
⑤ 대중교통 이용 홍보

W Construction work _____ _____ _____ _____ will begin next month. Therefore, _____ _____ _____, we'll close down the library from April 1 to May 31. You can check out books until next Friday. If you _____ _____ _____ _____ during the construction period, you can use the return box _____ _____ _____. Thank you for your understanding.

11 언급하지 않은 것 찾기

다음을 듣고, 남자가 Smart Cooking Center 에 대해 언급하지 않은 것을 고르시오.

① 설립 연도　② 강사 수　③ 수업 시간
④ 수업료　　⑤ 연락처

M If you want to be a good cook but _____ _____ _____ _____, sign up for a class at the Smart Cooking Center. The Smart Cooking Center has taught over 500 people how to cook _____ _____ _____ _____ in 2015. There are five certified cooking teachers at our center. You take any class _____ _____ _____ _____ _____. It's a good way to check out our classes. Each class is two hours long. For more details, call 535-7711. Thank you.

12 목적 파악

대화를 듣고, 여자가 전화를 건 목적으로 가장 적절한 것을 고르시오.

① 예약을 취소하기 위해서
② 메뉴를 변경하기 위해서
③ 창가 자리를 예약하기 위해서
④ 예약 인원을 변경하기 위해서
⑤ 대기자 명단에 이름을 올리기 위해서

(*Telephone rings.*)

M Hello. Star Restaurant. How may I help you?

W Hello. I _____ _____ _____ for tomorrow.

M May I have your name?

W Emily Choi.

M Let me check. (*Pause*) Yes, Ms. Choi, _____ _____ _____ _____ _____ _____, and you ordered the five-course meal for ten people.

W That's right. Can I change it to seven people, not ten?

M No problem, Ms. Choi. _____ _____ _____ _____ _____.

13 숫자 정보 파악

대화를 듣고, 여자가 지불해야 할 금액으로 가장 적절한 것을 고르시오.

① $30　　② $40　　③ $50
④ $60　　⑤ $70

Sound Clear ☆ **How about**
앞 단어의 끝 모음과 뒤 단어의 첫 모음이 만나 연음되어 [하워바웃]으로 발음된다.

W Hello. I'm looking for a suitcase. A big one.

M Okay. How about this one? It _____ _____ _____ _____ last year.

W Let me lift it. (*Pause*) It's not that heavy. How much is it?

M It's $40 _____ _____ _____. It was originally $50.

W That's good. And can you show me the backpack over there, too?

M Wonderful choice. It's $20, but _____ _____ _____ _____ if you buy it with the suitcase.

W Great! I'll buy _____ _____ _____.

14 관계 추론

대화를 듣고, 두 사람의 관계로 가장 적절한 것을 고르시오.

① 친구 – 친구　　② 의사 – 환자
③ 가수 – 작곡가　　④ 경찰관 – 시민
⑤ 담임 교사 – 학생

W Mr. Bernard, do you have a minute?

M Sure, Rachel. You look sick. Are you okay?

W I feel bad. I _____ _____ _____ _____ because I have a fever.

M Do you want to see a doctor?

W I think I should. So I _____ _____ _____ to leave school early.

M Do your parents know you are sick?

W Yes, I called my mom at lunch. She _____ _____ _____ _____ _____ if I got worse.

M Okay. I'll call your mother to let her know that you're leaving school now.

15 부탁한 일 파악

대화를 듣고, 여자가 남자에게 부탁한 일로 가장 적절한 것을 고르시오.

① 문서 스캔하기
② 스캐너 고치기
③ 이메일에 답장하기
④ 서비스 센터에 연락하기
⑤ 스마트폰으로 이메일 보내는 방법 보여 주기

W I have to scan this document right now, but the scanner _____ _____ _____.

M Why don't you contact the service center?

W It _____ _____ _____ _____.

M Oh, right. Today is Sunday.

W What should I do? I _____ _____ _____ _____ by today.

M I have an idea. You can take a picture of it and email it with your smartphone. 정답 단서

W _____ _____ _____ _____ _____ through my smartphone. Can you show me how to do it? 정답 단서

M Sure.

16 이유 파악

대화를 듣고, 여자가 이사를 한 이유로 가장 적절한 것을 고르시오.

① 넓은 집에 살고 싶어서
② 조용한 곳에 살고 싶어서
③ 통근 시간이 오래 걸려서
④ 이웃들이 마음에 안 들어서
⑤ 새로운 동네에서 살고 싶어서

Sound Clear ☆ **neighbors**
gh가 묵음이라서 [네이버스]로 발음된다.

M Lily, how was moving last weekend?

W It was really hard.

M I thought you liked the place _____ _____ _____ _____ _____.

W I did. That place was quiet and cozy, and my ☆ neighbors were good.

M Then _____ _____ _____ _____ ?

W Because it took me too long to go to work. 정답 단서

M I see. How do you like _____ _____ _____ ?

W I like it very much. It only takes 20 minutes _____ _____ _____ _____.

17 그림의 상황에 적절한 대화 찾기

다음 그림의 상황에 가장 적절한 대화를 고르시오.

① ② ③ ④ ⑤

① M Are you ready to order?
   W Yes. Grilled fish and potatoes, please.
② M Don't you think _____ _____ _____ _____ ?
   W Am I? I'll slow down.
③ M _____ _____ _____ _____ your steak?
   W Medium, please.
④ M Please _____ _____ _____ _____ _____.
   It can be dangerous.
   W Oops, I didn't see the line. Thank you.
⑤ M Excuse me. _____ _____ _____ _____ ?
   W It is to ride the train to Daejeon.

18 일치하지 않는 것 찾기 ✢

대화를 듣고, 여자가 다녀온 콘서트에 대한 내용으로 일치하지 않는 것을 고르시오.

① 아이돌 그룹들이 참여했다.
② 공원에서 열렸다.
③ 큰 스크린이 설치되어 있었다.
④ 표가 매진이었다.
⑤ 약 3만 명의 관객들이 왔다.

W Ron, I went to the Korean Dreamer Concert last Saturday!
M You did? I really wanted to go, too, but I _____ _____ _____ _____. How was it?
W It was great. I saw most of the top idol groups.
M Great! It was held at Central Stadium, right?
W Yes. There were _____ _____ _____ _____ _____, so I could see well.
M Good. I'm sure the stadium was crowded _____ _____ _____ _____ _____.
W Definitely. I heard there were about 30,000 people there.

19 마지막 말에 이어질 응답 찾기

대화를 듣고, 남자의 마지막 말에 이어질 여자의 말로 가장 적절한 것을 고르시오.

Woman: _____

① I don't like TV dramas.
② Can I change the channel now?
③ I know who your favorite actor is.
④ You're right. It's on channel thirteen.
⑤ I don't know his name. He's a new face.

Sound Clear ✩ **heard about it**
[d]와 [t]가 각각 뒤에 나오는 모음과 연음되어 [헐더바우릿]으로 발음된다.

W Are you watching the drama *The Mirror*?
M No. _____ _____ _____ _____?
W It's a weekend drama. _____ _____ _____ _____. It's so interesting.
M Aha, I think I heard about it from my sister. Is it really good?
W Yeah. You should watch it. _____ _____ _____, _____ _____?
M I do. Who's the lead actor?
W I don't know his name. He's a new face.

20 마지막 말에 이어질 응답 찾기

대화를 듣고, 남자의 마지막 말에 이어질 여자의 말로 가장 적절한 것을 고르시오.

Woman: _____

① We didn't make it on time.
② I made an appointment at 6 p.m.
③ Your Internet connection is down.
④ I'm afraid you'll have to wait until tomorrow.
⑤ I'd like to connect my computer to the Internet.

(*Telephone rings.*)
W Fast Service Center. How may I help you?
M Hello. I _____ _____ _____ _____ my Internet.
W What's wrong with it?
M The connection is often interrupted and it is very slow. I _____ _____ _____ _____ _____ several times, but it doesn't help.
W _____ _____ _____ _____ _____ the problem?
M For the past few hours. Could you send _____ _____ _____ _____ today?
W I'm afraid you'll have to wait until tomorrow.

1.0배속

1.2배속

01 다음을 듣고, 베를린의 날씨로 가장 적절한 것을 고르시오.

① ② ③

④ ⑤

02 다음을 듣고, 여자의 지시대로 그린 그림으로 가장 적절한 것을 고르시오.

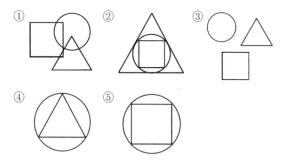

① ② ③

④ ⑤

03 대화를 듣고, 남자가 마지막에 느꼈을 심정으로 가장 적절한 것을 고르시오.

① happy   ② excited   ③ nervous
④ satisfied   ⑤ disappointed

04 대화를 듣고, 축제가 열리는 날짜를 고르시오.

① 9월 1일   ② 9월 8일   ③ 9월 15일
④ 9월 22일   ⑤ 9월 29일

05 대화를 듣고, 여자가 어젯밤에 한 일로 가장 적절한 것을 고르시오.

① 장보기   ② 청소하기   ③ 요리하기
④ 집들이하기   ⑤ 심야 영화 보기

06 대화를 듣고, 남자의 마지막 말의 의도로 가장 적절한 것을 고르시오.

① 감사   ② 기대   ③ 제안
④ 거절   ⑤ 축하

07 대화를 듣고, 여자가 내일 할 일로 가장 적절한 것을 고르시오.

① 숙제하기   ② 집안일하기
③ 사촌과 놀기   ④ 친척 집 방문하기
⑤ 친척 배웅하기

08 대화를 듣고, 두 사람이 식당에 대해 언급하지 <u>않은</u> 것을 고르시오.

① 분위기   ② 위생 상태
③ 음식의 맛   ④ 가격
⑤ 서비스

09 다음을 듣고, 남자가 하는 말의 내용으로 가장 적절한 것을 고르시오.

① 적절한 수면 시간
② 균형 잡힌 식단의 예
③ 겨울철 건강 유지법
④ 손을 깨끗이 씻는 방법
⑤ 규칙적인 생활의 중요성

10 다음을 듣고, 토마토에 대한 내용으로 일치하지 <u>않는</u> 것을 고르시오.

① 원산지 국가는 페루이다.
② 다양한 색의 토마토가 있다.
③ 기록상 가장 큰 토마토는 3.5kg이었다.
④ 스페인에서는 매년 토마토 축제가 열린다.
⑤ 토마토 축제에 15만 명 이상의 사람들이 모인다.

11 대화를 듣고, 두 사람이 이용할 교통수단을 고르시오.

① 버스　　　② 택시　　　③ 자전거
④ 지하철　　⑤ 자가용

12 대화를 듣고, 여자가 전화를 건 목적으로 가장 적절한 것을 고르시오.

① 숙제를 물어보기 위해서
② 약속 시간을 정하기 위해서
③ 할머니의 안부를 묻기 위해서
④ 제주도 여행을 계획하기 위해서
⑤ 개를 맡아 달라고 부탁하기 위해서

13 대화를 듣고, 두 사람이 만날 시각을 고르시오.

① 5:00 p.m.　② 5:10 p.m.　③ 5:20 p.m.
④ 5:30 p.m.　⑤ 5:40 p.m.

14 대화를 듣고, 두 사람의 관계로 가장 적절한 것을 고르시오.

① 간호사 – 환자　　　② 체육 교사 – 학생
③ 서점 직원 – 손님　　④ 공항 직원 – 탑승객
⑤ 영화관 직원 – 관람객

15 대화를 듣고, 여자가 남자에게 요청한 일로 가장 적절한 것을 고르시오.

① 빨래하기　　　② 일찍 귀가하기
③ 창문 닫기　　　④ 우산 가져다주기
⑤ 마중 나오기

16 대화를 듣고, 여자가 카메라를 사지 않은 이유를 고르시오.

① 가격이 비싸서
② 무게가 무거워서
③ 리모컨 기능이 없어서
④ 원하는 색상이 모두 팔려서
⑤ 디자인이 마음에 들지 않아서

17 다음 그림의 상황에 가장 적절한 대화를 고르시오.

①　　②　　③　　④　　⑤

18 다음을 듣고, 여자가 방과 후 영어 수업에 대해 언급하지 **않은** 것을 고르시오.

① 장소　　　② 일시　　　③ 수강 인원
④ 수업료　　⑤ 신청 방법

[19-20] 대화를 듣고, 여자의 마지막 말에 이어질 남자의 말로 가장 적절한 것을 고르시오.

19 Man: _____

① My order is late.
② Have a good day.
③ Here is my credit card.
④ No, that's it. Thank you.
⑤ I don't have time for dinner.

20 Man: _____

① Yes. I have a cat.
② I don't like animated movies.
③ Do you want to be a movie director?
④ I usually watch a movie every weekend.
⑤ Not yet. Do you want to watch it with me?

Dictation 18회

받아쓰기용

01 날씨 파악

다음을 듣고, 베를린의 날씨로 가장 적절한 것을 고르시오.

M Good morning. It's time for the weather report for Europe. London has ________ ________ ________ ________ ________ weather today. In Paris and Rome, ________ ________ ________ ________ ________ ________ has stopped, and partially cloudy but warm weather is expected. Berlin is expecting heavy snowfall, and it looks like it's going to ________ ________ ________ ________ ________ ________.

02 그림 정보 파악

다음을 듣고, 여자의 지시대로 그린 그림으로 가장 적절한 것을 고르시오.

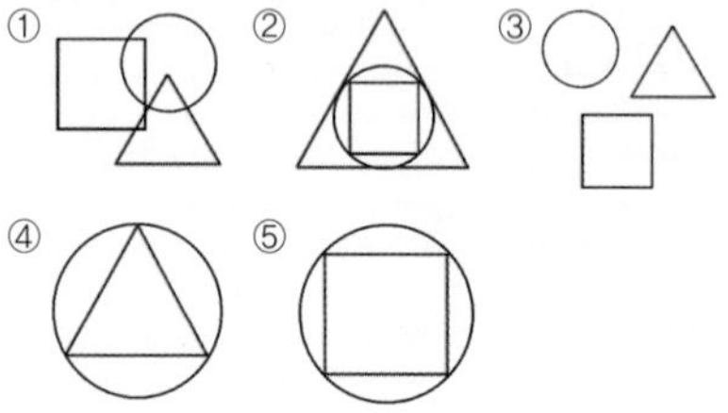

W Let's start drawing. We're going to draw some shapes. Listen carefully and ________ ________ ________ ________ ________. First, draw a big triangle on the paper with your pencil. Next, draw a circle ________ ________ ________ ________ ________ ________. The circle is smaller than the triangle. Finally, draw a square ________ ________ ________. The square is the smallest shape.

03 심정 추론

대화를 듣고, 남자가 마지막에 느꼈을 심정으로 가장 적절한 것을 고르시오.

① happy ② excited
③ nervous ④ satisfied
⑤ disappointed

Sound Clear☆ put it off
각 [t]가 모음 사이에서 약화되고 뒤 단어의 모음과 연음되어 [푸리로프]로 발음된다.

M I'm going camping with ________ ________ ________ ________ this weekend.
W Sounds exciting. Did you check the weather forecast?
M I did yesterday. It said ________ ________ ________ ________ ________ for the next few days.
W Well, I heard the forecast ________ ________ ________ ________. It has changed. It will rain all weekend.
M Oh, no. We are planning to set up a tent.
W Maybe you should put it off.
M ________ ________ ________ ________ ________. I hate rain.

04 특정 정보 파악

대화를 듣고, 축제가 열리는 날짜를 고르시오.

① 9월 1일 ② 9월 8일
③ 9월 15일 ④ 9월 22일
⑤ 9월 29일

W Hi, Mike. ________ ________ ________?
M Very good. I'm preparing for the school festival these days.
W Oh, I heard your short movie ________ ________ ________.
M Yeah. You should come and watch it.
W I will. Is the festival ________ ________ ________ ________ ________ ________ ________?
M It's on the ________ ________ ________ ________ ________.
W Today is September 15. So it's two weeks away.
M That's right. I'm so excited.

05　한 일 파악

대화를 듣고, 여자가 어젯밤에 한 일로 가장 적절한 것을 고르시오.

① 장보기　　　② 청소하기
③ 요리하기　　④ 집들이하기
⑤ 심야 영화 보기

M　What did you do yesterday?
W　I _____ _____ _____ _____ _____. I woke up early and cleaned my house all morning.
M　What a great start!
W　In the afternoon, I _____ _____ _____ _____ _____ and cooked dinner for ten people.
M　For ten people? _____ _____ _____ _____?
W　I had a housewarming party last night. You know I moved to a new apartment. *정답 단서*
M　Oh, right. _____ _____ _____ _____ _____ the next time.
W　Sure, I will.

06　의도 파악　　🇬🇧

대화를 듣고, 남자의 마지막 말의 의도로 가장 적절한 것을 고르시오.

① 감사　　② 기대　　③ 제안
④ 거절　　⑤ 축하

W　Congratulations!
M　Thank you, Mrs. Dunphy. Thank you so much for coming to _____ _____ _____.
W　Here are some flowers for you.
M　They're beautiful.
W　I still remember _____ _____ _____ _____ _____ _____ in the classroom.
M　I do, too.
W　Now you're graduating from university! I'm so _____ _____ _____!
M　I am here because of you. _____ _____ _____ _____ _____.

07　할 일 파악

대화를 듣고, 여자가 내일 할 일로 가장 적절한 것을 고르시오.

① 숙제하기　　　② 집안일하기
③ 사촌과 놀기　　④ 친척 집 방문하기
⑤ 친척 배웅하기

Sound Clear ☆ **a lot of**
[t]가 모음 사이에서 약화되고 뒤 단어의 모음과 연음되어 [얼라러브]로 발음된다.

M　Do you have any plans for tomorrow?
W　Yes. My cousin is coming to visit me, so _____ _____ _____.
M　Great. What are you going to do?
W　I'll _____ _____ _____ _____ _____ in the city.
M　You must be excited.
W　Yes, I am. So I have a lot of _____ _____ _____ before he comes.
M　_____ _____?
W　I have to do my homework and household chores. *함정*

08 언급하지 않은 것 찾기

대화를 듣고, 두 사람이 식당에 대해 언급하지 않은 것을 고르시오.

① 분위기　　② 위생 상태
③ 음식의 맛　　④ 가격
⑤ 서비스

M ＿＿＿＿ ＿＿＿＿ ＿＿＿＿ ＿＿＿＿ the restaurant tonight?
W I really liked the atmosphere there.
M ＿＿＿＿ ＿＿＿＿. I liked the food, too.
W Yes. The steak was so good, and the cake was the best.
M And it ＿＿＿＿ ＿＿＿＿ ＿＿＿＿ ＿＿＿＿, was it?
W No, it wasn't. The service was good, too. ＿＿＿＿ ＿＿＿＿ ＿＿＿＿ ＿＿＿＿ ＿＿＿＿ there tonight.
M You're welcome. Let's go there again soon.

09 주제 파악

다음을 듣고, 남자가 하는 말의 내용으로 가장 적절한 것을 고르시오.

① 적절한 수면 시간
② 균형 잡힌 식단의 예
③ 겨울철 건강 유지법
④ 손을 깨끗이 씻는 방법
⑤ 규칙적인 생활의 중요성

M Okay, students. Let's wrap up now and review ＿＿＿＿ ＿＿＿＿ ＿＿＿＿ ＿＿＿＿ to stay healthy throughout the winter. First, you should get enough sleep. A good night's sleep ＿＿＿＿ ＿＿＿＿ ＿＿＿＿. Second, eat well. Try to have a healthy, balanced diet every day. Third, wash your hands frequently. ＿＿＿＿ ＿＿＿＿ ＿＿＿＿ ＿＿＿＿ to wash your hands when you come back home from outside.

10 일치하지 않는 것 찾기 🇬🇧

다음을 듣고, 토마토에 대한 내용으로 일치하지 않는 것을 고르시오.

① 원산지 국가는 페루이다.
② 다양한 색의 토마토가 있다.
③ 기록상 가장 큰 토마토는 3.5kg이었다.
④ 스페인에서는 매년 토마토 축제가 열린다.
⑤ 토마토 축제에 15만 명 이상의 사람들이 모인다.

Sound Clear ☆ **tomato**
미국식은 [토메이로]로, 영국식은 [토마토]로 발음된다.

W Today, I'll ＿＿＿＿ ＿＿＿＿ ＿＿＿＿ ＿＿＿＿ ＿＿＿＿ about tomatoes. Tomatoes originally come from Peru, and ＿＿＿＿ ＿＿＿＿ ＿＿＿＿ ＿＿＿＿ ＿＿＿＿. They can be yellow, pink, purple, black, and even white! The largest tomato on record ＿＿＿＿ ＿＿＿＿ ＿＿＿＿ ＿＿＿＿ 3.5 kilograms. A tomato festival ＿＿＿＿ ＿＿＿＿ ＿＿＿＿ ＿＿＿＿ in Spain, where people throw more than 150,000 tomatoes at one another.

11 특정 정보 파악

대화를 듣고, 두 사람이 이용할 교통수단을 고르시오.

① 버스　　② 택시　　③ 자전거
④ 지하철　　⑤ 자가용

M It's time to go home.
W I'm ＿＿＿＿ ＿＿＿＿ ＿＿＿＿ ＿＿＿＿. Can we take a taxi?
M It's not ＿＿＿＿ ＿＿＿＿ ＿＿＿＿ ＿＿＿＿ ＿＿＿＿ here. What about taking the subway? It's really fast.
W The subway station is far from here.
M You're right. Why don't we take a bus? There's a ＿＿＿＿ ＿＿＿＿ ＿＿＿＿ ＿＿＿＿ ＿＿＿＿.
W Good idea. It takes a long time, but at least we can sit and ＿＿＿＿ ＿＿＿＿ ＿＿＿＿.
M Let's go.

12 목적 파악

대화를 듣고, 여자가 전화를 건 목적으로 가장 적절한 것을 고르시오.

① 숙제를 물어보기 위해서
② 약속 시간을 정하기 위해서
③ 할머니의 안부를 묻기 위해서
④ 제주도 여행을 계획하기 위해서
⑤ 개를 맡아 달라고 부탁하기 위해서

Sound Clear ☆ **What's up?**
앞 단어의 끝 자음과 뒤 단어의 모음이 만나 연음되어 [왓첩] 또는 [왓썹]으로 발음된다.

(*Cellphone rings.*)
M Hi, Lisa. What's up?
W Hi, Mason. I called to _____ _____ _____ _____.
M What is it?
W My parents and I will visit my grandmother in Jeju-do tomorrow. _____ _____.
M I'm sorry to hear that.
W So _____ _____ _____, will you take care of Mimi my dog?   정답 단서
M Okay, but I've never taken care of a dog before.
W I'll tell you _____ _____ _____ _____ _____.
Thank you so much.
M All right. Talk to you later.

13 숫자 정보 파악

대화를 듣고, 두 사람이 만날 시각을 고르시오.

① 5:00 p.m.   ② 5:10 p.m.
③ 5:20 p.m.   ④ 5:30 p.m.
⑤ 5:40 p.m.

M Hey, _____ _____ _____ _____ _____ after school today?
W Of course. We need to finish our group project.
M _____ _____ _____ is okay for me. What about you?
W I have a club meeting at 5:00.
M How long will it take?
W _____ _____ _____ _____. About 10 to 15 minutes, I guess.
M Then let's meet at the library at 5:30. _____ _____   정답 단서
_____.
W Okay. See you then.

14 관계 추론

대화를 듣고, 두 사람의 관계로 가장 적절한 것을 고르시오.

① 간호사 – 환자
② 체육 교사 – 학생
③ 서점 직원 – 손님
④ 공항 직원 – 탑승객
⑤ 영화관 직원 – 관람객

W Are there any tickets left for *Alice in Wonderland* at 4:15?
M There are _____ _____ _____ _____. How many tickets do you need?
W Oh, no. We need three. When is _____ _____ _____
_____?
M At 6:30.
W That's too late. What about *Jungle Book* at 4:30?
M There are three seats on the _____ _____ _____
_____ _____ _____.
W That's okay with me. Here's my credit card. How long is the movie?
M _____ _____ _____ _____ _____ _____.

15 요청한 일 파악

대화를 듣고, 여자가 남자에게 요청한 일로 가장 적절한 것을 고르시오.

① 빨래하기 ② 일찍 귀가하기
③ 창문 닫기 ④ 우산 가져다주기
⑤ 마중 나오기

Sound Clear☆ **supermarket**

'슈퍼마켓'은 실제로 [수펄마킷]에 가깝게 발음된다.

(*Cellphone rings.*)

M Hi, Mom. Where are you?

W I'm ________ ________ ________ ________ from the ☆supermarket. Are you home?

M Yes. I'm doing my homework.

W Good. I called you because it ________ ________ ________ ________.

M Do you want me to ________ ________ ________ ________?

W No, I brought one. Will you just close the windows? 정답 단서

M Sure. I'll ________ ________ ________ ________.

W Thanks. See you soon.

16 이유 파악

대화를 듣고, 여자가 카메라를 사지 않은 이유를 고르시오.

① 가격이 비싸서
② 무게가 무거워서
③ 리모컨 기능이 없어서
④ 원하는 색상이 모두 팔려서
⑤ 디자인이 마음에 들지 않아서

M Did you get the camera you wanted?

W No. I ________ ________ ________ looking for cameras, but I didn't buy one.

M What kind of camera do you want to buy?

W I want a camera that ________ ________ ________ ________ and a remote control. I also want it ________ ________ ________ ________ ________.

M You couldn't find one with those features?

W Actually, I found one that has all those features ________ ________ ________ ________. Black was sold out. 정답 단서

17 그림의 상황에 적절한 대화 찾기

다음 그림의 상황에 가장 적절한 대화를 고르시오.

① ② ③ ④ ⑤

① **W** Can I speak to Julia?
M ________ ________ ________ at the moment.

② **W** Please turn off the TV. I can't go to sleep.
M Why don't you close your bedroom door?

③ **W** Can you ________ ________ ________ for me?
M Sure. I can help you carry some books, too.

④ **W** How do you go to school?
M I usually ________ ________ ________ ________ ________.

⑤ **W** What's wrong? You don't look well.
M I ________ ________ ________.

18 언급하지 않은 것 찾기

다음을 듣고, 여자가 방과 후 영어 수업에 대해 언급하지 <u>않은</u> 것을 고르시오.

① 장소   ② 일시   ③ 수강 인원
④ 수업료   ⑤ 신청 방법

Sound Clear ☆ **textbook**
자음 세 개가 연속으로 나오면 중간 자음의 발음이 약화되어 [텍스북]으로 발음된다.

W Attention, students. This is an announcement about the after-school English class. ＿＿＿＿＿ ＿＿＿＿＿ ＿＿＿＿＿ ＿＿＿＿＿ in the English Zone on the third floor from 4 to 5 p.m. every Wednesday. The class and textbook are free. If you ＿＿＿＿＿ ＿＿＿＿＿ ＿＿＿＿＿ ＿＿＿＿＿, tell your homeroom teacher by this Friday. ＿＿＿＿＿ ＿＿＿＿＿ ＿＿＿＿＿ ＿＿＿＿＿ for more information.

---

19 마지막 말에 이어질 응답 찾기

대화를 듣고, 여자의 마지막 말에 이어질 남자의 말로 가장 적절한 것을 고르시오.

Man: ＿＿＿＿＿＿＿＿＿＿＿＿＿

① My order is late.
② Have a good day.
③ Here is my credit card.
④ No, that's it. Thank you.
⑤ I don't have time for dinner.

W Hi. ＿＿＿＿＿ ＿＿＿＿＿ ＿＿＿＿＿ ＿＿＿＿＿ to order?
M Hi. I'd like to get a double cheeseburger and a large coke.
W It will ＿＿＿＿＿ ＿＿＿＿＿ ＿＿＿＿＿ ＿＿＿＿＿ for a double cheeseburger. Is that okay with you?
M It's okay. (*Pause*) Oh, wait. I'll have orange juice ＿＿＿＿＿ ＿＿＿＿＿ ＿＿＿＿＿.
W Okay. Would you like to ＿＿＿＿＿ ＿＿＿＿＿ ＿＿＿＿＿?
M No, that's it. Thank you.

---

20 마지막 말에 이어질 응답 찾기

대화를 듣고, 여자의 마지막 말에 이어질 남자의 말로 가장 적절한 것을 고르시오.

Man: ＿＿＿＿＿＿＿＿＿＿＿＿＿

① Yes. I have a cat.
② I don't like animated movies.
③ Do you want to be a movie director?
④ I usually watch a movie every weekend.
⑤ Not yet. Do you want to watch it with me?

M What do you usually do ＿＿＿＿＿ ＿＿＿＿＿ ＿＿＿＿＿?
W I usually watch movies. I love watching movies.
M What kinds of movies do you like?
W I like ＿＿＿＿＿ ＿＿＿＿＿ ＿＿＿＿＿ ＿＿＿＿＿ ＿＿＿＿＿. What about you?
M I'm not really into movies like you. I only like animated movies.
W Oh, then did you ＿＿＿＿＿ ＿＿＿＿＿ ＿＿＿＿＿ ＿＿＿＿＿ ＿＿＿＿＿ with the cat as the main character?
M Not yet. Do you want to watch it with me?

Review Test

Word Check
영어는 우리말로, 우리말은 영어로 써 보기

01 recognize _____

02 scratch _____

03 volunteer _____

04 forum _____

05 grilled _____

06 participant _____

07 coincidence _____

08 unique _____

09 passionate _____

10 anniversary _____

11 certified _____

12 interrupt _____

13 그러므로 _____

14 설립하다 _____

15 기간 _____

16 노트북 컴퓨터 _____

17 충전하다 _____

18 광고하다 _____

19 허락 _____

20 (속도를) 늦추다 _____

21 외국의 _____

22 안락한 _____

23 확실히, 분명히 _____

24 연결 _____

Expression Check
알맞은 표현을 넣어 문장 완성하기

25 It took me too long to _____ _____ _____. 출근하는 데 시간이 너무 오래 걸려.

26 You can keep them _____ _____. 당신은 그것들을 오래 간직하실 수 있어요.

27 I _____ _____ to foreign participants in English. 나는 외국 참가자들에게 영어로 길을 안내했어.

28 She _____ _____ be taller than me. 그녀는 나보다 더 키가 컸었어.

29 Why don't you _____ _____ _____ on the homepage? 홈페이지에 글을 남겨 놓는 게 어때?

30 I saw _____ _____ the top idol groups. 나는 대부분의 톱 아이돌 그룹들을 봤어.

Answers p.98

Word Check 영어는 우리말로, 우리말은 영어로 써 보기

01	partially	13	언제든지
02	free time	14	추측하다
03	review	15	열, 줄
04	show time	16	(시간을) 보내다
05	owe	17	교과서
06	at least	18	특징
07	balanced	19	최근의
08	atmosphere	20	일, 행사
09	wrap up	21	신용 카드
10	on record	22	정보
11	except for	23	두 배의
12	carefully	24	리모컨

Expression Check 알맞은 표현을 넣어 문장 완성하기

25 Maybe you should _____ it _____. 너는 아마 그것을 미뤄야 할 것 같아.

26 I _____ _____ _____ many things. 나는 많은 것들을 하느라 바빴어.

27 Now you're _____ _____ university! 이제 네가 대학교를 졸업하다니!

28 I'm _____ tired _____ walk. 나는 너무 피곤해서 걸을 수가 없어.

29 My cousin is coming to visit me, so we'll _____ _____.
내 사촌이 날 보러 와서, 우리는 함께 시간을 보낼 거야.

30 Tomatoes originally _____ _____ Peru, and not all tomatoes are red.
토마토는 원래 페루가 원산지이고, 모든 토마토가 빨간 것은 아닙니다.

PART

3

고난도
모의고사
19-20회

1.0배속 1.2배속

01 다음을 듣고, 울산의 오늘 날씨로 가장 적절한 것을 고르시오.

① 　② 　③

④ 　⑤

02 대화를 듣고, 남자가 완성한 스티커로 가장 적절한 것을 고르시오.

① 　② 　③

④ 　⑤

03 대화를 듣고, 남자가 마지막에 느꼈을 심정으로 가장 적절한 것을 고르시오.
① proud　② relaxed　③ scared
④ nervous　⑤ depressed

04 대화를 듣고, 남자가 웹툰 박람회에서 한 일로 가장 적절한 것을 고르시오.
① 강의 듣기　② 사진 찍기
③ 만화책 보기　④ 작가 만나기
⑤ 웹툰 그리기

05 대화를 듣고, 여자가 받은 선물을 고르시오.
① 책　② 옷　③ 카메라
④ 바이올린　⑤ 휴대 전화

06 대화를 듣고, 여자의 마지막 말의 의도로 가장 적절한 것을 고르시오.
① 동의　② 불평　③ 감사
④ 거절　⑤ 부탁

07 대화를 듣고, 두 사람이 대화하는 장소로 가장 적절한 곳을 고르시오.
① 학교　② 호텔　③ 영화관
④ 문구점　⑤ 백화점

08 대화를 듣고, 두 사람의 관계로 가장 적절한 것을 고르시오.
① 점원 – 손님　② 경찰관 – 시민
③ 은행원 – 고객　④ 주차 요원 – 운전자
⑤ 매표소 직원 – 관객

09 대화를 듣고, 여자가 불꽃 축제에 대해 언급하지 <u>않은</u> 것을 고르시오.
① 날짜　② 장소　③ 기념품
④ 입장료　⑤ 주차비

10 대화를 듣고, 남자가 읽고 있는 기사의 내용으로 가장 적절한 것을 고르시오.
① 햄버거의 유래　② 수제 햄버거 맛집
③ 온실가스의 유해성　④ 지구 온난화 대책
⑤ 지구 온난화 유발 요인

11 다음을 듣고, 미술 강좌에 대한 내용으로 일치하지 <u>않는</u> 것을 고르시오.
① 4세 이상의 어린이들을 대상으로 한다.
② 6월 1일부터 7월 31일까지 열린다.
③ 6세 이상 어린이 강좌는 5시에 시작한다.
④ 강좌 시간은 50분이다.
⑤ 홈페이지에서 등록할 수 있다.

12 대화를 듣고, 여자가 한국에 온 목적으로 가장 적절한 것을 고르시오.

① 여행하기 위해서
② 한국인 친구를 만나기 위해서
③ 할머니 댁을 방문하기 위해서
④ 사촌의 결혼식에 참석하기 위해서
⑤ 한국에서 결혼식을 올리기 위해서

13 대화를 듣고, 남자가 지불해야 할 금액으로 가장 적절한 것을 고르시오.

① $10   ② $15   ③ $18
④ $20   ⑤ $25

14 대화를 듣고, 남자가 대화 직후에 할 일로 가장 적절한 것을 고르시오.

① 도서관 가기   ② 친구 만나기
③ 공연 예매하기   ④ 숙제 제출하기
⑤ 뮤지컬 관람하기

15 대화를 듣고, 남자가 여자에게 부탁한 일로 가장 적절한 것을 고르시오.

① 제과점 들르기   ② 지도 그리기
③ 초콜릿 사 오기   ④ 역사 숙제 도와주기
⑤ 인터넷으로 자료 찾기

16 대화를 듣고, 여자가 학교 건물에 들어가지 못한 이유로 가장 적절한 것을 고르시오.

① 방학 기간이어서
② 출입문이 잠겨 있어서
③ 교실이 공사 중이어서
④ 학교의 학생이 아니어서
⑤ 선생님이 허락하지 않아서

17 다음을 듣고, 남자가 여행에 대해 언급하지 않은 것을 고르시오.

① 장소   ② 날짜   ③ 참가비
④ 참가 대상   ⑤ 신청 방법

18 다음 그림의 상황에 가장 적절한 대화를 고르시오.

①   ②   ③   ④   ⑤

[19-20] 대화를 듣고, 여자의 마지막 말에 이어질 남자의 말로 가장 적절한 것을 고르시오.

19 Man: _____

① Enjoy your backpacking trip!
② Why don't you make a list first?
③ It's my first time to travel by myself.
④ Where are you going to buy all of them?
⑤ Backpacking is fun, but it can be tough, too.

20 Man: _____

① He kept talking during the movie.
② I don't like the actors in that movie.
③ It's better to see a movie in the theater.
④ Charlie recommended his favorite movie to me.
⑤ It has a touching story, great acting, and stunning effects.

01 날씨 파악

다음을 듣고, 울산의 오늘 날씨로 가장 적절한 것을 고르시오.

①   ②   ③

M It's time for a weather update. People in Seoul are waking up to -4°C while Gangneung feels _____ _____ _____ _____ Seoul. The southern areas are a bit warmer, so the temperatures for Busan and Ulsan are _____ _____ _____ _____ _____ _____. However, clouds are coming up from the south, so it's raining in Busan now, and those thick clouds _____ _____ _____ _____ Ulsan, too. Tomorrow, those clouds will stay, and it will rain in Busan and Ulsan.

정답 단서
함정

02 그림 정보 파악 🇬🇧

대화를 듣고, 남자가 완성한 스티커로 가장 적절한 것을 고르시오.

①   ②   ③

④   ⑤

M Emma, can you help me with this?
W Oh, you're making custom stickers. What can I do for you?
M I chose this square design but don't know _____ _____ _____ _____.
W Hmm... how about drawing _____ _____ _____ _____ _____ ?
M Good idea. And I want to put a smile icon on the sticker.
W Then put it _____ _____ _____ _____ _____ _____.
M Okay. Don't you think it's too simple?
W Why don't you put your name _____ _____ _____ ?
M Oh, it looks good. Thank you for your help.

03 심정 추론

대화를 듣고, 남자가 마지막에 느꼈을 심정으로 가장 적절한 것을 고르시오.

① proud   ② relaxed   ③ scared
④ nervous   ⑤ depressed

Sound Clear ☆ campaign
g가 묵음이라서 [캠페인]으로 발음된다.

M Cindy, _____ _____ _____ _____.
W Yes, Dad. I'm so glad the school president election _____ _____ _____.
M Good job during the election ☆campaign.
W Thanks, Dad.
M So _____ _____ _____ _____ ?
W I thought I was going to lose because Eric _____ _____ _____ _____.
M Oh, really?
W But do you know what? I _____ _____ _____ _____ !
M That's my girl! Congratulations, student president!

04 한 일 파악

대화를 듣고, 남자가 웹툰 박람회에서 한 일로 가장 적절한 것을 고르시오.

① 강의 듣기 ② 사진 찍기
③ 만화책 보기 ④ 작가 만나기
⑤ 웹툰 그리기

Sound Clear ☆ **fair**

fair(박람회)와 fare(요금)은 [페어]로 발음이 같으므로 맥락을 통해 의미를 파악해야 한다.

M The webtoon fair was ________ ________.

W Why? You waited for it for so long.

M I thought I could ________ ________ ________ ________ ________ to draw webtoons, but I couldn't.

W Didn't you say there was a booth for it?

M Yes, but it was too crowded. I ________ ________ ________ ________ ________ ________.

W What about your favorite writer's lecture?

M ________ ________ ________. It was canceled.

W Oh, no.

M So there was nothing to do but ________ ________ ________ ________ ________.

05 특정 정보 파악

대화를 듣고, 여자가 받은 선물을 고르시오.

① 책 ② 옷 ③ 카메라
④ 바이올린 ⑤ 휴대 전화

M Julia, ________ ________ ________ ________ ________.

W Wow, it's from Grandpa! What is it?

M I don't know. ________ ________ ________ ________ ________. He loves taking pictures.

W I don't think so. The box is too big for a camera. Maybe a violin? He knows I want to learn it.

M Come on. ________ ________ ________!

W Okay. (*Pause*) Wow! This is ________ ________ ________ ________! Look at this color.

M That's pretty. You'll look good in that red coat. ________ ________ ________.

W It suits me perfectly. I'm going to call Grandpa right now.

06 의도 파악

대화를 듣고, 여자의 마지막 말의 의도로 가장 적절한 것을 고르시오.

① 동의   ② 불평   ③ 감사
④ 거절   ⑤ 부탁

Sound Clear ☆ **travel**

[t]와 [r]이 연달아 나와 [츄레블]로 발음된다.

W Honey, _____ _____ _____ _____ _____.
M Okay. Would you like to go to Jeju-do?
W Again? We went there last year. I want to travel abroad.
M Then how about Japan? _____ _____ _____ _____.
W Good idea. I'll check on plane tickets tomorrow. I hope _____ _____ _____ _____ _____.
M I'll ask my Japanese friend for traveling tips. What else do you want me to do?
W _____ _____ _____ _____ _____, can you book a rental car?

07 장소 추론

대화를 듣고, 두 사람이 대화하는 장소로 가장 적절한 곳을 고르시오.

① 학교   ② 호텔   ③ 영화관
④ 문구점   ⑤ 백화점

W Excuse me. _____ _____ _____ _____ _____?
M No, that's just a regular ballpoint pen. These ones over here are erasable.
W Oh, thank you. And do you have paper clips?
M Yes, we do.
W How much is _____ _____ _____ _____ _____?
M A box of paper clips is $4.
W _____ _____ _____ _____, please. I'd like to buy a file folder, too.
M We _____ _____ _____ _____ _____. Follow me, please.

08 관계 추론

대화를 듣고, 두 사람의 관계로 가장 적절한 것을 고르시오.

① 점원 – 손님
② 경찰관 – 시민
③ 은행원 – 고객
④ 주차 요원 – 운전자
⑤ 매표소 직원 – 관객

M Excuse me, ma'am. Is this your car?
W Yes, it is. Is there a problem?
M You _____ _____ _____ _____ _____ here. Didn't you see the sign?
W Oh, I'm sorry. But I have to _____ _____ _____ at the supermarket. It won't take long.
M If you don't move your car now, I'll have to _____ _____ _____ _____ _____.
W Okay. Where can I park?
M There's _____ _____ _____ _____ across the street.
W I'll move my car now.

대화를 듣고, 여자가 불꽃 축제에 대해 언급하지 않은 것을 고르시오.

① 날짜　　　② 장소　　　③ 기념품
④ 입장료　　⑤ 주차비

W Peter, let's go to the fireworks festival. _____ _____ _____ _____ _____ _____.

M Good. When is it?

W It's on Saturday, October 3. It'll be at Riverside Park.

M _____ _____ _____ _____ _____?

W No, it's free. But we need to pay for parking. It costs $5 per hour.

M There is going to be _____ _____ _____ _____. Wouldn't taking the subway be better?

W The subway will be really crowded, and the subway station is not close to the park. I think _____ _____ _____ _____ _____.

M Okay.

---

10 주제 파악

대화를 듣고, 남자가 읽고 있는 기사의 내용으로 가장 적절한 것을 고르시오.

① 햄버거의 유래
② 수제 햄버거 맛집
③ 온실가스의 유해성
④ 지구 온난화 대책
⑤ 지구 온난화 유발 요인

> **Sound Clear** ☆ **got it**
> [t]가 모음 사이에서 약화되고 뒤 단어의 모음과 연음되어 [가릿]으로 발음된다.

W Hey, Jake. What are you doing?

M I'm _____ _____ _____ on global warming and hamburgers.

W Global warming and hamburgers? _____ _____ _____ _____.

M Listen. To make hamburgers, _____ _____ _____, _____ _____?

W Of course.

M To get beef, we raise cows. To raise cows, _____ _____ _____ to make fields for them.

W Okay. Now I understand.

M And cows also _____ _____ _____ _____ _____.

W Now I got it. The more hamburgers we eat, the warmer the Earth gets.

11 일치하지 않는 것 찾기

다음을 듣고, 미술 강좌에 대한 내용으로 일치하지 <u>않는</u> 것을 고르시오.

① 4세 이상의 어린이들을 대상으로 한다.
② 6월 1일부터 7월 31일까지 열린다.
③ 6세 이상 어린이 강좌는 5시에 시작한다.
④ 강좌 시간은 50분이다.
⑤ 홈페이지에서 등록할 수 있다.

M The Oakwood Art Center wants to _____ _____ _____ _____ _____ _____ for young children. Children who are four years old or older can sign up for a class. Classes are _____ _____ _____ _____ _____ _____. Classes for those who are four or five years old start at four o'clock. Classes for those _____ _____ _____ _____ _____ _____ start at five o'clock. Each class is 50 minutes long. You can sign up at the office. 정답 단서

12 목적 파악

대화를 듣고, 여자가 한국에 온 목적으로 가장 적절한 것을 고르시오.

① 여행하기 위해서
② 한국인 친구를 만나기 위해서
③ 할머니 댁을 방문하기 위해서
④ 사촌의 결혼식에 참석하기 위해서
⑤ 한국에서 결혼식을 올리기 위해서

M Miranda, is that you? I'm glad to see you again!
W Wow, Homin! Long time, no see. _____ _____ _____ _____ _____, right?
M Yes. Time really flies. _____ _____ _____ _____ to Korea?
W Do you remember my cousin Sarah?
M _____ _____ _____ _____ _____? We used to play at your grandma's house together.
W Right. _____ _____ _____ soon, so I'm going to attend her wedding. Her husband is Korean.
M Wow! Please say congratulations to her.
W Okay, I will.

13 숫자 정보 파악

대화를 듣고, 남자가 지불해야 할 금액으로 가장 적절한 것을 고르시오.

① $10 ② $15 ③ $18
④ $20 ⑤ $25

M Hello. One adult and three children, please.
W It's $10 for an adult and $5 for a child _____ _____ _____ _____ _____. How old are your children?
M _____ _____ _____ _____ _____ _____ _____, and the other is two years old.
W Children under four years old get in for free. So you only need to _____ _____ _____ _____.
M Okay. So $10 for me and $10 for two children, right?
W That's correct. Do you 정답 단서 _____ _____ _____ _____? You can get a 10% discount with it.
M No, I don't have one. 한정 Here's my credit card.

14 할 일 파악

대화를 듣고, 남자가 대화 직후에 할 일로 가장 적절한 것을 고르시오.

① 도서관 가기 ② 친구 만나기
③ 공연 예매하기 ④ 숙제 제출하기
⑤ 뮤지컬 관람하기

Sound Clear☆ **student hall**
자음 세 개가 연속으로 나오면 중간 자음의 발음이 약화되어 [스튜던-홀]로 발음된다.

M Hi, Wilma. Where are you going?
W I'm going to the ☆student hall to ________ ________ ________ ________.
M Oh, is it today?
W Yeah. My best friend Carol ________ ________ ________ ________ ________. Why don't you go with me?
M I'm afraid I can't. I'm going to the library ________ ________ ________ ________ ________.
W Come on. It'll be over at five. That's not that late.
M But ________ ________ ________ ________ ________, too.
W You can do your homework later.
M The homework is ________ ________. Enjoy the musical!

15 부탁한 일 파악

대화를 듣고, 남자가 여자에게 부탁한 일로 가장 적절한 것을 고르시오.

① 제과점 들르기
② 지도 그리기
③ 초콜릿 사 오기
④ 역사 숙제 도와주기
⑤ 인터넷으로 자료 찾기

W Ryan, are you doing your homework?
M Yes, Mom. The history homework ________ ________ ________ ________. I had to find a lot of information on the Internet.
W You have already done a lot. Do you need some help?
M It's okay. I can ________ ________ ________ ________ ________.
By the way, where are you going?
W To the bakery. There's ________ ________ ________.
M Can you buy me some chocolate on your way home? I need ________ ________ ________ ________ ________.
W Of course.

16 이유 파악

대화를 듣고, 여자가 학교 건물에 들어가지 못한 이유로 가장 적절한 것을 고르시오.

① 방학 기간이어서
② 출입문이 잠겨 있어서
③ 교실이 공사 중이어서
④ 학교의 학생이 아니어서
⑤ 선생님이 허락하지 않아서

M Hey, are you ________ ________ ________ ________ ________?
W Oh, yes. I left a book in my classroom, so I want to get it.
M You ________ ________ ________ ________ ________ right now.
W Why not? Students can enter the school anytime during vacation.
M Workers are ________ ________ ________. There is lots of construction going on.
W Oh, I think I heard about that from my homeroom teacher. When will the construction be finished?
M ________ ________ ________ ________. Why don't you come again then?
W Okay, I will. Thank you.

17 언급하지 않은 것 찾기

다음을 듣고, 남자가 여행에 대해 언급하지 않은 것을 고르시오.

① 장소 ② 날짜 ③ 참가비
④ 참가 대상 ⑤ 신청 방법

Sound Clear ☆ **scheduled**
미국식은 [스케쥴드]로, 영국식은 [셰쥴드]로 발음된다.

M The Korea Heritage Group would like to invite you on a trip to Dokdo. Dokdo is a Korean island ________ ________ ________ ________ ________. You can explore its beautiful nature. There will also be a forum during the trip, so you can ________ ________ ________ ________ of Dokdo. The trip is ☆scheduled from May 3 to 6. Anyone can participate ________ ________ ________ ________ ________ ________ staying in Korea. Sign up at KoreaHG.com and don't miss this great opportunity.

18 그림의 상황에 적절한 대화 찾기

다음 그림의 상황에 가장 적절한 대화를 고르시오.

① ② ③ ④ ⑤

① **W** ________ ________ ________ ________ would you like to have?
M I want to have a hamster.
② **W** Can I bring this juice inside the theater?
M No. You ________ ________ ________ ________ ________.
③ **W** Let's eat something after the show.
M Good idea. I know ________ ________ ________ ________ ________.
④ **W** Look at the baby monkey over there.
M It's so small and cute.
⑤ **W** Excuse me. Please do not ________ ________ ________.
M I'm sorry. I ________ ________ ________ again.

대화를 듣고, 여자의 마지막 말에 이어질 남자의 말로 가장 적절한 것을 고르시오.

Man: _____

① Enjoy your backpacking trip!
② Why don't you make a list first?
③ It's my first time to travel by myself.
④ Where are you going to buy all of them?
⑤ Backpacking is fun, but it can be tough, too.

W Dad, do you know _____ _____ _____ _____ _____?

M It's under your bed. Are you packing for your backpacking trip?

W Yes, I am. I'm _____ _____ _____ at the same time.

M _____ _____. I'm worried, too.

W Don't worry, Dad. I'll call you every day.

M Okay. Is there anything _____ _____ _____ _____ _____?

W Can you help me pack? I don't know _____ _____ _____ _____ _____ for the trip.

M Why don't you make a list first?

대화를 듣고, 여자의 마지막 말에 이어질 남자의 말로 가장 적절한 것을 고르시오.

Man: _____

① He kept talking during the movie.
② I don't like the actors in that movie.
③ It's better to see a movie in the theater.
④ Charlie recommended his favorite movie to me.
⑤ It has a touching story, great acting, and stunning effects.

M Have you seen the movie *New Road*?

W I haven't been to the theater _____ _____ _____ _____ _____. I'm so busy with my work.

M That's too bad. Sometimes you _____ _____ _____ _____ _____.

W I know. Anyway, is that a good movie?

M Oh, yes. It's Charlie Kim's new movie.

W Really? I have seen _____ _____ _____ _____ _____.

M Then I bet you'll like this one very much. I would say it's one of the best in movie history.

W _____ _____ _____ _____ _____?

M It has a touching story, great acting, and stunning effects.

1.0배속   1.2배속

01 다음을 듣고, 일요일의 날씨로 가장 적절한 것을 고르시오.

①
②
③
④
⑤

02 대화를 듣고, 남자가 구입할 식탁으로 가장 적절한 것을 고르시오.

03 다음을 듣고, 남자가 바르셀로나에서 하는 일을 고르시오.

① 택시 운전   ② 통역
③ 관광 안내   ④ 식당 운영
⑤ 도시 환경 정비

04 대화를 듣고, 남자가 어제 한 일로 가장 적절한 것을 고르시오.

① 벽화 그리기   ② 동생 돌보기
③ 사생 대회 나가기   ④ 보육원 봉사하기
⑤ 초등학교 동창 만나기

05 대화를 듣고, 여자의 심정으로 가장 적절한 것을 고르시오.

① grateful   ② worried   ③ relieved
④ frustrated   ⑤ satisfied

06 대화를 듣고, 남자의 마지막 말의 의도로 가장 적절한 것을 고르시오.

① 거절   ② 감사   ③ 수락
④ 항의   ⑤ 경고

07 대화를 듣고, 남자가 내일 할 일로 가장 적절한 것을 고르시오.

① 쇼핑하기   ② 결혼식 가기
③ 모임 나가기   ④ 피아노 수업 가기
⑤ 피아노 연주회 가기

08 다음을 듣고, 여자가 하는 말의 내용으로 가장 적절한 것을 고르시오.

① 대기 오염의 원인   ② 마스크 착용법 안내
③ 주차장 폐쇄 공지   ④ 미세 먼지 대응 조치
⑤ 미세 먼지의 원인

09 대화를 듣고, 두 사람이 꽃 가게에 대해 언급하지 않은 것을 고르시오.

① 위치   ② 휴무일
③ 문 닫는 시간   ④ 꽃 가격대
⑤ 할인 판매 시간대

10 대화를 듣고, 리빙 디자인 전시회에 대한 내용으로 일치하지 않는 것을 고르시오.

① 이번 주 일요일이 마지막 날이다.
② 최신 유행의 가구들이 전시된다.
③ 할인 가격으로 가구를 판매한다.
④ New Street Yard에서 열린다.
⑤ 입장권은 현장에서만 판매한다.

11 대화를 듣고, 두 사람의 관계로 가장 적절한 것을 고르시오.

① 아빠 – 딸
② 식당 종업원 – 손님
③ 식당 종업원 – 주방장
④ 주방장 – 음식 칼럼니스트
⑤ 식당 주인 – 아르바이트생

12 대화를 듣고, 두 사람이 경기장에 도착할 시각을 고르시오.

① 6:20 p.m.　② 6:30 p.m.　③ 6:50 p.m.
④ 6:55 p.m.　⑤ 7:10 p.m.

13 다음을 듣고, 미세 플라스틱에 대한 내용으로 일치하지 <u>않는</u> 것을 고르시오.

① 5밀리미터 이하의 아주 작은 크기이다.
② 필요에 의해 의도적으로 생산되기도 한다.
③ 생활용품에 사용하는 것은 금지되어 있다.
④ 크기가 작아서 수집되기가 어렵다.
⑤ 바다로 흘러들어 해양 생물을 위협한다.

14 대화를 듣고, 남자가 전화를 건 목적으로 가장 적절한 것을 고르시오.

① 음악 수업을 신청하기 위해서
② 음악 교사로 지원하기 위해서
③ 지원 자격을 문의하기 위해서
④ 유치원생들을 만나 보기 위해서
⑤ 유치원 수업을 참관하기 위해서

15 대화를 듣고, 여자가 어젯밤에 늦게 잔 이유로 가장 적절한 것을 고르시오.

① 친구와 전화하느라고
② 공포 영화를 보느라고
③ 방학 숙제를 하느라고
④ 컴퓨터 게임을 하느라고
⑤ 낮에 본 영화가 계속 떠올라서

16 대화를 듣고, 남자가 여자에게 요청한 일로 가장 적절한 것을 고르시오.

① 물 가져다주기
② 메뉴판 가져다주기
③ 창가 자리로 바꿔 주기
④ 식사를 빨리 가져다주기
⑤ 음식을 싱겁게 요리해 주기

17 다음 그림의 상황에 가장 적절한 대화를 고르시오.

①　②　③　④　⑤

18 대화를 듣고, 재활용 축제에 대한 내용으로 일치하지 <u>않는</u> 것을 고르시오.

① 재활용에 대해 배울 수 있다.
② 재활용품으로 만든 물건을 사고팔 수 있다.
③ 남자가 만든 물건이 판매될 예정이다.
④ 금요일부터 일요일까지 열린다.
⑤ 공원에서 열린다.

[19-20] 대화를 듣고, 여자의 마지막 말에 이어질 남자의 말로 가장 적절한 것을 고르시오.

19 Man: _____

① I'm so hungry now.
② I can't chew anything right now.
③ Okay. I'm afraid I might have a cavity.
④ Sorry, but I already went to the dentist.
⑤ It's important to brush your teeth after eating.

20 Man: _____

① The blue light affects your sleep.
② I don't use my smartphone in bed.
③ I'll use my smartphone more often.
④ I thought it could only damage my eyes.
⑤ The noise makes me wake up during the night.

01 날씨 파악

다음을 듣고, 일요일의 날씨로 가장 적절한 것을 고르시오.

① ② ③

④ ⑤

Sound Clear ☆ **Southern**

south(남쪽)의 th는 [θ]로 소리 나서 [싸우스]로 발음되지만, southern(남쪽의)의 th는 [ð]로 소리 나서 [써던]으로 발음된다.

W This week, the weather is going to be unpleasant. This evening, _____ _____ _____ _____ _____, and by tomorrow at noon, a line of showers and thunderstorms will approach the metropolitan areas in Southern Florida. If you're _____ _____ _____ _____ _____ of Florida, they will reach you on Friday morning. But by Saturday, the thunderstorms _____ _____ _____ _____ _____, and it will be sunny during the weekend.
정답 단서

02 그림 정보 파악

대화를 듣고, 남자가 구입할 식탁으로 가장 적절한 것을 고르시오.

① ② ③

④ ⑤

W Welcome to Sweet Home Furniture. May I help you?
M Yes, please. I'm _____ _____ _____ _____ _____.
W We have many different kinds of tables. What kind of table _____ _____ _____ _____ _____?
M I'd like a wooden table for two people.
W Okay. This dark one is the most popular one in our shop. It _____ _____ _____ _____.
M Actually, I like the bright one over there.
W Oh, that one is popular 정답 단서 _____ _____ _____ _____. We have round and square ones in that color.
M I'll take a round one.
정답 단서

03 특정 정보 파악 ✠

다음을 듣고, 남자가 바르셀로나에서 하는 일을 고르시오.

① 택시 운전   ② 통역
③ 관광 안내   ④ 식당 운영
⑤ 도시 환경 정비

M Do you have only one day to stay in Barcelona? One day seems short because Barcelona is a city you _____ _____ _____ _____ _____ _____. But don't worry. From Barcelona's most favorite landmark to _____ _____ _____ _____ _____ _____, I will recommend the best things you can do in a day. _____ _____ _____ _____ _____, you can make the most of your 24 hours in Barcelona.

04 한 일 파악

대화를 듣고, 남자가 어제 한 일로 가장 적절한 것을 고르시오.

① 벽화 그리기
② 동생 돌보기
③ 사생 대회 나가기
④ 보육원 봉사하기
⑤ 초등학교 동창 만나기

M How was your volunteer work yesterday?

W You know I like children. I _____ _____ _____ _____ near my house. I had a great time.

M What did you do there?

W I _____ _____ _____ _____ _____ and played with them on the playground. What about you?

M I painted a wall at an elementary school.

W That sounds interesting. _____ _____ _____ _____ _____ _____?

M Yes. Look at these pictures before and after we painted. It was not easy, but _____ _____ _____ _____ _____.

---

05 심정 추론

대화를 듣고, 여자의 심정으로 가장 적절한 것을 고르시오.

① grateful
② worried
③ relieved
④ frustrated
⑤ satisfied

Sound Clear ☆ **certainly**
1음절에 강세가 있고, tain은 [튼]으로 약하게 소리 나서 [썰튼리]로 발음된다.

W Hello. I _____ _____ _____ for *The Lion King* at 7:30.

M Okay. Could you show me your ticket?

W Sure. (*Pause*) I can't find my ticket.

M _____ _____ _____, ma'am.

W I certainly put the ticket in my pocket. I guess I _____ _____ _____.

M If you bought the ticket online, you can show me the booking confirmation message.

W I erased _____ _____ _____ _____ recently.

M Then I'm afraid there's no other way I can help you.

W I can't believe this. I _____ _____ _____ _____ _____ for two hours to watch the musical.

대화를 듣고, 남자의 마지막 말의 의도로 가장 적절한 것을 고르시오.

① 거절　　② 감사　　③ 수락
④ 항의　　⑤ 경고

W Dave, do you have any plans for the weekend?

M I'll _____ _____ _____ _____ _____. There will be perfect weather for fishing.

W That sounds great. Do you often go fishing?

M Yes. _____ _____ _____ _____. You never know _____ _____ _____ _____ when you catch fish.

W Actually, I've always wanted to go fishing.

M Have you? You can join me _____ _____ _____.

W Thank you, but I have plans tomorrow. How about next weekend?

M I _____ _____ _____ _____ _____, but I can go again if you want to join me.

대화를 듣고, 남자가 내일 할 일로 가장 적절한 것을 고르시오.

① 쇼핑하기　　　② 결혼식 가기
③ 모임 나가기　　④ 피아노 수업 가기
⑤ 피아노 연주회 가기

W I _____ _____ _____ _____ _____ to my friend's wedding.

M How about your brown dress? You look good in that dress.

W It's old. I want to go shopping and _____ _____ _____. Do you want to go with me?

M Sure. _____ _____ _____ _____.

W I'm not. I have plans with my co-workers. What about tomorrow?

M _____ _____ _____ _____ _____ _____. I have a piano lesson in the afternoon. What about Saturday afternoon? *정답 단서*

W That's fine with me. See you on Saturday.

다음을 듣고, 여자가 하는 말의 내용으로 가장 적절한 것을 고르시오.

① 대기 오염의 원인
② 마스크 착용법 안내
③ 주차장 폐쇄 공지
④ 미세 먼지 대응 조치
⑤ 미세 먼지의 원인

W As most of the country is suffering from _____ _____ _____ _____ _____, the South Korean government passed emergency measures to reduce fine dust yesterday. The government _____ _____ _____ _____ _____ _____ *정답 단서* _____ during weekdays in Seoul. The government has also banned old diesel cars from all roads. The government advises citizens to _____ _____ _____ _____ and to refrain from outdoor activities.

09 언급하지 않은 것 찾기

대화를 듣고, 두 사람이 꽃 가게에 대해 언급하지 <u>않은</u> 것을 고르시오.

① 위치　　　　② 휴무일
③ 문 닫는 시간　④ 꽃 가격대
⑤ 할인 판매 시간대

W Excuse me. Where is Amore Flower Shop?
M It's _____ _____ _____ _____ in Miller's Mall.
W Thank you. Did you just buy those roses from there?
M Yes, but I'm afraid it's closed now. I bought these _____
_____ _____ _____.
W Really? Isn't it open _____ _____ _____ _____?
It's Tuesday.
M That is true, but _____ _____ _____ _____.
The shop closes at six.
W Oh, my. I need to come back tomorrow.
M _____ _____ _____ _____. You can get a 10%
discount from five to six.
W That's good. Thank you for the tip.

10 일치하지 않는 것 찾기

대화를 듣고, 리빙 디자인 전시회에 대한 내용으로 일치하지 <u>않는</u> 것을 고르시오.

① 이번 주 일요일이 마지막 날이다.
② 최신 유행의 가구들이 전시된다.
③ 할인 가격으로 가구를 판매한다.
④ New Street Yard에서 열린다.
⑤ 입장권은 현장에서만 판매한다.

Sound Clear ☆ **exhibition**
h가 묵음이라서 [엑시비션]으로 발음된다.

W This Sunday is the last day of the living design exhibition.
M _____ _____ _____ _____ is that?
W We can see trendy home furniture and _____ _____
_____ _____ _____.
M Do you want to go there?
W Yes. I'm interested in finding out about _____ _____
_____ _____. And you?
M Hmm... where is it being held?
W At New Street Yard.
M Okay. Let's go and have lunch at Jimmy's Restaurant _____
_____ _____ _____ _____.
W Good idea! I'll reserve tickets on the homepage.
정답 단서

11 관계 추론 ✳

대화를 듣고, 두 사람의 관계로 가장 적절한 것을 고르시오.

① 아빠 – 딸
② 식당 종업원 – 손님
③ 식당 종업원 – 주방장
④ 주방장 – 음식 칼럼니스트
⑤ 식당 주인 – 아르바이트생

Sound Clear ☆ **pumpkin**
자음 세 개가 연속으로 나오면 중간 자음의 발음이 약화되어 [펌킨]으로 발음된다.

M How did you like the food today?
W I _____ _____ _____ _____. The sweet pumpkin pasta was especially impressive.
M Thank you. Sweet pumpkin pasta is _____ _____ _____ _____ _____ at my restaurant.
W It was the best pasta _____ _____ _____.
M I'm glad you liked my food.
W I'd like to ㆍ정답 단서ㆍ _____ _____ _____ _____ _____ _____ _____ in my next food column.
M Thank you very much. I'm looking forward to it. ㆍ정답 단서ㆍ

12 숫자 정보 파악

대화를 듣고, 두 사람이 경기장에 도착할 시각을 고르시오.

① 6:20 p.m.
② 6:30 p.m.
③ 6:50 p.m.
④ 6:55 p.m.
⑤ 7:10 p.m.

M What time does the game start?
W It will _____ _____ _____ _____.
M We don't have much time.
W _____ _____ _____ _____ _____ to the stadium?
M How about taking the subway? The roads will be crowded at this time.
W Let me see. (*Pause*) There's a subway at 6:20. _____ _____ _____ _____ _____ on time?
M It will take thirty minutes by subway, and we need to _____ _____ _____ _____ from the station.
W Then we can arrive before the game starts. Let's take that one.

13 일치하지 않는 것 찾기

다음을 듣고, 미세 플라스틱에 대한 내용으로 일치하지 <u>않는</u> 것을 고르시오.

① 5밀리미터 이하의 아주 작은 크기이다.
② 필요에 의해 의도적으로 생산되기도 한다.
③ 생활용품에 사용하는 것은 금지되어 있다.
④ 크기가 작아서 수집되기가 어렵다.
⑤ 바다로 흘러들어 해양 생물을 위협한다.

W Microplastics are _____ _____ _____ _____ which are five millimeters in size or less. They are made when bigger pieces of plastic _____ _____ _____ _____, or they are made on purpose for toothpaste, body scrubs, or many other items we use every day. ㆍ정답 단서ㆍ Because of their small sizes, _____ _____ _____ and flow into the ocean. As a result, they are threatening not only millions of sea animals _____ _____ _____ _____.

14 목적 파악

대화를 듣고, 남자가 전화를 건 목적으로 가장
적절한 것을 고르시오.

① 음악 수업을 신청하기 위해서
② 음악 교사로 지원하기 위해서
③ 지원 자격을 문의하기 위해서
④ 유치원생들을 만나 보기 위해서
⑤ 유치원 수업을 참관하기 위해서

Sound Clear ☆ **résumé**

résumé(이력서)는 [레쥬메이]로, resume
(재개하다)은 [리쥼]으로 발음된다.

(*Telephone rings.*)

W Nancy Brown. Rainbow Music Center.

M Hello. This is David Jackson. I _____ _____ _____
that your center is looking for a teacher.

W That's right, Mr. Jackson. Do you _____ _____ _____
_____ five-year-old children?

M Yes, I do. Indeed, I have worked _____ _____ _____
_____ _____ at a kindergarten. I like kids.

W That's good. Can you visit the center for an interview
tomorrow?

M No problem. Just tell me _____ _____ _____ _____
_____ _____ _____.

W Please come to our offices at 21 Seymour Street by 10 a.m.
and send your résumé by email today.

M Okay. See you tomorrow.

15 이유 파악

대화를 듣고, 여자가 어젯밤에 늦게 잔 이유로
가장 적절한 것을 고르시오.

① 친구와 전화하느라고
② 공포 영화를 보느라고
③ 방학 숙제를 하느라고
④ 컴퓨터 게임을 하느라고
⑤ 낮에 본 영화가 계속 떠올라서

M Tina, wake up! It's _____ _____ _____ _____
_____.

W Dad, can I skip the lesson today?

M You can't. If you skip today's lesson, you'll want to skip the
lesson again.

W I won't. Please _____ _____ _____ _____. I went
to bed at 3 a.m.

M Why? Did you _____ _____ _____ late?

W No, I didn't.

M Then why? It's vacation, so you _____ _____ _____.

W I watched a scary movie during the day, and the scenes
_____ _____ _____ _____ in my head.

M I told you it was not a good idea to watch it.

16 요청한 일 파악

대화를 듣고, 남자가 여자에게 요청한 일로 가장 적절한 것을 고르시오.

① 물 가져다주기
② 메뉴판 가져다주기
③ 창가 자리로 바꿔 주기
④ 식사를 빨리 가져다주기
⑤ 음식을 싱겁게 요리해 주기

M Do you _____ _____ _____ _____ _____, please?
W Sure. Are you here _____ _____ _____ _____?
M For lunch.
W I see. Follow me, please. (*Pause*) Are you okay with this table?
M It's good. Thank you.
W _____ _____ _____ _____ with the menu.
M Excuse me, but would you bring me some water first, please? I'm so thirsty.
W No problem. I'll bring _____ _____ _____ _____ _____ _____ _____ _____ right away.
M Thank you very much.

17 그림의 상황에 적절한 대화 찾기

다음 그림의 상황에 가장 적절한 대화를 고르시오.

① ② ③ ④ ⑤

① M I'd like to order a T-bone steak, please.
　W How would you like your steak?
② M _____ _____ _____ _____ every day?
　W The reason is that I want to be healthier.
③ M You look good in your new jacket.
　W Thanks. I _____ _____ _____ yesterday.
④ M Happy anniversary! I hope you like the roses.
　W Oh, _____ _____ _____ _____ _____. Thank you so much.
⑤ M Would you like something to drink?
　W I'd like a cup of coffee _____ _____ _____ _____ _____ _____ _____.

18 일치하지 않는 것 찾기

대화를 듣고, 재활용 축제에 대한 내용으로 일치하지 <u>않는</u> 것을 고르시오.

① 재활용에 대해 배울 수 있다.
② 재활용품으로 만든 물건을 사고팔 수 있다.
③ 남자가 만든 물건이 판매될 예정이다.
④ 금요일부터 일요일까지 열린다.
⑤ 공원에서 열린다.

M _____ _____ _____ _____ _____ the recycling festival. What about you?
W Recycling festival? What kind of festival is it?
M The festival _____ _____ _____ _____ _____. You can learn about recycling and buy goods _____ _____ _____ _____.
W Sounds interesting. What are you going to do at the festival?
M I'll _____ _____ _____ there. I make bags from old clothes.
W That's cool. I want to go and look around.
M It's going to be held _____ _____ _____ _____ at Grand Park. See you there.

19 마지막 말에 이어질 응답 찾기

대화를 듣고, 여자의 마지막 말에 이어질 남자의 말로 가장 적절한 것을 고르시오.

Man: _____

① I'm so hungry now.
② I can't chew anything right now.
③ Okay. I'm afraid I might have a cavity.
④ Sorry, but I already went to the dentist.
⑤ It's important to brush your teeth after eating.

> **Sound Clear** ☆ **numb**
> b가 묵음이라서 [넘]으로 발음된다.

M How do you feel?
W I feel better, but my mouth is still ☆numb.
M _____ _____ _____ _____ _____?
W No, I can't. My dentist said that I must not eat for a couple of hours.
M When do you _____ _____ _____ _____ again?
W Tomorrow afternoon.
M It's almost time for me to _____ _____ _____ _____, too.
W _____ _____ _____ _____ _____ _____ tomorrow then?
M Okay. I'm afraid I might have a cavity.

20 마지막 말에 이어질 응답 찾기

대화를 듣고, 여자의 마지막 말에 이어질 남자의 말로 가장 적절한 것을 고르시오.

Man: _____

① The blue light affects your sleep.
② I don't use my smartphone in bed.
③ I'll use my smartphone more often.
④ I thought it could only damage my eyes.
⑤ The noise makes me wake up during the night.

W _____ _____ _____ _____ for school this morning?
M I _____ _____ _____ _____ _____. It's very hard to get up early every morning.
W Do you sleep deeply every night?
M Not really. I often wake up _____ _____ _____ _____ _____ _____.
W Hmm... do you use your smartphone before going to bed?
M Yeah, I usually watch webtoons or use social media in bed.
W That might be the reason. _____ _____ _____ _____ _____ _____ can disturb a sound sleep.
M I thought it could only damage my eyes.

Review Test

Word Check

영어는 우리말로, 우리말은 영어로 써 보기

01	fireworks	13	해외로
02	get married	14	지울 수 있는
03	spread	15	선거
04	article	16	국제적인
05	exhausted	17	회장
06	parking lot	18	박람회
07	campaign	19	파괴하다
08	remodel	20	어울리다, 잘 맞다
09	inform	21	렌터카
10	attend	22	지구 온난화
11	hot spring	23	평균의
12	heritage	24	탐험하다

Expression Check

알맞은 표현을 넣어 문장 완성하기

25 Sometimes you need to _____ _____ _____. 너는 가끔은 좀 쉬어야 해.

26 Why don't you _____ _____ _____ first? 우선 목록을 작성하는 게 어떠니?

27 The history homework is _____ me _____. 저는 역사 숙제 때문에 미치겠어요.

28 I can finish it _____ _____ _____. 저 혼자 그것을 끝낼 수 있어요.

29 You _____ not _____ _____ park here. 당신은 이곳에 주차를 하시면 안 됩니다.

30 I thought I could _____ _____ some new software.
나는 새로운 소프트웨어를 시험해 볼 수 있을 거라고 생각했어.

Answers p.111

Word Check
영어는 우리말로, 우리말은 영어로 써 보기

01 confirmation _____

02 goods _____

03 government _____

04 shut down _____

05 unpleasant _____

06 grateful _____

07 frustrated _____

08 affect _____

09 thrilling _____

10 co-worker _____

11 on purpose _____

12 reduce _____

13 금지하다 _____

14 둔한, 감각이 없는 _____

15 보호의 _____

16 최신 유행의 _____

17 면접 _____

18 경기장 _____

19 아주 작은 _____

20 손상을 주다 _____

21 거르다, 빼먹다 _____

22 충치 _____

23 권고하다 _____

24 치약 _____

Expression Check
알맞은 표현을 넣어 문장 완성하기

25 Please let me _____ _____. 조금 더 자게 해 주세요.

26 I often wake up _____ _____ _____ _____ the night. 나는 밤중에 자주 깨.

27 The scenes replayed _____ _____ _____ in my head. 그 장면들이 머릿속에 되풀이되어요.

28 I'll bring a glass of water _____ _____ the menu right away.
지금 메뉴판과 함께 물 한 잔을 가지고 오겠습니다.

29 You can _____ _____ _____ _____ your 24 hours in Barcelona.
바르셀로나에서 당신의 24시간을 최대한 활용하세요.

30 Most of the country is _____ _____ high levels of fine dust.
전국 대부분 지역이 높은 수준의 미세 먼지로 고통받고 있다.

Word List

□ weather report	일기 예보
□ turn into	~로 바뀌다
□ pay attention to	~에 주의를 기울이다
□ safety	안전
□ either *A* or *B*	A나 B 둘 중 하나
□ package	소포
□ garbage	쓰레기
□ elderly	연세가 드신
□ physical examination	건강 검진
□ regularly	규칙적으로
□ register	등록하다
□ article	(신문·잡지의) 글, 기사
□ abandoned	버려진, 유기된
□ suffer	고통받다
□ report	신고하다, 알리다
□ animal shelter	동물 보호소
□ make a reservation	예매하다, 예약하다
□ convenient	편리한
□ competition	경연 대회
□ sign up	신청하다
□ hand in	제출하다
□ application form	신청서
□ remind	상기시키다
□ return	반납하다
□ throw trash	쓰레기를 버리다
□ belongings	소지품
□ discount	할인
□ bill	지폐
□ receipt	영수증
□ change	거스름돈
□ check out	(호텔에서) 체크아웃하다
□ recommend	추천하다
□ get a refund	환불을 받다
□ stranger	(어떤 곳에) 처음 온 사람
□ have a cold	감기에 걸리다
□ take medicine	약을 먹다
□ see a doctor	병원에 가다
□ stay healthy	건강을 유지하다
□ make a change	변화를 주다, 바꾸다
□ be satisfied with	~에 만족하다

□ (just) around the corner	바로 코앞인, 임박한
□ center	가운데
□ nervous	초조한
□ author	작가
□ book signing	책 사인회
□ autograph	(유명인의) 사인
□ allow	허락하다
□ have a reservation	예약이 되어 있다
□ have a seat	자리에 앉다
□ trim	(머리를) 다듬기; 다듬다
□ perm	파마
□ these days	요즘
□ dormitory	기숙사
□ snore	코를 골다
□ do household chores	집안일을 하다
□ come over	들르다, 오다
□ wash the dishes	설거지하다
□ vacuum	진공청소기로 청소하다
□ lecture	강연, 강의
□ fine dust	미세 먼지
□ society	사회
□ serious	심각한
□ environmentalist	환경 운동가
□ give a big hand	큰 박수를 보내다
□ thrilling	아주 신나는, 흥분되는
□ the Net(= the Internet)	인터넷
□ make a reservation	예약하다
□ celebrate	축하하다, 기념하다
□ decorate	장식하다
□ organic	유기농의
□ symptom	증상
□ have a runny nose	콧물이 나오다
□ have a sore throat	목이 따끔거리다
□ have a fever	열이 나다
□ pill	알약
□ be in trouble	어려움에 처하다
□ presentation	발표
□ graduation	졸업
□ participate	참가하다
□ lose weight	체중을 줄이다

실전 모의고사 03 회

☐ heavy rain	폭우
☐ the day after tomorrow	내일모레
☐ exhibition	전시회
☐ find out	발견하다, 알아내다
☐ erase	지우다
☐ back up	(파일 등을) 백업하다
☐ recover	복구하다
☐ search for	~을 찾다
☐ depressed	우울한
☐ be stressed out	스트레스를 받다
☐ sunbathe	일광욕하다
☐ go hiking	등산하다
☐ be mad at	~에게 화가 나다
☐ leave a comment	댓글을 남기다
☐ laugh at	(~을 보고) 웃다, 비웃다
☐ be born	태어나다
☐ work as	~로서 일하다
☐ expert	전문가
☐ environment	환경
☐ information	정보
☐ print	출력하다
☐ out of order	고장이 난
☐ except	~을 제외하고
☐ take a look	보다
☐ overcook	너무 오래 익히다
☐ transfer	갈아타다, 환승하다
☐ homemade	집에서 만든, 수제의
☐ individually	각각 따로
☐ have a stomachache	배가 아프다
☐ dizzy	어지러운
☐ get well	(병이) 낫다
☐ neighborhood	지역, 인근
☐ far from	~에서 먼
☐ valid	유효한
☐ midnight	자정
☐ additional	추가의
☐ hesitate	망설이다
☐ be up all night	밤을 새다
☐ agree with	~에게 동의하다
☐ limit	제한하다

실전 모의고사 04 회

☐ partly	부분적으로
☐ temperature	온도, 기온
☐ recover	회복하다
☐ average	평균
☐ beard	턱수염
☐ wavy	웨이브가 있는, 물결 모양의
☐ win first(second) place	1위(2위)를 하다
☐ be proud of	~을 자랑스러워하다
☐ chance	기회
☐ professional	프로의, 전문적인
☐ be afraid of	~을 무서워하다
☐ look around	둘러보다
☐ entrance	입구
☐ endangered	멸종 위기에 처한
☐ itchy	가려운
☐ eye drop	안약
☐ treatment	치료, 처치
☐ fascinating	매력적인
☐ flight time	비행시간
☐ sign up for	~을 신청하다
☐ admission ticket	입장권
☐ onsite	현장에서
☐ give a lecture	강연하다
☐ teachers' office	교무실
☐ humidifier	가습기
☐ congested	붐비는, 혼잡한
☐ open a savings account	예금 계좌를 개설하다
☐ fill out	작성하다, 기입하다
☐ transfer money	송금하다
☐ be on a diet	다이어트 중이다
☐ gain weight	체중을 늘리다
☐ use up	다 써 버리다
☐ dodge ball	피구
☐ definitely	당연히, 틀림없이
☐ advanced	상급의
☐ election	선거
☐ vote for	~에게 투표하다
☐ responsible	책임감 있는
☐ pour	(비가) 마구 쏟아지다
☐ look on the bright side	긍정적으로 보다

Word List

실전 모의고사 05 회

☐ throughout	내내, ~ 동안 쭉
☐ last	지속되다
☐ heavily	심하게, 아주 많이
☐ lost and found	분실물 보관소
☐ by any chance	혹시
☐ handle	손잡이
☐ improve	개선되다, 나아지다
☐ as you know	너도 알다시피
☐ related to	~와 관련 있는
☐ row	줄
☐ prefer A to B	B보다 A를 선호하다
☐ pick up	~을 찾아오다
☐ rice noodles	쌀국수
☐ focus on	~에 집중하다
☐ handmade	수제의
☐ grocery	식료품점
☐ pack	팩, 상자
☐ offer	가격 할인, (팔 물건의) 제공
☐ belong to	~에 속하다
☐ in fact	사실은
☐ at least	적어도, 최소한
☐ be good at	~을 잘하다
☐ notice board	게시판
☐ manage	관리하다
☐ sold out	매진된, 다 팔린
☐ available	이용할 수 있는
☐ generous	후한, 관대한
☐ support	지지
☐ transfer	전학 가다
☐ farewell party	송별회
☐ throw a party	파티를 열다
☐ count on	~을 믿다(확신하다)
☐ weigh	무게가 ~이다
☐ humid	습한
☐ turn off	~을 끄다
☐ air conditioner	에어컨
☐ messy	지저분한, 엉망인
☐ bother	신경 쓰이게 하다
☐ turn down the volume	볼륨을 줄이다
☐ look forward to	~을 기대하다

실전 모의고사 06 회

☐ nationwide	전국적인
☐ be covered with	~로 덮여 있다
☐ due to	~ 때문에
☐ stand for	~을 상징하다
☐ serious	진지한, 농담이 아닌
☐ go on a date	데이트하러 가다
☐ a couple of	둘의, 두어 개의
☐ the number-one movie	1위 영화
☐ spectacular	장관을 이루는, 극적인
☐ be into	~에 관심이 많다, ~을 좋아하다
☐ show off	자랑하다
☐ annual	연례의, 매년의
☐ staff member	직원
☐ take part in	~에 참여(참가)하다
☐ entry fee	참가비
☐ participant	참가자
☐ souvenir	기념품
☐ repair	수리하다
☐ as soon as possible	가능한 한 빨리
☐ approach	다가오다
☐ save	절약하다
☐ get a discount	할인을 받다
☐ come to	(총계가) ~이 되다
☐ share	공유하다, 나누다
☐ opinion	의견
☐ sprain	삐다, 접지르다
☐ get better	(병이) 나아지다
☐ try on	입어 보다
☐ post office	우체국
☐ away from	~에서 떨어져 있는
☐ donation	기부
☐ drive	(조직적인) 운동
☐ break open	부수고 열다
☐ canned food	통조림 식품
☐ unused	사용하지 않은
☐ exhausted	기진맥진한
☐ work out	운동하다
☐ historical	역사적인
☐ take place	일어나다
☐ the Middle Ages	중세 시대

실전 모의고사 07 회

□ thick clouds	무겁게 드리운 구름
□ A as well as B	B뿐만 아니라 A도
□ lecture room	강의실
□ citizen	시민
□ check out	(도서관 등에서) 대출하다
□ medium	중간의
□ on sale	할인 중인
□ search for	~을 찾다
□ wait in line	줄을 서서 기다리다
□ valuable	소중한, 가치 있는
□ in life	인생에서
□ be able to	~할 수 있다
□ unfortunately	유감스럽게도, 불행하게도
□ do one's best	최선을 다하다
□ in case	~할 경우에 대비해서
□ contact	연락하다
□ management office	관리 사무소
□ convenient	편리한
□ crowded	붐비는, 혼잡한
□ make an appointment	예약을 하다
□ put down	적어 두다, (목록 등에) 이름을 올리다
□ stay	계속[그대로] 있다
□ original	원래의
□ backache	요통
□ slip	미끄러지다
□ hike	하이킹하다
□ apply	(약 등을) 바르다
□ ease	(고통 등이) 가라앉히다
□ pain	통증
□ look good on	~에게 잘 어울리다
□ crawl	기어가다
□ creepy	소름이 끼치는, 오싹한
□ frightened	매우 놀란, 겁먹은
□ bug spray	살충제
□ immediately	즉시
□ relieve	덜어 주다, 완화하다
□ extremely	극도로, 매우
□ recommend	추천하다
□ not only A but also B	A뿐만 아니라 B도

실전 모의고사 08 회

□ atmosphere	대기
□ dry	건조한
□ prevent	예방하다
□ walk past	~을 지나치다
□ ponytail	말총머리(하나로 묶은 머리)
□ short-sleeved	반소매의, 짧은 소매의
□ striped	줄무늬의
□ shorts	반바지
□ make a presentation	발표를 하다
□ move to	~로 이사하다
□ unpack	(짐을) 풀다
□ arrange	정리하다
□ fever reducer	해열제
□ body temperature	체온
□ above	~을 넘는, ~보다 많은
□ instruction	(제품 등의) 설명
□ tropical	열대의
□ flesh	과육
□ Southeast Asia	동남아시아
□ public transportation	대중교통
□ deliver	배달하다
□ purify	정화하다
□ keep ~ in mind	~을 명심하다
□ housekeeping	(호텔 등의) 시설 관리과
□ property	소유물
□ parking lot	주차장
□ rush hour	러시아워, 출퇴근 혼잡 시간
□ traffic	교통(량)
□ male	남성의
□ extra-large	(치수) 특대의
□ article	(신문·잡지의) 글, 기사
□ do ~ a favor	~의 부탁을 들어주다
□ on one's way home	집에 오는 길에
□ dry cleaner's	세탁소
□ wallet	지갑
□ bump into	~에(게) 부딪히다
□ walk a dog	개를 산책시키다
□ crispy	바삭바삭한
□ talented	재능 있는
□ party	일행, 단체

Word List

☐ die down	잦아들다
☐ foggy	안개가 낀
☐ ordinary	평범한, 보통의
☐ get off	내리다
☐ be late for	~에 늦다, 지각하다
☐ pay for	~을 지불하다
☐ probably	아마
☐ have a suntan	햇볕에 피부를 태우다
☐ go surfing	파도타기를 하다
☐ audition	오디션을 실시하다
☐ instrument	악기
☐ lead singer	리드 보컬
☐ get a refund	환불을 받다
☐ through	~을 통해서
☐ policy	정책, 방침
☐ get a good night's sleep	숙면을 취하다
☐ provide	제공하다
☐ late fee	연체료
☐ overdue	기한이 지난
☐ length	길이
☐ be on vacation	휴가 중이다
☐ trim	다듬다, 손질하다
☐ duty-free	면세의
☐ hand out	나눠 주다
☐ arrival card	입국 신고서
☐ in-flight	기내의
☐ shortly	곧
☐ ingredient	재료
☐ checkout counter	계산대
☐ sneakers	운동화
☐ information desk	안내 데스크
☐ afford	(~을 살) 여유가 되다
☐ both A and B	A와 B 둘 다
☐ fitness center	피트니스 센터, 헬스클럽
☐ at a discounted price	할인 가격으로
☐ contact number	연락처
☐ address	주소
☐ charge	요금
☐ schedule	일정
☐ keep ~ing	~을 계속하다(반복하다)

☐ blow away	불어 날리다
☐ polka dot	물방울무늬
☐ plain	무늬가 없는
☐ neckline	목둘레선, 네크라인
☐ electronics	전자 기기
☐ vacuum cleaner	진공청소기
☐ warranty	품질 보증 (기간)
☐ rather	차라리
☐ cancel	취소하다
☐ storm	폭풍
☐ go to a movie	영화 보러 가다
☐ breakfast included	조식 포함의
☐ sometimes	가끔, 때때로
☐ issue	(정기 간행물의) 호
☐ go cycling	자전거 타러 가다
☐ flat	바람이 빠진
☐ typically	일반적으로, 대체로
☐ colorful	화려한, 다채로운
☐ on the other hand	반면
☐ moth	나방
☐ tell the difference	구별하다, 분간하다
☐ feel chilly	으슬으슬 춥다, 오한이 나다
☐ symptom	증상
☐ grand opening	개장, 개업
☐ eat out	외식하다
☐ occasion	일, 행사
☐ possible	가능한
☐ extra fee	추가 요금
☐ buy one, get one free	하나를 사면, 하나가 공짜
☐ eye drop	안약
☐ student ID card	학생증
☐ gallery	미술관
☐ work of art	미술품
☐ on display	전시된
☐ useful	유용한
☐ brochure	책자
☐ detail	세부 사항
☐ exhibit	전시, 전시품
☐ take care of	~을 돌보다
☐ by oneself	스스로, 혼자

실전 모의고사 11 회

☐ be back	돌아오다
☐ pattern	무늬
☐ nowadays	요즘
☐ surround	둘러싸다
☐ on business	업무로, 사업차
☐ put off	미루다, 연기하다
☐ exam	시험
☐ miss	놓치다
☐ get ready	준비하다
☐ in a hurry	서둘러
☐ niece	(여자) 조카
☐ particular	특정한, 특별한
☐ recommend	추천하다
☐ awesome	굉장한
☐ travel around	여기저기 여행하다
☐ impressive	인상 깊은
☐ traditional	전통의, 전통적인
☐ reasonable	(가격이) 적정한, 너무 비싸지 않은
☐ gratitude	감사
☐ participate in	～에 참가하다
☐ for a while	잠시 동안
☐ mild fever	미열
☐ flu	독감
☐ vaccination	예방 접종
☐ medicine	약
☐ booking number	예약 번호
☐ print	인쇄하다
☐ absolutely	전적으로, 틀림없이
☐ only if	～할 경우에 한해
☐ celebrate	축하하다, 기념하다
☐ customer service center	고객 서비스 센터
☐ cut in line	새치기하다
☐ stand in line	줄을 서다
☐ endless	끝없는
☐ (just) around the corner	바로 코앞인, 임박한
☐ encourage	격려하다, 권장하다
☐ take part in	～에 참여(참가)하다
☐ on one's own	혼자서
☐ seriously	진지하게, 진심으로

실전 모의고사 12 회

☐ across the nation	전국적으로
☐ average	평균 ～이 되다
☐ tropical night	열대야
☐ possibility	가능성
☐ isolated	외딴, 격리된
☐ make an announcement	발표를 하다, 안내 방송을 하다
☐ video chat	화상 채팅을 하다
☐ sold out	매진된, 다 팔린
☐ closed for repairs	수리를 위해 휴업하는
☐ on holiday	휴가 중에
☐ business trip	출장
☐ come to	(총계가) ～이 되다
☐ according to	～에 따라
☐ exchange rate	환율
☐ school cafeteria	학교 식당
☐ affect	영향을 미치다
☐ amount	양
☐ tend to	～하는 경향이 있다
☐ concentrate	집중하다
☐ lack	부족, 결핍
☐ behavior	행동
☐ mood	기분
☐ impressed	감동받은
☐ major in	～을 전공하다
☐ depressed	침울한, 의기소침한
☐ physical examination	신체검사
☐ chill	오한, 한기
☐ apologize for	～에 대해 사과하다
☐ inconvenience	불편
☐ refund	환불
☐ make a copy	복사하다
☐ instructions	(제품 등의) 사용 설명서
☐ go wrong	(일이) 잘못되다
☐ pollution	오염
☐ threaten	위협하다
☐ take action	조치를 취하다
☐ social network	소셜 네트워크, 사회 연결망
☐ talk behind one's back	～의 험담을 하다
☐ misunderstanding	오해

Word List

☐ fine dust	미세 먼지
☐ warning	경고
☐ clear out	(~을 없애고) 청소하다
☐ completely	완전히
☐ vertical	세로의
☐ air cleaner	공기 청정기
☐ exactly	정확히
☐ complain	항의하다
☐ annoyed	짜증이 난
☐ ashamed	부끄러운
☐ in person	직접
☐ recognize	알아보다
☐ except	~을 제외하고는
☐ separate	분리하다
☐ recycling bin	재활용품 수거함
☐ take out	꺼내다
☐ irresponsible	무책임한
☐ care about	~에 마음을 쓰다, 관심을 가지다
☐ environment	환경
☐ approach	다가가다
☐ destination	목적지
☐ belongings	소지품
☐ create	창작하다
☐ unusual	특이한
☐ ice sledding	얼음 썰매 타기
☐ certain	특정한
☐ professional	전문적인; 프로, 전문가
☐ delivery fee	배달료
☐ pain relief patch	파스
☐ saying	속담, 격언
☐ keep ~ away	~을 멀리하다
☐ lose weight	체중을 줄이다
☐ low in calories	칼로리가 낮은
☐ get one's autograph	~의 사인을 받다
☐ work out	운동하다
☐ be famous for	~로 유명하다
☐ remind A of B	A에게 B를 생각나게 하다
☐ break a habit	습관을 고치다
☐ answer a phone call	전화를 받다

☐ worldwide	전 세계적인
☐ pour	(비가) 마구 쏟아지다
☐ landscape	풍경, 풍경화
☐ stream	개울, 시내
☐ peaceful	평화로운
☐ relaxed	마음 편한
☐ convenience store	편의점
☐ main entrance	정문
☐ the first basement level	지하 1층
☐ wakeup call	모닝콜
☐ climax	클라이맥스, 절정
☐ be disappointed with	~에 실망하다
☐ stay healthy	건강을 유지하다
☐ overlook	간과하다
☐ little by little	조금씩
☐ successful	성공한
☐ housewarming party	집들이
☐ vegetarian	채식주의자
☐ stop by	~에 들르다
☐ intermediate	중급의; 중급자
☐ advanced	상급의
☐ depend on	~에 달려 있다, ~에 의해 결정되다
☐ apply to	~에 적용되다
☐ charge	요금
☐ purchase	구입, 구매
☐ staff member	직원
☐ autobiography	자서전
☐ childhood	유년기
☐ overcome	극복하다
☐ call A B	A를 B라고 부르다
☐ application form	신청서
☐ be used to	~에 익숙하다
☐ lost	길을 잃은
☐ student council	학생회
☐ as long as	~하기만 하면
☐ sneeze	재채기하다
☐ examine	진찰하다
☐ have an allergy to	~에 알레르기가 있다
☐ vaccinate	예방 주사를 맞히다

실전 모의고사 15 회

☐ full moon	보름달
☐ score a goal	골을 넣다
☐ first half	전반전
☐ brand-new	아주 새로운, 신품의
☐ wireless	무선의
☐ vacuum cleaner	진공청소기
☐ break down	고장 나다
☐ make a mistake	실수를 하다
☐ practical	실용적인
☐ graduation ceremony	졸업식
☐ graduate from	~을 졸업하다
☐ literary work	문학 작품
☐ release	(영화 등을) 개봉하다
☐ astronaut	우주 비행사
☐ female	여성의
☐ transfer	전학 가다
☐ hometown	고향
☐ relative	친척
☐ make it	시간 맞춰 가다
☐ set	준비가 된
☐ appearance	외관, 겉모습
☐ turn in	~을 돌려주다(반납하다)
☐ gather	모으다
☐ material	자료
☐ edit	편집하다
☐ a big deal	대단한 것
☐ air conditioner	에어컨
☐ in that case	그런 경우에는, 그렇다면
☐ switch	바꾸다
☐ admission fee	입장료
☐ New Year's Day	설날
☐ tasty	맛있는
☐ bow	절하다
☐ similar	비슷한
☐ custom	관습
☐ Thanksgiving Day	추수 감사절
☐ pollution	오염
☐ hardly	거의 ~ 않다(없다)
☐ serious	심각한
☐ issus	문제

실전 모의고사 16 회

☐ through	(기간·범위) ~까지
☐ partly	부분적으로
☐ amusement park	놀이공원
☐ even worse	게다가, 설상가상으로
☐ national	국립의
☐ unfortunately	유감스럽게도, 불행하게도
☐ get a high score	높은 점수를 받다
☐ disappointing	실망스러운
☐ main character	주인공
☐ announcement	발표, 알림
☐ delay	미루다, 연기하다
☐ local time	현지 시각
☐ inconvenience	불편
☐ cause	야기하다
☐ construction	공사
☐ apologize for	~에 대해 사과하다
☐ sign-up	(서명에 의한) 등록, 가입
☐ used	중고의
☐ be in good condition	보존 상태가 좋다
☐ submit	제출하다
☐ revise	수정하다
☐ feedback	피드백, 의견
☐ edition	(출간 횟수를 나타내는) 판, 호
☐ get one's autograph	~의 사인을 받다
☐ make one's day	~을 행복하게 하다
☐ campsite	캠핑장
☐ have a barbecue	바비큐 파티를 하다
☐ credit card	신용 카드
☐ give ~ a bath	~을 목욕시키다
☐ dryer	드라이어
☐ get wet	젖다
☐ watch out	주의하다
☐ washing machine	세탁기
☐ detergent	세제
☐ frequently	자주
☐ out of order	고장 난
☐ package	소포
☐ scale	저울
☐ express mail	속달 우편
☐ regular mail	보통 우편

Word List

☐ go on a picnic	소풍을 가다
☐ hardly	거의 ~ 않다(없다)
☐ recognize	알아보다
☐ used to	~하곤 했다
☐ scratch	긁힌 자국
☐ leave a message	메시지를 남기다
☐ relieved	안도하는
☐ forum	포럼, 토론회
☐ give directions	길을 안내하다
☐ foreign	외국의
☐ participant	참가자
☐ unique	독특한
☐ coincidence	우연의 일치
☐ passionate	열정적인
☐ be into	~에 관심이 많다, ~을 좋아하다
☐ ask ~ a favor	~에게 부탁을 하다
☐ take out the trash	쓰레기를 내다 버리다
☐ sign up for	~을 신청하다
☐ since	~부터(이후)
☐ found	설립하다
☐ certified	검증된, 보증된
☐ for free	무료로
☐ detail	세부 사항
☐ expand	확장하다
☐ period	기간
☐ discounted price	할인가
☐ be connected to	~에 연결되다
☐ laptop computer	노트북 컴퓨터
☐ charge	충전하다
☐ advertise	광고하다
☐ permission	허락
☐ leave school early	학교를 조퇴하다
☐ get worse	더 나빠지다
☐ scan	스캔하다
☐ grilled	구운
☐ definitely	확실히, 분명히
☐ lead actor	주연 배우
☐ new face	신인
☐ interrupt	방해하다, 중단시키다

☐ partially	부분적으로
☐ triangle	세모, 삼각형
☐ put off	미루다, 연기하다
☐ prepare for	~을 준비하다
☐ short movie	단편 영화
☐ be busy ~ing	~하느라 바쁘다
☐ occasion	일, 행사
☐ graduate from	~을 졸업하다
☐ owe	신세 지다, 빚지다
☐ hang out	~와 어울려 시간을 보내다
☐ do household chores	집안일을 하다
☐ atmosphere	분위기
☐ wrap up	마무리 짓다
☐ review	복습하다
☐ balanced	균형 잡힌
☐ diet	식사, 식습관
☐ frequently	자주
☐ originally	원래
☐ come from	~에서 오다
☐ on record	기록상, 공표된
☐ take place	개최되다
☐ one another	서로
☐ too ~ to ...	너무 ~해서 …할 수 없는
☐ subway station	지하철역
☐ far from	~에서 먼
☐ while	~하는 동안에
☐ away	자리에 없는
☐ take care of	~을 돌보다
☐ row	열, 줄
☐ on one's way home	집에 가는 길에
☐ do one's homework	숙제를 하다
☐ remote control	리모컨
☐ feature	특징
☐ except for	~을 제외하고는
☐ at the moment	바로 지금
☐ attention	주의, 주목
☐ after-school	방과 후의
☐ textbook	교과서
☐ animated movie(film)	애니메이션
☐ recent	최근의

고난도 모의고사 19 회

☐	southern	남쪽의
☐	average	평균의
☐	spread	펼치다
☐	custom	주문 제작한
☐	fair	박람회
☐	try out	~을 시험해 보다
☐	booth	(전시장 등의) 부스
☐	suit	어울리다, 잘 맞다
☐	perfectly	완벽히
☐	abroad	해외로
☐	hot spring	온천
☐	rental car	렌터카
☐	erasable	지울 수 있는
☐	be allowed to	~하는 것이 허용되다
☐	parking ticket	주차 위반 딱지
☐	public	공공의
☐	fireworks	불꽃놀이
☐	admission fee	입장료
☐	article	(신문·잡지의) 글, 기사
☐	global warming	지구 온난화
☐	destroy	파괴하다
☐	forest	숲, 삼림
☐	greenhouse gas	온실가스
☐	inform	알리다
☐	get married	결혼하다
☐	be over	끝나다
☐	due	~하기로 되어 있는(예정된)
☐	drive ~ crazy	~을 미치게 하다
☐	on one's own	혼자, 혼자 힘으로
☐	concentrate	집중하다
☐	remodel	개조하다
☐	heritage	(국가·사회의) 유산
☐	be located in	~에 위치하다
☐	explore	탐험하다
☐	no wonder	당연하다, 그도 그럴 것이
☐	take a break	잠시 휴식을 취하다
☐	previous	이전의
☐	bet	틀림없다, 분명하다
☐	stunning	굉장히 멋진
☐	effect	효과

고난도 모의고사 20 회

☐	unpleasant	불쾌한, 불편한
☐	thunderstorm	뇌우
☐	shower	소나기
☐	approach	접근하다
☐	metropolitan area	대도시권
☐	northern	북쪽의
☐	pass through	~을 빠져나가다
☐	married couple	부부
☐	confirmation	확인
☐	frustrated	좌절한
☐	childcare center	보육원, 탁아소
☐	worth it	그만한 가치가 있는
☐	landmark	랜드마크, 상징물
☐	experienced	경험 있는, 능숙한
☐	make the most of	~을 최대한 활용하다
☐	thrilling	아주 신나는
☐	suffer from	~로 고통받다
☐	emergency measure	비상 대책
☐	advise	권고하다
☐	refrain from	~을 삼가다
☐	find out about	~을 알게 되다, 파악하다
☐	trend	동향, 추세
☐	reserve	예약하다
☐	on time	제시간에
☐	microplastic	미세 플라스틱
☐	on purpose	고의로, 일부러
☐	flow into	~로 흘러들다
☐	as a result	결과적으로
☐	threaten	위협하다
☐	have experience ~ing	~한 경험이 있다
☐	indeed	사실
☐	sleep in	늦잠을 자다, 더 자다
☐	over and over	반복해서, 되풀이하여
☐	along with	~와 함께
☐	goods	상품
☐	numb	둔한, 감각이 없는
☐	dental checkup	치과 검진
☐	cavity	충치
☐	damage	손상을 주다
☐	affect	영향을 미치다

대한민국 대표 영단어 뜯어먹는 시리즈

개정판 **중학 영단어 시리즈** ▶ 새 교육과정 중학 영어 교과서 완벽 분석

날짜별 음원
QR 제공

예비중 ~ 중학 1학년
중학 기초 영단어 1200개
+ 기능어 100개

중학 1~3학년
중학 필수 영단어 1200개
+ 고등 기초 영단어 600개
+ Upgrading 300개

중학 1~3학년
중학 필수 영숙어 1000개
+ 서술형이 쉬워지는 숙어 50개

개정판 **수능 영단어 시리즈** ▶ 새 교육과정 고등 영어 교과서 및 수능 기출문제 완벽 분석

날짜별 음원
QR 제공

예비고 ~ 고등 3학년
수능 필수 영단어 1800개
+ 수능 1등급 영단어 600개

고등 2~3학년
수능 주제별 영단어 1800개
+ 수능필수 어원 90개
+ 수능 적중 어휘 150개

예비고 ~ 고등 3학년
수능 빈도순 영숙어 1200개
+ 수능 필수 구문 50개

LISTENING CLEAR

중학영어듣기 모의고사 20회

ANSWERS

2

동아출판

LISTENING CLEAR

중학영어듣기 모의고사 20회

2

01 ②	**02** ④	**03** ⑤	**04** ⑤	**05** ①
06 ①	**07** ⑤	**08** ④	**09** ③	**10** ④
11 ③	**12** ③	**13** ⑤	**14** ④	**15** ⑤
16 ④	**17** ⑤	**18** ③	**19** ⑤	**20** ④

01 ②

W Good morning. This is today's weather report. It will snow in the Gangwon area from morning to night. It will snow in Seoul in the afternoon. The expected amount of snow is up to three centimeters in Gangwon-do and about one centimeter in Seoul. It will rain in Busan, and the rain might turn into snow late at night. It will rain all day in Jeju-do. Please pay attention to your safety.

여 안녕하세요. 오늘의 일기 예보입니다. 강원 지역은 아침부터 밤까지 눈이 내리겠습니다. 서울은 오후에 눈이 내리겠습니다. 예상 적설량은 강원도는 3cm까지이며, 서울은 약 1cm입니다. 부산은 비 소식이 있으며, 밤늦게 비가 눈으로 바뀔 가능성이 있습니다. 제주도는 하루 종일 비가 올 것입니다. 안전에 주의하십시오.

해설 제주도는 하루 종일 비가 올 것이라고 했다.

어휘 weather report 일기 예보   expected 예상되는   amount 양   up to ~까지   turn into ~로 바뀌다   all day 하루 종일   pay attention to ~에 주의를 기울이다   safety 안전

02 ④

W What are you doing?
M I'm looking for a backpack for my nephew. Will you help me choose one?
W Sure. What about the one with stripes?
M It's not bad, but I'm thinking of something cute.
W How old is he?
M He's eight years old.
W Then either the dinosaur-shaped one or the monkey-shaped one is best.
M I think he will like the dinosaur one better. I'll buy it.

여 뭐 하고 있어?
남 내 조카를 위한 책가방을 찾고 있어. 고르는 걸 도와줄래?
여 그래. 줄무늬가 있는 건 어때?
남 나쁘지 않은데, 나는 귀여운 걸 생각 중이야.
여 조카가 몇 살인데?
남 8살이야.
여 그럼 공룡 모양 가방이나 원숭이 모양 가방이 제일 좋겠다.
남 내 조카는 공룡 모양 가방을 더 좋아할 것 같아. 이걸로 사야겠어.

해설 남자는 조카가 공룡 모양 가방을 더 좋아할 것 같아서 그것을 사겠다고 했다.

어휘 look for ~을 찾다   nephew (남자) 조카   choose 고르다, 선택하다   stripe 줄무늬   either A or B A나 B 둘 중 하나   dinosaur 공룡   -shaped ~ 모양의   monkey 원숭이

03 ⑤

M Mom, I'm home. Is there a package for me?
W No, there isn't anything. What are you expecting?
M I ordered a book online, and it should be here today.
W When did you order it?
M Yesterday.
W Well, then maybe you should wait a little longer.
M They said it would take only one day. I don't understand why it didn't come today.

남 엄마, 저 집에 왔어요. 저한테 소포 온 것 있어요?
여 아니, 아무것도 없어. 뭘 기다리고 있니?
남 제가 온라인으로 책을 주문했는데, 오늘 여기에 와 있어야 해요.
여 언제 주문했는데?
남 어제요.
여 글쎄, 그럼 조금 더 기다려야 할 것 같구나.
남 하루밖에 걸리지 않는다고 했어요. 왜 오늘 안 왔는지 이해할 수가 없네요.

해설 남자는 오늘 배송되어야 할 책이 도착하지 않아서 언짢을 것이다.

어휘 package 소포   expect (오기로 되어 있는 것을) 기다리다   order 주문하다   a little longer (시간) 좀 더   take (시간이) 걸리다   scared 무서워하는   satisfied 만족하는

04 ⑤

W Where did you visit to do volunteer work yesterday?
M I visited the park near my house.
W Did you pick up garbage and fallen leaves and branches?
M No. I helped paint a fence at the park. What about you?
W I did volunteer work at a nursing home.
M What did you do there?
W I helped elderly people take a walk.
M Sounds good.

여 어제 어디에서 자원봉사 활동을 했니?
남 나는 우리 집 근처의 공원에 갔어.
여 쓰레기와 낙엽과 나뭇가지를 주웠니?
남 아니. 공원에서 울타리를 칠하는 걸 도왔어. 너는?
여 난 양로원에서 자원봉사 활동을 했어.
남 그곳에서 뭘 했는데?
여 어르신들이 산책하시는 것을 도왔어.
남 좋네.

해설 여자는 자원봉사 활동으로 양로원에서 어르신들이 산책하시는 것을 도왔다고 했다.

어휘 volunteer work 자원봉사 활동   pick up ~을 줍다   garbage 쓰레기   fallen leaves 낙엽   branch 나뭇가지

fence 울타리   nursing home 양로원   elderly 연세가 드신
take a walk 산책하다

어휘 article (신문·잡지의) 글, 기사   abandoned 버려진,
유기된   suffer 고통받다   on the streets 길거리에서   report
신고하다, 알리다   animal shelter 동물 보호소

05 ①

M Hi, Jane. I'm sorry I'm late.
W That's okay.
M Are you all right? You look worried.
W I'm a little worried. It's my first time to have a
   physical examination.
M Just relax. Everything will be fine because you
   exercise regularly.
W But I don't anymore. I haven't been to the gym for
   two months.
M Oh, don't worry so much. Let's go to the desk and
   register first.

남 안녕, Jane. 늦어서 미안해.
여 괜찮아.
남 너 괜찮아? 걱정이 있는 것 같아.
여 나는 조금 걱정돼. 건강 검진을 받는 게 처음이거든.
남 마음을 편하게 가져. 너는 규칙적으로 운동하니까 다 괜찮을
   거야.
여 하지만 이제는 안 해. 두 달 동안 체육관에 가지 않았어.
남 오, 너무 걱정하지 마. 일단 데스크에 가서 등록하자.

해설 건강 검진을 받을 수 있고 데스크에서 등록하는 절차가 있는
곳은 병원이다.

어휘 worried 걱정스러워하는   physical examination 건강
검진   exercise 운동하다   regularly 규칙적으로   gym
체육관   register 등록하다

06 ①

W Hi, Kevin. What are you doing?
M I'm reading an article about abandoned animals.
W You mean street dogs and cats.
M Yeah. Many of them suffer and die on the streets.
   It's really sad.
W Maybe we can do something to help them.
M What do you think we can do?
W When we find abandoned animals, we can report
   them to animal shelters.
M That's a good idea.

여 안녕, Kevin. 뭐하고 있어?
남 버려진 동물들에 관한 기사를 읽고 있어.
여 거리에 떠돌아다니는 개와 고양이를 말하는 거구나.
남 그래. 많은 동물들이 길거리에서 고통받다가 죽어. 정말 슬픈
   일이야.
여 아마 우리가 그 동물들을 돕기 위해 뭔가 할 수 있을 거야.
남 우리가 뭘 할 수 있을까?
여 버려진 동물들을 발견했을 때, 그 동물들을 동물 보호소에 신고
   할 수 있어.
남 좋은 생각이야.

해설 남자는 버려진 동물들을 발견하면 동물 보호소에 신고할 수
있다는 여자의 말에 동의했다.

07 ⑤

W Look at this poster! I want to watch this play.
M Me, too! Why don't we make an online reservation
   now?
W Good. How about Saturday, the 12th?
M Let me see. (Pause) There aren't any seats left on
   the 12th.
W How about the next day?
M I have a family gathering on that day.
W How about a week later? There are lots of seats
   available on Sunday.
M Okay. The 20th is fine for me, too.

여 이 포스터 좀 봐! 나 이 연극 보고 싶어.
남 나도! 지금 온라인으로 예매하는 게 어때?
여 좋아. 12일 토요일은 어떠니?
남 어디 보자. (잠시 후) 12일에는 남아 있는 자리가 없어.
여 그 다음날은 어때?
남 난 그날 가족 모임이 있어.
여 일주일 후는 어때? 일요일에는 자리가 많이 있어.
남 그래. 나도 20일이 좋아.

해설 12일에는 극장에 자리가 없고 13일에는 남자가 가족 모임이
있어서 두 사람은 20일 일요일에 연극을 보기로 했다.

어휘 play 연극   make a reservation 예매하다, 예약하다
online 온라인의   seat 자리   left 남아 있는(leave의 과거분사)
gathering 모임   lots of 많은   available 이용할 수 있는

08 ④

M Mom, are you visiting Grandfather this Saturday?
W Yes. I'll leave early in the morning to take the train.
M Did you already buy a ticket?
W No, not yet. I think I'll buy one at the station.
M Why don't you use the mobile app to buy your
   ticket? It's really convenient.
W Great. Will you download the app for me?
M Sure. I'll do it right away.

남 엄마, 이번 주 토요일에 할아버지 댁에 가세요?
여 그래. 기차를 타기 위해 아침에 일찍 나갈 거란다.
남 표를 이미 사셨어요?
여 아니, 아직. 역에서 사려고 해.
남 휴대 전화 앱을 사용해서 표를 사시는 게 어때요? 정말 편리해요.
여 잘됐구나. 앱을 다운로드해 주겠니?
남 네. 바로 해 드릴게요.

해설 여자가 앱을 다운로드해 달라고 하자 남자는 바로 하겠다고
했다.

어휘 leave 떠나다   take the train 기차를 타다   station 역
mobile(= mobile phone) 휴대 전화   app 앱, 애플리케이션
convenient 편리한   download 다운로드하다   right away
즉시, 바로

09 ③

W Do you know there's a band competition on September 13?

M Yes. I'll sing and Mike will play the keyboard. I'm looking for a guitarist and a drummer.

W Can I join you? I can play the guitar.

M Really? Great! Then we only need a drummer.

W Let's ask some other people in our class. When is the deadline to sign up?

M By this Friday. We need to hand in an application form to the music teacher.

W I see. I'm sure we'll find a drummer before then.

여 너 9월 13일에 밴드 경연 대회가 있는 거 알고 있니?

남 응. 나는 노래를 부르고 Mike는 키보드를 연주할 거야. 나는 기타리스트와 드러머를 찾고 있어.

여 내가 함께해도 될까? 나 기타 칠 수 있어.

남 정말? 좋지! 그럼 우린 드러머만 있으면 되겠다.

여 우리 반 애들한테 물어보자. 신청 기한이 언제지?

남 이번 주 금요일까지야. 음악 선생님께 신청서를 내야 해.

여 알았어. 나는 우리가 그 전까지 드러머를 찾을 수 있을 거라고 확신해.

해설 두 사람은 밴드 경연 대회의 참가자 수는 언급하지 않았다.

어휘 competition 경연 대회 look for ~을 찾다 deadline 기한, 마감 일자 sign up 신청하다 hand in 제출하다 application form 신청서

10 ④

W May I have your attention, please? Thank you for visiting the library today. We'd like to remind all of you that the library is going to close in 30 minutes. Please return the books to the book carts nearest you. Please throw your trash in the trash cans. Make sure you take all your belongings with you when you leave. Thank you for spending time with us here today.

여 주목해 주십시오. 오늘 저희 도서관을 방문해 주셔서 감사합니다. 30분 후에 도서관이 문을 닫을 것임을 여러분께 상기시켜 드리고자 합니다. 책을 가장 가까운 책 카트로 반납해 주십시오. 쓰레기는 쓰레기통에 버려 주십시오. 나가실 때 모든 소지품을 챙겼는지 확인해 주십시오. 오늘 저희 도서관에서 시간을 보내 주셔서 감사합니다.

해설 도서관 폐관 시간을 상기시키는 안내 방송이다.

어휘 attention 주의, 주목 remind 상기시키다 return 반납하다 throw trash 쓰레기를 버리다 trash can 쓰레기통 belongings 소지품 spend (시간을) 보내다

11 ③

W Hi. I'd like to buy these two books.

M All right. These books are $4 each.

W Can I get a bookstore membership discount?

M Yes, you can. Please show me your membership card.

W Here you are.

M Okay. You get a $1 discount on each book.

W Great. Here's a $10 bill.

M Here are your receipt and change.

여 안녕하세요. 이 책 두 권을 사고 싶어요.

남 알겠습니다. 책은 각각 4달러입니다.

여 서점 회원 할인을 받을 수 있나요?

남 네. 회원 카드를 저에게 보여 주세요.

여 여기 있어요.

남 네. 한 권당 1달러씩 할인받으십니다.

여 좋아요. 여기 10달러 지폐를 드릴게요.

남 여기 영수증과 거스름돈 있습니다.

해설 4달러짜리 책 두 권을 각각 1달러씩 할인받았으므로 총 6달러를 지불해야 한다.

어휘 each 각각(의) bookstore 서점 membership 회원 discount 할인 bill 지폐 receipt 영수증 change 거스름돈

12 ③

W What are you going to order?

M A double cheeseburger and a coke. What about you?

W I'm not sure. What do you recommend?

M I heard the fried chicken here is very good, especially the spicy kind. Try it.

W Well, I had some chicken last night. I want something different.

M The tomato spaghetti is good, too. Do you like spaghetti?

W I do. I'll order that then.

여 뭐 주문할 거야?

남 더블 치즈버거랑 콜라. 너는?

여 모르겠어. 넌 뭘 추천하니?

남 여기 특히 매운맛 프라이드치킨이 아주 맛있다고 들었어. 먹어 봐.

여 글쎄, 나 어젯밤에 치킨 먹었거든. 다른 거 먹고 싶어.

남 토마토 스파게티도 괜찮아. 스파게티 좋아해?

여 응. 그럼 그거 시켜야겠다.

해설 남자가 토마토 스파게티를 추천하자 여자는 그것을 주문하겠다고 했다.

어휘 order 주문하다 recommend 추천하다 especially 특히 spicy 매운 kind 종류 different 다른

13 ⑤

M African elephants are the world's largest land animal. They can reach 3 meters tall and weigh about 6,000 kilograms. Because of their massive size, they need to eat a lot of food. They can eat as much as 150 kilograms of food a day, which includes grasses, fruits, and trees. They are famous for their very large ears. The large ears cover their shoulders and keep them cool under the hot African sun.

남 아프리카코끼리는 세계에서 가장 큰 육지 동물입니다. 그들은 3미터까지 자랄 수 있고, 무게는 약 6,000킬로그램이 나갑니다. 거대한 크기 때문에, 그들은 먹이를 많이 먹어야 합니다. 그들은 하루에 150킬로그램만큼의 먹이를 먹을 수 있는데, 그 먹이로는 풀, 과일, 나무가 포함됩니다. 그들은 아주 큰 귀로 유명합니다. 큰 귀가 그들의 어깨를 덮어서 뜨거운 아프리카 태양 아래에서 시원하게 지내도록 해 줍니다.

해설 아프리카코끼리의 큰 귀가 어깨를 덮어서 뜨거운 태양으로부터 시원하게 지내도록 해 준다고 했다.

어휘 land animal 육지 동물 reach ~에 이르다 weigh 무게가 ~이다 massive 거대한 a lot of 많은 include 포함하다 be famous for ~로 유명하다 cover 덮다 shoulder 어깨 keep 유지하다, (~한 상태로) 있게 하다

14 ④

W Good morning. How can I help you?
M I'd like to check out now. Here is my key.
W Okay. Please wait a moment, and I'll give you your receipt. (*Pause*) Here you are.
M Thank you. Can you recommend a gift shop near here?
W We have a souvenir shop on the second floor. You can find many special items there.
M That's good to know. Thank you.
W You're welcome. Enjoy shopping and have a safe trip back home.

여 안녕하세요. 어떻게 도와 드릴까요?
남 지금 체크아웃하려고 합니다. 여기 열쇠를 드릴게요.
여 알겠습니다. 잠시만 기다려주시면 영수증을 드리겠습니다. (잠시 후) 여기 있습니다.
남 고맙습니다. 여기 근처의 기념품 가게를 추천해 주시겠어요?
여 2층에 기념품 가게가 있습니다. 그곳에서 특별한 물건들을 많이 찾으실 수 있을 거예요.
남 알게 되어 좋네요. 고맙습니다.
여 천만에요. 즐거운 쇼핑하시고 댁까지 안전한 여행하십시오.

해설 호텔 프런트 직원과 체크아웃하는 투숙객 사이의 대화이다.

어휘 check out (호텔에서) 체크아웃하다 receipt 영수증 recommend 추천하다 gift(souvenir) shop 기념품 가게 special 특별한 item 물건 safe 안전한 trip 여행

15 ⑤

(*Cellphone rings.*)
W Hello, Hajun. What's up?
M Hey, I'm calling you because you didn't answer my message.
W Oh, I'm sorry. I didn't see your message. What was it about?
M I'm worried about my English essay because I'm poor at grammar. I need your help.
W Well, there's a website that can check your grammar for you.
M Oh, that will help. Can you send me the address?

W Sure. I'll send you the link right away.
M Thanks a lot.

(*휴대 전화가 울린다.*)
여 안녕, 하준아. 무슨 일이야?
남 야, 네가 내 메시지에 답을 안 해서 전화하는 거야.
여 아, 미안해. 메시지 못 봤어. 뭐에 대한 거였니?
남 내가 문법을 못해서 영어 과제가 걱정돼. 네 도움이 필요해.
여 음, 네 문법을 점검해 줄 수 있는 웹 사이트가 있어.
남 오, 도움이 될 것 같아. 주소를 보내 줄 수 있어?
여 물론이야. 지금 바로 링크를 보내 줄게.
남 정말 고마워.

해설 남자는 여자에게 문법을 점검해 주는 웹 사이트 주소를 보내 달라고 요청했다.

어휘 message 메시지 be worried about ~을 걱정하다 essay (짧은 논문 형태의) 과제물 be poor at ~을 못하다 grammar 문법 address 주소 link (웹 사이트) 링크

16 ④

W Charles, you look upset. Anything wrong?
M I wanted to get a refund for this sweater, but I couldn't.
W Why not? Didn't you bring your receipt?
M Of course, I did.
W Then what was the problem?
M The person said there are no refunds or exchanges on discounted items.
W Right. You bought it with a discount coupon, didn't you?
M Yes. But the cashier didn't tell me that when I bought it.

여 Charles, 너 기분이 안 좋아 보여. 무슨 일 있어?
남 이 스웨터를 환불받고 싶었는데, 못 받았어.
여 왜? 영수증 안 가져갔니?
남 물론 가져갔지.
여 그럼 뭐가 문제였던 거야?
남 할인 품목에 대해서는 환불이나 교환이 안 된대.
여 맞아. 너 그거 할인 쿠폰으로 샀잖아, 그렇지 않니?
남 응. 그런데 내가 이걸 살 때 계산대 직원이 말해 주지 않았어.

해설 남자는 할인 쿠폰으로 스웨터를 샀기 때문에 환불을 받지 못했다고 했다.

어휘 upset 속상한 get a refund 환불을 받다 bring 가져가다 receipt 영수증 refund 환불 exchange 교환 discounted 할인된 coupon 쿠폰 cashier 계산원

17 ⑤

① W Do you mind if I open the window?
  M No, not at all. Go ahead.
② W How many more stops should I go to get to Grand Park?
  M I'm sorry, but I'm a stranger here.
③ W Your eyes are red. Are you all right?
  M I'm just a little tired.

④ W How was your trip to London?
　M It was great. I visited many places.
⑤ W Can you tell me how to get to the subway
　　 station?
　M Go straight down this street and turn left at the
　　 corner.

① 여 제가 창문을 열어도 될까요?
　남 물론이죠. 그러세요.
② 여 Grand Park까지 가려면 몇 정거장 더 가야 합니까?
　남 죄송하지만 저도 이곳이 처음입니다.
③ 여 너 눈이 빨개. 괜찮아?
　남 난 그냥 좀 피곤해.
④ 여 런던 여행은 어땠어?
　남 좋았어. 난 많은 곳을 방문했어.
⑤ 여 지하철역까지 어떻게 가는지 말씀해 주시겠어요?
　남 이 길을 따라 쭉 가다가 모퉁이에서 왼쪽으로 도세요.

해설 지하철역으로 가는 길을 묻고 답하는 상황이다.

어휘 mind 언짢아하다, 상관하다　stop 정거장　get to ~에
도착하다　stranger (어떤 곳에) 처음 온 사람　a little 조금
tired 피곤한　trip 여행　visit 방문하다　subway station
지하철역　go straight 똑바로 가다　corner 모퉁이

18 ③

W I have a terrible cold.
M Did you take any medicine?
W Yes. I'm also taking vitamin C.
M Are you getting enough rest?
W That's the problem. I have a lot of work to do every
　day.
M Getting enough rest is important. You also need to
　drink a lot of water.
W Okay. I'll try. If I don't get better soon, I'll go to see
　a doctor.
M Yeah. You probably should.

여 나 심한 감기에 걸렸어.
남 약은 먹었니?
여 응. 비타민 C도 먹고 있어.
남 너 충분히 쉬고 있어?
여 그게 문제야. 난 매일 할 일이 많아.
남 충분히 쉬는 것도 중요해. 그리고 물도 많이 마셔야 해.
여 알았어. 노력할게. 빨리 낫지 않으면, 병원에 가 볼 거야.
남 그래. 아마 그래야 할 거야.

해설 두 사람은 감기를 낫게 하기 위한 방법으로 과일을 먹는 것은
언급하지 않았다.

어휘 have a cold 감기에 걸리다　terrible 지독한, 심한　take
medicine 약을 먹다　get rest 쉬다　enough 충분한　get
better 나아지다　see a doctor 병원에 가다　probably 아마

19 ⑤

W What's your favorite food?
M Hamburgers. I eat one for lunch every day.
W Every day? That's not good for your health.

M I know. But I love eating them, and I'm still healthy.
W But you might not stay healthy. You should make
　some changes.
M What do you mean by that?
W Eat more fruits and vegetables and less fast food.

여 네가 제일 좋아하는 음식이 뭐니?
남 햄버거. 나는 매일 점심으로 햄버거를 먹어.
여 매일? 그건 네 건강에 좋지 않아.
남 알아. 하지만 난 햄버거 먹는 걸 정말 좋아하고 아직 건강해.
여 그래도 건강을 유지할 수 없을 거야. 너는 변화를 줘야 해.
남 그게 무슨 뜻이니?
여 과일과 채소를 더 많이 먹고 패스트푸드를 덜 먹으렴.

해설 여자가 남자의 식습관을 지적하며 변화해야 한다고 하자 남
자가 그게 무슨 뜻인지 물었으므로, 건강한 식습관에 대해 조언하
는 응답이 가장 적절하다.
① 내가 가장 좋아하는 음식은 샐러드야.
② 내 말이 바로 그거야.
③ 너는 매일 운동해야 해.
④ 네가 방금 한 말을 이해하지 못하겠어.

어휘 health 건강　still 여전히　stay healthy 건강을 유지하다
make a change 변화를 주다, 바꾸다　mean 의미하다
exactly 정확히, 바로　vegetable 채소

20 ④

M Hi, Julie. Did you go to the musical yesterday?
W Yes, I did.
M How was it? Did you like it?
W I really enjoyed it, but I was not satisfied with my
　seat.
M What was wrong with it?
W It was hard to see the actors from my seat.
M Oh, then were you able to hear their voices well?
W Luckily, yes. I'll never forget their voices.

남 안녕, Julie. 어제 뮤지컬 보러 갔었니?
여 응, 갔었어.
남 뮤지컬은 어땠어? 좋았니?
여 정말 재미있게 봤는데, 자리는 만족스럽지 못했어.
남 뭐가 문제였는데?
여 내 자리에서 배우들을 보기가 힘들었어.
남 오, 그럼 그들의 목소리는 잘 들을 수 있었니?
여 응, 다행히. 난 그들의 목소리를 잊지 못할 거야.

해설 남자가 배우들의 목소리를 잘 들을 수 있었는지 물었으므로
이에 대한 긍정 또는 부정의 응답이 와야 한다.
① 정말 좋은 시간을 보냈어.
② 그건 내가 제일 좋아하는 뮤지컬이었어.
③ 나는 이미 표를 샀어.
⑤ 나는 곧 또 다른 뮤지컬을 보러 갈 계획이야.

어휘 be satisfied with ~에 만족하다　seat 자리　actor
배우　be able to ~할 수 있다　voice 목소리　luckily
다행히도　never 절대 ~ 않다　forget 잊다

01 ③	**02** ⑤	**03** ①	**04** ④	**05** ④
06 ⑤	**07** ①	**08** ②	**09** ⑤	**10** ②
11 ④	**12** ④	**13** ④	**14** ②	**15** ③
16 ⑤	**17** ⑤	**18** ⑤	**19** ④	**20** ②

01   ③

M Welcome to the weather forecast. Today is December 23, and Christmas is just around the corner. It will be cloudy and windy today, and we'll have the same conditions tomorrow. On Christmas, however, it will be sunny all day. There will be no white Christmas this year.

남 일기 예보입니다. 오늘은 12월 23일로, 크리스마스가 임박했습니다. 오늘은 구름이 끼고 바람이 많이 불겠으며 내일도 같을 것입니다. 그러나 크리스마스 당일에는 하루 종일 맑겠습니다. 올해는 화이트 크리스마스가 없을 것입니다.

해설 크리스마스에는 하루 종일 맑을 것이라고 했다.

어휘 weather forecast 일기 예보   Christmas 크리스마스 (just) around the corner 바로 코앞인, 임박한   conditions (물리적) 환경, (특정 시기의) 날씨   all day 하루 종일

02   ⑤

W Hello. How may I help you?
M I'm looking for a smartphone case.
W Okay. How about this striped one?
M Actually, it's for my younger sister. I don't think she wants a striped phone case.
W I see. What about this one with the big heart in the center?
M I think that's too simple.
W Then how about this one with three small hearts and the word "HAPPY" below?
M Oh, that's cute. I'll take it.

여 안녕하세요. 무엇을 도와드릴까요?
남 스마트폰 케이스를 찾고 있어요.
여 네. 이 줄무늬 케이스는 어떠세요?
남 사실은, 제 여동생을 위한 거예요. 여동생이 줄무늬 핸드폰 케이스를 원할 것 같지 않아요.
여 알겠습니다. 가운데에 큰 하트가 있는 이건 어떠세요?
남 너무 단순한 것 같아요.
여 그럼 작은 하트 세 개와 아래에 'HAPPY'라는 단어가 있는 이건 어떠세요?
남 오, 귀엽네요. 이걸로 할게요.

해설 남자는 작은 하트 세 개 아래에 'HAPPY'라고 적혀 있는 케이스를 사겠다고 했다.

어휘 look for ~을 찾다   striped 줄무늬의   heart 하트 center 가운데   simple 단순한   below 아래에

03   ①

W How was your audition for the student singing club?
M I passed it.
W Good for you! But you don't look happy. What's the matter?
M My best friend, Somin, failed the audition.
W Oh, didn't you two practice together all the time?
M Yeah. She is the one who taught me how to sing well.
W I know.
M She has to wait six months for the next audition. That's too long.

여 학생 노래 동아리 오디션은 어땠니?
남 나 합격했어.
여 잘됐다! 그런데 기뻐 보이지 않는구나. 무슨 일이야?
남 내 가장 친한 친구 소민이가 오디션에 떨어졌어.
여 오, 너희 둘이 줄곧 같이 연습하지 않았어?
남 응. 그녀는 나한테 노래를 잘 부르는 법을 가르쳐 준 사람이야.
여 알고 있어.
남 그녀는 다음 오디션까지 6개월을 기다려야 해. 그건 너무 길어.

해설 남자는 자신만 오디션에 붙고, 함께 연습하며 자신을 도와준 친구는 오디션에 떨어져 미안한 심정일 것이다.

어휘 audition 오디션   pass (시험 등에) 합격하다   fail (시험 등에) 떨어지다   practice 연습하다   all the time 내내, 줄곧 teach(-tought-taught) 가르쳐 주다   scared 무서워하는 nervous 긴장한, 초조해하는   satisfied 만족하는

04   ④

M Sue, how was the book fair last weekend?
W It was so great. You know, Suzanne Jones, my favorite author.
M You said she is your role model. Did you meet her?
W Yes! She was having a book signing at the fair.
M Great. Did you get her autograph?
W Yes! I waited for an hour, but it was worth it.
M Awesome. Did you take a picture with her, too?
W No. The line was too long, so they didn't allow pictures.

남 Sue, 지난 주말에 도서 박람회 어땠니?
여 정말 좋았어. 너 Suzanne Jones 알지, 내가 가장 좋아하는 작가.
남 그녀가 너의 롤 모델이라고 얘기했잖아. 그녀를 만났니?
여 응! 그녀가 박람회장에서 책 사인회를 하고 있었어.
남 좋다. 그녀의 사인을 받았니?
여 응! 한 시간 동안 기다렸지만 그럴 만한 가치가 있었어.
남 멋지다. 그녀와 사진도 찍었니?
여 아니. 줄이 너무 길어서 사람들이 사진을 못 찍게 했어.

해설 여자는 자신이 가장 좋아하는 작가의 사인을 받았다고 했다.

어휘 book fair 도서 박람회   author 작가   role model 롤 모델   book signing 책 사인회   autograph (유명인의) 사인 worth it 그만한 가치가 있는   allow 허락하다

05 ④

M Hello. I <u>have a reservation</u> for 2 p.m.
W Your name is?
M Steve Kim.
W Okay, Mr. Kim. <u>Have a seat here</u>, please. (*Pause*) So how do you want your hair done?
M I just want a trim.
W <u>How about a perm</u>? Perms for men are popular these days.
M Not this time. Keep the same hairstyle and just trim it, please.

남 안녕하세요. 오후 2시에 예약되어 있어요.
여 성함이 어떻게 되시죠?
남 Steve Kim입니다.
여 네, Kim 씨. 이쪽에 앉으세요. (*잠시 후*) 자, 머리를 어떻게 해 드릴까요?
남 그냥 다듬어 주세요.
여 파마는 어떠세요? 요즘 남성 파마가 인기 있어요.
남 이번엔 안 할래요. 같은 헤어스타일을 유지하고 그냥 다듬어 주세요.

해설 예약자 이름을 확인하고 헤어스타일에 관한 대화를 나누며 머리를 다듬을 수 있는 곳은 미용실이다.

어휘 have a reservation 예약이 되어 있다   have a seat 자리에 앉다   trim (머리를) 다듬기; 다듬다   perm 파마 popular 인기 있는   these days 요즘   keep 유지하다

06 ⑤

W You look very tired. What's wrong?
M <u>I can't sleep well</u> these days.
W Why not?
M I'm staying in the school dormitory, but my roommate <u>snores very loudly</u>.
W That sounds terrible. Have you talked to him about it?
M I have. He <u>feels bad about it</u>, but there is not much he can do.
W Why don't you use earplugs? They will help.

여 너 무척 피곤해 보여. 무슨 일 있어?
남 나 요즘 잠을 잘 못 자.
여 왜?
남 나는 학교 기숙사에서 지내고 있는데, 내 룸메이트가 코를 엄청 시끄럽게 골아.
여 괴롭겠다. 그것에 대해 그에게 이야기해 봤니?
남 했지. 그도 그것에 대해 미안해 하는데, 그가 할 수 있는 게 별로 없어.
여 귀마개를 사용하는 게 어때? 도움이 될 거야.

해설 룸메이트가 코를 시끄럽게 골아서 잠을 잘 못 잔다는 남자에게 여자는 귀마개를 사용해 보라고 제안했다.

어휘 these days 요즘   stay 머무르다, 지내다   dormitory 기숙사   roommate 룸메이트   snore 코를 골다   loudly 시끄럽게   earplugs 귀마개   help 도움이 되다

07 ①

W What are you making, Dad?
M I'm making fruit salad for the picnic. Is there <u>anything you want to eat</u>?
W Um, I want an egg sandwich.
M I can <u>make one for you</u>. Bring me some boiled eggs, the mayonnaise, and some bread.
W Okay. (*Pause*) I have <u>the boiled eggs and mayo</u> here, but there's no bread left. I'll go out to get some now.
M Great. Thanks.

여 뭘 만들고 계세요, 아빠?
남 소풍을 위해 과일 샐러드를 만들고 있어. 먹고 싶은 것이 있니?
여 음, 달걀 샌드위치를 먹고 싶어요.
남 내가 만들어 줄 수 있어. 삶은 달걀, 마요네즈, 그리고 빵 좀 가져오렴.
여 네. (*잠시 후*) 삶은 달걀과 마요네즈는 여기 있는데, 남아 있는 빵이 없어요. 지금 나가서 좀 사 올게요.
남 좋아. 고맙구나.

해설 남아 있는 빵이 없어서 여자는 나가서 빵을 사 오겠다고 했다.

어휘 fruit 과일   picnic 소풍   boiled 삶은   mayonnaise (=mayo) 마요네즈   bread 빵   left 남아 있는(leave의 과거분사)

08 ②

M Honey, <u>are you busy now</u>?
W No, I'm just reading. Why?
M We have to <u>do some household chores</u>. My parents are coming over.
W You're right. I'll wash the dishes.
M <u>You don't have to</u>. I already did them.
W Then what do you want me to do?
M Will you vacuum the house? <u>I'll buy some food</u> at the store.
W Okay. I'll do that now.

남 여보, 지금 바빠요?
여 아니요, 그냥 책 읽고 있어요. 왜요?
남 우리 집안일을 좀 해야 해요. 부모님이 오실 거예요.
여 맞아요. 내가 설거지를 할게요.
남 그럴 필요 없어요. 내가 이미 했어요.
여 그럼 내가 뭘 하면 좋겠어요?
남 진공청소기로 집을 청소해 줄래요? 나는 가게에 가서 음식을 좀 살게요.
여 알았어요. 지금 할게요.

해설 남자가 진공청소기로 집을 청소해 달라고 부탁하자 여자는 지금 하겠다고 답했다.

어휘 do household chores 집안일을 하다   parents 부모   come over 들르다, 오다   wash the dishes 설거지하다   already 이미, 벌써   vacuum 진공청소기로 청소하다

09 ⑤

M Welcome to today's special lecture. Nowadays, many people are worrying about fine dust, one of our society's serious problems. I hope today's lecture can help you understand the issue better. Julie Parker is an environmentalist who has been studying this issue both in China and Korea. Let's give a big hand for today's guest lecturer, Julie Parker.

남 오늘의 특별 강연에 오신 것을 환영합니다. 요즘, 많은 분들이 우리 사회의 심각한 문제 중 하나인 미세 먼지에 대해 걱정하고 계시죠. 오늘의 강연을 통해 여러분이 이 문제를 더 잘 이해할 수 있기를 바랍니다. Julie Parker는 중국과 한국에서 이 문제를 연구해 온 환경 운동가입니다. 오늘의 초청 강사인 Julie Parker를 큰 박수로 맞이해 주십시오.

해설 남자는 미세 먼지에 관한 강연이 이어질 것이라고 안내하며 초청 강사를 소개하고 있다.

어휘 lecture 강연, 강의　nowadays 요즘　worry about ~에 대해 걱정하다　fine dust 미세 먼지　society 사회　serious 심각한　issue 쟁점, 문제　environmentalist 환경 운동가　give a big hand 큰 박수를 보내다　guest 게스트, (프로그램 등에) 초대 받은 사람　lecturer 강연자, 강사

10 ②

W Eric, have you ever tried skydiving?
M Yes, I have. Actually, I did it last month.
W Really? How was it?
M It was so thrilling! You must try it.
W Awesome. I really want to try it.
M Check out "Freefall Skydiving" on the Net. You can make a reservation on the website.
W Cool. Send me the address later.
M I will. Oh, don't forget to download a discount coupon, too.
W That's a good tip. Thanks.

여 Eric, 너 스카이다이빙을 해 본 적 있니?
남 응, 해 봤어. 사실, 지난달에 했어.
여 정말? 어땠어?
남 정말 짜릿했어! 너도 꼭 해 봐.
여 멋지다. 나도 정말 해 보고 싶어.
남 인터넷에서 'Freefall Skydiving'을 찾아봐. 웹사이트에서 예약할 수 있어.
여 좋다. 나중에 나한테 주소 보내 줘.
남 그럴게. 참, 할인 쿠폰을 다운로드하는 것도 잊지 마.
여 그거 좋은 팁이다. 고마워.

해설 남자는 스카이다이빙을 한 장소는 언급하지 않았다.

어휘 skydive 스카이다이빙을 하다　thrilling 아주 신나는, 흥분되는　check out 확인하다, 조사하다　the Net(= the Internet) 인터넷　make a reservation 예약하다　address 주소　forget to ~하는 것을 잊다　discount coupon 할인 쿠폰　tip 조언, 팁

11 ④

W How can we celebrate Mom and Dad's wedding anniversary?
M Why don't we make a photo album for them?
W That's a great idea. They will love it.
M Let's write a letter and make a special cake, too.
W Make a cake? Won't that be hard?
M I have baked a cake with my baking club. I think I can do it.
W Good. Then I will decorate the house with balloons.
M Fantastic.

여 엄마 아빠 결혼기념일을 어떻게 축하할까?
남 부모님을 위한 사진첩을 만드는 게 어때?
여 그거 좋은 생각이다. 아주 좋아하실 거야.
남 편지를 쓰고 특별한 케이크도 만들자.
여 케이크를 만들자고? 어렵지 않을까?
남 나 제빵 동아리에서 케이크를 구워 봤어. 내가 할 수 있을 것 같아.
여 좋아. 그럼 나는 풍선으로 집을 장식할게.
남 아주 좋아.

해설 케이크는 남자가 직접 만들기로 했다.

어휘 celebrate 축하하다, 기념하다　wedding anniversary 결혼기념일　photo album 사진첩　hard 어려운　bake 굽다　decorate 장식하다　balloon 풍선

12 ④

(*Telephone rings.*)
M Best T-shirt. How may I help you?
W Hello. I want to change my order.
M Your name, please?
W Michelle Miller. I ordered thirty Wonder Woman T-shirts.
M Okay, let me check. (*Typing sound*) How do you want to change it?
W I want to order twenty, not thirty.
M All right. Your order has been changed. Anything else?
W That's it. Thank you.

(*전화벨이 울린다.*)
남 Best T-shirt입니다. 무엇을 도와드릴까요?
여 안녕하세요. 제 주문을 변경하고 싶어요.
남 성함이 어떻게 되시죠?
여 Michelle Miller입니다. 저는 Wonder Woman 티셔츠 30개를 주문했어요.
남 네, 확인해 보겠습니다. (*타이핑하는 소리*) 어떻게 바꾸고 싶으세요?
여 30개가 아니라 20개를 주문하고 싶어요.
남 알겠습니다. 주문이 변경되었습니다. 또 다른 건요?
여 그게 다예요. 고맙습니다.

해설 여자는 티셔츠 주문 수량을 30개에서 20개로 변경하기 위해 전화했다.

어휘 change 변경하다　order 주문; 주문하다　T-shirt 티셔츠

check 확인하다   else 또 다른, 그 밖의

13 ④

M Hi. I'd like to buy some kiwis. How much are they?
W A pack of kiwis is $8. There are ten kiwis in a pack.
M I'll take one pack.
W Okay. Anything else?
M How much are the apples?
W These are $1 each, and those organic ones are twice as expensive.
M I'll buy the organic ones. Five organic apples, please.
W So a pack of kiwis and five organic apples, right?
M That's correct. Here you are.

남 안녕하세요. 키위를 사고 싶은데요. 얼마예요?
여 키위 한 팩에 8달러입니다. 한 팩에 키위 10개가 있어요.
남 한 팩 살게요.
여 네. 다른 건요?
남 사과는 얼마인가요?
여 이 사과들은 각 1달러이고 저기 유기농 사과들은 두 배 비싸요.
남 유기농 사과를 살게요. 유기농 사과 5개 주세요.
여 그러니까 키위 한 팩과 유기농 사과 5개군요, 맞지요?
남 맞아요. 여기 있습니다.

해설 키위는 한 팩에 8달러이고 유기농 사과는 한 개에 2달러이다. 남자는 키위 한 팩과 유기농 사과 5개를 사겠다고 했으므로 총 18달러를 지불해야 한다.

어휘 pack 팩, 상자   else 또 다른, 그 밖의   each 각각   organic 유기농의   twice 두 배로   expensive 비싼   correct 맞는, 정확한

14 ②

M Hi. I think I've got a cold. Could you give me something for it?
W What are your symptoms?
M I have a runny nose and a sore throat.
W Do you have a fever?
M No, I don't.
W Okay. I can give you these pills. Take two three times a day.
M All right. How much is it?
W It's $5.

남 안녕하세요. 제가 감기에 걸린 것 같아요. 뭔가 좀 주시겠어요?
여 증상이 어떤가요?
남 콧물이 나오고 목이 따끔거려요.
여 열이 있나요?
남 아니요, 안 나요.
여 그러시군요. 이 알약을 드릴게요. 하루 세 번 두 알씩 드세요.
남 알겠습니다. 얼마인가요?
여 5달러입니다.

해설 남자가 감기에 걸린 것 같다고 하자 여자는 남자의 증상을 묻고 약을 복용하는 방법을 설명하고 있으므로, 두 사람은 약사와 환자의 관계이다.

어휘 cold 감기   symptom 증상   have a runny nose 콧물이 나오다   have a sore throat 목이 따끔거리다   have a fever 열이 나다   pill 알약

15 ③

(Cellphone rings.)

M Hello, Mom. It's me. I'm in big trouble.
W Oh, Martin, what's wrong?
M I saved my presentation file on my USB, but I left it at home. It's on my desk.
W Oh, do you want me to bring it to school?
M Can you just email me the file? The file name is "Science Project."
W No problem. I'll do it right away.
M Thank you so much, Mom.

(휴대 전화가 울린다.)

남 여보세요, 엄마. 저예요. 저 큰일 났어요.
여 오, Martin, 무슨 일이니?
남 제 USB에 발표 파일을 저장했는데 집에 두고 왔어요. USB는 책상 위에 있어요.
여 아, 내가 학교로 USB를 가져다줄까?
남 그냥 이메일로 파일을 보내 주실 수 있어요? 파일명은 'Science Project'예요.
여 그래. 지금 바로 할게.
남 정말 고마워요, 엄마.

해설 남자는 USB에 저장된 파일을 이메일로 보내 달라고 부탁했다.

어휘 be in trouble 어려움에 처하다   save 저장하다   presentation 발표   leave(-left-left) 두고 오다   bring 가져다주다   email 이메일을 보내다   right away 즉시, 바로

16 ⑤

M Susan, what club are you in?
W I'm in the book club. I like reading.
M What kinds of books do you read in the club?
W We read all kinds of books, but mostly novels.
M Did you join so you would read more books?
W No. I joined it because I like to discuss the books I read with others.
M It sounds like the perfect club for you.

남 Susan, 너 무슨 동아리에 있니?
여 나는 독서 동아리에 있어. 난 독서를 좋아해.
남 동아리에서는 무슨 종류의 책을 읽니?
여 우리는 모든 종류의 책을 읽지만, 주로 소설을 읽어.
남 너는 더 많은 책을 읽으려고 가입했니?
여 아니. 나는 내가 읽은 책에 대해 다른 사람들과 토론하는 것을 좋아해서 가입했어.
남 너에게 딱 맞는 동아리인 것 같다.

해설 여자는 자신이 읽은 책에 대해 다른 사람들과 토론하는 것을 좋아해서 독서 동아리에 가입했다고 했다.

어휘 club 동아리   kind 종류   mostly 주로   novel 소설   join 가입하다   discuss 토론하다   others 다른 사람들   sound like ~처럼 들리다   perfect 완벽한

17 ⑤

W Hello, students. The graduation music festival for this year is going to be held on February 15 in the auditorium. This festival is for everyone who will graduate from Narae Middle School this year. All third-grade students will participate. Each class will do a singing and dancing performance. It must be less than five minutes. Prepare well and see you at the festival!

여 안녕하세요, 학생 여러분. 올해의 졸업 음악 축제는 2월 15일에 강당에서 열릴 것입니다. 이 축제는 올해 나래 중학교를 졸업하는 모두를 위한 것입니다. 모든 3학년 학생들이 참여할 것입니다. 각 학급은 노래와 춤 공연을 할 것입니다. 공연은 반드시 5분 이내여야 합니다. 준비 잘 하시고 축제에서 만나요!

해설 여자는 졸업 음악 축제에 참가하는 학급 수는 언급하지 않았다.

어휘 graduation 졸업   festival 축제   be held 열리다, 개최하다   auditorium 강당   graduate from ~을 졸업하다   participate 참가하다   performance 공연   less than ~보다 더 적은   prepare 준비하다

18 ⑤

① W Have you been to Namsan Seoul Tower?
  M No, I haven't.
② W Let's take a picture here.
  M Good. Let me use my smartphone camera.
③ W Can I take pictures during the concert?
  M I'm sorry. You're not allowed to do that.
④ W What do you do in your free time?
  M I usually watch Korean dramas.
⑤ W Is it okay to take pictures here?
  M No. Taking pictures is not allowed in this museum.

① 여 너는 남산서울타워에 가 본 적이 있니?
  남 아니, 없어.
② 여 여기에서 사진 찍자.
  남 좋아. 내 스마트폰 카메라를 사용할게.
③ 여 콘서트 중에 사진을 찍어도 되나요?
  남 죄송합니다. 그러실 수 없습니다.
④ 여 너는 여가 시간에 무엇을 하니?
  남 나는 보통 한국 드라마를 시청해.
⑤ 여 여기에서 사진을 찍어도 되나요?
  남 아니요. 이 박물관에서는 사진 촬영이 허용되지 않습니다.

해설 박물관에서 사진 촬영을 금지하는 상황이다.

어휘 have been to ~에 가 본 적이 있다   take a picture 사진을 찍다   during ~ 동안   be allowed to ~하는 것이 허용되다   free time 여가 시간   usually 보통, 대개   museum 박물관

19 ④

M I'm planning to learn sign language. Are you interested in joining me?
W Sign language? What for?

M I think it'll be useful for my volunteer work next semester.
W Where are you going to learn it?
M At the community center. There is a class for it.
W Sounds like it's a good chance. Can I take the class?
M Sure. Sign up before Wednesday.

남 나는 수화를 배울 계획이야. 나랑 함께할래?
여 수화? 무엇 때문에?
남 다음 학기 봉사 활동에 유용할 것 같아.
여 어디에서 배울 거니?
남 주민 회관에서. 수화 수업이 있어.
여 좋은 기회일 것 같네. 나도 수업을 들어도 될까?
남 물론이지. 수요일 전에 신청해.

해설 여자가 자신도 수화 수업을 들을 수 있는지 물었으므로 이에 대한 긍정 또는 부정의 응답이 와야 한다.
① 나는 그것을 기대하고 있어.
② 넌 영어를 배워야 해.
③ 아니. 그녀는 못 올 것 같아.
⑤ 수화는 배우기 어려워.

어휘 be planning to ~할 계획이다   sign language 수화   be interested in ~에 관심이 있다   useful 유용한   volunteer work 자원봉사 활동   semester 학기   community center 주민 회관   chance 기회   take a class 수업을 듣다   look forward to ~을 기대하다   sign up 신청하다   difficult 어려운

20 ②

W I don't want to cook. Let's just order something.
M Good idea. What do you want to eat?
W I feel like fried chicken or hamburgers.
M Well, you know, I'm trying to lose weight.
W All right. Then what should we eat?
M How about bibimbap? It's lighter and healthier.
W Okay. Do you know the number for the delivery service?
M No. We'll have to look it up.

여 요리하기 싫다. 뭐 시켜 먹자.
남 좋아. 뭐 먹고 싶어?
여 난 프라이드치킨이나 햄버거를 먹고 싶어.
남 글쎄. 너도 알다시피 나 살 빼는 중이잖아.
여 알겠어. 그럼 뭘 먹어야 하지?
남 비빔밥 어때? 더 가볍고 건강에도 더 좋잖아.
여 그래. 너 배달 서비스 번호 알고 있어?
남 아니. 우리는 그것을 찾아봐야 해.

해설 여자가 배달 서비스의 번호를 아는지 물었으므로 이에 대한 긍정 또는 부정의 응답이 와야 한다.
① 나도 쌀국수를 더 좋아해.
③ 너는 살 뺄 필요 없어.
④ 죄송합니다. 전화 잘못 거셨어요.
⑤ 알겠습니다. 30분 이상 걸릴 겁니다.

어휘 cook 요리하다   order 주문하다   feel like ~을 하고

〔갖고〕 싶다   lose weight 체중을 줄이다   light 가벼운
healthy 건강에 좋은   delivery 배달   prefer ~을 더 좋아하다
rice noodles 쌀국수   look up 찾아보다

Review Test
pp.42~43

Word Check
01회

01 예상되는	02 등록하다
03 줄무늬	04 소포
05 (신문·잡지의) 글, 기사	06 자원봉사 활동
07 쓰레기	08 건강을 유지하다
09 (어떤 곳에) 처음 온 사람	10 신청하다
11 버려진, 유기된	12 환불을 받다
13 competition	14 safety
15 remind	16 take medicine
17 recommend	18 receipt
19 physical examination	20 available
21 suffer	22 belongings
23 elderly	24 voice

Expression Check

25 turn into	26 take a walk
27 make an, reservation	28 hand in
29 get better	30 was, satisfied with

Word Check
02회

01 하루 종일	02 오디션
03 수화	04 도서 박람회
05 아주 신나는, 흥분되는	06 (유명인의) 사인
07 기숙사	08 삶은
09 코를 골다	10 진공청소기로 청소하다
11 찾아보다	12 미세 먼지
13 these days	14 celebrate
15 performance	16 pack
17 organic	18 scared
19 symptom	20 presentation
21 lecture	22 wedding anniversary
23 correct	24 auditorium

Expression Check

25 around the corner	26 have a reservation
27 Check out	28 have, a sore throat
29 in, trouble	30 graduate from

실전 모의고사 03회
pp.44~51

01 ①	02 ④	03 ③	04 ②	05 ①
06 ④	07 ③	08 ②	09 ④	10 ③
11 ①	12 ⑤	13 ④	14 ③	15 ③
16 ③	17 ④	18 ④	19 ③	20 ⑤

01 ①

W Good morning. This is Sandra Kim with the weather forecast. Today will be clear and sunny all day long. It's perfect weather for a picnic. But tomorrow, it will be cloudy in the morning, and we expect heavy rain in the afternoon. So don't forget to bring your umbrella when you go out. The rain will continue until the day after tomorrow.

여 안녕하세요. 일기 예보의 Sandra Kim입니다. 오늘은 하루 종일 맑고 화창한 날이 되겠습니다. 소풍 가기에 완벽한 날씨입니다. 하지만 내일 오전에는 흐릴 것이고, 오후에는 폭우가 예상됩니다. 그러므로 외출하실 때 우산 챙기시는 것을 잊지 마십시오. 비는 내일모레까지 계속되겠습니다.

해설 내일 오후에는 폭우가 예상된다고 했다.

어휘 weather forecast 일기 예보   perfect 완벽한   picnic 소풍   heavy rain 폭우   bring 가져가다   umbrella 우산   go out 외출하다, 나가다   continue 계속되다   until ~까지   the day after tomorrow 내일모레

02 ④

M Thank you for coming to our art exhibition.
W You're welcome. There are so many beautiful paintings.
M All of the members of the Maestro Art Club worked so hard.
W Which one is yours?
M I like nature, so I drew many flowers.
W Oh, is that one yours? The red flowers in the vase?
M No, that one's not mine. I drew a rose garden with a few butterflies.
W I found it. I like your painting!

남 저희 미술 전시회에 와 주셔서 감사합니다.
여 천만에요. 아름다운 그림들이 많이 있네요.
남 Maestro Art Club의 모든 회원들이 아주 열심히 작업했습니다.
여 어느 것이 당신의 그림인가요?
남 저는 자연을 좋아해서, 꽃을 많이 그렸어요.
여 오, 저것이 당신의 그림인가요? 꽃병에 있는 빨간 꽃들이요?
남 아니요, 저 그림은 제 것이 아니에요. 저는 나비가 몇 마리 있는 장미 정원을 그렸어요.
여 찾았어요. 당신의 그림이 마음에 들어요!

해설 남자는 나비가 있는 장미 정원을 그렸다고 했다.

어휘 exhibition 전시회   painting 그림   member 회원
work 작업하다   hard 열심히   nature 자연   vase 꽃병
garden 정원   a few 어느 정도, 조금   butterfly 나비

어휘 search for ~을 찾다   how to ~하는 방법   simple
간단한   enter 입력하다   key word 주제어   list 목록   show
up 나타나다   borrow 빌리다   up to ~까지   for ~ 동안

03 ③

W   Did you find out what was wrong with my computer?
M   Yes. It was a computer virus.
W   Thank you. Is my computer clean now?
M   Yes, but I'm afraid the virus erased everything on your computer.
W   Really? But I didn't back up any files. Can you recover any of them?
M   There's no way to recover any of the files.
W   Oh, no! There are so many important files that I need tomorrow!

여   제 컴퓨터의 문제가 무엇인지 알아내셨나요?
남   네. 컴퓨터 바이러스였어요.
여   고맙습니다. 이제 제 컴퓨터는 치료됐나요?
남   네, 그런데 유감스럽게도 바이러스가 고객님의 컴퓨터에 있던 모든 것을 지워 버렸어요.
여   정말이요? 저는 파일을 하나도 백업하지 않았는데요. 파일들 중 어느 하나라도 복원할 수 있나요?
남   어떤 파일도 복구할 수 있는 방법은 없어요.
여   오, 안 돼요! 내일 필요한 중요한 파일들이 많이 있단 말이에요!

해설 파일들을 백업해 두지 않았는데 컴퓨터 바이러스 때문에 모든 파일이 지워져서 여자는 좌절감을 느꼈을 것이다.

어휘 find out 발견하다, 알아내다   erase 지우다   back up (파일 등을) 백업하다   recover 복구하다   important 중요한   frustrated 좌절감을 느끼는   relieved 안도하는   curious 궁금해하는

04 ②

W   Excuse me. Can you help me find some books?
M   You can search for books on the computer.
W   I don't know how to use it.
M   It's very simple. Just enter a few key words, and a list of books will show up.
W   Oh, I see.
M   And the book code tells you where it is.
W   Thank you. How many books can I borrow?
M   You can borrow up to five books for two weeks.

여   실례합니다. 책 찾는 것 좀 도와주시겠어요?
남   컴퓨터에서 책을 검색하실 수 있어요.
여   사용하는 방법을 모르겠어요.
남   아주 간단해요. 주제어를 입력하면, 책 목록이 나타날 거예요.
여   아, 그렇군요.
남   그리고 책 코드를 보면 책이 어디에 있는지 알 수 있어요.
여   고맙습니다. 책을 몇 권 빌릴 수 있나요?
남   2주 동안 다섯 권까지 빌리실 수 있습니다.

해설 책을 찾는 방법과 대출 가능한 도서의 수에 대해 이야기하고 있으므로 도서관에서 이루어지는 대화이다.

05 ①

W   You don't look good. What's wrong?
M   I'm upset with my mom. She always tells me to study.
W   Most parents talk like that.
M   I think I study enough. I don't even have any free time on weekends. But my mom wants me to study more.
W   You must feel a little depressed.
M   I'm really stressed out about it. What should I do?
W   Why don't you tell your dad about how you feel?

여   너 기분이 안 좋아 보여. 무슨 일 있어?
남   나는 우리 엄마한테 화났어. 엄마는 항상 나에게 공부하라고 말씀하시거든.
여   대부분의 부모님들이 그렇게 말씀하시잖아.
남   내 생각에 난 충분히 공부를 하고 있어. 주말조차 자유 시간이 없어. 그런데 엄마는 내가 더 공부하기를 원하셔.
여   좀 우울하겠구나.
남   난 이것 때문에 정말 스트레스 받아. 내가 어떻게 해야 하지?
여   네가 어떤 기분인지 너희 아빠한테 말씀드려 보는 게 어때?

해설 엄마 때문에 스트레스를 받는다는 남자에게 여자는 아빠에게 이야기해 보라고 조언했다.

어휘 be upset with ~에게 화가 나다   most 대부분의   parents 부모   enough 충분히   even 심지어, ~조차   free time 자유 시간   depressed 우울한   be stressed out 스트레스를 받다

06 ④

M   Sandy, how was your trip?
W   I wanted to stay there longer. It was such a beautiful place.
M   Sounds good. What did you do there?
W   I spent most of my time sunbathing and swimming. I also went hiking in the mountains.
M   Wow, it seems like you had such a great time.
W   Yeah. But what I liked the most was the beautiful sunset. I'll never forget the setting sun.
M   Wonderful.

남   Sandy, 여행 어땠니?
여   그곳에 더 오래 있고 싶었어. 정말 아름다운 곳이었거든.
남   좋았겠다. 거기서 뭘 했니?
여   난 일광욕하고 수영하는 데 대부분의 시간을 보냈어. 그리고 하이킹도 했어.
남   우와, 좋은 시간을 보냈던 것 같네.
여   응. 그래도 내가 가장 좋았던 건 아름다운 석양이었어. 나는 그 석양을 절대 잊지 못할 거야.
남   멋지다.

해설 여자는 아름다운 석양이 가장 좋았다고 했다.

어휘 sunbathe 일광욕하다   go hiking 하이킹을 가다
mountain 산   (the) most 가장, 최고로   sunset(setting
sun) 일몰, 석양   never 절대 ∼ 않다   forget 잊다

07 ③

W You look so worried. What's up?
M One of my best friends is mad at me.
W What happened?
M I left a comment on her blog, and she didn't like it.
W What did you write?
M Nothing special. It was just a joke. I thought she would laugh at it.
W I think you should call or meet her to say sorry.
M You're right. I have to call her right now.

여 너 너무 걱정스러워 보여. 무슨 일이야?
남 내 가장 친한 친구들 중 한 명이 나한테 몹시 화가 났어.
여 무슨 일이 있었는데?
남 내가 그녀의 블로그에 댓글을 남겼는데, 그녀가 그걸 마음에 들어 하지 않았어.
여 뭐라고 썼는데?
남 특별한 건 아니야. 그냥 농담이었어. 나는 그녀가 그걸 보고 웃을 줄 알았어.
여 내 생각에 너는 그녀에게 전화를 하거나 만나서 미안하다고 해야 할 것 같아.
남 네 말이 맞아. 지금 당장 그녀에게 전화를 해야겠어.

해설 남자는 자신에게 화가 난 친구에게 지금 당장 전화해야겠다고 했다.

어휘 be mad at ∼에게 몹시 화가 나다   happen 일어나다, 생기다   leave a comment 댓글을 남기다   joke 농담
laugh at (∼을 보고) 웃다, 비웃다

08 ②

W Today, I'd like to introduce my cousin Grace. She was born in the U.S. She studied design at university and is now working as a wedding dress designer. She's very passionate about her job. She wants to have her own brand someday. She is outgoing, humorous, and very friendly to everyone. I like her very much.

여 오늘 저는 제 사촌인 Grace를 소개하려고 합니다. 그녀는 미국에서 태어났습니다. 그녀는 대학교에서 디자인을 공부했고 현재 웨딩드레스 디자이너로서 일하고 있습니다. 그녀는 그녀의 일에 대해 매우 열정적입니다. 그녀는 언젠가 자신만의 브랜드를 가지고 싶어 합니다. 그녀는 외향적이고 유머 감각이 있으며, 모든 사람들에게 아주 친절합니다. 저는 그녀를 아주 좋아합니다.

해설 여자는 사촌의 나이는 언급하지 않았다.

어휘 be born 태어나다   university 대학교   work as ∼로서
일하다   designer 디자이너   passionate 열정적인   own
자신의   someday 언젠가   outgoing 외향적인   humorous
유머 감각이 있는   friendly 친절한, 상냥한

09 ④

M Are you planning to learn how to snowboard this winter? It is very important to learn from an expert. We have snowboarding experts who have more than seven years of teaching experience. Join our snowboarding programs and learn the basics of snowboarding in a safe environment. For more information, visit our website at www.snowlover.com.

남 올겨울에 스노보드 타는 법을 배울 계획이신가요? 전문가에게 배우는 것이 아주 중요합니다. 저희는 7년 이상의 교습 경험이 있는 스노보드 전문가들을 보유하고 있습니다. 저희 스노보드 프로그램에 참여하셔서 안전한 환경에서 스노보드의 기초를 배우세요. 더 많은 정보를 원하시면, 저희 웹사이트 www.snowlover.com을 방문하세요.

해설 남자는 스노보드 강습 프로그램을 홍보하고 있다.

어휘 be planning to ∼할 계획이다   learn 배우다   how to
∼하는 방법   snowboard 스노보드를 타다   important 중요한
expert 전문가   experience 경험   basic 기초   safe 안전한
environment 환경   information 정보

10 ③

(Cellphone rings.)
M Hi, Jina. What's up?
W Hey, Brian. Have you seen my text?
M No, I haven't. What was it about?
W Can you print my homework? My printer is out of order.
M No problem. Send it to me by email. When do you need it?
W By tomorrow morning. I have to submit it in English class.
M Okay. I'll bring it to school tomorrow.
W Thank you.

(휴대 전화가 울린다.)
남 안녕, 지나야. 무슨 일이야?
여 야, Brian. 내 문자 메시지 봤어?
남 아니, 못 봤어. 뭐에 대한 것이었는데?
여 내 숙제를 출력해 줄 수 있니? 내 프린터가 고장 났어.
남 문제없어. 나한테 이메일로 보내 줘. 언제 필요한 거야?
여 내일 아침까지. 영어 수업 시간에 제출해야 해.
남 알았어. 내일 학교에 가지고 갈게.
여 고마워.

해설 여자는 프린터가 고장 나서 남자에게 자신의 숙제를 출력해 달라고 부탁하기 위해 전화했다.

어휘 text 문자 메시지   print 출력하다   homework 숙제
out of order 고장이 난   submit 제출하다

11 ①

M Excuse me. Could you take this watch out? I want to take a closer look.

W Sure. This is the newest model, the GX34.
M It's pretty fancy. How much is this?
W It's $100.
M Do you have a cheaper one?
W The GX23 here is $80. This one is a little bigger than the GX34.
M It's okay. I'll take the GX23.
W Okay. Are you a member of our shop? You can get 10% off.
M That's good to hear. Here's my membership card.

남 실례합니다. 이 손목시계 좀 꺼내 주시겠어요? 더 가까이에서 보고 싶어요.
여 물론입니다. 이것은 가장 최신 모델인 GX34예요.
남 꽤 멋지네요. 얼마예요?
여 100달러예요.
남 더 저렴한 것도 있나요?
여 여기 GX23은 80달러입니다. 이건 GX34보다 약간 커요.
남 괜찮아요. GX23을 살게요.
여 알겠습니다. 저희 가게 회원이신가요? 10퍼센트 할인을 받으실 수 있어요.
남 좋네요. 여기 제 회원 카드요.

해설 남자는 80달러인 손목시계를 골랐는데 회원가로 10퍼센트 할인을 받을 수 있으므로, 72달러를 지불해야 한다.

어휘 take out 꺼내다   watch 손목시계   take a look 보다   closer 더 가까운(close의 비교급)   pretty 꽤   fancy 멋진   cheap 저렴한   a little 조금   member 회원   off 할인되어   membership card 회원 카드

12 ⑤

M Welcome to ABC Animal Kingdom, the largest zoo in the country. Many different animals from all over the world welcome you. In a special animal exhibit, you can see pandas from China until June 23. On weekends, you can take part in our special programs such as the Safari Bus Tour or the Baby Animal Encounters. We are open from 10 a.m. to 6 p.m. every day except Mondays. Have fun on your adventure at the zoo. Thank you.

남 국내에서 가장 큰 동물원인 ABC Animal Kingdom에 오신 것을 환영합니다. 세계 각국에서 온 많은 다양한 동물들이 당신을 환영합니다. 특별한 동물 전시장에서는, 6월 23일까지 중국에서 온 판다를 보실 수 있습니다. 주말에는, '사파리 버스 투어'나 '아기 동물 만나기'와 같은 특별한 프로그램에 참여하실 수 있습니다. 우리 동물원은 월요일을 제외하고 매일 오전 10시부터 오후 6시까지 개장합니다. 동물원에서 여러분의 모험을 즐기세요. 고맙습니다.

해설 동물원은 월요일에는 개장하지 않는다고 했다.

어휘 kingdom 왕국   country 나라   different 각각 다른, 각양각색의   welcome 환영하다   exhibit 전시회   take part in ~에 참여하다   such as ~와 같은   encounter 만남, 접촉   except ~을 제외하고   adventure 모험

13 ④

W Excuse me.
M Yes. How may I help you?
W I ordered my steak medium, but this one is overcooked.
M Oh, I'm sorry. I'll get you a new one.
W Thank you. And the people at the table next to me are too loud.
M Do you want to change your table?
W That would be nice.
M Just wait a moment, please. I'll come back in a minute.

여 저기요.
남 네. 무엇을 도와드릴까요?
여 스테이크를 중간 굽기로 주문했는데, 이건 너무 익었어요.
남 아, 죄송합니다. 새것을 가져다드릴게요.
여 고맙습니다. 그리고 제 옆 테이블에 있는 사람들이 너무 시끄러워요.
남 자리를 옮기시겠어요?
여 그게 좋겠어요.
남 잠시만 기다려 주세요. 곧 돌아오겠습니다.

해설 식당에서 여자가 음식과 자리에 대한 불만 사항을 이야기하고 있고 남자가 이에 응대하고 있으므로, 두 사람은 식당 종업원과 손님의 관계이다.

어휘 order 주문하다   medium (스테이크가) 중간 정도로 구워진   overcook 너무 오래 익히다   next to ~ 옆에   loud 시끄러운   come back 돌아오다   in a minute 곧, 즉시

14 ③

W Dad, can I go to a bookstore today? I want to buy some books.
M Are you going to the one in Gangnam Station?
W No. I'm going to Gwanghwamun.
M Why? The bookstore in Gangnam Station is nearer.
W I don't want to transfer from the subway to the bus.
M But it will take too long to get there.
W I don't mind at all. I will read a book in the subway.
M Okay. Take care.

여 아빠, 저 오늘 서점에 가도 돼요? 책을 좀 사고 싶어요.
남 강남역에 있는 서점으로 갈 거니?
여 아니요. 광화문으로 갈 거예요.
남 왜? 강남역에 있는 서점이 더 가깝잖아.
여 지하철에서 버스로 갈아타고 싶지 않아요.
남 그래도 거기 도착하는 데 너무 오래 걸릴 거야.
여 상관없어요. 저는 지하철 안에서 책을 읽을 거예요.
남 알았다. 조심해라.

해설 여자는 지하철에서 버스로 갈아타고 싶지 않아서 지하철만 타고도 갈 수 있는 서점에 간다고 했다.

어휘 bookstore 서점   nearer 더 가까운(near의 비교급)   transfer 갈아타다, 환승하다   not ~ at all 전혀 ~ 아닌   mind 상관하다, 신경 쓰다   subway 지하철

15 ③

W Are you busy now?
M Not really. Why?
W I'm going to volunteer at an elderly care center and bring some homemade cookies.
M How nice of you! Do you want me to help you bake the cookies?
W No. I've already baked them. Could you just help me wrap each cookie individually?
M Sure.

여 너 지금 바빠?
남 아니. 왜?
여 나 노인 복지 회관에 자원봉사를 하러 갈 건데 집에서 만든 쿠키를 좀 가져가려고 해.
남 너 참 착하구나! 내가 쿠키 굽는 걸 도와줄까?
여 아니. 내가 이미 다 구웠어. 쿠키를 각각 따로 포장하는 걸 도와줄 수 있어?
남 물론이지.

해설 여자는 남자에게 쿠키를 각각 따로 포장하는 것을 도와 달라고 부탁했다.

어휘 volunteer 자원봉사를 하다   elderly care center 노인 복지 회관   bring 가져가다   homemade 집에서 만든, 수제의   bake 굽다   wrap 포장하다   individually 각각 따로

16 ③

① W May I take your order?
  M I'd like to have a steak with a salad.
② W I have a stomachache and feel dizzy.
  M Take these pills three times a day.
③ W I hope you get well soon.
  M Thanks. The doctor said I have to stay here for another week.
④ W May I help you?
  M I'm looking for a present for my girlfriend.
⑤ W Excuse me. Is there a hospital near here?
  M Sorry. I don't know this neighborhood well.

① 여 주문하시겠어요?
  남 샐러드와 스테이크 주세요.
② 여 배가 아프고 어지러워요.
  남 하루에 세 번 이 알약을 드세요.
③ 여 네가 곧 낫기를 바라.
  남 고마워. 의사 선생님이 내가 일주일 더 있어야 한다고 하셨어.
④ 여 무엇을 도와드릴까요?
  남 제 여자 친구한테 줄 선물을 찾고 있어요.
⑤ 여 실례합니다. 이 근처에 병원이 있나요?
  남 죄송합니다. 저도 이 동네를 잘 몰라요.

해설 병문안을 온 사람과 입원한 환자 사이의 대화가 가장 적절하다.

어휘 have a stomachache 배가 아프다   dizzy 어지러운   pill 알약   get well (병이) 낫다   look for ~을 찾다   present 선물   neighborhood 지역, 인근

17 ④

W Let's get something to eat before the movie starts.
M Sounds good.
W I have coupons for a seafood buffet restaurant. Do you like seafood?
M I love seafood. That place is not too far from the theater. Let's go.
W Oh, wait. These coupons are only valid at lunchtime.
M That means we can't use them. It's 5 p.m. now.
W Yeah. What about the pizza place next to the theater?
M All right then.

여 영화가 시작하기 전에 뭘 좀 먹자.
남 좋아.
여 나한테 해산물 뷔페 쿠폰이 있어. 해산물 좋아해?
남 해산물 아주 좋아해. 그곳은 극장에서 많이 멀지도 않네. 가자.
여 아, 잠깐만. 이 쿠폰은 점심시간에만 유효해.
남 그럼 우리는 사용할 수 없다는 뜻이네. 지금 오후 5시야.
여 그러네. 영화관 옆에 있는 피자집은 어때?
남 그럼 어쩔 수 없지.

해설 쿠폰은 점심시간에만 유효한데 점심시간이 지나 쿠폰을 사용할 수 없어서 두 사람은 뷔페에 가지 못한다.

어휘 coupon 쿠폰   seafood 해산물   buffet restaurant 뷔페식당   far from ~에서 먼   theater 극장   valid 유효한   lunchtime 점심시간   mean 의미하다   next to ~ 옆에

18 ④

W The Summer Night Party is on Saturday, August 1, between 7 p.m. and midnight. It will be held in the main plaza of our resort. Anyone staying in our resort can attend the party for free. Please show us your room key at the entrance. Enjoy the live music with free snacks and drinks. If you need any additional information, please do not hesitate to contact our reception desk.

여 Summer Night Party가 8월 1일 토요일 오후 7시와 자정 사이에 있습니다. 이 파티는 저희 리조트의 메인 광장에서 열립니다. 저희 리조트에서 숙박하시는 분은 누구나 무료로 파티에 참석하실 수 있습니다. 입구에서 저희에게 방 열쇠를 보여 주십시오. 무료 간식과 음료와 함께 라이브 음악을 즐기세요. 추가 정보가 필요하시면, 주저하지 마시고 프런트에 연락하세요.

해설 여자는 경품 행사에 대해서는 언급하지 않았다.

어휘 between A and B A와 B 사이에   midnight 자정   be held 열리다, 개최되다   plaza 광장   resort 리조트   attend 참석하다   for free 무료로   entrance 입구   live 라이브의   additional 추가의   information 정보   hesitate 망설이다   reception desk 접수처, 프런트

19 ③

M Are you interested in baseball?

W Yes. I'm a big fan of the Black Eagles.
M Me, too! That's my favorite baseball team.
W They will play the Blue Hats this weekend for the league championship.
M I know. Why don't we go to the game together?
W Great. Let's meet at 5.
M That's too late. Let's meet at 4.

남 너 야구에 관심 있니?
여 응. 나는 Black Eagles의 열혈 팬이야.
남 나도! Black Eagles는 내가 제일 좋아하는 야구 팀이야.
여 이번 주말에 Blue Hats랑 리그 챔피언십 경기가 있어.
남 알아. 우리 같이 경기 보러 가는 게 어때?
여 좋아. 5시에 만나자.
남 너무 늦어. 4시에 만나자.

해설 약속 시간을 제안하는 말에 대한 응답이 와야 한다.
① 그 말을 들으니 유감이구나.
② 너는 할 수 있을 거라고 확신해.
④ 그 경기는 이미 시작했어.
⑤ 미안하지만 안 돼. 난 숙제를 해야 돼.

어휘 be interested in ~에 관심이 있다   big fan 열혈 팬
league (스포츠 경기의) 리그   championship 선수권 대회

20 ⑤

M I'm worried about my little brother. He uses his smartphone too much.
W How old is he?
M He's only eleven. Last night, he was up all night playing with his phone.
W He should find a way to control himself.
M I agree with you.
W He can download a smartphone control app. It'll help him limit his phone time.
M That's a good idea. Then he'll use his phone less.

남 나는 남동생 때문에 걱정이야. 그는 스마트폰을 너무 많이 써.
여 남동생이 몇 살인데?
남 겨우 열한 살이야. 어젯밤에 그는 스마트폰을 가지고 노느라 밤을 샜어.
여 그는 스스로를 조절하는 방법을 찾아야겠네.
남 네 말에 동의해.
여 그는 스마트폰 조절 앱을 다운로드할 수 있어. 그 앱이 휴대 전화 사용 시간을 제한하는 데 도움을 줄 거야.
남 좋은 생각이다. 그럼 그는 스마트폰을 덜 쓰겠네.

해설 여자가 스마트폰 사용을 제어하는 앱을 다운로드할 것을 제안했으므로 이와 관련된 응답이 와야 한다.
① 다음 기회에.
② 넌 다음에 더 잘할 수 있어.
③ 내가 뭘 해야 할지 모르겠어.
④ 내가 너라면, 난 병원에 갈 거야.

어휘 be worried about ~에 대해 걱정하다   be up all night 밤을 새다   way 방법   control 조절하다; 조절   agree with ~에게 동의하다   limit 제한하다

---

01 ④	02 ③	03 ⑤	04 ⑤	05 ③
06 ④	07 ⑤	08 ③	09 ⑤	10 ④
11 ⑤	12 ③	13 ②	14 ②	15 ④
16 ①	17 ③	18 ③	19 ⑤	20 ①

01 ④

M Good morning. It is a warm but partly cloudy Sunday. However, it will rain starting tomorrow morning, and the temperature will drop to -5°C during the day. The rain will turn into snow at night, and it will snow on Tuesday. Please be careful on the icy roads. The cold will be gone on Wednesday with temperatures recovering to average, and there will be sunny skies.

남 안녕하세요. 오늘은 따뜻하지만 부분적으로 구름이 낀 일요일입니다. 하지만 내일 아침부터는 비가 오겠고, 낮 동안에 기온이 영하 5°C로 떨어지겠습니다. 밤에는 비가 눈으로 바뀌겠으며, 화요일에는 눈이 내리겠습니다. 빙판길을 조심하세요. 수요일에는 평년 기온을 회복하면서 추위가 풀리겠고, 하늘은 맑겠습니다.

해설 화요일에는 눈이 내릴 것이라고 했다.

어휘 partly 부분적으로   temperature 기온   drop 떨어지다   during ~ 동안   turn into ~로 변하다   be careful 조심하다   icy 얼음으로 덮인   road 길   recover 회복하다   average 평균

02 ③

M Julie, who is your homeroom teacher this year?
W Mr. Brown, my math teacher.
M Mr. Brown? I don't know him.
W He's right over there with some other teachers. He's wearing glasses.
M There are two men wearing glasses. Do you mean the man with a beard?
W No, he's the science teacher.
M Now I can see him. He has wavy hair, and he's wearing a black suit, right?
W That's right.

남 Julie, 올해 네 담임 선생님은 누구시니?
여 수학 선생님이신 Brown 선생님이야.
남 Brown 선생님? 나는 그분을 몰라.
여 저기 다른 선생님들과 같이 계셔. 안경을 쓰고 계셔.
남 안경 쓴 남자분이 두 분 계신데. 턱수염 있는 분을 말하는 거야?
여 아니, 그분은 과학 선생님이셔.
남 이제 알겠다. 웨이브가 있는 머리에 검정색 정장을 입고 계신 분이구나, 맞지?
여 맞아.

해설 여자의 올해 담임 선생님은 안경을 쓰고, 웨이브가 있는 머리에 검정색 정장을 입고 있는 남자라고 했다.

어휘 homeroom teacher 담임 선생님   math 수학   wear 입다, 쓰다   glasses 안경   beard 턱수염   science 과학   wavy 웨이브가 있는, 물결 모양의   suit 정장

03 ⑤

W Peter, did you get the results of the singing contest?
M I won second place.
W Really? Congratulations! You must be very proud of yourself.
M Not really, but thanks.
W Why aren't you happy? Because you didn't win first place? Second place is also great!
M Only the first-place winner will have a chance to meet some professional singers.
W Oh, I see.

여 Peter, 노래 경연 대회 결과는 나왔어?
남 나는 2위를 했어.
여 정말? 축하해! 네 자신이 매우 자랑스럽겠다.
남 별로 그렇지는 않지만, 고마워.
여 왜 기뻐하지 않는 거야? 1위를 못했기 때문에? 2위도 대단한 거야!
남 1위를 한 사람만 프로 가수들을 만날 수 있는 기회를 가질 수 있단 말이야.
여 아, 그렇구나.

해설 노래 경연 대회에서 1위를 한 사람에게만 프로 가수들을 만날 수 있는 기회가 주어지는데 남자는 2위를 해서 결과에 만족하지 않는다.

어휘 result 결과   contest 경연 대회   win first(second) place 1(2)위를 하다   be proud of ~을 자랑스러워하다   chance 기회   professional 프로의, 전문적인   ashamed 부끄러운   confused 혼란스러운   unsatisfied 만족하지 않은

04 ⑤

W I went to Udo with my family last week.
M Oh, do you mean the island that is close to Jeju-do?
W That's right. Have you been there?
M I've been there, too. I went horse riding there.
W Great! I wanted to do that, but I couldn't. My younger sister was afraid of it.
M So what did you do there? Cycling?
W We rode an electric scooter and looked around the island. The island is so beautiful.

여 나는 지난주에 가족들이랑 우도에 갔었어.
남 아, 제주도에서 가까운 섬 말하는 거니?
여 맞아. 거기 가 봤니?
남 나도 가 봤어. 난 거기에서 말을 타러 갔었어.
여 좋았겠다! 나도 하고 싶었지만, 못 했어. 내 여동생이 무서워해서.
남 그래서 넌 거기에서 뭘 했어? 자전거 타기?

여 우리는 전동 스쿠터를 타고 섬을 둘러봤어. 그 섬은 정말 아름다워.

해설 여자는 전동 스쿠터를 타고 섬을 둘러봤다고 했다.

어휘 island 섬   close 가까운   go horse riding 말을 타러 가다   be afraid of ~을 무서워하다   cycle 자전거를 타다   electric 전기의, 전동의   scooter 스쿠터   look around 둘러보다

05 ③

M Excuse me, ma'am. How tall is your child?
W About 110 centimeters. Is anything wrong?
M Children under 150 centimeters in height cannot enter the main pool. You and your child should play in the kid's zone.
W Oh, I didn't know that.
M And even children must wear a swimming cap. There's a rental shop next to the entrance.
W I got it. Thank you.

남 실례합니다. 부인. 아이의 키가 몇인가요?
여 약 110센티미터예요. 문제 있나요?
남 키가 150센티미터 이하인 어린이들은 메인 수영장에 들어갈 수 없습니다. 부인과 아이께서는 키즈 존에서 노셔야 합니다.
여 아, 몰랐어요.
남 그리고 어린이들도 수영모를 착용해야 합니다. 입구 옆에 대여점이 있습니다.
여 알겠습니다. 고맙습니다.

해설 신장에 따른 수영장 입장 제한과 수영모 착용에 대한 대화가 이루어지는 곳은 수영장이다.

어휘 child(pl. children) 어린이   under ~ 미만의   height (사람의) 키   enter 들어가다   main 가장 큰, 주된   pool 수영장   kid 아이   zone 구역   even ~조차   swimming cap 수영모   rental shop 대여점   entrance 입구

06 ④

W Thomas, are you interested in going to this photo exhibition?
M What is it about?
W It's about endangered animals all around the world.
M Oh, I'm interested in that issue. Are you going there?
W Yes, with Min tomorrow. Do you want to join us? I have a spare ticket.
M Tomorrow? When will the exhibition end?
W This Sunday, but Min and I only have time to go tomorrow.
M Maybe next time. I have to work on a group project tomorrow.

여 Thomas, 이 사진전에 가는 거 관심 있니?
남 뭐에 관한 사진전이야?
여 전 세계의 멸종 위기 동물들에 관한 거야.
남 오, 나 그 문제에 관심 있어. 너는 거기 갈 거니?
여 응, 내일 민이랑. 너도 같이 갈래? 나한테 표 한 장이 더 있어.

남 내일? 전시회가 언제 끝나?
여 이번 주 일요일, 그런데 민이랑 나는 내일만 갈 시간이 있어.
남 다음에 갈게. 나는 내일은 조별 과제를 해야 해.

해설 여자가 사진전에 함께 가자고 제안했으나 남자는 다른 일정이 있어서 다음에 가겠다고 했다.

어휘 photo exhibition 사진전 endangered 멸종 위기에 처한 be interested in ~에 관심이 있다 issue 문제, 사안 spare 여분의 work on 작업하다 project 과제, 프로젝트

07 ⑤

W Many people experience itchy eyes <u>from time to time</u>. When your eyes are itchy, simply using eye drops <u>can be enough</u>. However, when eye drops don't help your eyes feel better and your eyes are getting redder, <u>you'd better see an eye doctor</u> so that you can get proper treatment right away. <u>In any case</u>, do not touch red itchy eyes with your hands.

여 많은 사람들은 때로 눈이 가려운 증상을 경험합니다. 눈이 가려울 때는, 안약을 사용하는 것만으로도 충분할 수 있습니다. 그러나, 안약이 눈이 나아지는 데 도움이 되지 않고 눈이 점점 빨개진다면, 즉시 적절한 치료를 받을 수 있도록 안과에 가야 합니다. 어떤 경우에도, 빨갛고 가려운 눈을 손으로 만지지 마세요.

해설 여자는 눈이 가려울 때 필요한 조치와 주의 사항을 설명하고 있다.

어휘 experience 경험하다 itchy 가려운 from time to time 가끔, 때때로 eye drop 안약 see an eye doctor 안과에 가다 proper 적절한 treatment 치료, 처치 right away 곧바로, 즉시 case 경우 touch 만지다

08 ③

M We have to plan our summer vacation. Where are we going?
W We went to Korea last year, so I want to go <u>somewhere other than Asia</u> this time.
M How about South America? I think Brazil would be fascinating.
W Isn't it too far? The flight time will be very long.
M Okay. Is there a country you <u>have in mind</u>?
W I'd like to <u>travel around</u> either England or France. What do you think?
M England! It'll be so exciting to watch soccer games there!
W Great. Let's <u>look for plane tickets</u> first.

남 우리 여름휴가를 계획해야 해. 어디로 갈까?
여 작년에 한국을 갔으니까, 이번엔 아시아가 아닌 곳으로 가고 싶어.
남 남미는 어때? 브라질이 매력적일 것 같은데.
여 너무 멀지 않아? 비행시간이 엄청 길 거야.
남 알았어. 생각해 둔 나라 있어?
여 난 영국이나 프랑스를 여행하고 싶어. 네 생각은 어때?
남 영국! 거기서 축구 경기를 보면 정말 신나겠다!

여 좋아. 우선 비행기 표를 찾아보자.

해설 여자가 영국이나 프랑스에 가고 싶다고 하자 남자는 영국에서 축구를 보고 싶다고 해서 영국으로 결정했다.

어휘 somewhere 어딘가에 other than ~ 외에 South America 남미 fascinating 매력적인 flight time 비행시간 have in mind ~을 염두에 두다(생각하다) either A or B A나 B 둘 중 하나 look for ~을 찾다

09 ⑤

M Semi, <u>can you help me find</u> some volunteer work?
W Sure. You can check the website called Volunteer Together.
M Volunteer Together?
W I can <u>check it out with you</u>. What kind of volunteer work do you want to do?
M Well, I like children. So I <u>want to do some work</u> with kids.
W How about this one? Reading English books to kids.
M That sounds interesting. <u>How can I sign up</u> for this volunteer work?
W You should call this number to sign up.
M Okay. I'll do that right now.

남 세미야, 자원봉사 활동 찾는 걸 좀 도와줄 수 있어?
여 물론이지. Volunteer Together라는 웹사이트를 확인해 봐.
남 Volunteer Together라고?
여 내가 너와 함께 확인해 줄게. 어떤 종류의 자원봉사 활동을 하고 싶어?
남 글쎄, 난 아이들을 좋아해. 그래서 아이들과 함께하는 활동을 하고 싶어.
여 이건 어때? 아이들에게 영어책 읽어 주기.
남 흥미로운데. 이 자원봉사 활동은 어떻게 신청하는 거야?
여 신청하려면 이 번호로 전화해야 해.
남 알았어. 지금 바로 해야겠다.

해설 남자는 지금 바로 전화해서 자원봉사 활동을 신청하겠다고 했다.

어휘 volunteer work 자원봉사 활동 called ~라는 이름의 sign up for ~을 신청하다 right now 지금 바로

10 ④

M Did you visit the air show yesterday? It was opening day.
W Yes, I did. It was really impressive. <u>Planes were flying upside down</u>!
M Awesome! What else did you see?
W <u>There was an exhibition</u> of drones.
M Great. How much is an admission ticket?
W It's $20 onsite, but <u>if you buy a ticket online</u>, it costs only $15.
M That's nice. I think I should go, too. When does the show end?
W It lasts for four days. It <u>closes in two days</u>.

남 어제 에어쇼 갔었어? 어제가 개막일이었잖아.

여 응, 갔었어. 정말 인상 깊었어. 비행기들이 거꾸로 날았어!

남 멋지다! 또 다른 건 뭘 봤어?

여 드론 전시회가 있었어.

남 좋았겠다. 입장권은 얼마야?

여 현장에서는 20달러인데, 온라인으로 입장권을 사면 15달러밖에 안 들어.

남 그거 좋다. 나도 가 봐야겠어. 쇼는 언제 끝나?

여 4일 동안 계속돼. 이틀 후에 폐막 해.

해설 여자는 에어쇼가 개최되는 장소는 언급하지 않았다.

어휘 opening day 개막일   impressive 인상 깊은   upside down 거꾸로   awesome 굉장한   exhibition 전시회   drone 드론   admission ticket 입장권   onsite 현장에서   cost (돈이) 들다   last 계속되다

11 ⑤

W Bentley, did you sign up for the meeting with the author event?

M The one that is next Wednesday at the student hall?

W It's not at the student hall but at the school library.

M Oh, is it? Who's coming?

W Julia Harrington. She'll give a lecture about her bestseller. There'll be a book-signing event, too.

M Do we sign up online?

W We did last year. But this year, you have to do it in the teachers' office.

M I see.

여 Bentley, 작가와의 만남 행사 신청했니?

남 다음 주 수요일에 학생회관에서 하는 거?

여 학생회관이 아니고 학교 도서관에서 해.

남 아, 그래? 누가 온대?

여 Julia Harrington. 그녀의 베스트셀러에 대해 강연할 거래. 책 사인회도 있을 거야.

남 온라인으로 신청하는 거니?

여 작년엔 그랬지. 하지만 올해는 교무실에서 해야 해.

남 알았어.

해설 작년에는 온라인으로 참가 신청을 했지만 올해는 교무실에서 신청해야 한다고 했다.

어휘 sign up for ~을 신청하다   author 작가   event 행사   student hall 학생회관   not A but B A가 아니라 B   library 도서관   give a lecture 강연하다   bestseller 베스트셀러   book-signing event 책 사인회   teachers' office 교무실

12 ③

(Telephone rings.)

M Hello. Front Desk. How may I help you?

W Hello. My room is too dry now.

M Did you turn on the humidifier?

W Yes, but it's still dry. I'd like to wet some towels and hang them up. So could you bring me some extra towels?

M Sure. How many towels do you need?

W I think two will be fine.

M Anything else?

W Not now. Thank you.

(전화벨이 울린다.)

남 안녕하세요. 프런트입니다. 무엇을 도와드릴까요?

여 안녕하세요. 제 방이 지금 너무 건조해요.

남 가습기를 켜셨나요?

여 네, 하지만 여전히 건조해요. 수건을 적셔서 걸어 두고 싶어요. 저에게 여분의 수건을 좀 가져다주실 수 있을까요?

남 물론입니다. 수건 몇 장이 필요하신가요?

여 두 장이면 될 것 같아요.

남 그 밖에 필요하신 건 없으신가요?

여 지금은 없어요. 감사합니다.

해설 여자는 방이 건조하여 수건을 적셔서 걸어 둘 수 있도록 수건을 더 가져다 달라고 요청하기 위해 전화했다.

어휘 dry 건조한   turn on ~을 켜다   humidifier 가습기   still 여전히   wet 적시다   towel 수건   hang up ~을 걸다   bring 가져다주다   extra 여분의   else 또 다른, 그 밖의

13 ②

(Telephone rings.)

W Fast and Safe Taxi Service. How may I help you?

M Hello. I need a taxi to take me to the airport tomorrow morning.

W Where and what time shall we pick you up?

M 215 K Street at 6:30, please. I need to be at the airport by 7:00.

W It's often congested there. Can we go there 15 minutes early?

M That would be great. Thank you.

(전화벨이 울린다.)

여 Fast and Safe Taxi Service입니다. 무엇을 도와드릴까요?

남 안녕하세요. 내일 아침에 저를 공항으로 데려다줄 택시가 필요해요.

여 어디로 몇 시에 모시러 갈까요?

남 K Street 215번지에 6시 30분이요. 저는 7시까지 공항에 가야 해요.

여 그곳은 자주 막힙니다. 15분 일찍 가도 될까요?

남 그게 좋겠네요. 고맙습니다.

해설 택시는 남자가 요청했던 시각인 아침 6시 30분보다 15분 일찍 도착하기로 했다.

어휘 take A to B A를 B로 데려다주다   airport 공항   pick up ~을 (차에) 태우러 가다   by ~까지   often 자주, 종종   congested 붐비는, 혼잡한   early 일찍

14 ②

M Hello. I'd like to open a savings account and put some money into it.

W Okay. Do you have another account with us?

M Yes, I do.

W Give me your ID card and fill out this form, please.

M Okay. (*Pause*) Here you are.

W Thank you. Would you like to transfer some money from your original account into your new one?

M Yes, please.

남 안녕하세요. 저는 예금 계좌를 개설하고 거기에 돈을 좀 입금하고 싶어요.

여 알겠습니다. 저희 은행에 다른 계좌가 있으신가요?

남 네, 있어요.

여 저에게 신분증을 주시고 이 양식을 작성해 주세요.

남 네. (*잠시 후*) 여기 있어요.

여 고맙습니다. 고객님의 원래 계좌에서 새로운 계좌로 송금하시겠어요?

남 네.

해설 예금 계좌를 개설하려는 고객과 은행원 사이의 대화이다.

어휘 open a savings account 예금 계좌를 개설하다
account 계좌 ID card 신분증 fill out 작성하다, 기입하다
form 서식, 양식 transfer money 송금하다 original 원래의

---

15 ④

W Hi, Michael. You look tired. Is everything okay?

M I didn't eat dinner. I'm just so hungry.

W Why? Are you on a diet?

M No, I'm not. You know I'm trying to gain weight.

W Are you too busy to eat?

M Nope. I have a medical checkup in the morning. I cannot eat anything the night before.

W I see. Eat a good meal after your checkup.

여 안녕, Michael. 피곤해 보이네. 괜찮아?

남 나 저녁을 안 먹었어. 그냥 너무 배가 고파.

여 왜? 다이어트 중이니?

남 아니. 나 체중 늘리려는 거 알잖아.

여 너무 바빠서 못 먹는 거야?

남 아니. 아침에 건강 검진이 있거든. 전날 밤에는 아무것도 먹을 수 없어.

여 그렇구나. 검진 후에 맛있는 거 먹어.

해설 남자는 내일 아침에 건강 검진을 받아야 해서 전날 밤에는 아무것도 먹을 수 없다고 했다.

어휘 be on a diet 다이어트 중이다 gain weight 체중을
늘리다 too ~ to ... 너무 ~해서 … 할 수 없는 busy 바쁜
medical checkup 건강 검진 the night before 그 전날 밤에

---

16 ①

(*Cellphone rings.*)

M Honey, I'm going home now. Is there enough dog food for Max?

W Yeah, I bought some last week.

M All right. I'll be right home.

W Hold on. We don't have any toothpaste left.

M Are you sure? Didn't you buy some from the market yesterday?

W No, I only bought toothbrushes. I realized today that we've used up the toothpaste. So can you pick

---

some up?

M Got it.

(*휴대 전화가 울린다.*)

남 여보, 나 지금 집에 가고 있어요. Max를 위한 개 사료는 충분히 있어요?

여 네, 지난주에 좀 샀어요.

남 알았어요. 바로 집으로 갈게요.

여 잠깐만요. 우리 치약이 남은 게 없어요.

남 정말요? 어제 시장에서 사지 않았어요?

여 아니요, 칫솔만 샀어요. 치약을 다 써 버린 걸 오늘 알았어요. 그러니 치약 좀 사 올래요?

남 알았어요.

해설 치약이 다 떨어져서 여자는 남자에게 치약을 사 오라고 했다.

어휘 enough 충분한 dog food 개 사료 toothpaste 치약
left 남아 있는(leave의 과거분사) market 시장 realize
깨닫다 use up 다 써 버리다 pick up ~을 사다

---

17 ③

M Attention, students. Next week is sports week at Hanguk Middle School. There is going to be a dodge ball tournament. Each class is going to play dodge ball every morning from 8:00 to 8:30 a.m. There'll be a final match next Friday at 3:00 p.m. The winning class will be given fried chicken as a prize. It's going to be a lot of fun.

남 학생 여러분, 주목해 주세요. 다음 주는 한국중학교의 체육 주간입니다. 피구 토너먼트가 있을 것입니다. 각 학급은 매일 오전 8시부터 8시 30분까지 피구 시합을 할 것입니다. 다음 주 결승전은 금요일 오후 3시에 있을 예정입니다. 우승하는 학급에게는 상품으로 프라이드치킨이 주어집니다. 아주 재미있을 거예요.

해설 남자는 준비물에 대해서는 언급하지 않았다.

어휘 dodge ball 피구 tournament 토너먼트 final match
결승전 prize 상품

---

18 ③

① **W** What is your favorite season?

　M It's definitely winter because I love winter sports.

② **W** When did you learn to ski?

　M When I was an elementary school student, my father taught me.

③ **W** Is that ski lift for beginners?

　M No, it's for advanced skiers. It goes directly to the top.

④ **W** I'm thinking of joining a sports club.

　M Oh, really? What sport do you like the most?

⑤ **W** Which do you prefer, skiing or snowboarding?

　M I prefer snowboarding.

① **여** 네가 가장 좋아하는 계절이 뭐야?

　남 나는 겨울철 운동을 정말 좋아하니까 당연히 겨울이지.

② **여** 너는 스키 타는 거 언제 배웠어?

남 내가 초등학생일 때, 아빠가 가르쳐 주셨어.
③ 여 저 스키 리프트는 초급자용인가요?
　남 아니요, 상급자용입니다. 그건 곧바로 정상으로 갑니다.
④ 여 나는 운동 동아리에 가입하는 것을 생각 중이야.
　남 오, 정말? 너는 어떤 운동을 가장 좋아해?
⑤ 여 너는 스키랑 스노보드 중에 뭘 더 좋아해?
　남 나는 스노보드를 더 좋아해.

해설 스키장에서 여자가 남자에게 리프트에 관한 질문을 하자 그에 대해 남자가 부정의 응답을 하는 상황이다.

어휘 definitely 당연히, 틀림없이　elementary school 초등학교　beginner 초급자　advanced 상급의　ski lift 스키 리프트　skier 스키 타는 사람, 스키어　directly 곧바로　top 정상　prefer ~을 더 좋아하다　snowboard 스노보드를 타다

19 ⑤

W Tomorrow is election day for the school president.
M Have you decided who you're going to vote for?
W Yes. I'm going to vote for Sandra.
M Can I ask you the reason?
W She was our class leader last year. She's very responsible. I'm sure she'll be a good school president, too.
M I see. I don't know her well, but my friends also said they're going to vote for her.
W Oh, really? What about you?
M I'm not sure. I haven't decided yet.

여 내일이 전교 회장 선거일이야.
남 누구 뽑을지 정했어?
여 응. 난 Sandra에게 투표할거야.
남 이유를 물어봐도 될까?
여 그녀는 작년에 우리 반 반장이었어. 그녀는 책임감이 강해. 나는 그녀가 훌륭한 전교 회장이 될 거라고 확신해.
남 그렇구나. 난 그녀를 잘 모르지만, 내 친구들도 그녀를 뽑을 거라고 하더라.
여 오, 정말이야? 너는?
남 모르겠어. 아직 못 정했어.

해설 여자가 누구에게 투표할 것인지 물었으므로 아직 결정하지 못했다는 응답이 가장 적절하다.
① 물론이지. 사람들은 온라인으로 투표할 수 있어.
② 선거는 내일이 아니야.
③ 내일 투표하는 것 잊지 마.
④ 내 생각에 너는 그녀를 뽑아야 해.

어휘 election 선거　president 회장　decide 결정하다　vote for ~에게 투표하다　reason 이유　class leader 반장　responsible 책임감 있는　forget to ~하는 것을 잊다　yet (부정문·의문문에서) 아직

20 ①

W It's pouring outside. We can't go on the walking tour.
M But walking along the Great Wall of China will surely be a great experience.

W In this rain? I don't think so. Let's look for some other things to do.
M Like what?
W What about taking a city bus tour?
M Isn't the traffic bad? Let's just do the walking tour with raincoats on. Look on the bright side.
W The bright side? What's good about walking in the rain?
M At least it'll be less crowded.

여 밖에 비가 엄청 오네. 우리 도보 관광 못 가겠다.
남 하지만 만리장성을 걷는 건 분명 대단한 경험일 텐데.
여 이 빗속에? 아닐 것 같은데. 할 만한 다른 걸 찾아보자.
남 어떤 거?
여 시내 관광 버스를 타는 건 어떠니?
남 교통 체증이 심하지 않아? 그냥 우비를 입고 도보 관광을 하자. 긍정적으로 생각해.
여 긍정적으로? 빗속을 걷는 게 뭐가 좋아?
남 적어도 덜 붐빌 거야.

해설 여자가 비를 맞으며 도보 관광을 하는 것의 장점이 무엇인지 물었으므로 이와 관련된 응답이 와야 한다.
② 모든 게 잘 될 거야.
③ 좋은 점을 생각할 수 있니?
④ 여행을 가는 건 위험할 거야.
⑤ 너는 우비를 입을 필요가 없어.

어휘 pour (비가) 마구 쏟아지다　walking tour 도보 관광　the Great Wall of China 만리장성　surely 분명히　experience 경험　look for ~을 찾다　traffic 교통(량)　raincoat 우비　look on the bright side 긍정적으로 보다　turn out ~인 것으로 드러나다(밝혀지다)　at least 적어도, 최소한　crowded 붐비는　dangerous 위험한

Word Check   03회

01 안도하는	**02** 모험
03 (파일 등을) 백업하다	**04** 복구하다
05 일광욕하다	**06** 주제어
07 ~까지	**08** 우울한
09 (~을 보고) 웃다, 비웃다	**10** 전시회
11 멋진	**12** 열정적인
13 outgoing	**14** expert
15 valid	**16** submit
17 encounter	**18** friendly
19 individually	**20** transfer
21 take out	**22** neighborhood
23 environment	**24** hesitate

Expression Check

25 search for	**26** upset with
27 stressed out	**28** out of order
29 working as	**30** up all night

Word Check   04회

01 여분의	**02** 전기의, 전동의
03 턱수염	**04** 부끄러운
05 혼란스러운	**06** 만족하지 않은
07 경험하다; 경험	**08** 대여점
09 멸종 위기에 처한	**10** 기온
11 거꾸로	**12** 가습기
13 close	**14** impressive
15 itchy	**16** onsite
17 treatment	**18** original
19 advanced	**20** pour
21 ID card	**22** election
23 responsible	**24** definitely

Expression Check

25 vote for	**26** sign up
27 hang, up	**28** other than
29 open a savings account	**30** used up

01 ⑤	02 ④	03 ②	04 ④	05 ③
06 ④	07 ④	08 ①	09 ⑤	10 ②
11 ③	12 ③	13 ⑤	14 ③	15 ④
16 ②	17 ③	18 ④	19 ①	20 ②

01   ⑤

M   Good morning. This is Jacob O'connell with your London weather report. Right now it's 10°C and very clear. We're expecting <u>blue skies throughout the day</u>. This good weather won't last long, however. There is <u>a chance of some rain</u> starting tonight. It will <u>rain heavily</u> tomorrow, and the temperature will drop to as low as 3°C.

남   안녕하세요. 런던 일기 예보의 Jacob O'connell입니다. 현재 기온은 10°C이고 아주 맑습니다. 온종일 파란 하늘을 볼 수 있을 것으로 예상됩니다. 그러나 이렇게 좋은 날씨는 오래가지 못하겠습니다. 오늘 밤부터 비가 올 가능성이 있습니다. 내일은 비가 많이 내릴 것이고, 기온은 3°C까지 떨어지겠습니다.

> **해설** 내일은 비가 많이 내릴 것이라고 했다.

> **어휘** throughout 내내, ~ 동안 쭉   last 지속되다   long 오래   chance 가능성   heavily 심하게, 아주 많이   temperature 기온   drop 떨어지다   as low as ~만큼 낮은

02   ④

(Telephone rings.)

W   J Mall Lost and Found. How may I help you?

M   <u>I lost my bag</u> this afternoon. Do you have it by any chance?

W   There are several bags here. Could you tell me <u>what it looks like</u>?

M   It is square, and it has a handle on the top.

W   <u>Does it have a strap</u>, too?

M   Yes. It has a long strap.

W   I think <u>your bag is here</u>.

M   What a relief! I will visit the mall tomorrow.

(전화벨이 울린다.)

여   J Mall 분실물 보관소입니다. 무엇을 도와드릴까요?

남   오늘 오후에 제 가방을 잃어버렸어요. 혹시 거기에 있을까요?

여   여기에 가방이 여러 개 있어요. 어떻게 생겼는지 말씀해 주시겠어요?

남   사각형이고, 윗면에 손잡이가 있어요.

여   끈도 있나요?

남   네. 긴 끈이 있어요.

여   고객님의 가방이 여기에 있는 것 같아요.

남   다행이네요! 내일 몰에 방문할게요.

> **해설** 남자의 가방은 사각형이고, 윗면에 손잡이가 있으며 긴 끈이 있다고 했다.

어휘 lost and found 분실물 보관소 lose(-lost-lost) 잃어버리다 by any chance 혹시 several 여러 개의 square 사각형의 handle 손잡이 top 위(윗면) strap 끈, 줄, 띠 relief 안심

03 ②

W Did something good happen to you?
M I've just finished *The Old Man and the Sea*.
W Do you mean the novel?
M You're right. I finished reading it in English.
W Really? Wasn't it hard to read?
M Well, it wasn't easy. It took me a whole month.
W You did a good job.
M I think my English has improved a lot. I'll try a more difficult book the next time.

여 너에게 무슨 좋은 일이 생겼니?
남 나는 〈노인과 바다〉를 막 끝냈어.
여 소설 말하는 거야?
남 맞아. 그것을 영어로 다 읽었어.
여 정말? 어렵지 않았니?
남 음, 쉽지 않았지. 한 달이 꼬박 걸렸어.
여 잘했네.
남 내 영어 실력이 많이 향상된 것 같아. 다음번에는 더 어려운 책을 시도해 볼 거야.

해설 남자는 꼬박 한 달 동안 영어로 된 소설책을 다 읽었다고 했고, 영어 실력이 많이 향상된 것 같다고 했으므로 뿌듯한 심정일 것이다.

어휘 finish 끝내다 mean 의미하다 novel 소설 whole 전체의 improve 개선되다, 나아지다 difficult 어려운 lonely 외로운 thankful 감사하는 disappointed 실망한

04 ④

W Dave, which club are you going to join?
M I'm not sure yet.
W Aren't you interested in playing computer games?
M Yeah, but as you know, there aren't any clubs related to computer games.
W What about the coding club? I'm thinking of joining it.
M What kind of club is it?
W You can learn basic programming skills and make your own games.
M That sounds interesting.

여 Dave, 너는 어느 동아리에 가입할 거야?
남 아직 확실하지 않아.
여 너 컴퓨터 게임하는 것에 관심 있지 않아?
남 응, 하지만 너도 알다시피 컴퓨터 게임과 관련된 동아리가 없어.
여 코딩 동아리는 어때? 난 거기에 들어갈까 생각 중이야.
남 그게 무슨 동아리니?
여 기초적인 프로그래밍 기술을 배울 수 있고 너만의 게임을 만들 수 있어.
남 그거 흥미롭구나.

해설 여자는 남자에게 코딩 동아리 가입을 생각 중이라고 했고, 남자도 코딩 동아리에 관심을 보였다.

어휘 yet (부정문·의문문에서) 아직 be interested in ~에 관심이 있다 as you know 너도 알다시피 related to ~와 관련 있는 learn 배우다 basic 기초적인 skill 기술 own 자신의 interesting 흥미로운

05 ③

M Hello. How may I help you?
W Hi. I'd like to change my seat. It's too close to the screen.
M Sure. Where do you want to sit?
W May I have a seat in the back?
M Let me see. (*Pause*) We have one seat in the back row, but it's right next to the door.
W That's okay with me. I prefer the back row to the front row.
M Okay. Here's your new ticket.

남 안녕하세요. 어떻게 도와드릴까요?
여 안녕하세요. 좌석을 바꾸고 싶어요. 스크린에서 너무 가까워요.
남 네. 어디에 앉고 싶으세요?
여 뒤쪽에 앉을 수 있나요?
남 볼게요. (잠시 후) 뒷줄에 자리가 하나 있는데, 문 바로 옆이에요.
여 괜찮아요. 전 앞줄보다 뒷줄이 좋아요.
남 네. 여기 새 관람권을 드릴게요.

해설 스크린에서 가까운 좌석을 뒷줄에 있는 좌석으로 바꾸며 새 관람권을 받는 상황이므로 영화관에서 이루어지는 대화이다.

어휘 seat 자리, 좌석 close 가까운 screen 스크린, 화면 have a seat 앉다 back 뒤쪽(의) row 줄 prefer *A* to *B* *B*보다 *A*를 선호하다 front 앞쪽(의) ticket 표

06 ④

W Mike, do you have a large backpack?
M I do. Do you need one?
W Yeah. May I borrow yours? I'm going hiking this week.
M Don't you have your own?
W I don't have a large one. I can't put all the things I need in it.
M Okay. When do you need it?
W This Friday. Thanks. Can I pick it up at your house in a few hours?
M Call me just before you get here.

여 Mike, 너 큰 배낭 있니?
남 응. 하나 필요해?
여 응. 네 것 좀 빌려도 될까? 이번 주에 하이킹을 가거든.
남 네 거 있지 않아?
여 난 큰 배낭은 없어. 내 배낭에는 내가 필요한 모든 것을 담을 수가 없어.
남 알았어. 언제 필요한데?
여 다음 주 금요일. 고마워. 몇 시간 후에 너희 집에서 그걸 가져가도 될까?

남 여기에 도착하기 전에 전화해.

해설 배낭을 빌리러 집에 가도 되는지 묻는 여자의 말에 도착하기 전에 전화하라고 답한 것은 배낭을 가지러 집에 와도 된다는 뜻이다.

어휘 backpack 배낭 borrow 빌리다 go hiking 하이킹을 가다 pick up ~을 찾아오다 in a few hours 몇 시간 후에

---

07 ④

M I'm hungry. Why don't we have an early dinner?
W Sure, but I want to have something light for dinner.
M Why? Are you on a diet?
W No. I had too much steak for lunch today.
M Then how about going to a Vietnamese restaurant?
W That's good. I will have rice noodles.
M Okay. I will have pineapple fried rice.

남 나 배고파. 우리 저녁을 일찍 먹는 게 어때?
여 그래, 그런데 난 저녁으로 가벼운 걸 먹고 싶어.
남 왜? 다이어트 중이야?
여 아니. 오늘 점심으로 스테이크를 너무 많이 먹었어.
남 그럼 베트남 음식점에 가는 건 어때?
여 그거 좋다. 나는 쌀국수를 먹을래.
남 그래. 나는 파인애플 볶음밥을 먹어야지.

해설 여자는 점심에 스테이크를 너무 많이 먹어서 저녁에는 가벼운 음식인 쌀국수를 먹을 것이라고 했다.

어휘 have a dinner 저녁을 먹다 early 이른 light 가벼운 be on a diet 다이어트 중이다 Vietnamese 베트남의 rice noodles 쌀국수 fried rice 볶음밥

---

08 ①

W What's wrong with you? You don't look good today.
M I'm worried about my English test next week.
W When is it?
M It's next Monday, but I can't focus on studying because I have a headache.
W Oh, dear. I think you haven't slept well lately.
M Yeah, maybe. What can I do?
W Why don't you get some sleep first and then study?
M Okay. I'll follow your advice.

여 무슨 일 있어? 너 오늘 기분이 안 좋아 보여.
남 다음 주 영어 시험이 걱정돼.
여 시험이 언제인데?
남 다음 주 월요일인데, 머리가 아파서 공부에 집중할 수 없어.
여 오, 저런. 최근에 잠을 충분히 안 잤나 보네.
남 응, 아마도. 어떻게 하지?
여 먼저 잠을 좀 자고 나서 공부하는 게 어때?
남 알았어. 네 조언을 따를게.

해설 여자가 남자에게 먼저 잠을 자고 나서 공부하는 것이 어떤지 조언하자 남자는 여자의 조언에 따르겠다고 했다.

어휘 be worried about ~을 걱정하다 focus on ~에 집중하다 because ~ 때문에 headache 두통 lately 최근에 get some sleep 잠을 자다 first 먼저, 우선 follow 따르다 advice 조언, 충고

---

09 ⑤

M I keep getting pimples! How come you have such clean skin?
W Well, I take time to wash my face every night.
M Is that all? Do you use regular soap when you wash your face?
W Actually, I use handmade soap that my mom made.
M Can I try some?
W Sure. I also don't eat fast food at all.
M Really? Please give me more tips.
W I always try to keep my skin not too dry.

남 나 여드름이 자꾸 나! 너는 어떻게 그렇게 깨끗한 피부를 가지고 있니?
여 글쎄, 나는 매일 밤 세수하는 데 시간을 들여.
남 그게 다야? 세수할 때 일반 비누를 사용하니?
여 사실, 나는 우리 엄마가 만드신 수제 비누를 사용해.
남 나도 좀 얻을 수 있을까?
여 물론이야. 그리고 나는 패스트푸드를 전혀 안 먹어.
남 정말? 좀 더 조언해 줘.
여 나는 항상 피부가 너무 건조하지 않게 하려고 노력해.

해설 여자는 오일을 사용하는 것은 언급하지 않았다.

어휘 pimple 여드름 how come 어떻게, 왜 skin 피부 regular 보통의 soap 비누 handmade 수제의 not ~ at all 전혀 ~ 하지 않은 tip 조언 dry 건조한

---

10 ②

W Welcome to Fresh Grocery. Now our special discount time will begin for the next twenty minutes. In the fruit section, buy one pack of cherries and get a second pack for half price. In the vegetable section, all potatoes and sweet potatoes are 40% off. Hurry up and don't miss these special offers.

여 Fresh Grocery에 오신 것을 환영합니다. 지금부터 20분 동안 특별 할인 시간이 시작됩니다. 과일 코너에서는, 체리 한 팩을 사시면 두 번째 팩을 반값에 드립니다. 채소 코너에서는, 모든 감자와 고구마가 40퍼센트 할인됩니다. 서두르셔서 이 특가 판매를 놓치지 마세요.

해설 여자는 과일 코너와 채소 코너에서 곧 시작될 반짝세일에 대해 안내하고 있다.

어휘 grocery 식료품점 discount 할인 section 구역, 부문 pack 팩, 상자 half price 반값 sweet potato 고구마 miss 놓치다 offer 가격 할인, (팔 물건의) 제공

---

11 ③

W Josh, which club do you belong to?
M I have belonged to the tennis club since last year.
W Really? I didn't know you like tennis.
M In fact, I'm the leader of the club. I play tennis at least three times a week.
W You must be very good at it.
M I'm pretty good, but I still need to practice more.

W I'm also interested in playing tennis. Where do you play?

M I usually play in my school gym.

여 Josh, 너 무슨 동아리에 속해 있어?

남 난 작년부터 테니스 동아리에 속해 있어.

여 정말? 네가 테니스를 좋아하는지 몰랐어.

남 사실, 내가 그 동아리 회장이야. 난 적어도 일주일에 세 번 테니스를 쳐.

여 테니스를 아주 잘 치겠구나.

남 꽤 잘 하긴 한데, 아직 더 연습을 해야 해.

여 나도 테니스 치는 것에 관심이 있어. 넌 어디에서 치니?

남 보통 학교 체육관에서 쳐.

[해설] 남자는 테니스를 일주일에 최소 세 번 친다고 했으므로 테니스를 매일 연습한다고는 할 수 없다.

[어휘] belong to ~에 속하다   since ~부터(이후)   in fact 사실은   leader 대표, 지도자   at least 적어도, 최소한   be good at ~에 능숙하다, 잘하다   pretty 꽤   practice 연습하다   be interested in ~에 관심이 있다   usually 보통, 대개

12 ③

M Claire, what are you doing?

W I'm making a notice board.

M For what?

W It's for managing our housework. You don't care about the chores, and I'm the one who does all the housework.

M Sorry. I always forget.

W That's why I'm making this board. I will write down a list of chores you have to do every day.

M That will be helpful.

남 Claire, 뭐 하고 있어?

여 게시판을 만들고 있어.

남 왜?

여 우리 집안일을 관리하기 위해서야. 넌 집안일에 신경 쓰지 않고, 나 혼자 모든 집안일을 하잖아.

남 미안해. 항상 잊어버려.

여 그래서 내가 이 게시판을 만드는 거야. 네가 매일 해야 할 집안일 목록을 적어 놓을 거야.

남 그거 도움이 되겠네.

[해설] 여자는 매일 해야 할 집안일 목록을 적어 두기 위해서 게시판을 만들고 있다고 했다.

[어휘] notice board 게시판   manage 관리하다   housework 집안일   care about ~에 마음을 쓰다   chore (정기적으로 하는) 일, 가사   forget 잊어버리다   write down ~을 적다   a list of ~의 목록   helpful 도움이 되는

13 ⑤

W Are there any train tickets to Busan this evening?

M What time do you want to leave?

W Around 6:00 p.m.

M All the tickets from 6:00 p.m. to 8:00 p.m. are sold out.

W Then when is the earliest available train after 8:00?

M There is a train ticket for 8:30. Do you want to get that one?

W Yes, give me that one, please. How long does it take to Busan?

M It takes two hours and fifteen minutes.

여 오늘 저녁에 부산으로 가는 기차표가 있나요?

남 몇 시에 출발하기 원하세요?

여 저녁 6시쯤이요.

남 저녁 6시부터 8시까지는 모든 표가 매진이에요.

여 그럼 8시 이후에 탈 수 있는 가장 이른 기차는 언제인가요?

남 8시 30분에 기차표가 있어요. 그걸로 사시겠어요?

여 네, 그걸로 주세요. 부산까지는 얼마나 걸리죠?

남 2시간 15분 걸려요.

[해설] 여자는 8시 30분에 출발하는 기차를 탈 것이고, 부산까지 2시간 15분 걸린다고 했으므로 도착 시각은 10시 45분이다.

[어휘] train ticket 기차표   leave 출발하다   around 약, ~쯤   sold out 매진된, 다 팔린   earliest 가장 이른(early의 최상급)   available 이용할 수 있는

14 ③

W Hello, Josh. Nice to meet you. I'm Judy Baker with New Stars.

M Nice to meet you, too.

W Your new album is a big hit. Congratulations!

M Thank you very much. I can't believe it.

W You wrote every song on the album, didn't you?

M That's right.

W You're amazing. Do you want to say something to your fans?

M Thank you so much for your generous support. I love you all!

여 안녕하세요, Josh. 만나서 반갑습니다. 저는 New Stars의 Judy Baker입니다.

남 저도 만나서 반갑습니다.

여 새 앨범이 대단한 히트예요. 축하드려요!

남 정말 고맙습니다. 믿을 수가 없어요.

여 앨범에서 모든 곡을 쓰셨죠, 그렇지 않나요?

남 맞아요.

여 대단하시네요. 팬 분들께 한 마디 하시겠어요?

남 저를 많이 지지해 주셔서 정말 감사드립니다. 여러분 모두 사랑해요!

[해설] 새 음반을 낸 가수와 그 가수를 인터뷰하는 리포터 사이의 대화이다.

[어휘] hit 히트, 인기 작품   Congratulations! 축하해요!   amazing 놀라운   fan 팬   generous 풍부한   support 지지

15 ④

M Did you hear that Mike is going to transfer to another school?

W Really? I didn't know that. When is he going to leave?

M Next month.

W How about giving him a farewell party?

M That sounds nice. When will Mike be free?

W I'll ask him about it. Can you find a good place to throw a party?

M No problem. You can count on me.

남 Mike가 다른 학교로 전학 간다는 것 들었어?

여 정말? 몰랐어. 언제 간대?

남 다음 달에.

여 그에게 송별회를 해 주는 거 어때?

남 그거 좋겠다. Mike가 언제 시간이 될까?

여 내가 그에게 물어볼게. 너는 파티를 열 좋은 장소를 찾아봐 줄래?

남 문제없어. 내게 맡겨.

해설 여자는 남자에게 다음 달에 전학 가는 Mike의 송별회를 열 만한 좋은 장소를 찾아 달라고 요청했다.

어휘 transfer 전학 가다   leave 떠나다   farewell party 송별회   free 다른 계획이 없는, 한가한   throw a party 파티를 열다   count on ~을 믿다[확신하다]

16 ②

M Do you have any plans for next weekend?

W No. Why?

M I can give you two tickets for *The Phantom of the Opera* on Sunday afternoon.

W Wow, I have wanted to see it for a long time. Why aren't you going?

M I have to visit my grandpa. He is in the hospital.

W I'm sorry to hear that. Please let me pay for the tickets.

M You don't need to. I cannot go anyway.

남 다음 주말에 무슨 계획 있니?

여 없어. 왜?

남 일요일 오후의 〈오페라의 유령〉 관람권 두 장을 너에게 줄게.

여 우와, 나 오랫동안 그거 보고 싶었거든. 넌 왜 안 가?

남 나는 할아버지를 뵈러 가야 해. 입원 중이시거든.

여 그 말을 들으니 유감이다. 내가 관람권 값을 낼게.

남 그럴 필요 없어. 어차피 나는 못 가.

해설 남자는 할아버지의 병문안을 가야 해서 뮤지컬을 보러 갈 수 없다고 했다.

어휘 ticket 표   for a long time 오랫동안   in the hospital 입원 중인   pay for ~을 지불하다   anyway 어쨌든

17 ③

M Have you heard of blue whales? They are the largest animals in the world. They can grow to over 30 meters long. That's longer than three buses. They weigh more than 130 tons, and they can live for about 80 years. You may think they eat big fish because of their size, but that's not true. They eat tiny shrimp called krill.

남 대왕고래에 대해 들어 봤나요? 대왕고래는 세계에서 가장 큰 동물입니다. 대왕고래는 30미터까지 자랄 수 있습니다. 그것은 버스 세 대보다 긴 길이입니다. 대왕고래는 무게가 130톤 이상 나가고, 약 80년 동안 살 수 있습니다. 여러분은 대왕고래의 크기 때문에 큰 물고기들을 먹을 거라고 생각할지도 모르지만, 사실 그렇지 않습니다. 대왕고래는 크릴이라고 불리는 아주 작은 새우를 먹습니다.

해설 남자는 대왕고래의 서식지는 언급하지 않았다.

어휘 hear of ~에 대해 듣다   blue whale 대왕고래   grow 자라다   over ~이 넘는, ~ 이상   weigh 무게가 ~이다   more than ~보다 많이, ~ 이상   because of ~ 때문에   true 사실인   tiny 아주 작은   shrimp 새우

18 ④

① **W** Do you enjoy playing soccer?

  M Yes, I do. How about you?

② **W** This room is hot and humid.

  M Let me turn on the air conditioner.

③ **W** What do you think of exercising in the morning?

  M I think it's great.

④ **W** Your room is too messy.

  M Sorry, Mom. I will clean it.

⑤ **W** Let's go to the film festival tomorrow.

  M Thanks for asking, but I have to meet my uncle.

① **여** 너는 축구하는 것을 좋아하니?

  남 응. 너는 어때?

② **여** 이 방은 덥고 습해.

  남 내가 에어컨을 켤게.

③ **여** 아침에 운동하는 것에 대해 어떻게 생각해?

  남 아주 좋다고 생각해.

④ **여** 네 방이 너무 지저분하구나.

  남 죄송해요, 엄마. 청소할게요.

⑤ **여** 내일 영화 축제에 가자.

  남 물어봐 줘서 고맙지만, 난 삼촌을 뵈러 가야 해.

해설 방이 지저분하다고 지적하는 내용의 대화가 가장 적절하다.

어휘 humid 습한   turn on ~을 켜다   air conditioner 에어컨   think of ~에 대해 생각하다   exercise 운동하다   messy 지저분한, 엉망인   film 영화   festival 축제

19 ①

W Can you turn off the TV? The sound is bothering me.

M I'm sorry. I really can't. My favorite team is playing an important baseball game.

W But I'm getting ready for my science exam tomorrow.

M Why don't you close your door?

W I did, but the sound is still bothering me.

M Okay. I'll turn down the volume.

W Thanks. When will the game be over anyway?

M It's just beginning.

여 TV 좀 꺼 줄래? 소리가 신경 쓰여.

남 미안. 정말 안 되겠어. 내가 제일 좋아하는 팀이 중요한 야구 경기를 하고 있단 말이야.
여 하지만 난 내일 과학 시험을 준비하고 있다고.
남 문을 닫는 게 어때?
여 닫았어. 하지만 소리가 여전히 거슬려.
남 알았어. 볼륨을 줄일게.
여 고마워. 그런데 경기는 언제 끝나는데?
남 이제 막 시작이야.

[해설] 여자가 경기가 언제 끝나는지 물었으므로 이제 막 시작했다는 응답이 가장 적절하다.
② 난 야구를 좋아하지 않아.
③ 경기가 정말 지루해.
④ 나는 공부하는 데 집중해야 해.
⑤ 야구는 인기 있는 경기가 아니야.

[어휘] turn off ~을 끄다   sound 소리   bother 신경 쓰이게 하다   important 중요한   get ready for ~을 준비하다   still 여전히   turn down the volume 볼륨을 줄이다   be over 끝나다   beginning 시작, 초반   focus on ~에 집중하다

20 ②

W Are you going to travel this winter?
M Yes. I'm going to L.A. to meet my aunt.
W Wow, you must be looking forward to it.
M That's true.
W What are you going to do in L.A.?
M I'm going to go to Hollywood. It will be really exciting.
W Great. Will you take some pictures and send them to me?
M That will be no problem.

여 너는 이번 겨울에 여행할 예정이니?
남 응. 나는 이모를 만나러 로스앤젤레스에 갈 거야.
여 우와, 정말 기대되겠다.
남 맞아.
여 로스앤젤레스에서 뭐 할 거니?
남 할리우드에 갈 거야. 정말 신날 거야.
여 좋겠다. 사진 찍어서 나한테 보내 줄래?
남 문제없어.

[해설] 여자가 사진을 찍어서 보내 달라고 부탁했으므로 이에 대한 수락 또는 거절의 응답이 와야 한다.
① 물론이야. 그렇게 해.
③ 난 전에 로스앤젤레스에 가 본 적이 없어.
④ 내년 여름에는 유럽을 여행할 거야.
⑤ 우리 이모는 로스앤젤레스에 10년 동안 살고 계셔.

[어휘] travel 여행하다   look forward to ~을 기대하다   excriting 신나는, 흥미진진한   take a picture 사진을 찍다   Europe 유럽

01 ⑤	02 ⑤	03 ②	04 ③	05 ①
06 ③	07 ③	08 ②	09 ⑤	10 ②
11 ④	12 ③	13 ③	14 ①	15 ④
16 ①	17 ②	18 ②	19 ④	20 ②

01 ⑤

W Hello, everyone. This is the nationwide weather report. Seoul is sunny right now, and most of Gyeonggi-do is the same. However, the sky is covered with heavy clouds in Busan and Ulsan, and rain will start soon in Dokdo and Pohang. Lastly, Jeju-do is having strong winds due to a storm.

여 안녕하세요, 여러분. 전국 일기 예보입니다. 서울은 현재 화창하며 경기도의 대부분 지역도 마찬가지입니다. 하지만 부산과 울산에는 짙은 구름이 잔뜩 끼어 있고, 독도와 포항에는 곧 비가 내리겠습니다. 마지막으로, 제주도는 폭풍 때문에 강한 바람이 불고 있습니다.

[해설] 부산과 울산에는 구름이 잔뜩 끼어 있다고 했다.

[어휘] nationwide 전국적인   weather report 일기 예보   most of ~의 대부분   be covered with ~로 덮여 있다   heavy cloud 짙은 구름   due to ~ 때문에   storm 폭풍

02 ⑤

M Emma, what are you doing?
W I'm designing T-shirts for my family. We're going to wear them during our trip.
M Wow, that's nice. Did you draw these stars?
W Yes. These three stars stand for my family: Dad, Mom, and me.
M Cool. So what are you writing now?
W I'm going to write "We Are Family" below the stars.
M That's cute.

남 Emma, 뭐 하고 있어?
여 우리 가족을 위한 티셔츠를 디자인하고 있어. 우리는 여행하는 동안에 이 티셔츠를 입을 거야.
남 와, 좋겠다. 네가 이 별들을 그렸니?
여 응. 이 별 세 개는 우리 가족을 상징해. 아빠, 엄마, 그리고 나.
남 멋지다. 그래서 지금은 뭘 쓰고 있는 거야?
여 별들 아래에 'We Are Family'라고 적을 거야.
남 귀엽다.

[해설] 여자는 별 세 개가 아빠, 엄마, 자신(여자)을 의미한다고 했고, 그 아래에 'We Are Family'라고 쓸 것이라고 했다.

[어휘] design 디자인하다   during ~ 동안에   trip 여행   stand for ~을 상징하다   below ~ 아래에

03 ②

W Hey, did something good happen to you? You look different today.
M Do I? Actually, I've got a girlfriend!
W Are you serious? Let me guess. Is it Yumi?
M You're right! I thought she didn't like me, but she does.
W Amazing. I'm happy for you!
M Thanks. We'll go on our first date tomorrow. I can't wait!
W Good luck on your first date.

여 이봐, 무슨 좋은 일 생겼니? 너 오늘 좀 달라 보여.
남 그래? 사실, 나 여자 친구 생겼어!
여 정말이야? 내가 맞혀 볼게. 혹시 유미야?
남 맞아! 그녀가 날 좋아하지 않는다고 생각했는데, 날 좋아한대.
여 놀랍다. 네가 잘돼서 기쁘다!
남 고마워. 우리는 내일 첫 데이트를 할 거야. 정말 기다려져!
여 첫 데이트에 행운을 빌어.

해설 남자는 내일 여자 친구와 할 첫 데이트를 기대하며 신이 난 상태이다.

어휘 happen 일어나다, 생기다 different 다른 serious 진지한, 농담이 아닌 guess 추측하다 go on a date 데이트하러 가다 Good luck on ~. ~에 행운을 빌어요.

04 ③

W Kyle, you look tired. Are you okay?
M I'm fine. I just spent too much energy throughout the weekend.
W Right, you said you were going to the ice festival. How was it?
M I had so much fun. It was a great experience.
W What did you do? Skiing or ice skating?
M Neither. I went fishing on the ice.
W Sounds interesting. Did you catch anything?
M Yes. I caught a couple of fish.

여 Kyle, 너 피곤해 보여. 괜찮니?
남 괜찮아. 단지 주말 내내 너무 많은 에너지를 썼을 뿐이야.
여 맞다. 너 얼음 축제에 갈 거라고 말했지. 어땠니?
남 정말 재미있었어. 좋은 경험이었어.
여 뭐 했는데? 스키 타기나 스케이트 타기?
남 둘 다 아니야. 난 얼음낚시를 했어.
여 흥미로운걸. 뭘 좀 잡았니?
남 응. 물고기 두어 마리를 잡았어.

해설 남자는 얼음낚시를 했다고 했다.

어휘 spend(-spent-spent) (에너지 등을) 들이다, 쓰다 throughout 내내, ~ 동안 쭉 experience 경험 ice skate 스케이트를 타다 neither 어느 것도 ~ 아니다 catch(-caught-caught) 잡다 a couple of 둘의, 두어 개의

05 ①

M Excuse me. Can you help me find a book? It's a novel.
W The novels are in section B.
M I went there, but I couldn't find the book that I'm looking for.
W Oh, really? What's the title?
M *Demian*.
W Oh, *Demian* is one of our bestsellers. So it should be in the bestseller section.
M Where is it?
W It's right next to the front counter over there.

남 실례합니다. 책 찾는 것 좀 도와주시겠어요? 소설이에요.
여 소설은 B 구역에 있습니다.
남 거기에 가 봤는데, 제가 찾고 있는 책을 찾을 수 없었어요.
여 오, 정말요? 제목이 무엇이죠?
남 〈데미안〉이요.
여 아, 〈데미안〉은 저희 베스트셀러 중 하나입니다. 그래서 베스트셀러 부문에 있을 겁니다.
남 거기가 어디인가요?
여 저 앞에 있는 계산대 바로 옆입니다.

해설 남자가 찾는 소설책이 계산대 옆의 베스트셀러 부문에 있다고 했으므로 서점에서 이루어지는 대화이다.

어휘 novel 소설 section 구역, 부문 look for ~을 찾다 title 제목 bestseller 베스트셀러 front 앞쪽의 counter 계산대

06 ③

M Do you have any plans for tomorrow?
W Nothing special. How about you?
M Mike and I are going to watch a movie tonight. Do you want to join us?
W Maybe. What kind of movie are you going to watch?
M *The Avengers*. It's the number-one movie right now.
W Isn't it an action movie?
M Yes. People say that it's very spectacular, and there is also a message behind it.
W I'm afraid I don't really want to see it. I'm not into action movies.

남 내일 무슨 계획 있어?
여 특별히 없어. 너는?
남 Mike랑 나는 오늘 밤에 영화 보러 갈 거야. 같이 갈래?
여 글쎄. 어떤 종류의 영화를 볼 건데?
남 〈The Avengers〉. 현재 1위 영화야.
여 그건 액션 영화 아니니?
남 맞아. 사람들이 아주 스펙터클하고, 영화 이면에 메시지도 있다고 하더라.
여 미안한데 나는 별로 보고 싶지 않아. 난 액션 영화에 관심 없어.

해설 여자는 액션 영화에 관심이 없어서 영화를 보고 싶지 않다고 하면서 남자의 제안을 거절했다.

어휘 the number-one movie 1위 영화 action movie 액션 영화 spectacular 장관을 이루는, 극적인 behind ~ 뒤에, 이면에 be into ~에 관심이 많다, ~을 좋아하다

07 ③

W Brian, why do you have all those plastic bottles?
M I'm going to make water rockets with them.
W Water rockets?
M In my club, we do a small project every month. This month, the project is flying rockets.
W Oh, you mean your science club. Do you enjoy it?
M I really do. Why don't you join us?
W I'm sorry, I can't. I joined the volunteering club yesterday.

여 Brian, 그 플라스틱 병들을 왜 가지고 있는 거야?
남 이것들로 물 로켓을 만들 거야.
여 물 로켓이라고?
남 우리 동아리에서, 매달 작은 프로젝트를 하거든. 이번 달 프로젝트는 로켓 날리기야.
여 오, 네 과학 동아리 말이구나. 재미있니?
남 정말 재미있어. 너도 우리 동아리에 들어올래?
여 미안하지만 안 돼. 난 어제 봉사 활동 동아리에 가입했어.

해설 남자는 자신이 속한 과학 동아리에서 진행하는 로켓 날리기 프로젝트를 준비하고 있다고 했다.

어휘 plastic 플라스틱   bottle 병   project 프로젝트, 계획(된 일)   fly 날리다   mean 의미하다   join 가입하다   volunteer 자원봉사를 하다

08 ②

M The restaurant is not open yet.
W Dinner starts at 6:00. What time is it?
M It's 5:30. We have to wait for 30 minutes.
W Is there a coffee shop nearby that we can spend some time at?
M I don't think it's a good idea. We'll have dinner soon. How about taking a walk?
W It's cold outside. Why don't we go to the bookstore? It's on the second floor of this building.
M That's a good idea. We'll come back here at 6 o'clock.

남 식당이 아직 안 열었네.
여 저녁은 6시에 시작하나 봐. 지금 몇 시야?
남 5시 30분이야. 30분 더 기다려야 해.
여 이 근처에 시간을 보낼 수 있는 커피숍 있어?
남 그건 별로 좋은 생각이 아닌 것 같아. 곧 저녁 먹을 거잖아. 산책하는 게 어때?
여 밖은 추워. 서점에 가는 게 어때? 서점이 이 건물의 2층에 있어.
남 그거 좋은 생각이다. 6시에 여기로 돌아오자.

해설 식당이 30분 후에 문을 열어서 그때까지 두 사람은 서점에 가 있기로 했다.

어휘 yet (부정문·의문문에서) 아직   nearby 근처에   spend (시간을) 보내다   take a walk 산책하다   the second floor 2층   building 건물   come back 돌아오다

09 ⑤

M Hello, Potomac Swimming Pool users. The annual swimming contest is next Saturday. This is the right time to show off your swimming skills. If you haven't signed up, it's not too late. Please tell any staff member that you want to take part in the contest. The entry fee is 5,000 won per person. All participants will receive a free drink and a souvenir T-shirt. Sign up now and have fun!

남 안녕하세요, Potomac Swimming Pool 이용객 여러분. 연례 수영 대회가 다음 주 토요일에 있습니다. 이번이 바로 여러분의 수영 실력을 자랑할 때입니다. 신청하지 않으셨다면, 늦지 않았습니다. 대회에 참여하고 싶다고 아무 직원에게나 말씀해 주세요. 참가비는 인당 5,000원입니다. 모든 참가자 분들은 무료 음료와 기념 티셔츠를 받으실 것입니다. 지금 신청하고 즐거운 시간 보내세요!

해설 남자는 수영 대회 우승자의 상금은 언급하지 않았다.

어휘 swimming pool 수영장   annual 연례의, 매년의   show off 자랑하다   skill 실력   sign up 신청하다   staff member 직원   take part in ~에 참여(참가)하다   entry fee 참가비   participant 참가자   receive 받다   souvenir 기념품

10 ②

(Cellphone rings.)
M Hello. Is this Noelle Miller?
W Speaking. Who's this?
M Neil Smith, the air conditioner repairman. Can I visit your house around 2 p.m. tomorrow?
W I think I'll be outside my home at that time.
M Then how about the day after tomorrow?
W I want to get it repaired as soon as possible. Can you come tomorrow evening?
M I'm busy until 9 o'clock. Is that too late?
W 9 o'clock is fine. Thank you.

(휴대 전화가 울린다.)
남 여보세요. Noelle Miller 씨 되시나요?
여 네. 누구시죠?
남 에어컨 수리 기사 Neil Smith입니다. 내일 오후 2시쯤 댁에 방문해도 될까요?
여 그때는 제가 밖에 있을 것 같아요.
남 그럼, 내일모레는 어떠세요?
여 저는 가능한 한 빨리 수리 받고 싶어요. 내일 저녁에 오실 수 있나요?
남 저는 저녁 9시까지는 바빠요. 너무 늦나요?
여 9시 괜찮아요. 고맙습니다.

해설 에어컨 수리 기사인 남자는 고객의 집에 언제 방문하면 좋을지 일정을 잡기 위해 전화했다.

어휘 air conditioner 에어컨   repairman 수리 기사   around ~쯤   the day after tomorrow 내일모레   repair 수리하다   as soon as possible 가능한 한 빨리   until ~까지   late 늦은

11 ④

W The holiday season is fast approaching. So we at Home Furniture will offer our store members a chance to save up to 50% on our products. It will be on this Sunday, December 23, from 10 a.m. to 3 p.m. You can get a discount on all our furniture only if you are a member of our store. Don't miss this great chance. See you on that day.

여 휴가철이 빠르게 다가오고 있습니다. 그래서 저희 Home Furniture에서는 회원 분들께 제품을 50퍼센트까지 절약할 수 있는 기회를 제공하고자 합니다. 12월 23일 이번 주 일요일 오전 10시부터 오후 3시까지입니다. 저희 상점의 회원이시기만 하면, 모든 가구를 할인 받으실 수 있습니다. 이 굉장한 기회를 놓치지 마세요. 그날 뵙겠습니다.

[해설] 가구점에서 회원들을 대상으로 하는 할인 행사에 대한 공지이다.

[어휘] holiday 휴가　season 철, 시기　approach 다가오다　furniture 가구　offer 제공하다　member 회원　chance 기회　save 절약하다　up to ~까지　product 제품　get a discount 할인을 받다　only if ~일 경우에만　miss 놓치다

12 ③

M Haley, do you want to go shopping with me this afternoon?
W I'm sorry, but I can't. I'm going to meet my friends in the library.
M How about tomorrow then?
W I'm available only in the morning. I have a swimming class in the afternoon.
M Then I guess I have to go by myself this time.
W What about Saturday? I'm free this weekend.
M Okay. See you on Saturday.

남 Haley, 오늘 오후에 나랑 같이 쇼핑하러 갈래?
여 미안하지만 안 돼. 도서관에서 친구들을 만날 거야.
남 그럼 내일은 어때?
여 오전에만 시간이 있어. 오후에는 수영 수업이 있거든.
남 그럼 이번엔 나 혼자 가야겠다.
여 토요일은 어때? 나 이번 주말에 한가해.
남 그래. 토요일에 보자.

[해설] 여자는 내일 오후에 수영 수업이 있다고 했다.

[어휘] go shopping 쇼핑하러 가다　library 도서관　available 시간이 있는　by oneself 혼자　free 다른 계획이 없는, 한가한

13 ③

M I'd like four tickets for the first floor. I want all the seats to be next to one another.
W There are only two seats on the first floor still available.
M Then give me two on the first floor and two on the second floor, please.
W Okay. A ticket for the first floor is $50, and one for

the second floor is $30.
M Then it comes to $160.
W If you all are family members, you can get a 10% family discount.
M Yes, we are. That's good to hear.

남 1층에 표 네 장 주세요. 모든 좌석이 서로 붙어 있으면 좋겠어요.
여 1층에는 두 자리만 가능합니다.
남 그럼 1층에 두 장과 2층에 두 장을 주세요.
여 알겠습니다. 1층은 표 한 장에 50달러이고, 2층은 표 한 장에 30달러입니다.
남 그럼 160달러가 되네요.
여 모두 가족이시면, 10퍼센트 가족 할인을 받으실 수 있어요.
남 네, 가족이에요. 좋네요.

[해설] 1층과 2층 좌석 표를 두 장씩 달라고 했는데, 1층 좌석은 장당 50달러, 2층 좌석은 장당 30달러이므로 총 금액은 160달러이다. 여기에 가족 할인 10퍼센트를 받았으므로 남자는 144달러를 지불해야 한다.

[어휘] on the first(second) floor 1(2)층에　seat 자리, 좌석　one another 서로　still 아직　available 이용 가능한　come to (총계가) ~이 되다　family members 가족 구성원　get a discount 할인을 받다

14 ①

M Mrs. Wilson, are you feeling better?
W Yes, much better. I had a bad cold.
M I'm glad you got better. By the way, aren't our children too noisy sometimes?
W Ah, it's mostly okay. But when they run in the apartment at night, it's a little hard for me to rest.
M I'm really sorry. We will be more careful.
W Most of the time it's fine. Don't worry too much.
M Thank you for your understanding.

남 Wilson 씨, 좀 괜찮아요?
여 네, 훨씬 나아졌어요. 심한 감기였네요.
남 나아졌다니 다행이네요. 그런데, 우리 아이들 때문에 가끔 너무 시끄럽지는 않나요?
여 아, 대체로 괜찮아요. 그런데 밤에 아파트에서 아이들이 뛰어다닐 때는 제가 잠들기가 좀 힘들긴 하더라고요.
남 정말 죄송해요. 더욱 조심할게요.
여 대체로는 괜찮아요. 너무 걱정하지 마세요.
남 이해해 줘서 고마워요.

[해설] 서로의 안부를 묻고 층간 소음에 대해 이야기하는 것으로 보아 두 사람은 윗집과 아랫집에 사는 이웃이다.

[어휘] bad cold 심한 감기　get better 나아지다　by the way 그런데　noisy 시끄러운　sometimes 가끔　mostly 대부분　apartment 아파트　rest 휴식을 취하다, 자다　be careful 조심하다　understand 이해하다

15 ④

M Don't you think we need some decorations in our classroom?
W Yes, I do. Why don't we put flowerpots by the

window?

M That's good. I can bring some.

W Thanks. I'm also thinking of making a class library.

M A class library? Where are you going to get all the books?

W I can tell everyone to bring some books to share.

M Good idea.

W Can you tell our teacher about this and ask his opinion?

M No problem.

남 우리 교실을 좀 꾸며야 할 것 같지 않니?

여 응, 그래. 창문 옆에 화분을 두면 어때?

남 그거 좋다. 내가 좀 가져올게.

여 고마워. 그리고 난 학급 문고를 만드는 걸 생각 중이야.

남 학급 문고? 모든 책들을 어디에서 가져올 건데?

여 애들한테 함께 볼 책들을 몇 권 가져오라고 말 할 거야.

남 좋은 생각이다.

여 선생님께 학급 문고에 대해서 말씀 드리고 의견을 여쭤봐 줄 수 있어?

남 문제없어.

[해설] 여자는 남자에게 학급 문고를 만드는 것에 대해 담임 선생님께 의견을 여쭤봐 달라고 부탁했다.

[어휘] decoration 장식   classroom 교실   flowerpot 화분   by ~ 옆에   bring 가져오다   think of ~을 생각하다   share 공유하다, 나누다   opinion 의견

16 ①

W Have you finished your English essay?

M Yes. I finished it last night.

W Good. Why don't we go biking this afternoon?

M I'm afraid I can't.

W Why not? Come on! It's perfect weather today.

M Because of my ankle. As you know, I sprained it while playing soccer two days ago.

W Oh, does it still hurt?

M Yeah. I need to be careful until it gets better.

여 너 영어 과제 끝냈니?

남 응. 어젯밤에 끝냈어.

여 잘됐다. 오늘 오후에 나랑 자전거 타러 가는 게 어때?

남 미안하지만 안 돼.

여 왜? 이봐! 오늘 완벽한 날씨잖아.

남 내 발목 때문에. 너도 알다시피, 나는 이틀 전에 축구하다가 발목을 삐었어.

여 아, 발목이 아직 아프니?

남 응. 나아질 때까지는 조심해야 해.

[해설] 남자는 이틀 전에 축구를 하다가 발목을 삐어서 자전거를 타러 갈 수 없다고 했다.

[어휘] finish 끝내다   essay (짧은 논문 형태의) 과제물   go biking 자전거 타러 가다   ankle 발목   as you know 너도 알다시피   sprain 삐다, 접지르다   while ~하는 동안에   ago ~ 전에   still 아직   hurt 아프다   get better (병이) 나아지다

17 ②

① **W** May I try this on?

M I'm sorry, but you cannot try sweaters on.

② **W** Long time, no see. How have you been?

M I didn't have time to finish my work.

③ **W** How did you like the musical?

M I didn't like it. It was boring.

④ **W** Is there a post office nearby?

M Yes. One block away from here.

⑤ **W** Thank you for coming to my party.

M It's my pleasure.

① 여 이것 좀 입어 봐도 될까요?

남 죄송하지만, 스웨터는 입어 보실 수 없어요.

② 여 오랜만이야. 어떻게 지냈니?

남 일을 끝낼 시간이 없었어.

③ 여 뮤지컬은 어땠니?

남 별로였어. 지루했어.

④ 여 근처에 우체국이 있나요?

남 네. 여기에서 한 블록 떨어져 있어요.

⑤ 여 내 파티에 와 줘서 고마워.

남 천만에.

[해설] ② 오랜만에 만나서 어떻게 지냈는지 묻는 말에 일을 끝낼 시간이 없었다고 답하는 것은 어색하다.

[어휘] try on 입어 보다   boring 지루한   post office 우체국   nearby 근처에   away from ~에서 떨어져 있는

18 ②

M There is a donation drive next month.

W Oh, I almost forgot. It's for the whole month of May, right?

M Yes. What are you going to donate?

W I don't know. I can break open my piggy bank.

M You cannot donate money. You can only donate canned food or unused items.

W Oh, right. I need to think about it.

M When you bring something, you can put it in one of the donation boxes on each floor of our school.

W I got it.

남 다음 달에 기부 운동이 있어.

여 오. 거의 잊고 있었어. 5월 내내 하는 거 맞지?

남 응. 넌 뭘 기부할 거니?

여 모르겠어. 내 돼지 저금통을 깨도 되고.

남 돈은 기부할 수 없어. 통조림 식품이나 사용하지 않은 물건들만 기부할 수 있어.

여 아, 맞다. 생각 좀 해 봐야겠다.

남 뭔가 가져오면 우리 학교 각 층에 있는 기부함 중 하나에 넣으면 돼.

여 알았어.

[해설] 기부 운동은 5월 내내 열린다고 했다.

[어휘] donation 기부   drive (조직적인) 운동   whole 전체의   donate 기부하다   break open 부수고 열다   piggy bank 돼지 저금통   canned food 통조림 식품   unused 사용하지 않은   item 물건   floor 층

19 ④

W Semin, do you exercise regularly?
M No, but I feel like I should do something. I <u>get exhausted too easily</u> these days.
W Then you really <u>should start working out</u>.
M What kind of exercise do you think is good for me?
W How about tennis? I play it <u>three times a week</u>. It's a good sport.
M I'm not good at ball sports.
W <u>What about swimming then?</u>

여 세민아, 너는 규칙적으로 운동을 하니?
남 아니, 그런데 뭐 좀 하긴 해야 할 것 같아. 요즘 너무 쉽게 지쳐.
여 그럼 너는 정말 운동을 시작해야겠다.
남 어떤 운동이 나한테 좋을 것 같니?
여 테니스는 어때? 난 일주일에 세 번 쳐. 좋은 운동이야.
남 난 구기 종목은 잘 못하는데.
여 <u>그럼 수영은 어때?</u>

해설 남자가 운동을 추천해 달라고 했는데 구기 종목은 잘하지 못한다고 했으므로 수영을 제안하는 말이 가장 적절하다.
① 마음에 든다니 기뻐.
② 글쎄, 네 친구들과 함께 해 봐.
③ 나는 테니스 동아리에 가입하고 싶어.
⑤ 농구를 하는 게 어때?

어휘 exercise 운동하다; 운동   regularly 규칙적으로   exhausted 기진맥진한   easily 쉽게   these days 요즘   work out 운동하다   be good at ~을 잘하다

20 ②

M Jina, what kinds of books do you like?
W <u>I like historical novels</u>. How about you?
M So do I! Then you might like *The Garden*.
W I think <u>I've heard of that book</u>.
M The story takes place in the Middle Ages.
W That's interesting.
M I've already finished reading it. Do you want me to <u>lend you the book</u>?
W No thanks. I'm going to buy it.

남 지나야, 너는 어떤 종류의 책을 좋아해?
여 나는 역사 소설을 좋아해. 너는?
남 나도! 그럼 너는 〈The Garden〉을 좋아할 거야.
여 그 책을 들어 봤던 것 같아.
남 그 이야기는 중세 시대를 배경으로 해.
여 흥미로운데.
남 난 이미 다 읽었어. 책을 빌려줄까?
여 <u>고맙지만 괜찮아. 책을 살 거야.</u>

해설 남자가 여자에게 책을 빌려줄지 물었으므로 이에 대한 긍정이나 부정의 응답이 와야 한다.
① 너한테 책을 빌려줄 수 있어.
③ 왜냐하면 난 그걸 읽고 싶지 않기 때문이야.
④ 응. 나는 전에 그 작가를 만난 적이 있어.
⑤ 고맙지만, 너 먼저 다 읽어.

어휘 historical 역사적인   novel 소설   take place 일어나다   the Middle Ages 중세 시대   lend 빌려주다   author 작가

Review Test
pp.78~79

Word Check   05회

01 ~에 속하다	02 보통의
03 끈, 줄, 띠	04 개선되다, 나아지다
05 ~와 관련 있는	06 줄
07 베트남의	08 조언, 충고
09 여드름	10 내내, ~ 동안 쭉
11 구역, 부문	12 분실물 보관소
13 air conditioner	14 half price
15 bother	16 humid
17 support	18 available
19 farewell party	20 generous
21 messy	22 manage
23 in a few hours	24 cost

Expression Check

25 focus on	26 by any chance
27 for a long time	28 throw a party
29 pick, up	30 sold out

Word Check   06회

01 놓치다	02 ~ 아래에
03 진지한, 농담이 아닌	04 경험
05 장관을 이루는, 극적인	06 연례의
07 산책하다	08 직원
09 참가비	10 할인을 받다
11 서로	12 전국적인
13 approach	14 furniture
15 souvenir	16 noisy
17 unused	18 share
19 sprain	20 repair
21 nearby	22 donation
23 decoration	24 exhausted

Expression Check

25 is covered with	26 stand for
27 a couple of	28 I'm, into
29 working out	30 takes place

01	⑤	02	④	03	③	04	⑤	05	③
06	①	07	⑤	08	⑤	09	②	10	⑤
11	④	12	④	13	③	14	①	15	⑤
16	②	17	④	18	④	19	①	20	③

01 ⑤

W This is CKNY, and I'm Anita with the weather. Right now, it's very humid, and the sky is covered with thick clouds. There is a 70% chance of rain this afternoon. Don't forget your umbrella when you go out. Staring tomorrow morning, however, it's going to be clear, and we will be able to see blue skies all day.

여 CKNY 일기 예보의 Anita입니다. 현재 상당히 습하고, 하늘이 짙은 구름으로 드리워져 있습니다. 오늘 오후에는 강수 확률이 70퍼센트입니다. 외출하실 때 우산을 잊지 마세요. 하지만 내일 아침부터는 맑겠으며 하루 종일 파란 하늘을 볼 수 있겠습니다.

해설 내일 아침부터는 맑을 것이라고 했다.

어휘 humid 습한 be covered with ~로 덮여 있다 thick clouds 무겁게 드리운 구름 chance 가능성 go out 외출하다 be able to ~할 수 있다 all day 하루 종일

02 ④

M What can I do for you?
W I want to buy a mug. Which one is popular?
M Our mugs are all very popular, but this one with the big heart is the most popular.
W Well, I'm not sure.
M Do you want a mug with writing on it?
W I'd like a mug with writing as well as the heart.
M Okay. This one has "Love" written below the heart.
W I like it. I'll take that one.

남 무엇을 도와드릴까요?
여 머그 컵을 사고 싶어요. 어떤 게 인기 있나요?
남 저희 머그 컵은 모두 인기가 많은데, 큰 하트가 있는 이 머그 컵이 가장 인기 있어요.
여 음, 잘 모르겠네요.
남 머그 컵에 글자가 쓰여 있는 걸 원하세요?
여 하트도 있고 글씨도 있는 걸 원해요.
남 네. 이 머그 컵은 하트 아래에 'Love'라고 쓰여 있습니다.
여 이게 마음에 들어요. 이걸 살게요.

해설 여자는 하트 아래에 'Love'라는 글자가 쓰인 머그 컵을 사겠다고 했다.

어휘 mug 머그 컵 popular 인기 있는 heart 하트 writing (손으로 쓰거나 인쇄된) 글자(글씨) A as well as B B뿐만 아니라 A도 below ~ 아래에

03 ③

M Do you know there'll be a music festival this weekend?
W I didn't know that. Where will it be held?
M At Central Park. Several rock bands will play there.
W Are the Blue Boys playing there?
M Yes, they are.
W They're my favorite rock band.
M Do you want to go with me then?
W I'd love to. I'm really looking forward to it.

남 이번 주말에 음악 축제가 있는 거 알고 있니?
여 몰랐어. 어디서 하는데?
남 Central Park에서. 여러 록 밴드들이 거기에서 연주할 거야.
여 Blue Boys도 거기에서 연주하니?
남 응.
여 그들은 내가 제일 좋아하는 록 밴드야.
남 그럼 나랑 같이 갈래?
여 좋아. 정말 기대된다.

해설 여자는 남자와 함께 음악 축제에 가는 것이 정말 기대된다고 했으므로 신이 난 상태이다.

어휘 festival 축제 be held 열리다, 개최되다 several 여러, 몇몇의 look forward to ~을 기대하다 proud 자랑스러운 nervous 긴장한, 초조해하는

04 ⑤

M This place is huge.
W It has the largest number of books in the city.
M It has lecture rooms, too.
W Yes. I heard it has many classes for citizens.
M Do you come here often?
W Yes. I come here to check out books and to study.
M I see. I want to check out some books, but I need to get a card first.

남 이곳은 정말 규모가 크구나.
여 이 도시에서는 제일 많은 책을 소장하고 있대.
남 강의실도 있네.
여 응. 시민들을 위한 많은 수업이 있다고 들었어.
남 넌 여기 자주 오니?
여 응. 책을 빌리고 공부하러 여기에 와.
남 그렇구나. 나도 책을 좀 빌리고 싶은데, 먼저 카드를 만들어야겠다.

해설 책을 많이 소장하고 있고 시민들을 위한 강의실이 있으며 책을 대출할 수 있는 곳은 도서관이다.

어휘 huge 거대한 the number of ~의 수 city 도시 lecture room 강의실 citizen 시민 often 자주 check out (도서관 등에서) 대출하다 first 먼저, 우선

05 ③

W Excuse me. Do you have this dress in a medium size?
M Yes, here it is. Would you like to try this on?

W Actually, I tried it on yesterday. I'll take it.
M All right. It's $49.
W $49? Isn't it on sale?
M I'm sorry. The sale ended yesterday.
W Oh, my. Can you sell it at the sale price today? It is only one day later.
M I'm sorry. You have to wait for the next sale.

여 실례합니다. 이 원피스 중간 사이즈가 있나요?
남 네, 여기 있습니다. 입어 보시겠어요?
여 사실 어제 입어 봤어요. 이걸 살게요.
남 네. 49달러입니다.
여 49달러요? 세일 중 아닌가요?
남 죄송합니다. 세일은 어제 끝났어요.
여 오, 이런. 오늘도 세일 가격에 판매하실 수 있나요? 고작 하루 지났잖아요.
남 죄송합니다. 다음 세일을 기다리셔야 해요.

해설 오늘도 세일 가격으로 판매할 수 있는지 묻는 여자의 말에 남자가 다음 세일을 기다리라고 답한 것은 여자의 요청을 거절하겠다는 뜻이다.

어휘 medium 중간의   try on 입어 보다   on sale 할인 중인   end 끝나다   price 가격   wait for ~을 기다리다

06 ①

W David, I heard you are taking piano lessons.
M Yes, I am. They're really fun.
W I want to take some music lessons, too.
M Let's take piano lessons together.
W I can already play the piano. I want to play something else.
M Then what about the violin?
W The violin? I think it will be too difficult.
M How about the guitar? You can play and sing. You like singing.
W That's a good idea. I'll search for a teacher now.

여 David, 네가 피아노 수업을 듣고 있다고 들었어.
남 응. 정말 재미있어.
여 나도 음악 수업 듣고 싶어.
남 같이 피아노 수업 듣자.
여 난 이미 피아노를 칠 수 있어. 다른 걸 연주해 보고 싶어.
남 그럼, 바이올린은 어떠니?
여 바이올린? 너무 어려울 것 같아.
남 기타는 어때? 연주하면서 노래할 수 있어. 너 노래하는 거 좋아하잖아.
여 그거 좋은 생각이다. 지금 선생님을 찾아봐야겠어.

해설 여자는 기타를 배워 보라는 남자의 제안에 동의하며 선생님을 찾아보겠다고 했다.

어휘 take a lesson 수업을 듣다   together 같이   else 또 다른, 그 밖의   difficult 어려운   search for ~을 찾다

07 ⑤

M How about having lunch before watching the movie?

W Okay. What do you want to eat?
M Let's try the new Chinese restaurant over there.
W Sounds good. Oh, there is a line of people waiting.
M Yeah, we need to wait a bit.
W Then wouldn't it be better to buy movie tickets first?
M Good idea. I'll go and buy tickets.
W Okay. Then I'll be waiting in line.

남 영화 보기 전에 점심 먹는 게 어때?
여 그래. 뭐 먹고 싶어?
남 저기에 있는 새로운 중국 음식점에 가 보자.
여 좋아. 오, 대기하는 줄이 있네.
남 응, 좀 기다려야겠다.
여 그럼, 먼저 영화표를 사는 게 낫지 않을까?
남 좋은 생각이야. 내가 가서 영화표를 살게.
여 그래. 그럼 나는 줄을 서서 기다리고 있을게.

해설 여자는 식당 앞에서 줄을 서서 기다리고 남자는 영화표를 사 오기로 했다.

어휘 have lunch 점심을 먹다   line 줄   a bit 조금   ticket 표   wait in line 줄을 서서 기다리다

08 ⑤

M What are you reading?
W I'm reading *Great Expectations*.
M Is it a novel?
W Haven't you heard of *Great Expectations*? It's a novel written by Charles Dickens.
M No, I haven't. What's the story about?
W It is a story of a boy who learns valuable lessons in life.
M Sounds interesting. Let me borrow it after you read it.

남 너 뭐 읽고 있어?
여 〈위대한 유산〉을 읽고 있어.
남 그거 소설이야?
여 〈위대한 유산〉을 못 들어 봤니? Charles Dickens가 쓴 소설이야.
남 아니, 못 들어 봤는데. 무슨 이야기야?
여 인생에서 소중한 교훈을 배우는 한 소년에 관한 이야기야.
남 재미있겠다. 네가 읽은 다음에 나 좀 빌려줘.

해설 여자는 책의 출판 연도는 언급하지 않았다.

어휘 novel 소설   hear of ~에 대해 듣다   learn 배우다   valuable 소중한, 가치 있는   lesson 교훈, 가르침   in life 인생에서   borrow 빌리다

09 ②

M Due to repairs on the water pipe, you'll not be able to use the water starting at 2:30 p.m. tomorrow. Unfortunately, we're not sure when the repairs will be over. We will do our best to finish it as soon as possible. You should fill buckets of water to use at night in case the repairs take a long time.

If you have any questions, please contact the management office at 250-357-9433.

남 수도관 수리로 인해, 내일 오후 2시 30분부터 물을 사용하실 수 없습니다. 유감스럽게도, 수리가 언제 끝날지 확실하지 않습니다. 가능한 한 빨리 끝내도록 최선을 다하겠습니다. 수리가 오래 걸릴 경우에 대비해서 밤에 사용하실 물을 양동이에 채워 놓으세요. 질문이 있으시면, 관리 사무소인 250-357-9433으로 연락하시기 바랍니다.

해설 수도관 수리로 인해 단수가 있을 것임을 알리는 안내 방송이다.

어휘 due to ～ 때문에　repair 수리　water pipe 수도관　be able to ～할 수 있다　unfortunately 유감스럽게도, 불행하게도　be over 끝나다　do one's best 최선을 다하다　as soon as possible 가능한 한 빨리　fill 채우다　bucket 양동이　in case ～할 경우에 대비해서　contact 연락하다　management office 관리 사무소

10　⑤

W How do you get to school?
M I usually take the bus. It's more convenient than going to school by subway.
W Right. But sometimes I don't like to take the bus.
M Why not?
W It takes much longer than the subway because there are so many stops.
M You're right. And it's too crowded in the morning. It's hard to get a seat.
W Yeah, but one good thing is that buses run very late at night.
M I agree.

여 너는 학교에 어떻게 가니?
남 난 보통 버스를 타. 지하철로 등교하는 것보다 더 편해.
여 맞아. 그런데 가끔 난 버스 타는 게 싫어.
남 왜?
여 정류장이 너무 많아서 지하철보다 훨씬 오래 걸리잖아.
남 맞아. 그리고 아침에는 너무 혼잡해. 자리를 잡기가 힘들어.
여 응, 그래도 한 가지 좋은 점은 버스는 밤늦게 운행한다는 거야.
남 동의해.

해설 버스가 밤늦게까지 운행하는 것은 장점이라고 했다.

어휘 convenient 편리한　go to school 등교하다　subway 지하철　stop 정류장　crowded 붐비는, 혼잡한　get a seat 자리를 잡다　run 운행하다　agree 동의하다

11　④

(Telephone rings.)
M Hello. I made an appointment with Dr. Smith, but I have to change it.
W Can I have your name, please?
M My name is James Harper. I have an appointment at 3:00 p.m. on Wednesday.
W All right, Mr. Harper. When do you want to change it to?
M Is there an opening next Tuesday at 3 o'clock?

W 3 o'clock is not available, but 3:30 is available.
M 3:30 is okay.
W Okay. I will put you down for that time.

(전화벨이 울린다.)
남 안녕하세요. 제가 Smith 박사님 진료를 예약했는데, 변경해야 해서요.
여 성함을 말씀해 주시겠어요?
남 제 이름은 James Harper입니다. 수요일 오후 3시로 예약되어 있어요.
여 네. Harper 씨. 언제로 바꾸고 싶으세요?
남 다음 주 화요일 3시는 비어 있나요?
여 3시는 안 되지만, 3시 30분은 가능합니다.
남 3시 30분도 괜찮습니다.
여 알겠습니다. 그 시간으로 해 드릴게요.

해설 남자는 수요일로 예약된 진료를 다음 주 화요일로 변경하기 위해 전화했다.

어휘 make an appointment 예약을 하다　have an appointment 예약이 되어 있다　opening 빈자리　available 시간이 되는　put down 적어 두다, (목록 등에) 이름을 올리다

12　④

M Mina, are you coming to my party tomorrow?
W I'm going. Everyone is bringing something to eat, right?
M Yes, they are.
W What should I bring?
M Jenny said she would bring some salad, and I'll make some spaghetti.
W I see. Is there someone who is bringing a dessert?
M Yes, Jisu is making some cookies. Why don't you bring some ice cream?
W All right. I will.

남 미나야. 내일 내 파티에 올 거야?
여 갈 거야. 모두 먹을 걸 가져가야 하는 거 맞지?
남 응.
여 나는 뭘 가져가면 돼?
남 Jenny는 샐러드를 가져온다고 했고, 나는 스파게티를 좀 만들 거야.
여 그렇구나. 후식 가져오는 사람 있어?
남 응. 지수가 쿠키를 좀 만들 거야. 너는 아이스크림을 가져오는 게 어때?
여 그래. 그럴게.

해설 남자가 아이스크림을 가져올 것을 제안하자 여자는 그러겠다고 했다.

어휘 bring 가져가다[가져오다]　dessert 디저트, 후식

13　③

M Are you ready to order?
W Yes. I'd like a cup of coffee and a donut, please.
M Coffee and donuts are $1 each. Do you want anything else?
W The banana muffins look delicious. How much is

one?

M Muffins are usually $4 each, but they're only $3 each today.

W What about a piece of apple pie?

M It's $2.

W Hmm... I'll just stay with my original order. Here's a $5 bill.

M All right. Here's your change.

남 주문하시겠어요?

여 네. 커피 한 잔하고 도넛 한 개 주세요.

남 커피와 도넛은 각 1달러입니다. 다른 것도 하시겠어요?

여 바나나 머핀이 맛있어 보이네요. 하나에 얼마예요?

남 머핀은 보통 각각 4달러이지만, 오늘은 각각 3달러예요.

여 사과 파이 한 조각은요?

남 2달러예요.

여 음... 그냥 원래 주문대로 할게요. 여기 5달러 지폐 드릴게요.

남 알겠습니다. 거스름돈 여기 있습니다.

해설 여자는 각각 1달러인 커피 한 잔과 도넛 한 개를 주문하며 5달러짜리 지폐를 냈으므로, 거스름돈으로 3달러를 받을 것이다.

어휘 a cup of ~ 한 컵   each 각각   delicious 맛있는
a piece of ~ 한 조각   stay 계속(그대로) 있다   original
원래의   order 주문   bill 지폐   change 거스름돈

14 ①

M Hi. I need something for a backache.

W What happened?

M I hurt my back when I slipped while hiking today.

W Did you go to see a doctor?

M It's too late. My doctor's office is closed now, so I have to go tomorrow morning.

W I see. Apply this cream on your back several times a day. It will help ease the pain.

M Thank you.

남 안녕하세요. 제가 허리가 아파서 뭔가가 필요해요.

여 무슨 일이 있었나요?

남 오늘 하이킹을 하다가 미끄러져서 허리를 다쳤어요.

여 병원에는 가셨어요?

남 너무 늦었어요. 지금은 병원이 닫혀 있어서 내일 아침에 가야해요.

여 그렇군요. 하루에 여러 번 허리에 이 크림을 바르세요. 통증을 가라앉히는데 도움이 될 거예요.

남 고맙습니다.

해설 남자는 허리를 다친 환자이다. 여자는 남자에게 병원에 가 봤는지 물으며 허리에 바를 약을 주었으므로 의사가 아니라 약사이다.

어휘 backache 요통   back 허리   slip 미끄러지다   while
~하는 동안에   hike 하이킹하다   see a doctor 병원에 가다
doctor's office 의원, 병원   apply 바르다   several times
여러 번   ease (고통 등을) 가라앉히다   pain 통증

15 ⑤

M How would you like your hair done?

W I want to change my hairstyle, but I'm not sure

which style will look good on me.

M I think you will look lovely with short hair.

W Really? I've always had long hair. Could you show me some pictures of short hairstyles?

M Sure. I'll bring them right away.

W Thank you.

M Here you are. Take your time.

남 머리를 어떻게 해 드릴까요?

여 헤어스타일을 바꾸고 싶은데, 어떤 스타일이 저에게 어울릴지 모르겠어요.

남 짧은 머리를 하시면 매력적이실 것 같아요.

여 정말요? 저는 늘 긴 머리를 해 왔어요. 짧은 헤어스타일 사진을 보여 주실 수 있나요?

남 물론이죠. 바로 가지고 올게요.

여 고맙습니다.

남 여기 있어요. 천천히 보세요.

해설 여자는 남자에게 짧은 헤어스타일 사진을 보여 달라고 요청했다.

어휘 hairstyle 헤어스타일   look good on ~에게 잘 어울리다
lovely 사랑스러운, 매력적인   right away 즉시, 바로

16 ②

M I'm in 507. I'm quite upset!

W What is the problem, sir?

M There is a big brown bug in the room. It's crawling on my bed. It's so creepy.

W Oh, I'm sorry. You must be frightened. Would you like me to bring you some bug spray?

M No. Just give me another room. I don't want to stay in this room any longer.

W Okay. We'll give you another room immediately. Let me check now.

남 507호인데요. 정말 화가 나네요!

여 무슨 문제 있으신가요, 손님?

남 방에 큰 갈색 벌레가 있어요. 내 침대 위를 기어가고 있어요. 정말 소름 끼쳐요.

여 오, 죄송합니다. 많이 놀라셨겠네요. 살충제를 가져다 드릴까요?

남 아니요. 그냥 다른 방을 주세요. 이 방에 더 이상 머물고 싶지 않아요.

여 알겠습니다. 바로 다른 방을 드리겠습니다. 지금 확인해 볼게요.

해설 남자는 자신이 묵는 방에서 벌레가 나와 화가 났다.

어휘 quite 꽤   upset 화가 난   bug 벌레   crawl 기어가다
creepy 소름이 끼치는, 오싹한   frightened 매우 놀란, 겁먹은
bug spray 살충제   not ~ any longer 더 이상 ~ 아닌
immediately 즉시

17 ④

W Do you want to stay healthy? I'll give you some basic tips. First, eat more vegetables and less meat. Avoid food which is high in fat. Second, work out regularly. Doing 30 minutes of exercise every day is good for your health as well as helpful to relieve your stress. Third, if you smoke, stop smoking. It's not only extremely bad for your health, but it also hurts your family and friends' health.

여 건강을 유지하고 싶으신가요? 제가 여러분께 몇 가지 기초적인 조언을 드리겠습니다. 첫째, 채소를 많이 드시고 고기를 적게 드세요. 지방 함량이 높은 음식은 피하세요. 둘째, 규칙적으로 운동하세요. 매일 30분씩 운동하는 것은 스트레스 해소에 도움될 뿐 아니라 건강에도 좋습니다. 셋째, 흡연을 하신다면 금연하세요. 흡연은 여러분의 건강에 극도로 안 좋을 뿐 아니라 여러분의 가족과 친구들의 건강도 해칩니다.

해설 여자는 건강을 유지하기 위한 방법에 대해 말하고 있다.

어휘 stay healthy 건강을 유지하다 basic 기초적인 avoid 피하다 fat 지방 work out 운동하다 regularly 규칙적으로 A as well as B B뿐만 아니라 A도 relieve 덜어 주다. 완화하다 smoke 담배를 피우다 not only A but also B A뿐만 아니라 B도 extremely 극도로 hurt 해치다

18 ④

① W Would you like to order now?
   M Yes. I'm ready to order.
② W What are you going to cook?
   M I'm going to make an omelet.
③ W Do you know what to do next?
   M You should add some pepper.
④ W Can you pass me the salad bowl?
   M Sure. Here you are.
⑤ W Can you recommend a dish on the menu?
   M The mushroom cream pasta is one of our most popular items.

① 여 지금 주문하시겠어요?
   남 네. 주문할게요.
② 여 너는 뭘 요리할 거니?
   남 나는 오믈렛을 만들 거야.
③ 여 다음에 뭘 해야 하는지 알고 있니?
   남 너는 후추를 좀 넣어야 해.
④ 여 샐러드 그릇 좀 건네줄 수 있어?
   남 물론이지. 여기 있어.
⑤ 여 메뉴에서 요리를 하나 추천해 주실 수 있나요?
   남 버섯 크림 파스타가 가장 인기 있는 메뉴 중 하나입니다.

해설 샐러드 그릇을 건네 달라고 요청하고 그에 응답하며 건네주는 내용의 대화가 적절하다.

어휘 omelet 오믈렛 add 추가하다 pepper 후추 pass 건네주다 bowl (우묵한) 그릇 recommend 추천하다 dish 요리 mushroom 버섯 popular 인기 있는

19 ①

M I'd like to buy some flowers for my wife. It's her birthday.
W What flowers does your wife like?
M She loves roses.
W Roses come in various colors: red, pink, and yellow.
M I'd like some red roses. How much are they?

W You can get a dozen for only $20.
M That sounds good. I'll take one dozen.
W Very good. Would you like anything else?
M No, thank you.

남 아내에게 줄 꽃을 좀 사려고 해요. 아내의 생일이거든요.
여 아내 분께서 어떤 꽃을 좋아하세요?
남 장미를 좋아해요.
여 장미는 여러 색으로 나와요. 빨간색, 분홍색, 노란색이 있습니다.
남 빨간 장미로 할게요. 얼마인가요?
여 단 20달러에 열두 송이를 가져가실 수 있어요.
남 좋네요. 열두 송이를 살게요.
여 아주 좋아요. 다른 것은 필요 없으세요?
남 없어요. 고맙습니다.

해설 여자가 다른 것을 더 살 것인지 물었으므로 이에 대한 긍정 또는 부정의 응답이 와야 한다.
② 대부분의 여자들은 장미를 아주 좋아해요.
③ 그녀에게 생일 축하한다고 말해 줘.
④ 아내 분께서 아주 좋아하시겠어요.
⑤ 잘 선택하셨어요. 오늘 할인 중이거든요.

어휘 wife 아내 rose 장미 various 다양한 dozen 다스, 12개짜리 한 묶음 choice 선택 on sale 할인 중인

20 ③

W Jake, what are you looking for?
M I lost my new pen. I bought it yesterday!
W When did you last use it?
M I remember I used it in English class.
W And then?
M Then, I went to P.E. class. After that, it was lunch. And now I can't find it.
W It should be somewhere in the classroom. Did you look everywhere?
M Yes, but I couldn't find it.

여 Jake, 뭘 찾고 있어?
남 새 펜을 잃어버렸어. 어제 산 건데!
여 펜을 마지막으로 쓴 게 언제니?
남 영어 수업 시간에 펜을 쓴 게 기억 나.
여 그러고 나서?
남 그러고 나서, 체육 수업에 갔어. 그 후에는, 점심시간이었어. 그리고 지금은 펜을 못 찾겠어.
여 교실 어딘가에 있겠네. 다 찾아봤어?
남 응. 그런데도 못 찾았어.

해설 여자가 교실을 다 찾아봤는지 물었으므로 이에 대한 긍정 또는 부정의 응답이 와야 한다.
① 그건 1달러야.
② 아니. 난 이미 펜이 하나 있어.
④ 난 사전에서 그것을 찾아봤어.
⑤ 컴퓨터를 사용하는 건 어떠니?

어휘 look for ~을 찾다 lose(-lost-lost) 잃어버리다 last 마지막으로 remember 기억하다 P.E. class 체육 수업 look up (사전 등에서) 찾아보다 dictionary 사전

실전 모의고사 **08**회　　pp.88~95

01 ①	02 ③	03 ③	04 ④	05 ③
06 ②	07 ③	08 ⑤	09 ③	10 ⑤
11 ④	12 ⑤	13 ③	14 ①	15 ③
16 ⑤	17 ⑤	18 ③	19 ④	20 ①

01 ①

M Good morning. This is the weekly weather forecast. It will be rainy or snowy on Monday and Tuesday. On Wednesday, there will be a lot of clouds. The weather will be clear from Thursday until the end of the weekend. As the weather continues to be clear, the atmosphere will get dry. Please pay special attention to prevent fires.

남 안녕하세요. 주간 일기 예보입니다. 월요일과 화요일에는 비 또는 눈이 오겠습니다. 수요일에는 구름이 많이 끼겠습니다. 목요일부터 주말이 끝날 때까지는 맑겠습니다. 맑은 날씨가 지속됨에 따라 대기는 건조해질 것입니다. 화재 예방에 특별히 주의를 기울이시기 바랍니다.

해설 목요일부터 주말이 끝날 때까지 맑을 것이라고 했다.

어휘 weekly 주간의　a lot of 많은　until ~까지　continue 계속되다　atmosphere 대기　dry 건조한　pay attention to ~에 주의를 기울이다　special 특별한　prevent 예방하다

02 ③

W I can't believe my eyes! Did you see her?
M Who are you talking about?
W The young woman over there. She's my favorite singer, Kate. She has just walked past us.
M I don't know her. Do you mean the woman with sunglasses?
W No, the woman with the ponytail who is wearing a short-sleeved, striped T-shirt.
M Now I see her. She's wearing shorts and sneakers.
W That's her.

여 믿을 수가 없어! 그녀를 봤니?
남 누구 말하는 거야?
여 저쪽에 있는 젊은 여자. 내가 제일 좋아하는 가수 Kate야. 그녀가 방금 우리를 지나쳐 갔어.
남 난 그녀를 몰라. 선글라스 낀 여자 말하는 거니?
여 아니, 반팔 줄무늬 티셔츠를 입고 있고 머리를 하나로 묶은 여자 말이야.
남 이제 보인다. 반바지를 입고 운동화를 신고 있네.
여 바로 그녀야.

해설 여자는 자신을 지나쳐 간 Kate라는 여자 가수를 가리키며 말하고 있다. Kate는 선글라스를 끼지 않았고 머리를 하나로 묶었으며, 반팔 줄무늬 티셔츠와 반바지를 입고 운동화를 신고 있다고 했다.

어휘 walk past ~을 지나치다　sunglasses 선글라스

ponytail 말총머리(하나로 묶은 머리)　short-sleeved 반소매의, 짧은 소매의　striped 줄무늬의　shorts 반바지　sneakers 운동화

03 ③

W Andy, you don't look well. What's wrong?
M I was just thinking about my class presentation.
W Do you mean the presentation of the group project?
M Yes. I'm the presenter tomorrow. This is my first time to make a presentation in front of many people.
W Don't worry. You have practiced a lot. You'll do well.
M Thanks, but I feel like I'll forget what I need to say.

여 Andy, 너 별로 안 좋아 보여. 무슨 일 있어?
남 나는 그냥 우리 반 발표에 대해 생각하고 있었어.
여 조별 프로젝트 발표 말이니?
남 응. 내가 내일 발표자야. 나는 많은 사람들 앞에서 발표를 하는 게 이번이 처음이야.
여 걱정하지 마. 연습 많이 했잖아. 잘할 거야.
남 고마워. 그런데 내가 말해야 할 것을 잊어버릴 것 같은 느낌이야.

해설 남자는 내일 많은 사람들 앞에서 발표를 해야 해서 긴장하고 있다.

어휘 presentation 발표　presenter 발표자　make a presentation 발표를 하다　in front of ~ 앞에　practice 연습하다　a lot 많이　feel like ~한 느낌이 있다

04 ④

W Ron, how was your weekend?
M I visited my grandma. She moved to a new house last Saturday.
W Did you help unpack and arrange things?
M No, my parents did. Grandma is too old to do it all by herself.
W What did you do then?
M I planted some trees and flowers in the front yard with Grandma. She loves gardening.
W That's great.

여 Ron, 주말 어땠어?
남 난 할머니 댁을 방문했어. 할머니께서 지난주 토요일에 새 집으로 이사하셨거든.
여 짐을 풀고 정리하는 걸 도와드렸니?
남 아니, 우리 부모님이 하셨어. 할머니는 너무 연로하셔서 혼자서 다 하실 수 없어.
여 그럼 넌 뭘 했는데?
남 할머니랑 같이 앞마당에 나무와 꽃을 좀 심었어. 할머니께서 정원 가꾸는 것을 아주 좋아하시거든.
여 잘했네.

해설 남자는 할머니와 함께 앞마당에 나무와 꽃을 심었다고 했다.

어휘 move to ~로 이사하다　unpack (짐을) 풀다　arrange 정리하다　too ~ to ... 너무 ~해서 … 할 수 없는　by oneself 스스로, 혼자　plant 심다　front 앞의　yard 마당　garden 정원을 가꾸다

05 ③

M Can I have a fever reducer for babies? She's two years old.
W Yes, you can. Have her take this syrup when her body temperature is above 38°C.
M I got it.
W Read and follow all instructions on the label over here.
M Okay. Thanks a lot.

남 아기용 해열제 있나요? 아기는 두 살이에요.
여 네. 아기의 체온이 38°C가 넘으면 이 시럽을 먹이세요.
남 알겠습니다.
여 여기 상표에 있는 설명을 모두 읽고 따르세요.
남 네. 정말 고맙습니다.

해설 해열제를 구입하고 있으므로 약국에서 이루어지는 대화이다.

어휘 fever reducer 해열제 take (약을) 먹다 syrup 시럽 body temperature 체온 above ~을 넘는, ~보다 많은 follow 따르다 instruction (제품 등의) 설명 label 상표

06 ②

M Liz, why are you so late?
W I worked late on a school project.
M Really? You must be very tired.
W And extremely hungry.
M Didn't you have dinner yet?
W I had a sandwich, but it wasn't enough at all.
M Oh, no. There isn't much to eat at home right now.
W Then can you order some fried chicken while I change my clothes?

남 Liz, 왜 이렇게 늦었니?
여 학교 프로젝트로 늦게까지 작업했어요.
남 정말? 아주 피곤하겠구나.
여 그리고 엄청 배고파요.
남 아직 저녁 안 먹었니?
여 샌드위치를 먹긴 했는데, 전혀 충분하지 않았어요.
남 아, 이런. 지금 집에 별로 먹을 게 없는데.
여 그럼 제가 옷 갈아입는 동안 프라이드치킨을 주문해 주실래요?

해설 여자는 자신이 옷을 갈아입는 동안 프라이드치킨을 주문해 달라고 부탁했다.

어휘 extremely 극도로 yet (부정문·의문문에서) 아직 not ~ at all 전혀 ~가 아닌 enough 충분한 order 주문하다 while ~하는 동안에 change clothes 옷을 갈아입다

07 ③

W Today, I'd like to introduce a very interesting fruit, durian, to you. Durian is a tropical fruit. It grows only in humid, hot places. It can grow up to thirty centimeters long and usually weighs one to three kilograms. The flesh is used for many dishes in Southeast Asia. People call it the "King of Fruits." It has a strong smell, so many hotels and public transportation systems do not let people carry it.

여 오늘은 여러분께 아주 흥미로운 과일인 두리안을 소개하겠습니다. 두리안은 열대 과일입니다. 습하고 더운 곳에서만 자라죠. 두리안은 길이가 30센티미터까지 자랄 수 있고, 보통 무게는 1~3킬로그램이 나갑니다. 과육은 동남아시아의 많은 요리에 사용됩니다. 사람들은 두리안을 '과일의 왕'이라고 부릅니다. 두리안은 냄새가 고약해서 많은 호텔과 대중교통 시설에서는 사람들이 두리안을 가지고 다니지 못하게 합니다.

해설 여자는 두리안의 색깔은 언급하지 않았다.

어휘 introduce 소개하다 interesting 흥미로운 tropical 열대의 grow 자라다 humid 습한 up to ~까지 weigh 무게가 ~이다 flesh 과육 dish 요리 Southeast Asia 동남아시아 call A B A를 B라고 부르다 smell 냄새 public transportation 대중교통 carry 가지고 다니다

08 ⑤

W Dad, it's Mom's birthday today. Do you have any special plans?
M Of course. I ordered a cake and flowers. I'll pick up the cake at 5 o'clock.
W What about the flowers?
M They'll be delivered to our home.
W Sounds like a perfect plan. Is there anything I can do?
M Can you call her and check when she'll be home from work?
W Okay. I'll do that right away.

여 아빠, 오늘이 엄마 생신이에요. 특별한 계획 있으세요?
남 물론이지. 나는 케이크와 꽃을 주문했단다. 5시에 케이크를 찾아올 거야.
여 꽃은요?
남 꽃은 집으로 배달될 거야.
여 완벽한 계획인 것 같네요. 제가 할 수 있는 일이 있나요?
남 엄마에게 전화해서 퇴근해서 언제 집에 오는지 확인해 줄래?
여 네. 지금 바로 할게요.

해설 여자는 엄마에게 전화해서 언제 집에 오는지 확인해 달라는 아빠의 요청에 응하며 지금 바로 하겠다고 했다.

어휘 special 특별한 plan 계획 order 주문하다 pick up ~에서 찾아오다 deliver 배달하다 work 직장

09 ③

M Mom, I'll make you French toast for breakfast.
W That sounds good. Do you know how to make it?
M Of course. It's very easy to make. Do we have enough bread, eggs, and milk?
W Yes. You also need butter to put on the pan.
M I know it. Do you want me to add some sugar on top?
W No. It will make the toast too sweet.
M Okay. Wait for a few minutes, Mom.

남 엄마, 제가 아침으로 프렌치토스트를 만들어 드릴게요.

여 그거 좋겠는걸. 그걸 어떻게 만드는지 아니?

남 물론이죠. 만들기 아주 쉬워요. 빵이랑 달걀이랑 우유가 충분히 있나요?

여 응. 그리고 팬에 올릴 버터도 필요해.

남 알아요. 토스트 위에 설탕을 뿌려 드릴까요?

여 아니. 토스트가 너무 달 거야.

남 알겠어요. 조금만 기다리세요, 엄마.

해설 여자가 토스트에 설탕을 넣고 싶지 않다고 하자 남자는 알았다고 했다.

어휘 French toast 프렌치토스트(우유와 달걀을 섞어 푼 것에 식빵을 적셔 프라이팬에 구운 것) enough 충분한 put on 올려 놓다 pan 프라이팬 add 추가하다 sugar 설탕 top 위, 윗면 for a few minutes 잠시 동안

10 ⑤

M Plants can purify the air at your home and they are also good for decorations. Then what can you do to keep your plants healthy? First, do not water your plants too often. Too much water can kill your plants. Second, let your plants get enough sunlight during the day. Third, do not move your plants around a lot. Keep these things in mind.

남 식물은 집의 공기를 깨끗하게 해 주고 장식에도 좋습니다. 그럼 식물을 잘 기르기 위해서 무엇을 할 수 있을까요? 첫째, 식물에 너무 자주 물을 주지 마세요. 너무 많이 물을 주면 식물이 죽을 수 있습니다. 둘째, 식물이 낮 동안에 충분히 햇빛을 받을 수 있도록 하세요. 셋째, 식물을 여기저기에 많이 옮기지 마세요. 이 사항들을 명심하세요.

해설 남자는 식물을 잘 기르기 위한 세 가지 방법을 말하고 있다.

어휘 plant 식물 purify 정화하다 air 공기 decoration 장식 keep 유지하다 healthy 건강한 water 물을 주다 kill 죽이다 sunlight 햇빛 day 낮 move around 여기저기 움직이다, 돌아다니다 keep ~ in mind ~을 명심하다

11 ④

M Are you going to take any classes during vacation?

W I haven't decided yet. What about you?

M I'll take a Chinese class for beginners at school.

W Sounds interesting. When is it?

M It's from Monday to Friday, and it starts on the first day of vacation.

W How many hours each day?

M The class lasts for an hour at 9 every morning, and the class is free.

W Great! I'm in.

남 너는 방학 동안에 수업 들을 거야?

여 아직 결정하지 못했어. 너는?

남 난 학교에서 초급 중국어 수업을 들을 거야.

여 재미있겠다. 언제야?

남 월요일부터 금요일까지이고, 방학 첫째 날에 시작해.

여 하루에 몇 시간이야?

남 수업은 매일 아침 9시에 한 시간 동안 하고, 무료야.

여 좋다! 나 들을래.

해설 중국어 수업은 아침 9시에 한 시간씩 한다고 했다.

어휘 take a class 수업을 듣다 during ~ 동안 vacation 방학 decide 결정하다 yet (부정문·의문문에서) 아직 Chinese 중국어 beginner 초급자 hour 시간 last 지속하다 for ~ 동안 free 무료의

12 ⑤

(Telephone rings.)

M Green Wood Hotel. How may I help you?

W Hello. My name is Linda Brown. I checked out of Room 1307 two hours ago.

M Yes, Ms. Brown. Is there anything wrong?

W I think I left my ring in the room. Was a ring found in the room?

M I will check with lost and found and call you back. Our housekeeping staff takes all lost property to the lost and found desk.

W Okay. Thank you. Call me at this number, please.

(전화벨이 울린다.)

남 Green Wood Hotel입니다. 무엇을 도와드릴까요?

여 안녕하세요. 제 이름은 Linda Brown입니다. 두 시간 전에 1307호를 체크아웃했어요.

남 네, Brown 씨. 무슨 문제 있으신가요?

여 제가 방에 반지를 두고 온 것 같아요. 방에서 반지가 발견되었나요?

남 분실물 보관소에 확인해 보고 다시 전화 드리겠습니다. 저희 객실 관리 직원들은 모든 유실물들을 분실물 보관소 접수처로 가져 갑니다.

여 알겠습니다. 고맙습니다. 이 번호로 전화 주세요.

해설 여자는 자신이 묵었던 방에 반지를 두고 나온 것 같아서 발견된 반지가 있는지 물어보기 위해 전화했다.

어휘 check out (호텔에서) 체크아웃하다 leave(-left-left) 두고 오다 ring 반지 find(-found-found) 발견하다 lost and found 분실물 보관소 housekeeping (호텔 등의) 시설 관리과 staff 직원 take A to B A를 B로 가지고 가다 lost 잃어버린 property 소유물 desk 접수처, 프런트

13 ③

M It's already 6:30.

W Really? We're going to be late for dinner. Are you going to drive?

M No. The restaurant doesn't have a parking lot. Let's take a taxi.

W It's rush hour, so there may be a traffic jam. How about taking the subway?

M The subway station isn't really close to our house.

W But I think the subway is the fastest way we can get there. We can't take a taxi or bus because of the rush hour traffic.

M You're right. Let's hurry.

남 벌써 6시 30분이네.

여 정말? 우리 저녁 식사에 늦겠다. 너 운전할 거야?

남 아니. 식당에 주차장이 없어. 택시 타자.

여 러시아워라서 차가 막힐 거야. 지하철을 타는 게 어때?

남 지하철역은 우리 집에서 별로 가깝지 않잖아.

여 그래도 지하철이 우리가 그곳에 갈 수 있는 가장 빠른 방법인 것 같아. 교통 혼잡 때문에 택시나 버스는 못 타.

남 네 말이 맞네. 서두르자.

해설 식당에 주차장이 없어서 자가용을 못 가져가고, 교통 체증이 있을 시간이라 택시나 버스보다는 지하철을 타기로 했다.

어휘 be late for ～에 늦다, 지각하다   drive 운전하다
parking lot 주차장   take a taxi 택시를 타다   rush hour
러시아워, 출퇴근 혼잡 시간   traffic 교통(량)

14   ①

M Excuse me. I need some help.

W What can I do for you?

M Do you have jogging pants for males in a large size?

W Yes. They're right over here. These pants come in both black and gray.

M I like the black ones. Can I try these on?

W Sure. The fitting room is over there. These pants run small, so try on an extra-large, too.

M Okay. Thank you.

남 실례합니다. 도움이 좀 필요해요.

여 무엇을 도와드릴까요?

남 남자 조깅용 바지 큰 사이즈 있나요?

여 네. 바로 여기에 있습니다. 이 바지는 검은색과 회색으로 나와요.

남 검은색이 마음에 드네요. 입어 봐도 될까요?

여 물론이죠. 탈의실은 저쪽에 있습니다. 이 바지는 작게 나왔으니 특대 사이즈도 입어 보세요.

남 알겠습니다. 고맙습니다.

해설 옷 가게 점원과 조깅용 바지를 사러 온 손님 사이의 대화이다.

어휘 jogging 조깅   pants 바지   male 남성   large (치수)
대형의   both A and B A와 B 둘 다   try on 입어 보다
fitting room 탈의실   run small (옷 등이) 작게 나오다
extra-large (치수) 특대의

15   ③

M What are you doing?

W I'm posting an article on my blog. Where are you going?

M I'm going to the supermarket to get some groceries. Do you need anything?

W Not really. But could you do me a favor?

M Sure. What is it?

W On your way home, can you pick up my clothes from the dry cleaner's? I had my shirts cleaned.

M Okay. No problem.

남 너 뭐 하고 있어?

여 내 블로그에 기사 한 편을 올리고 있어. 너 어디 가?

남 식료품을 좀 사러 슈퍼마켓에 가려고. 뭐 필요한 것 있니?

여 없어. 그런데 부탁 하나 들어줄 수 있어?

남 그래. 뭔데?

여 집에 오는 길에, 세탁소에서 내 옷 좀 찾아올 수 있어? 내 셔츠를 세탁 맡겼거든.

남 알았어. 문제없어.

해설 여자는 남자에게 집에 오는 길에 자신이 세탁소에 맡긴 옷을 찾아와 달라고 부탁했다.

어휘 post 게시하다   article (신문·잡지의) 글, 기사   blog
블로그   groceries 식료품   do ～ a favor ～의 부탁을
들어주다   on one's way home 집에 오는 길에   pick up
～에서 찾아오다   dry cleaner's 세탁소

16   ⑤

W Harry, where are you going?

M I'm going to the library.

W Are you going to return some books?

M No. I just checked these out.

W Then why are you going there?

M I lost my wallet. I think I dropped it when I bumped into someone in the library.

W Do you want me to go with you? I can help you find it.

M Really? Thank you.

여 Harry, 너 어디 가?

남 도서관에 가고 있어.

여 책 반납할 거야?

남 아니. 방금 이것들을 대출했어.

여 그럼 도서관에 왜 가는데?

남 내가 지갑을 잃어버렸거든. 도서관에서 누군가에게 부딪혔을 때 그걸 떨어뜨린 것 같아.

여 내가 같이 가 줄까? 네가 지갑 찾는 걸 도와줄 수 있어.

남 정말? 고마워.

해설 남자는 잃어버린 지갑을 찾으러 도서관에 가고 있다고 했다.

어휘 library 도서관   return 반납하다   check out (도서관
등에서) 대출하다   lose(-lost-lost) 잃어버리다   wallet 지갑
drop 떨어뜨리다   bump into ～에(게) 부딪히다

17   ⑤

① M Can I come in?

   W Sure. Go ahead.

② M What's your favorite animal?

   W Dogs are my favorite.

③ M How often do you walk your dog?

   W Three times a week.

④ M Is this your painting?

   W Yes. Do you like it?

⑤ M Excuse me. We do not allow dogs inside.

   W Oh, I'm sorry. I didn't see the sign.

① 남 들어가도 될까요?

   여 물론이죠. 어서 들어오세요.

② 남 당신이 제일 좋아하는 동물이 뭐예요?

여 저는 개를 제일 좋아해요.
③ 남 당신은 얼마나 자주 개를 산책 시키나요?
　여 일주일에 세 번이요.
④ 남 이것은 당신의 그림인가요?
　여 네. 마음에 드세요?
⑤ 남 실례합니다. 내부에 개를 데리고 들어가실 수 없습니다.
　여 아, 죄송합니다. 표지판을 못 봤어요.

해설 개를 데리고 안으로 들어갈 수 없다는 내용의 대화가 적절하다.

어휘 come in 들어가다　favorite 가장 좋아하는 (것)　walk a dog 개를 산책시키다　painting 그림　allow 허락하다, 허가하다　inside 내부에, 안으로　sign 표지판

18 ③

M Emily, can you <u>recommend a good place</u> for desserts?
W My favorite around here is Jackie's Bakery.
M Where is it?
W It's on Baker Street. It's <u>right across from the post office</u>.
M It's close. Why is it your favorite?
W Because the waffles there are so good. They're crispy on the outside and <u>very soft inside</u>. You should try one.
M Oh, I can't wait! What time does it open?
W It opens from 8 a.m. to 7 p.m.

남 Emily, 디저트가 괜찮은 장소를 추천해 줄 수 있어?
여 이 근처에서 내가 가장 좋아하는 곳은 Jackie's Bakery야.
남 그게 어디야?
여 Baker Street에 있어. 우체국 바로 맞은편이야.
남 가깝네. 왜 거기가 네가 가장 좋아하는 곳이니?
여 왜냐하면 거기 와플이 너무 맛있거든. 밖은 바삭바삭하고 안은 아주 부드러워. 너도 먹어 봐야 해.
남 오, 정말 기대돼! 거기 몇 시에 열어?
여 아침 8시부터 저녁 7시까지 열어.

해설 여자는 제과점의 분위기는 언급하지 않았다.

어휘 recommend 추천하다　dessert 디저트, 후식　across from ~의 맞은편에　waffle 와플　crispy 바삭바삭한　outside 바깥쪽　soft 부드러운　inside 안쪽　try 먹어 보다

19 ④

W Mike, I <u>have just read</u> your short story in the school newspaper.
M Oh, did you? What did you think?
W It is a really interesting story. <u>You're a talented writer</u>!
M Thank you.
W I didn't know <u>you wrote short stories</u>.
M It is my favorite hobby.
W <u>When did you first begin writing</u> short stories?
M <u>I started writing them when I was 9.</u>

여 Mike, 나 방금 학교 신문에서 네 단편 소설을 읽었어.
남 아, 그랬어? 어떻게 생각해?

여 정말 재미있는 이야기야. 너 재능 있는 작가더라!
남 고마워.
여 난 네가 단편 소설을 쓰는지 몰랐어.
남 그건 내가 가장 좋아하는 취미야.
여 언제 처음으로 단편 소설을 쓰기 시작했니?
남 나는 아홉 살 때 글을 쓰기 시작했어.

해설 언제 처음 단편 소설을 쓰기 시작했는지 물었으므로 시작한 시기를 답해야 한다.
① 응. 나는 독서를 아주 좋아해.
② 나는 어젯밤에 일찍 잠들었어.
③ 너는 어떤 종류의 이야기를 좋아하니?
⑤ 이 책에는 100개도 넘는 이야기들이 있어.

어휘 short story 단편 소설　newspaper 신문　interesting 재미있는, 흥미로운　talented 재능 있는　writer 작가　hobby 취미　first 처음으로　begin(start) 시작하다　more than ~보다 많은, ~ 이상의

20 ①

W Rose Restaurant. How may I help you?
M Hi. I would like to <u>make a reservation</u>.
W <u>For which day</u> are you making the reservation?
M It's for Friday.
W What time would you like to come?
M Is 7 p.m. available?
W We have <u>only one table available</u> at 7. How many people will be <u>in your party</u>?
M <u>There will be four of us.</u>

여 Rose Restaurant입니다. 무엇을 도와드릴까요?
남 안녕하세요. 예약을 하고 싶습니다.
여 어느 날짜에 예약하시겠어요?
남 금요일이요.
여 몇 시에 오실 건가요?
남 저녁 7시 가능한가요?
여 7시에는 딱 한 테이블 남아 있습니다. 일행이 몇 분이세요?
남 저희는 네 명이에요.

해설 몇 명이 식사를 하러 올 것인지 물었으므로 인원수를 답해야 한다.
② 저희는 7시에 도착할 것입니다.
③ 제 이름은 Henry Johnson입니다.
④ 저희는 토요일에 점심을 먹고 싶어요.
⑤ 괜찮은 디저트를 추천해 주실 수 있나요?

어휘 make a reservation 예약을 하다　available 이용할 수 있는　only 유일한, 단 하나의　party 일행, 단체　arrive 도착하다　recommend 추천하다　dessert 디저트, 후식

Word Check

07회

01 붐비는, 혼잡한	**02** 다스, 12개짜리 한 묶음
03 중간의	**04** 수업을 듣다
05 편리한	**06** 소름이 끼치는, 오싹한
07 규칙적으로	**08** 유감스럽게도, 불행하게도
09 연락하다	**10** 여러, 몇몇의
11 디저트, 후식	**12** ~ 한 조각
13 go out	**14** backache
15 avoid	**16** valuable
17 crawl	**18** bill
19 right away	**20** extremely
21 apply	**22** bowl
23 pain	**24** frightened

Expression Check

25 waiting in line	**26** on sale
27 as well as	**28** Due to
29 look good on	**30** as soon as possible

Word Check

08회

01 과육	**02** 계속되다
03 말총머리(하나로 묶은 머리)	**04** 반소매의, 짧은 소매의
05 발표	**06** 발표자
07 (치수) 특대의	**08** 해열제
09 (짐을) 풀다	**10** 열대의
11 배달하다	**12** 대기
13 purify	**14** beginner
15 dry cleaner's	**16** property
17 public transportation	**18** arrange
19 post	**20** sign
21 crispy	**22** prevent
23 talented	**24** party

Expression Check

25 walked past	**26** Keep, in mind
27 feel like	**28** pay, attention to
29 wasn't, at all	**30** bumped into

01 ③	**02** ③	**03** ④	**04** ④	**05** ⑤
06 ②	**07** ③	**08** ④	**09** ⑤	**10** ④
11 ④	**12** ①	**13** ⑤	**14** ④	**15** ⑤
16 ③	**17** ④	**18** ③	**19** ⑤	**20** ⑤

01 ③

M So this is what the weather will look like this weekend. We'll <u>have lots of showers</u> on Friday and Saturday. It will also be quite windy on these days. On Saturday night, <u>the winds will die down</u>, and the showers will stop. And on Sunday, it's going to be quite foggy. Fog can <u>make driving difficult</u>, so please be careful.

남 그러면 이번 주말의 날씨가 어떨지 말씀드리겠습니다. 금요일과 토요일에는 잦은 소나기 소식이 있습니다. 바람도 강하게 불겠습니다. 토요일 밤에는 바람이 잔잔해지고, 소나기가 그치겠습니다. 그리고 일요일에는 안개가 상당히 짙게 끼겠습니다. 안개 때문에 운전하기가 어려울 수 있으므로 주의하시기 바랍니다.

해설 일요일에는 안개가 짙게 낄 것이라고 했다.

어휘 weekend 주말 lots of 많은 shower 소나기 quite 꽤, 상당히 die down 잦아들다 foggy 안개가 긴 fog 안개 driving 운전 difficult 어려운 careful 조심하는

02 ③

M Hi. I'd like to buy a teddy bear for my daughter.
W <u>We have various kinds</u>. Which one would you like?
M I guess a teddy bear with a ribbon will be good.
W Here's one with a ribbon <u>around its neck</u>.
M Well, I think it's too ordinary. Do you have one <u>with clothes or accessories</u>?
W Yes, we do. This one is <u>wearing a dress</u>, and that one over there is wearing a hat.
M I'll take the one with the hat. That's cute.

남 안녕하세요. 제 딸을 위해 곰 인형을 사고 싶어요.
여 저희는 다양한 종류가 있답니다. 어느 것을 원하세요?
남 리본을 맨 곰 인형이 좋을 것 같아요.
여 여기 목에 리본을 맨 곰 인형이 있어요.
남 글쎄요, 너무 평범한 것 같네요. 옷을 입었거나 액세서리를 한 것도 있나요?
여 네, 있어요. 이건 원피스를 입고 있고, 저기에 있는 것은 모자를 쓰고 있어요.
남 모자를 쓴 걸로 할게요. 귀엽네요.

해설 남자는 모자를 쓴 곰 인형을 사겠다고 했다.

어휘 teddy bear 곰 인형, 테디 베어 daughter 딸 various 다양한 ribbon 리본 ordinary 평범한, 보통의 clothes 옷 accessory 액세서리 dress 원피스 hat 모자

03 ④

W Wait a minute. Where are we now?

M Oh, no. I think we got off at the wrong stop.

W Didn't you say this was the right stop?

M I thought so, but we had to go three more stops. I'm sorry.

W That's okay. But the next bus comes in 15 minutes. I think we'll be late for the concert.

M If we take a taxi, we'll arrive there on time. I'll pay for the ride.

W We won't be late then. Thank you.

여 잠깐. 우리 지금 어디에 있는 거지?

남 아, 이런. 우리 잘못 내린 것 같아.

여 여기가 맞는 정류장이라고 하지 않았어?

남 그렇게 생각했는데, 우리는 세 정거장 더 가야 했네. 미안해.

여 괜찮아. 그런데 다음 버스는 15분 후에 와. 우리 콘서트에 늦을 것 같아.

남 택시를 타면 제시간에 도착할 수 있을 거야. 내가 택시비를 낼게.

여 그러면 늦지 않겠다. 고마워.

해설 콘서트에 늦을 것이라고 걱정했으나 택시를 타고 가면 제때에 도착할 수 있으므로 여자는 안도했을 것이다.

어휘 get off 내리다   wrong 틀린   stop 정류장   right 맞는 in ~ 후에   be late for ~에 늦다, 지각하다   arrive 도착하다 on time 제시간에   pay for ~을 지불하다   ride 타기, 승차

04 ④

M Jane, you look better than ever.

W Do I? The reason is probably that I have a suntan.

M Oh, now I see that. Did you go hiking during the weekend?

W No one would hike in such hot weather. I went to the beach.

M And you swam all day.

W No. I went surfing.

M Really? I've always wanted to try that. Take me there with you the next time you go.

W Okay.

남 Jane, 너 그 어느 때보다 좋아 보인다.

여 그래? 아마 내가 햇볕에 타서 그럴 거야.

남 아, 지금 보니 그러네. 주말 동안에 하이킹했니?

여 이렇게 더운 날씨엔 아무도 하이킹하지 않아. 난 바닷가에 갔었어.

남 그리고 너는 하루 종일 수영했구나.

여 아니. 나는 파도타기를 했어.

남 정말? 나도 늘 그걸 해 보고 싶었는데. 다음번에 갈 때 나도 데려가 줘.

여 그래.

해설 여자는 바닷가에 가서 파도타기를 했다고 했다.

어휘 reason 이유   probably 아마   have a suntan 햇볕에 피부를 태우다   go hiking 하이킹을 가다   such 이와 같은, 이러한   beach 바닷가   all day 하루 종일   go surfing 파도타기를 하다   try ~을 해 보다

05 ⑤

M Hello. Is your band auditioning for new members?

W That's right. Come on in. (Pause) I'm Beth. What's your name?

M I'm Daniel. I'm in the first grade. I play the guitar. Do you want to hear me play it?

W Oh, there already is a guitarist in our band. Can you play any other instruments?

M No. I only play the guitar and sing.

W That's great. We need a lead singer, too. Are you interested?

M Yeah, sure.

W Good. Let me hear you sing.

남 안녕하세요. 밴드 신입 회원 오디션을 하고 있나요?

여 맞아. 들어와. (잠시 후) 나는 Beth야. 네 이름은 뭐니?

남 저는 Daniel이에요. 1학년이에요. 저는 기타를 쳐요. 제가 연주하는 걸 들어 보실래요?

여 아, 우리 밴드에는 이미 기타리스트가 있어. 다른 악기를 연주할 수 있니?

남 아니요. 저는 기타만 치고 노래를 불러요.

여 잘됐다. 우리 리드 보컬도 필요하거든. 관심 있니?

남 네, 그럼요.

여 좋아. 그럼 네가 노래 부르는 걸 들어 볼게.

해설 남자가 학교 밴드에 들어가기 위해서 오디션을 보러 온 상황이므로 두 사람이 대화하는 장소로 밴드 동아리방이 가장 적절하다.

어휘 audition 오디션을 실시하다   member 회원   the first grade 1학년   guitarist 기타리스트   instrument 악기   lead singer 리드 보컬   interested 관심 있는

06 ②

M Excuse me. Can I get a refund for a musical ticket? I bought it through an app.

W Yes. Please give me your phone.

M Here you are.

W I am sorry, but you cannot get a refund on the day of the concert.

M Really? I didn't know that.

W The refund policy is written below the ticket image. Look here.

M Oh, well, who can read such small letters?

W I'm sorry, but it's the policy.

남 실례합니다. 뮤지컬 관람권을 환불받을 수 있나요? 앱으로 샀는데요.

여 네. 제게 전화기를 주세요.

남 여기 있습니다.

여 죄송합니다만, 공연 당일은 환불을 받으실 수 없습니다.

남 정말요? 저는 몰랐는데요.

여 관람권 이미지 아래에 환불 규정이 쓰여 있어요. 여기를 보세요.

남 오, 이런, 이렇게 작은 글씨를 누가 읽을 수 있나요?

여 죄송합니다만, 이것이 규정입니다.

해설 여자가 '죄송합니다만, 이것이 규정입니다.'라고 한 것은 남자의 환불 요청을 거절한 것으로 해석할 수 있다.

07 ③

W Today, we had Dr. Baker with us in the studio. He gave us several tips for getting a good night's sleep. Don't go to bed with the TV on. Don't think too much before bedtime. Don't play games before you go to sleep and turn off your cell phone when you go to bed. Dr. Baker, thank you for providing useful advice to our listeners.

여 오늘 저희는 스튜디오에 Baker 박사님을 모셨습니다. 박사님께서 숙면을 취하기 위한 몇 가지 조언을 해 주셨습니다. TV를 켜고 잠자리에 들지 마세요. 취침 시간 전에 너무 많은 생각을 하지 마세요. 잠자기 전에 게임을 하지 말고 잠자리에 들 때는 휴대 전화를 끄세요. Baker 박사님, 저희 청취자들께 유용한 조언을 주셔서 감사드립니다.

해설 강연을 마무리하는 사회자의 맺음말을 통해 Dr. Baker가 숙면을 취하기 위한 조언을 주제로 강연했음을 알 수 있다.

어휘 studio 스튜디오   several 여러, 몇몇의   get a good night's sleep 숙면을 취하다   bedtime 취침 시간   go to sleep 잠자리에 들다   turn off ~을 끄다   cell phone 휴대 전화   provide 제공하다   useful 유용한   advice 조언   listener 청취자

08 ④

M I want to return these two books.
W Okay. (Pause) These are two days late.
M Oh, I didn't know that. Do I have to pay a late fee?
W You don't have to, but you may not borrow a book for four days.
M For four days?
W Yes. You can't check out books for the number of days that each book is overdue.
M Oh, I see.

남 이 책 두 권을 반납할게요.
여 네. (잠시 후) 이 책들은 이틀 연체되었네요.
남 아, 몰랐어요. 연체료를 내야 하나요?
여 그러실 필요는 없지만, 4일 동안 책을 빌리실 수 없어요.
남 4일 동안이요?
여 네. 각각의 책이 연체된 날짜만큼 책을 빌리실 수 없거든요.
남 아, 그렇군요.

해설 남자는 책 두 권을 이틀 연체했는데 각 책을 연체한 기간만큼 책을 대출할 수 없기 때문에 4일 동안 책을 대출할 수 없다고 했다.

어휘 return 반납하다   pay 지불하다   late fee 연체료   borrow 빌리다   for ~ 동안   check out (도서관 등에서) 대출하다   the number of ~의 수   each 각각의   overdue 기한이 지난

09 ⑤

W I have no idea what to buy Mary for her birthday. Do you have any good ideas?
M What about buying her some books? She likes reading.
W Well, I'd like to buy something more special.
M How about a concert ticket? She said she likes rock music.
W That's a good idea. Do you know her favorite band?
M No. I think her roommate Rebecca might know though.
W I guess so. I'll call her and ask right now.

여 나는 Mary의 생일에 그녀에게 무엇을 사 줘야 할지 모르겠어. 좋은 생각 있니?
남 책을 좀 사 주는 게 어때? 그녀는 독서를 좋아하잖아.
여 글쎄. 나는 더 특별한 것을 사고 싶어.
남 콘서트 표는 어때? 그녀가 록 음악을 좋아한다고 했어.
여 그거 좋은 생각이다. 그녀가 제일 좋아하는 밴드를 알고 있니?
남 아니. 하지만 그녀의 룸메이트인 Rebecca는 알 것 같아.
여 그렇겠네. 지금 그녀에게 전화해서 물어볼게.

해설 여자는 지금 Rebecca에게 전화해서 Mary가 가장 좋아하는 밴드를 알고 있는지 물어보겠다고 했다.

어휘 special 특별한   ticket 표   rock music 록 음악   favorite 가장 좋아하는   roommate 룸메이트   might ~일지도 모른다   though 그렇지만, 하지만

10 ④

M You have an iguana as a pet, don't you?
W Yes. Why?
M I want to have one, too. Can you give me some tips?
W Hmm... if you want a baby iguana, choose a green one. That means it is young.
M Interesting.
W And they can grow up to two meters long and weigh about ten kilograms.
M That's amazing. Is there anything I should know?
W You need to feed it fresh fruit and vegetables every day.

남 너 애완동물로 이구아나를 기르지, 그렇지 않니?
여 응. 왜?
남 나도 이구아나를 기르고 싶어서. 조언 좀 줄 수 있니?
여 음… 만약 새끼 이구아나를 원한다면, 초록색인 것을 골라. 그게 어리다는 뜻이거든.
남 흥미롭다.
여 그리고 이구아나는 2미터까지 자랄 수 있고 무게는 10킬로그램 정도 나갈 수 있어.
남 그거 놀랍다. 내가 알아야 할 것이 있니?
여 이구아나에게 매일 신선한 과일과 채소를 줘야 해.

해설 여자는 이구아나의 수명은 언급하지 않았다.

어휘 iguana 이구아나   pet 애완동물   tip 조언   choose 선택하다, 고르다   young 어린   grow 자라다   up to ~까지

weigh 무게가 ~이다   about 약, ~쯤   feed 먹이를 주다
fruit 과일   vegetable 채소

11 ④

M Hello. Do you have an appointment?
W No. I had my hair cut here yesterday, but it's not the same length on both sides.
M Do you remember the hair stylist's name?
W Yes. Her 58
name was Rosie.
M Oh, she's on vacation today. Can I trim your sides for you?
W Sure. Just make sure they are the same length, please.
M All right. Please sit here.

남 안녕하세요. 예약하셨나요?
여 아니요. 제가 어제 여기서 머리를 잘랐는데, 양쪽 길이가 같지 않아요.
남 미용사 이름을 기억하시나요?
여 네. Rosie였어요.
남 아, Rosie는 오늘 휴가입니다. 제가 손질해 드려도 될까요?
여 그럼요. 길이가 같아지게만 해 주세요.
남 알겠습니다. 여기에 앉으세요.

해설 여자는 어제 머리를 잘랐는데 양쪽 길이가 맞지 않아 다시 손질을 요청하러 미용실에 갔다.

어휘 have an appointment 예약이 되어 있다   have one's hair cut 머리를 자르다   same 같은   length 길이   both 양쪽의, 둘 다의   hair stylist 미용사   be on vacation 휴가 중이다   trim 다듬다, 손질하다   make sure 반드시 ~ 하다

12 ①

M Julie, do you want to have dinner before the concert starts?
W That sounds good to me. Let's go to the Italian restaurant next to the concert hall.
M Good. What time should we meet?
W The concert starts at 8 o'clock. So how about meeting at 6:30?
M Maybe we should meet a little earlier than that. The restaurant might be crowded.
W I see. Will it be okay if we meet two hours before the concert starts?
W I guess it'll be fine. See you then.

남 Julie, 콘서트 시작하기 전에 저녁 먹을래?
여 그거 좋겠다. 콘서트홀 옆에 있는 이탈리아 음식점에 가자.
남 좋아. 우리 몇 시에 만나야 하지?
여 콘서트가 8시에 시작돼. 그러니까 6시 30분에 만나는 게 어때?
남 그것보다는 조금 더 일찍 만나야 할 것 같아. 음식점이 붐빌 수도 있잖아.
여 그러네. 콘서트가 시작되기 두 시간 전에 만나면 괜찮을까?
남 괜찮을 것 같아. 그때 보자.

해설 콘서트는 8시에 시작되는데 두 사람은 콘서트가 시작되기 두

시간 전에 만나기로 했으므로 6시에 만날 것이다.

어휘 have dinner 저녁을 먹다   before ~ 전에   Italian 이탈리아의   next to ~ 옆에   concert hall 콘서트홀   maybe 아마   a little 조금   earlier 더 일찍(early의 비교급)   crowded 붐비는, 혼잡한

13 ⑤

W Excuse me. Could you bring me one more blanket? It's a bit cold here.
M Sure. Wait a moment, please. (Pause) Here you are. Would you like anything else?
W Not for now. Thank you. By the way, when do you sell duty-free items?
M After we hand these out. Have you filled out your arrival card?
W Yes, I have.
M Okay. We'll begin our in-flight duty-free sales shortly.
W Thank you.

여 실례합니다. 저에게 담요를 하나 더 가져다주시겠어요? 여기가 좀 춥네요.
남 네. 잠시만 기다려 주세요. (잠시/ 후) 여기 있습니다. 다른 것도 필요하신가요?
여 지금은 아니에요. 고맙습니다. 그런데, 면세품을 언제 판매하시나요?
남 저희가 이것들을 나눠 드린 후에요. 입국 신고서는 작성하셨나요?
여 네.
남 알겠습니다. 곧 기내 면세 판매를 시작하겠습니다.
여 고맙습니다.

해설 입국 신고서 작성과 기내 면세품 판매에 대해 이야기하고 있으므로 비행기 승무원과 탑승객 사이의 대화이다.

어휘 blanket 담요   a bit 조금   sell 판매하다   duty-free 면세의   item 물품   hand out 나눠 주다   fill out 작성하다, 기입하다   arrival card 입국 신고서   in-flight 기내의   sale 판매   shortly 곧

14 ④

W Let's see. Did we buy everything?
M I think so. Oh, do you want to buy some cookies, too?
W I think homemade cookies are better. I'll bake some for you.
M That's great. Do we have everything at home?
W No. We need flour, sugar, and butter. Oh, we also need eggs.
M Let's get some chocolate chips, too.
W Good! Will you get the eggs? I'll get the other ingredients.
M Okay. Let's meet at the checkout counter.

여 어디 보자. 우리 모두 샀지?
남 그런 것 같아. 아, 쿠키도 좀 살까?

여 집에서 만든 쿠키가 더 나은 것 같아. 내가 좀 구워 줄게.
남 좋아. 집에 모든 게 있나?
여 아니. 우리는 밀가루, 설탕, 그리고 버터가 필요해. 아, 달걀도 필요해.
남 초콜릿 칩도 좀 사자.
여 좋아! 너는 달걀을 가져올래? 난 다른 재료들을 가져올게.
남 그래. 계산대에서 만나자.

해설 여자는 남자에게 달걀을 가져와 달라고 요청했다.

어휘 everything 모든 것   homemade 집에서 만든, 수제의   bake 굽다   flour 밀가루   sugar 설탕   chip 조각   other 다른   ingredient 재료   checkout counter 계산대

---

15 ⑤

M Jane, did you buy the sneakers I recommended?
W No, I didn't.
M Why not? You really wanted to buy them.
W I did. I went to all of the shoe stores in town, but none of them had my size.
M Why don't you just order them online?
W When I buy sneakers, I always try them on.
M I see. I hope you find the sneakers in your size soon.

남 Jane, 내가 추천한 운동화 샀어?
여 아니, 못 샀어.
남 왜? 정말 사고 싶어 했잖아.
여 그랬지. 시내에 있는 모든 신발 가게에 갔었는데, 어느 곳도 내 사이즈의 신발이 없었어.
남 그냥 온라인으로 주문하는 게 어때?
여 난 운동화를 살 땐, 항상 신어 보거든.
남 그렇구나. 네 사이즈의 운동화를 곧 찾길 바라.

해설 여자는 시내의 모든 신발 가게에 가 보았으나 자신에게 맞는 크기의 신발이 없었다고 했다.

어휘 sneakers 운동화   recommend 추천하다   shoe store 신발 가게   in town 시내에   none 아무도 ~ 않다(없다)

---

16 ③

① **W** How much are these headphones?
   M They're $70.
② **W** Who's your favorite musician?
   M I love Taylor Swift.
③ **W** Would you turn down the volume?
   M Sure, no problem. I'm sorry.
④ **W** Can I borrow your pen for a moment?
   M Of course. Go ahead.
⑤ **W** Can I borrow some headphones from the library?
   M Ask at the information desk.

① **여** 이 헤드폰은 얼마예요?
   남 70달러입니다.
② **여** 네가 가장 좋아하는 뮤지션은 누구니?
   남 나는 Taylor Swift를 정말 좋아해.
③ **여** 볼륨 좀 줄여 주시겠어요?
   남 그럼요, 문제없어요. 죄송합니다.

---

④ **여** 잠깐 네 펜을 빌려도 될까?
   남 물론이지. 그렇게 해.
⑤ **여** 도서관에서 헤드폰을 빌릴 수 있어?
   남 안내 데스크에 물어봐.

해설 음악 소리를 줄여 달라고 요청하는 내용의 대화가 적절하다.

어휘 headphone 헤드폰   musician 뮤지션, 음악가   turn down the volume 볼륨을 줄이다   borrow 빌리다   for a moment 잠시 동안   library 도서관   information desk 안내 데스크

---

17 ④

M Let's write Mom a letter for Mother's Day.
W Of course. That's what we do every year. But I want to make it more special this time.
M Why don't we make breakfast for her?
W Good. While she's having breakfast, let's sing her favorite song.
M Sure, we can do that. How about buying some flowers?
W Flowers are good. What about ordering a cake, too?
M We can't afford to buy both flowers and a cake.
W You're right. Let's just get some flowers.

남 어머니의 날에 엄마한테 편지 쓰자.
여 당연하지. 우리가 매년 하는 거잖아. 그런데 난 이번에는 더 특별하게 하고 싶어.
남 엄마를 위해 아침상을 차리는 건 어때?
여 좋아. 엄마가 아침 식사를 하고 계실 때, 엄마가 제일 좋아하시는 노래를 불러 드리자.
남 그래, 그건 할 수 있어. 꽃을 좀 사는 건 어때?
여 꽃 괜찮다. 케이크도 주문하는 건 어때?
남 우리는 꽃과 케이크를 둘 다 살 여유가 없어.
여 네 말이 맞네. 그냥 꽃만 좀 사자.

해설 두 사람은 꽃과 케이크를 둘 다 살 여유가 없어서 꽃만 사기로 했다.

어휘 write ~ a letter ~에게 편지를 쓰다   Mother's Day 어머니의 날   special 특별한   make breakfast 아침을 차리다   order 주문하다   afford (~을 살) 여유가 되다   both A and B A와 B 둘 다

---

18 ③

M Do you want to stay fit? Come and join our fitness center. We're open 24 hours a day, 7(seven) days a week. For our members, we provide yoga classes at a discounted price. We have a large sauna for you to use, too. If you sign up before the end of this month, you can get a 30% discount. So hurry up.

남 좋은 체격을 유지하고 싶으신가요? 저희 피트니스 센터에 오셔서 등록하세요. 저희는 하루 24시간 일주일 내내 열려 있습니다. 회원 분들께는, 요가 강좌를 할인 가격으로 제공해 드립니다. 저희는 여러분이 사용하실 수 있는 넓은 사우나도 갖추고 있습니다. 이번 달 말까지 등록하시면, 30퍼센트 할인을 받으

실 수 있습니다. 그러니 서두르세요.

[해설] 회원들에게는 요가 강좌를 무료가 아니라 할인 가격으로 제공한다고 했다.

[어휘] fit (몸이) 건강한(탄탄한) fitness center 피트니스 센터, 헬스클럽 provide 제공하다 at a discounted price 할인 가격으로 sauna 사우나 sign up 등록하다 the end of ~의 말에 get a discount 할인을 받다 hurry up 서두르다

19 ⑤

M Thank you for shopping at Best Furniture.
W My pleasure. I really like my new sofa.
M Would you write your contact number and address here for the delivery?
W Okay. When can I expect it to be delivered?
M In three days. This Thursday.
W Can you make it on Wednesday?
M I'll check the schedule one more time.

남 Best Furniture에서 구입해 주셔서 고맙습니다.
여 별말씀을요. 저의 새 소파가 정말 마음에 들어요.
남 배송을 위해서 여기에 고객님의 연락처와 주소를 적어 주시겠어요?
여 네. 언제 배송되나요?
남 3일 후요. 이번 주 목요일입니다.
여 수요일로 해 주실 수 있을까요?
남 일정을 한 번 더 확인해 보겠습니다.

[해설] 여자가 더 빨리 배송해 줄 수 있는지 물었으므로 한 번 더 일정을 확인해 보겠다는 응답이 가장 적절하다.
① 정말 고맙습니다.
② 네. 주말은 괜찮아요.
③ 배송비는 25달러입니다.
④ 네. 목요일에 배송해 드릴게요.

[어휘] shop 사다, 쇼핑하다 furniture 가구 sofa 소파 contact number 연락처 address 주소 delivery 배송, 배달 expect 기대하다 deliver 배달하다 in ~ 후에 charge 요금 schedule 일정 one more time 한 번 더

20 ⑤

M Hi. I bought this smartphone yesterday.
W Is there a problem?
M It isn't working properly. It keeps turning off although it is fully charged.
W Will you hand it to me? I'll check it out.
M Here you are.
W (Pause) Hmm... it really does. I'll exchange it for a new one.
M I hope there's nothing wrong with the new one.

남 안녕하세요. 제가 어제 이 스마트폰을 샀는데요.
여 문제가 있나요?
남 제대로 작동이 안 돼요. 완전히 충전되어 있는데도 자꾸 꺼져요.
여 저한테 그것을 건네주시겠어요? 제가 확인해 보겠습니다.
남 여기요.

여 (잠시 후) 음… 정말 그러네요. 새것으로 교환해 드릴게요.
남 새것에는 아무 문제가 없으면 좋겠네요.

[해설] 남자의 스마트폰에 문제가 있어서 여자가 새것으로 바꿔 준다고 했으므로 새것에는 문제가 없으면 좋겠다는 말이 이어지는 것이 가장 적절하다.
① 방문해 주셔서 고맙습니다.
② 돈을 환불해 드릴게요.
③ 아니요. 저는 돈을 내고 싶지 않아요.
④ 불편을 끼쳐서 죄송합니다.

[어휘] work 작동하다 properly 제대로, 적절하게 keep ~ing ~을 계속하다(반복하다) turn off 꺼지다 although 비록 ~임에도 fully 완전히 charge 충전하다 hand 건네주다 exchange A for B A를 B로 교환하다 refund 환불하다 inconvenience 불편, 애로 pay for ~을 지불하다

01 ④	02 ②	03 ⑤	04 ③	05 ②
06 ⑤	07 ④	08 ②	09 ④	10 ④
11 ⑤	12 ②	13 ③	14 ⑤	15 ③
16 ③	17 ③	18 ②	19 ⑤	20 ②

01 ④

W Hello. I'm Amanda Jones. Here is the weather for next week. Tomorrow will be <u>warmer than today</u> with lots of sunshine nationwide. On Tuesday and Wednesday, however, it will be cold again. Thursday will be very windy, so please don't <u>let your hat blow away</u>. On Friday and Saturday, it will be cloudy, and <u>we're expecting snow</u>.

여 안녕하세요. Amanda Jones입니다. 다음 주 날씨입니다. 내일은 전국적으로 많은 햇살 가운데 오늘보다 더 따뜻하겠습니다. 하지만 화요일과 수요일에는 다시 추워지겠습니다. 목요일은 바람이 아주 많이 불 것이므로, 모자가 날아가지 않게 주의하시기 바랍니다. 금요일과 토요일에는 흐리겠으며, 눈이 올 것으로 예상됩니다.

해설 목요일에는 바람이 아주 많이 불 것이라고 했다.

어휘 warmer 더 따뜻한(warm의 비교급)   lots of 많은 sunshine 햇살   nationwide 전국적으로   again 다시   blow away 불어 날리다   expect 예상하다

02 ②

W Look at this sweater. The polka dots on it are so cute! I will buy this.

M Don't you already <u>have a similar one</u>?

W Oh, that one has smaller polka dots. It's totally different.

M <u>How about the plain one</u> over there?

W That's too simple. I also don't like V-shaped necklines.

M All right. <u>Buy what you want</u>.

W Okay. I'll buy the one I picked out first.

여 이 스웨터 좀 봐. 물방울무늬가 정말 귀여워! 나 이거 살래.

남 너 이미 비슷한 거 가지고 있지 않아?

여 아, 그건 더 작은 물방울무늬야. 완전히 달라.

남 저쪽에 있는 무늬 없는 스웨터는 어때?

여 저건 너무 단순해. 그리고 나는 브이넥은 안 좋아해.

남 알았어. 네가 원하는 걸 사.

여 응. 내가 처음에 고른 걸 살래.

해설 여자는 브이넥을 좋아하지 않는다고 했고 자신이 처음에 고른 것을 사겠다고 했으므로, 목둘레선이 둥글고 물방울무늬가 있는 스웨터를 구입할 것이다.

어휘 polka dot 물방울무늬   similar 비슷한   totally 완전히

different 다른   plain 무늬가 없는   V-shaped 'V' 자 모양의 neckline 목둘레선, 네크라인   pick out 고르다

03 ⑤

(*Telephone rings.*)

M Hello. Lion Electronics Service Center.

W Hi. My vacuum cleaner doesn't work. I hope I can <u>get it repaired</u> for free.

M When did you buy the product?

W I bought it about <u>a year and a half</u> ago.

M I'm afraid that all our products only have a one-year warranty.

W Only one year? That's too short.

M I'm sorry. <u>It's our policy</u>.

W I don't want to spend any money to repair it. I'd rather <u>buy a new one</u>.

(전화벨이 울린다.)

남 안녕하세요. Lion Electronics Service Center입니다.

여 안녕하세요. 제 진공청소기가 작동하지 않아요. 무상으로 수리받고 싶어요.

남 제품을 언제 구입하셨나요?

여 약 1년 반 전에 샀어요.

남 죄송합니다만 저희 모든 제품은 품질 보증 기간이 1년입니다.

여 겨우 1년이라고요? 너무 짧네요.

남 죄송합니다. 저희 방침이 그렇습니다.

여 저는 이걸 고치는 데 돈을 쓰고 싶지 않아요. 차라리 새 제품을 사겠어요.

해설 품질 보증 기간이 너무 짧다고 불평하며 유상으로 수리하는 대신 차라리 새것을 사겠다고 한 것으로 보아 여자는 짜증이 난 상태이다.

어휘 electronics 전자 기기   vacuum cleaner 진공청소기 work 작동하다   repair 수리하다   for free 무상으로 product 제품   about 약, ~쯤   half 절반   ago ~ 전에 warranty 품질 보증 (기간)   policy 정책, 방침   spend (돈을) 쓰다   rather 차라리

04 ③

M How was your weekend?

W <u>It was terrible</u>.

M What happened?

W I planned to go to an outdoor concert, but it was canceled <u>because of the storm</u>.

M Oh, yeah. It was a heavy storm. So did you just <u>stay at home</u>?

W No, I went to a movie. But <u>the movie was so boring</u>.

M That's too bad.

남 주말 어땠어?

여 형편없었어.

남 무슨 일 있었어?

여 야외 콘서트에 갈 계획이었는데, 폭풍 때문에 취소되었어.

남 아, 맞아. 강한 폭풍이었지. 그래서 그냥 집에 있었던 거야?

여 아니, 영화 보러 갔어. 그런데 영화가 너무 지루했어.

남 그거 참 안 됐다.

05 ②

M Good afternoon. What can I help you with?
W Good afternoon. My name is Linda Johnson. I made a reservation last week.
M Hold on a moment, please. (*Pause*) Okay, Ms. Linda Johnson. You booked a single room with a mountain view with breakfast included for a three-night stay.
W That's correct.
M Your room is 501. Here's your key.
W Thank you.

남 안녕하세요. 무엇을 도와드릴까요?
여 안녕하세요. 제 이름은 Linda Johnson입니다. 지난주에 예약했어요.
남 잠시만 기다려 주세요. (잠시 후) 네, Linda Johnson 씨, 산 전망의 1인용 객실을 조식 포함으로 3박 예약하셨군요.
여 맞습니다.
남 객실은 501호입니다. 여기 열쇠 있습니다.
여 고맙습니다.

06 ⑤

M What are you going to do this weekend, Rachel?
W I don't have any plans, but I'll probably read some books. I like reading.
M Do you also like watching movies?
W Sometimes I do.
M Then how about going to a movie with me?
W Is there a good new one to watch?
M A new movie about the Olympics is going to open this weekend.
W Well, I'm not a big sports fan. I will just read at home.

남 이번 주말에 뭐 할 거야, Rachel?
여 아무 계획 없는데, 아마 책을 좀 읽을 것 같아. 난 독서를 좋아하거든.
남 너 영화 보는 것도 좋아해?
여 가끔은 좋아해.
남 그럼 나랑 같이 영화 보러 가는 게 어때?
여 볼만한 괜찮은 새 영화가 있어?

남 올림픽에 대한 새 영화가 이번 주말에 개봉해.
여 글쎄, 나는 그다지 스포츠 열혈 팬이 아니라서. 그냥 집에서 책 읽을래.

07 ④

M Do you know this magazine?
W Yes. I buy it regularly because of the travel section.
M Oh, do you? Their travel section has a lot of useful information.
W I know. I think it's better than any other travel guidebooks. What's your favorite section?
M My favorite section is the cartoon section. The stories are so creative and interesting.
W I agree.
M I'm already waiting for the next issue.

남 너 이 잡지 알아?
여 응. 난 여행 부문 때문에 정기적으로 그걸 구매해.
남 아, 그래? 이 잡지의 여행 부문에 유용한 정보가 많지.
여 맞아. 다른 어떤 여행 안내서보다 더 좋은 것 같아. 네가 가장 좋아하는 부문은 뭐야?
남 내가 가장 좋아하는 부문은 만화 부문이야. 이야기가 아주 창의적이고 흥미로워.
여 동의해.
남 난 벌써 다음 호를 기다리고 있어.

08 ②

M Do you want to go cycling with me?
W I'd like to, but I can't. One of my tires is flat.
M You can use my sister's bike. I think that will be okay with her. I'll call and ask her.
W Thanks. By the way, where are we going?
M I'm thinking of riding around the lake. What do you think?
W That'll be nice.
M Okay. I'll call you right back after I ask my sister.

남 나랑 자전거 타러 갈래?
여 그러고 싶지만, 안 돼. 내 타이어 하나가 바람이 빠졌어.
남 우리 누나 자전거 써도 돼. 누나가 괜찮아 할 거야. 내가 누나에게 전화해서 물어볼게.
여 고마워. 그런데, 우리 어디로 가?
남 난 호수 주위를 빙 둘러서 타는 걸 생각 중이야. 네 생각은 어때?

여 그거 좋겠다.
남 그래. 내가 누나한테 물어보고 바로 전화할게.

해설 남자는 여자가 누나의 자전거를 써도 되는지 누나에게 전화해서 물어보겠다고 했다.

어휘 go cycling 자전거 타러 가다　tire 타이어　flat 바람이 빠진　think of ~을 생각하다　ride (자전거 등을) 타다　around 주위에, 둘레에　lake 호수

09 ④

M Butterflies are typically larger and have more colorful patterns on their wings. We can see them in the daytime. On the other hand, moths are typically smaller with dark-colored wings, and they fly at night. The easiest way to tell the difference between them is to look at their antennae because they look very different.

남 나비는 일반적으로 더 크고 날개에 더 화려한 무늬가 있습니다. 우리는 낮에 나비를 볼 수 있습니다. 반면에, 나방은 일반적으로 더 작고 어두운 색상의 날개가 있으며, 밤에 날아다닙니다. 나비와 나방은 더듬이가 아주 다르게 생겼기 때문에 나비와 나방을 구분하는 가장 쉬운 방법은 더듬이를 보는 것입니다.

해설 남자는 나비와 나방의 차이점을 설명하고 있다.

어휘 butterfly 나비　typically 일반적으로, 대체로　colorful 화려한, 다채로운　pattern 무늬　wing 날개　daytime 낮　on the other hand 반면에　moth 나방　dark-colored 어두운 색의　tell the difference 구별하다, 분간하다　look at ~을 보다　antenna(pl. antennae) 더듬이　different 다른

10 ④

W Dad, I don't feel well today.
M Oh, dear. What's wrong?
W I have a fever and feel chilly.
M You must have a cold. Do you have any other symptoms?
W I have a sore throat and a runny nose, too. But I just took some medicine. I'll be fine.
M It sounds like you have a bad cold. Let's go to see a doctor. I'll take you there.
W Okay. Thank you, Dad.

여 아빠, 저 오늘 몸이 안 좋아요.
남 오, 저런. 어디가 안 좋아?
여 열이 나고 으슬으슬 추워요.
남 감기에 걸렸구나. 또 다른 증상이 있니?
여 목이 아프고 콧물도 나요. 그래도 방금 약을 좀 먹었어요. 괜찮을 거예요.
남 심한 감기에 걸린 것 같구나. 병원에 가 보자. 내가 데려다줄게.
여 네. 고마워요, 아빠.

해설 여자는 기침이 나는 증상은 언급하지 않았다.

어휘 have a fever 열이 나다　feel chilly 으슬으슬 춥다, 오한이 나다　have a cold 감기에 걸리다　symptom 증상　have a sore throat 목이 아프다　have a runny nose 콧물이 나다　take medicine 약을 먹다　bad cold 심한 감기　see a doctor 병원에 가다

11 ⑤

M A new Japanese restaurant opened yesterday.
W I heard that, too. It's next to the bank, right?
M Yes. It is having a grand opening special for a week. It's offering 20% off all menu items.
W Oh, that's great! I love Japanese food. Why don't we eat out for dinner?
M The special is only for lunch.
W How about going there for lunch tomorrow?
M Okay. Let's meet at 12 in front of the restaurant.

남 어제 새로운 일식당이 개점했어.
여 나도 들었어. 은행 옆에 있는 것 맞지?
남 응. 일주일 동안 개점 특별 판매를 한대. 모든 메뉴를 20퍼센트 할인해 줘.
여 오, 그거 좋은데! 나 일본 요리 정말 좋아하거든. 저녁에 먹으러 가는 게 어때?
남 할인 행사는 점심에만 해.
여 내일 점심은 어때?
남 좋아. 식당 앞에서 12시에 만나자.

해설 할인 행사는 점심에만 한다고 했다.

어휘 Japanese 일본의　next to ~ 옆에　grand opening 개장, 개업　special (상점·식당의) 특별 상품, 특별 할인가　eat out 외식하다　in front of ~ 앞에

12 ②

W Sweetie, what are you doing in the kitchen?
M I'm making sandwiches, Mom.
W You just had lunch. Are you still hungry?
M No, I'm not. I will take them to Tommy's.
W What's the occasion?
M There'll be a party, and everyone needs to bring some food or drinks to share.
W I see. Let me know if you need my help.

여 얘야, 부엌에서 뭐 하고 있니?
남 저는 샌드위치를 만들고 있어요, 엄마.
여 너 방금 점심 먹었잖아. 아직 배고프니?
남 아니요. 샌드위치를 Tommy네 집에 가져갈 거예요.
여 무슨 일인데?
남 파티가 있는데, 모두가 나눠 먹을 음식이나 음료를 가져가야 하거든요.
여 그렇구나. 내 도움이 필요하면 알려 주렴.

해설 남자는 친구의 집에서 하는 파티에 음식이나 음료를 가져가야 해서 샌드위치를 만들고 있다고 했다.

어휘 kitchen 부엌　have lunch 점심을 먹다　still 아직　hungry 배고픈　take A to B A를 B로 가져가다　occasion 일, 행사　bring 가져가다　drink 음료　share 나누다, 공유하다

13 ③

W I'd like to have these clothes cleaned, please.
M Two shirts and one coat. Is that right?
W Yes. How much is it?
M It's $3 for each shirt and $7 for the coat. You can pick them up in three days.
W Is there any chance I can get them back by tomorrow?
M It's possible, but there is a $3 extra fee for quick service.
W Okay. I'll pick them up tomorrow.

여 이 옷들을 세탁 맡기고 싶어요.
남 셔츠 두 장과 코트 한 벌이네요. 맞나요?
여 네. 얼마예요?
남 셔츠는 한 장에 3달러이고 코트는 7달러입니다. 3일 후에 찾아 가시면 됩니다.
여 혹시 내일까지 찾아가는 게 가능한가요?
남 가능합니다만, 빠른 서비스로 3달러 추가 요금이 있습니다.
여 알겠습니다. 내일 찾아 갈게요.

해설 셔츠 두 장에 6달러, 코트 한 벌에 7달러, 빠른 서비스 추가 요금 3달러를 합하여 여자는 총 16달러를 지불해야 한다.

어휘 clothes 옷 clean 세탁하다 each 각각의 pick up ~에서 찾아오다 in ~ 후에 chance 가능성 by ~까지 possible 가능한 extra fee 추가 요금 quick 빠른

14 ⑤

W May I take your order?
M Yes. I'd like to have two hamburgers and French fries, please.
W Anything to drink?
M A large coke and a coffee, please.
W We have a special event on ice cream. If you buy one, you get one free.
M Then I'd like to have an ice cream instead of coffee.
W Okay. For here or to go?
M For here.

여 주문하시겠어요?
남 네. 햄버거 두 개랑 감자튀김 주세요.
여 마실 건요?
남 콜라 큰 것과 커피 주세요.
여 저희는 아이스크림 행사를 하고 있어요. 하나를 사시면, 다른 하나는 무료로 받으실 수 있어요.
남 그럼 커피 대신에 아이스크림으로 할게요.
여 알겠습니다. 여기서 드실 건가요 아니면 가져가실 건가요?
남 여기서 먹을 겁니다.

해설 음식 주문을 받으며 아이스크림 1+1 행사를 안내하는 음식점 직원과 손님 사이의 대화이다.

어휘 French fries 감자튀김 large 큰 coke 콜라 special 특별한 event 행사 buy one, get one free 하나를 사면, 하나가 공짜 instead of ~ 대신에

15 ③

W I can't read my book anymore. My eyes are too dry.
M Are you wearing contact lenses?
W No, I'm not.
M Why don't you try putting in some eye drops?
W I did that several times, but my eyes didn't get better.
M How about seeing an eye doctor? You may have another problem.
W Maybe I should. Will you make an appointment for me?
M Sure, I will.

여 더 이상 책을 못 읽겠어. 눈이 너무 건조해.
남 콘택트렌즈 끼고 있어?
여 아니.
남 안약을 좀 넣어 보는 게 어때?
여 여러 번 해 봤는데, 내 눈이 나아지질 않아.
남 안과에 가는 게 어때? 다른 문제가 있을 수도 있잖아.
여 그래야 할 것 같아. 나를 위해서 예약 좀 해 줄래?
남 그래, 그럴게.

해설 여자는 눈이 건조해서 안약을 여러 번 넣었지만 나아지지 않자 남자에게 안과 진료를 예약해 달라고 부탁했다.

어휘 not ~ anymore 더 이상 ~ 않다 dry 건조한 contact lenses 콘택트렌즈 eye drop 안약 several times 여러 번 get better 나아지다 see an eye doctor 안과에 가다 problem 문제 make an appointment 예약을 하다

16 ③

M May I buy a ticket for the Picasso exhibit?
W Sure. It's $30.
M Okay. Oh, wait. The sign says, "50% Discount for Students."
W That's right. Are you a student?
M Yes, I am.
W Do you have your student ID card?
M No. I don't have it right now.
W Sorry, but you need to show me your student ID to get a discount.

남 피카소 전시회 표 한 장을 살 수 있나요?
여 네. 30달러입니다.
남 네. 아, 잠깐만요. 표지판에 '학생은 50퍼센트 할인'이라고 적혀 있네요.
여 맞아요. 학생이신가요?
남 네.
여 학생증을 가지고 계신가요?
남 아니요. 지금은 없어요.
여 죄송하지만, 할인을 받으시려면 저에게 학생증을 보여 주셔야 합니다.

해설 학생 할인을 받으려면 여자에게 학생증을 보여 줘야 하는데 남자는 학생증을 가지고 있지 않아서 할인을 받지 못한다.

어휘 exhibit 전시회 sign 표지판 discount 할인 student ID card 학생증 show 보여 주다

17 ③

① **W** What do you do for a living?
  M I work as an art teacher.
② **W** We have to get new shoes for Tom.
  M Yeah. He is growing so fast.
③ **W** How long does it take to go to school?
  M It's 7:20.
④ **W** I'm calling to book a plane ticket to London.
  M What day do you want to leave?
⑤ **W** Try on these pants. These are your size.
  M Okay, thanks.

① **여** 직업이 무엇인가요?
  남 저는 미술 교사로 일해요.
② **여** Tom의 새 신발을 사야 해요.
  남 그래요. 그는 아주 빨리 자라고 있어요.
③ **여** 학교 가는 데 얼마나 걸려?
  남 7시 20분이야.
④ **여** 런던으로 가는 비행기 표를 예매하려고 전화했습니다.
  남 어느 날짜에 출발하기를 원하세요?
⑤ **여** 이 신발을 신어 보세요. 이게 당신의 사이즈예요.
  남 네, 감사합니다.

해설 ③ 학교 가는 데 시간이 얼마나 걸리는지 묻는 말에 현재 시각을 답하는 것은 어색하다.

어휘 work as ~로서 일하다　grow 자라다　book 예약하다, 예매하다　leave 출발하다　try on 입어 보다, 신어 보다

18 ②

W Hello, everyone. Thank you for visiting Getty Gallery. Renoir's special exhibition is being held only in our gallery. There are over seventy works of art on display. We have useful programs you can enjoy, such as workshops and audio-guided tours. If you're interested, please see the brochure for the details. We hope you enjoy the exhibits. Thank you.

여 안녕하세요, 여러분. Getty Gallery를 방문해 주셔서 감사합니다. 르누아르 특별 전시회는 오직 저희 미술관에서만 개최됩니다. 70점 이상의 미술품이 전시되어 있습니다. 저희 미술관에는 워크숍과 오디오 가이드 투어와 같이 여러분이 즐기실 수 있는 유용한 프로그램들이 마련되어 있습니다. 관심 있으시다면, 자세한 사항은 책자를 봐 주세요. 즐거운 관람하시기를 바랍니다. 감사합니다.

해설 미술관 관람객에게 전시회에 대해 간략히 설명하고 관내 프로그램을 알리는 안내 방송이다.

어휘 gallery 미술관　exhibition 전시회　be held 열리다, 개최되다　work of art 미술품　on display 전시된　useful 유용한　such as ~와 같은　brochure 책자　detail 세부 사항　exhibit 전시, 전시품

19 ⑤

M Anna, what are you going to do during vacation?
W I'm going to Florida. My uncle's family lives there.

M Cool! I want to go there.
W I'm so excited to be going.
M How long are you going to stay there?
W About three weeks.
M Do you have any plans there?
W I will go to Disney World with my cousins.

남 Anna, 방학 동안에 뭐 할 거니?
여 플로리다에 갈 거야. 그곳에 삼촌의 가족들이 살아.
남 좋겠다! 나도 거기 가고 싶다.
여 가게 되어서 너무 신나.
남 그곳에 얼마나 머물 거야?
여 3주 정도.
남 그곳에서 무슨 계획 있어?
여 사촌들이랑 Disney World에 갈 거야.

해설 플로리다에서 무엇을 할 것인지 물었으므로 그곳에서의 계획을 말하는 응답이 와야 한다.
① 나는 여행하는 것을 좋아하지 않아.
② 나는 여기에 세 달 동안 머물 거야.
③ 나는 전에 미국에 가 본 적이 없어.
④ 나는 일주일 후에 학교로 돌아가야 해.

어휘 during ~ 동안에　vacation 방학　excited 신이 난　stay 머무르다　about 약, ~쯤　plan 계획　cousin 사촌　travel 여행하다

20 ②

M Honey, how was Mike today?
W He was much better. He seems fine now.
M Is he in bed now?
W Not yet, but he's ready for bed. Could you take care of him now?
M Okay, I will. You should get some rest.
W Thank you. I think he'll be happy if you read him a book before he goes to bed.
M No problem. Just tell me his favorite book.
W He likes the book *Gorilla*.

남 여보, 오늘 Mike 어땠어요?
여 훨씬 좋아졌어요. 지금은 괜찮아 보여요.
남 지금 자고 있어요?
여 아직요, 하지만 잘 준비는 됐어요. 이제 당신이 Mike 좀 돌봐줄래요?
남 네, 그럴게요. 당신은 좀 쉬어요.
여 고마워요. 자기 전에 당신이 책을 읽어 주면 Mike가 아주 좋아할 거예요.
남 문제없어요. Mike가 가장 좋아하는 책만 말해 줘요.
여 그는 〈Gorilla〉라는 책을 좋아해요.

해설 Mike가 가장 좋아하는 책을 말해 달라고 했으므로 책의 제목을 답해야 한다.
① 내 취미는 소설을 읽는 거예요.
③ 그는 혼자 독서하는 것을 좋아해요.
④ 이제 내가 그를 돌볼 수 있어요.
⑤ 그는 한 시간 전에 잠이 들었어요.

어휘 seem ~인 것 같다　be in bed 자고 있다　take care

of ~을 돌보다　get rest 휴식을 취하다　go to bed 잠자리에 들다　favorite 가장 좋아하는　novel 소설　by oneself 스스로, 혼자

Review Test

pp.114~115

Word Check `09회`

01 다듬다, 손질하다	**02** 제대로, 적절하게
03 콘서트홀	**04** 오디션을 실시하다
05 악기	**06** 리드 보컬
07 ~을 통해서	**08** 재료
09 평범한, 보통의	**10** 연체료
11 피트니스 센터, 헬스클럽	**12** 곧
13 reason	**14** provide
15 duty-free	**16** in-flight
17 delivery	**18** bedtime
19 foggy	**20** information desk
21 overdue	**22** flour
23 contact number	**24** quite

Expression Check

25 turn down	**26** had, cut
27 filled out	**28** for a moment
29 both, and	**30** die down

Word Check `10회`

01 창의적인	**02** 고르다
03 물방울무늬	**04** 무늬가 없는
05 품질 보증 (기간)	**06** 비슷한
07 일, 행사	**08** 취소하다
09 휴식을 취하다	**10** 개장, 개업
11 추가 요금	**12** 전시된
13 policy	**14** typically
15 useful	**16** information
17 rather	**18** guidebook
19 on the other hand	**20** flat
21 cartoon	**22** breakfast included
23 detail	**24** product

Expression Check

25 blow away	**26** for free
27 going to a movie	**28** in front of
29 take, to	**30** take care of

실전 모의고사 11회

pp.116~123

01 ④	**02** ④	**03** ⑤	**04** ⑤	**05** ③
06 ②	**07** ④	**08** ⑤	**09** ③	**10** ④
11 ④	**12** ③	**13** ②	**14** ④	**15** ⑤
16 ③	**17** ③	**18** ④	**19** ①	**20** ⑤

01 ④

W Good morning. This is the weekend weather forecast. It's raining hard right now, and the rain will continue until tonight. However, tomorrow, on Saturday, the rain will stop, and it'll be sunny all day. You can enjoy the sunlight only on Saturday because the rain will be back again on Sunday morning.

여 좋은 아침입니다. 주말 일기 예보입니다. 현재 비가 많이 내리고 있으며, 이 비는 오늘 밤까지 계속되겠습니다. 하지만 내일인 토요일에는 비가 그치고, 하루 종일 맑겠습니다. 오직 토요일에만 햇빛을 즐기실 수 있겠는데요, 일요일 아침에는 다시 비 소식이 있기 때문입니다.

해설 일요일 아침에는 다시 비가 올 것이라고 했다.

어휘 weekend 주말　weather forecast 일기 예보　hard 심하게, 많이　continue 계속되다　until ~까지　sunlight 햇빛　be back 돌아오다　again 다시

02 ④

M Hello. How may I help you?
W I want to buy a plate.
M Okay. Do you like flower patterns?
W Yes, I do. Can you recommend one to me?
M All right. This one with one big flower is very popular nowadays.
W Not bad, but I think it's too simple.
M Then how about this one with two flowers and small dots surrounding them?
W That's nice. I'll take it.

남 안녕하세요. 무엇을 도와드릴까요?
여 저는 접시를 사고 싶어요.
남 네. 꽃무늬를 좋아하시나요?
여 네. 하나 추천해 주시겠어요?
남 알겠습니다. 큰 꽃 한 송이가 있는 이 접시가 요즘 아주 인기 있답니다.
여 나쁘진 않은데, 너무 단순한 것 같아요.
남 그럼 작은 점들이 꽃 두 송이를 둘러싸고 있는 이 접시는 어떠세요?
여 좋네요. 그걸로 할게요.

해설 남자가 작은 점들이 꽃 두 송이를 둘러싸고 있는 모양의 접시를 권하자 여자는 마음에 들어 하며 사겠다고 했다.

어휘 plate 접시   pattern 무늬   recommend 추천하다
popular 인기 있는   nowadays 요즘   simple 단순한   dot
점   surround 둘러싸다

03 ⑤

M Judy, do you have any special plans for this weekend?
W Yes. I'm going to Busan with my family.
M That sounds like fun. But you don't look happy.
W Well, last night, my dad said he couldn't come. He has to go to Japan on business.
M Why don't you put off the trip?
W We can't cancel all the hotels and trains. So it's a family trip without Dad.
M That's too bad he can't join you.

남 Judy, 이번 주말에 특별한 계획 있니?
여 응. 가족들과 부산에 갈 거야.
남 재미있겠다. 그런데 너 별로 안 기뻐 보여.
여 그게, 어젯밤에 아빠가 못 가신다고 하셨거든. 일본으로 출장 가셔야 해.
남 여행을 미루는 게 어때?
여 모든 호텔과 기차를 다 취소할 수 없어. 그래서 아빠 없는 가족 여행인 셈이지.
남 아버지가 같이 못 가신다니 정말 안됐다.

해설 여자는 해외 출장 때문에 아빠가 가족 여행을 함께 할 수 없게 되어서 실망한 상태이다.

어휘 on business 업무로, 사업차   put off 미루다, 연기하다
trip 여행   cancel 취소하다   without ~ 없이   join 함께하다

04 ⑤

W Jake, why didn't you come to baseball practice yesterday?
M My mom didn't let me go.
W Why? What did you do?
M She got upset because of my poor grade in math. She thinks it happened because I spent too much time playing baseball.
W Oh, no!
M So she made me take an online math class after school yesterday.
W You must do better on the next exam.

여 Jake, 어제 야구 연습에 왜 안 왔어?
남 엄마가 못 가게 하셨어.
여 왜? 너 뭐 했는데?
남 엄마가 내 형편없는 수학 점수 때문에 화가 나셨거든. 엄마는 내가 야구하는 데 시간을 너무 많이 보내서 그렇다고 생각하셔.
여 오, 저런!
남 그래서 어제 방과 후에 엄마가 수학 인터넷 강의를 들으라고 시키셨어.
여 너 다음 시험엔 더 잘해야겠다.

해설 남자는 엄마가 수학 인터넷 강의를 들으라고 해서 야구 연습에 못 갔다고 했다.

어휘 practice 연습   let (~을 하도록) 허락하다   poor
형편없는   grade 점수   happen 일어나다, 발생하다
spend(-spent-spent) (시간을) 보내다   take a class 수업을
듣다   online 온라인의   exam 시험

05 ③

W This place is huge, isn't it?
M Yes. I heard that it's the largest one in the country.
W I can see that. Hey, look at this. This whole tunnel is all made of glass.
M Wow, it's amazing. I feel like I'm deep in the ocean.
W Me, too. Let's keep going. The map says we get to the Whale Zone at the end of this tunnel.
M Okay. Maybe we can see the whale sharks there.
W I want to see them. Let's go.

여 여기 정말 크다, 그렇지 않니?
남 응. 우리나라에서 제일 큰 곳이라고 들었어.
여 그런 것 같네. 야, 이것 좀 봐. 이 터널 전체가 유리로 만들어져 있어.
남 와, 멋지다. 마치 내가 바닷속 깊은 곳에 있는 것 같아.
여 나도. 계속 가 보자. 이 터널 끝에서 Whale Zone에 갈 수 있다고 지도에 쓰여 있어.
남 그래. 아마 그곳에서 고래상어를 볼 수 있을 거야.
여 나 고래상어 보고 싶어. 가 보자.

해설 유리로 만들어진 터널에서 바닷속에 있는 것 같다고 했고, 고래상어를 보러 가자고 했으므로 수족관에서 이루어지는 대화이다.

어휘 place 장소   huge 거대한   country 나라   whole
전체의   tunnel 터널   be made of ~로 만들어지다   glass
유리   ocean 바다   whale 고래   zone 지역, 구역   whale
shark 고래상어

06 ②

M Mom, can you help me? I missed the school bus.
W You missed the school bus again?
M I went to bed late last night because of my homework.
W You said the same thing a week ago.
M But that's the truth. Can you take me to school? Mom, please.
W Promise me this will be the last time.
M Okay. It will never happen again.
W All right. I'll get ready in a hurry.

남 엄마, 저 좀 도와주시겠어요? 저 학교 버스를 놓쳤어요.
여 학교 버스를 또 놓쳤다고?
남 숙제 때문에 어젯밤에 늦게 잤단 말이에요.
여 너 일주일 전에도 똑같이 말했잖니.
남 하지만 사실인걸요. 학교에 데려다주실 수 있어요? 엄마, 제발요.
여 이번이 마지막일 거라고 약속하렴.
남 네. 다시는 이런 일이 일어나지 않을 거예요.
여 알았어. 서둘러서 준비할게.

해설 서둘러서 준비하겠다는 말은 학교에 데려다 달라는 남자의 요청을 수락하겠다는 뜻이다.

어휘 miss 놓치다   again 다시   because of ~ 때문에
truth 사실   promise 약속하다   last 마지막의   get ready
준비하다   in a hurry 서둘러

07 ④

W Dad, I'd like to go to the soccer shop this weekend.
M What do you need to buy?
W I need a soccer ball and soccer shoes.
M A soccer ball? Yours is still good.
W No, look at this. It's flat.
M You can just put air into it. You don't need a new one.
W Okay, but I really need new shoes. The ones I have are too small now.
M I see. I'll buy you some shoes.

여 아빠, 저 이번 주말에 축구 용품점에 가고 싶어요.
남 사야 할 것이 뭔데?
여 축구공이랑 축구화가 필요해요.
남 축구공? 네 축구공은 아직 괜찮은걸.
여 아니에요. 이것 보세요. 바람이 빠졌어요.
남 공기를 넣으면 된단다. 새것은 필요 없어.
여 알겠어요, 하지만 새 신발은 정말 필요해요. 제가 갖고 있는 것은 이제 너무 작거든요.
남 그렇구나. 신발은 사 줄게.

해설 여자는 축구공과 축구화가 필요하다고 했는데, 축구공은 바람을 넣어서 다시 사용하기로 해서 남자는 여자에게 축구화만 사 주기로 했다.

어휘 soccer shoes 축구화   flat 바람이 빠진   air 공기

08 ⑤

M Hello. I'd like to buy a birthday cake for my niece.
W Okay. Do you have anything particular in mind?
M Not really. Can you recommend one to me?
W All right. How about this chocolate cake with nuts? It's very popular.
M It looks delicious. I'll take it. Oh, wait.
W Yes?
M She might have a nut allergy. Let me check by calling my sister.
W Sure. Go ahead.

남 안녕하세요. 제 여자 조카를 위해 생일 케이크를 사고 싶어요.
여 네. 특별히 생각해 두신 것 있으세요?
남 아니요. 저에게 하나 추천해 주실 수 있을까요?
여 알겠습니다. 견과류가 들어간 이 초콜릿 케이크는 어떠신가요? 아주 인기 있답니다.
남 맛있어 보이네요. 그걸로 할게요. 아, 잠시만요.
여 네?
남 조카가 견과류 알레르기가 있을 수도 있어요. 여동생에게 전화해서 물어볼게요.
여 네. 그러세요.

해설 남자는 조카에게 견과류 알레르기가 있을 수도 있으니 여동생에게 전화해서 확인해 보겠다고 했다.

어휘 niece (여자) 조카   have ~ in mind ~을 염두에 두다
〔생각하다〕   particular 특정한, 특별한   recommend 추천하다
nut 견과류   allergy 알레르기

09 ③

M Sylvia, what did you do during your winter vacation?
W I went to Spain with my family.
M That's awesome! How long was the trip?
W It was 10 days. We traveled around many beautiful cities.
M That's quite long! Which city was the most impressive?
W Barcelona. There were many unique buildings designed by Gaudi.
M How did you like Spanish food?
W Excellent. I loved the seafood dishes the most.

남 Sylvia, 겨울 방학 동안에 뭐 했니?
여 가족들이랑 스페인에 갔어.
남 멋지다! 여행 기간은 얼마나 되었니?
여 10일이었어. 우리는 많은 아름다운 도시를 여행했어.
남 꽤 길다! 어느 도시가 가장 인상 깊었어?
여 바르셀로나. 가우디가 디자인한 독특한 건물들이 많이 있었어.
남 스페인 음식은 어땠어?
여 훌륭했어. 나는 해산물 요리를 가장 좋아했어.

해설 여자는 여행 경비는 언급하지 않았다.

어휘 awesome 굉장한   travel around 여기저기 여행하다
impressive 인상 깊은   unique 독특한   building 건물
design 디자인하다, 설계하다   Spanish 스페인의   seafood
해산물

10 ④

M One of the most important parts of traveling is to see how people in different countries live. Therefore, in order to see how Korean people live, you should visit several Korean traditional markets. In the markets, you can try popular Korean street foods such as *tteokbokki* and *sundae*. You can also buy various traditional Korean souvenirs at reasonable prices. So make sure you visit traditional markets during your trip!

남 여행의 가장 중요한 부분 중 한 가지는 다른 나라 사람들이 어떻게 사는지 보는 것이죠. 그러므로, 한국 사람들이 어떻게 사는지 보기 위해서, 여러분은 한국 전통 시장 여러 군데를 방문하셔야 합니다. 시장에서, 여러분은 떡볶이와 순대와 같은 한국의 유명한 길거리 음식을 맛볼 수 있습니다. 또한 다양한 전통적인 한국 기념품을 적정한 가격에 구입하실 수 있죠. 그러니 여행하시는 동안에 반드시 전통 시장을 방문해 보세요!

해설 남자는 한국의 전통 시장에서 경험할 수 있는 것에 대해 이야기하며 전통 시장을 홍보하고 있다.

어휘 important 중요한   part 부분   different 다른   in order to ~하기 위해서   several 몇몇의, 여러 개의   traditional

전통의, 전통적인   street food 길거리 음식   such as ~와 같은   various 다양한   souvenir 기념품   reasonable (가격이) 적정한, 너무 비싸지 않은   make sure 반드시 ~ 하다

11 ④

W Attention, students. We are going to <u>have a special event</u> next week called A Week of Thanks. A Week of Thanks is a week when you <u>express your gratitude to others</u> who help you. There will be a special box <u>on each floor</u> of our school. Write thank-you cards to your friends and teachers and put them in the box. The cards <u>will be delivered</u> on Friday afternoon. We hope every student participates in the event.

여 학생 여러분. 주목해 주십시오. 다음 주에 A Week of Thanks 라는 특별한 행사가 열립니다. A Week of Thanks는 여러분을 도와주는 사람들에게 감사함을 표현하는 주입니다. 학교의 각 층에 특별한 상자가 있을 것입니다. 친구들과 선생님께 감사 카드를 써서 상자에 넣으세요. 카드는 금요일 오후에 배달될 것입니다. 모든 학생들이 행사에 참여하길 바랍니다.

해설 친구들과 선생님께 감사 카드를 써서 상자에 넣으라고 했다.

어휘 express 표현하다   gratitude 감사   others 다른 사람들   deliver 배달하다   participate in ~에 참가하다

12 ③

M Tom told me that you are going to stay in Jeju-do for a while.
W Yes. <u>I'm leaving tomorrow</u>.
M How long are you going to stay there?
W <u>About a month</u>. I'm not sure.
M That's quite long. Why are you going to <u>stay there for so long</u>?
W I'm going there to see my grandma. She lives in Jeju-do.
M Didn't you see her last month for her eightieth birthday?
W Right. But now, she's <u>sick in the hospital</u>. I'm so worried about her.

남 네가 잠시 동안 제주도에서 지낼 거라고 Tom이 말하더라.
여 응. 내일 떠나.
남 거기서 얼마나 있을 거니?
여 한 달쯤. 잘 모르겠어.
남 꽤 오래 가 있는구나. 왜 그렇게 오랫동안 가 있는 거야?
여 할머니 뵈러 가. 할머니가 제주도에 사시거든.
남 할머니 팔순 생신으로 지난달에 뵙지 않았어?
여 맞아. 하지만 이번엔 할머니가 편찮으셔서 입원해 계셔. 할머니가 너무 걱정돼.

해설 여자는 할머니가 편찮으셔서 한 달 정도 제주도에 가 있을 것이라고 했다.

어휘 for a while 잠시 동안   leave 떠나다   about 약, ~쯤   in the hospital 입원하여   be worried about ~에 대해 걱정하다

13 ②

M Hello. How much is a ticket for the museum?
W It's $30 <u>for an adult</u>.
M How about a child?
W <u>It's half the price</u> of an adult ticket.
M I see. Two adults and two children, please.
W All right. Today is Culture Day, so you also get 10% off <u>from the total price</u>.
M Good. <u>I'm so lucky</u>. Here's my card.

남 안녕하세요. 박물관 표 가격이 얼마인가요?
여 어른은 30달러입니다.
남 어린이요?
여 어른 표의 절반 가격입니다.
남 그렇군요. 어른 두 장, 아이 두 장 주세요.
여 알겠습니다. 오늘은 문화의 날이라서 총액에서 10퍼센트를 할인받으실 수 있어요.
남 잘됐네요. 아주 운이 좋아요. 여기 제 카드 있습니다.

해설 어른 입장권은 30달러, 어린이 입장권은 15달러이므로 각 두 장씩 구입하면 총 90달러이다. 여기에 문화의 날 할인 10퍼센트를 받았으므로, 남자는 총 81달러를 지불해야 한다.

어휘 museum 박물관   adult 성인, 어른   half 절반의   price 가격   off 할인되어   total 총, 전체의   lucky 운이 좋은

14 ④

W Hello. <u>What brings you here</u>?
M She doesn't eat well and keeps sleeping.
W How long has she <u>had these symptoms</u>?
M It's been two days.
W <u>Let me take a look</u>. (*Pause*) She has a mild fever. I think she has a cold. Has she had a dog flu vaccination shot?
M Yes. She had one last month.
W Okay. I'm going to <u>give her some medicine</u>.

여 안녕하세요. 여기에 무슨 일로 오셨나요?
남 얘가 잘 먹지를 못하고 계속 잠만 자요.
여 이런 증상이 생긴 지 얼마나 되었나요?
남 이틀 되었어요.
여 한번 볼게요. (잠시 후) 미열이 있네요. 감기에 걸린 것 같아요. 개 독감 예방 접종은 했나요?
남 네. 한 달 전에 맞았어요.
여 알겠습니다. 약을 좀 줄게요.

해설 개 독감 예방 접종이라는 말을 통해 대화 초반부터 she라고 지칭한 대상이 강아지임을 알 수 있으므로, 동물 병원에 온 강아지 주인과 수의사 사이의 대화이다.

어휘 keep ~ing 계속 ~하다   symptom 증상   take a look 보다   mild fever 미열   have a cold 감기에 걸리다   flu 독감   vaccination 예방 접종   shot 주사 (한 대)   medicine 약

15 ⑤

M The movie starts in 10 minutes. We <u>arrived on time</u>.
W Yeah. Do you need popcorn or anything?

M I want a small popcorn and a coke.

W Okay. I'll buy them. Why don't you get the movie tickets?

M Sure, but from where?

W The ticket machines are over there. Enter the booking number, and the tickets will be printed.

M All right.

남 영화가 10분 후에 시작해. 우리 제시간에 도착했어.

여 그러게. 팝콘이나 뭐 필요해?

남 난 팝콘 작은 거랑 콜라를 먹고 싶어.

여 알았어. 내가 살게. 너는 영화표를 받는 게 어때?

남 그래. 그런데 어디에서 받지?

여 저쪽에 표 판매기가 있어. 예약 번호를 입력하면 표가 출력될 거야.

남 알았어.

[해설] 여자는 자신이 팝콘과 콜라를 사는 동안 남자에게 영화표를 출력해 달라고 요청했다.

[어휘] arrive 도착하다   on time 제시간에   machine 기계   enter 입력하다   booking number 예약 번호   print 인쇄하다

16 ③

M Carol, you like operas, don't you?

W Absolutely. Why?

M I have tickets for an opera at the opera house this Saturday. Why don't you go with me?

W At the opera house? Aren't the tickets expensive?

M I bought them at a good price. Can you go?

W I'd love to, but only if it's before dinner.

M Oh, no! The opera starts at 7 p.m. Is that due to your science homework?

W No. We're having a family dinner party to celebrate my brother's graduation.

남 Carol, 너 오페라 좋아하지, 그렇지 않니?

여 당연하지. 왜?

남 이번 주 토요일에 오페라 하우스에서 하는 오페라 표가 있거든. 나랑 같이 가는 게 어떠니?

여 오페라 하우스에서? 표가 비싸지 않아?

남 괜찮은 가격에 샀어. 갈 수 있어?

여 가고 싶지만, 저녁 전에만 돼.

남 오, 안 돼! 오페라는 저녁 7시에 시작해. 네 과학 숙제 때문이니?

여 아니. 우리 오빠의 졸업을 축하하기 위해 가족 저녁 파티를 할 거야.

[해설] 오페라는 저녁 7시에 시작하는데 여자는 저녁에 오빠의 졸업을 축하하는 가족 파티가 있어서 오페라를 보러 갈 수 없다고 했다.

[어휘] opera 오페라   absolutely 전적으로, 틀림없이   expensive 비싼   only if ~할 경우에 한해   due to ~ 때문에   celebrate 축하하다, 기념하다   graduation 졸업

17 ③

① W Did you call the customer service center?

　 M Yes, but the line was busy every time.

② W How long does it take?

M Look. The sign says it's a 30-minute walk from here.

③ W Hey, you just cut in line.

　 M Oops, I didn't know. Sorry.

④ W I hope we won't have to stand in line for a long time.

　 M I couldn't agree with you more.

⑤ W Look at those endless cars.

　 M Yeah, traffic is terrible today.

① 여 고객 서비스 센터에 전화해 봤어?

　 남 응. 그런데 매번 통화 중이야.

② 여 시간이 얼마나 걸릴까?

　 남 봐. 표지판에는 여기서부터 도보로 30분이라고 쓰여 있어.

③ 여 저기요, 방금 새치기하셨는데요.

　 남 앗, 몰랐어요. 죄송합니다.

④ 여 우리가 오랫동안 줄을 안 서도 되면 좋겠다.

　 남 네 말에 전적으로 동의해.

⑤ 여 저 끝없는 차들을 봐.

　 남 그러게, 오늘 길 진짜 많이 막힌다.

[해설] 여자가 남자에게 새치기했다고 지적하는 내용의 대화가 가장 적절하다.

[어휘] customer service center 고객 서비스 센터   the line is busy 통화 중이다   sign 표지판   cut in line 새치기하다   stand in line 줄을 서다   for a long time 오랫동안   agree with ~에게 동의하다   endless 끝없는   traffic 교통(량)

18 ④

W The 10th Sejong Marathon is just around the corner. On Sunday, March 24, more than 20,000 runners will be racing along Sejong Street. There are five-kilometers, ten-kilometers, and half-marathon courses. If you want to participate, sign up online at www.sejongmarathon.com by Friday, March 1. We encourage you to take part in this event. Thank you.

여 제10회 세종 마라톤이 임박했습니다. 3월 24일 일요일에 2만 명 이상의 주자들이 세종로를 따라 경주할 것입니다. 5km, 10km, 그리고 하프 마라톤 코스가 있습니다. 참가하고 싶으시다면, 3월 1일 금요일까지 www.sejongmarathon.com에서 온라인으로 등록하세요. 여러분이 이 행사에 참가하시기를 바랍니다. 감사합니다.

[해설] 여자는 마라톤의 참가 자격은 언급하지 않았다.

[어휘] marathon 마라톤   (just) around the corner 바로 코앞인, 임박한   race 경주하다   along ~을 따라   course (경주·경기의) 코스   participate 참가하다   sign up 등록하다   encourage 격려하다, 권장하다   take part in ~에 참가하다

19 ①

W What are you doing?

M I'm making a doghouse for Max.

W Wow. Are you building it on your own?

M Yeah. It's almost finished now. It took me almost

two weeks.

W Awesome. It looks warm and cozy.

M Thanks, but I think it's too simple.

W Hmm... why don't you put some stickers on it?

M Good idea. I'll do that.

여 뭐 하고 있어?

남 Max를 위한 개집을 만들고 있어.

여 와. 너 혼자 만들고 있는 거야?

남 응. 이제 거의 끝났어. 거의 2주나 걸렸네.

여 대단하다. 따뜻하고 아늑해 보여.

남 고마워. 그런데 너무 단순한 것 같아.

여 음… 개집에 스티커를 좀 붙이는 게 어때?

남 좋은 생각이야. 그렇게 할게.

해설 여자가 스티커를 붙이는 것이 어떤지 제안했으므로 이에 대한 수락 또는 거절의 응답이 와야 한다.

② 장갑은 좋은 선물이 되겠네.

③ 응. 더 따뜻해질 것 같아.

④ 넌 이것들을 더 가늘게 만들어야 해.

⑤ 나는 내 집도 나 혼자 만들었어.

어휘 doghouse 개집 build 짓다, 만들어 내다 on one's own 혼자서 almost 거의 cozy 아늑한 thin 얇은, 가는 be oneself 혼자, 스스로

20 ⑤

W I can't believe it's already time to go home.

M Oh, I didn't know it was this late.

W Thank you for inviting me to dinner tonight.

M My pleasure. I had a great time, too.

W Dinner was really good.

M I'm glad you liked it.

W You're an excellent cook. Seriously, you could open a restaurant.

M Thank you for saying that.

여 벌써 집에 갈 시간이라는 게 믿기지 않네요.

남 오, 이렇게 늦은지 몰랐어요.

여 오늘 저녁 식사에 저를 초대해 줘서 고마워요.

남 천만에요. 저도 아주 즐거웠습니다.

여 저녁 식사가 굉장히 맛있었어요.

남 마음에 드셨다니 기쁘네요.

여 당신은 훌륭한 요리사예요. 진심으로 식당 하나 차리셔도 되겠어요.

남 그렇게 말씀해 주셔서 고맙습니다.

해설 여자가 남자에게 요리를 아주 잘한다고 칭찬했으므로 이에 대한 응답으로 감사를 표현하는 말이 가장 적절하다.

① 저는 이 식당이 마음에 들어요.

② 아니요. 그러시면 안 돼요.

③ 당신은 언제나 환영입니다.

④ 저는 그에게 동의하지 않아요.

어휘 already 이미, 벌써 invite 초대하다 pleasure 기쁨, 즐거움 excellent 훌륭한 cook 요리사 seriously 진지하게, 진심으로 open 개업하다

01 ②	02 ③	03 ①	04 ⑤	05 ②
06 ②	07 ②	08 ④	09 ③	10 ⑤
11 ①	12 ③	13 ⑤	14 ③	15 ②
16 ②	17 ⑤	18 ②	19 ⑤	20 ④

01 ②

W Good morning. Today is Monday, July 21. The weather is going to be pleasant after a month of rain. Across the nation, it will be hot and humid during the workweek and on Saturday. The temperature could average 30°C. You will experience tropical nights from Thursday to Saturday. On Sunday, there is a possibility of isolated showers in northern Gyeonggi-do and in northern Gangwon-do.

여 좋은 아침입니다. 오늘은 7월 21일입니다. 한 달 동안의 비 끝에 날씨는 쾌적할 것으로 보입니다. 전국적으로, 주중과 토요일에는 덥고 습하겠습니다. 기온은 평균 30°C가 될 것입니다. 목요일부터 토요일까지는 열대야를 경험하실 것입니다. 일요일에는 경기도 북부와 강원도 북부에 국지적인 소나기 가능성이 있습니다.

해설 주중과 토요일에는 무덥고 습할 것이라고 했다.

어휘 pleasant 쾌적한 across the nation 전국적으로 humid 습한 workweek 주중 temperature 기온 average 평균 ~이 되다 experience 경험하다 tropical night 열대야 possibility 가능성 isolated 외딴, 격리된 shower 소나기 northern 북부의

02 ③

M I lost my son just a minute ago. He is a 6-year-old boy who has short, curly hair.

W What's his name?

M Mike Robinson.

W What is he wearing?

M He is wearing a long-sleeved striped shirt, jeans, and glasses.

W Okay, Mr. Robinson. We will make an announcement right away.

남 방금 전에 제 아들을 잃어버렸어요. 짧은 곱슬머리를 한 6살짜리 남자 아이예요.

여 아드님 이름이 무엇인가요?

남 Mike Robinson이요.

여 무엇을 입고 있나요?

남 긴 소매 줄무늬 셔츠와 청바지를 입고 있고 안경을 썼어요.

여 네, Robinson 씨. 지금 바로 안내 방송을 하겠습니다.

해설 남자는 짧은 곱슬머리에 긴소매 줄무늬 셔츠와 청바지를 입고 안경을 쓴 자신의 아들을 찾고 있다.

어휘 lose(-lost-lost) 잃어버리다   a minute ago 방금 전에 curly 곱슬곱슬한   long-sleeved 긴소매의   striped 줄무늬의 make an announcement 발표를 하다, 안내 방송을 하다

03 ①

M Is it true that you're moving to Daegu?
W Yes. I was going to tell you soon. It was a sudden decision.
M Why are you moving there?
W My mother got a new job there.
M Oh, I'll miss you a lot.
W Me, too. But we can video chat any time, and you can visit me during summer vacation.
M You're right. Things will change, but we'll still be good friends.
W Of course.

여 너 대구로 이사하는 게 사실이야?
여 응. 네게 곧 말하려고 했어. 갑작스러운 결정이었어.
남 왜 거기로 이사하는 거야?
여 우리 어머니께서 그곳에서 새 직장을 구하셨거든.
남 오, 네가 많이 보고 싶을 거야.
여 나도. 그래도 우리는 언제든지 화상 채팅을 할 수 있고, 네가 여름 방학 동안에 나한테 놀러 오면 되잖아.
남 맞아. 상황이 바뀌어도 우리는 여전히 좋은 친구일 거야.
여 물론이지.

해설 여자가 갑자기 이사를 가게 되어 서로가 많이 보고 싶을 것이라고 했으므로 두 사람은 슬픈 심정일 것이다.

어휘 move 이사하다   sudden 갑작스러운   decision 결정 miss 그리워하다   a lot 많이   video chat 화상 채팅을 하다 during ~ 동안   still 여전히

04 ⑤

W What did you do last Saturday?
M Nothing special. I just stayed at home.
W Why? Weren't you feeling well?
M No. Actually, I went to the theater with my brother, but all the tickets were sold out.
W That's too bad.
M So we went to the art museum next to the park, but it was closed for repairs.
W Oh, that's bad timing.
M We went back home and played board games until midnight.

여 지난주 토요일에 뭐 했어?
남 특별한 건 없었어. 그냥 집에 있었어.
여 왜? 몸이 좋지 않았던 거야?
남 아니. 사실 우리 형이랑 극장에 갔는데, 표가 다 매진이었어.
여 그것 참 안됐구나.
남 그래서 공원 옆에 있는 미술관에 갔는데, 미술관이 수리 중이라 닫혀 있었어.
여 오, 가는 날이 장날이구나.
남 우리는 집으로 돌아와서 자정이 될 때까지 보드게임을 했어.

해설 영화를 보러 갔지만 표가 매진이었고, 미술관에 갔지만 수리 중이라 문이 닫혀 있어서 남자는 집에 돌아와 보드게임을 했다고 했다.

어휘 theater 극장   sold out 매진된, 다 팔린   closed for repairs 수리를 위해 휴업하는   timing 시기, 타이밍   until ~까지   midnight 자정, 한밤중

05 ②

W Good afternoon, sir. How may I help you?
M Good afternoon. I'd like to exchange some U.S. dollars into Korean won.
W How much money would you like to exchange?
M $500. Here you are.
W Okay. Are you going to Korea on holiday?
M No, I'm going on a business trip.
W I see. It comes to 600,000 won according to today's exchange rate.
M Thank you.

여 안녕하세요, 손님. 무엇을 도와드릴까요?
남 안녕하세요. 미국 달러를 한국 원화로 환전하고 싶습니다.
여 돈을 얼마나 바꾸시겠어요?
남 500달러요. 여기 있습니다.
여 네. 한국에 휴가 가시는 거예요?
남 아니요, 출장 가는 거예요.
여 그러시군요. 오늘의 환율에 따라 60만원이 됩니다.
남 고맙습니다.

해설 미국 달러를 한국 원화로 바꿨으므로 은행에서 이루어지는 대화이다.

어휘 exchange A into B A를 B로 교환하다   on holiday 휴가 중에   business trip 출장   come to (총계가) ~이 되다 according to ~에 따라   exchange rate 환율

06 ②

W Time really flies. It's already December.
M December? Is it December 1 today?
W Yes. Why?
M I totally forgot. Tom's birthday party is tomorrow.
W Isn't Tom's birthday December 3?
M Right, but he will go on a trip with his family on his birthday.
W Oh, I remember that.

여 시간 정말 빠르다. 벌써 12월이야.
남 12월? 오늘 12월 1일이야?
여 응. 왜?
남 완전히 잊고 있었네. Tom의 생일 파티가 내일이잖아.
여 Tom의 생일은 12월 3일 아니야?
남 맞아, 그런데 Tom은 생일에 가족들과 여행을 갈 거야.
여 아, 기억나.

해설 오늘이 12월 1일인데 내일 Tom의 생일 파티가 있다고 했으므로, Tom의 생일 파티를 하는 날은 12월 2일이다.

어휘 fly (시간이) 아주 빨리 가다   totally 완전히   forget

(-forgot-forgotten) 잊다   go on a trip 여행을 가다
remember 기억하다   present 선물

07 ②

W I'd like to talk about the school cafeteria during
lunchtime. There are some problems with the
cafeteria. All the students come at the same time,
so it is very crowded. Most students have to wait
for a long time to get their food. But then they
have to eat quickly so that others can sit down. In
addition, when three or four students want to sit
together, it is difficult to find a table.

여 저는 점심시간 동안의 학교 식당에 대해 이야기하려고 합니다.
학교 식당에는 몇 가지 문제점이 있습니다. 모든 학생들이 동시
에 와서, 아주 혼잡합니다. 대부분의 학생들은 음식을 받기 위
해 오랫동안 기다려야 합니다. 하지만 그러고 나서 학생들은 다
른 사람들이 자리에 앉을 수 있도록 밥을 빨리 먹어야 하죠. 게
다가, 서너 명이 함께 앉고 싶을 경우에는 테이블을 찾기가 힘
듭니다.

해설 여자는 학교 식당의 음식에 대해서는 언급하지 않았다.

어휘 school cafeteria 학교 식당   lunchtime 점심시간
at the same time 동시에   crowded 혼잡한, 붐비는   for
a long time 오랫동안   quickly 빠르게   so that ~하도록
others 다른 사람들   in addition 게다가   difficult 어려운

08 ④

W This mall is huge! Have you been here before?
M No. It's my first time here, too. I'm so excited.
W Me, too. Where should we go first? Clothing
stores?
M Actually, I'm a little hungry. How about going to the
food court before shopping?
W Sure. Let's check where the food court is.
M There's a floor map over there. Let's check it out.
W Okay.

여 이 쇼핑몰은 규모가 크구나! 전에 여기에 와 본 적 있어?
남 아니. 나도 여긴 처음이야. 너무 신난다.
여 나도. 어디부터 갈까? 옷 가게?
남 사실 난 좀 배가 고파. 쇼핑하기 전에 푸드 코트에 가는 것은
어때?
여 그래. 푸드 코트가 어디에 있는지 확인해 보자.
남 저기 층별 안내도가 있네. 확인해 보자.
여 그래.

해설 두 사람은 층별 안내도를 보며 푸드 코트의 위치를 확인하기
로 했다.

어휘 mall 쇼핑몰   huge 거대한   excited 신난, 들뜬
clothing store 옷 가게   a little 조금, 약간   food court 푸드
코트   floor map 층별 안내도   check ~ out ~을 확인하다

09 ③

M Sleep affects everything. The amount of sleep
can affect how well you learn. Students who
sleep well tend to score higher on tests. However,
students who get less sleep have a harder time
concentrating in class. A lack of sleep can also
affect your behavior and mood. Therefore, it's
important to get enough sleep. Turn off the lights
and go to bed at the same time every day.

남 잠은 모든 것에 영향을 미칩니다. 잠의 양은 여러분이 얼마나
잘 학습하는지에 영향을 미칠 수 있습니다. 잠을 푹 자는 학생
들은 시험에서 더 높은 점수를 받는 경향이 있습니다. 그러나
잠을 더 적게 잔 학생들은 수업 시간에 집중하는데 더 어려움
을 겪습니다. 수면 부족은 행동과 기분에도 영향을 미칠 수 있
습니다. 따라서, 충분히 잠을 자는 것은 중요합니다. 불을 끄고
매일 같은 시간에 잠자리에 드십시오.

해설 남자는 수면이 성적뿐 아니라 행동과 기분에도 영향을 미친
다고 설명하며 충분한 수면의 중요성에 대해 이야기하고 있다.

어휘 affect 영향을 미치다   amount 양   tend to ~하는
경향이 있다   score (시험 등에서) 점수를 받다   less 더
적은(little의 비교급)   have a hard time ~ing ~하는 데
어려움을 겪다   concentrate 집중하다   lack 부족, 결핍
behavior 행동   mood 기분   important 중요한   enough
충분한   turn off ~을 끄다

10 ⑤

W You're very good at playing the piano. I was so
impressed.
M Thank you. I practice the piano every day. I enjoy
playing it.
W How long have you played the piano?
M I've played the piano for eight years. My mom
taught me how to play when I was five.
W Oh, so she plays it really well, too.
M Yes. She majored in piano in university.
W Oh, I see.

여 넌 피아노를 아주 잘 치는구나. 정말 감동받았어.
남 고마워. 나는 매일 피아노를 연습해. 피아노 치는 걸 좋아해.
여 얼마나 오랫 동안 피아노를 쳤니?
남 8년 동안 피아노를 쳤어. 내가 다섯 살 때 우리 엄마가 피아노
치는 법을 가르쳐 주셨거든.
여 오, 그래서 어머니께서도 피아노를 잘 치시는구나.
남 응. 대학교에서 피아노를 전공하셨어.
여 아, 그렇구나.

해설 대학교에서 피아노를 전공한 사람은 남자가 아니라 남자의
어머니이다.

어휘 be good at ~을 잘하다   impressed 감동받은
practice 연습하다   teach(-taught-taught) 가르쳐 주다
how to ~하는 방법   major in ~을 전공하다   university
대학교

11 ①

(*Cellphone rings.*)

M　Hello, Mina.

W　Hey, Tom. It seems you have a bad cold. Are you okay?

M　I feel much better now. Thanks. I went to see a doctor and got some rest all day.

W　It's good to hear that. By the way, I called you because of the math homework. You have to solve the questions on page 26.

M　Page 26? Okay. Thanks.

W　You're welcome. Take care and see you tomorrow!

(*휴대 전화가 울린다.*)

남　안녕, 미나야.

여　얘, Tom. 너 심한 감기에 걸린 것 같다. 괜찮아?

남　지금은 훨씬 나아졌어. 고마워. 난 병원에 갔다가 하루 종일 쉬었어.

여　다행이다. 그건 그렇고, 수학 숙제 때문에 전화했어. 넌 26쪽 문제들을 풀어야 해.

남　26쪽? 알았어. 고마워.

여　천만에. 몸조심하고 내일 보자!

[해설] 여자는 남자에게 수학 숙제를 알려 주기 위해 전화했다.

[어휘] seem ~인 것 같다　bad cold 심한 감기　see a doctor 병원에 가다　get rest 쉬다　all day 하루 종일　because of ~ 때문에　homework 숙제　solve 풀다　question 문제　take care 몸조심하다

12 ③

W　Jack, why are you depressed?

M　Mom, I'm one of the shortest in my class.

W　Did you have a physical examination at school?

M　Yes. Tony is five centimeters taller than me. He was shorter than me last year.

W　How tall is he now?

M　He is 165 centimeters. He grew ten centimeters last year, but I grew only two centimeters.

W　Don't worry. You will be much taller next year.

여　Jack, 왜 시무룩해 있니?

남　엄마, 제가 우리 반에서 가장 키가 작은 사람들 중 한 명이에요.

여　학교에서 신체검사를 했니?

남　네. Tony가 저보다 5cm 더 커요. 그는 작년에 저보다 작았어요.

여　지금 그 애는 키가 몇인데?

남　그는 165cm예요. 그는 작년보다 10cm 자랐는데, 저는 고작 2cm 자랐어요.

여　걱정하지 마. 내년에는 훨씬 더 클 거야.

[해설] 현재 키가 165cm인 Tony가 남자보다 5cm 크다고 했으므로, 남자의 현재 키는 160cm이다.

[어휘] depressed 침울한, 의기소침한　physical examination 신체검사　last year 작년　grow(-grew-grown) 자라다　only 겨우, 단　next year 내년

13 ⑤

M　Hello, Ms. Lee. I have a fever, and I have the chills.

W　I see. Let me take your temperature.

M　Okay.

W　(*Pause*) Oh, you have a high fever. Since when have you had a fever?

M　For a couple of hours, I think.

W　Take this pill, and you'd better go to the hospital right away. There's a bad flu going around these days.

M　Do you mean I should leave school early?

W　Yes, after telling your homeroom teacher.

남　안녕하세요. Lee 선생님. 저 열이 나고 으슬으슬 추워요.

여　그렇구나. 체온을 재 볼게.

남　네.

여　(*잠시 후*) 오, 고열이 있구나. 언제부터 열이 났니?

남　두 시간 정도 된 것 같아요.

여　이 약을 먹고, 지금 당장 병원에 가 보는 게 좋겠구나. 요즘 독감이 유행하고 있거든.

남　학교를 조퇴하라는 말씀이세요?

여　그래, 담임 선생님께 말씀드리고 나서.

[해설] 열이 나서 여자를 찾아온 남자에게 여자는 담임 선생님께 말씀드린 후 당장 병원에 가는 것이 좋겠다고 했으므로, 보건 교사와 학생 사이의 대화이다.

[어휘] have a fever 열이 나다　chill 오한, 한기　temperature 체온　since ~부터　a couple of 두어 개의　pill 알약　had better ~하는 것이 좋겠다　flu 독감　these days 요즘　leave school early 학교를 조퇴하다　homeroom teacher 담임 선생님

14 ③

W　I can't imagine even one day without my smartphone.

M　Living without a smartphone isn't bad.

W　What do you mean?

M　A week ago, my smartphone was broken, so I had to spend the whole day without it.

W　How was it?

M　I enjoyed it. I had more free time and focused more on my work.

W　Really? I feel so bored even when my battery's dead.

M　Why don't you try spending a day without your smartphone?

W　Hmm... I'll think about it.

여　나는 스마트폰 없는 단 하루도 상상할 수가 없어.

남　스마트폰 없는 생활도 나쁘지는 않아.

여　무슨 말이야?

남　일주일 전에 내 스마트폰이 고장 났거든. 그래서 하루 종일 스마트폰 없이 보내야 했어.

여　어땠어?

남　나는 즐거웠어. 자유 시간도 더 많이 생겼고 일도 더 집중할 수 있었어.

여 정말? 나는 배터리가 나갔을 때조차도 너무 심심하던데.
남 스마트폰 없이 하루만이라도 보내 보는 게 어때?
여 음… 생각해 볼게.

15 ②

W May I help you?
M Yes. I bought this bag yesterday, but the zipper
   doesn't work.
W I apologize for your inconvenience. Would you like
   a refund?
M No. I'd like to exchange it for another one. I want
   the same color and style.
W I'm afraid this is the last one in that color. We have
   it in gray and navy blue.
M Then I'll go with the gray one.
W All right. Here it is. Make sure the zipper works well.

여 무엇을 도와드릴까요?
남 네. 제가 어제 이 가방을 샀는데 지퍼가 안 돼요.
여 불편함을 겪게 해 드려서 죄송합니다. 환불을 원하시나요?
남 아니요. 다른 걸로 교환하고 싶어요. 같은 색상과 스타일을 원
   해요.
여 죄송하지만 이 색상으로는 이것이 마지막 물건입니다. 회색과
   짙은 남색은 있습니다.
남 그럼 회색으로 할게요.
여 알겠습니다. 여기 있습니다. 지퍼가 잘 되는지 확인해 보세요.

16 ②

W Excuse me. Where can I make copies?
M The copy machine is next to the entrance on the
   first floor.
W Do I need a card to use it?
M No, you can just pay in cash. There's a
   coin-exchange machine next to the copy machine.
W How much is it?
M Color copies cost fifty cents per page, and black
   and white copies cost ten cents per page.
W Can you show me how to use the machine?
M The instructions are posted on the machine. Just
   follow them.

여 실례합니다. 어디에서 복사하나요?
남 복사기는 1층 출입구 옆에 있습니다.
여 복사기를 사용하려면 카드가 필요한가요?

남 아니요, 그냥 현금으로 내시면 됩니다. 복사기 옆에 동전 교환
   기가 있습니다.
여 얼마인가요?
남 컬러 복사는 장당 50센트이고, 흑백 복사는 장당 10센트입니
   다.
여 복사기 사용법을 알려 주실 수 있어요?
남 기계에 사용 설명서가 붙어 있습니다. 그대로 따라하시면 됩니
   다.

17 ⑤

① W I don't know how to use this.
  M It's very simple. I'll tell you how.
② W What are you planning to do this weekend?
  M I'm planning to go on a picnic.
③ W Is it okay if I take a picture?
  M Sure. Go ahead.
④ W How do I get to the museum?
  M Go straight two blocks and turn right.
⑤ W I'm so nervous. What if something goes wrong?
  M Don't worry. You'll do well.

① 여 이것을 어떻게 사용하는지 모르겠어요.
  남 아주 간단해요. 제가 알려 드릴게요.
② 여 이번 주말에 무엇을 할 계획인가요?
  남 소풍을 갈 계획이에요.
③ 여 사진을 찍어도 될까요?
  남 물론이에요. 그러세요.
④ 여 박물관에 어떻게 가나요?
  남 두 블록을 곧장 간 후 오른쪽으로 도세요.
⑤ 여 정말 긴장돼요. 뭔가 잘못되면 어쩌죠?
  남 걱정하지 마요. 당신은 잘할 거예요.

18 ②

M I like your hat. Where did you get it?
W I bought it from bestclothes.com. It has all kinds of
  clothes and accessories.
M Cool. Does it deliver quickly?
W Yes. It delivers everything within twenty-four hours.
M Wow, that's surprising. How about the prices?
W The prices are reasonable. It also has the best
  customer service.

M I should check out the site.

남 네 모자가 마음에 든다. 어디에서 샀니?

여 bestclothes.com에서 샀어. 그 사이트에는 온갖 종류의 옷과 액세서리들이 있어.

남 멋지다. 배송을 빨리 해 주니?

여 응. 모든 물건을 24시간 이내에 배송해 줘.

남 와, 그거 놀랍다. 가격은 어때?

여 가격은 적당해. 그리고 고객 서비스도 아주 좋아.

남 그 사이트를 확인해 봐야겠어.

해설 여자는 주문이 간편하다는 점은 언급하지 않았다.

어휘 kind 종류 clothes 옷 accessory 액세서리 deliver 배달하다 quickly 빨리 within ~ 이내에 surprising 놀라운 reasonable (가격이) 적당한, 너무 비싸지 않은 check out ~을 확인하다

19 ⑤

W Plastic pollution is terrible these days. Every year a huge amount of plastic is thrown away.

M Yes. I've heard that.

W It threatens humans and animals' lives. We need to take action.

M What can we do?

W We have to stop using all kinds of plastic. For example, we shouldn't use plastic straws.

M Good idea. I think we should share all our ideas on our social networks.

W Okay. I'll post about straws then.

여 요즘 플라스틱 오염이 심각해. 매년 엄청난 양의 플라스틱이 버려지고 있어.

남 응. 나도 들었어.

여 이것이 인류와 동물들의 삶을 위협하고 있어. 우리는 조치를 취해야 해.

남 우리가 무엇을 할 수 있을까?

여 모든 종류의 플라스틱 사용을 멈춰야 해. 예를 들면, 우리는 플라스틱 빨대를 사용하면 안 돼.

남 좋은 생각이야. 소셜 네트워크에 우리의 생각을 공유해야 할 것 같아.

여 그래. 그럼 내가 빨대에 대해 글을 올릴게.

해설 남자가 소셜 네트워크에 플라스틱 오염을 줄이기 위한 방안을 공유해야 한다고 말했으므로, 이에 수긍하며 글을 올리겠다고 응답하는 것이 가장 적절하다.
① 난 참을 수가 없어.
② 정말 놀랍다!
③ 널 봐서 정말 기뻐.
④ 우리는 그러면 안 돼.

어휘 plastic 플라스틱 pollution 오염 terrible 심한 these days 요즘 amount 양 throw away 버리다 threaten 위협하다 human 인간, 사람 take action 조치를 취하다 stop ~ing ~하는 것을 그만두다 for example 예를 들어 straw 빨대 share 공유하다 social network 소셜 네트워크, 사회 연결망 post 올리다, 게시하다

20 ④

W Dad, I don't want to go to school tomorrow.

M What happened to you?

W My friend Rachel talked about me behind my back today. I thought we were good friends.

M That's too bad. Did you ask her why she did that?

W No. I didn't want to talk to her.

M There must be a misunderstanding. Why don't you tell her how you feel?

W Maybe you're right. I'll call her.

여 아빠, 저 내일 학교에 가기 싫어요.

남 무슨 일 있었니?

여 오늘 제 친구 Rachel이 저의 험담을 했어요. 우리는 좋은 친구라고 생각했는데 말이죠.

남 그것 참 안됐구나. 그 애가 왜 그랬는지 물어봤니?

여 아니요. 전 그 애랑 이야기하고 싶지 않아요.

남 오해가 있었던 것이 분명해. 그 애에게 네가 어떤 기분인지 이야기하는 게 어떻겠니?

여 아빠 말씀이 맞는 것 같아요. 그 애에게 전화할게요.

해설 남자가 여자의 기분이 어떤지 친구에게 말해 보라고 제안했으므로 이에 대한 수락 또는 거절의 응답이 와야 한다.
① 물론이죠. 제시간에 갈 거예요.
② 전 정말 그것에 대해 궁금해요.
③ 힘내세요. 상황이 더 나아질 거예요.
⑤ 걱정하지 마세요. 그녀는 곧 회복될 거예요.

어휘 talk behind one's back ~의 험담을 하다 misunderstanding 오해 curious 궁금한 get well (병이) 나아지다

Word Check   11회

01 요즘	02 참가하다
03 미열	04 업무로, 사업차
05 접시	06 전체의
07 잠시 동안	08 준비하다
09 특정한, 특별한	10 굉장한
11 다양한	
12 (가격이) 적정한, 너무 비싸지 않은	
13 gratitude	14 cozy
15 vaccination	16 truth
17 grade	18 surround
19 impressive	20 endless
21 encourage	22 graduation
23 build	24 seriously

Expression Check

25 by myself	26 only if
27 cut in line	28 put off
29 is, made of	30 stand in line

Word Check   12회

01 극장	02 평균 ~이 되다
03 긴소매의	04 열대야
05 화상 채팅을 하다	06 위협하다
07 시기, 타이밍	08 ~에 따라
09 환율	10 전적으로, 틀림없이
11 옷 가게	12 층별 안내도
13 affect	14 straw
15 concentrate	16 behavior
17 impressed	18 pleasant
19 copy machine	20 possibility
21 refund	22 pollution
23 chill	24 midnight

Expression Check

25 on holiday	26 majored in
27 apologize for	28 tend to
29 behind my back	30 at the same time

실전 모의고사 13회   pp.134~141

01 ④	02 ①	03 ②	04 ④	05 ④
06 ③	07 ③	08 ①	09 ③	10 ②
11 ③	12 ①	13 ⑤	14 ②	15 ④
16 ③	17 ⑤	18 ③	19 ⑤	20 ⑤

01 ④

M I'm Mitch with the weekly weather report. The city still has a fine dust warning, but starting on Tuesday night, strong winds will help clear out the dust completely. So the temperature will go down on Wednesday, but you can enjoy fresh air and sunlight throughout the day. A bit of rain is expected on Thursday morning, and there's a chance of it turning into snow on Friday.

남 주간 일기 예보의 Mitch입니다. 도시는 여전히 미세 먼지 경보가 내려져 있지만, 화요일 밤부터는 강한 바람이 먼지를 완전히 걷어 낼 것입니다. 따라서 수요일에 기온은 내려가겠으나, 종일 맑은 공기와 햇빛을 즐기실 수 있겠습니다. 목요일 오전에는 약간의 비가 예상되고요, 금요일에는 비가 눈으로 바뀔 가능성이 있습니다.

해설 수요일에는 기온은 떨어지지만 종일 맑은 공기와 햇살을 즐길 수 있을 것이라고 했다.

어휘 weekly 주간의   fine dust 미세 먼지   warning 경고   clear out (~을 없애고) 청소하다   completely 완전히   temperature 기온   fresh 상쾌한, 산뜻한   throughout the day 온종일   a bit of 약간의   expect 예상하다   chance 가능성   turn into ~으로 변하다

02 ①

M I'd like to buy an apron for my son.
W Okay. How about this one with stars on it?
M Do you have a simpler one?
W Yes. This one has a big star in the middle.
M I think the star is too big. I would also prefer a darker color.
W Then what about the one with vertical stripes hanging over there?
M That's nice. I'll take it.
W Okay. I hope your son likes it.

남 아들을 위한 앞치마를 사고 싶어요.
여 네. 별들이 있는 이것은 어떠세요?
남 더 단순한 것 있나요?
여 네. 이것은 가운데에 큰 별이 있어요.
남 별이 너무 큰 것 같아요. 그리고 더 어두운 색이면 좋겠어요.
여 그럼 저쪽에 걸려 있는 세로 줄무늬가 있는 건 어떠세요?
남 좋네요. 그걸 살게요.
여 알겠습니다. 아드님이 좋아하길 바라요.

남자는 세로 줄무늬가 있는 앞치마를 사기로 했다.

apron 앞치마   son 아들   simple 단순한   in the middle 가운데에   prefer ~을 더 좋아하다   dark 어두운   vertical 세로의   stripe 줄무늬   hang 걸리다

03 ②

M Would you turn on the air cleaner? The air in here is not fresh.
W It's already on. I think there is a problem.
M Do you know what the problem is?
W I think we need to change the filter.
M Didn't we get it changed last month?
W You're right. Exactly three weeks ago.
M A filter should last longer. I'll call the customer service center.
W You need to complain strongly.

남 공기 청정기 좀 켜 줄래요? 여기 공기가 좋지 않아요.
여 이미 켜져 있어요. 문제가 있는 것 같아요.
남 문제가 뭔지 알아요?
여 필터를 교체해야 할 것 같아요.
남 우리 지난달에 필터 교체하지 않았어요?
여 맞아요. 정확히 3주 전에요.
남 필터는 더 오래 가야 하잖아요. 내가 고객 서비스 센터에 전화할게요.
여 당신 강력히 항의해야 해요.

필터를 최근에 교체했는데도 공기 청정기가 제대로 작동하지 않아서 남자가 고객 센터에 전화하겠다고 했고, 여자도 강력히 항의하라고 했으므로 두 사람 모두 짜증이 난 상태이다.

turn on ~을 켜다   air cleaner 공기 청정기   fresh 상쾌한, 산뜻한   filter 필터   exactly 정확히   last 유지되다   customer service center 고객 서비스 센터   complain 항의하다   strongly 강하게, 강경히   pleased 기쁜   annoyed 짜증이 난   ashamed 부끄러운   depressed 낙담한

04 ④

M How was your weekend, Jenny?
W It was a perfect weekend. I met Brian in person!
M Brian the singer?
W Yes. Look at this picture. I took some pictures with him.
M Wow, it's really him. Where did you go?
W I went to Wilson's Department Store. He was shopping alone.
M Weren't there many people around him?
W No one recognized him except me. He was covering his face with his hat.

남 주말 어땠어, Jenny?
여 완벽한 주말이었어. 나 Brian을 직접 만났어!
남 가수 Brian?
여 응. 이 사진 좀 봐. 나 그와 함께 사진 찍었어.
남 와, 정말 그 사람이네. 너 어디 갔던 거야?
여 Wilson's Department Store에 갔었어. 그가 혼자 쇼핑하고

있더라.
남 그 사람 주변에 사람들이 많이 있지 않았어?
여 나 빼고 아무도 그를 못 알아봤어. 그가 모자로 얼굴을 가리고 있었거든.

여자는 백화점에 갔다가 유명한 가수를 만나 함께 사진을 찍었다고 했다.

perfect 완벽한   in person 직접   take a picture 사진을 찍다   department store 백화점   alone 혼자서   no one 아무도 ~않다   recognize 알아보다   except ~을 제외하고   cover 가리다

05 ④

W Customer number 26. Please come to counter B.
M Hi. I want to send this to Japan.
W What are the items inside? You cannot send food, drugs, plants, sprays, and so on.
M They're clothes.
W Okay. You can choose either airmail or ship delivery.
M I'll go with airmail. How long will it take to get there?
W It will arrive in three to five days.

여 26번 손님. B 카운터로 와 주세요.
남 안녕하세요. 저는 이걸 일본으로 보내고 싶어요.
여 안에 든 물건은 무엇인가요? 음식, 약, 식물, 스프레이 등은 보내실 수 없어요.
남 옷이에요.
여 네. 항공 우편과 선박 배송 중에 선택하실 수 있어요.
남 항공 우편으로 할게요. 도착하는 데 얼마나 걸릴까요?
여 3일에서 5일 후에 도착합니다.

해외로 소포를 보낼 수 있는 곳은 우체국이다.

customer 손님, 고객   item 물건   inside ~ 안에   drug 약   plant 식물   spray 스프레이   clothes 옷   choose 선택하다, 고르다   either A or B A 또는 B 둘 중에 하나   airmail 항공 우편   ship 배, 선박   delivery 배송   arrive 도착하다   in ~ 후에

06 ③

M Look at the trash can!
W Some people haven't separated their trash.
M Shall we separate it?
W Yes. The recycling bins are right there.
M Will you take out the paper and plastic? I'll take out the cans and bottles.
W Okay. I don't understand why people are so irresponsible.
M Me neither. They should care about the environment.
W I couldn't agree with you more.

남 이 쓰레기통 좀 봐!
여 어떤 사람들이 쓰레기를 분리하지 않았네.
남 우리가 이 쓰레기를 분리할까?
여 그래. 재활용품 수거함이 바로 저기에 있어.

남 네가 종이와 플라스틱을 꺼내 줄래? 나는 캔과 병을 꺼낼게.
여 알았어. 사람들이 왜 이렇게 무책임한지 이해가 안 가.
남 나도 그래. 그 사람들은 환경에 대해 더 신경 써야 해.
여 네 말에 전적으로 동의해.

[해설] I couldn't agree with you more.는 상대방의 말에 전적으로 동의한다는 뜻이다.

[어휘] trash can 쓰레기통   separate 분리하다   trash 쓰레기   recycling bin 재활용품 수거함   take out 꺼내다   plastic 플라스틱   bottle 병   irresponsible 무책임한   care about ~에 마음을 쓰다, 관심을 가지다   environment 환경   agree with ~에게 동의하다

07 ③

M Ladies and gentlemen, our train is approaching the platform. We'll arrive at Gwangmyeong Station shortly. If this is your destination, please be prepared to get off the train. This train's final destination is Seoul Station. Please take all your belongings with you when you get off the train. Thank you for traveling with us and have a good day.

남 신사 숙녀 여러분, 우리 열차는 플랫폼에 다가가고 있습니다. 곧 광명역에 도착합니다. 이곳이 여러분의 목적지라면, 열차에서 내릴 준비를 하시기 바랍니다. 이 열차의 종착지는 서울역입니다. 열차에서 내리실 때 소지품을 모두 잘 챙기시길 바랍니다. 저희와 함께 여행해 주셔서 감사드리며 좋은 하루 보내십시오.

[해설] 승객들에게 곧 도착할 역과 하차 시 주의 사항을 알리는 안내 방송이다.

[어휘] approach 다가가다   platform (기차역의) 플랫폼   arrive 도착하다   shortly 곧   destination 목적지   be prepared to ~할 준비를 하다   get off 내리다, 하차하다   final 마지막의   belongings 소지품   travel 여행하다

08 ①

M Why do you have all these boxes and cans?
W I'm working on an art project. I need to create an artwork using them.
M What are you going to make?
W I have no idea.
M How about searching the Internet for ideas?
W I did, but it wasn't helpful. I want to make something very unusual.
M Then how about visiting the Eco Design Expo? That might be helpful.
W That's a good idea. I'll go there tomorrow.

남 왜 이 상자들과 캔들을 가지고 있어?
여 난 미술 프로젝트를 하는 중이야. 이것들을 사용해서 미술품을 만들어야 해.
남 뭐를 만들 건데?
여 모르겠어.
남 아이디어를 위해 인터넷을 찾아보는 게 어때?
여 찾아봤는데, 도움이 안 됐어. 난 아주 특이한 걸 만들고 싶어.

남 그럼 친환경 디자인 박람회를 방문하는 게 어때? 도움이 될 것 같은데.
여 좋은 생각이야. 내일 거기에 가 봐야겠다.

[해설] 남자가 친환경 디자인 박람회에 가 보라고 제안하자 여자는 내일 가 보겠다고 했다.

[어휘] project 프로젝트   create 창작하다   artwork 미술품   search 찾다   helpful 도움이 되는   unusual 특이한   eco design 에코 디자인(친환경을 고려한 디자인)   expo 박람회

09 ③

M Do you know about the Hwacheon Sancheoneo Ice Festival?
W I have no idea. What is it?
M It's a winter festival held in Hwacheon in January. You can do various winter activities such as ice fishing and ice sledding.
W That sounds interesting. Have you visited the festival before?
M No. But I'm going there this weekend. Do you want to go with me?
W I'd love to. But how can we get there? We can't drive.
M There's a shuttle bus at Myeongdong Station.
W Great. That's convenient.

남 너 화천 산천어 얼음 축제에 대해 아니?
여 몰라. 그게 뭐야?
남 화천에서 1월에 열리는 겨울 축제야. 얼음낚시나 얼음 썰매 타기와 같은 다양한 겨울철 활동들을 할 수 있어.
여 재미있겠다. 너는 전에 그 축제에 가 본 적이 있니?
남 아니. 하지만 이번 주말에 갈 거야. 나랑 같이 갈래?
여 좋아. 그런데 우리가 거기에 어떻게 갈 수 있지? 우리는 운전 못 하잖아.
남 명동역에 셔틀 버스가 있어.
여 잘됐다. 그거 편리하네.

[해설] 남자는 축제의 입장료는 언급하지 않았다.

[어휘] festival 축제   hold(-held-held) 열다, 개최하다   various 다양한   activity 활동   such as ~와 같은   ice fishing 얼음낚시   ice sledding 얼음 썰매 타기   drive 운전하다   shuttle bus 셔틀 버스   convenient 편리한

10 ②

W What do you want to be in the future?
M I want to be a professional mountain climber. My dream is to climb Mt. Everest. What about you?
W I don't have a certain dream. I don't know what I want to do in the future.
M Think of what you like to do.
W Hmm... I enjoy singing, but I don't know if I'm really good at it.
M Practice every day, and you will be a professional someday.
W I'll have to think about it. Thanks.

여 너는 장래 희망이 뭐야?

남 나는 전문 산악인이 되고 싶어. 내 꿈은 에베레스트산을 오르는 거야. 너는?

여 나는 특정한 꿈이 없어. 나는 미래에 뭘 하고 싶은지 모르겠어.

남 네가 하기 좋아하는 것을 생각해 봐.

여 음… 나는 노래하는 걸 좋아하긴 한데, 내가 정말 노래를 잘하는지는 모르겠어.

남 매일 연습하면 언젠가는 프로가 될 거야.

여 생각 좀 해 봐야겠다. 고마워.

해설 남자가 여자에게 좋아하는 것을 생각해 보라고 하자, 여자는 노래하는 것을 즐긴다고 했다.

어휘 professional 전문적인; 프로, 전문가   mountain climber 산악인   climb 오르다   certain 특정한   be good at ~을 잘하다   practice 연습하다   someday 언젠가

11 ③

M Hello. I'm Jinho. Nice to meet you!

W My name is Jennifer. Nice to meet you, too.

M My family's house is your homestay. I'll take you there now.

W Thank you. I'm really looking forward to meeting everyone.

M It's your first time in Korea. Where do you want to visit the most?

W Gyeongbokgung Palace. I'm interested in the traditional buildings of every country I visit.

M Good. Gyeongbokgung Palace is near our house.

W That's great.

남 안녕. 나는 진호야. 만나서 반가워!

여 내 이름은 Jennifer야. 나도 만나서 반가워.

남 우리 가족의 집이 네가 홈스테이 할 곳이야. 내가 지금 너를 그곳으로 데리고 갈게.

여 고마워. 나는 모두를 만나는 것이 정말 기대돼.

남 너는 한국 방문이 처음이잖아. 가장 가고 싶은 곳은 어디야?

여 경복궁. 나는 내가 방문하는 모든 나라의 전통적인 건물에 관심이 있거든.

남 잘됐네. 경복궁은 우리 집 근처에 있어.

여 좋다.

해설 남자의 말에서 여자는 한국에 처음 방문했음을 알 수 있다.

어휘 homestay 홈스테이(외국인이 체류 중인 나라의 일반 가정에서 생활하는 것)   look forward to ~을 기대하다   palace 궁전   be interested in ~에 관심이 있다   traditional 전통적인   building 건물   near ~에서 가까이

12 ①

M What are you reading?

W I'm reading a book about Chinese culture.

M Chinese culture? I didn't know you're interested in China.

W I'm not really interested in China. I'm reading it because I have to.

M Why?

W I need to prepare for a presentation about Chinese culture next week.

M I see. Do your best.

남 너 뭘 읽고 있어?

여 중국 문화에 대한 책을 읽고 있어.

남 중국 문화? 네가 중국에 관심이 있는지 몰랐네.

여 그다지 중국에 관심이 있는 건 아니야. 읽어야 해서 읽고 있는 거야.

남 왜?

여 다음 주에 있을 중국 문화에 대한 발표를 준비해야 하거든.

남 그렇구나. 열심히 해.

해설 여자는 다음 주에 있을 중국 문화에 대한 발표를 준비하기 위해서 책을 읽는 것이라고 했다.

어휘 culture 문화   be interested in ~에 관심이 있다 prepare for ~을 준비하다   presentation 발표   do one's best 최선을 다하다

13 ⑤

(Telephone rings.)

W Han's Chicken. How may I help you?

M I want to order one fried chicken. I'm at 213 Green Road.

W Okay. Do you want the original recipe or the spicy one?

M Is the price the same?

W The original is 14,000 won. You have to pay 1,000 won more for the spicy one.

M I'll have the spicy one. Is there a delivery fee?

W Yes, it's 1,000 won.

M I see. Please deliver it quickly.

(전화벨이 울린다.)

여 Han's Chicken입니다. 무엇을 도와드릴까요?

남 프라이드치킨 한 마리를 주문하고 싶어요. Green Road 213 번지입니다.

여 네. 기본 맛을 원하시나요, 아니면 매운맛을 원하시나요?

남 가격이 같은가요?

여 기본 맛은 14,000원입니다. 매운맛은 1,000원을 더 내셔야 해요.

남 매운맛으로 할게요. 배달료가 있나요?

여 네, 1,000원입니다.

남 알겠습니다. 빨리 배달해 주세요.

해설 매운맛 치킨은 기본 맛보다 1,000원이 더 비싸서 15,000원이고 배달료가 1,000원이므로, 남자는 총 16,000원을 지불해야 한다.

어휘 order 주문하다   fried chicken 프라이드치킨   original 원래의   recipe 조리법   spicy 매운   price 가격   same 같은 delivery fee 배달료   deliver 배달하다   quickly 빨리

14 ②

W What's wrong, Michael?

M My ankle hurts. I think I sprained it while jumping rope.

W Oh, no. Do you want me to put an ice pack on your ankle?

M I already did that, but it still hurts.

W Let's go to see a doctor right away.

M I think just putting on some pain relief patches will do. Could you please get some patches for me?

W I see. But if it still hurts tomorrow, you should see a doctor.

M Okay, I will.

여 무슨 문제 있니, Michael?

남 발목이 아파요. 줄넘기를 하다가 발목을 삔 것 같아요.

여 오, 저런. 발목에 얼음주머니를 올려 줄까?

남 이미 해 봤는데, 여전히 아파요.

여 그럼 지금 바로 병원에 가 보자.

남 제 생각에는 파스를 좀 붙이면 될 것 같아요. 저를 위해 파스를 좀 사다 주실래요?

여 알았어. 하지만 내일도 계속 아프면, 병원에 가야 해.

남 네, 그럴게요.

해설 남자는 여자에게 파스를 사다 달라고 부탁했다.

어휘 ankle 발목   sprain 삐다, 접지르다   while ~하는 동안에   jump rope 줄넘기를 하다   ice pack 얼음주머니   pain relief patch 파스

15 ④

W Apples are one of the most popular fruits in the world. There are several reasons apples are so popular. First, they are good for your health. Remember the saying, "An apple a day keeps the doctor away." Second, apples can be grown all over the world. Third, they taste good. Lastly, they are effective at helping people lose weight because they are low in calories.

여 사과는 세계에서 가장 인기 있는 과일 중 하나입니다. 사과가 그렇게 인기 있는 데는 몇 가지 이유가 있습니다. 첫째, 사과는 건강에 좋습니다. '하루에 사과 한 알이면 의사가 필요 없다.'라는 속담을 기억하세요. 둘째, 사과는 전 세계에서 재배될 수 있습니다. 셋째, 사과는 맛이 좋습니다. 마지막으로, 사과는 칼로리가 낮아서 체중 감량에 효과적입니다.

해설 여자는 사과가 인기 있는 여러 가지 이유에 대해 말하고 있다.

어휘 popular 인기 있는   fruit 과일   several 몇몇의, 여러 개의   reason 이유   health 건강   remember 기억하다   saying 속담, 격언   keep ~ away ~을 멀리하다   grow(-grew-grown) 재배하다   all over the world 전 세계에   taste 맛이 ~하다   effective 효과적인   lose weight 체중을 줄이다   low in calories 칼로리가 낮은

16 ③

M Did you hear that there'll be a special lecture at the community center today?

W No, I didn't. What's the lecture about?

M Jordan Peterson will talk about happiness.

W Wow, isn't he the writer of the book 12 Rules for

Life? I'll go and get his autograph.

M I will go, too. I've always wanted to meet him.

W Why?

M I want to ask him how to be a good writer.

W Then today will be a great chance for you.

남 오늘 주민 회관에서 특강이 있을 거라는 소식 들었니?

여 아니. 뭐에 대한 강연인데?

남 Jordan Peterson이 행복에 대해 이야기한대.

여 우와, ⟨12 Rules for Life⟩의 작가 아니니? 가서 그의 사인을 받아야겠다.

남 나도 갈 거야. 그를 항상 만나고 싶었거든.

여 왜?

남 그에게 어떻게 훌륭한 작가가 될 수 있는지 묻고 싶어.

여 그럼 오늘이 너에게 좋은 기회가 되겠다.

해설 남자는 훌륭한 작가가 되는 방법을 물어보고 싶어서 작가를 만나고 싶다고 했다.

어휘 lecture 강의   community center 주민 회관   happiness 행복   writer 작가   rule 규칙   life 인생   get one's autograph ~의 사인을 받다   chance 기회

17 ⑤

① W What's wrong? You look tired today.
   M I think I caught a cold.
② W What do you think of this umbrella?
   M It looks okay, but it's heavy.
③ W I don't feel well these days. What should I do?
   M I think you should work out regularly.
④ W What do you want to eat for dinner?
   M I want to eat seafood spaghetti.
⑤ W Would you share your umbrella with me? I don't have one.
   M Sure, I can.

① 여 무슨 일이야? 너 오늘 피곤해 보여.
   남 난 감기에 걸린 것 같아.
② 여 이 우산에 대해 어떻게 생각해?
   남 괜찮아 보이는데, 무거워.
③ 여 요즘 몸이 좀 안 좋아. 내가 무엇을 해야 할까?
   남 나는 네가 규칙적으로 운동해야 한다고 생각해.
④ 여 저녁으로 뭐 먹고 싶어?
   남 해물 스파게티를 먹고 싶어.
⑤ 여 나랑 우산을 같이 쓸 수 있니? 나는 우산이 없어.
   남 물론, 그럴 수 있지.

해설 우산을 같이 쓰자고 요청하는 내용의 대화가 가장 적절하다.

어휘 catch a cold 감기에 걸리다   feel well 건강 상태가 좋다   these days 요즘   work out 운동하다   regularly 규칙적으로   seafood 해산물   spaghetti 스파게티   share (다른 사람과) 함께 쓰다

18 ③

W Eva Armisen is a Spanish artist. She is famous for her childlike style. The characters in her artwork all have happy and sweet smiles on their faces.

They remind us of the joy in the small and simple moments in our everyday lives. The subjects of her artwork are family, love, and togetherness.

여 에바 알머슨은 스페인 예술가입니다. 그녀는 아이 같은 화풍으로 유명합니다. 그녀의 작품 속의 인물들은 모두 얼굴에 행복하고 달콤한 미소를 띠고 있습니다. 그들은 우리에게 일상생활에서 작고 소박한 순간의 기쁨을 생각하게 합니다. 그녀의 작품의 주제는 가족, 사랑, 그리고 함께함입니다.

해설 여자는 에바 알머슨의 유년 시절에 대해서는 언급하지 않았다.

어휘 artist 화가, 예술가   be famous for ~로 유명하다   childlike 아이 같은   character 등장인물   artwork 미술품   remind *A* of *B* A에게 B를 생각나게 하다   moment 순간   everyday life 일상생활   subject 주제   togetherness 함께함, 유대감

19 ⑤

W Hey, what are you writing down?
M I'm working on my habit tracker.
W Habit tracker? I've never heard of it. What is it?
M It's a list for checking my habits every day.
W Sounds interesting. Why are you doing that?
M It helps me to break my bad habits and build good ones.
W Who taught you about this?
M My homeroom teacher last year.

여 얘, 뭘 적고 있니?
남 내 습관 기록지를 적고 있어.
여 습관 기록지라고? 그것에 대해 들어 본 적이 없는데. 그게 뭐야?
남 매일 내 습관을 체크하는 목록이야.
여 흥미롭네. 그걸 왜 하는 거야?
남 내 나쁜 습관을 고치고 좋은 습관을 만들도록 도와주거든.
여 이것에 대해 누가 가르쳐 준 거야?
남 작년 우리 담임 선생님께서.

해설 여자가 습관 기록지에 대해 가르쳐 준 사람이 누구인지 물었으므로 이에 대한 응답이 와야 한다.
① 그분은 내게 많은 것을 가르쳐 주셨어.
② John이 그걸 하는 걸 본 것 같아.
③ 이걸 어떻게 하는지 너에게 가르쳐 줄게.
④ 나는 내 나쁜 습관을 고치고 싶어.

어휘 habit 습관   tracker 추적기   list 목록   break a habit 습관을 고치다   build 만들다   teach(-taught-taught) 가르쳐 주다   homeroom teacher 담임 선생님

20 ⑤

(*Telephone rings.*)
M Hello.
W Hello. This is Cheryl. Is David at home?
M No, he's out. He left his phone here.
W I see. That's why he didn't answer either my phone calls or text messages.
M Do you want to leave a message?
W Yes, please. He has my tablet PC, but I need it

tomorrow.
M Your tablet PC?
W Yes. Would you please tell him to bring it tomorrow?
M Okay. I'll tell him when he comes back.

(*전화벨이 울린다.*)
남 여보세요.
여 여보세요. 저 Cheryl인데요. David가 집에 있나요?
남 아니, 그는 외출했어. David가 휴대 전화를 여기에 두고 갔구나.
여 그렇군요. 그래서 제 전화도 안 받고 문자 메시지에도 답을 하지 않았던 거군요.
남 메시지를 남겨 줄까?
여 네, 부탁드려요. 그가 제 태블릿 피시를 가지고 있는데, 저는 내일 그게 필요해요.
남 네 태블릿 피시라고?
여 네. David한테 내일 태블릿 피시를 가지고 오라고 말씀해 주시겠어요?
남 그래. 그가 돌아오면 말할게.

해설 여자가 내일 자신의 태블릿 피시를 가지고 오라고 David에게 말해 달라고 부탁했으므로, 그가 집에 돌아오면 말하겠다는 응답이 가장 적절하다.
① 나는 태블릿 피시가 없어.
② 도와줘서 고마워.
③ 그래. 너에게 내 공책을 빌려줄게.
④ 그는 전화를 받지 않았어.

어휘 leave(-left-left) 두고 가다   answer a phone call 전화를 받다   either *A* or *B* A 또는 B 둘 중 하나   text message 문자 메시지   leave a message 메시지를 남기다   lend 빌려주다   come back 돌아오다

01 ③	02 ④	03 ⑤	04 ③	05 ②
06 ⑤	07 ④	08 ④	09 ③	10 ⑤
11 ⑤	12 ①	13 ③	14 ③	15 ⑤
16 ③	17 ⑤	18 ④	19 ③	20 ⑤

01 ③

W Good morning. I'm Clara with the worldwide weather report. We won't have a clear winter sky here in Seoul because of the high level of fine dust. Due to the thick rain clouds across Japan, rain is pouring in Tokyo at this moment. In London, because of the heavy snow, many flights have been canceled. Finally, in Moscow, it is windy today. That's all for today.

여 좋은 아침입니다. 세계 일기 예보의 Clara입니다. 여기 서울은 높은 수준의 미세 먼지로 인해 겨울 하늘이 맑지 않겠습니다. 일본 전역에 걸친 짙은 비구름으로 인해, 지금 이 순간 도쿄에는 비가 마구 쏟아지고 있습니다. 런던은 폭설로 인해 많은 항공편이 취소되었습니다. 마지막으로, 오늘 모스크바에는 바람이 많이 붑니다. 오늘은 여기까지입니다.

해설 런던에 폭설이 내려서 많은 항공편이 취소되었다고 했다.

어휘 worldwide 전 세계적인   level 수준   fine dust 미세 먼지   due to ~ 때문에   thick (안개·연기 따위가) 짙은   rain cloud 비구름   across 가로질러   pour (비가) 마구 쏟아지다   moment 순간   because of ~ 때문에   heavy snow 폭설   flight 항공편   cancel 취소하다   windy 바람이 많이 부는

02 ④

M Hello. How can I help you?
W I'd like to buy a painting for my living room.
M What kind of painting are you looking for?
W I'm looking for a landscape painting.
M All right. How about this one? Doesn't this stream look peaceful?
W Yes, it does. But one with a sky would be better.
M Then you'll like this one. A clear sky is over the sunflower field.
W That is beautiful. I'll take it.

남 안녕하세요. 어떻게 도와드릴까요?
여 거실에 놓을 그림을 하나 사고 싶은데요.
남 어떤 종류의 그림을 찾고 계세요?
여 풍경화를 찾고 있어요.
남 알겠습니다. 이건 어떠세요? 이 개울이 평화로워 보이지 않으세요?
여 네, 그러네요. 그런데 하늘이 있는 그림이 더 좋겠어요.
남 그럼 이것이 마음에 드실 거예요. 해바라기 들판 위에 맑은 하늘이 있어요.

여 아름답네요. 그걸 살게요.

해설 여자는 해바라기 들판 위에 맑은 하늘이 있는 그림을 사겠다고 했다.

어휘 painting 그림   living room 거실   look for ~을 찾다   landscape 풍경, 풍경화   stream 개울, 시내   peaceful 평화로운   sunflower 해바라기   field 들판

03 ⑤

M I can't believe this! I think I'll get a free gift! I won a prize!
W Are you serious?
M Yes, look at this email. I won first prize in a shopping mall event.
W Let me see. Well, did you check the date here?
M What date?
W It says the gifts are given until January 3. Wasn't that a week ago?
M Oh, my! Did I miss it? No way!

남 믿을 수 없어! 나 경품을 받을 것 같아! 나 당첨됐어!
여 정말이야?
남 응. 이 이메일 좀 봐. 쇼핑몰 행사에서 내가 일등에 당첨되었어.
여 어디 보자. 음. 너 여기에 있는 날짜 확인했니?
남 무슨 날짜?
여 경품은 1월 3일 전까지만 증정된다고 쓰여 있어. 일주일 전 아니야?
남 오, 이런! 내가 놓친 거야? 안 돼!

해설 일등에 당첨되어 경품을 받을 줄 알았는데 경품 증정 기간이 지난 것을 알고 남자는 실망했을 것이다.

어휘 believe 믿다   free gift 경품   win a prize 상을 타다, 당첨되다   serious 진심인   date 날짜   until ~까지   miss 놓치다   satisfied 만족한   frightened 겁먹은   relaxed 마음 편한   disappointed 실망한

04 ③

M I went to Sky Mall last weekend. There are lots of big stores there.
W Oh, the mall opened recently. Did you buy anything?
M No. I went there to watch the movie *Enemy*.
W Is there a theater in the mall?
M Yeah. It's on the ninth floor.
W That's good. Can you recommend a good restaurant there?
M Try the seafood restaurant on the eighth floor. People say the food there is very good.

남 나 지난 주말에 Sky Mall에 갔었어. 거기에 큰 상점들이 많더라.
여 오, 그 쇼핑몰이 최근에 개장했지. 뭔가 샀어?
남 아니. 난 거기에 영화 〈Enemy〉를 보러 갔었어.
여 쇼핑몰 안에 영화관도 있어?
남 응. 9층에 있어.
여 좋네. 거기에 있는 괜찮은 식당을 추천해 줄 수 있니?
남 8층에 있는 해산물 식당에 가 봐. 사람들이 그 집 음식이 정말

맛있대.

해설 남자는 새로 개장한 쇼핑몰에 있는 영화관에서 영화를 봤다고 했다.

어휘 mall 쇼핑몰   lots of 많은   store 가게   open 개업하다   recently 최근에   theater 영화관   floor 층   recommend 추천하다   restaurant 식당   seafood 해산물

05 ②

M Excuse me. Is there a convenience store nearby?
W Yes. At the main entrance, turn right and it's on the corner of this block.
M I see. When does breakfast start in the morning?
W It's from 7:30 to 10:30. The restaurant is on the first basement level.
M Okay. Can I have a wakeup call tomorrow at 8:30?
W Of course. What is your room number?
M I'm staying in 905. Thank you.

남 실례합니다. 근처에 편의점이 있나요?
여 네. 정문에서 오른쪽으로 도시면 이 블록의 모퉁이에 있습니다.
남 그렇군요. 아침에 조식은 언제 시작하나요?
여 7시 30분부터 10시 30분까지입니다. 식당은 지하 1층에 있습니다.
남 네. 내일 8시 30분에 모닝콜을 걸어 줄 수 있을까요?
여 물론입니다. 방 번호가 어떻게 되시죠?
남 905호에 묵고 있어요. 고맙습니다.

해설 남자가 여자에게 조식 시간을 물어보고 모닝콜을 부탁하고 있으므로 호텔에서 이루어지는 대화이다.

어휘 convenience store 편의점   nearby 근처에   main entrance 정문   corner 모퉁이   breakfast 아침 식사   the first basement level 지하 1층   wakeup call 모닝콜   stay 머무르다

06 ⑤

W Junho, is there anything wrong? You look down.
M Never mind. I'm fine.
W Come on. What are friends for?
M Well, I feel bad because of my musical audition. I was so nervous that I made a terrible mistake at the climax of the song.
W Oh, I'm sorry to hear that.
M I'm so disappointed with myself.
W Don't be. I'm sure you'll do better the next time.

여 준호야, 무슨 일 있어? 기분이 안 좋아 보여.
남 신경 쓰지 마. 괜찮아.
여 에이, 말해 봐. 친구 좋다는 게 뭐니?
남 음, 난 뮤지컬 오디션 때문에 기분이 안 좋아. 너무 긴장해서 노래의 클라이맥스에서 끔찍한 실수를 했거든.
여 아, 정말 유감이다.
남 난 내 자신이 정말 실망스러워.
여 그러지 마. 난 네가 다음번엔 잘할 거라 확신해.

해설 뮤지컬 오디션에서 실수를 해서 낙담한 남자에게 여자는 다

음번엔 잘할 거라고 위로하고 있다.

어휘 down 우울한   because of ~ 때문에   audition 오디션   so ~ that … 너무 ~해서 …하다   nervous 긴장한   make a mistake 실수를 하다   climax 클라이맥스, 절정   be disappointed with ~에 실망하다

07 ④

M People are interested in staying healthy. Many of them exercise regularly and have an annual physical checkup. However, they seem to overlook the importance of what they eat. I think having healthy food is the most effective way to stay healthy. Eat as many fruits and vegetables as possible. Eat fish instead of meat. If you eat lots of unhealthy food, it's important to change your diet little by little. Then, you'll be successful.

남 사람들은 건강을 유지하는 것에 관심이 있습니다. 많은 사람들이 규칙적으로 운동을 하거나 매년 건강 검진을 받지요. 하지만 먹는 것의 중요성은 간과하고 있는 것 같아요. 저는 건강한 음식을 먹는 것이 건강을 유지하는 가장 효과적인 방법이라고 생각합니다. 되도록 많은 과일과 채소를 드세요. 고기 대신에 생선을 드세요. 건강에 해로운 음식을 많이 먹는다면, 조금씩 식단을 바꾸는 것이 중요합니다. 그러면, 당신은 성공하실 겁니다.

해설 남자는 건강에 좋은 음식을 먹는 것이 건강을 유지하는 가장 효과적인 방법이라고 말하고 있다.

어휘 stay healthy 건강을 유지하다   exercise 운동하다   regularly 규칙적으로   have a physical checkup 건강 검진을 받다   annual 매년의   seem ~인 것 같다   overlook 간과하다   importance 중요성   effective 효과적인   way 방법   as many as possible 되도록 많이   instead of ~ 대신에   unhealthy 건강에 해로운   diet 식사, 식습관   little by little 조금씩   successful 성공한

08 ④

W David, what kind of food would be good for the housewarming party?
M How about *bulgogi*? Our friends like Korean food, you know.
W But Sarah is a vegetarian.
M Oh, you're right. Then how about potato pizza? Pizza's everyone's favorite.
W Not bad. But I want to prepare a Korean dish.
M Hmm... what about *japchae*? We can make it without meat.
W That's a good idea. Let's make it.

여 David, 집들이에 어떤 음식이 좋을까?
남 불고기는 어때? 너도 알다시피 우리 친구들이 한국 음식을 좋아하잖아.
여 하지만 Sarah가 채식주의자잖아.
남 아, 맞다. 그럼 감자 피자는 어때? 피자는 모두들 가장 좋아하는 음식이잖아.
여 나쁘진 않은데. 난 한국 요리를 준비하고 싶어.

남 음… 잡채는 어때? 고기 없이 만들 수 있어.
여 좋은 생각이다. 그걸 만들자.

해설 남자가 잡채를 만드는 것은 어떤지 제안하자 여자가 좋은 생각이라고 동의했다.

어휘 housewarming party 집들이 vegetarian 채식주의자 favorite 가장 좋아하는 것 prepare 준비하다 dish 요리 without ~ 없이 meat 고기

09 ③

M What are you going to cook for dinner?
W I'm going to make spaghetti. (*Pause*) Oh, we don't have enough onions.
M Let me get some from the grocery store.
W Thanks. And take these eggs to the Smiths next door. I borrowed some from them last week.
M Okay. I'll stop by before I go to the market.
W Don't forget to say thank you for the pancakes they gave us last weekend, too.
M I will. I'll help you cook when I get home.

남 저녁 요리 하실 거예요?
여 스파게티를 만들 거야. (잠시 후) 오, 양파가 충분하지 않네.
남 식료품점에서 좀 사 올게요.
여 고마워. 그리고 옆집 Smith 씨 댁에 이 달걀들 좀 가져다주렴. 지난주에 그들에게서 좀 빌렸었거든.
남 네. 가게에 가기 전에 들르게요.
여 지난 주말에 주신 팬케이크도 고마웠다고 말하는 거 잊지 말고.
남 그럴게요. 제가 집에 오면 요리하시는 걸 도와드릴게요.

해설 남자는 양파를 사러 가기 전에 달걀을 가져다주러 옆집에 들르겠다고 했다.

어휘 enough 충분한 onion 양파 grocery store 식료품점, 슈퍼마켓 next door 옆집에 borrow 빌리다 stop by ~에 들르다 forget to ~하는 것을 잊다

10 ⑤

M Hello. I'd like to take a swimming lesson.
W We have beginner, intermediate, and advanced classes.
M I'll take the class for beginners.
W The beginner's class starts at eleven in the morning every Tuesday and Thursday.
M Okay. How much does it cost?
W It's $50 per month, but there's a 10% discount when you sign up for three months or more.
M I'll sign up for three months.
W Okay. We give you this towel as a gift when you first sign up, too.
M Good. Thanks.

남 안녕하세요. 저는 수영 강좌를 듣고 싶어요.
여 초급, 중급, 상급 수업이 있습니다.
남 초급자 수업을 들을게요.
여 초급자 수업은 매주 화요일과 목요일 아침 11시에 시작합니다.
남 네. 비용이 얼마예요?

여 한 달에 50달러인데, 3개월 이상 등록하시면 10퍼센트 할인됩니다.
남 3개월 등록할게요.
여 알겠습니다. 처음 등록하실 때 사은품으로 이 수건도 드려요.
남 좋네요. 고맙습니다.

해설 여자는 수영에 필요한 준비물은 언급하지 않았다.

어휘 beginner 초보자 intermediate 중급의; 중급자 advanced 상급의 cost (비용이) ~ 들다 discount 할인 sign up 등록하다 towel 수건 first 처음으로

11 ⑤

M There's a big sale on laptops at ABC Electronics. Don't you need a new one?
W I do! How much of a discount is the store offering?
M It depends on the product, but most models are 30 to 50% off. Discounts apply to online sales only.
W Fantastic. For how long does the sale last?
M For three days starting today.
W What about the delivery fee?
M There's no charge for purchases over $500.
W I got it. I think I should order one right away.

남 ABC Electronics에서 대대적인 노트북 할인 판매를 해. 너 새것 필요하지 않아?
여 필요해! 그 가게는 할인을 얼마나 해 준대?
남 제품에 따라 다르지만, 대부분의 모델은 30~50퍼센트 할인이야. 할인은 온라인 판매에만 적용돼.
여 엄청 좋다. 할인 판매를 얼마 동안이나 하니?
남 오늘부터 3일 동안이야.
여 배송료는 어떤데?
남 500달러 이상 구매하면 무료야.
여 알았어. 지금 당장 하나 주문해야겠다.

해설 500달러 이상의 제품을 구매하면 배송비가 무료라고 했다.

어휘 sale 할인 판매 electronics 전자 제품 discount 할인 offer 제공하다 depend on ~에 달려 있다, ~에 의해 결정되다 product 제품 most 대부분의 off 할인되어 apply to ~에 적용되다 last 지속되다 delivery fee 배송료 charge 요금 purchase 구입, 구매 over ~ 이상의

12 ①

M Hello. AP Service Center. How may I help you?
W Hello. You fixed my smartphone last night.
M Is there still a problem?
W No, no. I left my shopping bag, and I'm here to pick it up.
M Oh, I see. What does your bag look like?
W It's a paper bag with a white jacket in it.
M Okay. Let me check if one of our staff members put it in the back.

남 안녕하세요. AP Service Center입니다. 무엇을 도와드릴까요?
여 안녕하세요. 어젯밤에 제 스마트폰을 수리해 주셨는데요.

남 아직 문제가 있나요?
여 아니요. 제가 쇼핑백을 두고 가서 찾으러 왔어요.
남 아, 알겠습니다. 가방이 어떻게 생겼나요?
여 안에 흰 재킷이 들어 있는 종이 가방이에요.
남 네. 저희 직원 중 한 명이 가방을 뒤쪽에 두었는지 확인해 보겠습니다.

해설 여자는 어제 두고 간 쇼핑백을 찾으러 왔다고 했다.

어휘 fix 수리하다   still 여전히   leave(-left-left) 두고 오다
pick up ~을 찾아오다   staff member 직원

13 ③

W Hi. I'd like to order a chicken curry and a salad, please.
M Do you want to add extra toppings on your curry?
W Yes. One cheese topping, please.
M The total is $22. Anything else?
W I'll have a large sweet potato chips and a medium coke. I'll use this free-drink coupon, too.
M Then it's only $8 for the chips.
W Okay. Here's my card.

여 안녕하세요. 닭고기 카레와 샐러드 주문할게요.
남 카레에 토핑을 추가하시겠어요?
여 네. 치즈 토핑 주세요.
남 총 22달러입니다. 또 다른 건요?
여 고구마튀김 큰 것과 중간 크기의 콜라 하나요. 이 무료 음료 쿠폰을 사용할게요.
남 그럼 고구마튀김만 해서 8달러입니다.
여 네. 여기 제 카드요.

해설 치즈 토핑을 얹은 닭고기 카레와 샐러드는 22달러이다. 고구마튀김과 콜라를 추가로 주문했으나 무료 음료 쿠폰을 사용해서 고구마튀김 가격인 8달러만 추가되므로, 여자는 총 30달러를 지불해야 한다.

어휘 curry 카레   add 추가하다   extra 추가의   topping 토핑, 고명   total 총액   sweet potato 고구마   medium 중간의

14 ③

W Let me introduce my role model, Scarlet Choi. She not only dances in musicals but also designs dance performances for idol groups. I read her autobiography, *Dance Is My Life*. In the book, she wrote about her childhood and how hard her life was. She overcame difficulties by dancing. I could understand why people call her "Practice Queen."

여 저의 롤 모델 Scarlet Choi를 소개하겠습니다. 그녀는 뮤지컬에서 춤을 출 뿐 아니라 아이돌 그룹을 위해 춤 공연도 설계합니다. 저는 〈Dance Is My Life〉라는 그녀의 자서전을 읽었습니다. 그 책에서 그녀는 자신의 유년기에 대해 그리고 그녀의 삶이 얼마나 힘들었는지에 대해 썼습니다. 그녀는 춤으로 어려움을 극복했습니다. 저는 왜 사람들이 그녀를 '연습 여왕'이라고 부르는지 이해할 수 있었습니다.

해설 여자는 롤 모델의 나이는 언급하지 않았다.

어휘 role model 롤 모델(존경하며 본받고 싶은 사람)   not only A but also B A뿐만 아니라 B도   design 디자인하다, 설계하다   performance 공연   autobiography 자서전   childhood 유년기   overcome(-overcame-overcome) 극복하다   difficulty 어려움   call A B A를 B라고 부르다

15 ⑤

W Hello. I'd like to check out this book.
M Can I have your library card?
W I don't have one. It's my first visit here.
M You need a card to check out books. Would you like to make one?
W Yes.
M Do you see the computer over there? Fill out the application form on the library's homepage first.
W Okay.
M Then, print it and give it to me with your ID card.
W All right. Thanks.

여 안녕하세요. 이 책을 대출하고 싶어요.
남 도서관 카드를 주시겠어요?
여 없는데요. 저는 여기에 처음 방문했어요.
남 책을 대출하시려면 카드가 필요합니다. 하나 만드시겠어요?
여 네.
남 저쪽에 컴퓨터 보이시죠? 우선 도서관 홈페이지에서 신청서를 작성하세요.
여 알겠습니다.
남 그 다음에, 신청서를 인쇄하셔서 제게 신분증과 함께 주세요.
여 알겠습니다. 고맙습니다.

해설 여자는 책을 대출하려고 하고, 남자는 도서관 카드를 만드는 방법을 안내하고 있는 것으로 보아, 도서관 사서와 도서관 이용객 사이의 대화이다.

어휘 check out (도서관 등에서) 대출하다   library 도서관   fill out 작성하다, 기입하다   application form 신청서   print 인쇄하다   ID card 신분증

16 ③

W Do you have any plans for the holiday?
M I'm going to Gyeongju for a family trip.
W That's good. Have you finished preparing for it?
M I booked a hotel room, but I haven't decided what to eat there.
W Check out the app Yummy Time. It shows a list of the fine restaurants by region.
M That's good. Will you download the app for me? I'm not used to my new smartphone.
W Okay. Give me yours.

여 휴일에 무슨 계획 있어?
남 경주로 가족 여행을 갈 거야.
여 좋겠다. 여행 준비는 다 했어?
남 호텔은 예약했는데, 거기에서 뭘 먹을지는 아직 정하지 못했어.
여 Yummy Time이라는 앱을 확인해 봐. 지역별로 괜찮은 식당

의 목록을 보여 주거든.

남 그거 괜찮다. 나를 위해 앱을 다운로드해 줄래? 내가 새로운 스마트폰에 익숙하지 않아서.

여 알았어. 네 것 줘 봐.

해설 남자는 새로 산 스마트폰이 익숙하지 않다며 여자에게 앱을 다운로드해 달라고 했다.

어휘 plan 계획   holiday 휴일   trip 여행   prepare for ~을 준비하다   book 예약하다   list 목록   fine 질 높은, 좋은   by region 지역별로   be used to ~에 익숙하다

17 ⑤

M Why are you so late?
W I'm sorry. I missed the train.
M Did you get up late again?
W Not at all. I woke up at 7 a.m.
M Then why were you late? Was there a traffic jam on the way to the train station?
W Nope. On the way to the station, I met a boy who was lost.
M Oh, no.
W He was crying, so I took him to the nearest police station. It took me more than an hour.

남 왜 이렇게 늦었어?
여 미안해. 기차를 놓쳤어.
남 또 늦잠 잤어?
여 전혀 아니야. 나 아침 7시에 일어났어.
남 그럼 왜 늦었어? 기차역으로 가는 길에 교통 체증이 있었어?
여 아니. 역으로 가는 길에 길을 잃은 한 남자아이를 만났거든.
남 오, 저런.
여 남자아이가 울고 있어서 가장 가까운 경찰서로 데려다줬어. 한 시간 넘게 걸렸어.

해설 여자는 길을 잃고 울고 있는 아이를 만나서 경찰서에 데려다 주느라 기차를 놓쳤다고 했다.

어휘 miss 놓치다   get up late 늦잠을 자다   traffic jam 교통 체증   on the way to ~로 가는 길에   lost 길을 잃은   police station 경찰서   more than ~보다 많이

18 ④

① M Excuse me. The elevator is full now.
   W Oops, I'll get off.
② M Let's get some ice cream. Which flavor do you like?
   W I like vanilla. What about you?
③ M You cannot take that cart out of the building.
   W I didn't know that. I'm sorry.
④ M I'd like to exchange these jeans.
   W There is a fitting room on the second floor.
⑤ M Can you fix this copy machine?
   W I'm not sure. Let me take a look.

① 남 실례합니다. 엘리베이터가 만원이에요.
   여 어머, 내릴게요.
② 남 아이스크림 사 먹자. 무슨 맛 좋아해?

여 난 바닐라를 좋아해. 너는?
③ 남 건물 밖으로 카트를 가지고 가시면 안 돼요.
   여 몰랐어요. 죄송합니다.
④ 남 이 청바지를 교환하고 싶어요.
   여 2층에 탈의실이 있습니다.
⑤ 남 이 복사기를 고칠 수 있니?
   여 모르겠어. 한번 볼게.

해설 ④ 청바지를 교환하고 싶다고 했는데 탈의실의 위치를 알려 주는 것은 어색하다.

어휘 elevator 엘리베이터   full 가득한, 빈 공간이 없는   get off 내리다   flavor 맛   vanilla 바닐라   out of ~의 밖으로   building 건물   exchange 교환하다   jeans 청바지   fitting room 탈의실   fix 고치다   copy machine 복사기   take a look 보다

19 ③

W It's pouring outside. I don't have an umbrella.
M Me neither. What should we do? I don't think it will stop soon.
W Hmm... I've got an idea!
M Tell me.
W I heard the student council lends students umbrellas when it rains.
M Student council?
W Yes! As long as we leave our name and phone number.
M I didn't know that. I hope there are still some umbrellas left.
W I'm not sure. Let's hurry.

여 밖에 비가 쏟아지고 있어. 난 우산 없는데.
남 나도 없어. 어쩌지? 금방 그칠 것 같지 않아.
여 음… 좋은 생각이 있어!
남 말해 봐.
여 비가 올 때 학생회에서 학생들에게 우산을 빌려준다고 들었어.
남 학생회에서?
여 응! 이름이랑 전화번호를 남기기만 하면.
남 몰랐어. 우산이 아직 남아 있으면 좋겠다.
여 잘 모르겠네. 서두르자.

해설 남자가 우산이 아직 남아 있었으면 좋겠다고 했으므로 잘 모르겠으니 서두르자는 응답이 가장 적절하다.
① 네가 원할 때 언제든지.
② 난 그가 누구인지 몰라.
④ 물론이지. 너는 그것을 사도 돼.
⑤ 그것들을 사물함 옆에 둬.

어휘 pour (비가) 마구 쏟아지다   outside 밖에   student council 학생회   lend 빌려주다   as long as ~하기만 하면   leave(-left-left) 남기다   still 아직   locker 사물함

20 ⑤

W Hello. What seems to be the problem?
M I think I have a cold. I have a runny nose and keep sneezing.

W Okay. <u>Let me examine you first</u>.

M All right.

W Now I'll <u>check your body</u> temperature.

M Okay.

W You don't have a fever, and your nose looks fine. I don't think you have a cold.

M Then why do I <u>have these symptoms</u>?

W <u>I think you have an allergy to something</u>.

여 안녕하세요. 무엇이 문제인가요?

남 저는 감기에 걸린 것 같아요. 콧물이 나고 계속 재채기를 해요.

여 네. 우선 진찰을 해 볼게요.

남 알겠습니다.

여 이제 체온을 확인해 볼게요.

남 네.

여 열은 없으시고, 코도 괜찮아요. 감기에 걸리신 것 같진 않아요.

남 그럼 저에게 왜 이런 증상이 있나요?

여 뭔가에 알레르기가 있으신 것 같아요.

해설 남자가 감기가 아니라면 왜 자신에게 이런 증상이 있는지 물었으므로 감기 외의 다른 진단을 내리는 응답이 가장 적절하다.

① 감기에 걸리신 게 확실합니다.

② 저는 아직 예방 주사를 맞지 않았어요.

③ 지금 당장 병원에 가 보셔야 해요.

④ 그 이유는 당신이 계속 재채기를 하기 때문이에요.

어휘 have a cold 감기에 걸리다　have a runny nose 콧물이 나다　keep ~ing 계속 ~하다　sneeze 재채기하다　examine 진찰하다　body temperature 체온　have a fever 열이 나다　symptom 증상　vaccinate 예방 주사를 맞히다　have an allergy to ~에 알레르기가 있다

Review Test
pp.150~151

Word Check
13회

01 미세 먼지	**02** 완전히
03 문자 메시지	**04** 세로의
05 궁전	**06** 필터
07 항의하다	**08** 강하게, 강경히
09 알아보다	**10** ~을 제외하고
11 직접	**12** 항공 우편
13 separate	**14** lecture
15 approach	**16** warning
17 belongings	**18** destination
19 artwork	**20** irresponsible
21 effective	**22** saying
23 sprain	**24** character

Expression Check

25 either, or	**26** care about
27 keeps, away	**28** prepare for
29 remind, of	**30** break, habits

Word Check
14회

01 전 세계적인	**02** 자서전
03 풍경, 풍경화	**04** 평화로운
05 중요성	**06** 최근에
07 모닝콜	**08** 클라이맥스, 절정
09 채식주의자	**10** 겁먹은
11 ~에 들르다	**12** 조금씩
13 overlook	**14** intermediate
15 advanced	**16** overcome
17 purchase	**18** unhealthy
19 performance	**20** cancel
21 electronics	**22** examine
23 childhood	**24** sneeze

Expression Check

25 disappointed with	**26** fill out
27 used to	**28** depends on
29 not only, but also	**30** as long as

01 ④	02 ②	03 ③	04 ⑤	05 ②
06 ④	07 ②	08 ④	09 ③	10 ③
11 ④	12 ③	13 ⑤	14 ②	15 ⑤
16 ①	17 ③	18 ⑤	19 ③	20 ④

01 ④

W Good morning, listeners. It's finally the *chuseok* holiday. Today, clear but windy weather is expected. However, on *chuseok* morning, it will start to rain. So don't forget to take an umbrella on *chuseok*. The sky will clear up in the evening, and we'll be able to see the full moon at night.

여 좋은 아침입니다. 청취자 여러분. 드디어 추석 연휴입니다. 오늘은 맑지만 바람이 부는 날씨가 예상됩니다. 하지만 추석 아침에는 비가 내리기 시작할 것입니다. 그러니 추석에 우산 챙기는 것을 잊지 마세요. 저녁에는 하늘이 갤 것이고, 밤에는 보름달을 볼 수 있을 것입니다.

해설 추석 아침에는 비가 내리기 시작할 것이라고 했다.

어휘 finally 드디어   holiday 연휴   expect 예상하다   forget to ~하는 것을 잊다   clear up (날씨가) 개다   be able to ~할 수 있다   full moon 보름달

02 ②

W Hello. Do you have a hand mirror?

M Yes, we do. Which shape do you want, a square or a circle?

W I like square shapes better.

M Good. I'd like to recommend this one. Isn't the puppy cute?

W It's cute, but can you show me one that doesn't have any animal characters?

M Okay. What about this one? It has a big ribbon on the back.

W That's pretty. I'll take it.

여 안녕하세요. 손거울 있나요?
남 네, 있어요. 정사각형과 원형 중 어떤 모양을 원하세요?
여 저는 정사각형이 더 좋아요.
남 좋습니다. 이걸 추천 드리고 싶어요. 강아지가 귀엽지 않나요?
여 귀엽긴 한데, 동물 캐릭터가 없는 걸 보여 주시겠어요?
남 네. 이건 어떠세요? 뒷면에 큰 리본이 있어요.
여 예쁘네요. 이걸 살게요.

해설 여자는 정사각형 모양이면서 뒷면에 큰 리본이 있는 손거울을 사겠다고 했다.

어휘 hand mirror 손거울   shape 모양, 형태   square 정사각형   circle 원   recommend 추천하다   puppy 강아지   character 캐릭터   ribbon 리본   back 뒷면

03 ③

(*Cellphone rings.*)

W Hey, I'm almost home. How is the soccer game going?

M It's only the beginning of the first half, but we've just scored a goal!

W Really? Who did it?

M Marcus did it. He's a really good player.

W I can't believe I missed that.

M We had a good start. Come quickly and watch it with me.

W Okay. See you soon.

(휴대 전화가 울린다.)

여 이봐, 나 거의 집에 다 왔어. 축구 경기는 어떻게 되고 있어?
남 아직 전반전 시작인데, 방금 골 하나를 넣었어!
여 정말? 누가 넣었어?
남 Marcus가 넣었어. 그는 정말 훌륭한 선수야.
여 내가 그걸 놓쳤다니 믿을 수 없어.
남 시작이 좋아. 빨리 와서 나랑 같이 보자.
여 알겠어. 곧 봐.

해설 축구 경기의 전반전이 시작한 지 얼마 되지 않았는데 응원하는 팀이 한 골을 넣어서 남자는 신이 난 상태이다.

어휘 almost 거의   beginning 시작   first half 전반전   score a goal 골을 넣다   player 선수   miss 놓치다   quickly 빨리

04 ⑤

W Eric, how was the motor show?

M It was so much fun.

W It's good to hear that. Did you test-drive any brand-new cars?

M Sadly, no. I missed the event because of a traffic jam. I got there too late.

W That's too bad. Then what did you do?

M I met my favorite car designer and took some pictures with him.

W That's awesome.

여 Eric, 모터쇼 어땠어?
남 정말 재미있었어.
여 잘됐네. 신형 자동차를 시운전했니?
남 슬프게도, 아니. 교통 체증 때문에 그 행사를 놓쳤어. 거기에 너무 늦게 도착했거든.
여 그것 참 안됐다. 그럼 뭘 했어?
남 내가 가장 좋아하는 자동차 디자이너를 만나서 그와 함께 사진을 찍었어.
여 그거 굉장하다.

해설 남자는 모터쇼에서 자신이 가장 좋아하는 자동차 디자이너를 만나서 사진을 찍었다고 했다.

어휘 test-drive 시운전하다   brand-new 아주 새로운, 신품의   miss 놓치다   because of ~ 때문에   traffic jam 교통 체증   designer 디자이너   take a picture 사진을 찍다   awesome 굉장한

05 ②

M Hi. I'm looking for a wireless vacuum cleaner.
W Please come this way. (*Pause*) This model is <u>the latest one</u>.
M It looks good.
W It is very powerful but light. <u>Try lifting it</u>.
M It's not heavy at all, but it's <u>more expensive than I thought</u>.
W Aren't you interested in robot vacuum cleaners?
M I was using one, but it broke down. I'd like to try something different.
W I see. <u>Take your time</u> and look around.

남 안녕하세요. 저는 무선 청소기를 찾고 있어요.
여 이쪽으로 오세요. (잠시 후) 이 모델이 가장 최신 모델입니다.
남 좋아 보이네요.
여 아주 강력하지만 가벼워요. 한번 들어 보세요.
남 전혀 무겁지 않네요. 하지만, 제가 생각한 것보다 훨씬 비싸네요.
여 로봇 청소기에는 관심 없으세요?
남 하나 쓰고 있었는데, 고장 났어요. 다른 걸 써 보고 싶어요.
여 그러시군요. 천천히 둘러보세요.

해설 무선 청소기를 찾고 있는 남자에게 여자가 최신 모델을 소개하고 로봇 청소기도 권유한 것으로 보아, 가전제품 매장에서 이루어지는 대화이다.

어휘 look for ~을 찾다   wireless 무선의   vacuum cleaner 진공청소기   latest 최근의, 최신의   powerful 강력한   light 가벼운   lift 들다   not ~ at all 전혀 ~이 아닌   expensive 비싼   break down 고장 나다   take one's time 천천히 하다, 시간을 들이다   look around 둘러보다

06 ④

W Excuse me. I have waited for a long time, but I <u>haven't gotten my order yet</u>.
M Oh, let me check. Hold on a moment, please.
W Okay.
M Your food is ready now. Here you are.
W This is not <u>what I ordered</u>.
M Didn't you order a chicken salad?
W No. I ordered an avocado salad.
M I'm sorry. <u>Let me check again</u>.
W The service is so slow, and you make mistakes. I'm never coming here again.

여 저기요. 오래 기다렸는데, 제가 주문한 음식이 아직 안 나왔어요.
남 아, 확인해 보겠습니다. 잠시 기다려 주세요.
여 네.
남 음식이 지금 준비되었습니다. 여기 있습니다.
여 이건 제가 주문한 게 아닌데요.
남 닭고기 샐러드를 주문하지 않으셨나요?
여 아니요. 전 아보카도 샐러드를 시켰어요.
남 죄송합니다. 다시 확인해 보겠습니다.
여 서비스는 아주 느리고 당신은 실수를 하는군요. 여기에 다시는 오지 않을 거예요.

해설 여자는 식당의 서비스가 느린데다 종업원이 주문 실수도 해서 다시는 이곳에 오지 않겠다고 불평하고 있다.

어휘 wait 기다리다   for a long time 오랫동안   yet (부정문·의문문에서) 아직   order (식당에서) 주문한 음식(음료); 주문하다   hold on 기다리다   avocado 아보카도   make a mistake 실수를 하다   never 결코 ~ 않다   again 다시

07 ②

M I want to <u>buy some gifts</u> for my family. Can you recommend anything?
W <u>What is the gift for</u>?
M It's just a New Year's gift.
W <u>How kind of you</u>! Desk calenders might be good.
M We already have several calendars at home.
W Then <u>what about diaries</u>? They're practical and not very expensive.
M That sounds good. I'll buy them.

남 난 우리 가족을 위해 선물을 사고 싶어. 뭔가 추천해 줄 수 있니?
여 무슨 선물인데?
남 그냥 새해 선물이야.
여 넌 정말 친절하구나! 탁상용 달력이 좋을 것 같아.
남 우리 집에 이미 달력 몇 개가 있어.
여 그럼 다이어리는 어때? 실용적이고 별로 비싸지 않잖아.
남 그거 좋겠다. 그걸 사야겠어.

해설 여자의 제안에 따라 남자는 다이어리를 사겠다고 했다.

어휘 recommend 추천하다   desk calendar 탁상용 달력   already 이미, 벌써   several 몇몇의, 여러 개의   diary 다이어리   practical 실용적인

08 ④

W Tomorrow is Lisa's graduation ceremony.
M I know. I can't believe she <u>is graduating from</u> elementary school.
W Time really flies. Let's buy some flowers tomorrow morning.
M Sure. Where should we <u>have lunch after the ceremony</u>?
W Charley's Steak House is her favorite place. Let's go there.
M Great. I think we need to make a reservation. <u>There'll be lots of people</u>.
W Okay. I'll get right on it.

여 내일이 Lisa의 졸업식이에요.
남 알아요. Lisa가 초등학교를 졸업한다니 믿을 수가 없어요.
여 시간 정말 빠르죠. 내일 아침에 꽃을 좀 사요.
남 그래요. 졸업식 후에 점심을 어디에서 먹을까요?
여 Charley's Steak House가 Lisa가 가장 좋아하는 곳이에요. 거기에 가요.
남 좋아요. 예약을 해야 할 것 같아요. 사람들이 많을 거예요.
여 알겠어요. 지금 바로 할게요.

해설 남자가 식당을 예약해야 할 것 같다고 하자 여자는 지금 바로 하겠다고 했다.

어휘 graduation ceremony 졸업식   believe 믿다   graduate from ~을 졸업하다   elementary school 초등학교

make a reservation 예약하다　get right on ～을 바로
시작하다

09 ③

M Mom, can I sign up for the school literary tour?
W School literary tour? What is it?
M It's a tour to a place in a literary work. The author of this year is Lee Hyo-seok.
W Where is the tour going?
M To Bongpyeong.
W How many people are going?
M About thirty students and a teacher. Mom, please.
W Okay. You can go. How can you sign up?
M I can sign up on our school homepage. Thank you, Mom.

남 엄마, 저 학교 문학 여행을 신청해도 돼요?
여 학교 문학 여행? 그게 뭐니?
남 문학 작품 속의 장소로 가는 여행이에요. 올해의 작가는 이효석이에요.
여 여행을 어디로 가니?
남 봉평이요.
여 몇 명이 가는데?
남 학생 약 30명이랑 선생님 한 분이요. 엄마, 제발요.
여 그래. 가도 돼. 어떻게 신청하는 거야?
남 학교 홈페이지에서 신청할 수 있어요. 고마워요, 엄마.

해설 남자는 교통편은 언급하지 않았다.

어휘 sign up for ～을 신청하다　literary 문학의　tour 여행
literary work 문학 작품　author 작가

10 ③

W *Space Kingdom* will finally be released in a week! *Space Kingdom* is a story about the life of an astronaut in the future. Susan Smith plays the main character Wendy, a strong and powerful female hero. This is her first action movie, so many people are looking forward to watching her act. Let's visit the future by watching *Space Kingdom* this summer.

여 〈Space Kingdom〉이 드디어 일주일 후에 개봉됩니다. 〈Space Kingdom〉은 미래의 우주 비행사의 삶에 대한 이야기입니다. Susan Smith가 강하고 영향력 있는 여성 영웅인 주인공 Wendy의 배역을 맡았습니다. 이 영화는 그녀의 첫 액션 영화라, 많은 사람들이 그녀의 연기를 보는 것을 기대하고 있지요. 올여름 〈Space Kingdom〉을 보며 미래에 방문해 보세요.

해설 여자는 올여름 개봉할 신작 영화를 소개하고 있다.

어휘 finally 드디어　release (영화 등을) 개봉하다　astronaut
우주 비행사　play 연기하다, 배역을 맡다　main character
주인공　powerful 영향력 있는　female 여성의　hero 영웅
look forward to ～을 기대하다　act 연기

11 ④

M I'm transferring to another school next month.
W I heard about that. Where are you moving to?
M To Pohang. I've never been there.
W Really? My hometown is Pohang, and my relatives live there. It's a beautiful city.
M I heard Pohang is a good city to live in, but I'm worried because I don't have any friends there.
W I'm sure you will make lots of new friends. They'll like you.

남 나 다음 달에 다른 학교로 전학 가.
여 그 소식 들었어. 어디로 이사 가니?
남 포항으로. 난 거기에 한 번도 가 본 적이 없어.
여 정말? 내 고향이 포항이고 우리 친척들도 거기에 사셔. 포항은 아름다운 도시야.
남 포항이 살기 좋은 도시라고 들었지만, 거기에 친구가 한 명도 없어서 걱정돼.
여 네가 새 친구들을 많이 사귈 거라고 확신해. 그들은 널 좋아할 거야.

해설 포항에 친척들이 살고 있다고 말한 사람은 여자이다.

어휘 transfer 전학 가다　another 또다른　move 이사하다
hometown 고향　relative 친척　live 살다　city 도시
make a friend 친구를 사귀다

12 ③

(*Telephone rings.*)
W White Teeth Dental Clinic. What can I do for you?
M Hello. I have an appointment at 5 p.m. today.
W Could you tell me your name, please?
M My name is Robert Wilson. I'm afraid I can't make it today.
W Do you want to cancel your appointment?
M No. I want to change it to Thursday at the same time.
W All right. You're all set now. See you on Thursday.

(전화벨이 울린다.)
여 White Teeth Dental Clinic입니다. 무엇을 도와드릴까요?
남 안녕하세요. 오늘 오후 5시에 예약이 되어 있는데요.
여 성함을 말씀해 주시겠어요?
남 제 이름은 Robert Wilson입니다. 죄송하지만 제가 오늘 못 갈 것 같아요.
여 예약을 취소해 드릴까요?
남 아니요. 목요일 같은 시각으로 변경하고 싶어요.
여 알겠습니다. 변경되셨습니다. 목요일에 뵙겠습니다.

해설 남자는 치과 진료 예약을 같은 시간대의 목요일로 바꾸기 위해서 전화했다.

어휘 have an appointment 예약이 되어 있다　make it
시간 맞춰 가다　cancel 취소하다　change A to B A를 B로
바꾸다　set 준비가 된

13 ⑤

W Hi. I left my briefcase when I got off the subway.
M Which subway station did you <u>get off</u> at?
W Greenville Station.
M Do you remember when you got off?
W It was <u>about</u> <u>an</u> <u>hour</u> <u>ago</u>.
M Okay. Can you tell me <u>the</u> <u>appearance</u> <u>of</u> <u>your</u> <u>briefcase</u>?
W It's dark brown, and there's a small pocket on the back.
M All right. Please write down your name and number here. I'll call you <u>if</u> <u>it</u> <u>is</u> <u>turned</u> <u>in</u>.

여 안녕하세요. 제가 지하철에서 내릴 때 서류 가방을 두고 내렸어요.
남 어느 지하철역에서 내리셨나요?
여 Greenville역이요.
남 언제 내리셨는지 기억하세요?
여 약 한 시간 전이었어요.
남 네. 서류 가방의 외관을 말씀해 주실래요?
여 진한 갈색이고, 뒷면에 작은 주머니가 있어요.
남 알겠습니다. 여기에 이름과 전화번호를 적어 주세요. 물건이 들어오면 전화 드리겠습니다.

[해설] 여자가 지하철에 물건을 두고 내렸다고 하자 남자가 물건이 들어오면 연락을 준다고 했으므로, 분실물 보관소 직원과 지하철 이용객 사이의 대화이다.

[어휘] briefcase 서류 가방   get off 내리다   about 약, ~쯤
appearance 외관, 겉모습   dark 진한, 어두운   pocket
주머니   back 뒷면   turn in ~을 돌려주다(반납하다)

14 ②

M Maria, how was the musical yesterday?
W It was perfect except that I was late for it.
M You were late? How late were you?
W I <u>arrived</u> <u>at</u> <u>the</u> <u>theater</u> at 7:05. The musical started at 7.
M So you only missed the first five minutes.
W Actually, <u>they</u> <u>wouldn't</u> <u>let</u> <u>me</u> <u>in</u> until 7:15, so I missed the opening scene.
M Oh, no.
W But <u>except</u> <u>for</u> <u>that</u>, it was good.

남 Maria, 어제 뮤지컬 어땠어?
여 내가 늦은 것을 제외하고는 완벽했어.
남 늦었다고? 얼마나 늦었는데?
여 공연장에 7시 5분에 도착했어. 뮤지컬은 7시에 시작했고.
남 그럼 초반 5분만 놓친 거네.
여 사실은, 7시 15분까지 들여보내 주지 않더라고. 그래서 첫 장면을 놓쳤어.
남 오, 저런.
여 하지만 그걸 제외하고는 좋았어.

[해설] 뮤지컬은 7시에 시작했지만 여자는 공연장에 7시 5분에 도착했다고 했다.

[어휘] except ~을 제외하고   late 늦은   arrive 도착하다

theater 극장   miss 놓치다   actually 사실은   let ~ in ~을 들어오게 하다   until ~까지   opening 시작(첫) 부분   scene 장면

15 ⑤

W Noah, are you all ready for your presentation?
M Not yet. I <u>gathered</u> <u>all</u> <u>the</u> <u>materials</u>, but I haven't finished editing the video.
W Let me help you. I love making and editing videos.
M Do you? That's very sweet of you!
W It's not a big deal. So how do you <u>want</u> <u>me</u> <u>to</u> <u>edit</u> <u>it</u>?
M Can you <u>make</u> <u>it</u> <u>shorter</u> than 30 seconds?
W Sure. Just let me know <u>what</u> <u>cannot</u> <u>be</u> <u>edited</u> <u>out</u>.
M Okay. Thanks!

여 Noah, 발표는 다 준비했어?
남 아직. 자료들을 모두 모으긴 했는데 동영상 편집을 못 끝냈어.
여 내가 도와줄게. 난 동영상을 찍고 편집하는 걸 정말 좋아해.
남 그래? 너 정말 친절하구나!
여 별것 아니야. 그래서 내가 어떻게 편집하면 될까?
남 30초보다 더 짧게 만들 수 있어?
여 당연하지. 무엇을 잘라 내면 안 되는지만 알려 줘.
남 응. 고마워!

[해설] 남자는 여자에게 동영상을 더 짧게 편집해 달라고 부탁했다.

[어휘] be ready for ~할 준비가 되다   presentation 발표
gather 모으다   material 자료   edit 편집하다   video 동영상
a big deal 대단한 것   second 초   edit out ~을 잘라 내다

16 ①

W Mr. Lee, <u>do</u> <u>you</u> <u>have</u> <u>a</u> <u>minute</u>?
M Of course, Claire. What is it?
W Could you change my seat in the classroom?
M Do you have a problem with Soyun next to you?
W <u>Not</u> <u>at</u> <u>all</u>. She and I are doing great.
M Then why do you want to change your seat?
W I'm so cold in my seat. The air conditioner is too close.
M In that case, I'll see <u>if</u> <u>someone</u> <u>can</u> <u>switch</u> <u>seats</u> with you.

여 Lee 선생님, 시간 있으신가요?
남 물론이지, Claire. 무슨 일이니?
여 교실에서 제 자리를 바꿔 주실 수 있나요?
남 네 옆자리 소윤이와 무슨 문제 있니?
여 전혀요. 그녀와 저는 잘 지내고 있어요.
남 그럼 왜 자리를 바꾸고 싶은 거니?
여 제 자리가 너무 추워요. 에어컨이 너무 가까워요.
남 그렇다면, 누가 너와 자리를 바꿔 줄 수 있는지 알아보마.

[해설] 여자는 에어컨이 가까워 너무 추워서 자리를 바꾸고 싶다고 했다.

[어휘] seat 자리   next to ~ 옆에   air conditioner 에어컨
close 가까운   in that case 그런 경우에는, 그렇다면   if
~인지   switch 바꾸다

17 ③

M The 7th Korean Culture Festival is going to be held in Sejong Park this Saturday and Sunday. You can see a traditional Korean drum dance and the *Hanbok* fashion show. You'll also have a chance to try various Korean foods. The admission fee is 5,000 won. Come and be part of the festival!

남 제7회 한국 문화 축제가 이번 주 토요일과 일요일에 세종 공원에서 열릴 것입니다. 한국의 전통적인 북춤과 한복 패션쇼를 보실 수 있습니다. 그리고 다양한 한국 음식을 맛볼 수 있는 기회를 가지실 수 있습니다. 입장료는 5,000원입니다. 오셔서 축제의 일부가 되세요!

해설 남자는 축제가 열리는 시간은 언급하지 않았다.

어휘 culture 문화   festival 축제   be held 열리다, 개최되다
traditional 전통적인   drum 북   chance 기회   various
다양한   admission fee 입장료   part 부분

18 ⑤

① **M** Where are my glasses?
   W Didn't you put them on your desk?
② **M** Can you tell me where the shoe store is?
   W Take the escalator and go to the third floor.
③ **M** Excuse me. Can I try these pants on?
   W Sure. What size do you wear?
④ **M** What do you want for your birthday?
   W Well, can you buy me some new ballet shoes?
⑤ **M** These shoes are too small for me.
   W Try these on. They're bigger.

① **남** 내 안경이 어디에 있지?
   여 책상 위에 놓지 않았니?
② **남** 신발 가게가 어디에 있는지 말해 주실래요?
   여 에스컬레이터를 타고 3층으로 가세요.
③ **남** 저기요. 이 바지를 입어 봐도 될까요?
   여 그럼요. 사이즈가 어떻게 되시죠?
④ **남** 너 생일 선물로 뭐 받고 싶니?
   여 음, 새 발레화를 사 주실 수 있어요?
⑤ **남** 이 신발은 저에게 너무 작아요.
   여 이걸 신어 보세요. 이 신발이 더 커요.

해설 손님이 신발이 작다고 하자 점원이 더 큰 신발을 권하는 내용의 대화가 가장 적절하다.

어휘 glasses 안경   shoe store 신발 가게   escalator
에스컬레이터   floor 층   try on 입어 보다, 신어 보다   pants
바지   ballet 발레

19 ③

W How did you celebrate your first New Year's Day in Korea?
M I visited my homestay family's hometown and met their relatives.
W That's nice. Tell me more about it.
M I had *tteokguk* for breakfast. It was tasty.

W What did you do after breakfast?
M I bowed to my homestay parents and grandparents and got some money.
W That's interesting. Did you do anything else?
M We played *Yunnori* together.

여 넌 한국에서의 첫 설날을 어떻게 기념했니?
남 내 홈스테이 가족의 고향에 가서 그들의 친척들을 만났어.
여 좋네. 더 이야기해 봐.
남 아침으로 떡국을 먹었어. 맛있더라.
여 아침 후에는 뭐 했어?
남 내 홈스테이 부모님과 조부모님께 절을 하고 돈을 받았어.
여 그거 흥미롭다. 다른 것도 했어?
남 우리는 함께 윷놀이를 했어.

해설 여자가 설날에 또 무엇을 했는지 물었으므로 설날에 했던 일에 대한 응답이 와야 한다.
① 우리는 비슷한 관습이 있어.
② 그 게임은 정말 재미있어.
④ 나는 특별한 행사에 참여할 거야.
⑤ 우리는 추수 감사절에 푸짐한 저녁을 먹었어.

어휘 celebrate 기념하다, 축하하다   New Year's Day 설날
hometown 고향   relative 친척   tasty 맛있는   bow 절하다
parents 부모   grandparents 조부모   similar 비슷한
custom 관습   take part in ~에 참여(참가)하다
Thanksgiving Day 추수 감사절

20 ④

M The air pollution is terrible today.
W Yeah. I can't see the buildings across the river.
M I can hardly remember the last time I saw a clear sky.
W Right. I need to buy some more masks on my way home.
M Me, too. I have a sore throat.
W Even my eyes are sore. Do you know what tomorrow will be like?
M It'll be as terrible as it is today.

남 오늘 대기 오염이 심각하네.
여 응. 강 건너편에 있는 건물들이 안 보여.
남 마지막으로 맑은 하늘을 본 적이 언제인지 거의 기억나지 않아.
여 맞아. 난 집에 가는 길에 마스크를 더 사야겠어.
남 나도. 목이 따가워.
여 난 심지어 눈도 따가워. 내일은 어떨지 아니?
남 오늘만큼 심각할 거야.

해설 여자가 내일의 대기 상태를 아는지 물었으므로 오늘만큼 내일도 심각할 것이라는 응답이 가장 적절하다.
① 넌 병원에 가야 해.
② 괜찮아. 물어봐 줘서 고마워.
③ 대기 오염은 심각한 문제야.
⑤ 난 여름보다 겨울이 좋아.

어휘 pollution 오염   across ~의 맞은편에   hardly 거의
~ 않다(없다)   remember 기억하다   on one's way home
집에 가는 길에   have a sore throat 목이 아프다(따끔거리다)
even 심지어   serious 심각한   issue 문제

01 ①	02 ⑤	03 ⑤	04 ③	05 ④
06 ⑤	07 ①	08 ⑤	09 ②	10 ③
11 ④	12 ④	13 ③	14 ②	15 ①
16 ⑤	17 ②	18 ③	19 ④	20 ⑤

01 ①

M Welcome to this week's weather forecast. <u>From Monday through Wednesday</u>, the weather will be partly cloudy. On Wednesday afternoon, <u>the temperature will drop</u>. By Thursday, it will fall to -7°C, and it will begin to snow. The snow will <u>continue until Friday night</u>. Three inches of snow are expected.

남 이번 주의 일기 예보입니다. 월요일부터 수요일까지 부분적으로 흐리겠습니다. 수요일 오후에는 기온이 떨어질 것입니다. 목요일까지 영하 7°C로 떨어지고, 눈이 오기 시작하겠습니다. 눈은 금요일 밤까지 계속될 것입니다. 3인치의 눈이 예상됩니다.

해설 목요일에 눈이 내리기 시작해서 금요일 밤까지 눈이 계속될 것이라고 했다.

어휘 through (기간·범위) ~까지　partly 부분적으로　temperature 기온　drop 떨어지다　fall 떨어지다　continue 계속되다　until ~까지　inch 인치　expect 예상하다

02 ⑤

W I'd like to order a birthday cake for my mom.
M Okay. <u>Will you choose one</u> from these samples?
W I like this one with flowers.
M You have to choose <u>the shape of the cake</u>, too. It can be round or heart-shaped.
W I'd like a round one. Can you <u>put a message on it</u>, too?
M Sure. What message do you want me to write?
W Can you write "Happy Birthday" with flowers around it?
M No problem.

여 저희 엄마를 위한 생일 케이크를 주문하고 싶어요.
남 네. 이 샘플들 중에서 하나를 골라 보시겠어요?
여 꽃들이 있는 이게 마음에 들어요.
남 케이크 모양도 정하셔야 해요. 둥근 모양 또는 하트 모양입니다.
여 둥근 게 좋네요. 메시지도 올려 주실 수 있나요?
남 물론이죠. 무슨 메시지를 써 드릴까요?
여 'Happy Birthday'라고 써 주시고 꽃들을 글자 주변에 둘러 주세요.
남 문제없습니다.

해설 여자는 'Happy Birthday'라는 글자 주위에 꽃들이 장식된 둥근 모양의 케이크를 주문했다.

어휘 choose 선택하다　sample 샘플, 견본품　shape 모양, 형태　round 둥근　heart-shaped 하트 모양의　message 메시지　around 둘레에, 주위에

03 ⑤

W What did you do during the weekend?
M I went to Dream World, <u>the new amusement park</u>.
W Great! You really wanted to go there, didn't you?
M Yes, but it was <u>not as good as I thought</u>.
W Why? It has many fun rides.
M The lines were so long that I could <u>go on only two rides</u>. Even worse, those rides were boring.
W That's too bad.

여 주말 동안에 뭐 했어?
남 새로 개장한 놀이공원인 Dream World에 갔었어.
여 좋았겠다! 너 거기에 정말 가고 싶어 했잖아, 그렇지 않니?
남 응. 그런데 생각만큼 좋지는 않더라.
여 왜? 재미있는 놀이 기구들이 많잖아.
남 줄이 너무 길어서 난 놀이 기구를 겨우 두 개 탔어. 게다가 그 놀이 기구들은 지루했어.
여 그것 참 안 됐구나.

해설 새로 생긴 놀이공원에 갔는데 줄이 너무 길어 놀이 기구를 겨우 두 개 탔고, 심지어 그 놀이 기구들은 지루했다고 했으므로 남자는 실망했을 것이다.

어휘 amusement park 놀이공원　ride 놀이 기구　so ~ that ... 너무 ~해서 …하다　even worse 게다가, 설상가상으로　boring 지루한　satisfied 만족하는　disappointed 실망한

04 ③

W Welcome. How may I help you?
M Hi. <u>How can I get to</u> the National Art Museum?
W Do you see the bus stop across the street? Take bus number 17 there and <u>get off at the seventh stop</u>.
M I see. How often does the bus come?
W There's a bus <u>every twenty minute</u>.
M Okay. Thank you so much.
W You're welcome. Have a nice day.

여 어서 오세요. 무엇을 도와드릴까요?
남 안녕하세요. 국립 미술관에 어떻게 갈 수 있나요?
여 길 맞은편에 버스 정류장 보이시죠? 저기에서 17번 버스를 타고 일곱 번째 정류장에서 내리세요.
남 알겠습니다. 버스는 얼마나 자주 오나요?
여 버스는 20분마다 있습니다.
남 네. 정말 고맙습니다.
여 별말씀을요. 좋은 하루 보내세요.

해설 여자가 남자를 맞이하며 자신이 도울 것이 있는지 묻고, 남자는 국립 미술관으로 가는 길을 묻는 것으로 보아, 관광 안내소에서 이루어지는 대화이다.

어휘 national 국립의　art museum 미술관　bus stop 버스 정류장　across ~의 맞은편에　street 길　get off 내리다

05 ④

W Sam, <u>did you do well</u> on your math exam?
M Unfortunately, no. I don't feel good about it.
W Was it difficult?
M Yes, it was! And I couldn't <u>get a high score</u> on my science exam either.
W Don't be so upset.
M I <u>spent a lot of time studying</u>, so it's very disappointing.
W Final exams are all over. So just <u>let it go</u> and get some rest.

여 Sam, 수학 시험 잘 봤니?
남 불행하게도, 못 봤어. 난 기분이 좋지 않아.
여 어려웠어?
남 응! 그리고 난 과학 시험에서도 높은 점수를 받지 못했어.
여 너무 속상해 하지 마.
남 난 공부하는 데 시간을 많이 썼어. 그래서 아주 실망스러워.
여 기말고사는 다 끝났잖아. 그러니까 잊어버리고 좀 쉬어.

해설 수학 시험과 과학 시험을 잘 보지 못해서 낙담한 남자에게 여자는 기말고사는 끝났으니 잊어버리고 쉬라며 남자를 격려하고 있다.

어휘 math 수학 exam 시험 unfortunately 유감스럽게도, 불행하게도 difficult 어려운 get a high score 높은 점수를 받다 science 과학 upset 속상한 disappointing 실망스러운 be over 끝나다 get rest 쉬다

06 ⑤

M What's wrong, Jenny?
W My computer <u>suddenly stopped working</u>!
M Let me help you. (Typing sound) It's working now.
W Wow, thanks! I think you know a lot about computers.
M I'm good with computers. <u>It's not a big deal</u>.
W <u>Did someone teach you</u>?
M No. I want to be a computer engineer, so I read a lot of books about computers.
W Oh, I see.

남 무슨 일이야, Jenny?
여 내 컴퓨터가 갑자기 작동을 멈췄어!
남 내가 도와줄게. (타이핑하는 소리) 지금은 작동해.
여 와, 고마워! 너 컴퓨터에 대해 많이 알고 있는 것 같아.
남 난 컴퓨터를 잘해. 별것 아니야.
여 누군가가 너에게 가르쳐 줬니?
남 아니. 난 컴퓨터 엔지니어가 되고 싶어서 컴퓨터에 관한 책을 많이 읽어.
여 오, 그렇구나.

해설 남자는 컴퓨터 엔지니어가 되고 싶어서 컴퓨터에 관한 책을 많이 읽는다고 했다.

어휘 suddenly 갑자기 work 작동하다 a big deal 대단한 것 teach 가르쳐 주다 engineer 엔지니어, 기술자

07 ①

M Liz, are you going to your yoga class today?
W Not today. I have a class <u>every Tuesday and Thursday</u>.
M Then why don't you have dinner with me?
W <u>I'm afraid I can't</u>. Let's eat tomorrow.
M Tomorrow is fine. But why not today?
W My friend John is <u>the main character in a play</u>, so I'm going to watch it.
M I see. Have a great time.

남 Liz, 오늘 요가 수업에 가니?
여 오늘은 안 가. 매주 화요일과 목요일에 수업이 있어.
남 그럼 나랑 같이 저녁 먹는 게 어때?
여 미안하지만 안 돼. 내일 먹자.
남 내일 좋아. 그런데 왜 오늘은 안 돼?
여 내 친구 John이 연극에서 주인공이라서 그거 보러 가야 하거든.
남 그렇구나. 좋은 시간 보내.

해설 여자는 친구가 주연으로 나오는 연극을 보러 간다고 했다.

어휘 yoga 요가 have dinner 저녁 식사를 하다 main character 주인공 play 연극

08 ⑤

M Excuse me. I didn't hear the announcement. Was it about the plane for Chicago?
W Yes. The plane for Chicago at 9:00 a.m. is delayed <u>due to the heavy snowstorm</u>.
M Oh, no. What time is it going to leave now?
W At 10:30 a.m. from gate number 5.
M <u>What's the arrival time</u> in Chicago then?
W It <u>takes about thirteen hours</u>, so it will arrive at 9:30 p.m. local time.
M I see. Thank you.

남 실례합니다. 제가 안내 방송을 못 들었어요. 시카고행 비행기에 대한 방송이었나요?
여 네. 오전 9시 시카고행 비행기가 강한 눈보라 때문에 연착되었어요.
남 오, 이런. 이제 몇 시에 출발하나요?
여 오전 10시 30분에 5번 게이트에서요.
남 그럼 시카고 도착 시각은요?
여 약 13시간 걸려서 현지 시각으로 오후 9시 30분에 도착할 거예요.
남 알겠습니다. 고맙습니다.

해설 여자는 항공편의 목적지인 시카고의 날씨는 언급하지 않았다.

어휘 hear 듣다 announcement 발표, 알림 plane 비행기 delay 미루다, 연기하다 due to ~ 때문에 snowstorm 눈보라 leave 출발하다 arrival 도착 arrive 도착하다 local time 현지 시각

09 ②

M This is an announcement for all guests at the Windsor Hotel. We're very <u>sorry about any</u>

inconvenience caused by the construction of our new escalator. Please be careful near the construction areas on the first and second floors. The construction hours are from 10 a.m. to 4 p.m. There will be construction for the next three days. We apologize again for the inconvenience.

남 Windsor Hotel의 모든 고객님들께 안내 말씀 드립니다. 새로운 에스컬레이터 설치 관계로 불편을 드려 죄송합니다. 1층과 2층의 공사 구역 주변에서는 주의해 주시기 바랍니다. 공사 시간은 오전 10시부터 오후 4시까지입니다. 앞으로 사흘 동안 공사를 진행할 예정입니다. 불편을 드려 다시 사과드립니다.

해설 앞으로 사흘간 있을 호텔 내 에스컬레이터 공사에 대한 안내 방송이다.

어휘 guest 손님 inconvenience 불편 cause 야기하다 construction 공사 escalator 에스컬레이터 careful 조심하는, 주의하는 area 구역 apologize for ~에 대해 사과하다

10 ③

W Do you love taking pictures? Do you want to be better at it? Join our club. Any first grader can join. We'll give you many good tips on how to take better photographs. We meet every Wednesday after school. You don't have to pay anything. You just have to bring your camera. There is a sign-up paper in our club room. Please sign it before this Friday.

여 사진 찍는 것을 좋아하시나요? 사진을 더 잘 찍고 싶으신가요? 우리 동아리에 들어오세요. 1학년은 누구든 들어올 수 있습니다. 사진을 더욱 잘 찍는 방법에 대한 좋은 조언들을 많이 드리겠습니다. 우리는 방과 후 매주 수요일에 모입니다. 돈을 낼 필요는 없습니다. 그냥 본인의 카메라를 가져오세요. 우리 동아리 방에 가입 신청서가 있습니다. 이번 주 금요일 전에 서명해 주세요.

해설 매주 수요일 방과 후에 모인다고 했다.

어휘 take a picture(photograph) 사진을 찍다 first grader 1학년 학생 pay (돈을) 내다, 지불하다 sign-up (서명에 의한) 등록, 가입 sign 서명하다

11 ④

M Hi. I heard you buy used books.
W Yes, we do. We buy and sell used books.
M Then could you look at these books?
W Sure. (Pause) Wow, these books are in good condition.
M Yeah, I bought them only a few months ago. How about these magazines?
W Sorry. We don't buy magazines.
M Okay. Then how much can I get for the books?
W Let me check how much I can offer you.

남 안녕하세요. 중고 서적을 구입하신다고 들었습니다.

여 네. 저희는 중고 서적을 구입하고 판매합니다.
남 그럼 이 책들을 좀 봐 주실래요?
여 네. (잠시 후) 와, 이 책들 상태가 좋은데요.
남 그렇죠. 불과 몇 달 전에 구입한 것들이에요. 이 잡지들은 어떤가요?
여 죄송해요. 저희는 잡지는 구매하지 않아요.
남 알겠습니다. 그럼 책값으로 얼마를 받을 수 있나요?
여 얼마를 드릴 수 있을지 확인해 보겠습니다.

해설 남자는 서점에서 중고 서적을 구입한다는 말을 들었다며 여자에게 책 상태를 봐 달라고 했으므로, 중고 서적을 팔기 위해 서점에 간 것임을 알 수 있다.

어휘 used 중고의 look at ~을 보다, 살피다 be in good condition 보존 상태가 좋다 magazine 잡지 offer 제공하다

12 ④

W Minho, we need to submit our video by Sunday night.
M Do you mean the one for the school video contest?
W Yes. I think we need to hurry. We should revise our script.
M Did you ask the teacher to give us some feedback on the script?
W Yes. She already gave us some feedback by email.
M Okay. What did she tell us to do?
W I haven't read the email yet. I'll read it now.

여 민호야, 우리 일요일 밤까지 동영상을 제출해야 해.
남 학교 동영상 경연 대회를 위한 동영상을 말하는 거니?
여 응. 우리 서둘러야 할 것 같아. 대본을 수정해야 하잖아.
남 선생님께 대본에 대한 피드백을 달라고 부탁드렸니?
여 응. 선생님께서 이미 이메일로 피드백을 주셨어.
남 그래. 선생님께서는 우리가 뭘 하라고 하셨니?
여 나 아직 이메일을 못 읽었어. 지금 읽을게.

해설 여자는 선생님이 이메일로 주신 피드백을 아직 읽지 못했다며 지금 읽겠다고 했다.

어휘 submit 제출하다 video 동영상 contest 경연 대회 hurry 서두르다 revise 수정하다 script 대본 feedback 피드백, 의견 yet (부정문·의문문에서) 아직

13 ③

W How can I help you?
M Hi. I'm looking for some headphones. How much are these black ones?
W They are $79. They are the bestselling model at our store.
M They are a bit expensive for me.
W How about these ones then? They are similar to the black ones, and they are on sale.
M How much are they?
W They were originally $99, but there's a discount of $30 now. They are a very popular item.
M That's great. I'll take them.

여 무엇을 도와드릴까요?

남 안녕하세요. 저는 헤드폰을 찾고 있어요. 이 검은색 헤드폰은 얼마인가요?

여 79달러입니다. 그것이 우리 매장에서 가장 잘 팔리는 모델이에요.

남 저에게는 조금 비싸네요.

여 그럼 이건 어떠세요? 검은색 헤드폰과 비슷하고, 할인 중이에요.

남 얼마예요?

여 원래 99달러였지만, 지금은 30달러를 할인해 드려요. 아주 인기가 많은 제품이랍니다.

남 좋아요. 그걸로 살게요.

해설 원래 가격인 99달러에서 30달러가 할인된 가격으로 판매 중인 헤드폰을 사겠다고 했으므로, 남자가 지불해야 할 금액은 69달러이다.

어휘 look for ~을 찾다   headphone 헤드폰   bestselling 가장 많이 팔리는   a bit 조금, 약간   expensive 비싼   be similar to ~와 비슷하다   on sale 할인 중인   originally 원래   discount 할인   popular 인기 있는   item 물품

14 ②

W It is very nice to meet you! I'm a big fan of yours.

M Nice to meet you, too.

W I've been your fan since I read your first novel.

M Thank you so much.

W I brought the first edition of your first novel. Can I get your autograph on it?

M Of course. What is your name?

W I'm Helen.

M Here you are, Helen.

W Thanks. You made my day.

여 만나서 정말 반가워요! 저는 당신 작품의 열혈 팬이에요.

남 저도 만나서 반갑습니다.

여 당신의 첫 소설을 읽은 이후로 당신의 팬이었어요.

남 정말 고맙습니다.

여 당신의 첫 소설의 초판본을 가지고 왔어요. 여기에 사인을 해 주실 수 있을까요?

남 물론입니다. 성함이 어떻게 되세요?

여 Helen이에요.

남 여기 있어요, Helen.

여 고마워요. 덕분에 즐거운 하루가 됐어요.

해설 여자가 남자의 첫 번째 소설을 읽었을 때부터 남자의 팬이었다고 하며 사인을 해 달라고 요청한 것으로 보아, 작가와 독자 사이의 대화이다.

어휘 fan 팬   novel 소설   bring(-brought-brought) 가져오다   edition (출간 횟수를 나타내는) 판, 호   get one's autograph ~의 사인을 받다   make one's day ~을 행복하게 하다

15 ①

W David, do you have any plans for the weekend?

M Yes. I'm going to Gangwon-do with my family.

W Great! What are you going to do there?

M My family all loves hiking, so we'll hike in the mountains. We'll also swim at the beach.

W Sounds good. Where will you stay?

M We will set up a tent at a campsite.

W Are you going to cook, too?

M Yes. We're going to have a barbecue. And we'll eat some seafood at a restaurant there.

W Sounds fun. Have a great time.

여 David, 주말에 무슨 계획 있어?

남 응. 가족들과 강원도에 갈 거야.

여 좋겠다! 거기에서 뭘 할 거야?

남 우리 가족이 모두 등산을 정말 좋아해서 우린 등산을 할 거야. 그리고 해변에서 수영도 할 거야.

여 좋겠다. 어디에서 머무니?

남 캠핑장에서 텐트를 칠 거야.

여 요리도 할 거야?

남 응. 바비큐 파티를 할 거야. 그리고 거기에 있는 식당에서 해산물도 먹을 거야.

여 재미있겠다. 좋은 시간 보내.

해설 남자는 여행 계획으로 낚시는 언급하지 않았다.

어휘 hike 하이킹하다   beach 해변, 바닷가   set up 세우다   campsite 캠핑장   have a barbecue 바비큐 파티를 하다   seafood 해산물

16 ⑤

(Telephone rings.)

W Hello. What can I do for you?

M Hello. I'm calling about a delivery problem.

W What is the problem?

M My order is late. I paid for quick delivery, but my order hasn't arrived yet.

W I'm very sorry. I'll check it right away. What is your name?

M My name is James Park.

W Your order will arrive today. We'll refund the quick delivery fee on your credit card.

M I hope this does not happen again.

(전화벨이 울린다.)

여 안녕하세요. 무엇을 도와드릴까요?

남 안녕하세요. 배송 문제로 전화했습니다.

여 문제가 무엇인가요?

남 제가 주문한 것이 늦어서요. 빠른 배송 요금을 지불했는데 아직도 주문한 물건이 도착하지 않았어요.

여 정말 죄송합니다. 지금 확인하겠습니다. 성함이 어떻게 되시죠?

남 James Park입니다.

여 주문하신 상품은 오늘 도착할 예정입니다. 빠른 배송 요금은 신용 카드로 환불해 드리겠습니다.

남 다시는 이런 일이 없었으면 합니다.

해설 남자는 빠른 배송 요금을 지불했는데도 아직 물건을 받지 못해서 이를 항의하기 위해 전화했다.

어휘 call about ~일로 전화하다   delivery 배달, 배송   order 주문, 주문품   pay(-paid-paid) 지불하다   quick 빠른   arrive 도착하다   refund 환불하다   delivery fee 배송료   credit card 신용 카드

17 ②

M Amy, did you walk the puppies today?
W Yes, I did an hour ago. And I just gave some food to them.
M Good. Then I'll give them a bath now.
W All right. Do you need any help?
M No, thank you. I can do it by myself. Oh, can you bring me some towels?
W Sure. Don't you need the dryer, too?
M I already brought it to the bathroom. Thanks.

남 Amy, 오늘 강아지들을 산책시켰니?
여 응, 한 시간 전에 했어. 그리고 방금 먹이도 줬어.
남 좋아. 그럼 지금 목욕을 시켜야겠다.
여 그래. 내 도움이 필요하니?
남 고맙지만 아니야. 혼자 할 수 있어. 참, 수건을 좀 가져다줄 수 있니?
여 그래. 드라이어도 필요하지 않아?
남 그건 이미 화장실에 가져왔어. 고마워.

해설 남자는 여자에게 수건을 가져다 달라고 부탁했다.

어휘 walk 산책 시키다 puppy 강아지 give ~ a bath ~을 목욕시키다 by oneself 혼자, 스스로 dryer 드라이어 bathroom 화장실

18 ③

① W Take an umbrella with you, or you'll get wet.
  M Oh, is it raining? Okay.
② W Whose notebook is this?
  M It's Nancy's. Let me take it to her.
③ W Watch out! The floor is wet.
  M Oops! Thanks for letting me know.
④ W May I take your order now?
  M I need a little more time.
⑤ W Why didn't you call me last night?
  M I'm sorry. I lost my phone.

① 여 우산을 가져가세요, 그렇지 않으면 젖을 거예요.
  남 오, 비가 오고 있어요? 알겠어요.
② 여 이 공책은 누구 거예요?
  남 Nancy 거예요. 내가 그녀에게 가져다줄게요.
③ 여 조심하세요! 바닥이 젖었어요.
  남 아이쿠! 알려 주셔서 고마워요.
④ 여 지금 주문하시겠어요?
  남 좀 더 시간이 필요해요.
⑤ 여 어젯밤에 왜 나한테 전화 안 했어요?
  남 미안해요. 휴대 전화를 잃어버렸어요.

해설 바닥이 젖어 있으니 조심하라고 주의를 주는 내용의 대화가 가장 적절하다.

어휘 get wet 젖다 notebook 공책 watch out 주의하다 floor 바닥 wet 젖은 a little more 조금 더 lose(-lost -lost) 잃어버리다

19 ④

M It's my first time here. Can you tell me how to use the washing machine?
W Sure. Put your clothes and some detergent in the machine. Now, close the door and put in 50 cents here.
M Okay.
W Then, set the water temperature and push the start button.
M Is there anything else to do?
W Nope. It's pretty simple, isn't it?

남 나는 여기엔 처음 와 봐. 세탁기를 어떻게 사용하는지 말해 줄래?
여 그래. 세탁기에 옷과 세제를 넣어. 이제, 문을 닫고 여기에 50센트를 넣어.
남 알겠어.
여 그 다음, 수온을 맞추고 시작 버튼을 눌러.
남 해야 할 것이 더 있어?
여 아니. 꽤 간단하지, 그렇지 않니?

해설 남자가 해야 할 것이 더 있는지 물었으므로 이에 대한 긍정 또는 부정의 응답이 와야 한다.
① 난 그걸 자주 하지 않아.
② 넌 돈이 필요 없어.
③ 모든 기계가 고장 났어.
⑤ 난 기계를 어떻게 사용하는지 몰라.

어휘 how to ~하는 방법 use 사용하다 washing machine 세탁기 clothes 옷 detergent 세제 set (기기 등을) 맞추다, 조절하다 temperature 온도 push 누르다 frequently 자주 machine 기계 out of order 고장 난 simple 간단한

20 ⑤

W I'd like to send this package to Gwangju.
M Okay. Please put that on the scale. What's inside?
W Books.
M Do you want to send it by express or regular mail?
W How long does regular mail take?
M It usually takes three days.
W It's too long. I'll send it by express mail.

여 이 소포를 광주에 보내려고 합니다.
남 네. 소포를 저울 위에 올리세요. 안에 무엇이 있나요?
여 책이요.
남 속달 우편으로 보내시겠어요, 보통 우편으로 보내시겠어요?
여 보통 우편은 얼마나 걸리나요?
남 대개 3일 걸립니다.
여 너무 오래 걸리네요. 속달 우편으로 보낼게요.

해설 보통 우편은 3일이 소요된다고 했으므로, 너무 오래 걸리니 속달 우편으로 보내겠다는 말이 이어지는 것이 가장 적절하다.
① 광주는 여기에서 멀어요.
② 속달 우편 치고 너무 오래 걸리네요.
③ 죄송한데 너무 비싸네요.
④ 저희는 배송 서비스를 하지 않습니다.

어휘 package 소포 scale 저울 express mail 속달 우편 regular mail 보통 우편 far from ~에서 먼 delivery 배송

Word Check   15회

01 (영화 등을) 개봉하다	02 전반전
03 골을 넣다	04 아주 새로운, 신품의
05 친척	06 무선의
07 대단한 것	08 우주 비행사
09 바꾸다	10 문학의
11 절하다	12 작가
13 full moon	14 practical
15 female	16 ballet
17 appearance	18 admission fee
19 even	20 scene
21 edit	22 lift
23 graduation ceremony	24 hardly

Expression Check

25 look around	26 take part in
27 broke down	28 make mistakes
29 let, in	30 looking forward to

Word Check   16회

01 주의하다	02 피드백, 의견
03 샘플, 견본품	04 떨어지다
05 게다가, 설상가상으로	06 미술관
07 실망스러운	08 대단한 것
09 주인공	10 자주
11 현지 시각	12 공사
13 cause	14 detergent
15 scale	16 used
17 revise	18 submit
19 drop	20 originally
21 snowstorm	22 national
23 inconvenience	24 script

Expression Check

25 give, a bath	26 made, day
27 far from	28 in good condition
29 apologize, for	30 get, high score

실전 모의고사 17회   pp.170~177

01 ②	02 ⑤	03 ④	04 ②	05 ④
06 ②	07 ③	08 ⑤	09 ②	10 ②
11 ④	12 ④	13 ③	14 ⑤	15 ⑤
16 ③	17 ④	18 ②	19 ⑤	20 ④

01 ②

W Good morning. This is the weather forecast for this week. We're starting Monday with rain, but it will be sunny tomorrow. It is expected to continue until Friday. On Friday and Saturday, it will be cloudy and windy. So if you plan to go on a picnic this weekend, you need to wait until Sunday because we'll have clear skies on that day.

여 좋은 아침입니다. 이번 주의 일기 예보입니다. 비와 함께 월요일을 시작하고 있지만 내일은 맑을 것입니다. 이는 금요일까지 계속될 것으로 예상됩니다. 금요일과 토요일에는 흐리고 바람이 많이 불겠습니다. 따라서 이번 주말에 소풍을 갈 계획을 하신다면, 일요일에는 화창할 것이므로 일요일까지 기다리셔야겠습니다.

해설 화요일부터 금요일까지 계속해서 맑을 것이라고 했으므로, 목요일의 날씨는 맑을 것이다.

어휘 weather forecast 일기 예보   expect 예상하다 continue 계속되다   until ~까지   plan to ~할 계획이다   go on a picnic 소풍을 가다

02 ⑤

M Clara, is this you?
W Yes. I'm 15 years old in this picture.
M I can hardly recognize you. I've never seen you with short hair like this.
W Yeah, I didn't like long hair when I was young.
M And is this your younger sister Emma next to you?
W Right. She used to be taller than me.
M I can see that. You two are so cute in those dresses.

남 Clara, 이게 너니?
여 응. 사진 속의 나는 열다섯 살이야.
남 널 거의 못 알아보겠어. 난 이렇게 짧은 머리를 한 너를 본 적이 없어.
여 응, 나는 어렸을 때는 긴 머리를 좋아하지 않았어.
남 그리고 네 옆에 있는 건 네 여동생 Emma니?
여 맞아. 그녀는 나보다 키가 더 컸었어.
남 그러네. 너희 둘 다 원피스를 입으니 참 귀엽다.

해설 사진 속에서 여자는 짧은 머리를 했고, 여자보다 키 큰 여동생이 바로 옆에 있으며, 둘 다 원피스를 입고 있다고 했다.

어휘 hardly 거의 ~ 않다(없다)   recognize 알아보다   used to ~하곤 했다   dress 원피스

03 ④

M　The desk we ordered arrived this morning.
W　Good. Do you like it?
M　The color and the size are okay, but there's a big scratch on the top.
W　Really? We should ask them to exchange it.
M　Yes. So I called the customer center several times, but nobody answered the phone.
W　Oh, no. Why don't you leave a message on the homepage?
M　I already did! Nobody has answered that either.

남　우리가 주문한 책상이 오늘 아침에 도착했어.
여　잘됐네. 마음에 들어?
남　색상과 크기는 괜찮은데, 윗면에 크게 긁힌 자국이 있어.
여　정말? 바꿔 달라고 해야겠다.
남　응. 그래서 고객 센터에 여러 번 전화했는데, 아무도 전화를 받지 않아.
여　오, 이런. 홈페이지에 글을 남겨 놓는 게 어때?
남　벌써 했지! 그것에도 아무도 답을 하지 않았어.

[해설] 하자가 있는 제품이 배달되었는데 고객 센터에 전화 연결이 안 되고, 홈페이지에 글을 남겨도 답변이 없어 남자는 짜증이 났다.

[어휘] order 주문하다　arrive 도착하다　scratch 긁힌 자국　top 윗면　exchange 교환하다　customer center 고객 센터　several times 여러 번　nobody 아무도 ~ 않다　leave a message 메시지를 남기다　either (부정문에서) ~도　relieved 안도하는　pleased 기쁜

04 ②

W　Andy, what did you do last weekend?
M　I volunteered at the World Water Forum.
W　Oh, what is that?
M　It is a forum about water pollution, so people gave presentations on that issue.
W　What kind of volunteer work did you do there?
M　I gave directions to foreign participants in English.
W　Wow, that sounds interesting.

여　Andy, 지난 주말에 뭐 했니?
남　나는 World Water Forum에서 자원봉사를 했어.
여　오, 그게 뭐니?
남　수질 오염에 대한 포럼이어서, 사람들이 그 문제에 대해 발표를 했어.
여　너는 거기서 어떤 봉사 활동을 한 거야?
남　외국 참가자들에게 영어로 길을 안내했어.
여　와, 흥미로운걸.

[해설] 남자는 외국인 참가자들에게 영어로 길을 안내하는 봉사 활동을 했다고 했다.

[어휘] volunteer 자원봉사를 하다　forum 포럼, 토론회　pollution 오염　presentation 발표　issue 문제, 사안　give directions 길을 안내하다　foreign 외국의　participant 참가자

05 ④

M　Hi. I'm looking for something special for my wife.
W　Is it a special day?
M　Ah, yes. It's our wedding anniversary.
W　Happy anniversary! How about red roses? They are popular for wedding anniversaries.
M　Hmm... I'm not sure. I want something unique.
W　Then what about these dried flowers? You can keep them for long.
M　That sounds good. I'll take them.

남　안녕하세요. 제 아내를 위한 특별한 것을 찾고 있어요.
여　특별한 날인가요?
남　아. 네. 저희 결혼기념일이에요.
여　축하드려요! 빨간 장미는 어떠세요? 빨간 장미는 결혼기념일에 인기 있어요.
남　음… 잘 모르겠어요. 독특한 걸 원하는데요.
여　그럼 이 드라이플라워는 어떠세요? 오래 간직하실 수 있어요.
남　그게 좋겠네요. 그걸로 할게요.

[해설] 꽃을 구입하는 상황이므로 꽃 가게에서 일어나는 대화이다.

[어휘] look for ~을 찾다　wedding anniversary 결혼기념일　unique 독특한　keep 가지고 있다　for long 오랫동안

06 ②

W　Steve, do you know Ms. Taylor?
M　Yes. She was my homeroom teacher last year.
W　What a coincidence! She is my homeroom teacher this year!
M　Good for you! She's a really good teacher.
W　I like her class because she always brings interesting things to show us.
M　Me, too. She's the most passionate person I've ever met.
W　You can say that again.

여　Steve, 너 Taylor 선생님 아니?
남　응. 작년에 우리 담임 선생님이셨어.
여　이런 우연이! 그분이 올해 우리 담임 선생님이셔.
남　잘됐다! 그분은 정말 좋은 선생님이셔.
여　선생님이 언제나 우리에게 보여 줄 흥미로운 걸 갖고 오셔서 난 선생님 수업이 좋더라.
남　나도. 그분은 내가 만났던 사람 중에 가장 열정적인 분이셔.
여　네 말에 동의해.

[해설] You can say that again.은 상대방의 말에 동의하는 표현이다.

[어휘] homeroom teacher 담임 선생님　coincidence 우연의 일치　interesting 흥미로운　passionate 열정적인

07 ③

W　Have you decided on your school club?
M　Yes. I'll join the baseball club. What about you?
W　Well, I'm not sure yet.
M　You were in the math club last year, weren't you?

W Yeah, so I want to join a new club.
M Then why don't you join the music club? You're really into music these days.
W I love that idea. I'll do that.

여 너 학교 동아리 정했니?
남 응. 난 야구 동아리에 가입할 거야. 너는?
여 글쎄, 아직 잘 모르겠어.
남 넌 작년에 수학 동아리였지, 그렇지 않았어?
여 응. 그래서 새로운 동아리에 가입하고 싶어.
남 그럼 음악 동아리에 가입하는 게 어때? 너 요즘 음악에 관심이 정말 많잖아.
여 그 생각이 마음에 든다. 그렇게 해야겠어.

해설 음악 동아리에 가입하라는 남자의 제안을 듣고 여자는 그렇게 하겠다고 했다.

어휘 decide 결정하다   yet (부정문·의문문에서) 아직
be into ～에 관심이 많다, ～을 좋아하다   these days 요즘

08 ⑤

W Josh, what are you doing?
M I'm playing a game, Mom.
W Did you finish your English homework? You said you had a lot.
M Of course, I did. It was pretty easy.
W Good. Then can I ask you a favor?
M Sure. What is it?
W Can you stop playing and take out the trash? I have to prepare dinner right now.
M All right. I'll do it right away.

여 Josh, 뭐 하고 있니?
남 게임하고 있어요, 엄마.
여 영어 숙제는 다 했니? 숙제가 많다고 했잖아.
남 그럼요, 다 했죠. 꽤 쉬웠어요.
여 잘했구나. 그럼 부탁 하나 해도 될까?
남 네. 뭔데요?
여 게임 그만하고 쓰레기를 내다 버려 줄래? 난 지금 당장 저녁을 준비해야 해서.
남 알겠어요. 지금 바로 할게요.

해설 여자가 남자에게 게임을 그만하고 쓰레기를 내다 버려 달라고 부탁하자 남자는 바로 하겠다고 했다.

어휘 pretty 꽤   ask ~ a favor ～에게 부탁을 하다   take out the trash 쓰레기를 내다 버리다   prepare 준비하다

09 ②

M You bought wireless earphones!
W Yeah, they were on sale. I bought them at the discounted price of $80.
M Good deal! Do they only come in white?
W No, they come in two colors: white and black.
M I see. They're connected to your smartphone, right?
W Yes. They can also be connected to my laptop computer.

M How many hours does the battery last?
W If it is fully charged, it lasts for ten hours.

남 너 무선 이어폰을 샀구나!
여 응. 할인을 했거든. 할인가로 80달러에 샀어.
남 괜찮은데! 이어폰은 흰색으로만 나오니?
여 아니, 흰색과 검정색 두 가지 색상으로 나와.
남 그렇구나. 스마트폰이랑 연결되는 거 맞지?
여 응, 그리고 노트북과도 연결될 수 있어.
남 배터리는 몇 시간이나 지속되니?
여 완전히 충전하면 열 시간 동안 지속돼.

해설 여자가 구입한 무선 이어폰은 두 가지 색상으로 나온다고 했다.

어휘 wireless 무선의   earphone 이어폰   on sale 할인 중인
discounted price 할인가   be connected to ～에 연결되다
laptop computer 노트북 컴퓨터   battery 배터리   last
지속되다   fully 완전히   charge 충전하다

10 ②

W Construction work to expand the library will begin next month. Therefore, for safety reasons, we'll close down the library from April 1 to May 31. You can check out books until next Friday. If you want to return books during the construction period, you can use the return box outside the building. Thank you for your understanding.

여 도서관을 확장하기 위한 공사가 다음 달에 시작될 것입니다. 따라서 안전상의 이유로 4월 1일부터 5월 31일까지 도서관을 휴관할 것입니다. 다음 주 금요일까지는 도서를 대출하실 수 있습니다. 공사 기간 동안 도서를 반납하시려면 도서관 건물 밖에 있는 반납함을 이용하시면 됩니다. 이해해 주셔서 고맙습니다.

해설 여자는 도서관 확장 공사로 인한 휴관 기간과 공사 기간 동안 책을 반납하는 방법을 안내하고 있다.

어휘 construction 공사   expand 확장하다   library 도서관
therefore 그러므로   safety 안전   reason 이유   close
down 문을 닫다   check out (도서관 등에서) 대출하다   until
～까지   return 반납하다   during ～ 동안   period 기간

11 ④

M If you want to be a good cook but you don't know how, sign up for a class at the Smart Cooking Center. The Smart Cooking Center has taught over 500 people how to cook since it was founded in 2015. There are five certified cooking teachers at our center. You take any class for one day for free. It's a good way to check out our classes. Each class is two hours long. For more details, call 535-7711. Thank you.

남 훌륭한 요리사가 되고 싶지만 방법을 모르신다면, Smart Cooking Center에서 하는 수업에 등록하세요. Smart Cooking Center는 2015년에 설립된 이래로 500명 이상의 사람들에게 요리하는 방법을 가르쳐 왔습니다. 저희 센터에는 다섯 명의 검증된 요리 강사들이 있습니다. 당신은 하루 동안

무료로 어떠한 수업이라도 들으실 수 있습니다. 저희의 수업을 확인해 보실 수 있는 좋은 방법이지요. 각 수업은 두 시간입니다. 더 자세한 사항은 535-7711로 전화 주세요. 고맙습니다.

해설 남자는 수업료는 언급하지 않았다.

어휘 cook 요리사; 요리하다 sign up for ~을 등록하다 how to ~하는 방법 since ~부터(이후) found 설립하다 certified 검증된, 보증된 for free 무료로 detail 세부 사항

12 ④

(*Telephone rings.*)
M Hello. Star Restaurant. How may I help you?
W Hello. I booked a table for tomorrow.
M May I have your name?
W Emily Choi.
M Let me check. (*Pause*) Yes, Ms. Choi, we have you at eight o'clock, and you ordered the five-course meal for ten people.
W That's right. Can I change it to seven people, not ten?
M No problem, Ms. Choi. Your reservation has been changed.

(전화벨이 울린다.)
남 안녕하세요. Star Restaurant입니다. 무엇을 도와드릴까요?
여 여보세요. 제가 내일 테이블 하나를 예약했는데요.
남 성함이 어떻게 되시죠?
여 Emily Choi요.
남 확인해 보겠습니다. (잠시 후) 네, Choi 고객님, 8시에 예약되어 있으시고, 10인분의 다섯 가지 코스 요리를 주문하셨네요.
여 맞아요. 10명이 아니라 7명으로 바꿀 수 있을까요?
남 문제없습니다. Choi 고객님. 예약이 변경되었습니다.

해설 여자는 10명에서 7명으로 예약 인원을 변경하기 위해 전화했다.

어휘 book 예약하다 order 주문하다 course (식사의) 코스 meal 식사 change 변경하다 reservation 예약

13 ③

W Hello. I'm looking for a suitcase. A big one.
M Okay. How about this one? It was advertised on TV last year.
W Let me lift it. (*Pause*) It's not that heavy. How much is it?
M It's $40 at a discount. It was originally $50.
W That's good. And can you show me the backpack over there, too?
M Wonderful choice. It's $20, but it'll be half price if you buy it with the suitcase.
W Great! I'll buy both of them.

여 안녕하세요. 저는 여행 가방을 찾고 있어요. 큰 걸로요.
남 네. 이건 어떠세요? 작년에 TV에서 광고되었던 거예요.
여 한번 들어 볼게요. (잠시 후) 그렇게 무겁지 않네요. 얼마예요?
남 할인하여 40달러입니다. 원래 50달러였어요.
여 좋네요. 그리고 저쪽에 있는 배낭도 보여 주시겠어요?

남 탁월한 선택이십니다. 배낭은 20달러인데, 여행 가방과 함께 사시면 절반 가격입니다.
여 좋아요! 둘 다 살게요.

해설 여행 가방은 할인하여 40달러이고, 20달러인 배낭은 여행 가방과 함께 구입하면 절반 가격이라고 했는데 여자가 둘 다 구입한다고 했으므로, 총 50달러를 지불해야 한다.

어휘 look for ~을 찾다 suitcase 여행 가방 advertise 광고하다 lift 들다 heavy 무거운 at a discount 할인하여 originally 원래 backpack 배낭 choice 선택 half price 반값 both 둘 다

14 ⑤

W Mr. Bernard, do you have a minute?
M Sure, Rachel. You look sick. Are you okay?
W I feel bad. I can't focus on class because I have a fever.
M Do you want to see a doctor?
W I think I should. So I need your permission to leave school early.
M Do your parents know you are sick?
W Yes, I called my mom at lunch. She told me to talk to you if I got worse.
M Okay. I'll call your mother to let her know that you're leaving school now.

여 Bernard 선생님, 시간 있으세요?
남 물론이지, Rachel. 너 아파 보이는구나. 괜찮니?
여 몸이 안 좋아요. 열이 나서 수업에 집중할 수가 없어요.
남 병원에 가고 싶니?
여 그래야 할 것 같아요. 그래서 조퇴하려면 선생님의 허락이 필요해요.
남 부모님께서도 네가 아픈 걸 알고 계시니?
여 네, 점심시간에 엄마한테 전화했어요. 더 나빠지면 선생님께 말씀드리라고 하셨어요.
남 알았다. 너희 어머니께 전화드려서 네가 지금 학교를 나설 거라고 말씀드리마.

해설 여자는 조퇴하려면 남자의 허락이 필요하다고 했고, 남자는 여자의 어머니께 전화하여 여자가 조퇴하는 것을 알리겠다고 했으므로, 담임 교사와 학생 사이의 대화이다.

어휘 focus on ~에 집중하다 have a fever 열이 나다 permission 허락 leave school early 학교를 조퇴하다 parents 부모 get worse 더 나빠지다

15 ⑤

W I have to scan this document right now, but the scanner is not working.
M Why don't you contact the service center?
W It doesn't open on Sundays.
M Oh, right. Today is Sunday.
W What should I do? I need to email it by today.
M I have an idea. You can take a picture of it and email it with your smartphone.
W I've never sent an email through my smartphone.

Can you show me how to do it?
M Sure.

여 지금 이 문서를 스캔해야 하는데, 스캐너가 작동되지 않아.
남 서비스 센터에 연락하는 게 어때?
여 일요일엔 안 열잖아.
남 아, 맞다. 오늘이 일요일이지.
여 어떡하지? 오늘까지 이걸 이메일로 보내야 하는데.
남 방법이 있어. 네 스마트폰으로 그것의 사진을 찍어서 사진을 이메일로 보내면 돼.
여 난 내 스마트폰으로 이메일을 보내 본 적이 없어. 어떻게 하는지 내게 보여 줄 수 있니?
남 물론이지.

해설 여자는 스마트폰으로 이메일을 보내 본 적이 없어서 남자에게 어떻게 하는지 보여 달라고 부탁했다.

어휘 scan 스캔하다   document 문서   scanner 스캐너   work 작동되다   contact 연락하다   email 이메일을 보내다; 이메일   through ~을 통해   how to ~하는 방법

---

⑤ M Excuse me. What is this line for?
   W It is to ride the train to Daejeon.

① 남 주문하시겠습니까?
   여 네. 생선구이와 감자 주세요.
② 남 네가 너무 빨리 운전하고 있다고 생각하지 않아?
   여 내가? 속도 늦출게.
③ 남 스테이크를 어떻게 해 드릴까요?
   여 중간 정도 굽기로 해 주세요.
④ 남 노란선 뒤에서 기다리세요. 위험할 수 있습니다.
   여 어머, 선을 못 봤어요. 고맙습니다.
⑤ 남 실례합니다. 이 줄은 무슨 줄인가요?
   여 대전행 기차를 타기 위한 줄이에요.

해설 역무원이 승객에게 노란색 선 뒤에서 기다리라고 주의를 주는 내용의 대화가 적절하다.

어휘 grilled 구운   potato 감자   slow down (속도를) 늦추다   medium (스테이크가) 중간 정도로 구워진   behind ~의 뒤에   dangerous 위험한   ride 타다

---

16 ③

M Lily, how was moving last weekend?
W It was really hard.
M I thought you liked the place you used to live in.
W I did. That place was quiet and cozy, and my neighbors were good.
M Then why did you move?
W Because it took me too long to go to work.
M I see. How do you like the new place?
W I like it very much. It only takes 20 minutes to get to my office.

남 Lily, 지난 주말에 이사는 어땠니?
여 너무 힘들었어.
남 난 네가 예전에 살던 곳을 좋아하는 줄 알았는데.
여 좋아했지. 그곳은 조용하고 안락하고, 이웃들도 좋았어.
남 그럼 왜 이사한 거야?
여 출근하는 데 시간이 너무 오래 걸려서.
남 그랬구나. 새로 이사 간 곳은 마음에 들어?
여 정말 마음에 들어. 사무실까지 가는 데 고작 20분 걸려.

해설 여자는 통근하는 데 시간이 너무 오래 걸려서 이사했다고 했다.

어휘 move 이사하다   used to ~하곤 했다   quiet 조용한   cozy 안락한   neighbor 이웃   go to work 출근하다   office 사무실

---

17 ④

① M Are you ready to order?
   W Yes. Grilled fish and potatoes, please.
② M Don't you think you're driving too fast?
   W Am I? I'll slow down.
③ M How would you like your steak?
   W Medium, please.
④ M Please wait behind the yellow line. It can be dangerous.
   W Oops, I didn't see the line. Thank you.

---

18 ②

W Ron, I went to the Korean Dreamer Concert last Saturday!
M You did? I really wanted to go, too, but I couldn't get a ticket. How was it?
W It was great. I saw most of the top idol groups.
M Great! It was held at Central Stadium, right?
W Yes. There were big screens above the stage, so I could see well.
M Good. I'm sure the stadium was crowded because it was sold out.
W Definitely. I heard there were about 30,000 people there.

여 Ron, 나 지난주 토요일에 Korean Dreamer Concert에 갔었어!
남 그랬어? 나도 정말 가고 싶었는데, 표를 못 구했어. 어땠니?
여 좋았어. 대부분의 톱 아이돌 그룹들을 봤어.
남 좋았겠다! Central Stadium에서 열렸던 거 맞지?
여 응. 무대 위에 큰 스크린이 있어서 잘 볼 수 있었어.
남 좋네. 콘서트가 매진이어서 경기장이 붐볐겠는데.
여 당연하지. 거기에 약 3만 명이 있었다고 들어.

해설 여자가 다녀온 콘서트는 경기장에서 열렸다고 했다.

어휘 most of ~의 대부분   be held 열리다, 개최되다   stadium 경기장   screen 스크린, 화면   above ~보다 위에   stage 무대   crowded 붐비는, 혼잡한   sold out 매진된, 다 팔린   definitely 확실히, 분명히

---

19 ⑤

W Are you watching the drama The Mirror?
M No. When is it on?
W It's a weekend drama. It's on channel thirteen. It's so interesting.
M Aha, I think I heard about it from my sister. Is it really good?

W Yeah. You should watch it. You like mysteries, don't you?

M I do. Who's the lead actor?

W I don't know his name. He's a new face.

여 너 드라마 〈The Mirror〉 보니?

남 아니. 언제 하는 건데?

여 주말 드라마야. 13번 채널에서 해. 정말 재미있어.

남 아하, 우리 누나한테 그것에 대해서 들은 것 같아. 그게 그렇게 재미있어?

여 응. 너도 봐야 해. 너 추리물 좋아하잖아, 그렇지 않니?

남 좋아하지. 주연 배우가 누구야?

여 난 그의 이름은 몰라. 그는 신인이야.

[해설] 남자가 드라마의 주연 배우가 누구인지 물었으므로 신인이라 이름은 잘 모른다는 응답이 가장 적절하다.

① 나는 TV 드라마를 좋아하지 않아.

② 이제 채널을 돌려도 돼?

③ 난 네가 가장 좋아하는 배우가 누구인지 알아.

④ 네 말이 맞아. 13번 채널에서 해.

[어휘] drama 드라마   channel (TV·라디오의) 채널   mystery 미스터리, 추리물   lead actor 주연 배우   new face 신인

20 ④

(Telephone rings.)

W Fast Service Center. How may I help you?

M Hello. I have a problem with my Internet.

W What's wrong with it?

M The connection is often interrupted and it is very slow. I turned my computer off and on several times, but it doesn't help.

W How long have you had the problem?

M For the past few hours. Could you send someone to fix it today?

W I'm afraid you'll have to wait until tomorrow.

(전화벨이 울린다.)

여 Fast Service Center입니다. 무엇을 도와드릴까요?

남 안녕하세요. 제 인터넷에 문제가 있어요.

여 어떤 문제인가요?

남 연결이 자주 끊기고 속도가 아주 느려요. 컴퓨터를 여러 번 껐다가 켜 봤지만, 도움이 되지 않아요.

여 얼마나 오랫동안 그 문제가 있었나요?

남 지난 몇 시간 동안이요. 오늘 고칠 사람을 보내 주실 수 있나요?

여 죄송하지만 내일까지 기다리셔야 해요.

[해설] 남자가 인터넷을 고칠 사람을 오늘 보내 줄 수 있는지 물었으므로 내일까지 기다려야 한다는 응답이 가장 적절하다.

① 우리는 시간 맞춰 가지 못했어요.

② 저는 오후 6시에 예약을 했어요.

③ 당신의 인터넷 연결이 다운되었어요.

⑤ 제 컴퓨터를 인터넷에 연결하고 싶어요.

[어휘] connection 연결   often 자주   interrupt 방해하다, 중단시키다   turn off ~을 끄다   turn on ~을 켜다   past 지난   fix 고치다   make it 시간 맞춰 가다   make an appointment 예약을 하다   down 작동이 안 되는, 다운된   connect A to B A를 B에 연결하다

01 ③	02 ②	03 ⑤	04 ⑤	05 ④
06 ①	07 ③	08 ②	09 ③	10 ⑤
11 ①	12 ⑤	13 ④	14 ⑤	15 ③
16 ④	17 ③	18 ③	19 ④	20 ⑤

01 ③

M Good morning. It's time for the weather report for Europe. London has sunny but cold and windy weather today. In Paris and Rome, a mix of rain and snow has stopped, and partially cloudy but warm weather is expected. Berlin is expecting heavy snowfall, and it looks like it's going to last for the next few days.

남 좋은 아침입니다. 유럽의 일기 예보입니다. 오늘 런던은 맑지만 춥고 바람이 많이 부는 날씨입니다. 파리와 로마에는 비와 눈이 섞여 내리던 것이 멈추고, 부분적으로 흐리지만 따뜻한 날씨가 예상됩니다. 베를린은 폭설이 예상되며, 앞으로 며칠 동안 지속될 것으로 보입니다.

[해설] 베를린은 앞으로 며칠 동안 폭설이 예상된다고 했다.

[어휘] weather report 일기 예보   Europe 유럽   mix 섞인 것, 혼합   partially 부분적으로   expect 예상하다   heavy snowfall 폭설   last 지속되다   for the next few days 앞으로 며칠 동안

02 ②

W Let's start drawing. We're going to draw some shapes. Listen carefully and do as I tell you. First, draw a big triangle on the paper with your pencil. Next, draw a circle in the middle of the triangle. The circle is smaller than the triangle. Finally, draw a square inside the circle. The square is the smallest shape.

여 그리기를 시작합시다. 우리는 몇 가지 모양을 그릴 것입니다. 잘 듣고 제가 여러분께 말하는 대로 하세요. 먼저, 연필로 종이에 큰 세모를 그립니다. 다음으로, 세모 중앙에 동그라미를 그립니다. 동그라미가 세모보다 작습니다. 마지막으로, 동그라미 안에 네모를 그립니다. 네모가 가장 작은 모양입니다.

[해설] 먼저 큰 세모를 그리고, 세모 안의 가운데에 동그라미를 그린 다음, 동그라미 안에 네모를 그리라고 했다.

[어휘] shape 모양, 형태   carefully 주의 깊게   triangle 세모, 삼각형   circle 동그라미, 원   middle 가운데   finally 마지막으로   square 네모, 정사각형   inside ~ 안에

03 ⑤

M I'm going camping with some of my friends this

weekend.

W Sounds exciting. Did you check the weather forecast?

M I did yesterday. It said there would be no rain for the next few days.

W Well, I heard the forecast a few minutes ago. It has changed. It will rain all weekend.

M Oh, no. We are planning to set up a tent.

W Maybe you should put it off.

M I guess I have to. I hate rain.

남 나 이번 주말에 몇몇 친구들하고 캠핑 갈 거야.
여 재미있겠다. 일기 예보는 확인해 봤어?
남 어제 확인했어. 앞으로 며칠 동안은 비가 안 온다고 하던데.
여 글쎄, 내가 몇 분 전에 예보를 들었거든. 예보가 바뀌었어. 주말 내내 비가 올 거야.
남 오, 이런. 우린 텐트를 칠 계획인데.
여 아마 미뤄야 할 것 같다.
남 그래야겠다. 난 비가 정말 싫어.

해설 주말 내내 비가 오는 것으로 일기 예보가 바뀌어 캠핑 계획을 미뤄야 하는 상황이므로 남자는 실망스러울 것이다.

어휘 go camping 캠핑을 가다   weather forecast 일기 예보   be planning to ~할 계획이다   set up 세우다   put off 미루다, 연기하다   hate 몹시 싫어하다

04 ⑤

W Hi, Mike. How's everything going?

M Very good. I'm preparing for the school festival these days.

W Oh, I heard your short movie will be showing.

M Yeah. You should come and watch it.

W I will. Is the festival during the fourth or the fifth week?

M It's on the last Thursday of this month.

W Today is September 15. So it's two weeks away.

M That's right. I'm so excited.

여 안녕, Mike. 잘 지내고 있어?
남 아주 잘 지내. 난 요즘 학교 축제를 준비하고 있어.
여 오, 네 단편 영화가 상영될 거라고 들었어.
남 응. 너도 와서 봐.
여 그럴게. 축제는 넷째 주에 하니 아니면 다섯째 주에 하니?
남 축제는 이번 달 마지막 목요일이야.
여 오늘이 9월 15일이니까 2주 후네.
남 맞아. 난 너무 신나.

해설 오늘이 9월 15일인데 축제는 2주 후라고 했으므로, 축제가 열리는 날짜는 9월 29일이다.

어휘 prepare for ~을 준비하다   festival 축제   these days 요즘   short movie 단편 영화   show 상영되다   during ~ 동안   away 떨어져

05 ④

M What did you do yesterday?

W I was busy doing many things. I woke up early and

cleaned my house all morning.

M What a great start!

W In the afternoon, I went to the grocery store and cooked dinner for ten people.

M For ten people? What was the occasion?

W I had a housewarming party last night. You know I moved to a new apartment.

M Oh, right. Invite me to your house the next time.

W Sure, I will.

남 어제 뭐 했어?
여 난 많은 것들을 하느라 바빴어. 일찍 일어나서 오전 내내 집을 청소했어.
남 훌륭한 시작이네!
여 오후에는 식료품점에 갔었고 저녁 10인분을 요리했어.
남 10인분? 무슨 일이었는데?
여 어젯밤에 집들이를 했거든. 나 새 아파트로 이사한 거 알잖아.
남 아, 맞다. 다음번에 나도 너희 집으로 초대해 줘.
여 응. 그렇게.

해설 여자는 어젯밤에 자신의 새 아파트에서 집들이를 했다고 말했다.

어휘 be busy ~ing ~ 하느라 바쁘다   wake up 일어나다   grocery store 식료품점, 슈퍼마켓   occasion 일, 행사   housewarming party 집들이   apartment 아파트   invite 초대하다

06 ①

W Congratulations!

M Thank you, Mrs. Dunphy. Thank you so much for coming to my graduation ceremony.

W Here are some flowers for you.

M They're beautiful.

W I still remember the day when we first met in the classroom.

M I do, too.

W Now you're graduating from university! I'm so proud of you!

M I am here because of you. I owe you a lot.

여 축하해!
남 고맙습니다. Dunphy 선생님. 제 졸업식에 와 주셔서 정말 감사드려요.
여 여기 너를 위한 꽃이란다.
남 예쁘네요.
여 난 아직도 우리가 처음 교실에서 만났던 날을 기억한단다.
남 저도요.
여 이제 네가 대학교를 졸업하다니! 네가 너무 자랑스럽구나!
남 선생님 덕분에 제가 여기에 있는걸요. 신세를 많이 졌습니다.

해설 남자는 상대방 덕분에 자신이 여기에 있는 것이고 신세를 많이 졌다는 말로 감사를 표현하고 있다.

어휘 graduation ceremony 졸업식   still 아직, 여전히   remember 기억하다   graduate from ~을 졸업하다   university 대학교   be proud of ~을 자랑스러워하다   owe 신세 지다, 빚지다   a lot 많이

07 ③

M Do you have any plans for tomorrow?
W Yes. My cousin is coming to visit me, so we'll hang out.
M Great. What are you going to do?
W I'll show him my favorite places in the city.
M You must be excited.
W Yes, I am. So I have a lot of work to do before he comes.
M Like what?
W I have to do my homework and household chores.

남 내일 무슨 계획 있니?
여 응. 내 사촌이 날 보러 와서. 함께 시간을 보낼 거야.
남 좋겠다. 뭐 할 거니?
여 나는 그에게 도시에서 내가 가장 좋아하는 곳을 보여 줄 거야.
남 신나겠다.
여 응. 그래서 그가 오기 전에 할 일이 많아.
남 어떤 거?
여 숙제와 집안일을 해야 해.

해설 여자는 사촌과 함께 시간을 보낼 것이라고 했다.

어휘 cousin 사촌   visit 방문하다   hang out 어울려 시간을 보내다   a lot of 많은   do one's homework 숙제를 하다   do household chores 집안일을 하다

08 ②

M How did you like the restaurant tonight?
W I really liked the atmosphere there.
M I agree. I liked the food, too.
W Yes. The steak was so good, and the cake was the best.
M And it was not really expensive, was it?
W No, it wasn't. The service was good, too. Thank you for taking me there tonight.
M You're welcome. Let's go there again soon.

남 오늘 밤 식당 어땠니?
여 나는 그곳의 분위기가 정말 마음에 들었어.
남 동의해. 난 음식도 좋았어.
여 응. 스테이크가 정말 맛있었고, 케이크는 최고였어.
남 그리고 가격이 별로 비싸지도 않아, 그렇지?
여 그래, 비싸지 않더라. 서비스도 좋았어. 오늘 밤 그곳에 날 데려가 줘서 고마워.
남 천만에. 조만간 또 가자.

해설 두 사람은 식당의 위생 상태는 언급하지 않았다.

어휘 atmosphere 분위기   agree 동의하다   expensive 비싼   take (사람을) 데려가다   again 다시

09 ③

M Okay, students. Let's wrap up now and review what we should do to stay healthy throughout the winter. First, you should get enough sleep. A good night's sleep makes everyone healthier. Second, eat well.

Try to have a healthy, balanced diet every day. Third, wash your hands frequently. Make it your habit to wash your hands when you come back home from outside.

남 자, 학생 여러분. 이제 마무리 짓고 겨울철에 건강을 유지하기 위해서 우리가 해야 할 일을 복습해 봅시다. 첫째, 잠을 충분히 자야 합니다. 충분한 수면은 모든 사람들을 더 건강하게 만듭니다. 둘째, 잘 먹어야 합니다. 매일 건강에 좋고 균형 잡힌 식사를 하려고 노력하세요. 셋째, 손을 자주 씻으세요. 밖에서 집에 돌아오면 손을 씻는 것을 습관으로 만드세요.

해설 겨울철에 건강을 유지하는 방법에 대해 말하고 있다.

어휘 wrap up 마무리 짓다   review 복습하다   stay healthy 건강을 유지하다   throughout 내내, ~ 동안 쭉   get enough sleep 잠을 충분히 자다   balanced 균형 잡힌   diet 식사   frequently 자주   habit 습관

10 ⑤

W Today, I'll tell you some interesting facts about tomatoes. Tomatoes originally come from Peru, and not all tomatoes are red. They can be yellow, pink, purple, black, and even white! The largest tomato on record was as heavy as 3.5 kilograms. A tomato festival takes place every year in Spain, where people throw more than 150,000 tomatoes at one another.

여 오늘, 저는 여러분에게 토마토에 관한 재미있는 사실을 이야기할 거예요. 토마토는 원래 페루가 원산지이고, 모든 토마토가 빨간 것은 아닙니다. 토마토는 노란색, 분홍색, 보라색, 검은색, 그리고 심지어 하얀색일 수도 있답니다! 기록상 가장 큰 토마토는 3.5 킬로그램만큼이나 무거웠습니다. 스페인에서는 매년 토마토 축제가 개최되는데, 이 축제에서 사람들은 서로에게 15만 개 이상의 토마토를 던진답니다.

해설 토마토 축제에서 사람들은 15만 개 이상의 토마토를 던진다고 했다.

어휘 fact 사실   originally 원래   come from ~에서 오다   on record 기록상, 공표된   festival 축제   take place 개최되다   throw 던지다   one another 서로

11 ①

M It's time to go home.
W I'm too tired to walk. Can we take a taxi?
M It's not easy to get a taxi here. What about taking the subway? It's really fast.
W The subway station is far from here.
M You're right. Why don't we take a bus? There's a bus stop across the street.
W Good idea. It takes a long time, but at least we can sit and get some rest.
M Let's go.

남 집에 갈 시간이야.
여 난 너무 피곤해서 걸을 수가 없어. 우리 택시 탈까?

남 여기에서는 택시를 잡기가 쉽지 않아. 지하철을 타는 건 어때? 정말 빠르잖아.

여 지하철역은 여기에서 멀어.

남 네 말이 맞네. 버스를 타는 건 어때? 길 건너에 버스 정류장이 있어.

여 좋은 생각이야. 오래 걸리지만 적어도 앉아서 쉴 수 있으니까.

남 가자.

해설 남자가 버스를 타자고 제안하자 여자는 버스를 타면 앉아서 쉴 수 있다며 좋은 생각이라고 했다.

어휘 too ~ to ... 너무 ~해서 ...할 수 없는   tired 피곤한 subway station 지하철역   far from ~에서 먼   bus stop 버스 정류장   across ~의 맞은편에   street 길   at least 적어도, 최소한   get rest 쉬다

12 ⑤

(Cellphone rings.)

M Hi, Lisa. What's up?

W Hi, Mason. I called to ask you a favor.

M What is it?

W My parents and I will visit my grandmother in Jeju-do tomorrow. She's sick.

M I'm sorry to hear that.

W So while we're away, will you take care of Mimi my dog?

M Okay, but I've never taken care of a dog before.

W I'll tell you everything you need to know. Thank you so much.

M All right. Talk to you later.

(휴대 전화가 울린다.)

남 안녕, Lisa. 무슨 일이야?

여 안녕. Mason. 너에게 부탁을 하려고 전화했어.

남 뭔데?

여 우리 부모님이랑 내가 내일 제주도에 할머니를 뵈러 가. 할머니께서 편찮으셔.

남 그 말을 들으니 유감이다.

여 그래서 우리가 가 있는 동안에, 네가 우리 개 Mimi를 돌봐 줄래?

남 그래. 그런데 난 전에 개를 돌봤던 적이 없어.

여 네가 알아야 할 것을 전부 알려 줄게. 정말 고마워.

남 알았어. 나중에 이야기하자.

해설 여자는 부모님과 함께 할머니가 계신 제주도에 가 있는 동안 자신의 개를 맡아 달라고 부탁하기 위해 전화했다.

어휘 ask ~ a favor ~에게 부탁을 하다   while ~하는 동안에 away 자리에 없는   take care of ~을 돌보다   later 나중에

13 ④

M Hey, are we going to meet after school today?

W Of course. We need to finish our group project.

M Anytime after five is okay for me. What about you?

W I have a club meeting at 5:00.

M How long will it take?

W It won't take long. About 10 to 15 minutes, I guess.

M Then let's meet at the library at 5:30. Don't be late.

W Okay. See you then.

남 얘, 오늘 방과 후에 우리 만나는 거야?

여 당연하지. 우리는 그룹 프로젝트를 끝내야 해.

남 나는 5시 이후면 언제든지 괜찮아. 너는?

여 나는 5시에 동아리 모임이 있어.

남 얼마나 걸리는데?

여 오래 걸리지 않을 거야. 내 생각에 10분에서 15분 정도.

남 그럼 5시 30분에 도서관에서 만나자. 늦지 마.

여 알았어. 그때 보자.

해설 5시에는 여자가 동아리 모임이 있다고 해서 두 사람은 5시 30분에 만나기로 했다.

어휘 finish 끝내다   anytime 언제든지   meeting 회의   take (시간이) 걸리다   guess 추측하다   library 도서관   late 늦은

14 ⑤

W Are there any tickets left for *Alice in Wonderland* at 4:15?

M There are only two seats left. How many tickets do you need?

W Oh, no. We need three. When is the next show time?

M At 6:30.

W That's too late. What about *Jungle Book* at 4:30?

M There are three seats on the right side of the first row.

W That's okay with me. Here's my credit card. How long is the movie?

M Two hours and five minutes.

여 4시 15분에 하는 〈이상한 나라의 앨리스〉 표 남았나요?

남 두 좌석만 남아 있습니다. 표가 몇 장 필요하세요?

여 오, 안 돼요. 저희는 3장이 필요해요. 다음 상영 시각은 언제인가요?

남 6시 30분이요.

여 너무 늦네요. 4시 30분에 하는 〈정글 북〉은 어떤가요?

남 첫 번째 줄 오른쪽에 세 자리가 있어요.

여 괜찮아요. 여기 제 신용 카드요. 영화 상영 시간이 얼마나 돼요?

남 2시간 5분입니다.

해설 영화표가 남아 있는지, 상영 시간은 얼마나 되는지 묻고 답하고 있으므로 영화관 직원과 관람객 사이의 대화이다.

어휘 ticket 표   seat 자리   left 남아 있는(leave의 과거분사) show time 상영 시각   row 열, 줄   credit card 신용 카드

15 ③

(Cellphone rings.)

M Hi, Mom. Where are you?

W I'm on my way home from the supermarket. Are you home?

M Yes. I'm doing my homework.

W Good. I called you because it started to rain suddenly.

M Do you want me to get you an umbrella?
W No, I brought one. Will you just close the windows?
M Sure. I'll do that right away.
W Thanks. See you soon.

(휴대 전화가 울린다.)

남 여보세요, 엄마. 어디에 계세요?
여 슈퍼마켓에서 집에 가는 길이야. 너 집이니?
남 네. 숙제하고 있어요.
여 잘했네. 갑자기 비가 와서 네게 전화했어.
남 우산을 가져다 드릴까요?
여 아니, 하나 가져왔어. 창문들 좀 닫아 줄래?
남 네. 지금 바로 할게요.
여 고마워. 곧 보자.

해설 여자는 남자에게 비가 오니 창문을 닫아 달라고 요청했다.

어휘 on one's way home 집에 가는 길에 supermarket 슈퍼마켓 do one's homework 숙제를 하다 suddenly 갑자기 window 창문

16 ④

M Did you get the camera you wanted?
W No. I spent all weekend looking for cameras, but I didn't buy one.
M What kind of camera do you want to buy?
W I want a camera that has a simple design and a remote control. I also want it to be light and black.
M You couldn't find one with those features?
W Actually, I found one that has all those features except for the color. Black was sold out.

남 원했던 카메라를 샀니?
여 아니. 주말을 온통 카메라를 찾는 데 보냈는데, 사지 않았어.
남 어떤 종류의 카메라를 사고 싶은데?
여 디자인이 단순하고 리모컨이 있는 카메라를 가지고 싶어. 또한 가볍고 검은색인 걸 원해.
남 그 특징들을 갖춘 카메라를 못 찾은 거야?
여 사실, 색상을 제외하고는 모든 특징을 가진 걸 찾았어. 검은색은 매진이었어.

해설 여자는 자신이 원했던 검은색 카메라가 품절이어서 카메라를 사지 않았다고 했다.

어휘 spend(-spent-spent) (시간을) 보내다 look for ~을 찾다 simple 단순한 design 디자인 remote control 리모컨 light 가벼운 feature 특징 except for ~을 제외하고는 sold out 매진된, 다 팔린

17 ③

① W Can I speak to Julia?
   M She's not here at the moment.
② W Please turn off the TV. I can't go to sleep.
   M Why don't you close your bedroom door?
③ W Can you hold the door for me?
   M Sure. I can help you carry some books, too.
④ W How do you go to school?
   M I usually ride my bike to school.

⑤ W What's wrong? You don't look well.
   M I have a headache.

① 여 Julia와 통화할 수 있을까요?
   남 그녀는 지금 여기에 없어요.
② 여 TV를 꺼 줘. 잠을 잘 수가 없어.
   남 네 침실 문을 닫는 게 어떠니?
③ 여 나를 위해 문을 잡아줄 수 있니?
   남 물론이야. 책 옮기는 것도 도와줄게.
④ 여 넌 어떻게 등교하니?
   남 난 보통 학교에 자전거를 타고 가.
⑤ 여 무슨 일 있어? 너 안 좋아 보여.
   남 난 머리가 아파.

해설 문을 잡아 달라고 부탁하고 이에 답하는 내용의 대화가 가장 적절하다.

어휘 speak to ~와 말하다 at the moment 바로 지금 turn off ~을 끄다 go to sleep 잠을 자다 hold 잡다 carry 나르다 ride one's bike 자전거를 타다 have a headache 머리가 아프다

18 ③

W Attention, students. This is an announcement about the after-school English class. The class will be held in the English Zone on the third floor from 4 to 5 p.m. every Wednesday. The class and textbook are free. If you want to take the class, tell your homeroom teacher by this Friday. Visit our school homepage for more information.

여 주목하세요, 학생 여러분. 방과 후 영어 수업에 대한 안내입니다. 수업은 3층에 있는 English Zone에서 매주 수요일 오후 4시부터 5시까지 열릴 것입니다. 수업과 교과서는 무료입니다. 수업을 듣고 싶으면 이번 주 금요일까지 담임 선생님께 말씀드리세요. 더 많은 정보를 보려면 우리 학교 홈페이지를 방문하세요.

해설 여자는 방과 후 영어 수업의 수강 인원에 대해서는 언급하지 않았다.

어휘 attention 주의, 주목 announcement 발표, 알림 after-school 방과 후의 be held 열리다, 개최되다 textbook 교과서 free 무료의 homeroom teacher 담임 선생님 information 정보

19 ④

W Hi. What would you like to order?
M Hi. I'd like to get a double cheeseburger and a large coke.
W It will take about seven minutes for a double cheeseburger. Is that okay with you?
M It's okay. (*Pause*) Oh, wait. I'll have orange juice instead of a coke.
W Okay. Would you like to order anything else?
M No, that's it. Thank you.

여 안녕하세요. 무엇을 주문하시겠어요?
남 안녕하세요. 더블 치즈버거와 콜라 큰 것 주세요.

여 더블 치즈버거는 7분 정도 걸릴 거예요. 괜찮으세요?

남 괜찮아요. (잠시 후) 아, 잠깐만요. 콜라 대신에 오렌지 주스로 할게요.

여 알겠습니다. 다른 것을 더 주문하시겠어요?

남 아니요, 그게 다예요. 고맙습니다.

해설 여자가 다른 것을 더 주문할 것인지 물었으므로 이에 대한 긍정 또는 부정의 응답이 와야 한다.

① 제가 주문한 음식이 늦네요.

② 좋은 하루 보내세요.

③ 여기 제 신용 카드요.

⑤ 저는 저녁 먹을 시간이 없어요.

어휘 double 두 배의   cheeseburger 치즈버거   coke 콜라   instead of ~ 대신에   order 주문한 음식   else 또 다른, 그 밖의   credit card 신용 카드

20 ⑤

M What do you usually do in your free time?

W I usually watch movies. I love watching movies.

M What kinds of movies do you like?

W I like almost all kinds of movies. What about you?

M I'm not really into movies like you. I only like animated movies.

W Oh, then did you watch the recent animated film with the cat as the main character?

M Not yet. Do you want to watch it with me?

남 너는 여가 시간에 보통 뭘 하니?

여 나는 보통 영화를 봐. 난 영화 보는 걸 아주 좋아해.

남 어떤 종류의 영화를 좋아하니?

여 나는 거의 모든 종류의 영화를 좋아해. 너는?

남 나는 너처럼 영화를 그렇게 좋아하지는 않아. 난 애니메이션만 좋아해.

여 오, 그럼 고양이가 주인공으로 나오는 최신 애니메이션 봤니?

남 아직 못 봤어. 나랑 같이 볼래?

해설 여자가 최근 개봉한 애니메이션을 봤는지 물었으므로 이에 대한 긍정 또는 부정의 응답이 와야 한다.

① 응. 나는 고양이를 길러.

② 난 애니메이션을 좋아하지 않아.

③ 너는 영화감독이 되고 싶니?

④ 나는 보통 주말마다 영화를 봐.

어휘 usually 보통, 대개   free time 여가 시간   almost 거의   be into ~에 관심이 많다, ~을 좋아하다   like ~처럼   animated movie(film) 애니메이션   recent 최근의   main character 주인공

01 ⑤	02 ④	03 ①	04 ②	05 ②
06 ⑤	07 ④	08 ②	09 ③	10 ⑤
11 ⑤	12 ④	13 ④	14 ①	15 ③
16 ③	17 ③	18 ⑤	19 ②	20 ⑤

01 ⑤

M It's time for a weather update. People in Seoul are waking up to -4°C while Gangneung feels twice as cold as Seoul. The southern areas are a bit warmer, so the temperatures for Busan and Ulsan are average for this time of year. However, clouds are coming up from the south, so it's raining in Busan now, and those thick clouds are spread all over Ulsan, too. Tomorrow, those clouds will stay, and it will rain in Busan and Ulsan.

남 최신 날씨 정보를 전해 드리는 시간입니다. 강릉은 서울보다 두 배 추운 가운데 서울 시민들은 영하 4도로 아침을 시작하고 있습니다. 남부 지방은 조금 더 따뜻하여, 부산과 울산은 평년 기온을 보이고 있습니다. 하지만, 남쪽에서 구름이 몰려오고 있어, 현재 부산은 비가 내리고 있으며, 울산 전역에도 짙은 구름이 뒤덮고 있습니다. 내일은 이 구름들이 계속 머무를 것이며, 부산과 울산에 비가 오겠습니다.

[해설] 오늘 울산은 구름이 잔뜩 끼었다고 했다.

[어휘] weather update 최신 날씨 정보 twice 두 배로 southern 남쪽의 area 지역 a bit 조금 temperature 기온 average 평균의 south 남쪽 thick cloud 무겁게 드리운 구름 spread(-spread-spread) 펼치다 all over 곳곳에 stay 머무르다

02 ④

M Emma, can you help me with this?
W Oh, you're making custom stickers. What can I do for you?
M I chose this square design but don't know what to do next.
W Hmm... how about drawing a circle inside the square?
M Good idea. And I want to put a smile icon on the sticker.
W Then put it in the middle of the circle.
M Okay. Don't you think it's too simple?
W Why don't you put your name below the smile?
M Oh, it looks good. Thank you for your help.

남 Emma, 이것 좀 도와줄래?
여 오, 너 주문 제작 스티커를 만들고 있구나. 어떻게 도와줄까?
남 이 정사각형 디자인은 골랐는데 그 다음에 뭘 해야 할지 모르겠어.

여 음… 정사각형 안에 원을 그리는 게 어때?
남 좋은 생각이야. 그리고 난 스티커에 스마일 아이콘을 넣고 싶어.
여 그럼 원의 가운데에 넣어 봐.
남 그래. 디자인이 너무 단순하다고 생각하지 않니?
여 스마일 아래에 네 이름을 넣는 게 어때?
남 오. 괜찮아 보이네. 도와줘서 고마워.

[해설] 남자는 정사각형 안에 원을 그린 후 원 안에 스마일 그림을 넣고, 그 아래에 자신의 이름을 넣어 스티커를 완성했다.

[어휘] custom 주문 제작한 sticker 스티커 choose(-chose -chosen) 선택하다, 고르다 square 정사각형 circle 원 icon 아이콘 middle 가운데 simple 단순한 below ~ 아래에

03 ①

M Cindy, you must be exhausted.
W Yes, Dad. I'm so glad the school president election is finally over.
M Good job during the election campaign.
W Thanks, Dad.
M So what was the result?
W I thought I was going to lose because Eric gave a great speech.
M Oh, really?
W But do you know what? I won in the end!
M That's my girl! Congratulations, student president!

남 Cindy, 너 아주 피곤하겠구나.
여 네, 아빠. 드디어 전교 회장 선거가 끝나서 정말 좋아요.
남 선거 운동 하느라 수고했어.
여 고마워요, 아빠.
남 그래서 결과는 어떻게 되었니?
여 Eric이 연설을 잘해서 저는 제가 질 거라고 생각했어요.
남 오, 정말이니?
여 그런데 그거 아세요? 결국엔 제가 이겼어요!
남 역시 내 딸이야! 축하한다, 학생회장!

[해설] 딸이 학생회장으로 당선된 것을 듣고 칭찬과 축하를 해 준 것으로 보아, 남자는 딸이 자랑스러울 것이다.

[어휘] exhausted 기진맥진한, 진이 빠진 president 회장 election 선거 be over 끝나다 finally 마침내 campaign 캠페인, 운동 result 결과 lose 지다 give a speech 연설을 하다 in the end 마침내, 결국

04 ②

M The webtoon fair was really disappointing.
W Why? You waited for it for so long.
M I thought I could try out some new software to draw webtoons, but I couldn't.
W Didn't you say there was a booth for it?
M Yes, but it was too crowded. I gave up waiting for my turn.
W What about your favorite writer's lecture?
M Don't even ask. It was canceled.
W Oh, no.

M So there was nothing to do but take a couple of pictures.

남 웹툰 박람회는 정말 실망스러웠어.
여 왜? 너 오랫동안 기다렸잖아.
남 나는 웹툰을 그리는 새로운 소프트웨어를 시험해 볼 수 있을 거라 생각했는데, 그러지 못했어.
여 그걸 위한 부스가 있었다고 하지 않았어?
남 응, 그런데 너무 붐볐어. 내 순서를 기다리는 걸 포기했지.
여 네가 제일 좋아하는 작가의 강의는 어땠어?
남 묻지도 마. 취소되었어.
여 오, 저런.
남 그래서 사진 몇 장 찍는 것 말고는 할 게 없었어.

해설 남자는 박람회에서 자신이 한 일이라고는 사진 몇 장을 찍은 것밖에 없다고 했다.

어휘 fair 박람회 disappointing 실망스러운 wait for ~을 기다리다 try out ~을 시험해 보다 booth (전시장 등의) 부스 crowded 붐비는, 혼잡한 give up ~ing ~하는 것을 포기하다 turn 차례, 순서 lecture 강의 cancel 취소하다 but ~ 외에 a couple of 몇 개의, 두서너 개의

05 ②

M Julia, a birthday present has arrived.
W Wow, it's from Grandpa! What is it?
M I don't know. It might be a camera. He loves taking pictures.
W I don't think so. The box is too big for a camera. Maybe a violin? He knows I want to learn it.
M Come on. Open it up!
W Okay. (Pause) Wow! This is just what I wanted! Look at this color.
M That's pretty. You'll look good in that red coat. Try it on.
W It suits me perfectly. I'm going to call Grandpa right now.

남 Julia, 생일 선물이 도착했구나.
여 와, 할아버지로부터 온 거네요! 뭐예요?
남 몰라. 카메라일 수도 있어. 할아버지가 사진 찍는 걸 아주 좋아하시잖니.
여 아닌 것 같아요. 카메라치고는 상자가 너무 커요. 아마 바이올린일까요? 할아버지는 제가 바이올린을 배우고 싶어 하는 걸 아시잖아요.
남 자, 어서. 열어 봐!
여 네. (잠시 후) 왜! 이건 딱 제가 원했던 거예요! 이 색깔 좀 보세요.
남 예쁘구나. 너에게 그 빨간 코트가 잘 어울릴 거야. 입어 보렴.
여 저한테 꼭 맞아요. 지금 바로 할아버지께 전화해야겠어요.

해설 빨간 코트가 여자에게 잘 어울릴 것이라는 남자의 말과 코트가 자신에게 꼭 맞는다는 여자의 말을 통해, 여자가 옷을 선물로 받았음을 알 수 있다.

어휘 present 선물 arrive 도착하다 maybe 아마도 try on 입어 보다 suit 어울리다, 잘 맞다 perfectly 완벽히

06 ⑤

W Honey, we should plan our vacation.
M Okay. Would you like to go to Jeju-do?
W Again? We went there last year. I want to travel abroad.
M Then how about Japan? You like hot springs.
W Good idea. I'll check on plane tickets tomorrow. I hope there are good seats left.
M I'll ask my Japanese friend for traveling tips. What else do you want me to do?
W If you aren't busy tomorrow, can you book a rental car?

여 여보, 우리 휴가를 계획해야 해요.
남 그래요. 제주도에 갈까요?
여 또요? 거기 작년에도 갔잖아요. 저는 해외여행을 가고 싶어요.
남 그럼 일본은 어때요? 당신 온천을 좋아하잖아요.
여 좋은 생각이에요. 내일 비행기 표를 확인해 볼게요. 좋은 좌석이 남아 있으면 좋겠네요.
남 내가 일본인 친구한테 여행 정보를 물어볼게요. 내가 했으면 하는 것이 또 있어요?
여 당신이 내일 바쁘지 않으면, 렌터카를 예약해 줄 수 있어요?

해설 여자는 남자에게 내일 바쁘지 않으면 렌터카를 예약해 줄 수 있는지 물었다.

어휘 plan 계획하다 vacation 휴가 travel 여행하다 abroad 해외로 hot spring 온천 seat 좌석 left 남아 있는 (leave의 과거분사) book 예약하다 rental car 렌터카

07 ④

W Excuse me. Is this an erasable pen?
M No, that's just a regular ballpoint pen. These ones over here are erasable.
W Oh, thank you. And do you have paper clips?
M Yes, we do.
W How much is this box of paper clips?
M A box of paper clips is $4.
W Give me two boxes, please. I'd like to buy a file folder, too.
M We have many kinds over there. Follow me, please.

여 저기요. 이게 지워지는 펜인가요?
남 아니요. 그건 그냥 일반 볼펜입니다. 이쪽에 있는 이것들이 지워지는 거예요.
여 오, 고맙습니다. 그리고 종이 클립 있나요?
남 네, 있습니다.
여 이 종이 클립 한 상자에 얼마예요?
남 종이 클립 한 상자는 4달러입니다.
여 두 상자 주세요. 파일 폴더도 사고 싶어요.
남 저쪽에 많은 종류가 있습니다. 저를 따라오세요.

해설 여자가 지워지는 펜, 종이 클립, 파일 폴더를 구매하고 있으므로 문구점에서 이루어지는 대화이다.

어휘 erasable 지울 수 있는 regular 일반적인, 보통의 ballpoint pen 볼펜 paper clip 종이 클립 file folder 파일 폴더, 서류철 follow 따라오다

08 ②

M Excuse me, ma'am. Is this your car?

W Yes, it is. Is there a problem?

M You are not allowed to park here. Didn't you see the sign?

W Oh, I'm sorry. But I have to pick up something at the supermarket. It won't take long.

M If you don't move your car now, I'll have to give you a parking ticket.

W Okay. Where can I park?

M There's a public parking lot across the street.

W I'll move my car now.

남 실례합니다. 부인. 이것이 부인의 차인가요?

여 네, 그렇습니다. 무슨 문제가 있나요?

남 이곳에 주차를 하시면 안 됩니다. 표지판 못 보셨나요?

여 아, 죄송합니다. 그런데 제가 슈퍼마켓에서 뭐 좀 사 와야 해서요. 오래 걸리지는 않을 거예요.

남 지금 차를 빼지 않으시면, 주차 위반 딱지를 끊겠습니다.

여 알겠습니다. 어디에 주차하면 되나요?

남 도로 건너편에 공영 주차장이 있습니다.

여 지금 차를 뺄게요.

해설 주차 금지 구역에 주차를 한 시민과 주차 단속을 하는 경찰관 사이의 대화이다.

어휘 be allowed to ~하는 것이 허용되다   park 주차하다
sign 표지판   parking ticket 주차 위반 딱지   public 공공의
parking lot 주차장   across ~의 맞은편에   street 길

09 ③

W Peter, let's go to the fireworks festival. I've been looking forward to it.

M Good. When is it?

W It's on Saturday, October 3. It'll be at Riverside Park.

M Is there an admission fee?

W No, it's free. But we need to pay for parking. It costs $5 per hour.

M There is going to be a lot of traffic. Wouldn't taking the subway be better?

W The subway will be really crowded, and the subway station is not close to the park. I think we'd better pay for parking.

M Okay.

여 Peter, 우리 불꽃 축제 가자. 나 그걸 기대하고 있었거든.

남 좋아. 언제야?

여 10월 3일 토요일이야. Riverside Park에서 해.

남 입장료가 있어?

여 아니, 무료야. 그런데 주차비는 내야 해. 한 시간에 5달러야.

남 교통량이 많을 거야. 지하철을 타는 게 낫지 않을까?

여 지하철도 무척 붐빌 거고, 지하철역이 공원에서 가깝지 않아. 차라리 주차비를 내는 게 나을 거야.

남 알았어.

해설 여자는 불꽃 축제의 기념품에 대해서는 언급하지 않았다.

어휘 fireworks 불꽃놀이   festival 축제   look forward to
~을 기대하다   admission fee 입장료   pay for ~을 지불하다
parking 주차   cost (비용이) 들다   per ~당   traffic 교통(량)
crowded 붐비는, 혼잡한   had better ~하는 것이 좋겠다

10 ⑤

W Hey, Jake. What are you doing?

M I'm reading an article on global warming and hamburgers.

W Global warming and hamburgers? I don't get it.

M Listen. To make hamburgers, we need beef, don't we?

W Of course.

M To get beef, we raise cows. To raise cows, we destroy forests to make fields for them.

W Okay. Now I understand.

M And cows also create lots of greenhouse gases.

W Now I got it. The more hamburgers we eat, the warmer the Earth gets.

여 얘, Jake. 뭐 하고 있어?

남 지구 온난화와 햄버거에 관한 기사를 읽고 있어.

여 지구 온난화와 햄버거? 무슨 말인지 모르겠어.

남 들어 봐. 햄버거를 만들려면 소고기가 필요해, 그렇지 않니?

여 물론이지.

남 소고기를 얻기 위해 우리는 소를 키워. 소를 키우려면 소를 위한 들판을 만들기 위해 우리는 숲을 파괴하지.

여 그렇지. 이제 이해가 되네.

남 소들은 온실가스도 많이 만들어 내.

여 이제 알겠어. 우리가 햄버거를 더 먹을수록, 지구는 더 따뜻해지는구나.

해설 남자는 햄버거를 많이 먹을수록 지구 온난화가 더욱 유발된다는 내용의 기사를 읽고 있다.

어휘 article (신문·잡지의) 글, 기사   global warming 지구
온난화   beef 소고기   raise 기르다   destroy 파괴하다
forest 숲, 삼림   field 들판   create 만들어 내다   lots of 많은
greenhouse gas 온실가스   Earth 지구

11 ⑤

M The Oakwood Art Center wants to inform you about its art classes for young children. Children who are four years old or older can sign up for a class. Classes are from June 1 to July 31. Classes for those who are four or five years old start at four o'clock. Classes for those who are six years old or older start at five o'clock. Each class is 50 minutes long. You can sign up at the office.

남 Oakwood Art Center는 여러분께 어린이들을 위한 미술 강좌에 대해 안내해 드리겠습니다. 4세 이상의 어린이들은 강좌를 등록할 수 있습니다. 강좌는 6월 1일부터 7월 30일까지입니다. 4세나 5세 어린이들을 위한 수업은 4시에 시작합니다. 6세 이상 어린이들을 위한 수업은 5시에 시작합니다. 각 수업은 50분씩입니다. 사무실에서 등록하실 수 있습니다.

사무실에서 등록할 수 있다고 했다.

inform 알리다   sign up for ~을 등록하다   each 각각의   office 사무실

12 ④

M Miranda, is that you? I'm glad to see you again!
W Wow, Homin! Long time, no see. It's been about five years, right?
M Yes. Time really flies. What brings you here to Korea?
W Do you remember my cousin Sarah?
M How can I forget her? We used to play at your grandma's house together.
W Right. She's getting married soon, so I'm going to attend her wedding. Her husband is Korean.
M Wow! Please say congratulations to her.
W Okay, I will.

남 Miranda, 너 맞아? 널 다시 보게 되다니 기쁘다!
여 와, 호민아! 오랜만이야. 5년 만이지, 그렇지?
남 응. 시간 정말 빠르다. 한국엔 무슨 일로 온 거야?
여 내 사촌 Sarah 기억해?
남 내가 그녀를 어떻게 잊겠어? 우리 같이 너희 할머니 댁에서 놀았잖아.
여 맞아. 그녀가 곧 결혼을 하거든. 그래서 난 그녀의 결혼식에 참석할 거야. 그녀의 남편이 한국 사람이거든.
남 와! 그녀에게 축하한다고 전해 줘.
여 응, 그렇게.

여자는 한국인 남자와 결혼하는 사촌의 결혼식에 참석하기 위해 한국에 왔다고 했다.

cousin 사촌   forget 잊다   used to ~하곤 했다   get married 결혼하다   attend 참석하다   wedding 결혼(식)   husband 남편   congratulations 축하 인사, 축하의 말

13 ④

M Hello. One adult and three children, please.
W It's $10 for an adult and $5 for a child aged four years or over. How old are your children?
M Two of them are eight years old, and the other is two years old.
W Children under four years old get in for free. So you only need to pay for two children.
M Okay. So $10 for me and $10 for two children, right?
W That's correct. Do you have a membership card? You can get a 10% discount with it.
M No, I don't have one. Here's my credit card.

남 안녕하세요. 어른 한 명과 아이 셋이요.
여 어른은 10달러이고 네 살이거나 그 이상 어린이는 5달러입니다. 자녀분들이 몇 살인가요?
남 두 명은 여덟 살이고, 한 명은 두 살이에요.
여 네 살 미만의 어린이들은 무료로 입장합니다. 그러니 아이 두 명 것만 내시면 됩니다.

남 네. 그럼 제 것 10달러와 아이 두 명 10달러, 맞죠?
여 맞습니다. 회원 카드를 가지고 계신가요? 그것으로 10퍼센트 할인을 받으실 수 있어요.
남 아니요, 없어요. 여기 제 신용 카드 드릴게요.

아이 셋 중 한 명은 두 살이라서 입장료가 무료이다. 어른 한 명에 10달러와 아이 두 명에 10달러를 합하여, 남자는 총 20달러를 지불해야 한다.

adult 어른, 성인   child 아이(pl. children)   age 나이가 들다   over ~ 이상   under ~ 미만의   for free 무료로   correct 정확한   membership card 회원 카드   get a discount 할인을 받다   credit card 신용 카드

14 ①

M Hi, Wilma. Where are you going?
W I'm going to the student hall to watch the school musical.
M Oh, is it today?
W Yeah. My best friend Carol is acting in the musical. Why don't you go with me?
M I'm afraid I can't. I'm going to the library to do my science homework.
W Come on. It'll be over at five. That's not that late.
M But the library closes at five, too.
W You can do your homework later.
M The homework is due tomorrow. Enjoy the musical!

남 안녕, Wilma, 너 어디에 가는 중이니?
여 나 학교 뮤지컬을 보러 학생회관에 가는 중이야.
남 아, 그게 오늘이니?
여 응. 내 제일 친한 친구 Carol이 뮤지컬에서 연기를 할 거야. 나랑 같이 가는 게 어때?
남 미안하지만 안 돼. 난 과학 숙제를 하러 도서관에 가는 중이야.
여 에이, 가자. 5시에 끝날 거야. 그렇게 늦지 않잖아.
남 하지만 도서관도 5시에 문을 닫는 걸.
여 숙제는 나중에 하면 되잖아.
남 숙제가 내일까지라서. 뮤지컬 재미있게 봐!

남자는 숙제를 하러 도서관에 간다고 했다.

student hall 학생회관   act (연극·영화에서) 연기하다   do one's homework 숙제를 하다   be over 끝나다   later 나중에   due ~하기로 되어 있는(예정된)

15 ③

W Ryan, are you doing your homework?
M Yes, Mom. The history homework is driving me crazy. I had to find a lot of information on the Internet.
W You have already done a lot. Do you need some help?
M It's okay. I can finish it on my own. By the way, where are you going?
W To the bakery. There's no bread left.
M Can you buy me some chocolate on your way home? I need something sweet to keep

concentrating.

W Of course.

여 Ryan, 숙제하고 있니?

남 네, 엄마. 저 역사 숙제 때문에 미치겠어요. 인터넷에서 많은 자료를 찾아야 했어요.

여 이미 많이 했네. 도움이 필요하니?

남 괜찮아요. 저 혼자 끝낼 수 있어요. 그런데, 어디 가세요?

여 제과점에. 남아 있는 빵이 없어서.

남 집에 오시는 길에 초콜릿 좀 사다 주실 수 있어요? 계속 집중하려면 단것이 필요해요.

여 물론이지.

[해설] 남자는 여자에게 제과점에서 집에 오는 길에 초콜릿을 사다 달라고 부탁했다.

[어휘] do one's homework 숙제하다   history 역사   drive ~ crazy ~을 미치게 하다   a lot of 많은   information 정보   on one's own 혼자, 혼자 힘으로   by the way 그런데   bakery 제과점   left 남아 있는(leave의 과거분사)   on one's way home 집에 오는 길에   keep ~ing 계속해서 ~하다   concentrate 집중하다

16   ③

M Hey, are you a student at this school?

W Oh, yes. I left a book in my classroom, so I want to get it.

M You cannot enter the school building right now.

W Why not? Students can enter the school anytime during vacation.

M Workers are remodeling the classrooms. There is lots of construction going on.

W Oh, I think I heard about that from my homeroom teacher. When will the construction be finished?

M Probably in a week. Why don't you come again then?

W Okay, I will. Thank you.

남 얘야, 이 학교 학생이니?

여 아, 네. 교실에 책을 두고 와서. 가지러 가려고요.

남 지금 당장은 학교 건물에 들어갈 수 없단다.

여 왜 안 돼요? 학생들은 방학 중에도 언제든지 학교에 들어갈 수 있잖아요.

남 인부들이 교실을 개조하고 있어. 공사가 한창 진행 중이란다.

여 아, 담임 선생님께 그것에 대해서 들은 것 같아요. 공사는 언제 끝나요?

남 아마 일주일 후에. 그때 다시 오는 게 어떻겠니?

여 네. 그럴게요. 고맙습니다.

[해설] 남자는 여자에게 교실이 공사 중이라서 학교 건물에 들어갈 수 없다고 했다.

[어휘] leave(-left-left) 두고 오다   enter 들어가다   building 건물   anytime 언제든지   during ~ 동안   vacation 방학   remodel 개조하다   construction 공사   homeroom teacher 담임 선생님   probably 아마   in ~ 후에

17   ③

M The Korea Heritage Group would like to invite you on a trip to Dokdo. Dokdo is a Korean island located in the East Sea. You can explore its beautiful nature. There will also be a forum during the trip, so you can learn about the history of Dokdo. The trip is scheduled from May 3 to 6. Anyone can participate if you are an international student staying in Korea. Sign up at KoreaHG.com and don't miss this great opportunity.

남 Korea Heritage Group이 독도 여행에 여러분을 초대합니다. 독도는 동해에 위치한 한국의 섬입니다. 여러분은 독도의 아름다운 자연을 탐험할 수 있습니다. 또한 여행 중에 포럼이 있어서, 독도의 역사에 대해 배우실 수 있습니다. 여행은 5월 3일부터 6일까지로 일정이 잡혀 있습니다. 한국에서 지내고 있는 외국 유학생이라면 누구든지 참여할 수 있습니다. KoreaHG.com에서 신청하시고 이 대단한 기회를 놓치지 마세요.

[해설] 남자는 여행의 참가비는 언급하지 않았다.

[어휘] heritage (국가·사회의) 유산   invite 초대하다   trip 여행   island 섬   be located in ~에 위치하다   East Sea 동해   explore 탐험하다   nature 자연   history 역사   forum 포럼, 토론회   schedule 일정을 잡다   participate 참여하다   international 국제적인   sign up 신청하다   opportunity 기회

18   ⑤

① **W** What kind of pet would you like to have?
   M I want to have a hamster.
② **W** Can I bring this juice inside the theater?
   M No. You can only bring in water.
③ **W** Let's eat something after the show.
   M Good idea. I know a good restaurant near here.
④ **W** Look at the baby monkey over there.
   M It's so small and cute.
⑤ **W** Excuse me. Please do not feed the animals.
   M I'm sorry. I won't do it again.

① **여** 넌 어떤 종류의 애완동물을 키우고 싶니?
   남 난 햄스터를 키우고 싶어.
② **여** 극장 안에 이 주스를 가지고 가도 되나요?
   남 아니요. 물만 가지고 가실 수 있어요.
③ **여** 공연 후에 뭐가 먹자.
   남 좋은 생각이야. 내가 이 근처에 괜찮은 식당을 알고 있어.
④ **여** 저쪽에 있는 새끼 원숭이 좀 봐.
   남 정말 작고 귀엽다.
⑤ **여** 실례합니다. 동물들에게 먹이를 주지 마세요.
   남 죄송합니다. 다시는 하지 않을게요.

[해설] 동물들에게 먹이를 주지 말라는 내용의 대화가 가장 적절하다.

[어휘] pet 애완동물   inside ~의 안에   theater 극장   bring in 들여오다   feed 먹이를 주다

19 ②

W Dad, do you know where my sleeping bag is?
M It's under your bed. Are you packing for your backpacking trip?
W Yes, I am. I'm excited but nervous at the same time.
M No wonder. I'm worried, too.
W Don't worry, Dad. I'll call you every day.
M Okay. Is there anything I can help you with?
W Can you help me pack? I don't know what I need to pack for the trip.
M Why don't you make a list first?

여 아빠, 제 침낭이 어디에 있는지 아세요?
남 네 침대 밑에 있어. 배낭여행 짐 싸는 거야?
여 네. 신나기도 하지만 동시에 긴장이 되기도 해요.
남 당연히 그렇겠지. 나도 걱정이 된단다.
여 걱정하지 마세요, 아빠. 매일 전화할게요.
남 그래. 내가 뭐 도와줄 거라도 있니?
여 짐 싸는 것 좀 도와주실래요? 여행을 위해 뭘 싸야 할지 모르겠어요.
남 우선 목록을 작성하는 게 어떠니?

해설 여자가 여행에 가져갈 짐으로 무엇을 싸야 할지 모르겠다고 했으므로 우선 목록을 작성해 보라고 제안하는 응답이 가장 적절하다.
① 즐거운 배낭여행 하렴!
③ 나 혼자 여행하는 것이 처음이야.
④ 그 모든 것을 어디에서 살 거니?
⑤ 배낭여행은 재미있지만, 힘들 수도 있어.

어휘 sleeping bag 침낭   pack (짐을) 싸다   backpacking trip 배낭여행   nervous 긴장한   at the same time 동시에   no wonder 당연하다. 그도 그럴 것이   make a list 목록을 작성하다   by oneself 혼자서   tough 힘든, 어려운

20 ⑤

M Have you seen the movie *New Road*?
W I haven't been to the theater for a couple of months. I'm so busy with my work.
M That's too bad. Sometimes you need to take a break.
W I know. Anyway, is that a good movie?
M Oh, yes. It's Charlie Kim's new movie.
W Really? I have seen all of his previous movies.
M Then I bet you'll like this one very much. I would say it's one of the best in movie history.
W What makes you say that?
M It has a touching story, great acting, and stunning effects.

남 〈New Road〉라는 영화 봤니?
여 나는 몇 달 동안 극장에 못 갔어. 일 때문에 너무 바빠.
남 그것 참 안됐다. 가끔은 좀 쉬어야지.
여 알고 있어. 그건 그렇고, 그거 괜찮은 영화니?
남 아, 응. Charlie Kim의 새 영화야.
여 정말? 나 그의 이전 영화는 전부 봤어.
남 그럼 넌 틀림없이 이 영화도 무척 좋아할 거야. 그건 영화 역사상 최고의 영화 중 하나야.

여 그렇게 말하는 이유가 뭐야?
남 감동적인 이야기, 훌륭한 연기, 그리고 굉장히 멋진 효과를 갖춘 영화거든.

해설 여자가 왜 그 영화를 최고라고 평가하는지 물었으므로 해당 영화의 좋은 요소들을 설명하는 응답이 가장 적절하다.
① 그는 영화 도중에 계속 이야기했어.
② 나는 그 영화 속 배우들이 마음에 안 들어.
③ 극장에서 영화를 보는 게 나아.
④ Charlie가 나한테 그가 가장 좋아하는 영화를 추천해 줬어.

어휘 a couple of 몇 개의, 두서너 개의   be busy with ~로 바쁘다   sometimes 가끔   take a break 잠시 휴식을 취하다   anyway 그건 그렇고   previous 이전의   bet 틀림없다. 분명하다   recommend 추천하다   touching 감동적인   stunning 굉장히 멋진   effect 효과

01 ②	02 ③	03 ③	04 ①	05 ④
06 ③	07 ④	08 ④	09 ④	10 ⑤
11 ④	12 ④	13 ③	14 ②	15 ⑤
16 ①	17 ④	18 ④	19 ③	20 ④

01 ②

W This week, the weather is going to be unpleasant. This evening, a few thunderstorms will form, and by tomorrow at noon, a line of showers and thunderstorms will approach the metropolitan areas in Southern Florida. If you're living in the northern parts of Florida, they will reach you on Friday morning. But by Saturday, the thunderstorms will pass through the area, and it will be sunny during the weekend.

남 이번 주는 날씨로 인한 불편함이 있겠습니다. 오늘 저녁에 뇌우가 형성될 것이며 내일 정오까지 플로리다 남부 대도시권에 소나기와 뇌우가 접근할 것입니다. 플로리다 북부에 살고 계시다면, 소나기와 뇌우는 금요일 오전에 도달하겠습니다. 그러나 토요일까지는 뇌우가 그 지역을 빠져나갈 것이며 주말 동안에는 맑겠습니다.

해설 토요일까지 뇌우가 지나가고 주말 동안에는 맑을 것이라고 했다.

어휘 unpleasant 불쾌한, 불편한   thunderstorm 뇌우   form 형성되다   noon 정오   shower 소나기   approach 접근하다, 다가오다   metropolitan area 대도시권   southern 남쪽의   northern 북쪽의   reach 이르다, 도달하다   pass through ~을 빠져나가다

02 ③

W Welcome to Sweet Home Furniture. May I help you?
M Yes, please. I'm looking for a dining table.
W We have many different kinds of tables. What kind of table do you have in mind?
M I'd like a wooden table for two people.
W Okay. This dark one is the most popular one in our shop. It has a traditional look.
M Actually, I like the bright one over there.
W Oh, that one is popular with young married couples. We have round and square ones in that color.
M I'll take a round one.

여 Sweet Home Furniture에 오신 것을 환영합니다. 도와드릴까요?
남 네. 저는 식탁을 찾고 있어요.
여 저희는 많고 다양한 종류의 식탁을 가지고 있어요. 어떤 종류의 식탁을 생각하고 계세요?
남 2인용의 나무로 된 식탁을 원해요.
여 알겠습니다. 이 어두운 색의 식탁이 저희 가게에서 가장 인기가 있답니다. 고전적인 스타일이죠.
남 사실, 저는 저쪽에 있는 밝은 색의 식탁이 좋아요.
여 오, 저것은 젊은 부부들에게 인기가 있답니다. 저 색상으로는 둥근 것과 사각형이 있어요.
남 둥근 것으로 할게요.

해설 남자는 나무로 만들어진 밝은 색의 둥근 식탁을 사겠다고 했다.

어휘 furniture 가구   look for ~을 찾다   dining table 식탁   have ~ in mind ~을 염두에 두다[생각하다]   wooden 나무로 된   dark 짙은, 어두운   popular 인기 있는   traditional 전통적인, 고풍의   look 스타일   actually 사실은   bright 밝은   married couple 부부   round 둥근   square 사각형의

03 ③

M Do you have only one day to stay in Barcelona? One day seems short because Barcelona is a city you could easily spend several days in. But don't worry. From Barcelona's most favorite landmark to a good place for local food, I will recommend the best things you can do in a day. With this experienced local guide, you can make the most of your 24 hours in Barcelona.

남 바르셀로나에서 머물 시간이 하루뿐인가요? 바르셀로나는 당신이 며칠도 거뜬히 머무를 만한 도시이기 때문에 하루는 짧은 것 같습니다. 하지만 걱정하지 마세요. 바르셀로나에서 가장 유명한 명소부터 현지 음식을 먹을 수 있는 좋은 장소까지, 당신이 하루에 할 수 있는 최고의 것들을 제가 추천해 드리겠습니다. 이 경험 많은 현지 가이드와 함께 바르셀로나에서 당신의 24시간을 최대한 활용하세요.

해설 남자는 자신을 경험이 풍부한 현지 가이드라고 자칭하며, 바르셀로나를 관광할 사람들을 대상으로 말하고 있다.

어휘 seem ~인 것 같다   easily 쉽게   several day 며칠   landmark 랜드마크, 상징물   local 현지의   recommend 추천하다   experienced 경험 있는, 능숙한   guide 가이드, 안내원   make the most of ~을 최대한 활용하다

04 ①

M How was your volunteer work yesterday?
W You know I like children. I visited a childcare center near my house. I had a great time.
M What did you do there?
W I read some books to children and played with them on the playground. What about you?
M I painted a wall at an elementary school.
W That sounds interesting. Do you have pictures of it?
M Yes. Look at these pictures before and after we painted. It was not easy, but it was really worth it.

남 어제 봉사 활동은 어땠니?
여 넌 내가 어린아이들을 좋아하는 거 알잖아. 난 우리 집 근처에 있는 보육원을 방문했어. 좋은 시간을 보냈지.

남 거기에서 뭘 했니?

여 아이들에게 책을 읽어 주고 놀이터에서 아이들과 함께 놀았어. 너는?

남 나는 초등학교에서 벽을 칠했어.

여 흥미롭다. 사진 있어?

남 응. 우리가 페인트를 칠하기 전과 후 사진들을 봐. 쉽진 않았지만, 정말 보람 있었어.

해설 남자는 어제 초등학교에서 벽화를 그렸다고 했다.

어휘 volunteer work 자원봉사 활동　childcare center 보육원, 탁아소　playground 놀이터, 운동장　paint 페인트를 칠하다　wall 벽　elementary school 초등학교　worth it 그만한 가치가 있는

05 ④

W Hello. I booked a ticket for *The Lion King* at 7:30.

M Okay. Could you show me your ticket?

W Sure. (*Pause*) I can't find my ticket.

M Take your time, ma'am.

W I certainly put the ticket in my pocket. I guess I dropped it somewhere.

M If you bought the ticket online, you can show me the booking confirmation message.

W I erased all my text messages recently.

M Then I'm afraid there's no other way I can help you.

W I can't believe this. I drove all the way here for two hours to watch the musical.

여 안녕하세요. 저는 7시 30분에 하는 〈라이온 킹〉 표를 예매했습니다.

남 네. 표를 보여 주시겠어요?

여 네. (잠시 후) 제 표를 찾을 수 없어요.

남 천천히 하세요, 부인.

여 분명히 표를 제 주머니에 넣었거든요. 어딘가에 떨어뜨린 것 같아요.

남 온라인으로 표를 구매하셨으면, 저에게 예약 확인 메시지를 보여 주셔도 됩니다.

여 저는 최근에 문자 메시지를 다 지웠어요.

남 그렇다면 죄송하지만 제가 도와드릴 방법이 없습니다.

여 믿을 수 없어요. 뮤지컬을 보려고 두 시간 동안 운전해서 여기까지 왔거든요.

해설 표를 분실하여 뮤지컬을 못 보게 되었으므로 여자는 좌절감을 느꼈을 것이다.

어휘 book 예약하다　take one's time 천천히 하다, 시간을 들이다　certainly 분명히　pocket 주머니　drop 떨어뜨리다　somewhere 어딘가에　confirmation 확인　text message 문자 메시지　recently 최근에　no ～가 없는　other 다른　way 방법　grateful 감사하는　relieved 안도하는　frustrated 좌절한　satisfied 만족한

06 ③

W Dave, do you have any plans for the weekend?

M I'll go fishing on a boat. There will be perfect weather for fishing.

W That sounds great. Do you often go fishing?

M Yes. I'm really into it. You never know how thrilling it is when you catch fish.

W Actually, I've always wanted to go fishing.

M Have you? You can join me if you want.

W Thank you, but I have plans tomorrow. How about next weekend?

M I wasn't planning to go then, but I can go again if you want to join me.

여 Dave, 주말 동안에 무슨 계획 있니?

남 배를 타고 낚시하러 갈 거야. 낚시하기에 완벽한 날씨일 거야.

여 좋겠다. 낚시하러 자주 가니?

남 응. 난 낚시를 정말 좋아해. 물고기를 잡을 때 얼마나 신이 나는지 너는 모를 거야.

여 사실, 나도 늘 낚시하러 가고 싶었어.

남 그랬어? 네가 원하면 나와 함께해도 좋아.

여 고맙지만, 내일은 내가 계획이 있어. 다음 주말은 어떠니?

남 그땐 갈 계획은 없었지만, 네가 나와 함께하고 싶다면 난 또 가도 돼.

해설 계획한 일은 아니지만 자신과 함께 낚시하러 가고 싶다면 또 갈 수 있다는 남자의 말은 다음 주말에 낚시를 하러 가자는 여자의 제안을 수락한 것이다.

어휘 go fishing 낚시하러 가다　be into ～에 관심이 많다, ～을 좋아하다　thrilling 아주 신나는, 흥분되는　catch 잡다　be planning to ～할 계획이다　again 다시

07 ④

W I don't know what to wear to my friend's wedding.

M How about your brown dress? You look good in that dress.

W It's old. I want to go shopping and get a new one. Do you want to go with me?

M Sure. I'm available this afternoon.

W I'm not. I have plans with my co-workers. What about tomorrow?

M Only in the morning or evening. I have a piano lesson in the afternoon. What about Saturday afternoon?

W That's fine with me. See you on Saturday.

여 내 친구 결혼식에 뭘 입어야 할지 모르겠어.

남 갈색 원피스는 어때? 너는 그 원피스가 잘 어울려.

여 그건 낡았어. 쇼핑 가서 새 옷을 살래. 나랑 같이 갈래?

남 그래. 난 오늘 오후에 시간 돼.

여 난 안 되는데. 내 동료들과 계획이 있어. 내일은 어때?

남 오전이나 저녁에만 돼. 오후에는 피아노 수업이 있거든. 토요일 오후는 어때?

여 난 괜찮아. 토요일에 보자.

해설 남자는 내일 오후에 피아노 수업이 있어서 오전이나 저녁에만 시간이 된다고 했다.

어휘 wedding 결혼(식)　dress 원피스　available 시간이 있는　co-worker 동료

08 ④

W As most of the country is suffering from high levels of fine dust, the South Korean government passed emergency measures to reduce fine dust yesterday. The government has shut down public parking lots during weekdays in Seoul. The government has also banned old diesel cars from all roads. The government advises citizens to put on protective masks and to refrain from outdoor activities.

여 전국 대부분 지역이 높은 수준의 미세 먼지로 고통받고 있는 가운데, 어제 한국 정부는 미세 먼지를 줄이기 위한 비상 대책을 가결했습니다. 정부는 평일 동안 서울의 공공 주차장들을 폐쇄했습니다. 정부는 또한 모든 도로에 노후된 경유 자동차들을 금지시켰습니다. 정부는 시민들에게 보호 마스크를 착용할 것과 실외 활동을 자제할 것을 권고하였습니다.

해설 한국 정부가 미세 먼지를 줄이기 위해 시행한 여러 가지 대책에 대해 말하고 있다.

어휘 most of ~의 대부분   suffer from ~로 고통받다   level 수준   fine dust 미세 먼지   government 정부   pass (법안 등을) 통과시키다, 가결하다   emergency measure 비상 대책   reduce 줄이다   shut down 닫다   public 공공의   parking lot 주차장   weekday 평일   ban 금지하다   advise 권고하다   citizen 시민   protective 보호의   refrain from ~을 삼가다   outdoor activity 야외 활동

09 ④

W Excuse me. Where is Amore Flower Shop?
M It's on the first floor in Miller's Mall.
W Thank you. Did you just buy those roses from there?
M Yes, but I'm afraid it's closed now. I bought these just before it closed.
W Really? Isn't it open every day except Mondays? It's Tuesday.
M That is true, but it's ten past six. The shop closes at six.
W Oh, my. I need to come back tomorrow.
M Visit there after five. You can get a 10% discount from five to six.
W That's good. Thank you for the tip.

여 실례합니다. Amore Flower Shop이 어디에 있나요?
남 Miller's Mall 1층에 있어요.
여 고맙습니다. 그 장미들을 거기에서 사신 거예요?
남 네, 하지만 유감스럽게도 지금은 문을 닫았어요. 제가 이것들을 가게가 닫기 직전에 샀거든요.
여 정말요? 월요일 빼고는 매일 열지 않아요? 오늘 화요일인데요.
남 맞아요, 그런데 지금 6시 10분이에요. 가게는 6시에 문을 닫아요.
여 오, 이런. 내일 다시 와야겠네요.
남 오후 5시 이후에 가 보세요. 5시부터 6시까지는 10퍼센트 할인을 받으실 수 있어요.
여 그거 좋네요. 조언해 주셔서 감사합니다.

해설 두 사람은 꽃의 가격대는 언급하지 않았다.

어휘 on the first floor 1층에   close 문을 닫다   open 문을 연(영업을 하는)   except ~을 제외하고   true 사실은   ten past six 6시 10분   get a discount 할인을 받다   tip 조언

10 ⑤

W This Sunday is the last day of the living design exhibition.
M What kind of exhibition is that?
W We can see trendy home furniture and purchase items at discounted prices.
M Do you want to go there?
W Yes. I'm interested in finding out about the latest furniture trends. And you?
M Hmm... where is it being held?
W At New Street Yard.
M Okay. Let's go and have lunch at Jimmy's Restaurant on the way back home.
W Good idea! I'll reserve tickets on the homepage.

여 이번 주 일요일이 리빙 디자인 전시회의 마지막 날이야.
남 그게 무슨 전시회야?
여 최신 유행의 가정용 가구들을 볼 수 있고 할인가로 물건들을 구입할 수 있어.
남 너 거기에 가고 싶어?
여 응. 난 최신의 가구 동향을 파악하는 데 관심이 있거든. 너는?
남 음… 어디에서 열리는 거야?
여 New Street Yard에서.
남 좋아. 갔다가 집에 돌아오는 길에 Jimmy's Restaurant에서 점심 먹자.
여 좋은 생각이야! 내가 홈페이지에서 입장권을 예약할게.

해설 홈페이지에서 입장권을 예약하겠다는 여자의 말을 통해 입장권은 온라인으로 판매한다는 것을 알 수 있다.

어휘 exhibition 전시회   trendy 최신 유행의   furniture 가구   purchase 구입하다   at a discount price 할인가로   be interested in ~에 관심이 있다   find out about ~을 알게 되다, 파악하다   latest 최근의, 최신의   trend 동향, 추세   be held 열리다, 개최되다   reserve 예약하다

11 ④

M How did you like the food today?
W I loved every single dish. The sweet pumpkin pasta was especially impressive.
M Thank you. Sweet pumpkin pasta is the most popular menu item at my restaurant.
W It was the best pasta I've ever had.
M I'm glad you liked my food.
W I'd like to write about the pasta and your restaurant in my next food column.
M Thank you very much. I'm looking forward to it.

남 오늘 식사 어떠셨어요?
여 모든 요리가 맛있었어요. 단호박 파스타가 특히 인상적이었어요.
남 고맙습니다. 단호박 파스타는 저희 식당에서 가장 인기 있는 요리랍니다.

여 제가 먹어 본 파스타 중에 최고였어요.
남 제 음식이 마음에 드셨다니 기쁩니다.
여 저의 다음 음식 칼럼에서 이 파스타와 당신의 식당에 대해 쓰고 싶어요.
남 정말 고맙습니다. 칼럼 기대하겠습니다.

해설 남자는 자신의 음식을 맛있게 먹어 주어 기쁘다고 했고, 여자는 파스타와 식당에 대해 칼럼을 쓸 것이라고 했으므로, 주방장과 음식 칼럼니스트 사이의 대화이다.

어휘 dish 요리　sweet pumpkin 단호박　especially 특히　impressive 인상적인　popular 인기 있는　column (신문·잡지의) 정기 기고란(칼럼)　look forward to ~을 기대하다

12 ④

M What time does the game start?
W It will start at seven o'clock.
M We don't have much time.
W Shall we take a taxi to the stadium?
M How about taking the subway? The roads will be crowded at this time.
W Let me see. (Pause) There's a subway at 6:20. Will it get us there on time?
M It will take thirty minutes by subway, and we need to walk for five minutes from the station.
W Then we can arrive before the game starts. Let's take that one.

남 경기가 몇 시에 시작하지?
여 7시에 시작해.
남 시간이 별로 없네.
여 경기장까지 택시 탈까?
남 지하철 타는 게 어때? 이 시간에는 도로가 혼잡할 거야.
여 어디 보자. (잠시 후) 6시 20분에 지하철이 있어. 그걸 타면 제 시간에 도착할 수 있을까?
남 지하철로 30분 걸리고, 역에서부터 5분 걸어가야 해.
여 그럼 경기가 시작하기 전에 도착할 수 있어. 그걸 타자.

해설 두 사람은 6시 20분에 지하철을 탈 것이고, 지하철로 30분, 지하철역에서 경기장까지 걸어서 5분 소요된다고 했으므로, 6시 55분에 경기장에 도착할 것이다.

어휘 stadium 경기장　road 도로　crowded 붐비는, 혼잡한　on time 제시간에　station 역　arrive 도착하다

13 ③

W Microplastics are tiny bits of plastic which are five millimeters in size or less. They are made when bigger pieces of plastic break into small pieces, or they are made on purpose for toothpaste, body scrubs, or many other items we use every day. Because of their small sizes, they cannot be collected and flow into the ocean. As a result, they are threatening not only millions of sea animals but also human health.

여 미세 플라스틱은 5밀리미터 이하의 아주 작은 플라스틱 조각입니다. 미세 플라스틱은 더 큰 플라스틱 조각이 부서져서 작은 조

각이 될 때 만들어지거나, 우리가 매일 사용하는 치약, 바디 스크럽, 또는 다른 많은 용품들에 쓰이기 위해 의도적으로 만들어집니다. 미세 플라스틱은 작은 크기 때문에 수집되지 못하고 바다로 흘러듭니다. 결과적으로, 미세 플라스틱은 수백만 마리의 해양 동물들뿐 아니라 인류의 건강을 위협하고 있습니다.

해설 미세 플라스틱은 우리가 사용하는 많은 생활용품에 들어 있다고 했다.

어휘 microplastic 미세 플라스틱　tiny 아주 작은　bit 작은 조각　piece 조각　break 부서지다　on purpose 고의로, 일부러　toothpaste 치약　scrub 문질러 씻기　because of ~ 때문에　collect 수집하다　flow into ~로 흘러들다　ocean 바다　as a result 결과적으로　threaten 위협하다　not only A but also B A뿐 아니라 B도　millions of 수백만의　human 인간, 사람　health 건강

14 ②

(Telephone rings.)
W Nancy Brown. Rainbow Music Center.
M Hello. This is David Jackson. I saw an advertisement that your center is looking for a teacher.
W That's right, Mr. Jackson. Do you have any experience teaching five-year-old children?
M Yes, I do. Indeed, I have worked as a part-time music teacher at a kindergarten. I like kids.
W That's good. Can you visit the center for an interview tomorrow?
M No problem. Just tell me where it is and at what time.
W Please come to our offices at 21 Seymour Street by 10 a.m. and send your résumé by email today.
M Okay. See you tomorrow.

(전화벨이 울린다.)
여 Rainbow Music Center의 Nancy Brown입니다.
남 안녕하세요. 저는 David Jackson입니다. 센터에서 교사를 구한다는 광고를 보았습니다.
여 맞아요, Jackson 씨. 5세 아이들을 가르쳐 본 경험이 있으신가요?
남 네. 사실, 저는 유치원에서 시간제 음악 교사로 일했습니다.
여 잘됐네요. 내일 면접을 보러 센터를 방문하실 수 있나요?
남 문제없습니다. 시간과 장소만 말씀해 주세요.
여 오전 10시까지 Seymore Street 21번지에 있는 저희 사무실로 와 주시고 이력서는 오늘 이메일로 보내 주세요.
남 알겠습니다. 내일 뵙겠습니다.

해설 남자는 음악 교사 구인 광고를 보고 음악 교사 자리에 지원하기 위해 전화했다.

어휘 advertisement 광고　look for ~을 찾다　have experience ~ing ~한 경험이 있다　indeed 사실　part-time 시간제의　kindergarten 유치원　kid 아이　interview 면접　office 사무실　résumé 이력서

15 ⑤

M Tina, wake up! It's time for your swimming lesson.
W Dad, can I skip the lesson today?
M You can't. If you skip today's lesson, you'll want to skip the lesson again.
W I won't. Please let me sleep in. I went to bed at 3 a.m.
M Why? Did you play computer games late?
W No, I didn't.
M Then why? It's vacation, so you weren't doing homework.
W I watched a scary movie during the day, and the scenes replayed over and over in my head.
M I told you it was not a good idea to watch it.

남 Tina, 일어나! 수영 수업 갈 시간이야.
여 아빠, 오늘 수업 빠지면 안 돼요?
남 안 돼. 오늘 수업을 빠지면, 수업을 또 빠지고 싶을 거야.
여 안 그럴 거예요. 조금 더 자게 해 주세요. 새벽 3시에 잤단 말이에요.
남 왜? 늦게까지 컴퓨터 게임했니?
여 아니요.
남 그럼 왜? 방학이라서 숙제도 안 했을 테고.
여 낮에 무서운 영화를 봤는데 머릿속에서 영화 장면이 계속 되풀이되어서요.
남 내가 그걸 보는 건 좋은 생각이 아니라고 말했잖니.

해설 여자는 어제 낮에 본 공포 영화의 장면이 머릿속에서 계속 떠올라서 새벽에 잠들었다고 했다.

어휘 skip 거르다, 빼먹다 sleep in 늦잠을 자다, 더 자다 scary 무서운 day 낮 scene 장면 replay 재생하다 over and over 반복해서, 되풀이하여

16 ①

M Do you have a table for one, please?
W Sure. Are you here for drinks or lunch?
M For lunch.
W I see. Follow me, please. (Pause) Are you okay with this table?
M It's good. Thank you.
W I'll be right back with the menu.
M Excuse me, but would you bring me some water first, please? I'm so thirsty.
W No problem. I'll bring a glass of water along with the menu right away.
M Thank you very much.

남 한 사람 자리 있나요?
여 물론입니다. 음료를 드실 건가요, 아니면 점심 식사인가요?
남 점심 식사요.
여 알겠습니다. 저를 따라오세요. (잠시 후) 이 자리 괜찮으세요?
남 좋아요. 고맙습니다.
여 메뉴판을 가지고 바로 다시 오겠습니다.
남 실례지만, 물부터 가져다주시겠어요? 너무 목이 말라서요.
여 문제없습니다. 지금 바로 메뉴판과 함께 물 한 잔을 가지고 오겠습니다.

남 정말 고맙습니다.

해설 남자는 목이 말라 물을 먼저 가져다 달라고 요청했다.

어휘 drink 음료 follow 따라오다 bring 가져오다 first 먼저, 우선 thirsty 목이 마른 a glass of water 물 한 잔 along with ~와 함께

17 ④

① **M** I'd like to order a T-bone steak, please.
  W How would you like your steak?
② **M** Why do you jog every day?
  W The reason is that I want to be healthier.
③ **M** You look good in your new jacket.
  W Thanks. I just bought it yesterday.
④ **M** Happy anniversary! I hope you like the roses.
  W Oh, red roses are my favorite. Thank you so much.
⑤ **M** Would you like something to drink?
  W I'd like a cup of coffee with milk and one teaspoon of sugar.

① 남 티본스테이크를 주문하겠습니다.
  여 스테이크를 어떻게 해 드릴까요?
② 남 너는 왜 매일 조깅을 하니?
  여 그 이유는 더 건강해지고 싶기 때문이야.
③ 남 너 새 재킷이 잘 어울린다.
  여 고마워. 어제 이걸 샀어.
④ 남 기념일 축하해요! 장미가 마음에 들었으면 좋겠어요.
  여 오, 빨간 장미는 제가 가장 좋아하는 꽃이에요. 정말 고마워요.
⑤ 남 마실 것 좀 드릴까요?
  남 우유와 설탕 한 티스푼을 넣은 커피 한 잔 주세요.

해설 남자가 여자에게 꽃을 건네자 여자가 기뻐하는 상황이다.

어휘 order 주문하다 T-bone steak 티본스테이크('T' 자 모양의 뼈가 붙은 스테이크) jog 조깅하다 reason 이유 anniversary 기념일 a cup of coffee 커피 한 잔 teaspoon 티스푼, 찻숟가락

18 ④

M I'm going to participate in the recycling festival. What about you?
W Recycling festival? What kind of festival is it?
M The festival has exhibitions and a market. You can learn about recycling and buy goods made from recycled items.
W Sounds interesting. What are you going to do at the festival?
M I'll sell handmade bags there. I make bags from old clothes.
W That's cool. I want to go and look around.
M It's going to be held from Saturday to Sunday at Grand Park. See you there.

남 나는 재활용 축제에 참가할 거야. 너는?
여 재활용 축제? 그건 무슨 종류의 축제니?
남 축제에는 전시회와 시장이 열려. 재활용에 대해 배울 수 있고 재활용품으로 만들어진 물건을 살 수 있어.

여 흥미롭네. 너는 축제에서 뭘 할 거야?
남 난 거기에서 수제 가방을 팔 거야. 나는 낡은 옷으로 가방을 만들어.
여 멋지다. 나도 가서 둘러보고 싶어.
남 축제는 Grand Park에서 토요일부터 일요일까지 열려. 거기서 보자.

해설 재활용 축제는 토요일부터 일요일까지 열린다고 했다.

어휘 participate in ~에 참여(참가)하다 recycling 재활용
festival 축제 exhibition 전시회 market 시장 goods
상품 recycle 재활용하다 sell 팔다 handmade 수제의
look around 둘러보다 be held 열리다, 개최되다

19 ③

M How do you feel?
W I feel better, but my mouth is still numb.
M Can you eat anything now?
W No, I can't. My dentist said that I must not eat for a couple of hours.
M When do you go to the dentist again?
W Tomorrow afternoon.
M It's almost time for me to get a dental checkup, too.
W Why don't you go with me tomorrow then?
M Okay. I'm afraid I might have a cavity.

남 상태가 좀 어때?
여 나아졌는데, 입이 여전히 감각이 없어.
남 지금은 뭐 좀 먹을 수 있어?
여 아니, 못 먹어. 치과 의사 선생님이 몇 시간 동안 먹으면 안 된다고 했어.
남 언제 다시 치과에 가니?
여 내일 오후에.
남 나도 치과 검진 받을 때가 거의 다 되었는데.
여 그럼 내일 나랑 같이 가는 게 어때?
남 그래. 나 충치가 있을까 봐 두려워.

해설 여자가 내일 자신과 함께 치과에 가자고 제안했으므로 이에 대한 수락 또는 거절의 응답이 와야 한다.
① 난 지금 너무 배고파.
② 난 지금 당장은 아무것도 씹을 수 없어.
④ 미안하지만, 난 이미 치과에 다녀왔어.
⑤ 먹고 난 후에 양치를 하는 게 중요해.

어휘 still 여전히 numb 둔한, 감각이 없는 dentist 치과 의사
a couple of hours 몇 시간 go to the dentist 치과에 가다
dental checkup 치과 검진 chew (음식을) 씹다 cavity
충치 important 중요한 brush one's teeth 양치를 하다

20 ④

W Why were you late for school this morning?
M I couldn't get up on time. It's very hard to get up early every morning.
W Do you sleep deeply every night?
M Not really. I often wake up in the middle of the night.
W Hmm... do you use your smartphone before going to bed?
M Yeah, I usually watch webtoons or use social media in bed.
W That might be the reason. The blue light from a smartphone can disturb a sound sleep.
M I thought it could only damage my eyes.

여 오늘 아침 학교에 왜 늦었니?
남 제시간에 못 일어났어. 아침마다 일찍 일어나는 게 너무 힘들어.
여 매일 밤 잠을 푹 자니?
남 아니 별로. 밤중에 자주 깨.
여 음… 잠자리에 들기 전에 스마트폰을 사용하니?
남 응, 보통 침대에서 웹툰을 보거나 소셜 미디어를 해.
여 그게 이유일 수 있어. 스마트폰에서 나오는 블루라이트가 숙면을 방해할 수 있거든.
남 나는 그것이 눈만 상하게 하는 줄 알았어.

해설 여자가 스마트폰에서 나오는 블루라이트가 숙면을 방해하는 원인인 것 같다고 했으므로, 블루라이트가 눈만 상하게 하는 줄 알았다는 말이 이어지는 것이 가장 적절하다.
① 블루라이트는 수면에 영향을 미쳐.
② 나는 침대에서 스마트폰을 사용하지 않아.
③ 나는 더 자주 스마트폰을 사용할 거야.
⑤ 그 소음이 밤중에 내가 깨게 해.

어휘 get up 일어나다 on time 제시간에 sleep deeply
잠을 깊이 자다 wake up (잠에서) 깨다 in the middle
of ~의 도중에 use social media 소셜 미디어를 사용하다
reason 이유 disturb 방해하다 sound sleep 숙면 affect
영향을 미치다 damage 손상을 주다 noise 소음

Review Test

pp.210~211

Word Check

19회

01 불꽃놀이	**02** 결혼하다
03 펼치다	**04** (신문·잡지의) 글, 기사
05 기진맥진한, 진이 빠진	**06** 주차장
07 캠페인, 운동	**08** 개조하다
09 알리다	**10** 참석하다
11 온천	**12** (국가·사회의) 유산
13 abroad	**14** erasable
15 election	**16** international
17 president	**18** fair
19 destroy	**20** suit
21 rental car	**22** global warming
23 average	**24** explore

Expression Check

25 take a break	**26** make a list
27 driving, crazy	**28** on my own
29 are, allowed to	**30** try out

Word Check

20회

01 확인	**02** 상품
03 정부	**04** 닫다
05 불쾌한, 불편한	**06** 감사하는
07 좌절한	**08** 영향을 미치다
09 아주 신나는, 흥분되는	**19** 동료
11 고의로, 일부러	**12** 줄이다
13 ban	**14** numb
15 protective	**16** trendy
17 interview	**18** stadium
19 tiny	**20** damage
21 skip	**22** cavity
23 advise	**24** toothpaste

Expression Check

25 sleep in	**26** in the middle of
27 over and over	**28** along with
29 make the most of	**30** suffering from

LISTENING CLEAR
중학영어듣기 모의고사 20회

2